HBJ SOCIAL STUDIES

THE UNITED STATES
ITS HISTORY AND NEIGHBORS

Titles in this series:

SENIOR PROGRAM ADVISERS

JOHN BARBINI
Director of Program Services
School District 54
Schaumberg, Illinois

PAUL S. HANSON
Social Studies Supervisor
Dade County Public Schools
Miami, Florida

CHERYL BILES MOORE
Director, Staff Development,
Research and Evaluation
Orange County Department of Education
Costa Mesa, California

DR. WILLIAM D. TRAVIS
Curriculum Coordinator
Pittsfield Public Schools
Pittsfield, Massachusetts

DONALD P. VETTER
Supervisor of Social Studies
Carroll County Public Schools
Westminster, Maryland

THOMAS GREGORY WARD
Social Studies Specialist
Fairfax County Schools, Area II
Fairfax, Virginia

ALICE WELLS
Curriculum Consultant
Cartwright School District No. 83
Phoenix, Arizona

SENIOR CONTENT SPECIALISTS

DR. BILIANA CICIN-SAIN
Associate Professor of Political Science
University of California
Santa Barbara, California

DR. IRVING CUTLER
Chairman, Geography Department
Chicago State University
Chicago, Illinois

DR. STEPHANIE ABRAHAM HIRSH
Consultant, Staff Development and
Free Enterprise Education
Richardson Independent School District
Richardson, Texas

DR. DONALD O. SCHNEIDER
Associate Professor of Social
Science Education
University of Georgia
Athens, Georgia

DR. PETER J. STEIN
Professor of Sociology
William Paterson College
New York, New York

SKILLS DEVELOPMENT

DR. H. MICHAEL HARTOONIAN
Madison, Wisconsin

HBJ SOCIAL STUDIES
THE UNITED STATES
ITS HISTORY AND NEIGHBORS

HBJ HARCOURT BRACE JOVANOVICH, PUBLISHERS

Orlando   New York   Chicago   Atlanta   Dallas

CLASSROOM CONSULTANTS

RUTH F. ADAMS
Lorraine Academy
Buffalo, New York

NANCY M. ATLEE
Eastvalley Elementary School
Marietta, Georgia

BEVERLY BALBI
Meadow Homes School
Concord, California

SISTER MARY ANDRÉ BECKER
St. John's Academy
Rensselaer, New York

MARGARET P. BENEDICT
Murray LaSaine Elementary School
Charleston, South Carolina

ROSE MARIE BRYAN
Jefferson Elementary School
South St. Paul, Minnesota

MARIANNE CASAREZ
Hillcrest Elementary School
Del Valle, Texas

PATRICIA R. DALTON
Montrose Elementary School
Henrico County Public Schools
Richmond, Virginia

RUTH J. DuBREUIL
Dunedin Elementary School
Dunedin, Florida

CAROL E. FENTON
Campbell Elementary School
Sandusky, Ohio

PAUL M. HOUSE
North Elementary School
Jonesboro, Arkansas

PRISCILLA IACANO
Bonita Canyon School
Irvine, California

DR. MAE JACKSON
Edison Elementary School
Eugene, Oregon

SANDRA K. JONES
Wesconnett Elementary School
Jacksonville, Florida

KEN KLAAS
Hearthwood Elementary School
Vancouver, Washington

ROBERT L. KLAGES
South Carroll High School
Winfield, Maryland

LARRY L. LUSBY
Pasadena I.S.D.
Genoa Elementary School
Houston, Texas

CATHY MARSH
A. G. Cox Grammar School
Winterville, North Carolina

TIMOTHY L. MATEER
East Petersburg Elementary School
East Petersburg, Pennsylvania

MARIE O. MATSUKAWA
Woodstock Elementary School
Salt Lake City, Utah

A. BETTY PADDOCK
Southern Blvd. School
Chatham, New Jersey

MARJO NELSON PRINZING
McLaughlin School
Muskegon, Michigan

LAURA TERRY, Ph.D.
Cynthia Heights Elementary School
Evansville, Indiana

SHIRLEY E. THORP
James Elementary School
Kansas City, Missouri

MARTHA SPARKS VANOVER
Roy H. Guess Elementary School
Beaumont, Texas

GERALDINE S. WELCH
Bevins Elementary School
Sidney, Kentucky

JULIAN C. WILLIAMS
Oliver Wendell Holmes
   Elementary School
Chicago, Illinois

JUANITA H. YANCEY
Melcher Elementary School
Kansas City, Missouri

WRITER

LORNA COGSWELL MASON
Castro Valley, California

READABILITY

DR. JEANNE BARRY
Jeanne Barry and Associates, Inc.
Oakland, California

AMERICAN INDIAN CONSULTANT

DR. WILLARD E. BILL
Supervisor of Indian Education
Office of the Superintendent of
   Public Instruction
Olympia, Washington

Requests for permission to make copies of any part of the work should be mailed to: Permissions, Harcourt Brace Jovanovich, Publishers, Orlando, Florida 32887.

For permission to reprint copyrighted material, grateful acknowledgment is made to the following sources:

Dial Books for Young Readers, a division of E. P. Dutton, Inc.: From *To Be A Slave* by Julius Lester. Copyright © 1968 by Julius Lester. *Joan Daves:* From *I Have A Dream* by Martin Luther King, Jr. Copyright © 1963 by Martin Luther King, Jr. *Pantheon Books, a division of Random House, Inc.:* From *Hard Times: An Oral History of the Great Depression* by Studs Terkel. Copyright © 1970 by Studs Terkel. *Peter Smith Publisher, Inc.:* From *The Journal of Madam Knight* by Madam Knight.

PHOTOGRAPH ACKNOWLEDGMENTS

Key: T, Top; B, Bottom; L, Left; C, Center; R, Right.

RESEARCH CREDITS: Black Star, © J. Mason, 1980: 7B. Click, Chicago, © James Rowan, 1981: 10B. © Terry Eiler, 1969: 14T. After Image, © Harvey Sherman, 1977: 14B. © Tony Linck: 25B. © Cahokia Mounds State Historical Site, drawing by Valerie Waldorf: 26B. © American Museum of Natural History, *Daily Life of Algonkian Indians*, A. A. Jansson: 42B. © American Museum of Natural History, #1171: 43T. Woodfin Camp & Associates, © Craig Aurness: 52BL. Woodfin Camp & Associates, © Daily Telegraph Magazine, C. Bonington, photographer: 53T. Woodfin Camp & Associates, © Roland & Sabrina Michaud: 74T. Peter Arnold, Inc. © S. J. Kraseman, 1973: 115C. Peter Arnold, Inc. © J. Davis: 115B. "This reproduction is based on a work copyrighted by the New England Mutual Life Insurance Company, 1943, renewed 1971, and is used through the courtesy of the proprietor.": 138T. John Hancock Mutual Life Insurance Company, © Doris Lee, 1951: 139B. © The White House Historical Association, photograph by The National Geographic Society: 279TL. © Smithsonian Institution, 1983: 294T. © American Museum of Natural History: 297B. © 1983, Los Angeles Times, reprinted by permission: 304TR. © 1964, NEA, Inc.: 304TL. © Wide World Photos, 1946: 465TR, 470TR. © The Bettman Archive, Inc., 1934: 471T. © The Bettman Archive, Inc., 1933: 471B. © United States Postal Service, 1981: 488T. © Peter Jaret: 494T, 495T. © Elliot Varner Smith: 492T, 492B, 493B, 495B. After-Image, © Elise M. Wenger, 1978: 500. © John deVisser, 1977: 506B. Black Star, © Jonathan Wenk, 1982: 512B. Langley in the Christian Science Monitor, © 1983: 519B. © Wide World Photos, 1980: 520B. After-Image, © David C. Oshner, 1979: 527T.

(Continued on page 566.)

Table of Contents

Maps and Globes

Charts, Graphs, Diagrams, and Timelines

INTRODUCTION: AMERICAN HISTORY AND GEOGRAPHY

As Americans, we share a common **heritage.** Our heritage includes ways of thinking, believing, and doing things. Our heritage comes to us from different times and different places in the past. It includes the kinds of food we eat and the language we speak. It includes the holidays we celebrate and the laws we live by.

This book is about our land and our heritage. The study of the past is called **history.** History is the means by which we learn of our heritage as a people and as a nation.

History is seeing the connections between things. The picture at the left shows these connections as places along a road. This is a picture history. It starts at the top with a view of the land and an Indian village. Then the picture history shows changes taking place. Along the road come settlers, building log cabins and starting farms. As you follow the road toward the present, you see buildings and towns getting larger. You see a railroad and then cars and trucks. The picture shows that the past is connected to the present. That is why we study history.

In the picture, things are shown in the order they happened. Something that happens is an **event.** One way we show connections in history is to put events in their proper place in time.

Scholars who study the past are **historians.** To understand life in times past, historians use many sources of information. They use diaries written by people long ago. They look through old newspapers. They read descriptions of past events. They study old account books in which people listed what they bought and sold. They look at old pictures and photographs. Using a variety of sources, historians piece together what life was like in the past. In this book you will be reading some of what they have learned.

Using Your Textbook

This book has been designed to help you learn. At the beginning of each lesson is a section called To Guide Your Reading. It includes a list of key words, people, and places. It also includes several questions to think about as you read. Each lesson ends with a Reading Check with several more questions.

Important words are printed in thicker letters called **boldface.** The meaning of a key word in boldface will always be found near the word.

In the back of your book there is a **glossary.** A glossary lists important words, with a definition and pronunciation of each. Also in the back of your book is an **index,** an alphabetical listing of important people, places, events, and topics. Each listing has page numbers telling its place in the book.

Another important section in the back includes maps of the United States and the world, information about each state, and a list of the Presidents.

Become familiar with all parts of your book. To do so will make learning easier.

1

REVIEWING MAPS AND GLOBES

You know that Earth is a **sphere**. A sphere is anything shaped like a ball. At one end of Earth is the **North Pole**. At the opposite end is the **South Pole**. Halfway between the North Pole and the South Pole is the **equator**. The equator is an imaginary line that circles the Earth. The equator is an equal distance from both the North Pole and the South Pole.

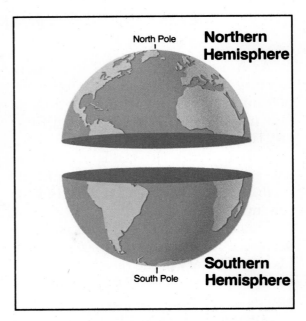

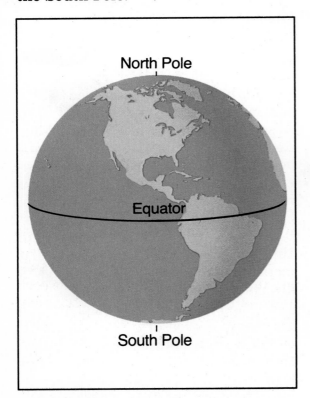

Half a sphere is a **hemisphere**. To describe locations on Earth, we make imaginary divisions of the Earth into hemispheres. If we divide Earth at the equator, then we are dividing it in two. One half is the Northern Hemisphere. The other half is the Southern Hemisphere.

Another way to divide Earth is with an imaginary line running through the North Pole and the South Pole. We divide Earth in this way into an Eastern Hemisphere and a Western Hemisphere.

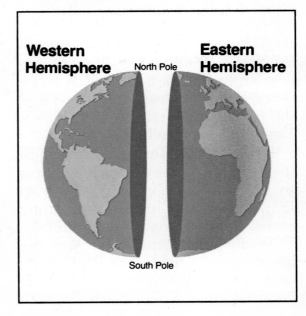

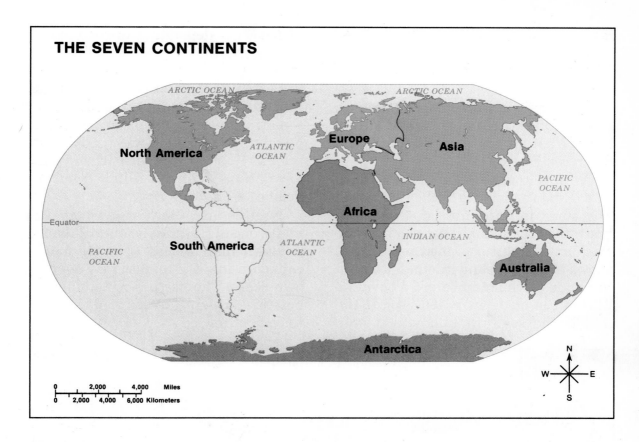

THE SEVEN CONTINENTS

Continents

The map above shows the seven **continents,** or great masses of land, in the world. The continents are North America, South America, Europe, Asia, Africa, Australia, and Antarctica. Our country is located in North America. Compare the map to the drawings on the opposite page. Is North America located in the Eastern Hemisphere or Western Hemisphere? in the Northern Hemisphere or Southern Hemisphere?

Reading Maps

Because the Earth is a sphere, a globe is the most accurate way to represent Earth. A globe is bulky, however, and cannot show small areas in much detail. Therefore, flat maps are used. Maps usually have several features in common. They include a title, a compass rose, a map scale, and often a map key.

The title of a map tells you the subject of the map. Many maps in this book show our country as it was in the past. Maps showing the past often have dates next to the title. When you look at a map, pay attention to both its title and its dates.

The **compass rose** shows you where north is on a map. By now you know the directions north, south, east, and west. Often, however, we need to describe places that are located in between these directions. For instance, we might want to describe a place that is between south and west. Another word for *between* is **intermediate.**

Intermediate directions are those between the four main directions. Intermediate directions are northeast, southeast, southwest, and northwest. Look at the compass rose on the map below. Find the intermediate directions. What intermediate direction best describes Florida?

A **map scale** compares a distance on a map to a distance in the real world. The scale is important if you are to know the real distance between points. Each map in this book has a scale that shows both miles and kilometers. Find the scale on the map below. Above the line is the scale in miles. Below the line is the scale in kilometers. Map scales vary depending on how much area is shown.

Maps may also have keys. A map key explains the **symbols** on the map. A symbol is something that stands for something else. Symbols on a map may be colors or special marks. Look at the map key below. How does the symbol for national capital differ from the symbol for a large city?

On this map there are two smaller maps, one of Hawaii and one of Alaska. A small map within a larger one is called an **inset.** An inset may have its own scale. The use of insets makes it possible to show far-apart places next to each other.

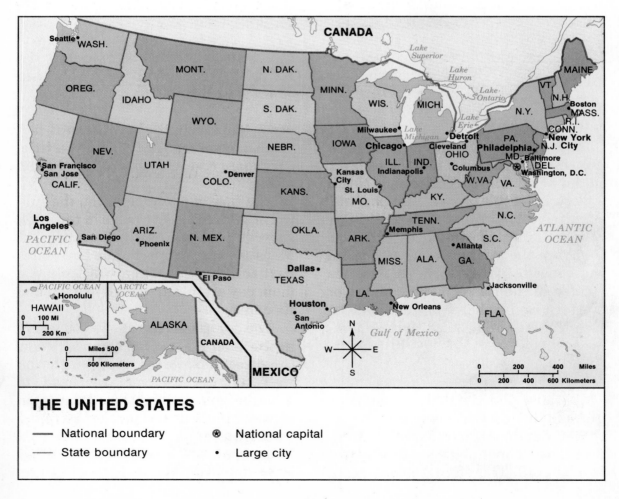

THE UNITED STATES

— National boundary   ⊛ National capital

-- State boundary   • Large city

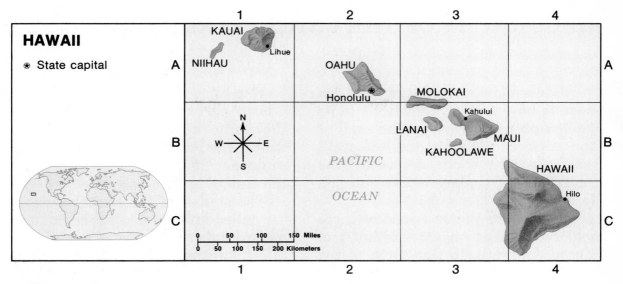

Using a Grid

People often use a system of imaginary lines to locate places on a map. The map above of the state of Hawaii has lines running in both a vertical and a horizontal direction. These lines cross to form a **grid,** a pattern of squares. Look at the square in the upper left-hand corner. Above the square is the number *1*. To the side of the square is the letter *A*. This combination of letter and number identifies this square as *A-1*. Where is square *A-2*? Can you find square *C-3*? In what square is the city of Honolulu? Is there land located in square B-1?

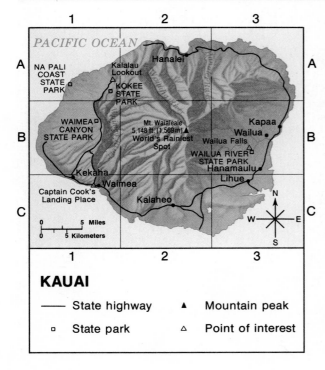

KAUAI

—— State highway ▲ Mountain peak

▫ State park △ Point of interest

Questions to Answer

Review your map skills by answering the following questions. Use the map of the Hawaiian island of Kauai (KOU•eye) to answer the following questions.

1. Is the distance from Waimea (C-1) to Kalaheo (C-2) closer to 10 miles or 100 miles?
2. What is the symbol for point of interest?
3. Is Kokee State Park north or south of Waimea Canyon State Park?
4. Is Waimea in the northeast, northwest, or southwest part of the island of Kauai?
5. In what grid square is the world's rainiest spot?

GEOGRAPHY OF THE UNITED STATES

To learn about America's past, you need to have a basic knowledge of its **geography.** Geography is the study of the surface of Earth and the ways people use the Earth. A study of the geography of a place starts with its location.

The United States is one of three major countries on the continent of North America. To the north of the United States is Canada. To the south of the United States is Mexico.

Water forms a natural boundary for a large part of the United States. On the east is the Atlantic Ocean. On the west is the Pacific Ocean. Much of the southeastern United States borders on the Gulf of Mexico.

The shapes of the Earth's surface are called **landforms.** There are four major kinds of landforms: mountains, hills, plateaus, and plains. All of these landforms, plus smaller landforms, are found in the United States.

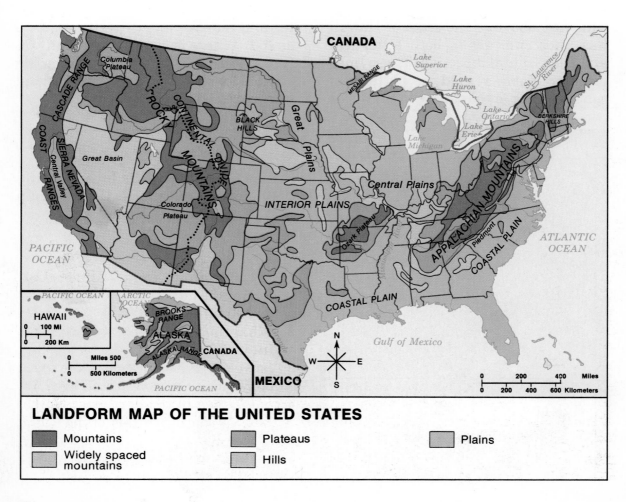

LANDFORM MAP OF THE UNITED STATES

- Mountains
- Widely spaced mountains
- Plateaus
- Hills
- Plains

Mountains

There are three major mountain areas of the United States.

In the East are the **Appalachian Mountains.** This large chain of mountains extends from Maine to the northern parts of Georgia and Alabama. Parts of the Appalachian Mountains have their own names. Among them are the Allegheny Mountains, the Blue Ridge Mountains, the Adirondack Mountains, the Catskill Mountains, and the Green Mountains.

The **Rocky Mountains** lie in the interior of the United States. These mountains extend from Alaska through Canada as far south as New Mexico. The Rocky Mountains are sometimes called the "backbone" of North America. Parts of the Rocky Mountains also have their own names. Among them are the Teton Range, the Front Range, and the Wasatch Range.

On the Pacific coast there are other groups of mountains. These extend generally in a north and south direction. The mountains in this area include the **Coast Ranges,** mountains that hug the Pacific coast. About 100 to 150 miles (about 161 to 241 km) inland from the Coast Ranges are two other mountain ranges. These are the **Sierra Nevada,** in California, and the **Cascade Range,** in Oregon and Washington.

The mountains near the Pacific Coast include many **volcanoes.** A volcano is a mountain formed by hot rocks, ashes, and gas. These materials rise from the interior of the Earth to the surface. When this happens, we say a volcano **erupts.** A volcano that is erupting or likely to erupt is an **active volcano.** There are about 60 volcanoes in the western United States, including Hawaii, that may erupt sometime in the future.

The eruption of Mount St. Helens in 1980 sent ashes and gas thousands of feet into the sky. The eruption started forest fires and caused floods that resulted in widespread damage to the surrounding area.

Hills

Hills are not as high as mountains. They are generally rounded at the top. Hills can have their own names. The Berkshire Hills in Massachusetts and the Black Hills in South Dakota are examples. There is often an area of gently rolling hills at the base of mountains. These gentle hills are called a **piedmont,** or **foothills.** The Appalachian Piedmont is on the eastern side of the Appalachian Mountains.

Valleys

Valleys are low places between mountains or hills. Valleys come in all sizes. Some are very small and narrow. Some are large. The Central Valley in California is 500 miles (about 800 km) long and about 100 miles (about 160 km) across.

Streams and rivers usually run through valleys. During floods, they deposit **silt,** a mud composed of fine bits of rock and soil. Silt creates fertile soil in the valleys. Valleys can be important farming areas.

Valleys are important as main transportation routes. It is easier to travel through a river valley than up and down mountains and hills. Roads and railroads usually follow valleys.

Plains

Plains are regions of flat or gently rolling land. Plains do not have steep hills or valleys. There are two major plain regions in the United States: the

The central valley of California is one of the nation's richest agricultural areas. Vegetables, rice, sugar beets, cotton and many kinds of fruit are among the products raised here.

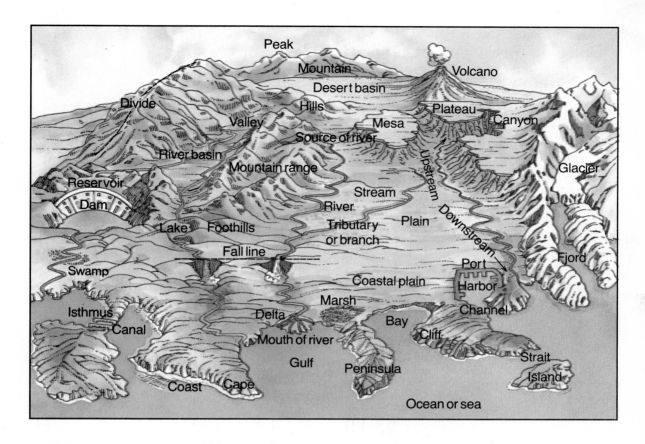

GEOGRAPHIC DICTIONARY

basin a land area mostly surrounded by higher land

bay a small area of ocean partly surrounded by land

canal a waterway dug across land for transportation or irrigation

canyon a narrow valley with high, steep sides

cape a point of land that extends into a body of water

channel a narrow waterway connecting two bodies of water; the deepest part of a waterway

continent one of the Earth's seven main land masses

delta a rich soil deposit, usually triangle-shaped, at a river's mouth

divide a high ridge of land between areas with different river basins

fall line the point where a river forms a waterfall as it drops to lower land

fjord a narrow inlet of the sea between high, steep banks

foothill a low hill at the base of a mountain

glacier a large mass of slow-moving ice spread over a land surface

gulf a large area of ocean partly surrounded by land

harbor a sheltered area along a seacoast where ships can anchor

highland a region of hills, mountains, or plateaus

hill a small, raised part of the land, lower than a mountain

isthmus a narrow strip of land connecting two larger land areas

lowland a low, mostly level land area

marsh an area of low, wet land

mesa a flat-topped hill with steep sides, common in dry areas

mountain range a group or chain of mountains

mouth (of river) the place where a river or stream empties into a larger body of water

peak the pointed top of a mountain

peninsula land surrounded by water on three sides

plain a large area of flat or gently rolling land

plateau an area of high, flat land

port a city or place where ships arrive and depart

prairie a broad, grassy plains region

rain forest a woodland with rain much of the year and marked by a dense growth of trees and plants

reservoir a lake where a large water supply is stored

source (of river) the place where a stream or river begins

strait a narrow water passage between two larger bodies of water

stream a small body of flowing water

swamp low, wet land

tributary a river or stream that flows into another river

tundra a broad, treeless plain in a polar region

valley low land between mountains or hills

volcano a hill or mountain formed when melted rock is forced through the Earth's surface

9

Coastal Plain and the **Interior Plains.** The Coastal Plain is found along the coasts of the Atlantic Ocean and the Gulf of Mexico.

The Interior Plains are located between the Appalachian Mountains and the Rocky Mountains. In this area the plains are divided into two kinds, depending on the amount of rainfall. They are the **Central Plains** and the **Great Plains.** The Central Plains receive more than 20 inches (about 51 cm) of rainfall a year. Sometimes this area is called the Tall-Grass Prairie. The Great Plains receive less than 20 inches (about 51 cm) of rainfall. This area has short grass and few trees.

Ripe grass waves in the wind in this picture taken on the Tall Grass Prairie.

Most American farming takes place on the plains. For this reason, crop names have also been given to plains regions. The southern part of the Coastal Plain is called the **Cotton Belt.** Much corn is grown on the Central Plains and therefore they are also called the **Corn Belt.** The Great Plains are often called the **Wheat Belt.**

Plateaus

Plateaus are another major landform of the United States. A plateau is high flat land. Plateaus rise sharply above neighboring land on at least one side. Some plateaus rise sharply on all sides and have level tops. Such plateaus are then called **tablelands,** or **mesas.** One major plateau region in the United States is the Columbia Plateau in the Northwest. Others are the Colorado Plateau in the Southwest and the Ozark Plateau in the Southeast.

Rivers and Waterways

Rain and snow that does not sink into the ground is called **runoff.** East of the Rocky Mountains, the water in rivers goes to the Atlantic Ocean or the Gulf of Mexico. West of the Rocky Mountains, the runoff ends up in the Pacific Ocean. The division line follows the **crest,** or high point, of the Rocky Mountains. This line is called the **Continental Divide.**

Rivers are an important part of American life. Big rivers provide transportation. When dams are built across rivers, the water's force turns machinery to make electricity. Rivers provide water for farming, for manufacturing, and for everyday use.

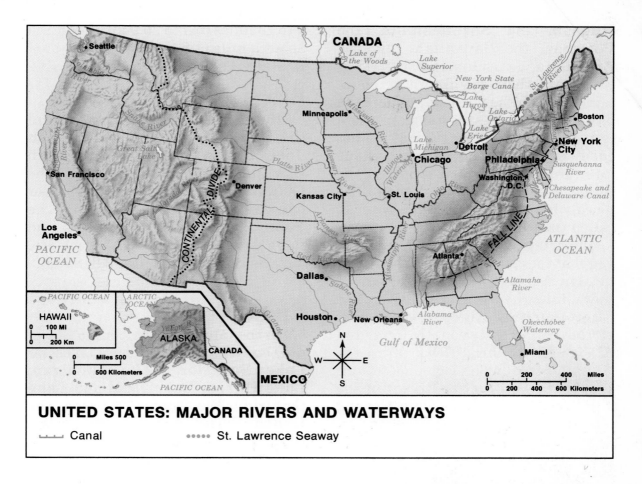

UNITED STATES: MAJOR RIVERS AND WATERWAYS

⊔⊔ Canal   ••••• St. Lawrence Seaway

The largest river in the United States is the **Mississippi River.** It runs 2,348 miles (3,780 km) from its source in Lake Itasca, Minnesota, to the Gulf of Mexico. As it leaves Lake Itasca, the Mississippi is a small stream. When it reaches the Gulf of Mexico, it is a vast river, nearly a mile (1.6 km) wide.

Near its mouth at the Gulf of Mexico, the Mississippi begins to drop silt. The river drops its load of silt in a pattern the shape of a triangle. This triangular piece of land near a river mouth is called a **delta.** A delta has rich soil and makes good farmland.

Streams and rivers that flow into other rivers are called **tributaries.** Tributaries of the Mississippi include the **Missouri River,** the **Ohio River,** the **Arkansas River,** the **Red River,** and the **Tennessee River.**

A river and its tributaries are called a **river system.** The Mississippi river system **drains,** or collects water, from a huge area. The area drained by a river is called a **basin.** The Mississippi River basin extends from the Rocky Mountains to the Appalachian Mountains. It covers one-eighth of North America.

Rivers of the East

On the eastern side of the Appalachian Mountains, the rivers run to the Atlantic Ocean. These rivers include the **Connecticut,** the **Delaware,** the

Hudson, the **Susquehanna,** the **Potomac,** the **Savannah,** and the **Altamaha** (OL•tuh•muh•hah). They first make their way from the mountains through the piedmont. Where the piedmont meets the coastal plain, there is a hard stone layer. Rivers cannot easily **erode,** or wear away, this stone layer. Instead, the rivers drop over the stone layer to the plains below. The place where these waterfalls occur is called the **fall line.**

Important rivers of the Southeast begin at the southern end of the Appalachian Mountains. They flow from there into the Gulf of Mexico. The **Chattahoochee River** serves as part of the border between Georgia and Alabama. It then flows into the **Apalachicola** (ap•uh•lach•uh•KOH•luh) **River.** The **Tombigbee River** and the **Alabama River** join before flowing into Mobile Bay on the Gulf of Mexico.

Rivers of the Southwest

The major river of the Southwest is the **Rio Grande.** The Rio Grande flows from its source in Colorado to the Gulf of Mexico. For much of its length, the river serves as the border between the United States and Mexico.

Another major river of the Southwest is the **Colorado River.** Its basin extends from the Rocky Mountains to the Sierra Nevada. The Colorado River has cut its way through layers and layers of earth and rock to reach the Gulf of California. The places where rivers cut deep through the land are called **canyons,** or **gorges.** The Grand Canyon of the Colorado is one of the world's natural wonders. It extends 217 miles (about 349 km) through Arizona. It is

4 to 13 miles (6.4 to 20.9 km) wide and about a mile (1.6 km) deep.

Rivers of the West

In California the major rivers are the **Sacramento River** and the **San Joaquin** (san wah•KEEN) **River.** Both flow into San Francisco Bay. The **Columbia River** serves as the border between Washington and Oregon. The **Yukon River** begins in Canada and flows through Alaska to the Bering Sea, a distance of 1,770 miles (2,848 km).

Great Lakes

In the interior of the United States are the **Great Lakes.** These lakes are **Lake Superior, Lake Michigan, Lake Huron, Lake Erie,** and **Lake Ontario.** The border between the United States and Canada passes through these lakes. The Great Lakes are connected to each other. Together they form the largest body of fresh water in the world. The **St. Lawrence River** flows from the Great Lakes in a northeasterly direction before emptying into the Atlantic Ocean.

The Great Lakes provide an important transportation network. Ships can travel between the Great Lakes and the Atlantic Ocean in two ways. One is to use the St. Lawrence River. The other is to travel through the New York State Barge Canal System to the Hudson River. The canal system connects Lake Erie with the Hudson River.

Ships can also travel between the Great Lakes and the Gulf of Mexico by using the Illinois Waterway. The Illinois Waterway connects Lake Michigan with the Mississippi River.

Regions of the United States

The United States is a huge country. For this reason, it is often easier to talk about **regions.** Regions are parts of the country that are alike in some way. For instance, Maine, Vermont, New Hampshire, Massachusetts, Connecticut, Rhode Island, New York, Pennsylvania, New Jersey, Delaware, and Maryland all have things in common. These states share similar landforms and resources. They are all located in the northeastern part of our country. Sometimes we want to speak of all these states together. Calling the region the Northeast is much easier than naming the states one by one.

The states of Minnesota, Wisconsin, Illinois, Michigan, Indiana, and Ohio form the Great Lakes region. These states all border one of the Great Lakes. They also share a similar history because of their location.

Look at the map below. It shows you seven regions of the United States. In which region do you live?

Climate of the United States

Look at the world map on pages 550-551. Find the United States. As you can see, most of our country is in the middle of North America. This says something about the **climate,** or long-range weather, of the United States. It is between the extreme cold of the North Pole and the constant heat of the equator. The climate of most of the United States is well suited for growing many crops.

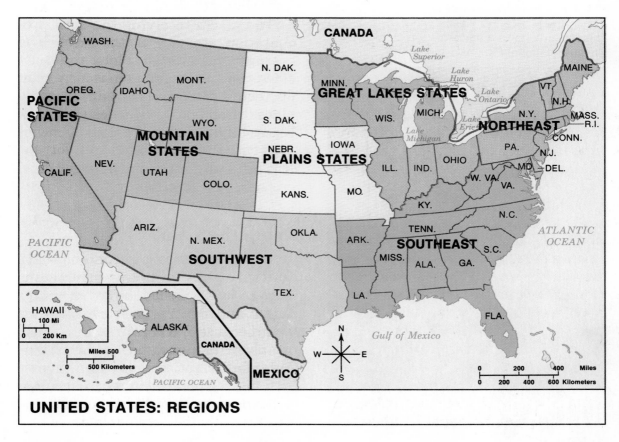

UNITED STATES: REGIONS

Navajo herders take their sheep to water in a desert at Monument Valley, Utah.

This picture shows a thick rain forest in Olympic National Park, Washington.

Temperature is an important part of climate. Generally, the northern part of the United States is cooler than the southern part. In winter the northern part of the United States can be freezing cold. Freezing temperatures are rare in the most southern parts of the United States. The weather in places along the ocean is not as severe as in places farther inland. Near the ocean it is usually not as hot in summer or as cold in winter. Precipitation also affects climate.

Most of the eastern United States has an annual precipitation between 20 and 60 inches (50 and 150 cm). The western half of the United States has a variable precipitation. Those places that receive an average of less than 10 inches (25 cm) of precipitation a year are called **deserts.**

The places receiving the most precipitation are also in the West. The average precipitation along the coast of Oregon and Washington is more than 60 inches (152 cm) a year. In some places it equals 150 inches (381 cm). Places that receive more than 80 inches (203 cm) a year are often rain forests. It is difficult for people to live or grow crops in rain forests.

Using the Land

In our country's past, most people lived only where there was enough rain to grow crops. Today, however, many desert and dry regions are farming areas because of **irrigation.** Irrigation means bringing water to farmland. Water for irrigation comes from rivers, from underground wells, or from dams.

Dams have been built on most rivers of the West. These dams serve two

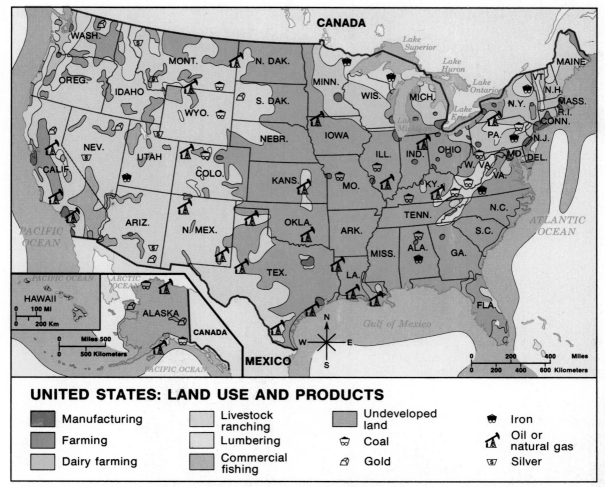

UNITED STATES: LAND USE AND PRODUCTS

- Manufacturing
- Farming
- Dairy farming
- Livestock ranching
- Lumbering
- Commercial fishing
- Undeveloped land
- Coal
- Gold
- Iron
- Oil or natural gas
- Silver

purposes. They make electricity, and they store water in large lakes called **reservoirs** (REZ·uhv·wahrs). Water can then be directed from the reservoir to the farmland by pipes and canals. Reservoirs also supply water for people living in cities and towns.

The use of dams, reservoirs, and irrigation has made it possible to increase the amount of food grown. It has also made possible the growth of large cities in dry areas.

Look at the map above. It shows the main products and uses of land in the United States today. Notice that most of our country is used to produce food, minerals, or manufactured goods.

Questions to Answer

Review geography by answering the following questions.

1. What are the four major landforms?
2. What are the three major mountain areas of the United States?
3. What are the two major types of plains in the United States?
4. What is a plateau?
5. What is the Continental Divide?
6. Why are rivers an important part of American life?
7. How long is the Mississippi River?
8. What is a river system?
9. What is climate?
10. What are the two purposes of dams?

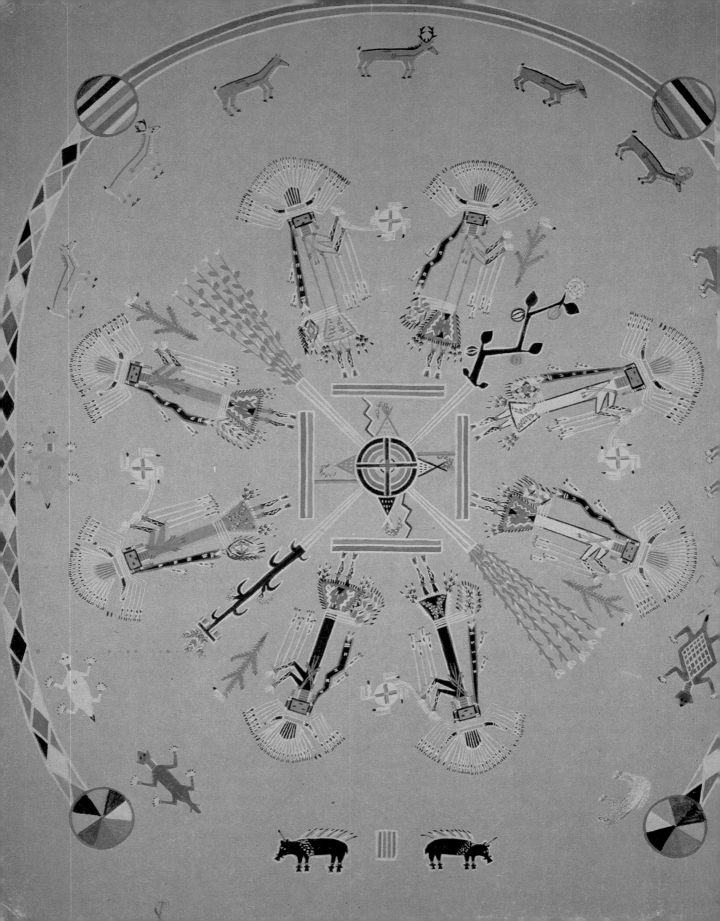

UNIT ONE

THE FIRST AMERICANS

The American Indians lived in North and South America for thousands of years before the first Europeans came. The heritage of the American Indians can be found in their art, their stories, and their customs. The sandpainting at the left is an example of Indian art. This is a religious picture that shows holy people bearing gifts of corn and plants. It shows plants, people, and animals all as part of the world.

The American Indians were the first farmers of the Western Hemisphere. They developed corn and potatoes from wild plants. In this painting you can see the importance of both plants and animals to the Indians. Knowing about the American Indians is important to understanding the heritage of the Americas and of our nation.

Key Dates and Events

70,000–10,000 years ago
The last Ice Age

40,000–20,000 years ago
Ancestors of American Indians cross from Asia to North America

10,000 years ago
Big animals disappear

People begin hunting and gathering

By 7,000 years ago
People of the Americas were farming

4,000 years ago
Eskimos come to North America

300 B.C.–A.D. 900
Height of Maya civilization

A.D. 600
Hohokam build irrigation canals

A.D. 1200
Height of Mississippian culture

A.D. 1276
Drought starts in Southwest

A.D. 1438–1532
Height of Inca civilization

A.D. 1570
League of Iroquois formed

CHAPTER 1

Passage to a New World

The first people to come to North and South America were hunters of large animals. In time many of these first Americans began to farm and to live in communities. Scientists have learned about these people from the objects they made. The spear point of the hunter, a beautiful pot, a stone carving—each of these tells its own story.

18

1. STONE AGE PEOPLE FROM ASIA

To Guide Your Reading

Look for these important words:

Key Words
- glaciers
- Ice Age
- mammoths
- strait

- land bridge
- migration
- Stone Age
- flint

Places
- Bering Strait

Look for answers to these questions:

1. Why could people and animals move from Asia to North America during the Ice Age?
2. What kinds of tools did these first Americans use?
3. What happened when the big animals disappeared?

Thousands of years ago sheets of ice nearly two miles thick were creeping over the northern parts of North America. These sheets of ice, called **glaciers** (GLAY•shuhrs), covered most of what is now Canada. This was the time of the last **Ice Age.** It lasted from about 70,000 years ago to about 10,000 years ago.

All sorts of animals roamed North America at the time of the Ice Age. There were huge, hairy elephants called **mammoths.** There were giant bison, similar to the buffalo, with horns 6 feet (1.8 m) across. Giant ground sloths were as large as cows or even elephants. In the wet meadowlands lived giant beavers as big as bears. Elsewhere there were bears as big as horses. In the skies flew giant vultures.

The most common animals in North America were camels and horses. Other grass-eating animals were the buffalo, deer, moose, caribou, and elk. Tigers, lions, wolves, coyotes, and cougars hunted these animals.

At the peak of the Ice Age, so much water turned into ice that the level of the oceans dropped. More land was uncovered. Today 55 miles (89 km) of sea separate North America from Asia at the **Bering Strait.** A **strait** is a narrow passageway between two large bodies of water. During the last Ice Age, however, a **land bridge** a thousand miles (1,609 km) wide connected the two continents. The land bridge was free of ice. Grass grew there. Herds of animals from Asia came to graze. Following the animals across the land bridge were the people. They depended on the animals for their food, clothing, and shelter. Where the animals went, they went also. These people were the ancestors of American Indians.

This movement of people and animals from Asia to North America is called a **migration.** The migration of people and animals took place over a period lasting 20,000 years.

The migrating animals and people crossed the land bridge, then moved

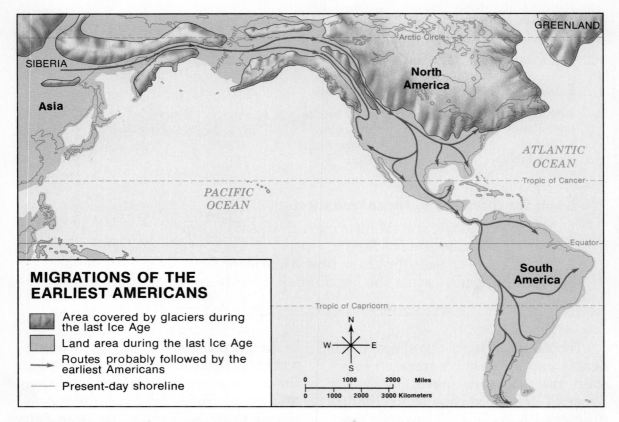

MIGRATIONS OF THE
EARLIEST AMERICANS

- Area covered by glaciers during the last Ice Age
- Land area during the last Ice Age
- → Routes probably followed by the earliest Americans
- — Present-day shoreline

south along an ice-free passageway between two glaciers. These first Americans knew how to use fire. Without it, they might not have survived the cold of the Far North. With fire they could keep warm, and they could cook meat.

In time some of these hunting peoples went as far south as the tip of South America. Others moved into the eastern parts of both North and South America.

The first Americans who came all had straight black hair and copper-colored skin. In other ways they were different from one another. They did not all speak the same language. Neither did they all look alike. Some were short and some were tall. Others were of medium height. Some had long heads, and others had round heads.

These hunting people used stone and bone to make their tools. For this reason we sometimes give the name **Stone Age** to the time in which they lived. During the Stone Age **flint** was the stone most often used for tools. Flint can be as hard as steel, yet it can be chipped easily. The hunters made scrapers, knives, and spear points from it. They also shaped bone into tools. They made spear shafts from splinters of the leg bones of mammoths.

Using spears, these earliest Americans worked together to hunt animals many times larger than themselves. With knives they cut up the animals they had killed. With scrapers of bone or flint, they cleaned animal skins. With bone needles and strips of rawhide, the hunters made clothing and footwear.

Scientists Solving Puzzles

For many years scientists did not agree on how long the Indians had been in America. Then they found proof that the ancestors of American Indians had been in North America for at least 10,000 years. In the early 1900s a cowboy found a pit full of old animal bones near Folsom, New Mexico. In 1926 scientists looking at the pit found a stone spear point buried among some animal rib bones. Scientists knew that the rib bones were those of a giant bison. They also knew that the animal had vanished from the earth 10,000 years ago. They concluded therefore that people must have been in America at least 10,000 years ago.

Early American hunters chipped flint, quartz, and obsidian into spear points. These spear points were found in Arizona buried among the bones of mammoths.

Since 1926 scientists have found many more tools made by early people. Most of them now agree that people were in North America more than 20,000 years ago. Some scientists think people have been here for 40,000 years. Scientists continue to work to fill in the missing pieces of the story of the earliest Americans.

Big Animals Disappear

About 10,000 years ago the early American hunters had to change their way of life. This was because most of the big animals such as mammoths disappeared. Camels and horses also disappeared from the Western Hemisphere. Scientists do not know why so many animals vanished. Some think that a changing climate bringing warmer weather was a reason. Some think that the hunters destroyed the animals. "Man was the most terrible tiger," one scientist has said.

As the big animals disappeared, the hunters began to develop new tools for hunting smaller animals. They began to gather the roots and seeds of plants. People near the sea began to gather shellfish. For several thousand years people lived by both hunting and gathering.

Reading Check

1. Where was the land bridge connecting North America and Asia?
2. What is a migration?
3. How do we know people were in North America at least 10,000 years ago?
4. How did people change their ways when the big animals disappeared?

21

THE MAMMOTHS

A favorite game animal of early hunters was the mammoth. It was the largest animal on earth. Great herds of mammoths roamed North America.

A mammoth looked like an elephant, but it was even bigger. Try to imagine its size. A male mammoth stood 16 feet (5 m) at the shoulder, about as tall as a two-story house. That is much bigger than today's largest elephant, which stands about 13 feet (4 m). The mammoth was 7 feet (2 m) wide and walked on legs 18 inches (46 cm) thick. It grew long, curved tusks 8 to 9 feet (2.4 to 2.7 m) long.

These gigantic animals were peaceable. Their favorite food was the new green leaves of trees. The mammoths were big enough to fight off the fierce saber-toothed tigers. Yet hunters working together were often able to kill these huge beasts. We know this because stone spear points have been found among mammoth bones.

In the arctic parts of North America, Asia, and Europe, people hunted another kind of mammoth. This mammoth was covered with hair 20 inches (50.8 cm) long. We call it the Wooly Mammoth.

There are places in the Far North where the ground never thaws. For that reason parts of mammoth bodies, not just mammoth bones, have been found. Dogs have been known to eat mammoth meat frozen for thousands of years.

Finding a whole mammoth is rare. Scientists were thrilled in 1977 when Russian goldminers uncovered a whole baby mammoth. Scientists named the baby Dima. Forty thousand years ago Dima had become separated from his mother. With only three baby teeth, he could not survive by eating grass. Starving, he fell into a pit and there died. His body froze and then was covered by landslides.

When a Russian scientist first saw the frozen baby mammoth, he said: "I put my hand on the dark skin and felt the chill of centuries long gone. It was as if I had touched the Stone Age."

2. FARMING AND SETTLED LIFE

To Guide Your Reading

Look for these important words:

Key Words
- agriculture
- surplus
- specialize
- civilizations
- Mayas

- Incas
- Aztecs
- Mound Builders
- mounds
- culture
- Hopewell

- obsidian
- mica
- Mississippian

Places
- Cahokia

Look for answers to these questions:

1. How did knowledge of farming change life for people?
2. What is a civilization? What is a culture?
3. What cultures developed in eastern North America?

Ancestors of the American Indians began to experiment with planting seeds about 7,000 years ago. The Indian farmers started with a small wild grass with only a few seeds on it. By always planting the best-looking seeds, the farmers slowly developed corn. Gradually they learned more and more about **agriculture,** or farming.

Once people learned how to raise food plants, they were able to settle down in one place. They did not always have to search for food to survive. Early farmers found that planting, weeding, watering, and harvesting crops did not take all their time. There was time left over for doing other things. The farming people began to use this time to build homes, to make new tools, and to make pottery.

The development of agriculture also resulted in a **surplus** of food. A surplus is an amount more than what is needed. People with a surplus of grain traded their surplus for other things, such as flint or salt.

Having a surplus also meant that not everyone had to farm. With agriculture, one person could grow the food for several. The result was that people could **specialize.** *To specialize* means to spend most of your time doing one kind of job. If there is extra food, then some people do not have to spend time raising or finding food. They can spend time instead making pots or weaving.

Agriculture made possible the development of **civilizations.** A civilization usually has large cities, complex government, and highly developed arts and sciences. The **Mayas,** Indian peoples of Central America and Mexico, developed a civilization over 1,000 years ago. They had a government and laws. They built huge temples and pyramids. They knew how to make objects of great beauty. They studied the skies and developed a very accurate calendar. They had a system of writing.

Later the **Incas** in Peru and the **Aztecs** in Mexico developed major

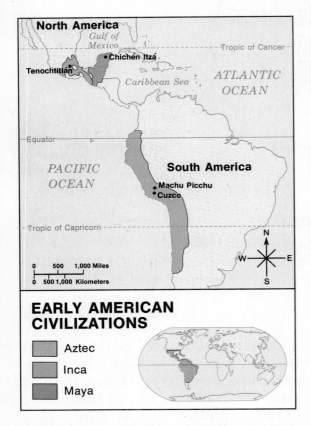

EARLY AMERICAN CIVILIZATIONS

- Aztec
- Inca
- Maya

civilizations. Both were important at the time the first Europeans arrived in the Americas. Both depended on agriculture.

The Mound Builders

Agriculture was also important to the way of life of Indians living in what is now the United States. In the eastern half of our country lived the **Mound Builders.** They made large **mounds,** or heaps of earth. Some mounds were miles long. Some of these mounds were for burials. Others were built as bases for temples and living quarters. Still other mounds had no purpose that we can discover.

The Mound Builders lived in villages and towns. They could do so because a surplus of food made it pos-

sible to specialize. There were those who designed and built mounds. Some farmed or hunted. Others worked at crafts. Still others were warriors or traders. A few were rulers.

The way of life shared by a group of people is called a **culture.** The people in a culture usually speak the same language, follow similar customs, use similar tools, and have similar beliefs.

Scientists have divided the Mound Builders into several cultures. They include the Hopewell culture and the Mississippian culture.

The Hopewell Culture

The people of the **Hopewell** culture farmed in the Illinois and Ohio river valleys from about 200 B.C. to A.D. 500, about 700 years. The Hopewell people were also great traders. They traveled great distances to get the objects they valued. Some went to the Rocky Mountains to get grizzly-bear teeth and **obsidian** (uhb•SID•ee•un). Obsidian is a glassy, black, volcanic rock that makes excellent arrow points, knives, and scrapers.

Some Hopewell traders went to the Gulf of Mexico for sea-turtle shells and shark teeth. Others went to the Great Lakes region to get copper nuggets to hammer into ornaments. From Florida the traders brought back alligator teeth.

The Hopewell people made beautiful pipes in the shapes of animals and birds. They wove a cloth using thread made from soft bark. The people wore clothing made of leather, fur, or cloth. They decorated their clothing with freshwater pearls and ornaments made of copper and **mica** (MY•kah). Mica is a clear rock that comes apart in thin sheets.

In their mounds the Hopewell people buried their important dead. They placed with them objects the dead had used in everyday life. Most of what we know about the Hopewell people comes from studying objects found in the burial mounds.

The Hopewell culture gradually disappeared. We do not know why. It is possible that it was destroyed by more warlike cultures.

Those Hopewell people living west of Lake Michigan in time created another mound-building culture. These Mound Builders liked to build their mounds in the shapes of animals and birds. Some of these animal-and-bird shapes are so large that the only way to see one as a whole is from an airplane!

The Mississippian Culture

Another group of Mound Builders was the **Mississippian** culture. Most of their mounds had a square base, sloping sides, and a flat top. Such mounds were pyramids built without the familiar pointed top. Located in the southern part of the Mississippi valley, the Mississippian culture was most active about A.D. 1200. Its biggest center was at **Cahokia** (kuh•HOH•kee•uh), near present-day St. Louis, Missouri. Other centers were in present-day Oklahoma, Alabama, and Georgia.

Mound Builders constructed this giant serpent at least 1,300 years ago. Located in southern Ohio, the Serpent Mound is about a quarter of a mile long. Do you see the small mound in the snake's open jaws?

This picture shows Cahokia as it may have looked 800 years ago. The great flat-topped pyramid is Monks Mound, the largest earth pyramid in the world. Notice the number of farms surrounding the city. Farming made possible large communities like Cahokia.

Scientists think that at one time Cahokia was a city of 30,000 people. The community had about 100 mounds, including the largest earth pyramid in the world. The large pyramid at Cahokia is 100 feet (30.5 m) tall, as high as a ten-story building.

Some of the mounds at Cahokia were used for burials. Others were platforms for religious temples and for houses of important people.

Along Cahokia Creek was a large marketplace for traders and craftsworkers. The traders came in canoes heavy with furs, shells, mica, flint, and copper. The craftsworkers included toolmakers, potters, weavers, jewelers, and leather workers. Some people mined flint nearby and turned it into knives and hoe blades. Others boiled water from a salt spring in order to get salt.

Cahokia was a busy community as late as A.D. 1500. Then its people left. We do not know the reasons.

Reading Check

1. What is a surplus?
2. What does it mean to specialize?
3. What are the features of a civilization?
4. Name at least three ways the Hopewell culture and the Mississippian culture were alike. Name at least three ways they were different.

3. EARLY PEOPLE OF THE SOUTHWEST

To Guide Your Reading

Look for these important words:

Key Words
- Anasazi
- dwellings
- drought
- Hohokam
- archaeologists
- archaeology
- artifacts
- radiocarbon dating

Look for answers to these questions:

1. Where did the Anasazi live?
2. In what ways did the Anasazi use wild plants?
3. Where did the Hohokam live?
4. How do scientists learn about people in the past?

Among the great sandstone cliffs of the Southwest are the ghost towns of another early people. We know these people as the **Anasazi** (ahn•uh•SAH•zee)—*the old ones*. The Anasazi built their communities in what is called the Four Corners. This is where the borders of four states—Utah, Colorado, New Mexico, and Arizona—meet. In this region rivers have carved deep canyons through pinkish-red sandstone. Mesas extend beyond the canyons. The Anasazi built their homes on the mesas, on the canyon floors, and in the canyon walls. Their homes were like apartment houses, with rooms built on top of other rooms. They used mud bricks and wooden beams to build these **dwellings,** or homes.

The Anasazi raised corn, squash, beans, sunflowers, and cotton on the mesas or on the canyon floor. When necessary, they climbed up and down the cliffs by using toeholds cut in the rock. Today some of their dwellings can be reached only by people using rock-climbing equipment. It is hard to imagine people carrying babies and baskets of food up and down such cliffs.

The Anasazi made use of wild plants. The pinyon tree provided nuts. It also gave resin (REZ•uhn) for waterproofing baskets. The yucca plant supplied soft

The yucca plant provided food, soap, and fiber for Indians of the southwest.

27

fibers for weaving baskets and hard fibers for needles. The fruit of the yucca plant was good to eat. Its root yielded a soap.

In the Anasazi culture the men farmed, hunted, and wove cotton blankets. The women made pottery, prepared food, and repaired the houses.

A **drought,** a long period of no rain, started in A.D. 1276. The years of drought made growing food impossible. By A.D. 1300 the Anasazi had left their homes in the Four Corners. Many moved across the Continental Divide to settle in the Rio Grande valley of present-day New Mexico. They were probably the ancestors of today's Pueblo Indians.

The Hohokam Culture

Indians in the **Hohokam** (hoh. HOH.kum) culture learned that the secret of living in the desert was irrigation. Starting in A.D. 600 these people built miles of irrigation canals in the Gila (HEE.luh) River area of central Arizona. Their only tools were dig-

Centuries ago, a group of Anasazi Indians built their homes in this large natural cave. The site is now a part of Mesa Verde National Park.

ging sticks and baskets to carry away the dirt. Digging such canals must have taken a great deal of cooperation among the people.

The canals provided enough water to irrigate crops. Food was plentiful. The Hohokam had time for other things. Some made beautiful pottery. Others must have spent hours playing ball games. Large ball courts have been found in Hohokam ruins.

The Hohokam lived successfully in the Southwest for more than 1,000 years. Then about A.D. 1400 their culture disappeared. No one knows exactly what happened. Their descendents may be the Pima and Papago Indians of Southern Arizona.

Hohokam potters used repeated designs when they made these beautiful pots.

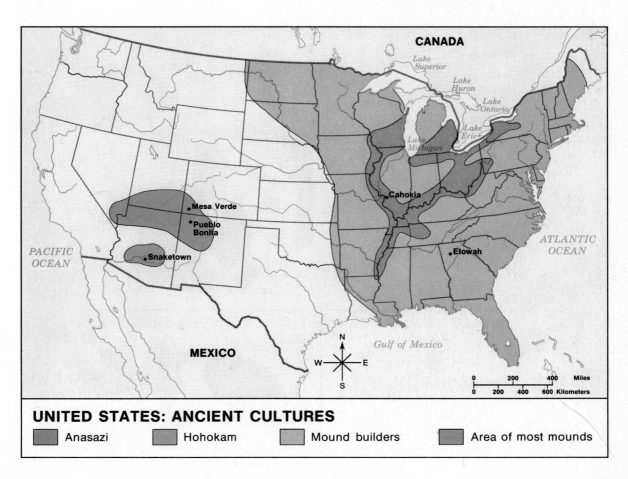

UNITED STATES: ANCIENT CULTURES

- Anasazi
- Hohokam
- Mound builders
- Area of most mounds

ARCHAEOLOGISTS AT WORK

1   Artifacts, Level 1

Arrowhead

Spanish gold coin

Broken pot

Rusted metal knife

2   Artifacts, Level 2

Broken pot

Copper ornament

Pipe

Obsidian knife blade

Level 1

Level 2

Level 3

Level 4

3   Artifacts, Level 3

Fish hook

Arrowhead

Broken pot

Bone hoe

4   Artifacts, Level 4

Chipped flint

Spear point

Bone scraper

Charcoal

30

Learning from Remains

Early people left no written records. How then do we know about those who lived long ago? Some did leave spear points and pottery, bits of which survive. Others left their mounds, their irrigation ditches, their cliff houses. From those remains scientists learn about the people who lived in the past.

The scientists who study remains to learn about the past are called **archaeologists** (ahr•kee•AHL•uh•juhsts). Their science is **archaeology** (ahr•kee•AHL•uh•gee).

To study the distant past, archaeologists dig into the earth. They choose to dig in places where people might have lived or camped. They search carefully for bones, weapons, tools, and pieces of pottery that early cultures may have left behind. Objects used by people in the past are called **artifacts.**

When archaeologists find artifacts, they try to figure out how old they are. One way to do this is to figure the age of the layer of earth where each artifact was found. Generally, objects near the surface were made more recently than objects buried farther down. An archaeologist may find a pot 2 feet (61 cm) below the ground and a spear 6 feet (183 cm) below the ground. The archaeologist figures that the person who made the pot lived more recently than the person who used the spear.

What if an arrowhead is found near some pottery? The archaeologist figures that the same people who used the pottery also hunted. Seeds, bones, and shells that are found give clues as to what people ate.

Archaeologists use other methods to find out the exact age of an object. One such method is counting tree rings.

If you look at the cut surface of a sawed-off tree, you will see many rings. Each ring represents one year of that tree's growth. Scientists count and compare the rings on pieces of wood. By working backward from a known year, they have a kind of calendar of tree rings. An archaeologist who finds an ancient piece of wood can figure out from tree rings the year the tree was cut down. Using tree rings to date objects works quite well in the dry climate of the Southwest. There, tree rings have been used to date artifacts 2,000 years old.

Archaeologists also use a technique called **radiocarbon dating.** All plants, animals, and human beings on earth contain radiocarbon. When a living thing dies, the radiocarbon within it begins to disappear very slowly and regularly. By measuring the radiocarbon in an object, scientists can figure out its approximate age. Radiocarbon dating works best for objects between 500 and 50,000 years old.

Archaeologists are the great detectives of science. They work slowly and carefully, putting their clues together to solve each new puzzle. With each archaeological conclusion, we come nearer to understanding the mysteries of the past.

Reading Check

1. What were the natural features of the area where the Anasazi lived?
2. Why could the Hohokam grow food in the desert?
3. Name two methods archaeologists use to date objects.
4. What examples of cooperation can you find in the Anasazi and Hohokam cultures?

31

SKILLS FOR SUCCESS

USING TIMELINES TO UNDERSTAND DATES

Why is it important to understand dates? When you talk about your own life, it is easy to say that something happened 5 years ago. When you talk about events in history, it is different. Saying that something happened 183 years ago or 310 years ago is awkward. It is easier to talk about events if you can say that something happened in 1500 or 1860. Understanding dates helps you understand time.

An easy way to think about time is to look at a **timeline.** A timeline is a diagram that shows a certain period of time. It may look something like a ruler. Important events are marked on a timeline at the points when they happened. Look at timeline *A* below.

This timeline shows a **decade,** a period of ten years. The space between each pair of dates is a year. The timeline begins with 1960 and ends with 1970. As you can see, the earliest date is on the left of the timeline. The most recent date is on the right. The decade of 1960–1970 can also be called the 1960s.

Three important events in the history of space travel are shown on timeline *A*. The earliest event shown is the date that the first person was launched into space. This happened in April, 1961. The line for this event is just to the right of the mark that begins the year 1961. The next line shows the date the first spacecraft landed on the moon. This

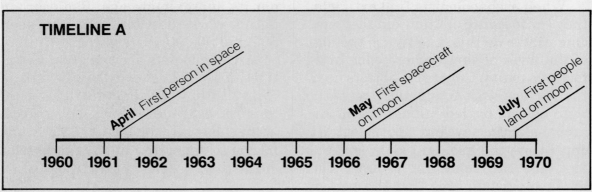

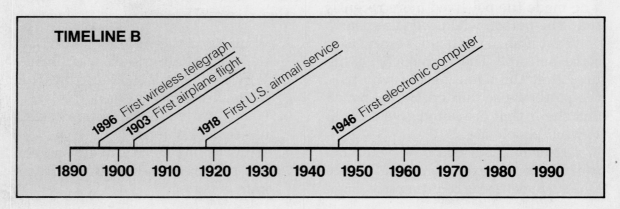

line is to the right of the mark that begins the year 1966. What is the most recent event shown on this timeline?

Timeline *A* shows a period of ten years. Imagine trying to use the same kind of timeline to show a period of 1,000 years. It would have to be 100 times longer than this timeline. How can one make a timeline covering many years without using a piece of paper several feet long?

One kind of timeline can show decades. Look at timeline *B*. It is read from left to right, just as timeline *A* was. On this timeline, only every tenth year is shown. The space between each pair of dates is a decade. Look at the first decade on the left. It begins with the year 1890. A line to the right of the the mark for the year 1890 shows the date of the first wireless telegraph. This line is a little more than halfway between the two marks. This line represents the year 1895. From left to right, read the dates and

descriptions of the events shown on the timeline. Which event is the earliest? Which is the most recent?

Another kind of timeline can show centuries. A **century** is a period of 100 years. Now look at timeline *C* below.

The earliest date shown on this timeline is 1500. The space between the first two dates covers a period of 100 years. The earliest event shown on this timeline is Ponce de León's landing in Florida in 1513. What is the next event? Read the timeline from left to right. What two events happened after the Civil War?

When we talk about modern times, we often refer to the time we live in as the *twentieth century*. Timeline *D* below shows how centuries are counted. The years between 1000 and 1100 are known as the *eleventh century*. The years between 1100 and 1200 are the *twelfth century*. What is the name of the century between 1800 and 1900?

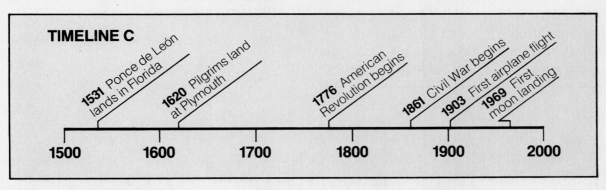

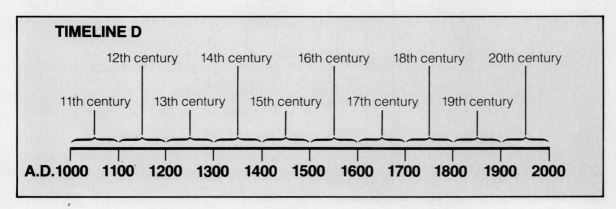

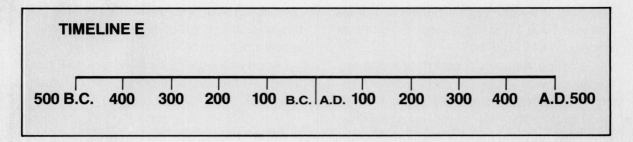

TIMELINE E

| 500 B.C. | 400 | 300 | 200 | 100 B.C. | A.D. 100 | 200 | 300 | 400 | A.D. 500 |

All of the dates you have been reading could be written with the letters A.D. before them. We measure years backward and forward from the birth of Jesus Christ. Years labeled A.D. come *after* the birth of Christ. The letters A.D. stand for *anno Domini,* Latin words meaning "in the year of the Lord."

Events that took place before the birth of Jesus Christ are always labeled B.C. This stands for "before Christ." A date followed by the letters B.C. tells how many years something happened before the birth of Christ. In other words, an event happening in 45 B.C. took place 45 years *before* the birth of Christ. Look at timeline *E* above.

Scientists tell us that the Hopewell culture existed from 200 B.C. to A.D. 500. How many centuries is that? How many years?

How many centuries are there between 300 B.C. and A.D. 200? If an event took place 2,500 years ago, did it happen before or after the birth of Christ?

Not all timelines are horizontal, or go across the page. Some timelines are vertical. Vertical timelines are read from top to bottom, with the earliest date at the top. Look at timeline F. What is the first event on this timeline? What is the most recent event?

CHECKING YOUR SKILLS

Answer the following questions. Use the information in this lesson to help you.

1. What is the definition of each of these words?
   timeline
   decade
   century
   A.D.
   B.C.

2. Find timeline C on page 33. This timeline shows the years from 1500 to 2000. How many years does the space between each pair of blocks stand for?

3. In what year did the Pilgrims land at Plymouth?

4. In what century did the Pilgrims land?

5. The first 100 years after the birth of Christ are called the first century A.D. What would the 100 years before the birth of Christ be called?

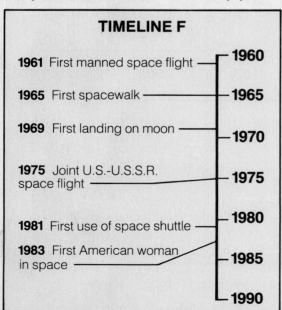

TIMELINE F

1961 First manned space flight — **1960**

1965 First spacewalk — **1965**

1969 First landing on moon — **1970**

1975 Joint U.S.-U.S.S.R. space flight — **1975**

1981 First use of space shuttle — **1980**

1983 First American woman in space — **1985**

1990

CHAPTER 1 REVIEW

WORDS TO USE

Write down the words below. Next to each word, write the correct definition from the list that follows.

1. **agriculture**
2. **archaeologist**
3. **archaeology**
4. **artifact**
5. **civilization**
6. **culture**
7. **flint**
8. **migration**
9. **specialize**
10. **surplus**

a. An amount more than what is needed

b. A kind of stone used by early hunters for spear points and knives

c. Farming

d. A way of life that has large cities, complex government, and highly developed arts and sciences

e. To spend most of one's time at one kind of job

f. The movement of people or animals from one place to another

g. The way of life shared by a group of people

h. An object used by people in the past

i. The scientific study of artifacts and remains

j. A scientist who studies objects to learn about the past

FACTS TO REVIEW

1. Why were people and animals able to roam from Asia to North America during the Ice Age?

2. What materials did early hunters use to make their tools?

3. How did farming make possible a settled life?

4. How do we know the Hopewell people were great traders?

5. What are the outstanding remains of Mississippian culture?

IDEAS TO DISCUSS

1. Imagine that you are with archaeologists who have just found two obsidian arrows and a carved, decorated clay pot. What do these objects tell you about the people who once used them?

2. Advanced Indian cultures depended on specialization. What kind of specialization is there in your community?

3. All human cultures depend on some kind of cooperation. What examples of this statement can you find in this chapter? How is cooperation important today?

○ SKILLS PRACTICE

Using Timelines to Understand Dates
Answer these questions.

1. Which came more recently? 400 B.C. or A.D. 200?

2. What is the name of the present decade? present century?

3. In what century was the year 1492?

4. In what century was the year 1805?

CHAPTER 2

Major Indian Groups

About this chapter

When the Europeans came to the Western Hemisphere, they found all kinds of Indians. The Indians did not all look alike. They lived in different kinds of dwellings. They had different languages and customs. Some were warlike. Some were peace-loving. Indians also differed from one another because they had different customs and beliefs.

The American Indians lived in many different kinds of **natural environments.** A natural environment is the natural world around you, including the land, water, climate, plants, and animals. The Indians made the best use they could of the plants, animals, and natural features of the places where they lived.

1. INDIANS OF NORTH AMERICA

To Guide Your Reading

Look for these important words:

Key Words
- natural environment
- shamans

Look for answers to these questions:

1. What did Indian groups have in common?
2. In what ways did Indians learn from each other?
3. How did life change for the Indians after the Europeans came?

American Indians all had a form of religion. Many thought of the earth as a mother and of the sky as a father. Indians claimed land for their use, but they did not believe any person could own a part of Mother Earth. Many believed that all the parts of nature had spirits. They believed in living in harmony with these spirits.

The Indian groups had **shamans** (SHAY•muhns). Shamans were both priests and healers. Shamans could answer questions about disease, about life and death, about right and wrong. Shamans tried to explain to people why things happened the way they did. Shamans knew the stories of how the world came to be. Because there were many different Indian groups, there were many different stories.

The Indians had ceremonies that included dancing and singing to drums. Sometimes dances were held for important religious reasons, such as to pray for rain or good crops. Sometimes they were held before or after a battle.

Indians who lived near water used various types of canoes. By canoeing and by walking, the Indians were able to trade with each other. Many of our roads today follow ancient Indian trails.

Warfare was common among many Indian groups. Some fought only to protect the land they used. Others fought to get personal glory, territory, slaves, and wealth. Such ways were not limited only to Indians. For thousands of years people in all parts of the world have lived in conflict.

Learning from Each Other

For hundreds of years the American Indians had been learning from each other. They learned how to grow corn, how to build mounds, how to make pottery, how to weave cloth.

When the Europeans came, the Indians continued to learn. They quickly learned to use whatever helped them. They welcomed iron tools and eagerly traded for iron knives, kettles, and axes. The sheep, goats, cattle, and horses brought by the Europeans became the basis of new Indian cultures.

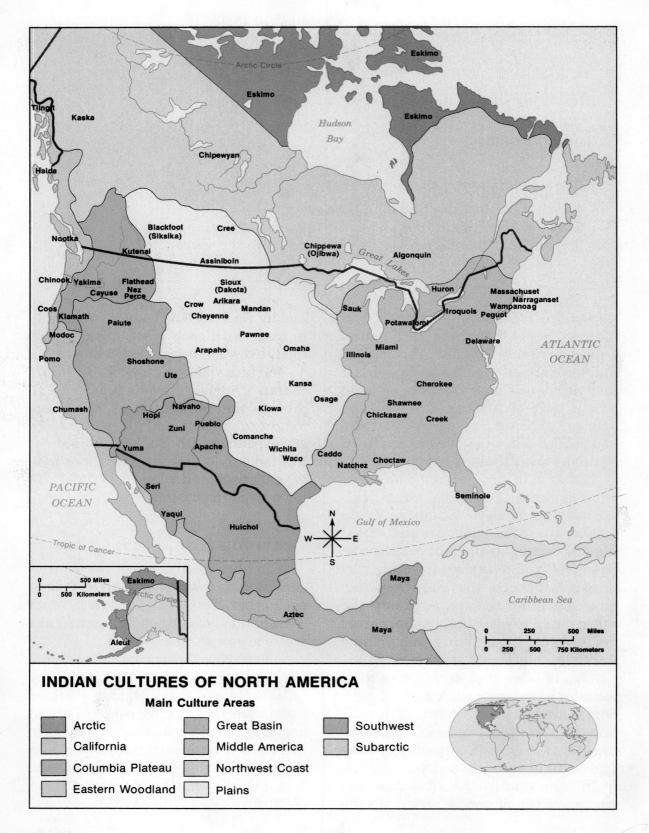

Tlingit
Kaska
Haida
Eskimo
Hudson Bay
Eskimo
Eskimo
Arctic Circle

Chipewyan

Nootka
Kutenai
Blackfoot (Siksika)
Cree
Assiniboin
Chippewa (Ojibwa)
Great Lakes
Algonquin

Chinook
Yakima
Cayuse
Flathead
Nez Perce
Sioux (Dakota)
Arikara
Crow
Cheyenne
Mandan
Sauk
Huron
Iroquois
Massachuset
Narraganset
Wampanoag
Peguot

Coos
Klamath
Modoc
Pomo
Paiute
Shoshone
Ute
Potawatomi
Miami
Illinois
Omaha
Pawnee
Delaware
ATLANTIC OCEAN

Chumash
Hopi
Navaho
Zuni
Pueblo
Apache
Kansa
Kiowa
Osage
Comanche
Wichita
Waco
Caddo
Natchez
Choctaw
Cherokee
Shawnee
Chickasaw
Creek

Yuma
Seri
Yaqui
Huichol
PACIFIC OCEAN
Tropic of Cancer
N
W E
S
Gulf of Mexico
Seminole

Eskimo
Arctic Circle
Aleut
0   500 Miles
0   500 Kilometers

Maya
Aztec
Maya
Caribbean Sea

0   250   500 Miles
0   250   500   750 Kilometers

INDIAN CULTURES OF NORTH AMERICA

Main Culture Areas

- Arctic
- California
- Columbia Plateau
- Eastern Woodland
- Great Basin
- Middle America
- Northwest Coast
- Plains
- Southwest
- Subarctic

Religion was important to all Indian cultures. Here, Iroquois dancers in the False-Face ceremony seek to cure a person suffering toothache.

Many Indian cultures did not survive the coming of the Europeans. One reason for this was that many Indians were forced to give up the land of their ancestors. This land was productive. Losing the land destroyed the foundation of many cultures. Another reason Indian cultures did not survive was disease. European diseases like measles, flu, and smallpox killed millions in North America.

With more advanced tools, the Europeans changed the land the Indians knew so well. The Indians could no longer live as their ancestors had. The history of American Indians for the last 300 years is a history of a people trying to keep their chosen ways. Many Indian cultures are now gone. Yet countless numbers of places—cities and towns, rivers and mountains—carry the names and memories of these first Americans.

Reading Check

1. What is a natural environment?
2. What is a shaman?
3. Name four ways in which the Indians learned from each other.
4. Why did many Indian cultures not survive the coming of Europeans?

39

SKILLS FOR SUCCESS

USING CULTURAL MAPS

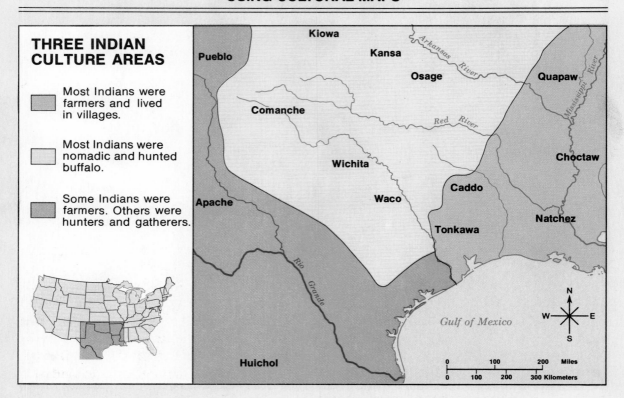

THREE INDIAN CULTURE AREAS

Most Indians were farmers and lived in villages.

Most Indians were nomadic and hunted buffalo.

Some Indians were farmers. Others were hunters and gatherers.

A cultural map shows the location of particular cultures. A culture is a group of people who share a similar way of life. On a cultural map, each culture is identified by a name placed in the center of its territory. Look at the cultural map below.

This map shows parts of Texas, New Mexico, and Oklahoma. On it are the names of the Indian groups who once lived there. Find the homelands of the Wichita group. Did the Kiowas live north or south of the Wichita?

A color key is used to show three regions on the map. Find the lands of the Waco Indians. As you can see, they are shaded green. The map key gives the meaning of green. It tells you that the Waco probably lived in forest villages as other Woodland Indians did.

CHECKING YOUR SKILLS

Use the cultural map above to answer these questions:

1. Did the Comanche Indians farm or hunt buffalo?

2. Would you expect to find buffalo hunters among the Hopis or among the Kiowas?

3. Does the map tell you whether or not the Apaches were farmers?

4. According to the map, were the Wichita Indians more like the Natchez Indians or more like the Comanches?

5. According to the map, how did Indians of the Southwest get their food? How does that compare to Indians of the Southeast?

40

2. WOODLAND INDIANS

To Guide Your Reading

Look for these important words:

Key Words
- palisade
- slash-and-burn
- extinct
- wigwams

- longhouses
- wampum
- league
- Six Nations
- Five Civilized Tribes

People
- Hiawatha

Look for answers to these questions:

1. How did the Woodland Indians use the forests around them?
2. How did the Woodland Indians clear land for farming?
3. What was life like in an Iroquois village?
4. What was life like among the Creek Indians?

When the first Europeans came to North America, they found the eastern part of the continent covered with vast forests. The Indians who lived in the forests of the Northeast and Southeast are called Woodland Indians.

The kinds of trees and shrubs varied from north to south, but everywhere they sheltered many kinds of animals. Swift deer, shy elk, and fat bears fed in the woods. In the streams and meadows were sleek beaver and muskrats. There were squirrels, opossums, and many birds, including wild turkeys.

The Woodland Indians made use of the trees for many things. They used trees and tree bark to make canoes and shelters. They used some trees for food. Nuts came from trees like the walnut and hickory. In the Northeast maple sugar was made from the sap of the maple tree.

The Woodland Indians were farmers, gatherers, and hunters. In the Northeast the Indians did more gathering and hunting than farming. In the Southeast the soil and climate were better for agriculture. There the Indians depended on farming for their food. In their fields, the Woodland Indians raised corn, beans, squash, and pumpkins.

Because they farmed, the Woodland Indians lived in villages. The villages of the Woodland Indians often included a community building for meetings and ceremonies. Surrounding each village was a wall made of sharpened tree trunks. Such a wall is a **palisade.** The fields lay outside the wall.

The Indians made clearings in the woods for their fields. They had no tools sharp or powerful enough to cut down trees. They killed a tree by cutting away a circle of bark in the fall. When spring came, the tree was dead, its leaves gone. The sun shone through the dead branches to the ground. Among the dead trees, the Indians planted crops.

After a year or two the Indians burned the dead trees. After several more years a field might be completely cleared. This method of agriculture is called **slash-and-burn.**

Some Indians used fish as a fertilizer. Others did not. Without fertilizer a field wore out in about ten years and no longer produced good crops. Then the village moved to a new location and started clearing new fields.

Although the Woodland Indians raised much of their food, they also gathered and hunted. They gathered nuts, berries, wild fruits, greens, and shellfish. They caught fish and hunted bear, beaver, porcupine, deer, and birds.

The most common food bird was the passenger pigeon, which traveled in flocks of hundreds of thousands. Sometimes so many flew overhead that the sky was dark for hours. At night they roosted in trees, weighing down the branches. There they were easy to catch and kill. Early white settlers also killed and ate great numbers of passenger pigeons. Today they are **extinct.** That means there is not one left.

Woodland Indians also hunted to get animal skins for clothing. Furry beaver and bear skins made warm robes, capes, and blankets. Scraped and tanned deerhide made soft buckskin for lighter clothes.

This scene shows daily life in an Algonquian village. At left, a woman prepares to skin a deer. What other activities do you see?

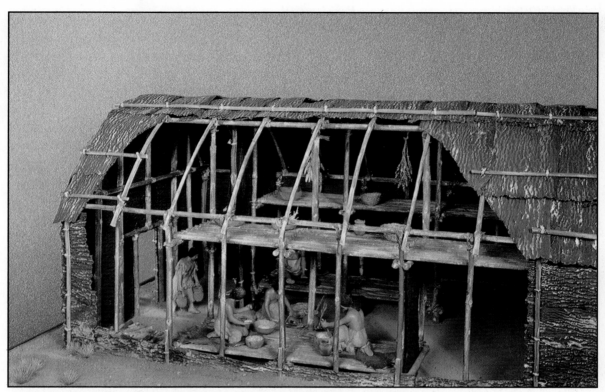

This cut-away model shows a cooking scene in an Iroquois longhouse.
Notice the high shelf for storage.

The Northeast Indians

The Woodland Indians of the Northeast included two main language groups, the Algonquian (al•GAHN•kwee•uhn) and the Iroquois (IR•uh•kwoy). The Algonquian lived along the Atlantic coast. In their villages they lived in round, bark-covered shelters called **wigwams.**

The Iroquois lived inland. Their dwellings are called **longhouses.** The Iroquois longhouses were made of poles covered with elm bark. Each longhouse had a hall down its middle with small, open rooms on each side. One family lived in each room. From eight to ten families lived in each longhouse. The families in each longhouse were related to the woman who was head of the longhouse.

Women were important in Iroquois culture. Women owned the longhouse, the farming tools, and the fields. Women did the farming. The women also decided which men would be chiefs.

Families cooked their meals on fires built in the main hall of the longhouse. On high shelves each family kept mats, baskets, buckets made of bark, pots, tobacco pipes, and wooden bowls. There might also be digging sticks for planting corn and snowshoes for getting around in the winter.

The shelves also held **wampum.** Wampum were beads made from porcupine quills or seashells. Wampum was woven into belts or strung into necklaces. The Iroquois used wampum to help them remember important events. They also used wampum as money.

This wampum belt was made in 1683 by Delaware Indians as a gift of peace.

The Iroquois were famous warriors. About 1570 the shaman **Hiawatha** (hy·uh·WAW·thuh) persuaded five of the Iroquois tribes to stop fighting each other and to unite in a **league.** A league is a union of people joined for a common purpose. By the middle of the 1600s the league used armies of 500 to 1,000 men to conquer its Indian neighbors. After a sixth group joined the league, it was called the **Six Nations.** The Iroquois became the most powerful of the Indian groups in the Northeast.

Indians of the Southeast

The Indian peoples of the Southeast also lived in farming villages. Their villages were scattered along the fertile coastal plain, in the foothills of the mountains, and along the rich valley of the Mississippi River.

The villages of the Southeastern Indians often contained as many as 100 dwellings built around a central square. The dwellings were made of a framework of poles and covered with grass or mud plaster. In the Deep South, where the weather was warm, dwellings were often roofed platforms. Wealthy families might have as many as four dwellings, to be used as storehouses, a summer house, and a winter house.

The Creek Indians of the Southeast divided their year into two seasons: winter and summer. The year started with the corn harvest in the month of Much Heat (August). The months that followed were Little Chestnut (September), Big Chestnut (October), Frost (November), Big Winter (December), and Little Winter (January). Their summer started with the month of Wind (February). The months after Wind were Little Spring (March), Big Spring (April), Mulberry (May), Blackberry (June), and Little Heat (July).

After the corn had been harvested in the fall, the Creek men went hunting. These hunting parties lasted as long as five and six months. The men returned in time to work the fields and plant the crops in the spring. Both men and women had to work in the fields. There were fines for those who tried to avoid work. The people worked and planted to songs in the morning. In the afternoons they played ball games. In the evenings they danced.

When summer came, war parties left to attack their enemies. The war parties often brought back captives. The captives became slaves, but children of slaves were born free.

This picture of the Algonquian village of Secoton, North Carolina, was painted about 1585. At the bottom right, Indians are performing a ceremonial dance. The three fields show newly sprouted corn, green corn, and ripe corn.

The Creek Indians in what are now Georgia and Alabama were organized into a league of towns. The towns were divided into red towns and white towns. The red towns supplied war leaders. The white towns were concerned with peaceful activities and supplied the principal chiefs.

After the arrival of white people, the Creeks, Choctaws (CHAHK•taws), Chickasaws, Cherokees, and Seminoles (SEM•uh•nohls) were called the **Five Civilized Tribes.** They quickly accepted parts of the culture of white settlers. Many raised animals, had large farms, and became Christians.

Reading Check

1. Name at least three ways in which the Woodland Indians used trees.
2. What is slash-and-burn agriculture?
3. What was wampum? Why was it important?
4. What did Creek men do during different seasons of the year?

45

3. INDIANS OF THE PLAINS

To Guide Your Reading

Look for these important words:

Key Words
- lodges
- sod
- nomads
- tepee
- travois

Look for answers to these questions:

1. In what ways did Indians of the Central Plains use their environment?
2. How did Indians live on the Great Plains?
3. Why was cooperation particularly important for the Great Plains Indians?

West of the great area of the woodlands were the grassy plains. Few trees grew there. In places, one could see for miles.

Among the Indians who lived on the tall-grass prairies of the Central Plains were the Sioux (SOO), the Mandans, the Pawnees, and the Wichitas. They were both farmers and hunters. They farmed the rich land in the river valleys. They hunted deer, elk, and buffalo.

In their villages these Indians lived in circular houses called **lodges.** Each lodge was built over a shallow pit. In the northern parts of the prairie, the lodges were covered with **sod.** Sod is the ground cover that includes both grass and grass roots. Such a house was warm and protected in the cold winters. In the southern parts of the prairie, the lodges were covered with grass, animal skins, or mats.

Some of the villages along the Missouri River often were trade centers for Indians from far places. Later they became centers for the trade between white people and Indians. The site of Pierre, South Dakota, for example, was capital of the Arikara (uh•RIK•uh•ruh) Indian nation for 400 years. It then became a fur-trading center for the French and Indians.

Indians of the Central Plains lived in lodges like the one in this picture. Here, women pound corn, weave, and tend to their children in front of the lodge.

Life for the Plains Indians depended on cooperation in hunting the buffalo. Here, Indians, disguising themselves in wolf skins, creep up on a herd of grazing buffalo.

The Plains Nomads

The people who lived on the Great Plains did not farm or live in villages. Here there were no rich river valleys. The roots of the short grass were very tough. It was impossible to dig the soil using a tool such as a digging stick.

Instead, the Indians on the Great Plains were hunters and **nomads.** Although nomads may have no fixed dwellings, they usually claim certain territory. The Indian nomads followed certain routes within this territory. Their route usually depended on the movement of the buffalo. Sometimes they sought ripening wild plums or berries.

Among the Plains nomads were people of the Kiowa, Comanche, Cheyenne, and Crow tribes. Their dwell-ings, their clothing, their food, even the fuel for their fires, came from the buffalo. For fuel the Plains nomads used dried buffalo droppings called chips.

The dwelling of the plains nomads was a **tepee.** It was made by lashing poles together to make a cone. Over the poles were hung skins that had been sewn together. Smoke from the buffalo-chip fire inside the tepee went out a smoke hole at the top. Blankets and robes of buffalo skins helped keep people warm inside the tepee.

Because Plains Indians could go miles and miles on the Plains without ever seeing a tree, they placed great value on wooden tepee poles. They transported the poles by turning them into a kind of carrier called a **travois** (truh•VOY). Two poles were fastened to

The buffalo provided food, clothing, and shelter for this Comanche village on the Great Plains. What activities are taking place here?

a harness on a dog. Belongings were hung between the poles. The ends of the pole dragged behind. Later the Indians used horses, which they called "big dogs," to do the same job.

For village dwellers, pottery was a big help for storing, cooking, and eating food. But pots break easily, and they can be heavy. For the nomads, pots were not a help. Instead, the nomadic Indians made containers of buffalo skins. They even cooked in skin pots.

In the nomadic way of life each person was an important part of the group. Everyone had to help, even babies. A crying baby might scare away buffalo or attract enemies. Mothers gently taught their babies not to cry.

A travois

Among the nomads, no person was born more important than anyone else. A man became a chief because he proved himself a good hunter and a good leader of people. He was a chief because his people chose him to be chief.

Anyone who did not follow the ways of the group was made to leave it. Sending a person out on the Plains alone was often a death sentence. Survival on the Plains depended on people working together.

Reading Check

1. Name the two ways the Central Plains Indians got their food.
2. What kind of person did the Plains nomads choose as chief?
3. Compare the Indian dwellings of the Central Plains with those of the Great Plains.
4. Why was it important that each member of a nomadic group cooperate?

4. HUNTERS AND GATHERERS

To Guide Your Reading

Look for these important words:

Key Words
- staple food
- assembly
- acorns

Places
- Great Basin
- Columbia Plateau

Look for answers to these questions:

1. Where is the Columbia Plateau? the Great Basin? California?
2. What did the Indians of these regions have in common?
3. What foods did different environments provide?

The Great Plains stop at the base of the Rocky Mountains. Indians rarely went into these high mountains, so the mountains were like a great fence between Indian groups.

In an area that stretched from the Rocky Mountains to the Pacific Ocean lived the Indians of California, of the Columbia Plateau, and of the Great Basin. They were all similar because their main foods came from gathering and hunting. They did not farm.

Indians of the Great Basin

The **Great Basin** lies between the Rocky Mountains and the Sierra Nevada Mountains. The valleys, mountains, and plateaus of the Great Basin receive little rainfall. This land can be beautiful, but harsh. The Indians of the Great Basin were the poorest Indians because the Great Basin is mostly desert. Animals and food plants are harder to find here than in other areas.

The Indians of the Great Basin included the Utes (YOOTS), the Shoshones (shu•SHOW•nees), and the Paiutes (PY•yoots). They lived in small family groups, moving often to look for food. In the summer they moved into the mountain valleys to get fruits and berries. In the fall they gathered nuts from the pine cones of the pinyon trees. They hunted rabbit and occasionally deer and antelope. They wore few clothes but used blankets made of rabbit skins to keep warm in winter. Their dwellings were huts made of brush. The women made fine baskets for gathering, storing, and cooking food.

The people of the Great Basin ate whatever they could catch. Besides rabbits, birds, and antelopes, they ate grasshoppers, prairie dogs, lizards, snakes, and mice.

Indians of the Plateau

The **Columbia Plateau** is east of the Cascade Mountains. It is a region of forests and many rivers. Indians there also lived by gathering, but they had a richer life than those of the Great Basin. Streams and rivers of the region were full of salmon and other fish. Salmon was their **staple food.** A staple food is the food that people depend on most for nourishment.

The Indians of the Plateau included the Nez Perce (nez•PUHRS), the Klamath, the Yakima (YAK•uh•mah), and the Flathead Indians. They lived in villages. Each village had a chief and an **assembly,** a lawmaking body. Any citizen, man or woman, could speak or vote in the assembly. Like the Plains Indians, the Indians of the Columbia Plateau chose leaders whom they respected. Both men and women served as chiefs and shamans.

California Indians

The Indians of California lived on the land between the Pacific Ocean and the Sierra Nevada. This land of broad river valleys and rolling hills was covered with grass and oak trees.

In this gentle land lived a patchwork of people speaking more than 100 different languages. All these people depended on gathering and hunting for their food.

The staple food of the California Indians was **acorns,** the nuts from oak trees. Oak trees were so plentiful that the Indians did not have to worry about what they would eat. In the fall they had only to gather enough acorns to get them through the year. The acorns were ground and soaked in water to get rid of bitterness. Then the mixture was turned into mush by cooking it in a basket with red-hot stones.

A Karok woman of California cooks acorn mush in a woven basket.

To their acorn diet the California Indians added all kinds of berries, greens, and roots. Those who lived close to the seashore gathered shellfish. In the fall the Indians hunted deer, elk, antelope, ducks, and geese.

Reading Check

1. How did the Indians of California, the Columbia Plateau, and the Great Basin get their food?
2. What kinds of foods did Indians of the Great Basin eat?
3. What was the staple food of the Indians of the Columbia Plateau? of the California Indians?
4. Why were the California Indians better off than Indians of the Great Basin?

50

5. THE SOUTHWEST AND NORTHWEST

To Guide Your Reading

Look for these important words:

Key Words
- springs
- hogans
- totems

- potlatches
- kayaks
- igloo

Places
- Arctic Plains

Look for answers to these questions:

1. How did the Indians in the Southwest make use of their natural environment?
2. In what ways did the Northwest Coast Indians use the resources of their environment?
3. What tools did the Eskimos develop to survive in the Far North?

The Southwest is a land of mountains and deserts, of high plateaus and deep canyons. The skies are usually sunny. There is little rainfall. Indian farmers of the Southwest learned long ago to make the desert bloom by using water.

Some used irrigation to get water from the rivers to their crops. Others built their villages near **springs.** Springs are places where underground water breaks through the earth's surface.

Indians of the Southwest who lived in villages and farmed were called Pueblo Indians. Pueblo is the Spanish word for *village*. The staple foods of these Indians were corn, beans, and squash. They raised turkeys for their feathers. They wove the feathers to make warm robes.

The men did the farming and wove cotton cloth. The women made pottery and wove baskets. Like the Iroquois, the women of many Pueblo groups owned the houses.

The Pueblo Indians believed in being peaceful. They fought only to protect themselves. One of the Pueblo groups is the Hopi (HOH•pee). In their language *Hopi* means "the peaceful."

Other Indian groups in the Southwest farmed but did not depend on their crops the way the Pueblo Indians did. These Indians also hunted and gathered. They included the Apaches and the Navajos.

The Navajos did not live in villages like the Pueblo Indians. Instead families lived in scattered dwellings called **hogans.** A hogan is a round or a six-sided dwelling made of logs and dried mud. A family might have several hogans to use during the year.

Sheep, which were brought by the first Europeans, became an important part of Navajo life. Navajos became known as good herders and weavers.

51

Indians of the Northwest

The coastal area between the Pacific Ocean and the Cascade Range was home to many Indian groups. The rainfall is heavy on the ocean coast. Great cedars grow in the forests. These trees grow so tall that they can block sunlight from the forest floor.

Like their neighbors on the Columbia Plateau, the Indians of the Northwest Coast depended on fish as a staple food. Salmon, halibut, cod, and shellfish were all abundant in the coastal waters. Some groups even went far out in the ocean to hunt whales.

The Northwest Coast Indians had leisure time, too. They developed crafts and arts. They were excellent wood-workers. In addition to making huge canoes of wood, they also made carved bowls and masks.

The Indians of the Northwest Coast believed in animal spirits called **totems.** They asked such totems as the eagle, beaver, raven, bear, and whale for protection. The masks they made for their religious ceremonies were made to look like these totems.

Family groups identified themselves with particular totems. A person could have many totems in his or her family history. To show family history, the Northwest Coast Indians carved totem poles. These were placed in front of their homes or in their burial places.

The Northwest Indians also made blankets of cedar bark and the hair of mountain goats. Their clothing was made of shredded cedar bark. In the winter they used furs and hides as robes.

The chiefs were wealthy people. Wealth was measured by the number of slaves and the number of things a person had. The wealthy people were expected to have great feasts to which many people came. These feasts were called **potlatches.** At a potlatch the host not only fed people but also gave them presents. Sometimes he gave away all his wealth. That made him even more respected.

Cedar trees tower behind this lodge and totem pole of Northwest Coast Indians.

Eskimos of the Far North

In the Far North, including Alaska, lived the Eskimos. Their ancestors probably crossed in boats from Asia about 4,000 years ago. The Eskimo culture replaced earlier cultures in the Far North. By 1,000 years ago, the

The Eskimos learned to live in a land of ice and snow. A thick fur coat and mittens keep this Eskimo warm as he builds an igloo of snow blocks.

Eskimo culture ranged across the Far North from Alaska to Greenland.

Life is difficult in the Far North. In winter there is no sun for several months. When there is sun, the sun's reflection off the ice can cause blindness. In winter, temperatures can go as low as −60°F (−51°C).

Much of the land is bare. Where there is soil, grass, flowers, and bushes grow. There are almost no trees. These parts of the Far North are called the **Arctic Plains.**

The Eskimos developed tools to live in this harsh climate. Those who lived near the ocean fished and hunted seals, walruses, and whales. To do so, they made strong fish hooks and harpoons. Those who lived inland hunted game animals with spears. For their clothing Eskimos used animal skins. Such skins could keep them warm in the coldest weather. Even their canoes, called **kayaks,** were covered with skin.

For their dwellings they used skins, stone, sod, or even chunks of snow. A house made of snow blocks is called an **igloo.**

To journey on the ice and snow, the Eskimos invented a dog-drawn sled. To protect their eyes from the sun, they invented goggles. Their goggles had tiny slits to see through. To get light in the dark winter, they burned fish oil in lamps. Like other early Americans, the Eskimos developed ways to live in their environment.

Reading Check

1. What group of Southwest Indians lived in villages? in hogans?
2. Name at least three ways in which the Northwest Indians used wood.
3. Why did Indians of the Northwest make totem poles?
4. What was the natural environment of the Eskimos?

SKILLS FOR SUCCESS

USING THE LIBRARY TO WRITE A REPORT

Suppose you want to find out more about American Indians and write a report on what you learn. Where do you start? A good place is the library.

Libraries have three main sections: those for fiction, nonfiction, and reference books.

Fiction books tell stories. Sometimes the stories are based on real events. Sometimes they are about imaginary people or events. Many people enjoy reading fiction. For information about a subject, however, nonfiction and reference books are best.

Nonfiction books give facts about real people and real things. All nonfiction books are organized on shelves by subject. Each subject has its own call number.

Reference books are collections of facts. A reference book has an *R* (for "reference") and a call number on its spine. Reference books are for use in the library. They may not be taken home.

Using the Card Catalog

To find a nonfiction book in the library, you have to know its **call number.** Call numbers and other information about books can be found in the card catalog. The card catalog lists every book in the library by **title,** by **author,** and by **subject.** Each card carries the call number of the book it lists. Look at the title card below.

Title Card

	Indians.
j970.1 T	**Tunis, Edwin.** Written and illustrated by Edwin Tunis. Revised edition. New York: Crowell, 1979. 157 p. illus.

The title card lists the call number in the upper left-hand corner. The first line lists the title. Look at an author card below. How does it differ from the title card?

Author Card

	Tunis, Edwin
j970.1 T	Indians. Written and illustrated by Edwin Tunis. Revised edition. New York: Crowell, 1979. 157 p. illus.

Below is a subject card. Notice that the subject is listed before the author or title.

Subject Card

	INDIANS OF NORTH AMERICA
j970.1 T	**Tunis, Edwin** Indians. Written and illustrated by Edwin Tunis. Revised edition. New York: Crowell, 1979. 157 p. illus.

Using Reference Books

To get information about a subject, you may need to use reference books. One of the most commonly used reference books is an **encyclopedia.** An encyclopedia has articles on a great many subjects. The articles in an encyclopedia are called **entries.** They are arranged alphabetically. Most encyclopedias consist of many books, or volumes.

To find out about American Indians in the encyclopedia, first use the **index.** The index is usually in the last volume of the encyclopedia.

Look at the index below. The main article about American Indians is in the I-J volume. The article begins on page 163. But there are also many other articles about American Indians in the encyclopedia. For example, there is an article about Indian foods beginning on page 337 of the E-F volume. Where in the encyclopedia can you look to find out about Indian masks? Will you find a picture or a map with this article?

Other useful reference materials are atlases, almanacs, magazines, and dictionaries.

An **atlas** is a book that contains many maps. There are different kinds of atlases. If you want to find information on a map, ask the librarian to help you find the right kind of atlas.

Almanacs are collections of facts, records, and general information. An almanac is an excellent source for information about the most recent years.

Magazine articles can be useful sources of information. Most libraries have an index listing magazine articles by subject. A librarian can help you find magazine articles or show you how to use the index.

A **dictionary** contains words listed in alphabetical order. Dictionaries explain the meanings and show the pronunciations of words. A dictionary is a good place to check on the spelling of a word.

Beginning a Report

You know that you can find information in nonfiction books and reference materials. Now think about what you have to do to write a report. First you want to find information on your subject. If your subject is American Indians, start by looking through books on the subject. Look at the pictures. Look at the tables of contents. Read what interests you. You will be learning about the subject while also finding out what information is available.

Now you must limit your subject. You cannot give every bit of available information about American Indians in one short report. One of your choices is to write a report about some part of Indian life. You could write about dwellings, food, clothing, or art. Another choice is to write about just one group of American Indians. You could write about the Anasazi or the Sioux or the Iroquois. If you find you still have too much information, limit your subject even more. Instead of writing about the Iroquois, you might choose to write just about longhouses.

Look through the books or articles to find information on your subject. Use the table of contents and the index to help you quickly find what you need.

As you read, make notes on index cards or pieces of paper. Use a different card or piece of paper for each **source.** A source is the author, the name of the book, and the page. Write your source in the upper right-hand corner of the card or paper.

If you copy down the exact words of your source, be sure to use quotation marks. If you use the quotation in your paper, be sure to tell the source.

Organizing Your Report

After you have found all your information, you will have to organize your report. The easiest way to do this is by putting your notes in order. Make a separate pile of note cards for each topic. Then decide which topic to write about first, which to write about next, and so on.

When you have notes that do not seem to fit, set them aside. You may end up using them, or you may throw them out. You do not have to use all the information you have gathered.

Writing the First Draft

The **first draft** is your first try at writing the report. As you write your first draft, write quickly. Do not worry about perfect spelling or penmanship yet. It is important to get your ideas down on paper before you forget them.

A report usually has three parts: an **introduction,** a **body,** and a **conclusion.** The first part is the introduction, or opening paragraph. This tells the reader what to expect in the report. When you write your introduction, keep it very simple. Write one or two sentences that tell what your report is about.

The body is the main part of the report. It gives the information you have gathered about the subject. The paragraphs in the body should follow the order in which you have organized your notes.

How do you write a paragraph for your report? Pick up your first pile of notes. Make sure they are all about the same topic. Begin each paragraph with a sentence that explains why the topic is important. This sentence is the topic sentence of the paragraph.

Write the rest of your report in the same way. Begin each paragraph with a topic sentence.

The third part of a report is the conclusion, or closing paragraph. It reminds the reader of what you have said in your report. It tells again why the subject you wrote about is important.

After you have finished your first draft, read it aloud to yourself. As you read, circle the words whose spelling you want to check. Underline any sentences that do not make very good sense. Then make your corrections on this first draft.

Next, share the first draft with another person. Ask if any part of the report is not clear. Use that person's suggestions to improve your paper.

Finishing the Report

Now copy the report over carefully, with all of the corrections and changes you have made.

The last thing to add is a **bibliography.** This is a list, in alphabetical order, of the sources of information you have used. List books by the author's last name. List encyclopedias by title and give the name of the article and volume.

CHECKING YOUR SKILLS

Answer the following questions.

1. What are the best kinds of books to use for finding information?

2. Where can you find the call number of a book titled *The Art of the Woodland Indians?*

3. Why is it important to limit your subject?

4. What is a way to organize notes before writing a report?

5. What are the three parts of a report?

6. What is a bibliography?

CLOSE-UP

AMERICAN INDIANS TODAY

Today more than one million Indians live in the United States. Another five million Americans may have Indian ancestors. Indians have made their mark on every part of American life and culture.

Many Indians live on special Indian lands that are called **reservations.** Some of these reservations are small. Some, like the Navajo reservation in Arizona, are quite large. The Navajo reservation is as big as the state of West Virginia.

Wherever they live in our country, most American Indians find themselves members of two cultures. They have ties to their Indian heritage. At the same time they are living and working in the society of modern America. For many Indians it has not been easy to be part of two worlds.

In the following pages, you will meet five modern-day American Indians. All five have a deep sense of the culture, history, and traditions of their ancestors. Each carries the strength of an Indian heritage to an occupation in the modern world.

Dan Namingha—Artist

The Hopi and Tewa Indians of the Southwest have long made some of the world's most beautiful pottery. Dan Namingha's family has been a part of this tradition. His great-great grandmother, Nampeyo (nam•PAY•yoh), was one of the greatest Hopi potters. His mother and grandmother are also well-known for their pottery.

When Dan Namingha was a child, he began to draw the graceful designs he saw on the pots around his home.

Dan Namingha works on one of his paintings.

57

His second-grade teacher noticed these drawings and knew that he had talent. Every day for five years she gave him art lessons.

These lessons paid off. When Dan Namingha was 16, he earned a scholarship to study art at the University of Kansas. He later studied art in both Santa Fe, New Mexico, and Chicago, Illinois. Today Dan Namingha is a successful artist. His paintings and sculpture have won many prizes.

Dan Namingha uses strong colors to show his feelings about the Hopi and the Southwest. Sometimes he paints from memories of stories his grandmother used to tell. He also tries to picture scenes from his childhood. "A lot of my paintings are of a feeling I had at the moment I saw something," Mr. Namingha says.

Dan Namingha now lives with his wife and two sons on a Tewa reservation in New Mexico. He works in a studio that he built with his own hands. There he draws from the past to communicate to the present.

Hoksina Wayagobi checks the cattle on his ranch.

Hoksina Wayagobi—Rancher

Some years ago Joe Day lost control of his car on an icy Montana road. The car flipped into a snowbank. Badly injured, Joe Day lay for several hours waiting for help. As he lay there, Joe Day thought about his life and how close he had come to death. He decided he wanted very much to be alive, to make more out of life. He knew he needed to get closer to his Indian heritage. He was part Sioux and part Assiniboine (uh•SIN•uh•boyn).

Joe Day recovered from that terrible accident. Today he goes by his Indian name, Hoksina Wayagobi (HOK•shi•nah wa•YAH•guh•bee). He owns his own cattle ranch, the 5,000-acre (2,023.5-ha) Thunderbird Ranch in eastern Montana. "I came out of that experience a different man," he says. "I guess before I didn't know the meaning of Indian self-respect, not really."

Now Hoksina Wayagobi is an active supporter of Indian rights in Montana. He and Emily, his wife, are active in tribal affairs at the Fort Peck Indian Reservation.

Running a cattle ranch is hard work. Hoksina Waya-gobi makes the Thunderbird Ranch successful with constant attention to the land. He makes sure that he never has too many cattle grazing. Too many cattle would ruin the grassland. He checks his fences and water systems almost every day. Like his ancestors, Hoksina Wayagobi cares about the land. "If we take care of the earth," he says, "the earth will take care of us."

Adele Little Dog—School Principal

Tucked away on the Standing Rock Sioux Reservation in South Dakota is the small town of Little Eagle. There is an elementary school in Little Eagle. The principal of this school is Adele Little Dog, a Sioux Indian.

A few years ago Adele Little Dog was worried about the education the children of Little Eagle were receiving. She knew that there were problems with Indian education all over America. Only 1 of 100 Indian children had Indian teachers. Indians were dropping out of school twice as often as other youths. Indian children were not learning how to read and write.

These days Adele Little Dog is much more hopeful about the future. A 1972 law, the Indian Education Act, provides money to train Indians as teachers. It also provides money to help Indian schools pay for field trips, hire tutors, and perform other activities.

When Mrs. Little Dog's son Dana was 10 years old, he had no Indian teachers. By the time Dana entered high school, the situation was quite different. "Now our people are trained as certified teachers," says Mrs. Little Dog. "We have Sioux teachers who understand our children." She hopes that, as a result, the children will do better in school.

Adele Little Dog knows how important education is to the well-being of American Indians. She feels that the millions of dollars being spent on Indian education will also be of great benefit to all Americans. "We are spending money," she says, "on our future, and I can't think of a better way to spend it."

Adele Little Dog helps a Sioux student with his work.

59

George Horse Capture works to further understanding of Plains Indian culture.

George Horse Capture—Museum Curator

In Cody, Wyoming, the Buffalo Bill Historical Center focuses on Western life and history. One of the museums in the Center tells about Plains Indians. The curator, or person in charge, of the museum is George P. Horse Capture, a member of the Gros Ventre (GROH VAHN•truh) tribe.

The Plains Indian Museum tells the story of the great buffalo-hunting tribes. Inside you can see war bonnets, shields, painted buffalo skulls, blankets, and necklaces made of grizzly bear claws.

The tepee room has a 50-foot-high ceiling. The beautifully decorated tepees seem to reach up to the heavens. One of the tepees has a special blue and white design. The maker of the tepee was told in a dream that the special design would bring him luck in buffalo hunts.

Mr. Horse Capture and other Indians helped design the museum building. The entrance faces east, toward the rising sun, just as the Indians placed their lodges. The building is shaped like a circle. "Nature is round," explains George Horse Capture. "The world, the seasons, even the ages of man from childhood to childhood, are round."

George Horse Capture has worked to build a place where people can learn about the culture of Plains Indians, past and present. Among those who come are busloads of Indian children. "It is a time of wonderment and appreciation when they come," Mr. Horse Capture says.

Ella Ground—Teacher

American Indian languages have given much to our culture. Of our 50 states, 25 take their names from Indian words. The many Indian words now used in English include *raccoon, moose, squash,* and *moccasin.*

Today, many of the Indian languages are dying out because Indian children are not learning to speak them. This worries many Indian leaders. They fear that the loss of Indian languages will mean the loss of Indian cultures.

In Buffalo, New York, many Mohawk and Seneca children attend the Native American School, No. 19. This is a public school. The school staff wanted these children to stay in touch with the culture and language of their heritage. They asked Ella Ground, then 72 years old, to teach the Seneca children. Mrs. Ground is a Seneca and the clan mother of the Hawk Clan.

At first Mrs. Ground tried to turn the job down. Most people her age are retired. She had never taught before. She only knew how to speak the Seneca tongue, not how to read or write it. She was shy and did not want to be in front of people. But Ella Ground knew that the Seneca language *was* in danger of dying out. At last she agreed to try teaching one day a week.

In 1976 Ella Ground started teaching at the Native American School. Soon she was teaching as many as ten classes a day! Her students learn by speaking the Seneca language. The Seneca language is part of the Iroquois language group. "What is—deer?" she says to the class. A sixth-grade Seneca girl responds with the correct answer: "Neoge (nee•UH•geh)."

Thanks to Ella Ground, dozens of young Seneca Indians are keeping the flame of their language and culture alive. "I want to see the children learn," says Ella Ground. "That's what keeps me going."

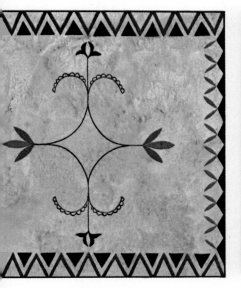

Ella Ground teaches the Seneca language to students in Buffalo, New York.

CHAPTER 2 REVIEW

WORDS TO USE

Explain the meaning of each term below. Then use each term in a complete sentence.

1. **extinct**
2. **league**
3. **natural environment**
4. **nomads**
5. **palisades**
6. **shaman**
7. **sod**
8. **staple food**
9. **totems**
10. **wampum**

FACTS TO REVIEW

1. How did the Woodland Indians clear fields for their crops?

2. In what important way were the Iroquois and Algonquian alike? Name two ways in which they were different.

3. Why is Hiawatha remembered as an important person?

4. Who were the "Civilized Tribes"? Why were they called that?

5. Describe two main groups of Plains Indians.

6. Describe the staple foods of Indians of the Columbia Plateau and California. What did the Great Basin Indians eat?

7. In what ways were the Navajos and the Hopis different?

8. How did the Northwest Coast Indians use their environment?

9. How did Eskimos meet their needs for clothing, transportation, and housing?

10. Which group of Indians used kayaks? travois? wampum?

IDEAS TO DISCUSS

1. Indian ways were often a result of different natural environments. Choose two Indian groups from different natural environments. Compare and contrast how each group made use of its natural environment.

2. In what way was the life of a nomad different from the life of a person who lived in a village? What were some of the advantages and disadvantages of nomadic life? Which kind of life would you prefer?

3. What are some examples of cooperation among Indian groups? Why is cooperation important to any group? What are examples of cooperation in your life?

4. People everywhere express their ideas and beliefs in art. Look at the pictures of Indian art in this unit. Which art do you like best? Why?

◯ SKILLS PRACTICE

Using Cultural Maps Use the map on page 38 to answer the following questions.

1. How did the Kansa Indians get their food?

2. Is it likely the Natchez Indians were farmers? Why?

3. Were the Caddo Indians or Choctaw Indians more likely to see buffalo? Why?

4. Name the Indian tribe south of the Rio Grande.

5. Did the Comanches hunt buffalo?

UNIT 1 REVIEW

WORDS TO REMEMBER

Number your paper from 1 to 10. Use the terms below to complete the sentences that follow. Write the correct term next to each number.

agriculture
archaeologists
cultures
league
migration

natural environments
nomads
shamans
specialize
staple food

1. There was a _____ of both animals and people across the land bridge.

2. Experimenting with seeds led to the development of _____.

3. A surplus of food makes it possible for people to _____.

4. Scientists who study objects to learn about the past are _____.

5. The Indians of North America lived in many different _____.

6. Indian leaders who acted as priests and healers are called _____.

7. Many Indian _____ did not survive the coming of the Europeans.

8. The Iroquois formed a _____ of Indians called the Six Nations.

9. Plains Indians who depended on the buffalo for food, shelter, and clothing were _____.

10. Fish was a _____ for Indian groups that lived close to rivers and streams.

FOCUS ON MAIN IDEAS

1. What route did the first Americans follow from Asia to America?

2. Name at least four food plants the American Indians developed.

3. Describe how agriculture makes settled life possible.

4. How do we know about ancient Indian cultures?

5. Describe at least three ways in which the Woodland Indians made use of their environment.

6. What was the difference between the nomads of the Great Plains and the hunting-and-gathering Indians of the Great Basin?

7. Identify the staple foods of:

   a. the Indians of the Southwest
   b. the Indians of California
   c. the Indians of the Columbia Plateau
   d. the Indians of the Northwest Coast
   e. the Eskimos

8. Why was the shaman important in Indian cultures?

9. Describe the natural environment of the people who lived in:

   a. an igloo
   b. a skin tepee
   c. a longhouse
   d. a round lodge
   e. a brush hut
   f. a pueblo

10. Explain the purpose of each of these things: wampum, palisade, travois, totem pole, kayak.

ACTIVITIES

1. **Research/Writing** Choose one North American Indian group that interests you. Go to your school or public library to find information. Write a report describing where the group lived, its food, its dwellings, and its crafts.

2. **Research/Art** Find out more about the arts and crafts of the American Indians. Make some examples of Indian arts or crafts. Share them with the class.

3. **Reading** Read legends or stories as told by an American Indian group. Retell one of the stories in your own words.

4. **Acting Out** Together with some fellow students, select an Indian story or legend. Act out the legend for the class.

5. **Acting** With several fellow students, each pretend you belong to a different Indian group. You all meet at a trading village and exchange information about how each of you lives. Discuss your dwellings, your food, your clothing, your natural environment, and your arts and crafts.

6. **Art** On pages 39 and 43 are pictures of dioramas. A diorama shows a real-life scene by using objects and figures. Choose an Indian group you have studied and make a small diorama showing a scene of life for that group.

◯ SKILLS REVIEW

1. Using the Library to Write a Report

Read each statement below. On a piece of paper write whether it is true or false. If it is false, re-write to make the statement true.

a. Books that give facts and information are fiction books

b. An encyclopedia has articles on many subjects.

c. The best place to find the call number of a book is the card catalog.

d. You should limit your topic after you have written the first draft.

e. When you read, you should take notes on cards or pieces of paper.

f. It is important to write down the author or title of a book you use.

g. You should organize your notes before you begin to write your report.

h. Most reports have two parts: an introduction and a body.

i. You should show your first draft to another person for suggestions to improve it.

j. The last thing you add to your report is a bibliography.

2. Using a Timeline
Look at the timeline below to answer the following questions.

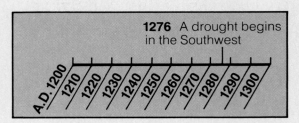

a. What is the number of years between A.D. 1200 and A.D. 1300 called?

b. What is the name for the number of years between 1240 and 1250?

c. What letters are used to show that a date occurred after the birth of Christ?

d. In what decade did a drought begin in the Southwest?

e. What is the name of the century starting in A.D. 1200?

YOUR STATE'S HISTORY

Important events have happened in your state, maybe even in your home town. The Your State's History activities in each unit review will help you discover the history of your home state while you learn the history of your country. You may want to use a special notebook for the activities of this section. You can find information for many of these activities in books about your state.

There were many American Indian cultures in what is now the United States. These cultures differed from each other in their foods. They differed in the materials they used for clothing, tools, and dwellings. They differed in their language and arts.

The following activities can help you learn about Indian cultures in your state.

LEARNING ABOUT INDIAN CULTURE

1. Find out which Indian groups lived in your state before Europeans came to America. Write the names of the groups in your notebook. In the library learn more about one of these groups. In your notebook write about how that group lived.

2. Make an Indian culture map of your state. Show where different cultures lived. Show whether they were primarily nomads, hunters and gatherers, or farmers living in villages.

3. Indians used wild plants and animals for food, clothing, and medicine. Find out how Indians from your state used wild plants and animals. If possible, bring to class some of the wild plants and explain how the Indians used them.

4. Many city and state museums have exhibits about Indian life as it was. Is there such a museum in your area? Where is it? Visit the museum and then report on what you learned.

5. In the picture below a Hopi woman weaves a basket as her ancestors did. What arts and crafts did Indians in your state do? Learn about one of these arts or crafts. Share what you learned with the class.

LEARNING ABOUT GEOGRAPHY

6. Many places in the United States have Indian names. Make a list of the places in your state that have Indian names. Can you find out what any of the names mean?

LONGE · ISLELAND ·

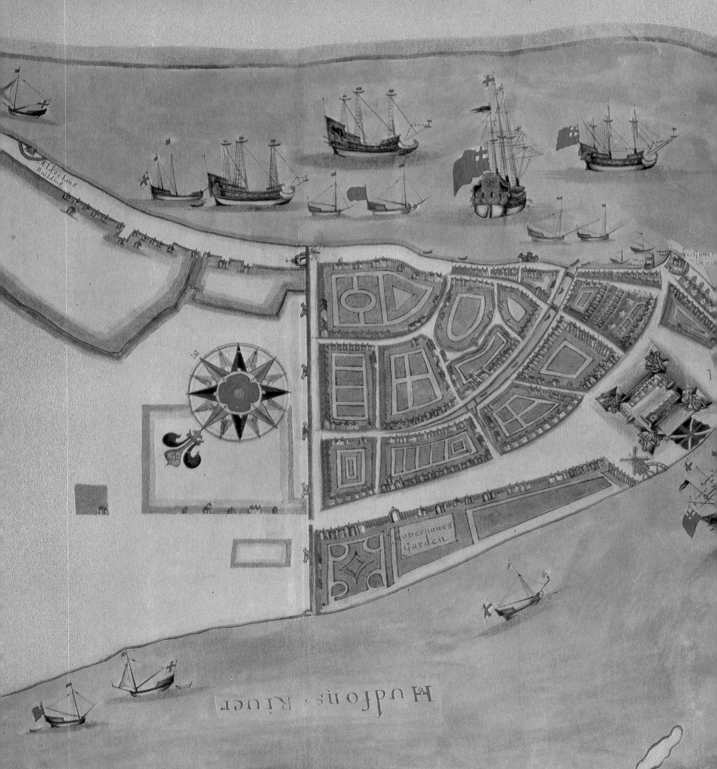

Governours Garden

Hudsons River

UNIT TWO

DISCOVERY, EXPLORATION, AND SETTLEMENT

The armor of a Spanish soldier shines in the sun. French fur traders glide down a river in a birchbark canoe. English families arrive on the *Mayflower*. The Dutch build windmills on Manhattan Island. These were the signs of the beginning of European settlement in North America. The Spanish, the French, the English and the Dutch were not the first Europeans to come to North America. However, they were the ones who changed the course of its history.

The first Europeans who came were looking either for wealth or for a passageway to Asia. Then came explorers who were interested in learning what the land and people were like. Last came the settlers, people who planned to make their homes in the newly found lands. The first settlements were small and usually built near a harbor. You can see this in the early map of the settlement that became New York City.

In this unit you will learn about how Europeans explored and then settled in North America.

Key Dates and Events

About 1,000 years ago
Leif Ericson sails to North America

1492
Christopher Columbus reaches America

1519
Ferdinand Magellan voyages around the world

Hernando Cortés invades Mexico

1534
Jacques Cartier makes first voyage to Canada

1540–1542
Coronado explores the American Southwest

1541
Hernando de Soto finds the Mississippi River

1585
The English settle at Roanoke

1607
The English settle at Jamestown

1609
Henry Hudson explores the Hudson River

1620
The Pilgrims land at Plymouth

1630
The Puritans found Boston

CHAPTER 3

Europeans Come to America

The telling of history depends on written records. Scientists can learn much by studying the remains of the past, but history begins with the written record. This chapter begins with the voyage to North America by Leif (LAYF) Ericson. We do not know for certain that he was the first European to come to North America. There may have been many others. However, we begin with Leif Ericson because his story was written down.

Almost 500 years passed between Leif Ericson's voyage to America and the voyage of Christopher Columbus. Columbus's voyage of discovery was an amazing journey—the result of his skills, knowledge, and imagination. Columbus opened the way for still other European explorers.

1. LEIF ERICSON SAILS TO VINLAND

To Guide Your Reading

Look for these important words:

Key Words
- Vikings
- navigators
- sagas

People
- Leif Ericson

Places
- Iceland
- Greenland
- Vinland
- Newfoundland

Look for answers to these questions:

1. Who were the Vikings?
2. Who was Leif Ericson?
3. Where was Vinland?
4. How do we know about Leif Ericson?

The European discovery of North America started with a storm and a story.

One summer about a thousand years ago a young man named Bjarni Herjulfsson (BYAHR•nee HER•yahlf•suhn) was sailing from a port in **Iceland** to **Greenland.** He was captain of a cargo boat. On his voyage a terrible Arctic storm arose. Strong winds and high waves tossed the boat about for days.

When the storm was over, Bjarni could see a low, flat land covered with trees. This was the Atlantic coast of North America. His sailors wanted to stop and explore, but Bjarni was stubborn. He had been told that Greenland had glaciers. This land did not have glaciers, so it could not be Greenland. He decided to sail north until he found glaciers. At last he came to Greenland.

Greenland had been discovered and settled some years before by Eric the Red. Bjarni's story was told during the long winter evenings by settlers in Greenland. Among those who heard Bjarni's story were Eric the Red and his son, **Leif Ericson.** They decided they would try to find the land Bjarni had seen. They bought Bjarni's boat and prepared it for the voyage. On the day they were to leave, Eric the Red fell from his horse and hurt his leg.

"I am not meant to discover more countries than this one we now live in," said Eric. "This is as far as we go together." Leif alone was to command the voyage.

The Vikings

For the men who set out on that voyage of discovery, travel was a way of life. They were members of a group of people sometimes called **Vikings** and sometimes called Norsemen. The Vikings first lived in the region of what is now known as Scandinavia. Scandinavia today includes the countries of Norway, Sweden, and Denmark.

Several hundred years before the time of Leif Ericson, many Vikings left their homeland in boats searching for adventure, riches, and new lands to settle. Some settled in Iceland, a large island in the north Atlantic. Icelanders became famous for the woolen cloth they wore. They traded it for the things they did not have, such as grain, wood, and iron.

The Vikings were good **navigators.** That means they knew how to find their way on the seas. They were also excellent boatbuilders. They had learned to build a type of cargo boat that was good for ocean travel. This boat had a large sail, and it could carry such trade goods as furs and grain. It could also carry families of settlers and their livestock.

It was in such a boat that Leif Ericson and his crew of about 30 men set out to find the land Bjarni had described. Leif hoped to return to Greenland with his boat full of lumber.

Few trees grew in Greenland, yet the Viking settlers needed wood. They needed wood to build their boats. They needed wooden beams to support the sod roofs of their houses. They needed wood for furniture. Wood was so valuable that when Eric the Red moved from one place to another, he took apart his house and carried its wood with him.

Arrival at Vinland

Leif Ericson and his crew found the land Bjarni described. Leif called it **Vinland.** The land had fine grassland and berry vines. The Icelandic word

His hand at the rudder, Ericson steers toward Vinland. The ship has a strong crew at the oars, and a single sail to catch the wind.

Remains of a Viking settlement have been found at L'Anse Aux Meadows in Newfoundland. There these Viking dwellings have been rebuilt.

vin can mean either "grassland" or "wine." We do not know whether Leif Ericson meant "grassland" or "wineland" when he called it Vinland. Leif Ericson spent the winter in Vinland before returning to Greenland with a cargo of wood and berries.

The next person to lead a voyage to Vinland was Leif's brother Thorvald. One day Thorvald and his men came upon a small group of Indians asleep under their skin boats. They attacked, killing eight of the nine Indians. The ninth Indian escaped, returning with a large war party. In the battle that followed, Thorvald was killed.

Leif Ericson's sister Freydis was a leader of one of the last groups to visit Vinland. On this trip she caused 35 of her companions to be killed. She then returned home rich in furs and lumber. Leif Ericson was horrified at her evil deeds.

The stories about the deeds of the Vikings are called **sagas.** We now know the sagas about Leif Ericson are based on truth. Archaeologists have discovered the remains of a Viking settlement in **Newfoundland,** Canada. As a result, we know Vikings lived there about 1,000 years ago.

The Viking discovery of North America was forgotten. Dim memories of Vinland remained only in the sagas. Almost 500 years passed before Europeans again came to North America.

Reading Check

1. How long ago did Leif Ericson visit North America?
2. How did Leif Ericson know about another land?
3. What did Leif Ericson hope to find?
4. Why do we believe the sagas are based on truth?

SKILLS FOR SUCCESS

USING HISTORICAL MAPS

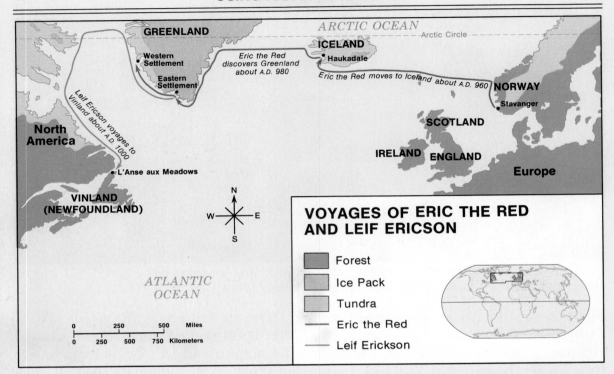

VOYAGES OF ERIC THE RED AND LEIF ERICSON

Forest
Ice Pack
Tundra
Eric the Red
Leif Erickson

A **historical map** gives information about a past event or period of time. It can show where past events took place. Historical maps can show cities and nations that existed at a particular time in the past.

The map above shows the routes of Eric the Red and Leif Ericson. Some historical maps give dates in the title. On this map the dates are next to the routes.

Like other maps, historical maps have keys that explain colors or symbols on the map. Look at the key for this map.

Leif Ericson sailed to a place he called Vinland. Vinland is on the map, but its present name, Newfoundland, appears in parentheses. Historical maps often show past names for places.

Historical maps may show natural features because natural features can be

important to explaining past events. On this map three natural features are shown: forest, ice pack, and tundra. Tundra describes the treeless plains of the far North. The map shows these features to help you understand why finding lumber was so important to the settlers of Greenland.

CHECKING YOUR SKILLS

Use the map to answer these questions.

1. What land did Eric the Red leave in A.D. 960?

2. When did Eric the Red move to Iceland?

3. When did Leif Ericson make his voyage?

4. Would it have been easier for the Greenland Vikings to voyage east rather than west to find lumber? Why or why not?

2. EUROPEANS LOOK TO ASIA

To Guide Your Reading

Look for these important words:

Key Words
- logs
- compass
- charts
- navigation
- caravel

People
- Marco Polo
- Great Khan
- Prince Henry
- Bartholomew Dias
- Vasco de Gama

Places
- Venice
- China
- Middle East
- Arabia
- Africa
- India
- Indies
- Portugal

Look for answers to these questions:

1. Why were Europeans interested in Asia?
2. Who was Marco Polo?
3. Why did Europeans desire to find an ocean route to Asia?
4. Why were the Portuguese the first to explore the Atlantic Ocean?

Most Europeans took little note of the Viking discovery. They were looking east toward Asia, not toward the west.

The trees of North America were valuable to the Vikings who lived on Greenland. Most Europeans, however, were not interested in trees. They desired gold, silk, perfumes, spices, and jewels. These things came from Asia.

Travel to Asia was very difficult. To get there, it was necessary to cross burning hot deserts and climb steep mountains. Robbers and bandits were a constant danger.

One traveler to Asia was **Marco Polo.** He was about 17 years old in 1271 when he left his home in **Venice,** Italy. He left with his father and uncle, who were merchants. It took them 4 years

to reach Beijing (Peking), the capital city of **China.** It was another 24 years before the travelers came home, their pockets full of jewels.

Marco Polo wrote a book about his adventures and the amazing things he had seen. He described the power and wealth of the ruler of China, who was called the **Great Khan.** On one New Year's Day celebration the Khan's subjects gave him 100,000 white horses. Marco Polo reported that 5,000 elephants were in this New Year's parade. Each elephant wore beautiful trappings worked with gold and silk.

Marco Polo did not visit Japan, which he called Cipangu (chy•PAN•goo). However, he did describe what others said about the palace of the ruler of Cipangu. "The entire roof is covered

This market in the Middle East today is little changed from markets Marco Polo might have visited. Which foods do you recognize?

with a plating of gold," Marco Polo wrote. "Many of the apartments have small tables of pure gold."

At the time many people who heard Marco Polo's stories thought he was making them up. Years later, however, his stories excited Europeans who had begun to wonder what the rest of the world was like.

Trade in the Middle East

Most European traders did not go all the way to China as Marco Polo did. Instead they traveled to such cities in the Middle East as Damascus and Alexandria. There they met other traders, who came with goods from **Arabia** and **Africa.** The traders also carried goods from **India,** China, and the **Indies** (the islands of Southeast Asia). The Europeans particularly desired spices such as pepper, cinnamon, cloves, and nutmeg. In exchange, the Europeans sold cloth, glassware, swords, wheat, furs, and timber.

We use many words that come from the Arabic (AR•uh•bik) language. The words name some of the objects traders bought in the markets at Damascus. Among them are *artichoke, spinach, orange, jar, apricot, syrup, cotton, sugar,* and *coffee.*

The Italian merchants of Venice and Genoa (JEN•uh•wuh) tried to keep the Middle East trade for themselves. If they could control the trade, then they could charge high prices. Other Europeans did not like this situation. They wished there were ways to get goods from the East without depending on the Italians or the Arabs. Could there be another route to Asia besides the route through the Middle East?

74

Prince Henry of Portugal

Henry, a prince of **Portugal,** hoped to find a water route to Asia. To do so, **Prince Henry** knew he must learn more about the oceans. In his search for knowledge, Prince Henry helped prepare the way for a new age.

To most Europeans the Atlantic Ocean was a great unknown. They called it the Sea of Darkness. Many believed that it was inhabited by giant sea monsters that could swallow ships whole. They were afraid to sail south. There, they believed, the sea boiled and the sun would roast their skins. They were also afraid to sail west because they might not find winds to bring them home again.

Prince Henry wanted to find out the truth. He encouraged ship captains to keep **logs,** daily records about a ship's journey. Logs included information on winds, ocean currents, and the shapes of coastlines. One of the most important tools that captains used was the **compass,** an instrument for finding directions. The compass was first used in Asia. By the 1400s European sailors had begun to depend on the compass.

Henry talked to the captains returning from voyages. He listened carefully to their stories. Their bits of information began to fit together like the pieces in a jigsaw puzzle. Henry and his scholars began to make **charts,** or maps, of the coastlines and the ocean. Prince Henry's efforts led to a science of **navigation.** *Navigation* means figuring out a ship's direction and location and the distance it travels.

In these years the Portuguese developed an ocean-going sailboat called a **caravel** (KAR•uh•vel). It used three sails. It could travel well either

Sailors once feared terrible creatures like this would destroy their ships.

As the sails catch the wind, the ship moves forward at an angle. Zigzagging, the ship holds a course into the wind.

SAILING INTO THE WIND
Wind Direction

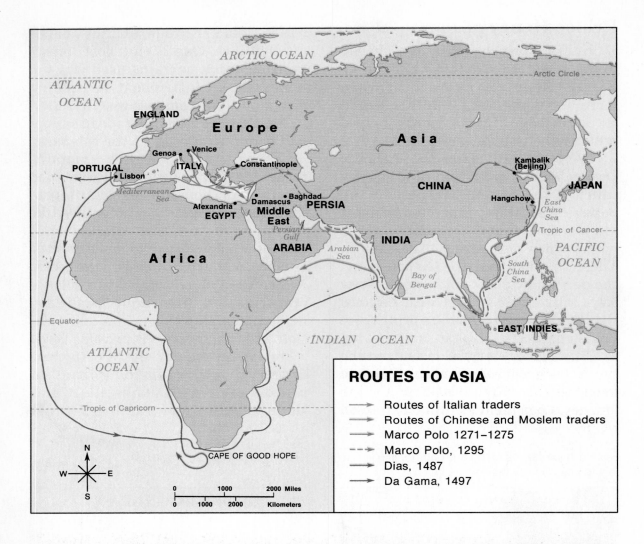

ROUTES TO ASIA

→ Routes of Italian traders
→ Routes of Chinese and Moslem traders
→ Marco Polo 1271–1275
--→ Marco Polo, 1295
→ Dias, 1487
→ Da Gama, 1497

into the wind or with the wind. This was a major achievement. Before the invention of the caravel, ships could sail into the wind only with great difficulty. On the caravel, sailors were not so afraid to go far from home. Even with winds against them, they knew they could return home.

The Portuguese explored farther and farther down the African coast. Prince Henry died in 1460 before the Portuguese crossed the equator. Yet he had laid the foundation for the great discoveries. **Bartholomew Dias,** a Portuguese captain, reached the southern tip of Africa in 1487. Ten years later **Vasco da Gama,** also a Portuguese sea captain, went around Africa to India. He found the new route to Asia that Prince Henry had dreamed of.

Reading Check

1. Where did Marco Polo travel?
2. Where did the traders from Venice meet Arab traders?
3. Why did Prince Henry have an interest in navigation?
4. How did Prince Henry begin to learn the truth about the Atlantic Ocean?

SKILLS FOR SUCCESS

FINDING DIRECTIONS

Imagine you are a Viking at sea. From your small boat there is no land to be seen. Wherever you look, you can see only the cold, gray waves of the Atlantic. How do you know in which direction you are sailing?

Using the Sun

The Vikings used the sun to find directions during the day. They knew, as you do, that the sun rises in the east and sets in the west. Therefore, if you head toward the sun in the late afternoon, you are moving westward. If the late afternoon sun is at your back, in which direction are you facing?

The farther one lives from the equator, the more the position of the sun varies with the seasons. In northern parts of the world, the sun sets southwest in winter and northwest in summer. If you want to use the sun to find direction, you must learn its position in every hour of every day in every season. That is what the Vikings did.

Using the Stars

Early sailors such as the Vikings found their direction at night by using the stars. One important star is the North Star. Because it always shines from the direction of the North Pole, it also has the name **Polaris** (puh•LAR•uhs), the pole star.

To find the North Star, you must first be able to locate two star patterns, the **Big Dipper** and the **Little Dipper.** Like the hands of a clock, these star patterns rotate around the North Star. To locate the North Star, first find the two stars forming the "cup" opposite the handle of the Big Dipper. Those stars are always in a straight line with the North Star. Notice that the North Star is in the handle of the Little Dipper.

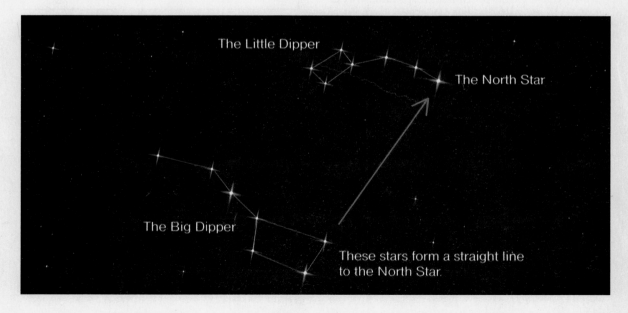

The Little Dipper

The North Star

The Big Dipper

These stars form a straight line to the North Star.

Using a Compass

How do you tell directions if you can't see the stars or sun? The invention of the compass solved this problem. With a compass sailors could find their direction in any weather, day or night. The compass is still an important tool.

The most important part of a compass is its magnetic needle. This needle will always line up in a north-south direction, with one end pointing north. Most compasses have the directions printed on them.

When you use a compass, you must make sure it is not near large metal objects. These can make the compass needle point in a false direction. Hold the compass steady until the needle is still. Then slowly turn your body until the needle points to the letter *N* on the compass. You and your compass will be facing north.

Orienting Maps

To use a map to go somewhere, you must first **orient** (OHR•ee•uhnt) the map. *To orient* means to line up in the right direction. One way to orient a map is to figure your direction from the position of the sun. If it is three o'clock in the afternoon, the sun is in the west. Turn your map so that west on the map lines up with the sun.

A better way to orient a map is to use a compass. With a compass you can make sure that north on the map is really pointing toward the North Pole. You can use a compass to do this. First, line up the needle and the *N* on the compass to find out which direction is north. Then turn the map so that *N* on the map is also pointing in the same direction as the compass needle. Now your map is oriented.

Look at the map on this page. Imagine that you are standing where the map shows you are. The street you are on runs east and west. You know this because *N* on the compass rose points in the same direction as north on the compass you're holding. You see a big street on your left that runs north and south. What street is that? You want to walk to the courthouse. Is it north or south of where you are? Should you turn right or left when you reach Main Street?

CHECKING YOUR SKILLS

Answer the following questions.

1. How can you figure out which way is west in the late afternoon?

2. How can you figure out which way is north at night?

3. You want to use a compass to orient yourself. When you hold it up, the needle is pointing to the letter *W* on the compass face. What should you do?

4. You want to orient your street map with the compass. What should you do?

3. CHRISTOPHER COLUMBUS

To Guide Your Reading

Look for these important words:

Key Words
- expedition

People
- Christopher Columbus
- King Ferdinand
- Queen Isabella
- Amerigo Vespucci

Places
- Spain
- West Indies
- Caribbean Sea
- Cuba
- Hispaniola

Look for answers to these questions:

1. What people and experiences shaped Columbus's ideas?
2. Why did Queen Isabella pay for Columbus's voyage?
3. How did Columbus and his men live at sea?
4. What discoveries did Columbus make?

Christopher Columbus is one of the most famous persons in history. His fame comes from his discovery in 1492 of a world unknown to Europeans.

The son of a weaver, Columbus was born in Genoa, Italy. Genoa was an important port, full of activity. The comings and goings of the port attracted him. As soon as Columbus was old enough, he went to sea. He began as a deckhand on a merchant ship and worked himself up to captain.

In May 1476 five Genoese merchant ships, including that of Columbus, were off the coast of Portugal. The Portuguese thought they were enemy warships and attacked. Columbus's ship sank. Columbus was wounded and six miles (9.7 km) from land. Holding onto an oar, he paddled the best he could to the shore and to safety. After coming ashore, Columbus went to Lisbon, the largest city in Portugal. His brother, a mapmaker, lived there.

Columbus was then 25 years old. Like most people of his time, he had never learned to read and write. Now, living in Lisbon, Columbus began to study. He learned to read and write. He learned mapmaking from his brother. Then he married Dona Felipa, the daughter of a Portuguese sea captain. The sea captain had many books. He also had charts and logs he had kept on his voyages.

The books included the writings of Marco Polo and of Ptolemy (TAHL‧uh‧mee), an ancient Greek. Ptolemy described the world as round. He believed that Asia stretched much farther east than it does. Mapmakers began to make world maps based on the ideas of Ptolemy, travelers like Marco Polo, and the Portuguese explorers.

At that time Portugal was the country most advanced in the science of navigation. But Portugal made that

This portrait is thought to be the best likeness of Columbus. No one painted his picture while he was alive because his importance was not then understood.

information available only to Portuguese sailors. It was Columbus's good fortune that he could use his father-in-law's library.

Columbus read the books and studied the sea charts in the library. He learned that the Portuguese had sailed far south along the African coast. A new idea began to take shape in his head. He asked himself: If the Portuguese could sail so far south, was it possible that he could sail as far west and find Asia?

Columbus took his idea to the king of Portugal. The king was interested, even though he considered Columbus "to be a big talker, and full of fancy and imagination." The king, however, turned Columbus down in order to continue the exploration of the African coast.

Help from Queen Isabella

Disappointed, Columbus went to **Spain** to see **King Ferdinand** and **Queen Isabella.** He hoped they would pay for an **expedition.** An expedition is a journey or voyage taken for a special reason.

Queen Isabella was a well-read, intelligent, and active ruler. She was also deeply religious. Isabella was interested in Columbus's arguments that one could reach Asia by sailing west. If it were true, then Spain would have much to gain by supporting Columbus. Spain would get wealth and riches. Spain would become as important as Portugal in ocean exploration. Spain could lead the way in bringing Christianity to millions of Asians.

Spain was fighting a war. Isabella didn't have the money just then to support Columbus. She told him to wait, and wait he did for six years. With the coming of peace to Spain in 1492, Ferdinand and Isabella were able to support Columbus. That year Columbus made the voyage that opened up a new world to the Europeans.

On Board Ship

Three little ships commanded by Christopher Columbus set sail from Palos on the coast of Spain. The time was eight o'clock in the morning on August 3, 1492. The ships were the *Niña,* the *Pinta,* and the *Santa Maria.* Columbus sailed in the *Santa Maria,* the largest of the ships.

The only cabin on the *Santa Maria* was the small one that Columbus used. The 40 sailors on board slept on the deck under the stars. They cooked their food of salted meat, fish, lentils, and chick-peas over an open fire in a box of sand.

The sailors measured time with a half-hour sandglass. Every half-hour the sand ran out, and the glass had to be turned.

In his cabin Columbus kept a careful log. There he recorded the weather, what the sailors saw, the latitude, and his estimates of the distance traveled. These records would help him to repeat the voyage.

More than 30 days passed at sea with no sight of land. The sailors were restless and afraid. Would they ever reach land? they asked themselves. Would they ever see home again?

On October 10 the men complained to Columbus about the long voyage. They told him they could bear it no longer. Columbus reminded them of the riches they might find. It was no use to complain, he told them, because he planned to stay on his course. The sailors grumbled angrily at this. They began to talk among themselves about throwing Columbus into the sea.

The next day, October 11, the sailors saw a carved stick in the water and a piece of cane. From these signs they knew land to be near. Land! They rejoiced and gave thanks to God.

Columbus Finds Land

On October 12 the ships anchored safely off an island Columbus named San Salvador. The people of this new land came forth shyly to greet the Spaniards. The Spanish gave them red caps and glass beads. "At this they were greatly pleased and became so entirely our friends that it was a wonder to see," Columbus wrote. The island people in turn gave parrots, spears, and balls of cotton yarn to the Spaniards.

Columbus believed he had reached Asia and was now in the Indies. For this reason he called the people *Indians*. We use that name to this day to refer to the first people of the Americas. We use the name **West Indies** to refer to the islands Columbus visited. The West Indies are located in the **Caribbean** (kar·uh·BEE·uhn) **Sea.**

Columbus had come to find gold, not parrots and cotton, so he sailed on. He visited the big island of **Cuba.** He thought Cuba must be Cipangu, Marco Polo's name for Japan. Disappointed to find no palaces roofed in gold, he sailed on.

Columbus and his sailors next came to an island he named **Hispaniola** (his·puhn·YOH·luh). Columbus called Hispaniola a "marvel." He thought its plains and mountains beautiful. He praised the loveliness of its houses and villages and the politeness of its people. Today Hispaniola is divided into the nations of Haiti (HAIT·ee) and the Dominican Republic.

While sailing off the coast of Hispaniola on Christmas Day, the *Santa Maria* was wrecked on a reef. People of Hispaniola helped Columbus's crew to carry the ship's cargo to shore. Columbus's despair about his ship turned to delight when he found that the people had pieces of gold and gold ornaments. They willingly traded this gold for such trinkets as little bells.

Columbus did not find Cipangu or the Court of the Great Khan. He did find fertile lands and friendly people. He saw enough gold to hope for more. Columbus decided that he must return to Spain with news of his discoveries.

Land at last! Christopher Columbus and his crew come ashore at San Salvador on October 12, 1492. Columbus claims the land for Spain.

The *Niña* and *Pinta* set a course for home. At sea they ran into terrible storms. At last, on March 15, the storm-tossed boats entered the port of Palos. As proof of his discoveries, Columbus brought back gold ornaments, parrots, and six captive Indians.

All Europe was excited by the news of Columbus's discoveries. The Portuguese, the English, the French, and the Spanish all soon sent out expeditions of discovery. Columbus made three more voyages himself. He lived out his life believing that he had sailed west to Asia.

Another ocean traveler, **Amerigo Vespucci** (ahm•uh•REE•goh ve•SPOO•chee), may have been the first to realize a new continent had been found. He called it a "new world." It was in honor of Amerigo Vespucci that a German mapmaker proposed that the new land be called America.

Reading Check

1. In what country did Columbus learn reading, writing, and mapmaking?
2. Who paid for Columbus's expedition?
3. What was life like on the *Santa Maria?*
4. Why were Europeans excited when Columbus returned from his first voyage?

4. FIRST VOYAGE AROUND THE WORLD

To Guide Your Reading

Look for these important words:

Key Words
- astronauts
- astronomy
- journal
- scurvy

People
- Ferdinand Magellan
- Vasco Núñez de Balboa
- Lapu Lapu
- Juan Sebastián del Cano

Places
- Isthmus of Panama
- Pacific Ocean
- Strait of Magellan
- Philippine Islands

Look for answers to these questions:

1. What was Ferdinand Magellan's goal?
2. How did Magellan use the knowledge gained by others?
3. What hardships did Magellan and his men experience?
4. What did Europeans learn from Magellan's voyage?

Columbus did not find the Indies by sailing west, but his dream did not die. **Ferdinand Magellan** made it come true.

Magellan grew up in Portugal. Boys and girls today hear about **astronauts,** the explorers of the moon and outer space. Magellan grew up hearing about the explorers of the ocean.

As a young man, Magellan studied both geography and **astronomy.** Astronomy is the study of the stars. An understanding of the stars was needed for navigation on the seas.

Magellan was eager to travel. When he was 25 years old, he was able to go on a Portuguese ship to India. There he helped the Portuguese set up trading posts. Magellan became a good sailor and navigator.

After ten years Magellan returned to Portugal with an idea. He too wanted to reach the Indies by sailing west. He started studying all the charts and logs he could find. From these he learned that Columbus did not reach the Indies.

He also learned that **Vasco Núñez de Balboa** had crossed the **Isthmus of Panama** in 1513 and seen a vast ocean. Balboa called it the South Sea. Magellan later called it the **Pacific Ocean.** *Pacific* means peaceful.

Magellan thought that he could find a way to the ocean Balboa had seen. Then he could sail to Asia. When the king of Portugal refused Magellan's request for money, Magellan went to Spain. The king of Spain, who was the grandson of Ferdinand and Isabella, agreed to pay for the voyage.

Some historians say this was the greatest sea voyage ever made. Magellan set sail in August 1519. He was in command of five ships. On those ships were 240 men, the youngest being 14 years old.

Antonio Pigafetta, an Italian, went with Magellan. He kept a **journal,** a daily record of what he saw. From that journal comes much of our information about Magellan's voyage. Magellan's journal of the voyage was lost.

The five ships crossed the Atlantic Ocean. Near the tip of South America, Magellan found the waterway to the Pacific Ocean. We now call that waterway the **Strait of Magellan.**

Hardships of the Voyage

Magellan, like Columbus, thought the world smaller than it was. He was not prepared for the terrible journey that lay ahead. Pigafetta wrote of the trip across the Pacific:

They were three months and twenty days without eating fresh food, and they ate biscuit, and when there was no more of that they ate the crumbs which were full of worms.

Pigafetta wrote that the sailors were so hungry that they boiled leather for four or five days and then ate it. They even ate sawdust. A man who caught a mouse could sell it for a gold coin. Men died of **scurvy** because they had no fruit or vegetables. Scurvy is a disease caused by lack of vitamin C.

Finally, land was sighted. It was a large island, probably Guam. Magellan wanted to rest there, but the people on the island stole what little the sailors had. Still hungry, sick, and weak, the men sailed on. They then came to the **Philippine Islands.**

There Magellan found friendly people who offered them rice, coconuts, oranges, and bananas. With these foods, the sick men got well and grew strong again. Chiefs whom Magellan met promised to obey the king of Spain.

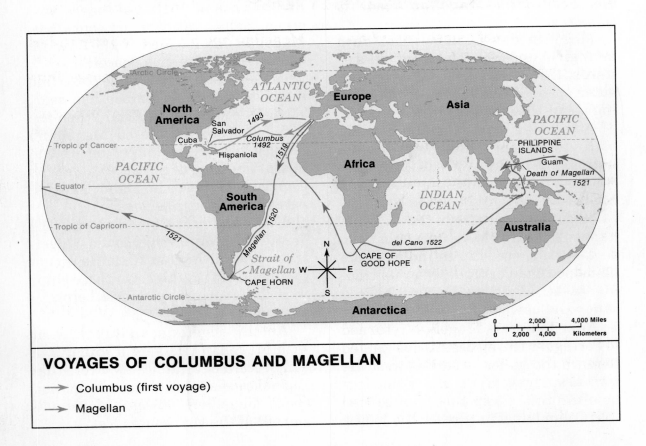

VOYAGES OF COLUMBUS AND MAGELLAN

→ Columbus (first voyage)

→ Magellan

Lisbon, Portugal, hums with activity as caravels take on supplies before voyages of exploration. A similar scene could have been found in Seville, Spain, when Magellan left on his important voyage.

However, a chief named **Lapu Lapu** refused to promise to obey the king of Spain. Magellan decided he would show off the strength and power of the Spanish by attacking Lapu Lapu. This was a fatal mistake.

When the Spanish attacked, Lapu Lapu's men pushed them back into the sea. The big guns of the Spanish ships were too far away to help. Magellan was killed by a bamboo spear. Other sailors were killed or drowned.

Juan Sebastián del Cano commanded the voyage home. The trip around the rest of the world to Spain was full of hardship—shipwreck, disease, and hunger. Finally, on September 9, 1522, one ship and 18 starving men limped into the Spanish port of Seville.

Magellan and del Cano had proved that one could sail around the world.

Magellan had planned the trip to find riches like gold and spices. The Spanish found riches, but the richest thing they found was knowledge.

Magellan's voyage proved beyond all doubt that the world was round. It showed that there was more water than land on Earth. It proved that the world was larger than Columbus or even Magellan had thought. It proved that the lands Columbus found were not part of Asia but a new world.

Reading Check

1. Which European first sighted the Pacific Ocean?
2. Where is the Strait of Magellan?
3. Name three hardships faced by Magellan's crew.
4. Why was the voyage of Magellan important?

CLOSE-UP

PLANTS OF THE NEW WORLD

The world experienced great changes after 1492. The voyages of exploration took Europeans to parts of the world where they had never been. The voyages were like bridges between the old and new worlds. People, ideas, and things began to move from their native places across these bridges.

The Europeans were very interested in the plants they found in the new world. Many of these plants had been grown by Indians for thousands of years. Christopher Columbus took home seeds and samples of plants from his first voyage. Within 50 years of Columbus's voyages, plants from the Western Hemisphere were being grown all over the world. These new-world plants became important foods in Europe, Africa, and Asia.

CORN   Columbus sent several men to explore the island of Cuba in 1492. They reported to him that the Indians "had a sort of grain they called maize which was baked, dried, and made into flour." Europeans continue to use the Indian word *maize* to identify what Americans today call corn. Corn was grown all over America wherever the Indians practiced agriculture. It grew very well and provided the Indians with much of their food. Because of this, it has been called "the grain that built a hemisphere." Corn was a valuable gift of American Indians to the world. It has become one of the most important foods for people and their livestock.

CHOCOLATE   Chocolate was a favorite drink of the Aztec and Mayan Indians of Mexico. Seeds of the cacao (kuh•KAOO) tree were roasted and ground, stirred in hot water, and flavored with vanilla and spices. The Aztec word for this drink was *xocoatl* (CHOH•awt•ahl). The Spanish found the Aztec chocolate drink too bitter, so they added sugar to it. Later, the English added milk. You know this drink as cocoa, hot chocolate, or chocolate milk.

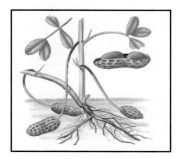

PEANUTS   A peanut is not really a nut. It is related to the bean and pea family. The pod of the peanut ripens underground. The peanut was first grown in South America. Soon after Columbus's time it was growing in Africa, India, and China. It is an important crop today in the southeastern United States. Peanuts are rich in protein, minerals, and vitamins.

BEANS   Beans have often been called the "poor person's meat" because they have so much food value. With corn and squash, beans made up the diet of many different Indian groups in the Western Hemisphere. The beans found in the new world are today grown all over the world. They include the string bean, the kidney bean, the lima bean, the navy bean, and the pinto bean. You can eat them as green beans, as baked beans, as chili beans, or as refried beans.

SQUASH   Squash was developed and grown by Indians in both South and North America for several thousand years. Our name for this vegetable comes from the Indians of Massachusetts, who called it *asquootasquash*. The Europeans shorted the word to the last syllable—*squash*. There are two basic kinds of squash: winter squash and summer squash. Winter squash has a hard outside and can keep for months. Summer squash, like zucchini, is eaten while it is still soft and tender.

87

POTATO   The potato was cultivated in the Andes Mountains by the people of Peru. The potato can grow in rocky soil and in cold places where grain crops cannot grow. The potato has become an important food crop for the world. The first Europeans to start cultivating the potato were poor people in Ireland. It was the major crop in Ireland in the 1600s. By the 1700s people in other northern European countries were eating several pounds of potatoes a day. Potatoes help people stay healthy because they are rich in vitamins and minerals.

PEPPER   There are two kinds of pepper. The black pepper that you sprinkle from a pepper shaker is from Asia. The other kind of pepper is a vegetable. The vegetable peppers used in the Americas included the chili pepper and the bell pepper. Vegetable peppers come in different colors, from red to yellow to green. Some are mild in taste. Others are so hot that just one bite can bring tears to your eyes. All are very high in vitamin C. The vegetable pepper is as important today to the foods of Mexico as it was in Aztec times. It has also become an important food in Asia and Europe.

TOMATO   The Aztecs called this food *tomatl* (toh•MAHT•ul). Like the potato, the tomato may have first been grown in Peru. It was likely a weed that started growing in the corn fields. The Indians began to cultivate it and combine it with chili peppers to make a sauce. When the tomato was first introduced to Europe, it was not quickly accepted as a food plant. Many people thought it poisonous. They used it only for decoration in their gardens. Only in the last 100 years has the tomato become an important food crop in many countries. It is high in both vitamin A and vitamin C. The tomato is used as a fresh vegetable, as a juice, or in sauces.

88

CHAPTER 3 REVIEW

WORDS TO USE

Explain the meaning of each word listed below. Then use each word in a complete sentence.

1. **astronomy**
2. **compass**
3. **expedition**
4. **journal**
5. **navigation**

FACTS TO REVIEW

1. What were the Greenland Vikings looking for in North America?

2. Why did Europeans want to find a water route to Asia?

3. In what ways did Prince Henry encourage navigation?

4. What new idea did Columbus have?

5. Name three reasons Queen Isabella was interested in helping Columbus.

6. How did Indians of the Caribbean show good will toward the Spaniards?

7. How did America get its name?

8. How were Magellan and Columbus alike? How were they different?

9. What did Balboa discover?

10. What knowledge did the voyage of Magellan and del Cano bring to the world?

IDEAS TO DISCUSS

1. People learn from the experiences of others. What examples of this idea can you find in the chapter you have just read?

2. What new inventions and scientific knowledge made exploration possible? Who are our modern-day explorers? What inventions have made their explorations possible?

3. We know that the Vikings visited America 500 years before Columbus. Why do we consider Columbus so important?

4. Which voyager would you like to have sailed with?

◯ SKILLS PRACTICE

1. **Finding Directions** Answer the following questions:

   a. If you turn your back to the sun at three o'clock in the afternoon, what general direction are you facing?

   b. If you face a rising sun, what general direction is to your left? to your right?

   c. In which direction does the compass needle point?

   d. You wish to orient the map on page 84 so that east on the map is true east. How can you do this with a compass?

   e. With a map and a flashlight, how could you orient yourself on a clear night?

2. **Using Historical Maps** Make your own historical map using an outline map of the world. Show the discovery voyages of da Gama, Dias, Columbus (the first voyage), and Magellan. Use a color for each voyage. Tell the dates of each.

CHAPTER 4

Spanish Exploration and Settlement

In 1519 the Spanish began to explore the mainland of the Americas. Hernando Cortés (kawr•TEZ) led the way with his conquest of the Aztec Indians in Mexico. Looking for gold and riches, the Spanish continued their exploration. They settled parts of South America, Central America, and the southern part of what is now the United States. Spain no longer controls any of these areas. Yet they all reflect a Spanish heritage in both language and culture.

1. CORTÉS CONQUERS MEXICO

To Guide Your Reading

Look for these important words:

Key Words
- conquistador
- legend
- Quetzalcoatl
- viceroy

People
- Hernando Cortés
- Montezuma
- Marina

Places
- New Spain
- Tenochtitlán
- Mexico City

Look for answers to these questions:

1. Who ruled the Aztecs?
2. What was the Aztec capital like?
3. How did Cortés conquer Mexico?

The Spanish came to the new world for gold, glory, and God.

Hernando Cortés was one of the most famous of the Spanish explorers. Cortés conquered the Aztecs of Mexico. He was a **conquistador,** the Spanish word for *conqueror.*

Like Magellan, Cortés had heard about the famous trips of Columbus while he was growing up in Spain. When he was 19 years old, Cortés had sailed to Hispaniola. He dreamed of finding both adventure and gold. His chance came in 1519. In that year he led an expedition to conquer Mexico.

Before leaving, Cortés spoke. He told his men: "We are about to begin a just and good war which will bring us fame. Almighty God will give us victory. I shall make you in a very short time the richest of all men who have crossed the seas."

Horses Win a Battle

The Spanish landed first near Tabasco, a Mayan village on the east coast of Mexico. The Tabascan Indians fought the invaders, throwing clubs and spears and shooting deadly arrows. Despite the steel armor and swords of the Spanish, the brave Indians might have won. But when the Spanish rode horses into the battle, the Indians fled. They were terrified because they had never seen horses before. To them a man on a horse was one huge monster.

The Indians at Tabasco then made peace with Cortés. While the Indian leaders and Cortés were exchanging gifts, the horses began to neigh. The Indians asked Cortés what they were saying. Cortés answered that the horses were scolding him for not punishing the Indians. The Indians then begged pardon of the horses. They offered them roses and turkeys to eat.

From Tabasco, Cortés went north along the coast to found the town of Vera Cruz. He called the land he was exploring **New Spain.** Leaving Vera Cruz, Cortés started across the mountains to **Tenochtitlán** (tay•NOCH•tee•TLAHN), capital city of the Aztecs.

The Aztec ruler was **Montezuma.** Montezuma ruled over 11 million people. Many of them belonged to other Indian groups that the Aztecs had conquered.

Cortés had with him 400 soldiers, 16 horses, 10 cannon, and 13 guns. Even with superior weapons, how could he hope to conquer this large country?

The answer is that he had help.

Cortés had the help of a woman named **Marina.** Marina knew several Indian languages. Through her Cortés could talk with the Indians. A soldier with Cortés wrote, "Marina was a person of the greatest importance and was obeyed without question by the Indians throughout New Spain."

Cortés also had the help of Indians who were unhappy with Aztec rule. They gave food to the Spanish. They even helped Cortés fight the Aztecs.

The Legend of Quetzalcoatl

Perhaps the greatest help Cortés had was an Aztec **legend.** A legend is a story about the past. It may or may not be true. This legend was about an important god named **Quetzalcoatl** (ket•sahl•KWAHT•uhl). Quetzalcoatl was an Indian god of wind and light. He was also the god of wisdom and knowledge.

About 500 years before Cortés, a famous king also named Quetzalcoatl ruled. He had light skin and a beard. Then this king left, sailing to the east. He promised to return in the year of One Reed. In the Aztec calendar One Reed came every 52 years. For 500 years the Indians had watched the east coast looking for their god-king's return. Cortés arrived in the year of One Reed.

Montezuma may have believed Cortés was Quetzalcoatl. He sent presents to Cortés as Cortés was journeying toward Tenochtitlán. Montezuma asked Cortés not to come to Tenochtitlán. Hoping to encourage Cortés to turn back, Montezuma sent him even more presents. One of the gifts was a gold platter as big as a cart wheel. It weighed almost 200 pounds (90.7 kg). The presents of gold only made Cortés greedy for more, and he pushed on toward Tenochtitlán.

Arrival at Tenochtitlán

The Spanish were amazed at the powerful civilization that lay before them. In Tenochtitlán they saw great stone towers. They saw villages built along a network of canals. There were thousands of houses and many more thousands of people. There were beautiful palaces surrounded by gardens fragrant with flowers and fruit trees. Colorful birds flew from branch to branch. Some of the Spanish soldiers wondered if they were dreaming.

Montezuma welcomed Cortés and gave him a palace to live in. Four days later Cortés made Montezuma his prisoner. He hoped to rule the Aztecs by capturing their king.

The Spanish were shocked at the Aztec practice of human sacrifice to their gods. When the Spanish tried to stop an Aztec ceremony of sacrifice, fighting broke out. Montezuma tried to stop the fighting by speaking to his people. While he was talking, someone threw a stone at Montezuma's head and killed him.

The Spanish left Tenochtitlán but only after heavy fighting. Half of them

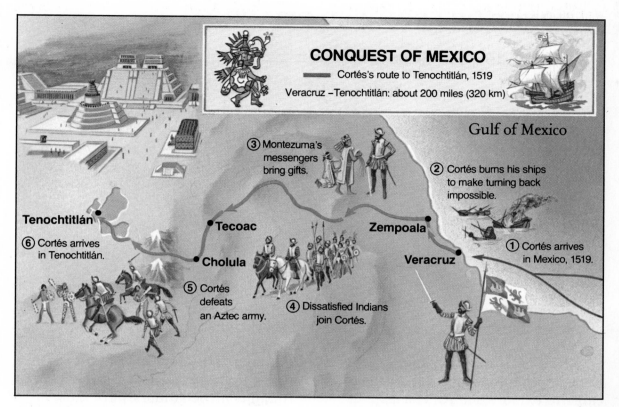

CONQUEST OF MEXICO

Cortés's route to Tenochtitlán, 1519

Veracruz – Tenochtitlán: about 200 miles (320 km)

Gulf of Mexico

③ Montezuma's messengers bring gifts.

② Cortés burns his ships to make turning back impossible.

Tenochtitlán
⑥ Cortés arrives in Tenochtitlán.

Tecoac

Zempoala

① Cortés arrives in Mexico, 1519.

Cholula

Veracruz

⑤ Cortés defeats an Aztec army.

④ Dissatisfied Indians join Cortés.

died. Many fell into the canals and drowned, dragged down by the weight of the gold they were carrying.

Cortés and his group found safety with the Indians who had helped them earlier. The next year, in 1521, Cortés returned to Tenochtitlán. With the help of 6,000 Indians, the Spanish destroyed the great city. Only by destroying the city did Cortés think he could break the power of the Aztecs, and he did.

On the ashes of Tenochtitlán the Spanish built the present-day **Mexico City.** Mexico City became the capital of New Spain.

Cortés was one of the bravest and most able of the Spanish conquistadors. After defeating the Aztecs, he set about ruling the country. He studied its resources and established peace as he understood it. He sent out other exploring expeditions.

The Spanish made the Indians of Mexico their slaves. They were forced to work in mines, to carry heavy loads, and to work the land. Millions died from disease and cruel treatment.

The king of Spain became afraid of the power of Cortés. He decided to strip Cortés of his power. He appointed one of his own representatives, called a **viceroy,** to govern Mexico. The king also took from Cortés his land and wealth. Cortés died poor in Spain in 1547.

Reading Check

1. What conquistador invaded Mexico?
2. Who was the ruler of the Aztecs?
3. How were Cortés and his men treated by the Aztecs?
4. How did Cortés finally achieve control over the Aztecs?

2. PONCE DE LEÓN AND PIZARRO

To Guide Your Reading

Look for these important words:

People
- Juan Ponce de León
- Francisco Pizarro
- Atahualpa
- Cabeza de Vaca

Places
- Florida
- Peru
- Cuzco
- Lima

Look for answers to these questions:

1. Why did Ponce de León go to Florida in 1521?
2. What people did Pizarro conquer? What methods did he use?
3. What led the Spanish to believe in the Seven Golden Cities?

Fired with the news of Cortés and his golden land, other Spaniards soon came to explore the Americas.

Juan Ponce de León had explored the coast of **Florida** in 1513 and claimed it for Spain. Some people said he was looking for a fountain of youth. Water from this fountain, it was said, would keep a person from growing old. After hearing of Cortés's conquest of Mexico, he returned to Florida in 1521. He hoped to establish a colony. Instead fierce Indians drove the Spanish back into the sea. Ponce de León died of an arrow wound from the battle. In Florida he had found death, not youth.

Pizarro in Peru

Francisco Pizarro (puh•ZAHR•oh), like many of the conquistadors, left a life of poverty in Spain to seek his fortune in the Americas. Pizarro had been with Balboa when Balboa first viewed the Pacific Ocean. Then he settled in Panama. There he heard rumors of a rich empire to the south. He longed to find out if the rumors were true.

Pizarro, shown here in the grand armor of a conqueror, began life as a poor man.

94

These Inca ruins high in the mountains of Peru are called Machu Picchu.

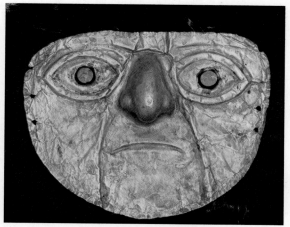

The Incas formed gold into beautiful masks, sculpture, and jewelry.

With the king of Spain's permission, Pizarro led an expedition to the coast of **Peru.** There, in 1532, his group of 180 men, with 27 horses, defeated the powerful Incas.

The Inca kingdom covered 3,000 miles (4,827 km) of the western coast of South America. At least 12 million people lived there. A network of roads and relay stations connected the towns. All the Indians paid taxes to the Inca ruler. Some paid in potatoes or corn. If people had gold, they paid in gold. They called gold "tears of the divine sun."

When Pizarro arrived in Peru, the ruler of the Incas was **Atahualpa** (aht•uh•WAHL•puh). Pizarro invited Atahualpa to visit him. Atahualpa came with about 3,000 followers. When Atahaulpa refused to become a Christian, Pizarro's men opened fire. They killed hundreds of Indians and captured Atahualpa. Atahualpa then offered to fill a large room with gold in return for his freedom. Pizarro agreed.

Indians came from all over the country with gifts of gold for the room. The gold had been beautifully crafted into all sorts of objects: eating utensils, birds, animals, necklaces. Pizarro had most of this fine work melted down into gold bars.

After two months Pizarro had received about 13,000 pounds (5,896 kg) of gold and 26,000 pounds (11,791 kg) of silver. He then had Atahualpa strangled to death. After Atahualpa's death, Pizarro took **Cuzco,** the Inca capital, without a struggle. He founded the new city of **Lima** on the coast. Inca land and wealth were divided among his supporters.

The conquistadors then began to quarrel with each other. Some backed Pizarro. Others backed Diego de Almagro. In this quarrel Almagro was killed, and his supporters were left poor and landless. Afraid for their lives and angry, Almagro's supporters charged into Pizarro's palace and killed him.

As he had done with Mexico, the king of Spain then decided to take control of Peru. Pizarro's brother killed the king's viceroy when he arrived. Two years later, however, he was killed by one of the king's men. The king of Spain was now in charge.

Cabeza de Vaca and his fellow survivors trudge across the desert. They were not so well clothed or armed as shown here.

Search for Golden Cities

The gold found in the new world encouraged the Spanish to believe in an old legend. This was the legend of the Seven Golden Cities. It told about seven bishops who had once left Spain. They were said to have crossed the ocean and to have founded seven cities of gold.

The Spanish had discovered more gold in Mexico and Peru than they dreamed possible. Why, they asked, could there not be even more? The Seven Golden Cities must surely exist.

Their hopes were raised by the story of **Cabeza de Vaca** (kuh•BAY•zuh day VAHK •uh). Cabeza de Vaca was one of four survivors of an expedition to Florida. After being shipwrecked on the east coast of Texas, the survivors had spent eight years living with different groups of Indians. They had wandered through what is now Texas, New Mexico, Arizona, and northern Mexico. At last, with Indian help, they had come to the Indian trail leading to Mexico City.

In Mexico City, Cabeza de Vaca gave a report to the viceroy. He said that the mountains he had crossed were rich in gold, iron, and copper. He also said that the Indians had told him of large cities to the north. Could these be the Seven Golden Cities? The Spaniards decided to find out.

Reading Check

1. Where did Ponce de León explore?
2. What was the Inca kingdom like?
3. What methods did Pizarro use to conquer the Incas?
4. Why did the story of Cabeza de Vaca raise Spanish hopes of finding the Seven Golden Cities?

THE ATTRACTION OF GOLD

 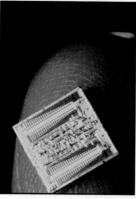  

The pictures above show gold in some of its many forms. At the far left are bars of gold bullion. Next is a gold computer microchip. You can judge its size from the finger holding it. The two pictures to the right show gold ornaments made by the Indians of Colombia and Peru before the Spanish Conquest.

"Get gold, in a fair way if possible, but get gold." So told King Ferdinand of Spain to the Spanish explorers who went off to the new world.

Why was gold so important?

For the Spanish who conquered the new world, gold meant wealth, power, and fame. Most of the Spanish conquistadors were not wealthy. If they could find gold, or take it from the Indians, they would be rich overnight. With gold they could buy land and horses. They could buy beautiful things. They could pay people to work for them. Gold has always been a kind of money.

From earliest times people have valued gold. It is easy to melt. It is easy to shape into objects. Gold can be hammered into sheets so thin that 1,000 sheets are no thicker than this page.

Gold never loses its beautiful yellow color. Gold does not rust like iron. Gold objects made thousands of years ago are still as bright as when they were made. Gold seems to last forever.

Gold is very useful in modern times. Because electricity passes through gold without changing it, gold is used in computers. Because gold reflects harmful rays of the sun, it is used in the windows of jet airplanes. Gold was in the helmets of American astronauts who walked on the moon.

Gold lasts. Some of the gold Pizarro found in Peru may be in jewelry worn today or in a jet flying overhead.

3. THE EXPEDITION OF CORONADO

To Guide Your Reading

Look for these important words:

People
- Francisco Coronado
- Friar Marcos
- Estéban
- Juan Cabrillo

- Hernando de Soto

Places
- Cibola

- Rio Grande River
- Quivira
- California
- Mississippi River

Look for answers to these questions:
1. What was the purpose of Coronado's expedition?
2. Did Coronado find what he was looking for?
3. Why do we remember Juan Cabrillo and Hernando de Soto?
4. What did the Spanish explorers in North America accomplish?

The viceroy of Mexico assigned **Francisco Coronado** the job of exploring the area north of Mexico. Coronado first sent out an advance group led by a priest, **Friar Marcos.** His guide was **Estéban.**

Estéban was a slave. He had been one of Cabeza de Vaca's fellow survivors. Estéban was very good at Indian languages. Many Indians thought he was a shaman because of a gourd rattle he carried.

Ahead of Friar Marcos went Estéban, shaking his rattle and demanding gifts of the Indians he met. When Estéban reached the Zuni Indian town of **Cibola,** the Zunis were insulted by his demands. They killed him.

When Friar Marcos learned of Estéban's death, he decided not go to Cibola himself. From a distance he viewed Cibola and then turned toward Mexico "with much more fear than food." When he was again in Mexico,

he reported that Cibola was "larger than the city of Mexico."

Those who heard Friar Marcos's report used it to feed their own dreams of riches. Soon the report was magnified, and it was told that Cibola was richer than Mexico City. With such a rumor, Coronado had no trouble finding people to go on an expedition.

Coronado Sets Off

In high spirits, the Coronado expedition started from Compostela in the winter of 1540. Going with Coronado were over 300 Spaniards, most of them on horseback. A few of them were women with their children. One woman, Francisca de Hozes, rode the whole way on horseback—a round trip of 7,000 miles (11,263 km).

Also in the expedition were some black servants and 1,300 Indians, including women and children. Coronado insisted that the Indians be treated well. They did not have to carry loads. Instead, the Indians took care of the horses and other animals. There were at least 600 horses and mules to carry baggage. About 550 horses were used for riding. A large herd of cattle and as many as 5,000 sheep provided food for the expedition.

The route Coronado followed was an old one, used by Indians for hundreds of years. It led north through upper Mexico into the valley of the **Rio Grande.** With so many animals, the expedition moved slowly. Eager to reach Cibola, Coronado and a small group of followers went ahead. They could hardly wait to see its wonders for themselves.

When Coronado and his men reached Cibola, what disappointment they felt! It was no grand city. It was a pueblo—a small village. But within the village, they knew, was food. Having brought little of their own food, the advance party was starving. After a brief battle, the people of Cibola withdrew, leaving the pueblo to Coronado. One of his men later wrote: "There we found something we prized more than gold or silver—namely, plentiful maize and beans, turkeys, and salt."

The Grand Canyon

From Cibola Coronado sent out a scouting party to the west. Led by Garcia López de Cárdenas, the party went as far as the Grand Canyon. They were the first Europeans to gaze into the deep canyon. From the rim they could see the Colorado River a mile (1.6 km) below them. The river looked like a watery ribbon. They spent three days trying to find a way down the canyon before turning back.

Francisco Coronado headed a huge expedition to find gold. He found no gold but learned much about the North American interior.

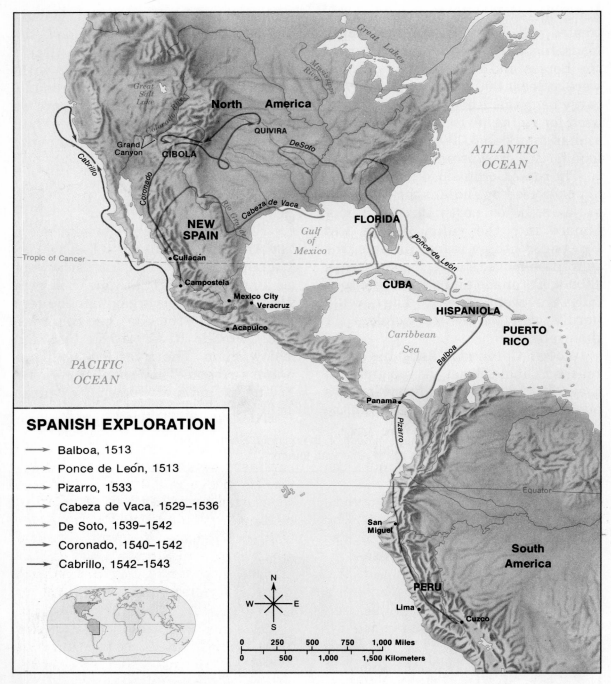

SPANISH EXPLORATION

→ Balboa, 1513
→ Ponce de León, 1513
→ Pizarro, 1533
→ Cabeza de Vaca, 1529–1536
→ De Soto, 1539–1542
→ Coronado, 1540–1542
→ Cabrillo, 1542–1543

Kansas and "The Turk"

The hope of a rich Cibola had led Coronado to the interior of North America. The hope of reaching a rich **Quivira** (kee•VEER•uh) kept him there for another year. Quivira was in the region we know as Kansas. Coronado wanted to go there because he had been told that it held a wealth of gold. It was also possible, he believed, that Quivira was ruled by Christians. Maybe it was one of the Seven Golden Cities.

100

The story of Quivira had been made up by an Indian from that region. The Spanish called this Indian "the Turk." He was a slave of a Pueblo Indian chief friendly to Coronado. Perhaps the Turk thought he could return to his home if the Spanish went to Quivira.

On their way to Quivira, the Spanish traveled through what is now New Mexico, Texas, Oklahoma, and Kansas. These flat plains were a new experience. "There is nowhere a stone, a hill, a tree, or a bush, or anything of the sort. But there are many excellent pastures with fine grass," wrote Pedro de Castañeda, one of the travelers. There were so many buffalo on the plains that Coronado said he never lost sight of them.

"Traveling in these plains is like voyaging at sea, for there are no roads other than cattle trails," Castañeda wrote. To keep track of their course, the Spaniards navigated the grassy plains with a compass. To keep track of distances, one person counted the footsteps taken each day.

What did Coronado find in Quivira? Only a small village of grass huts. The Wichita Indian village was located near the middle of present-day Kansas.

Soon after reaching Quivira, Coronado was badly injured in a fall from his horse. Weak, homesick, and very disappointed, Coronado led his followers back to Mexico. They had traveled as far on land as if they had crossed the Atlantic Ocean and back. It was a courageous journey.

Cabrillo in California

In 1542, the same year that Coronado returned to Mexico City, a Spanish

Eager for European goods, Indians along California's coast offered Juan Cabrillo fresh fish, water, and firewood.

expedition set forth from Mexico to explore the west coast of North America. In charge was **Juan Cabrillo,** a conquistador who had been with Cortes. Sailing north along the Pacific Coast, Cabrillo became the first Spanish explorer of **California.** Cabrillo discovered San Diego Bay and landed there. His expedition then made other landings near what are today Los Angeles and Santa Barbara. Early in 1543 Cabrillo died from a fall. The expedition continued without Cabrillo, sailing as far north as Oregon.

Hernando de Soto

Meanwhile, another Spanish explorer, **Hernando de Soto,** was looking in the Southeast for the Seven Golden

101

Full of hope they would soon find gold, de Soto and more than 300 men landed at Tampa Bay in Florida in 1539. Three years later, de Soto was dead of fever and his men gave up the search in despair.

Cities. De Soto had helped Pizarro conquer Peru. He hoped to find more of such wealth.

With more than 300 men and 200 horses, de Soto landed near Tampa Bay in Florida. He started north, looking for gold. He reached the Savannah River in Georgia. Finding no gold there, he turned west and crossed the lower Appalachian Mountains. His wanderings eventually brought him to the **Mississippi River.** De Soto and his men were the first Europeans to see the mighty Mississippi.

De Soto was a cruel man who made enemies of the Indians. After accepting their friendship and food, he would often take them as slaves.

After spending three fruitless years looking for gold, de Soto died of fever in 1542. He was buried in the Mississippi River. The Spaniards did not want the Indians to find his body and know they had lost their leader.

Most Spanish explorers in North America did not find gold. Some lost their lives. Others went home poor and disappointed. The explorers, however, did learn much about the continent. They learned about its geography and about the people who lived there. They claimed new lands for Spain.

Reading Check

1. What did Coronado hope to find in Cibola? What did he find?
2. How did the Spanish navigate on the plains?
3. Which Spaniard first explored California?
4. Why did Hernando de Soto spend three years wandering in the Southeast?

4. SPANISH SETTLEMENT

To Guide Your Reading

Look for these important words:

Key Words
- colony
- colonists
- missionaries

- missions
- presidio

People
- Bartolomé de las Casas

Places
- St. Augustine

Look for answers to these questions:

1. What did Bartolomé de las Casas do for the Indians?
2. What kinds of settlements did the Spanish establish in the Southwest and in California?
3. What changes did the Spanish way of life bring to North America?

After the first Spanish explorers had come to the new world, colonies were established. A **colony** is a settlement that is ruled by a faraway country. People who come from a mother country to live in a colony are called **colonists**.

Bartolomé de las Casas (bahr·TAHL·o·may day lahs KAHS·us) settled in Hispaniola in 1502 as a colonist. Like other Spanish settlers, he was given land. He was also given the right to force Indians to work on his land as slaves.

Las Casas first became a successful farmer and then a priest in the Roman Catholic Church. In time he grew concerned about the cruel treatment of the Indians. When he asked the Indians how they were, they always replied, "Hungry, hungry, hungry." Nine of every ten Indians on Hispaniola died from disease or overwork.

Las Casas announced he would no longer keep Indian slaves. He began to work to get better treatment for the Indians. He became known as the Protector of the Indians. Once he described how a captive Indian girl had found a gold nugget weighing 35 pounds (15.9 kg). The Spanish miners she worked

Las Casas, a thoughtful man, saw Indians as human beings with a right to fair treatment and freedom.

103

A SPANISH MISSION IN CALIFORNIA

River

Cornfields

Aqueduct

Vineyard

Olive trees

Olive crusher

Vegetable garden

Storerooms

Wash trough

Weaver

Indian village

Fruit orchard

Workshops

Patio

Candle making

Tallow maker

Priests' quarters

Cemetery

Church

Fountain

Majordomo's quarters

Mission cross

Tannery

for celebrated by roasting a pig. "But," Las Casas wrote, "the poor girl who found the nugget did not receive anything—not even a single bite of the pig."

The king of Spain listened to the words of Las Casas. In 1542 the king ruled that Indians could not be made slaves. In 1550 the king ordered that all conquests of Indian peoples be stopped.

Our Spanish Heritage

The Spanish once controlled most of the southern part of what is now the United States. As a result, many Spanish buildings, place names, and words have become part of our American heritage.

Visitors today can tour the fort built by the Spanish at **St. Augustine,** Florida, in 1565. St. Augustine is the oldest city founded by Europeans in the United States. San Antonio, Texas; Santa Fe, New Mexico; and San Diego, California, are all cities that were established by the Spanish.

Americans use Spanish words such as *canyon, key,* and *mesa* to describe landforms. The first cowboys were Spanish. Words like *lasso, corral, ranch,* and *rodeo* all come from the Spanish. Other words taken from Spanish are *alligator, mosquito,* and *tornado.*

Most Spanish settlement in what is now the United States took place in the Southwest and in California. The first to settle in these parts were usually Catholic **missionaries.** They were priests who hoped to convert the Indians to the Christian faith.

Besides their religion, the missionaries brought fruit trees, cattle, sheep, and horses. Their settlements were called **missions.** Missions included a church and the buildings necessary to farming and ranching. The missionaries forced many Indians to work on the mission lands against their will.

Soldiers usually accompanied the missionaries. Once a mission was established, the soldiers built a fort, called a **presidio** (pri•SEED•ee•oh). After the missionaries and soldiers had settled, then colonists came to settle on nearby lands.

The missionaries, soldiers, and colonists established a Spanish way of life where they settled. In Texas and California, cattle were particularly important to that way of life. The hides and animal fat were traded for manufactured goods from Mexico and Spain. In New Mexico, Spanish colonists found that sheep did well in the dry climate.

The animals introduced by the Spanish changed life for many Indians. The horses brought by colonists to New Mexico multiplied and formed into herds of wild mustangs. The Plains Indians quickly learned to tame these horses. They were soon using them for hunting buffalo and for warfare. The Indians of the Southwest started to herd sheep. They began weaving sheep's wool into beautiful garments and blankets for themselves.

Reading Check

1. Who was known as the Protector of the Indians?
2. Name four cities of the United States that were founded by the Spanish.
3. What animals did the Spanish introduce to North America?
4. How did Spanish settlers change life for the Indians?

SKILLS FOR SUCCESS

USING CHARTS AND TABLES

Reading an Organizational Chart

Some information is easiest to understand when it is shown in a drawing. The drawing below is an **organizational** (org•unuh•ZAY•shun•uhl) **chart.**

This chart shows how the Spanish government ruled Mexico. The person at the top of the chart is the most powerful. In this case the king of Spain ruled Spain and its possessions, including Mexico. He gave orders to the viceroy of Mexico. The viceroy passed the orders along to the governors of the different parts of Mexico. Each governor then passed orders down to the **alcaldes** (al•KAHL•days), the officials ruling in each town.

Power flows only in one direction on this chart, from top to bottom. The viceroy gives orders to the governor of a province. The governor of a province never gives orders to the viceroy. Could a governor give orders to another governor?

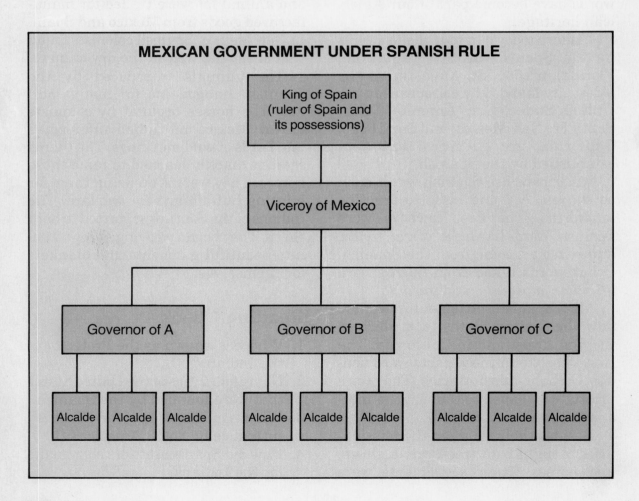

MEXICAN GOVERNMENT UNDER SPANISH RULE

King of Spain
(ruler of Spain and
its possessions)

Viceroy of Mexico

Governor of A

Governor of B

Governor of C

Alcalde Alcalde Alcalde

Alcalde Alcalde Alcalde

Alcalde Alcalde Alcalde

Reading a Flow Chart

Another useful chart is a **flow chart.** A flow chart shows the order in which tasks are done or something happens. An arrow on a flow chart points from one task to the next task, from beginning to end. Here is a flow chart that shows how one would organize an expedition.

Look at the top of the chart. The first task is making clear the purpose of the expedition. Follow the arrow to the next job. What is the next step in organizing an expedition? Read the rest of the steps in order. Do you buy supplies before or after you know how many people are coming? What is the last thing you do?

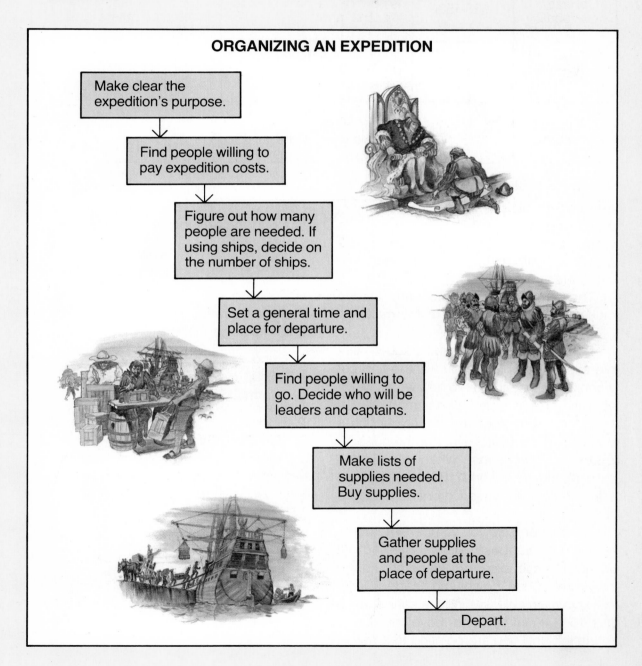

ORGANIZING AN EXPEDITION

Make clear the expedition's purpose.

Find people willing to pay expedition costs.

Figure out how many people are needed. If using ships, decide on the number of ships.

Set a general time and place for departure.

Find people willing to go. Decide who will be leaders and captains.

Make lists of supplies needed. Buy supplies.

Gather supplies and people at the place of departure.

Depart.

107

SPANISH EXPLORERS OF NORTH AMERICA

Explorer	Dates of Exploration	Achievements	Results
Hernando Cortés	1519-1535	Conquered the Aztecs of Mexico, discovered Lower (Baja) California	Claimed Mexico for Spain and settled it under Spanish rule
Cabeza de Vaca	1528-1536	Wandered through what is now Texas, New Mexico, Arizona, and northern Mexico	Brought back information and stories that interested others in this region
Hernando de Soto	1539-1542	Explored the Southeast; discovered the Mississippi River	Increased Spain's knowledge of North America; claimed land for Spain
Francisco Coronado	1540-1542	Explored the Southwest and the Interior Plains	Increased Spain's knowledge of North America; claimed land for Spain

Reading a Table

A **table** lists bits of information. This way of presenting information makes it easy for a reader to compare facts. The table below presents information about Spanish explorers.

The names of the explorers are listed in the first column. What kind of information is listed in the second column?

Each row across gives facts about a single explorer. Suppose you want to find out when Cortés explored the new world. Move your finger down the first column until you find Cortés's name. Then move your finger across the row until it is under the heading *Dates of Exploration*. When did Cortés explore the new world? Follow the same steps to find out when Coronado explored the Southwest.

A table can help you compare members of a group. Suppose you want to find out which of these explorers came first to the new world. Scan the column headed *Dates of Exploration* until you find the earliest date. It is 1513. Point to it and move your finger to the left until you are pointing to a name.

You can see that the earliest explorer was Ponce de León. Follow the same steps to find out who was the latest explorer.

CHECKING YOUR SKILLS

For each question below, decide whether the best answer is an organizational chart, a flow chart, or a table.

1. Suppose you want to explain how to make a kite. How can you best present this information?

2. Suppose you want to present facts about different states, such as when they became states, what their capitals are, and how many people live in each state. What is the best way to show this information?

3. Suppose you want to show the responsibilities of class or school officers. How can you best present this information?

4. What is the best way to present facts comparing the kinds of ships the Spanish used?

CHAPTER 4 REVIEW

WORDS TO USE

Use the words below to complete the sentences that follow.

colony
conquistadors
legend
missionaries
viceroy

1. The _____ invaded North and South America and claimed the land for Spain.

2. The _____ of Quetzalcoatl helped Cortés in the conquest of Mexico.

3. A _____ ruled New Spain in the name of the king.

4. Catholic _____ introduced Christianity to the Indians.

5. A _____ is a settlement ruled by a faraway country.

FACTS TO REVIEW

1. How did each of the following help Cortés conquer Mexico?

   a. Horses
   b. Legend of Quetzalcoatl
   c. Indians unhappy with Aztec rule

2. How were Hernando Cortés and Francisco Pizarro alike? different?

3. What was the purpose of the Coronado expedition?

4. Many Spanish explorers did not find gold, but what did they achieve?

5. How did Bartolomé de las Casas influence the king of Spain?

IDEAS TO DISCUSS

1. The king of Spain took away the land and the wealth of the conquistadors. How might the conquistadors have argued against the king's action? How might the king have answered?

2. What skills and abilities do you think the explorers needed? Why were their explorations important?

3. Were all Spanish explorers conquistadors? Were all conquistadors explorers? Explain your answers.

◯ SKILLS PRACTICE

1. **Making a Flow Chart**   Write the following sentences on slips of paper. Then arrange them in the order they happened. Paste the slips on a sheet of paper and add arrows to make a flow chart. Give a title to this chart.

   a. Montezuma welcomes Cortés to his palace.
   b. Cortés and his men begin to build Mexico City.
   c. Cortés journeys to Tenochtitlán.
   d. Cortés escapes to safety. The next year he returns to destroy Tenochtitlán.
   e. Cortés takes Montezuma prisoner and fighting breaks out.

2. **Making a Table**   Make your own table of Spanish explorers of North America. Start with the information in the table on page 108. Add these names to your table: Juan Ponce de León, Estéban, Juan Cabrillo.

CHAPTER 5

Northern Explorations

About this chapter

Other European nations followed Spain in exploring and settling the new world. Portugal claimed a large part of South America and named it Brazil. In the 1500s England, France, and Holland all sent expeditions to explore North America. These explorations then became the basis of their claims to parts of North America.

1. NEWFOUNDLAND AND CANADA

To Guide Your Reading

Look for these important words:

Key Words
- northwest passage
- translate

People
- John Cabot
- Giovanni Verrazano

- Jacques Cartier
- Donnaconna

Places
- Newfoundland
- Grand Banks

- France
- Canada
- St. Lawrence River
- Montreal
- Saguenay

Look for answers to these questions:

1. How did England benefit from John Cabot's voyage?
2. Why were the French interested in finding a new route to Asia?
3. What were the results of French explorations?

The first English expedition reached the new world in 1497. It was led by an Italian, Giovanni Caboto (jo·VAHN·ee kah·BOH·toh), who lived in England. The English called him **John Cabot** (CAB·uht). Cabot had heard about the voyages of Columbus. He wanted to sail west like Columbus. The king of England approved his idea. Cabot would claim any lands he found for England.

Cabot sailed from Bristol, England. His course across the Atlantic Ocean was far north of Columbus's course. He reached a large island he called **Newfoundland** and claimed it for England. Off the coast of Newfoundland the waters were very rich in fish. The English could simply lower baskets into the water and draw them up filled with fish. The name of this rich fishing area is the **Grand Banks.**

Cabot made another voyage in 1498, but he was lost at sea. The fishermen of Bristol, however, remembered the Grand Banks. In small but sturdy boats, they set out each spring to cross the stormy North Atlantic to catch codfish.

The Northwest Passage

The route around South America to Asia was long and difficult. Explorers hoped to find a **northwest passage,** a waterway leading to Asia through North America.

The king of **France** was one of those who wanted to find a northwest passage. Portugal was becoming powerful and rich from its trade with Africa and India. Spain too was growing wealthy from its conquests of Mexico and Peru. If France could discover a new route to Asia, perhaps it might also have a chance to get such wealth.

In 1524 the king of France sent an Italian, **Giovanni Verrazano** (ver·uh·ZAHN·oh), to find a northwest passage.

Verrazano first touched land on the coast of North Carolina. There, Verrazano wrote, an Indian approached the French. In his hand he held "a burning stick, as if to offer us fire." It was probably a peace pipe, but the Frenchmen had never seen or heard of tobacco. They responded by showing their "fire"—and fired a gun.

Verrazano then sailed northward, finding the harbors of present-day New York City and, later, Newport, Rhode Island. He went beyond Cape Cod before returning to France. A northwest passage did not exist, he told the king.

Jacques Cartier

Ten years later **Jacques Cartier** (ZHAHK kahr•tee•AY) tried again to find a northwest passage for France. Between 1534 and 1536 Cartier made the voyages that opened up North America to the French.

In 1534 Cartier explored the northern Atlantic coast of North America. The Hurons, an Iroquois tribe, were quite friendly to the French explorer. The chief of the Hurons, **Donnaconna,** placed great trust in him. Donnaconna let Cartier take his two teenage sons to France. Cartier wanted the young men to learn French so that they could **translate** for him. *To translate* means to change statements from one language to another.

Cartier returned to North America the next year. He brought the two young Hurons with him. They could now speak French. They told him of a great river

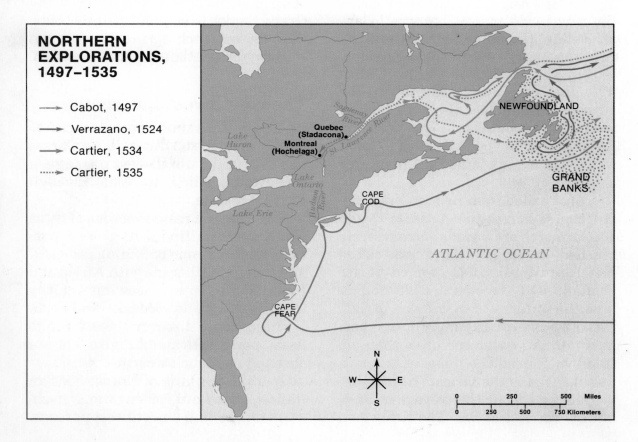

NORTHERN
EXPLORATIONS,
1497–1535

→ Cabot, 1497

→ Verrazano, 1524

→ Cartier, 1534

┈┈► Cartier, 1535

Quebec (Stadacona)
Montreal (Hochelaga)
Saguenay River
St. Lawrence River
NEWFOUNDLAND
Lake Huron
Lake Ontario
Lake Erie
Hudson River
CAPE COD
GRAND BANKS
CAPE FEAR
ATLANTIC OCEAN
N W E S
0 250 500 Miles
0 250 500 750 Kilometers

The Huron Indians boiled spruce needles to make a tea that cured the French of scurvy. The tea saved many lives.

that was the "road of **Canada**." Cartier then sailed up the **St. Lawrence River.** When Cartier arrived at the village of Hochelaga (HOCH•uh•lah•guh), 1,000 Hurons came to greet him. They brought gifts of corn bread. They brought their children for him to touch. Behind the village was a large hill. Cartier named it Mont Royal, which meant "Royal Mountain" in French. Mont Royal later became **Montreal** (mahn•tree•OL), today the largest city in Canada.

Cartier had hoped the St. Lawrence River would lead him to China. His hopes disappeared when he came on great rapids. No boat could travel through the fast, tumbling water of the rapids. The expedition was forced to turn back.

Cartier spent the winter in a fort he and his men built. By the middle of the winter the French were suffering terribly from scurvy. Their teeth were falling out. Their gums were rotting. Their arms and legs were swollen and painful.

The Hurons came to their rescue. They showed the French how to treat the scurvy. The treatment consisted of drinking a tea made by grinding and boiling the bark of an evergreen tree. At first, most of the sailors said they would rather die than drink the brew. The few who did, however, were completely cured in several days. After that, the others were eager to drink the bitter tea.

The Huron chief Donnaconna was eager to please Cartier. Donnaconna noticed that Cartier's eyes grew bright at the talk of gold and gems. Donnaconna started to tell stories about a make-believe place called **Saguenay** (SAHG•uh•nay). He said there were rubies, much gold, and even spices

Every spring European fishermen sailed to the Grand Banks to fish. Here, cod is cleaned, salted, and dried for the return voyage.

there. The Saguenay people, he said, had only one leg. Donnaconna's imagination grew. The people in Saguenay, he said, had wings instead of arms and flew from tree to tree. Saguenay must be a marvelous land indeed!

The French hoped to find Saguenay. With that aim, Cartier made a third voyage to Canada. He planned to build a settlement to use as a base for exploring Saguenay. When the Hurons understood that the French intended to settle, they became unfriendly. The severe winter and the unfriendliness of the Hurons discouraged the French. Forgetting about Saguenay, Cartier returned to France in the spring.

Yet French fishermen knew a good thing when they saw it. Like the English, they returned each summer to fish in the Grand Banks and at the mouth of the St. Lawrence River. They were soon joined by fishermen from other parts of Europe. The fishermen salted and dried their catch before returning to their homelands.

Some of the French fishermen found the Indians willing to trade furs. There were many kinds of fur in that region. Deer, bear, beaver, otter, and seal in large numbers lived in North America. The Europeans wanted the furs for their hats and coats. The Indians in turn liked the beads, hatchets, knives, and kettles of the French.

Reading Check

1. Who led the first English voyage to the new world?
2. Who first explored the St. Lawrence River?
3. Why did Cartier hope to find Saguenay?
4. After Cartier's voyages, why did the French return to North America?

114

BEAVERS

A beaver

A tree cut by beavers

A beaver lodge

The first French explorers in North America had looked for gold and diamonds. Later explorers decided the most precious resource was the furry, funny-looking beaver. Probably 100 million beavers then lived in North America. Before long, trapping beavers and trading fur skins became the biggest business in northern America.

Beavers belong to the rodent family, as do squirrels, mice, and rats. The average beaver is about 3 feet (1 m) long and weighs about 50 pounds (23 kg). Beavers have sharp teeth. They eat the bark and young buds of trees.

Beavers are excellent swimmers. They have large, flat tails that they use to steer through the water. They also slap their tails on the water to signal friends and warn of the presence of enemies. They live in groups and work together to build dams and shelters.

The early beaver trappers were interested in beavers for their fur. Beaver fur provides excellent protection against cold and moisture. It has been prized for centuries for hats and coats.

In the 1600s, trappers combed the eastern part of North America in search of beaver. In those early days a trapper could trade 12 beaver pelts for 1 musket. One pelt might bring 4 pounds (1.8 kg) of gun powder, a new kettle, or 1 pound (0.5 kg) of tobacco.

During the early 1800s fur trading spread west and became an even bigger business. Huge fortunes were made. Trappers called "mountain men" moved into the wildest reaches of the Rocky Mountains.

Soon some trappers were catching as many as 100 beavers a week. By the mid-1800s, too many beaver had been taken. Trapping beaver was no longer profitable.

Today, most states have laws protecting beavers. Beaver populations are higher than they were a century ago. Some trapping is still permitted to keep the population from growing too large. In North America most people now value live beavers as much as they used to value beaver skins.

2. ENGLAND CHALLENGES SPAIN

To Guide Your Reading

Look for these important words:

Key Words
• sea dogs

People
• Francis Drake

• Philip II
• Elizabeth I
• Sir Walter Raleigh
• John White

Places
• San Francisco Bay
• Roanoke Island
• Virginia

Look for answers to these questions:

1. Why could England challenge Spain's power in the new world?
2. Who was Francis Drake? Why did the Spanish call him a "dragon?"
3. Where were the first English settlements in North America? What happened to them?

As rich and powerful as Spain was in the 1500s, the mighty nation shook with anger at the name of one Englishman: **Francis Drake.** They called him *El Dragon,* Spanish for "the dragon."

Like the dragons of legend, Francis Drake struck quickly. He also loved gold—Spanish gold. Because of him, much Spanish treasure ended up in England.

England had found no gold in the new world. Nor had England found a northwest passage to Asia. England did not have Spain's wealth, but it was rich in another way. It had speedy ships and skilled ocean sailors. At first the English sailors went after the fish in the Grand Banks. Then they went after Spanish treasure ships.

Spain's king, **Philip II,** hoped to get control of England by marrying England's queen, **Elizabeth I.** Philip also hoped to make Spain the most powerful country in Europe. Elizabeth

let Philip's hopes for marriage grow. At the same time, she encouraged English sea captains to seize Spanish treasure.

English merchants and sea captains used their own money to build ships in hope of capturing Spanish treasure. When they succeeded, they had money to build more ships. The commanders of these English warships were called **sea dogs.** They were really pirates, but Elizabeth protected them because they were helping England.

Drake was the most famous of the English sea dogs. He had been born to a poor family in 1540. For a time the family lived near the king's shipyards. There, as a boy, Drake learned about ships and the sea. He first went to sea when he was 14 years old.

Drake's adventures as *El Dragon* started in 1570. In that year, as a new sea dog, he watched the comings and goings of the Spanish treasure ships in the Caribbean Sea. He learned about the geography of the area. He learned about the sea currents and islands. He found unknown harbors where he could hide his ships. The next year Drake the Dragon began his attacks on the Spanish.

Drake Finds Spanish Riches

Spain was so sure of itself that it was not prepared for Drake's daring. Drake and his men heard of a mule train on its way to a Spanish port in

Francis Drake's men pile Spanish gold, silver, and jewels at their leader's feet.

Panama. It consisted of 190 mules carrying gold and silver from the mines of Peru. Drake and his men made a surprise attack on the mule train. They carried away all the gold. There was so much silver that they had to leave it behind.

Then in 1577 Drake started his most famous voyage. In his ship the *Golden Hind,* Drake sailed through the Straits of Magellan to the Pacific Ocean. Off the coast of South America, Drake captured a Spanish treasure ship. It took four days for Drake's men to transfer the rich cargo to the *Golden Hind.* They had captured 13 chests of silver coins, 26 tons (23.6 T) of silver bars, and 80 pounds (36.3 kg) of gold. There were also countless boxes of jewels and pearls. The cargo was worth millions of dollars.

Drake did not want to follow the same route home. He was afraid that Spanish war ships would find him. He therefore sailed up the Pacific Coast.

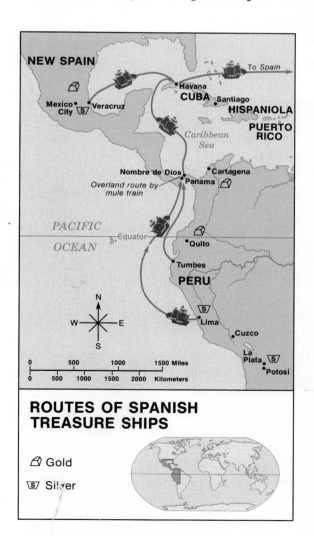

ROUTES OF SPANISH TREASURE SHIPS

⌂ Gold

⌂ Silver

117

He stopped near **San Francisco Bay** in California and claimed the land for England. He may even have gone as far north as Vancouver Island, Canada. He returned to England by sailing across the Pacific Ocean and around the world to England.

Drake was the first Englishman to sail around the world. Upon his return he was greeted as a hero. Queen Elizabeth gave him a special reward. She made him a knight. He was now known as Sir Francis Drake. The Spanish were furious.

Settling Roanoke Island

The Spanish treasure taken by sea dogs such as Drake increased England's power. With the treasure, England built a strong navy. A strong navy made England powerful. Some English people began to think of controlling land in the new world as Spain did. **Sir Walter Raleigh** (RAHL•ee) dreamed of an English settlement in North America. Hoping to find a good place for a settlement, Raleigh had sent out some ships to explore the Atlantic Coast. They visited **Roanoke Island** in 1584. The Indian queen who ruled that area warmly welcomed the English. Raleigh claimed the land for England, calling it **Virginia.**

The next year Raleigh sent a group of Englishmen to settle and build a fort on Roanoke Island. But the settlers did not expect to work. They expected the

After capturing Spanish treasure and sailing around the world, Francis Drake returned to England a hero. Here, on board the *Golden Hind,* Queen Elizabeth touches the kneeling Drake with a sword and makes him a knight.

At Roanoke in 1590, John White finds chests of rotting books and a mysterious message carved on a tree. "What does this mean?" he asks.

Indians to feed them. It is not surprising that relations between the English and the Indians soured. Francis Drake stopped by the settlement in 1586. Finding the colonists starving, he took them back to England with him.

In 1587 Raleigh sent a second group of people to colonize Roanoke Island. This group was led by **John White.** White's granddaughter, Virginia Dare, was the first English child born in the new world.

We do not know what happened to the second colony. White stayed only one summer before returning to England to get more supplies. Forced then to serve in the navy, he could not return until 1590. He found the colony deserted. Carved on a log was a single word: "CROATAN." Croatan was the name of a nearby island. White wanted

to search for the settlers, but a storm was coming. The ship's captain said they must leave immediately. They did so. White was never able to answer questions that we still ask. Were the settlers on Roanoke Island killed by the Indians? Did they leave to settle on Croatan? Did they join an Indian group?

Reading Check

1. What was a sea dog?
2. How did England benefit from the activities of sea dogs such as Francis Drake?
3. How did Sir Walter Raleigh help achieve English settlement in North America?
4. What questions remain about the fate of the second colony on Roanoke Island?

3. EXPLORERS OF THE INTERIOR

To Guide Your Reading

Look for these important words:

Key Words
- Spanish Armada

People
- Henry Hudson
- Samuel de Champlain

- Louis Joliet
- Jacques Marquette
- Robert La Salle

Places
- Chesapeake Bay

- Hudson River
- Hudson Bay
- Quebec
- New Orleans

Look for answers to these questions:

1. Why did Spain lose control over the new world?
2. What did Henry Hudson achieve?
3. Who encouraged French settlement of North America?
4. Why did the French get along with the Indians?

Spain was not as powerful as the world thought. The successful attacks of the English sea dogs on Spanish ships showed that. Philip II became angry that Elizabeth approved of the sea dogs. He decided to invade England. The Spanish gathered together a huge fleet of warships, called the **Spanish Armada.** In 1588 the Spanish Armada set out to conquer England. But the English, with the help of a storm, defeated the Spanish at sea. England's defeat of the Spanish Armada left Spain weak. Spain could no longer claim all the new world for itself.

Henry Hudson

European explorers continued to probe the North American coastline looking for a northwest passage. **Henry Hudson,** an Englishman, was one such explorer. He had spent most of his life looking for a new way to get to China. First he had tried to get there by find-ing a passage through Russia. Then he tried the North American coast.

On his first trip to North America in 1609, Hudson sailed as captain of a Dutch ship. He explored **Chesapeake Bay** and then New York harbor. He sailed up the river he named for himself—the **Hudson River.** On its shores he found Iroquois Indians who were willing to trade skins of beaver and otter. Hudson's voyage gave Holland claim to the Hudson River valley. Soon the Dutch were establishing fur trading posts along the river.

On his second voyage to North America in 1610 Hudson sailed for an English company. The company asked him to explore the northern part of Canada. Hudson explored the bay that also carries his name—**Hudson Bay.** The members of his crew, however, thought they were going to starve in that faraway place. They wanted to go home. They put Hudson, his young son, and seven others in a rowboat and

Hope now gone, Henry Hudson holds his son's hand. They and seven loyal crewmembers had been left stranded in a rowboat in Hudson Bay. From the background, can you tell why they probably did not survive?

sailed away. Hudson was never heard of again.

Samuel de Champlain

The French meanwhile had renewed their interest in Canada, the land rich in both furs and fish. In 1603 an expedition was sent to explore New France. Its geographer and mapmaker was **Samuel de Champlain** (duh sham·PLAYN). In 1608 he returned to establish the first successful French settlement in the new world at **Quebec** (kwi·BEK).

Champlain was known as a strong leader of men. He was also known for his fairness and politeness to defeated enemies. His leadership encouraged

French exploration and settlement of North America. For that reason he is called the Father of New France.

As the French explored the interior of North America, they set up trading posts. The French missionaries and fur traders got along well with most Indians. There were several reasons for this:

- The French learned the Indian languages.
- The traders were not interested in taking land from the Indians.
- The traders and the Indians treated each other like business partners, as equals. The Indians welcomed the iron tools they exchanged for furs. In the business of getting and selling furs, French traders and Indians depended on each other.

121

Exploring the Mississippi

The French continued to explore the rivers and lakes that led into the interior of North America. In 1673 one French expedition traveled across huge Lake Michigan, down the Wisconsin River, and then down the Mississippi River. Traveling in birchbark canoes, the explorers reached as far south as the mouth of the Arkansas River. After four months, the expedition had traveled about 2,500 miles (4,022 km).

This famous expedition was led by **Louis Joliet** (LOO•ee zhol•YAY), a fur trader born in Quebec, and **Jacques Marquette** (ZHAHK mahr•KET), a priest who knew many Indian languages.

Father Marquette described some of the wonders of the river journey.

> From time to time, we came upon monstrous fish, one of which struck our canoe with such violence that I thought that it was a great tree about to break the canoe to pieces. On another occasion, we saw on the water a monster with the head of a tiger, a sharp nose like that of a wildcat, with whiskers and straight, erect ears.

He may have seen a huge catfish.

Another French explorer, **Robert La Salle** (luh SAL), began his exploration of the Mississippi River in 1679. In Illinois La Salle established Fort

Explorers Marquette and Joliet head down the Mississippi. It is unlikely, though, that Marquette would have traveled standing up in a canoe.

The French built trading posts like this one at Fond-du-Lac, Wisconsin. Why do you suppose there is an Indian village across the river?

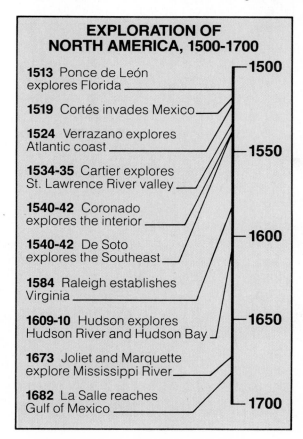

EXPLORATION OF NORTH AMERICA, 1500-1700

1500

1513 Ponce de León explores Florida

1519 Cortés invades Mexico

1524 Verrazano explores Atlantic coast

1550

1534-35 Cartier explores St. Lawrence River valley

1540-42 Coronado explores the interior

1600

1540-42 De Soto explores the Southeast

1584 Raleigh establishes Virginia

1609-10 Hudson explores Hudson River and Hudson Bay

1650

1673 Joliet and Marquette explore Mississippi River

1682 La Salle reaches Gulf of Mexico

1700

Crevecoeur (KREHV•kuhr). All kinds of problems delayed the expedition, but at last, in 1682, La Salle reached the mouth of the Mississippi. He claimed the Mississippi River basin for France.

The city of **New Orleans** was founded by the French in 1718. By that time the French had established small trading posts and villages throughout the Mississippi River valley. That is why many place names there are French—names such as St. Louis, Des Moines, Detroit, and Louisville.

Reading Check

1. What was the Spanish Armada?
2. What areas of North America did Henry Hudson explore?
3. Why is Samuel de Champlain known as the Father of New France?
4. What was the result of French exploration of the Mississippi River?

123

SKILLS FOR SUCCESS

USING LATITUDE AND LONGITUDE

To locate points on Earth, we use a system of imaginary lines. Lines that run in an east-west direction are called **lines of latitude.** Lines that run in a north-south direction are called **lines of longitude.**

Understanding Latitude

The equator is a line of latitude. Lines of latitude always remain the same distance from each other. For this reason lines of latitude are also called **parallels** (PAIR•uh•lels). Parallel lines never meet. They are always the same distance from each other.

Lines of latitude are useful for talking about locations. They make globes and maps easier to use. Look at the globe below.

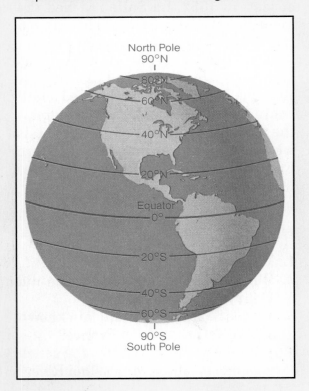

Find the equator on this globe. It is the thick red line around the middle of the globe. Notice that the equator is labeled 0°. This is read as *zero degrees.* (The symbol ° stands for degrees.) A **degree** is a unit of measure used to describe lines of latitude and lines of longitude.

Lines of latitude are also labeled according to direction. Find the red line just above the equator. This parallel is labeled *20°N*—in words, *twenty degrees north.* The *N* tells you that this parallel is north of the equator. The numeral tells you how far north.

Now find the red line above the one labeled *20°N.* This line is labeled *40°N (forty degrees north).* The greater the number of a parallel followed by *N,* the farther north it is. The parallel that is farthest north on this globe is the one labeled *80°N.* The North Pole is the point that is farthest north on Earth. Its latitude is *90°N.*

The parallels to the south of the equator are identified by the letter *S,* for *south,* following the degree number. Find the red line just below the equator. This line is labeled *20°S (twenty degrees south).* Which parallel is to the south of this one?

The greater the number of a parallel followed by *S,* the farther south it is. The parallel that is farthest south on this globe is labeled *80°S.* The South Pole is the point farthest south on Earth. It is labeled *90°S.*

The degree labels of parallels make it easy to talk about how far north or south something is. For example, if you say that the latitude of Austin, Texas, is 30°N, you are saying how far north the city is from the equator.

Most globes do not show every parallel. The globe pictured on page 124 shows every twentieth parallel—20°N, 40°N, 60°N, and so on. Some globes show only every fifteenth parallel—15°N, 30°N, 45°N, and so on. Often you need to look between parallels to find a place. Let's say you wanted to find a city with latitude 50°N on a globe showing every twentieth parallel. You would have to look halfway between the parallel labeled *40°N* and the parallel labeled *60°N*.

Understanding Longitude

When you look at a globe, you will also see lines running north-south. These are lines of longitude, or **meridians.**

Each meridian connects the North Pole and the South Pole. Meridians are numbered much as the parallels are numbered. Look at the globe below.

On this globe the meridians at the equator are 20 degrees apart. Find the line of longitude labeled **Prime Meridian.** It runs north-south near the city of London in Great

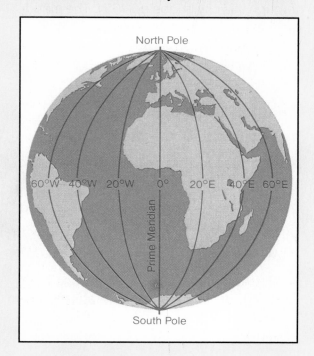

Britain. As you can see, this meridian is labeled *0° (zero degrees).*

The meridians to the west of the Prime Meridian are labeled in *degrees west longitude.* Find the meridian just to the west of the Prime Meridian. It is labeled *20°W (twenty degrees west).* The meridian just to the west of this one is labeled *40°W.* As you move west of the Prime Meridian, the numerals, followed by *W,* become greater.

The meridians to the east of the Prime Meridian are labeled in *degrees east longitude.* On this globe the meridian just to the east of the Prime Meridian is labeled *20°E (twenty degrees east).* What meridian on this globe is just to the east of the meridian labeled *20°E?* Again, as you progress farther east of the Prime Meridian, the numerals, followed by *E,* become greater.

The meridian on the opposite side of the globe from the Prime Meridian is called the **International Date Line.** This meridian is labeled *180°,* the greatest number of a meridian.

The degree labels of meridians are also used in talking about locations. For example, the city of Alexandria, Egypt, is near the meridian labeled *30°E.* Therefore, we say the longitude of Alexandria is 30°E.

As with parallels, most globes and maps do not show every meridian. This globe shows only every twentieth meridian. If you wanted to find a city at 70°W longitude, you would have to look halfway between the meridians 60°W and 80°W.

Locating Places on a Map

Together, the lines of latitude and longitude form a **grid.** A grid is a pattern of crossing lines. The grid makes it possible to talk about how far north or south something is and also about how far east or west it is. Neither latitude nor longitude alone is enough to find

125

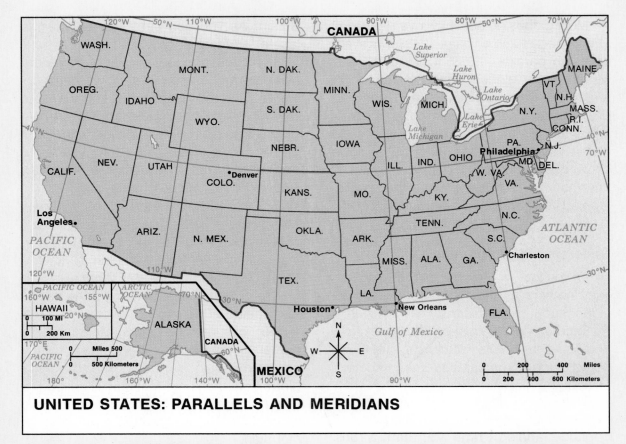

UNITED STATES: PARALLELS AND MERIDIANS

a place on a globe or map. Both are necessary.

The map on this page shows the mainland United States. It has a grid of parallels and meridians drawn over it.

Every fifth parallel is shown—from 25°N to 50°N. The entire United States lies north of the equator, so all the parallels are written with *N,* for *north.* Which meridians are shown? The United States lies west of the Prime Meridian, so all the meridians are written with *W,* for *west.*

Try using both parallels and meridians to find locations. At the side of the map, find the parallel 30°N. At the bottom of the map find the meridian 95°W. Trace these lines to the point at which they meet. The city of Houston, Texas, is not far from this point.

Now try finding the latitude and longitude of a city. Find Philadelphia, Pennsyl-

vania, on the map. The parallel that runs through this city is labeled *40°N.* The meridian that runs through it is labeled *75°W.* Philadelphia's location is 40°N latitude, 75°W longitude.

CHECKING YOUR SKILLS

Use the map to answer these questions.

1. What place on this map is located at about 35°N latitude and 90°W longitude?

2. How would you write the latitude and longitude for New Orleans?

3. What is the latitude of Denver, Colorado?

4. City A is located at 41°N latitude and 74°W longitude. City B is located at 44°N latitude and 100°W longitude. Which city is farther north? Which city is farther east?

CHAPTER 5 REVIEW

WORDS TO USE

Number your paper from 1 to 10. Write the name that best fits each description.

John Cabot   Louis Joliet
Jacques Cartier   Robert La Salle
Samuel de Champlain   Walter Raleigh
Francis Drake   Giovanni Verrazano
Henry Hudson   John White

1. With Jacques Marquette, he explored much of the Mississippi River.

2. He explored the St. Lawrence River area looking for a northwest passage.

3. This explorer claimed the Mississippi River basin for France.

4. He discovered the Grand Banks.

5. This man explored the Atlantic Coast of North America for France in 1524.

6. He was responsible for the first English settlements in North America.

7. This sea dog captured Spanish treasure for England.

8. This Englishman was in charge of the settlement at Roanoke Island.

9. This man explored for both Holland and England.

10. This explorer is also called the Father of New France.

FACTS TO REVIEW

1. How did the Hurons at first show good will to the Cartier expeditions?

2. How did fast ships and good sailors help England become powerful?

3. Why was the English victory over the Spanish Armada important?

4. Name three reasons why the French and most Indians remained on friendly terms.

5. How were Samuel de Champlain and Walter Raleigh alike?

IDEAS TO DISCUSS

1. Why did the English and French travel so far to fish in the Grand Banks? What might have been the results of finding this plentiful new food supply?

2. The fur trade was an important reason for both French and Dutch settlement in North America. How did trade benefit both the Europeans and Indians?

○ SKILLS PRACTICE

Latitude and Longitude   Use the map on page 126 to answer these questions.

1. What city is at 30°N latitude, 90°W longitude?

2. Which three states have northern borders at 35°N latitude?

3. What line of latitude forms the northern borders of New York and Vermont?

4. In what state would you be at 35°N latitude, 120°W longitude? at 65°N latitude, 145°W longitude?

CHAPTER 6

Settlement of the Atlantic Coast

The 1500s were spent in exploration of the Western Hemisphere. By 1600 Spain, France, and England all claimed parts of North America. The 1600s then became a century of settlement. As you have read, the Spanish were the first to settle in North America. Their first settlement on the Atlantic Coast was St. Augustine. In this chapter you will read about other early settlements on the Atlantic Coast.

1. COLONISTS SUCCEED AT JAMESTOWN

To Guide Your Reading

Look for these important words:

Key Words
- stock
- stock company
- profit
- prosper

People
- John Smith
- Powhatan
- Pocahontas
- John Rolfe

Places
- Jamestown

Look for answers to these questions:

1. How was Jamestown settled?
2. What problems did the colonists have to overcome?
3. How did John Smith help the Jamestown colony?
4. Why did the Jamestown colony at last succeed?

The English settlements at Roanoke Island failed, but the idea of settling a colony lived on. A group of English merchants decided to try again. To establish a new colony, they needed permission from the king of England. In the English view the king controlled all land claimed by England. With the permission of King James the group of London merchants organized the Virginia Company. The aim of these merchants was to start trading posts.

The Virginia Company was owned by many people. They each had given money to organize the company. In return, each had received shares of ownership in the company. These shares were called **stock.** This kind of company was a **stock company.** The Virginia Company hoped that in the long run it would make a **profit.** A profit is the money left over after expenses have been paid.

Two ships sent by the Virginia Company sailed into Chesapeake Bay early in 1607. They came to a large river, which they called the James River to honor their king. They settled on a shore of the James River in a place that would be easy to defend. They named the settlement **Jamestown.** They built there a small fort, a church, a storehouse, and some houses.

The 1607 English settlement at Jamestown succeeded—but just barely.

Establishing a settlement so far from home took lots of money and careful planning. Ships had to transport people and goods across the Atlantic Ocean. People had to have food. Shelters had to be built. All kinds of work had to be done. Help was necessary when hard times came.

Jamestown was in a marshy area, full of mosquitoes. It was not a healthy place to settle. Nearby there were thick forests. The waters, then as now, were rich in sea life.

The 105 men and boys who arrived to settle Jamestown hoped to find gold. These colonists were not used to working with their hands. They did not know how to farm or to fish. They simply were not prepared to take care of themselves. They depended on the Indians or on ships from England to provide food. Within a year, half had died of starvation, disease, or Indian attacks.

John Smith

Jamestown might have disappeared, like the settlement at Roanoke, but for **John Smith.** Smith had one of the most exciting and colorful lives of any man of his time. He was born in England, but before coming to America, he had been a soldier in Hungary. There he had been captured and sent as a slave to Turkey. Two years later he escaped on horseback to Russia. Smith was a soldier, an explorer,

John Smith was a man of both wisdom and courage. Without him, Jamestown would not have survived.

and a writer. Most of all, he was a bold and practical person.

On an expedition to explore the countryside around Jamestown, Smith was captured by Powhatan (pow•HAT•un) Indians. Their chief, also named **Powhatan,** sentenced him to death. The Indians prepared to kill him. Then, **Pocahontas** (poh•ku•HAHNT•us), the chief's 12-year-old daughter, held onto Smith and pleaded for his life. Powhatan listened to his daughter's pleas and spared Smith's life.

Friendly relations were then established between the Jamestown settlers and Powhatan's tribe. The Indians began to bring corn and turkeys to the English. Pocahontas herself brought food. Smith wrote that Pocahontas kept the colony from death, starvation, and "utter confusion."

Smith himself did much to keep the colony going. He declared that anyone who did not work would not eat. Every able person was soon busy—sawing wood, building houses, planting gardens, or hunting for food.

Even though Smith brought order for a while to Jamestown, the infant colony continued to have problems. Smith returned to England in 1609 to recover from a leg injury. The next winter was known as the "starving time." Of 490 persons in the colony, only 60 survived.

Jamestown might have met a sad fate had not the Virginia Company continued its support. The company hired more people to go to Jamestown to work. Not all were English. Some of the first were Poles, who knew how to make pitch, tar, and turpentine. These products were necessary for making and repairing ships.

Today, visitors imagine life in early Jamestown as they stroll down its streets. The buildings are copies of the original structures.

Land and Tobacco

The Jamestown colony began to **prosper,** or do well, when the colonists began to cultivate tobacco. Tobacco was a plant native to the Western Hemisphere. A Jamestown leader, **John Rolfe,** experimented with various types of tobacco and ways of drying it. By 1613 he had developed a tobacco that the English liked. The Virginians were soon sending shiploads of tobacco to England. There it became popular and sold for very high prices. The high prices encouraged settlers to plant more tobacco. They even planted it in the streets of Jamestown. Tobacco was used as money.

A turning point for the Jamestown colony came in about 1616. At that time the Virginia Company began to give land to settlers who had stayed seven years. Until then, there had been no private ownership of land. Everyone was supposed to work on company land. After receiving land of their own, the colonists worked harder. The Virginia colonists worked harder for themselves in one day than they did in a week for the company, John Smith said.

Reading Check

1. What problems did the first Jamestown settlers face?
2. How did Pocahontas help Jamestown?
3. Who made the Jamestown colonists work for their food?
4. Why was tobacco important to the success of the Jamestown colony?

2. THE GROWTH OF VIRGINIA

To Guide Your Reading

Look for these important words:

Key Words
- indentured servant
- House of Burgesses

Look for answers to these questions:

1. How did tobacco help Virginia prosper?
2. How was Virginia governed?
3. Why were Africans and women brought to Jamestown?
4. As Virginia grew, what happened to relations between settlers and Indians?

Tobacco encouraged the growth of Virginia. Stories of the money to be made by growing tobacco attracted more settlers. In Virginia a man could earn more money in a year than in several years in England. With help in the fields, he could become quite rich.

The high price of tobacco created a demand for people to work in the fields. A system was developed to provide workers for Virginia. In return for ocean passage, a person agreed to work for a period of time. At the end of that time, generally five to seven years, the person was free. Such a person was called an **indentured servant.**

Most indentured servants who first came to work in the Virginia tobacco fields were English men and boys. Later, both men and women came. For many it was a way to escape hard times, to start a new life.

By 1619 Virginia had about 1,000 settlers. The colony was still ruled by a governor appointed by the Virginia Company. The settlers had to obey company rules. This changed in 1619. In that year the Virginia Company said that the English in America would live under English laws. They would have the same rights as those in England. One of those rights was the right to establish and maintain a lawmaking assembly.

In Virginia the colonists elected people to represent them in the lawmaking assembly. This assembly was called the **House of Burgesses.** The House of Burgesses gave the Virginia colonists valuable experience in self-government. The Virginians still had a governor, but he now had to follow English law. That included sharing the ruling power with the House of Burgesses.

Africans and Women Come

In 1619 a Dutch trading ship arrived in Jamestown with a group of 20 Africans. For more than 100 years the Spanish had brought Africans as slaves to the new world. The African slaves worked in the fields and mines. However, the first Africans in Jamestown were treated not as slaves but as indentured servants. After serving the agreed number of years, they were freed like other indentured servants.

As more field workers were needed, black people were made indentured servants for life. By the middle of the 1600s, all black people coming to America were considered slaves. Slavery was made legal in Virginia in 1661.

Most of the early colonists had not planned to settle in Virginia for life. They hoped to make a fortune and return to England. Very few women had come. To encourage people to settle permanently in Virginia, the Virginia Company sent 90 women to Jamestown in 1619. When they stepped off the ship, many men were waiting to marry them.

Why would a woman go off to a distant place to marry someone she hardly knew? The answer must be the same as for the men who went. It was a chance for adventure and a new life. It was a way to leave behind a life that held little hope.

Relations with Indians

Since 1607, when Pocahontas saved John Smith's life, the Powhatans had remained suspicious of the English. Then, in 1614, John Rolfe married Pocahontas. The English thought the marriage would keep the Powhatans forever friendly.

Dutch traders sold the first Africans to Jamestown in 1619. For years to come, blacks torn from their homeland would be forced into slavery.

The new Powhatan chief saw English settlement as a threat. Here, in 1622, he leads a surprise attack against the Virginia colonists.

They were wrong. After Chief Powhatan died, the Powhatan Indians stopped being helpful. They did not like losing their fishing and hunting lands to the Virginia settlers. In 1622, to stop the growing colony, the Indians attacked and killed 347 people. Having lost about one-third of their people, the English started an all-out war against the Indians. They finally defeated the Powhatans and took over their lands.

This pattern was repeated many times in American history. Indians and settlers were generally friendly to each other at first. As more and more settlers pushed into Indian territory, friendly relations turned to bloody conflicts.

The King Takes Control

After the Indian attack of 1622, King James took away the rights of the Virginia Company. He took over direct responsibility for the colony. The king, of course, was on the other side of the Atlantic Ocean. He could not very well look after all the concerns and problems of the colonists. To represent him, the king appointed a governor for the colony. This governor, like the company governors since 1619, shared ruling power with the House of Burgesses.

Reading Check

1. What did an indentured servant agree to?
2. What was the House of Burgesses? Why was it important?
3. How did conditions change for blacks between 1619 and 1661?
4. How did relations between the Powhatan Indians and Jamestown settlers change? What was the reason?

3. THE PILGRIMS LAND AT PLYMOUTH

To Guide Your Reading

Look for these important words:

Key Words
- Pilgrims
- destination
- *Mayflower*
- compact
- Mayflower Compact

People
- Massasoit
- Squanto
- William Bradford
- Miles Standish

Places
- New England
- Cape Cod
- Plymouth

Look for answers to these questions:

1. Who were the Pilgrims? Why did they come to the new world?
2. What kind of government did the Pilgrims have?
3. How did Indians help the Pilgrims?
4. Why did the Plymouth colony survive and prosper?

The hope of making a profit from trade was the main reason the Virginia Company founded Jamestown. Religion was the main reason for another English colony.

In 1614 John Smith had explored the Atlantic Coast above the Hudson River. He named this area **New England.** We use the name today to speak of the states of Connecticut, Rhode Island, Massachusetts, New Hampshire, Vermont, and Maine.

Smith mapped the coastline of New England and named the places along the coast. Smith wrote about New England in glowing terms. He described the richness of the land and waters, the fine forests, the great fish catches. "Here every man may be master and owner of his own labor and land," Smith wrote. In America more people would seek this ideal than had ever come to seek gold.

Among those who read Smith's description of New England was a group of English people in Holland. This group had left Scrooby, England, in 1608 because they disapproved of the Church of England. At that time everyone had to belong to the Church of England. To practice religion as they wanted, the Scrooby group fled to Holland. We call them **Pilgrims.** A pilgrim is a person who makes a journey for a religious reason.

The Pilgrims in Holland could practice their religion freely. Still, they worried about their children losing their English ways. Finding a place of their own in the new world might solve the problem.

The Virginia Company gave the Pilgrims permission to settle near the Hudson River. This was to be their **destination,** the place they hoped to reach. The Pilgrims, however, had no money to pay for the voyage. London merchants agreed to pay for the voyage and provide workers. In turn, the Pilgrims agreed to repay the merchants in furs, fish, and lumber.

Finally the details of the agreement were worked out. The Pilgrims hired a ship, the **Mayflower,** to take them to their new home in the fall of 1620. About one-third of the 102 travelers on the *Mayflower* were Pilgrims. Others were their servants and people hired by the London merchants.

The *Mayflower* had a long and dreadful voyage lasting 66 days. Violent storms drove the Pilgrims off course, and they ended up far north of their destination. When the Pilgrims finally sighted land, they were at **Cape Cod** in Massachusetts. Reaching a harbor near the tip of Cape Cod, "they fell upon their knees and blessed the God of heaven, who had brought them over the vast and furious ocean."

The Mayflower Compact

The Pilgrims faced an immediate problem. Cape Cod was north of the land governed by the Virginia Company. They were in a place without government. Without government, there were no laws. To meet that problem, the Pilgrim leaders on the *Mayflower* made a **compact,** an agreement. All the men signed the **Mayflower Compact.** They agreed that "just and equal" laws would be made for the general good of the colony. They further agreed that they would obey these laws. In other words, they would govern themselves. We take this idea for granted. But when kings and queens ruled, it was a brave idea.

In a place without government, the Pilgrims agree to govern themselves. William Bradford leads the signing of the Mayflower Compact.

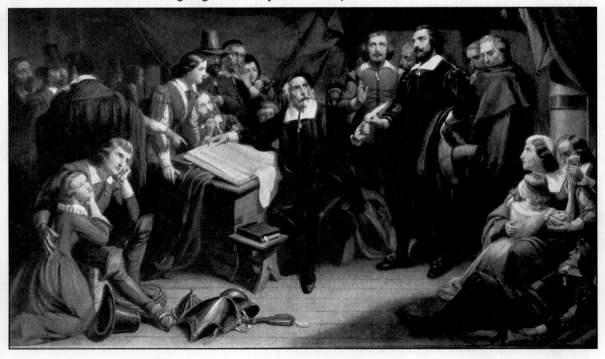

The Founding of Plymouth

Another major problem faced the Pilgrims. The windy shores of Cape Cod were not a good place to settle. For four weeks the Pilgrims explored the bay in the raw, cold winds. They finally chose to settle at the place John Smith had named **Plymouth.** It had a harbor, open fields nearby, and fresh stream water. The Pilgrims were especially pleased to find fresh water. The stream water of England and Holland was too polluted to drink. When they lived there, they drank beer instead of water.

Near the end of December, the colonists began sawing wood and making boards for the first building at Plymouth. They worked just as hard on December 25 as on other days. The Pilgrims did not celebrate Christmas because, they said, it was not mentioned in the Bible.

The Pilgrims faced a hard winter. They were weak from the stormy voyage. They were hungry from lack of proper food. For a long time they could build no adequate shelter against the cold and the wet weather. Half the group died from disease.

Help from Indians

When spring arrived, Pilgrim spirits rose. Those who had been sick started to get better. Best of all, help came. Although the Pilgrims had seen Indians, they had had no contact with them. Then one day an Indian walked into their midst and said, "Welcome, Englishmen." He asked for food and beer.

How surprised the English were! The Indian, whose name was Samoset, had learned some English from contacts

After landing at Plymouth, the Pilgrims huddled around fires for warmth.

with English fishermen. Several days later, **Massasoit** (mas•uh•SOH•it), the chief of the Wampanoag (WAMP•uhn•oh•ahg) Indians, accompanied Samoset on a visit to the Pilgrims. Massasoit and the Pilgrim leaders worked out an agreement to maintain peaceful relations. The peace lasted for 50 years.

Among the Indians with Massasoit was an English-speaking Indian named **Squanto.** Squanto had been kidnapped years before to be sold as a slave in Spain. He had escaped and spent several years in England before returning to his native land.

When Squanto arrived home, he discovered that his whole tribe, the Pawtuxet (paw•TUX•et), had died. They

137

Samoset startles the Plymouth colonists with an English greeting. Stepping forward to meet him are Miles Standish and William Bradford. Soon the settlers learn they have good friends among their Indian neighbors.

had probably died of the plague (PLAYG), a terrible disease carried by fleas and rats. There were no rats in the new world until European ships started making visits. The land that once had many Indians on it now lay empty. This was the land the Pilgrims had settled.

Squanto showed the Pilgrims how to plant corn and catch fish. Because he knew both languages, Squanto also helped keep Pilgrim-Indian relations smooth. Squanto helped the colonists survive.

The Plymouth colony also survived because it had strong leaders. One of

them was **William Bradford.** Bradford, an English farmer, had gone with the Pilgrims to Holland and then to Plymouth. He was elected governor of Plymouth in 1621. He was to be reelected 30 times before his death in 1656. Most of what we know about Plymouth comes from Bradford's history of Plymouth colony.

Another strong leader was **Miles Standish.** Standish was a military man. He was responsible for the defense of the colony. His firm but fair dealings with Indians contributed to peace at Plymouth.

The First Thanksgiving

The Pilgrims harvested their first crops in the fall of 1621. Governor Bradford thought the Pilgrims should have a celebration. He sent men to the forest to shoot turkeys so that they might "rejoice together" in a "special manner." Fish, clams, oysters, and lobsters were gathered. Women baked corn bread.

The Pilgrims invited their Indian neighbors to come. Imagine their surprise when 90 Indians showed up! The Pilgrims did not have food for so many. Massosoit quickly understood the situation. He sent some of his braves to the woods to get deer. With five deer added to the feast, there was enough for all. The Indians and Pilgrims spent three days feasting and having contests. It was the first Thanksgiving. We do not know the exact day of this feast.

The Pilgrims Prosper

When the Pilgrims first arrived in Plymouth, everyone worked for the community. That meant that there was no private ownership of land. The harvest was divided equally among the families. People began to complain about this because some were working

This recent painting shows the first Thanksgiving celebration. How does it show friendship between the Pilgrims and the Indians?

Children visiting Plymouth today experiment with the old quill pens used by early colonists. William Bradford used such a pen to write down his history of Plymouth colony.

harder than others. In 1623 the land was divided among the settlers. They learned the same lesson the settlers in Jamestown had learned. People work harder on their own land. "The women now went willingly to the fields," wrote Bradford. Until then the women had claimed "weakness and inability" to do work in the fields, Bradford wrote in his history.

Although there was now private ownership of land, the ideal of people sharing with one another remained strong. Because meadowland was scarce, it was owned by the group as a whole. Everyone could use it. Each year certain people were appointed to catch the small fish that went up the streams. These were then distributed to all farmers for fertilizer. When wood was cut for the winter, it was also distributed to each family.

Others from England soon joined the small colony. One of them was Abraham Pearce. Historians think Pearce may have been among the Africans sent to Jamestown in 1619. He served as an indentured servant. Then he went to England as a free man and from there to the Plymouth colony.

The Pilgrims at Plymouth began to prosper with their fishing, farming, and fur trading. When the next wave of settlers arrived, the Pilgrims had a surplus of goods. They then sold milk, meat, and produce to the new settlers.

Reading Check

1. What was the Mayflower Compact?
2. Where did the Pilgrims settle?
3. How did Squanto help the Pilgrims?
4. How did the Pilgrims share their resources?

4. BOSTON AND NEW AMSTERDAM

To Guide Your Reading

Look for these important words:

Key Words
- Puritans
- inflation

People
- Peter Stuyvesant

Places
- Massachusetts Bay Colony
- Boston
- New Netherland
- Manhattan

- New Amsterdam
- New Sweden
- New York

Look for answers to these questions:

1. Who were the Puritans? What were their reasons for coming to America?
2. Where did the Dutch settle? How was their settlement ruled?
3. How did the English gain control of New Amsterdam?

The Pilgrims were poor people who started their settlement with fewer than 100 colonists. The later settlement of **Massachusetts Bay Colony** at **Boston** was quite different. Here, in 1630, 15 ships arrived carrying more than 1,000 settlers. These settlers, as the Pilgrims did, disapproved of many practices of the Church of England. They did not separate from the church, like the Pilgrims, but wished to make it more "pure." For this reason, these people are called **Puritans.** Like the Pilgrims, the Puritans hoped to establish a community where they could put Christian ideals into practice.

The Puritans had other reasons for coming to New England. In England itself Puritan farmers had found it harder and harder to make a living. Those who owned their land complained of high taxes. Farmers who rented land complained of rising rents. Yet the amount they received for their

John Winthrop, who led the Puritans from England to Boston, governed them for nearly 20 years.

crops stayed the same. Craftsmen also found it difficult to support their families. Prices were rising faster than wages. The same amount of money bought fewer goods. England was suffering from **inflation.**

The Puritan settlement in Boston was successful from the start and continued to grow. Many communities were soon established near Boston.

New Netherland

While the English were settling Virginia and New England, the Dutch started settlements along the Hudson River. They had claimed that area since Henry Hudson had explored the river for Holland. They named the area **New Netherland**.

In 1624 a Dutch company set up a trading post at Fort Orange. Fort Orange is the present-day Albany, capital of New York. In 1626 the company bought the island of **Manhattan** from the Indians and established a trading post called **New Amsterdam.** There they built a wall to keep out wolves and Indians. The street running alongside the wall was known as Wall Street. Wall Street is famous today as a center of banking and finance.

The Dutch company welcomed a variety of settlers. French, Danes, Italians, Spaniards, and Jews all found homes in New Amsterdam.

New Amsterdam prospered after the Dutch company appointed **Peter Stuyvesant** (STY•vuh•sunt) as governor. Stuyvesant had lost his right leg in a Dutch attack on a French fort. Thereafter he walked on a wooden leg called a peg leg. That gave him a nickname of Pegleg Peter.

New Amsterdam was a community of about 1,000 people in 1650. Notice the ships in the harbor and the windmills in the distance.

Peter Stuyvesant strides forward to meet the English who have landed. A harsh and unpleasant leader, Stuyvesant was unable to get the citizens of New Amsterdam to fight the English.

Stuyvesant was a powerful and stubborn governor. He ruled the Dutch colony as he chose. There were often strong disagreements between Stuyvesant and the citizens of New Amsterdam. The citizens wanted more say in government and disliked Stuyvesant's strong-handed rule.

In 1655 Stuyvesant took over the small colony of **New Sweden.** This Swedish colony was centered at Fort Cristina, in what is now Wilmington, Delaware.

Compared to the English colonies, there were few people in the Dutch colony of New Netherland. Knowing this, the king of England declared war on Holland. The king told his brother, the Duke of York, that he could have the Dutch colonies. In 1664 the Duke of York sailed into the harbor of New Amsterdam. Stuyvesant tried to get the citizens of New Amsterdam to fight the English. They refused, and Stuyvesant had to surrender without firing a shot. New Amsterdam was renamed **New York.** The English now controlled most of the Atlantic Coast of North America.

Reading Check

1. Where did the Puritans settle?
2. Why did the Puritans come to New England?
3. Why did the citizens of New Amsterdam disagree with Peter Stuyvesant?
4. Why was England able to take over New Netherland?

LOG CABINS

A broad ax

Imagine that it is the early 1600s. You have just come with your family to the new world. What do you do first? Chances are that first you build a shelter.

Most early English colonists knew how to build houses like those in their homelands. These houses were constructed of bricks, stone, or planks of sawed wood. Building homes of these materials took special tools as well as time. For settlers facing the coming of winter, time was often short. Tools were often scarce.

Many early settlers died from the freezing cold in poorly built houses. Solid, quickly built houses were needed until finer ones could be built.

In 1638 a new kind of building appeared on the American scene. In New Sweden, colonists from Sweden and Finland started building a type of structure common in their homeland. This was a log cabin. The only tool needed to build a log cabin was an ax. The only materials needed were plenty of tall, straight trees. Add to that a good deal of hard work, and the result was a sturdy home.

The square notch

The typical log cabin was built in six steps. First, a woodsman selected straight, smooth trees of about the same width. Then, steel ax flashing, he felled the trees and trimmed them to the right length. The logs were pulled by horses or dragged by hand to the building site. They were notched at the ends so they would fit together. Next, the logs were lifted into place. Finally, the cracks between the logs were "chinked." They were filled with mud, clay, or moss. Two people could complete a cabin like this in a couple of weeks.

Log cabins quickly became popular in Pennsylvania, Ohio, Kentucky, and Tennessee. In these areas where deep forests stretched as far as the eye could see, logs were readily available. One visitor to a Kentucky village in the 1700s exclaimed, "Almost every house in the settlement was built of logs."

The saddle notch

Building log cabins, settlers could make safe, warm homes for themselves in the wilderness of America.

SKILLS FOR SUCCESS

USING PHYSICAL MAPS

Reading a Relief Map

Maps show the shapes of countries and continents. Often they also show what the surface of the land is like. Look at the drawing below.

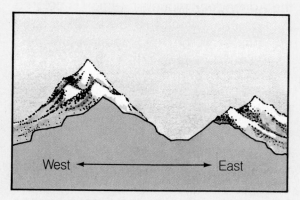

West ← → East

The drawing shows a cross section. A cross section shows what the land would look like if it were sliced. Imagine slicing a pear from top to bottom. The exposed part of the pear would be the cross section.

In the cross section the mountain range to the west is quite high. The mountain range to the east is lower. Between the mountain ranges is a valley.

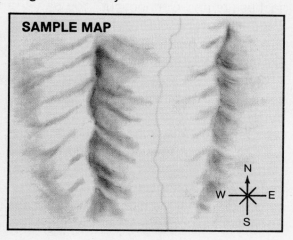

SAMPLE MAP

These landforms are also shown on the sample map. The top of the high mountain range is the heavily shaded area. The lightly shaded area near the eastern edge of the map is the lower mountain range. The valley, the lowest area, is not shaded.

This type of map is called a **relief map.** A relief map uses shading to show the shape of landforms. The relief map below shows part of the northeastern United States.

Find the darkly shaded area in the western part of the map. The shading tells you that this is a mountainous area. Which mountains are to the south of the Adirondack Mountains?

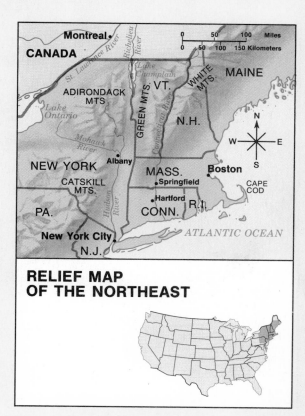

RELIEF MAP OF THE NORTHEAST

Find the Mohawk River on the map. It runs from west to east between the two mountain ranges. The land near this river is not shaded. This tells you that the land is lower than the mountainous lands to the north and south.

Find the Connecticut River on the map. Between what mountains does it flow?

Which states seem to have no mountains? According to this map, would you find mountains along the Maine seacoast? Why or why not?

Reading an Elevation Map

The relief map shows mountains. However, the map does not tell you *how high* the mountains are. For this information you must look at an **elevation map.** An elevation map shows the heights of land areas. The word *elevation* means height.

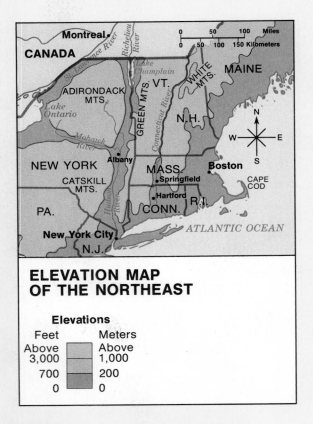

ELEVATION MAP OF THE NORTHEAST

Elevations

Feet	Meters
Above 3,000	Above 1,000
700	200
0	0

Most elevation maps use color to show elevations above sea level. Look at the elevation map below. The map key tells you which colors are used to show different elevations.

For example, dark green is used for land that is between sea level and 700 feet (200 m) high. You can see that the eastern part of Massachusetts is dark green. This tells you that the land is between 0 (sea level) and 700 feet (200 m) in elevation. Most of the Adirondack mountain region is colored light green. How high is this land? Is there any place on the map above 3,000 feet (1,000 m)? Where is it?

Finding Out Which Way Rivers Flow

You can use an elevation map to find out which way a river flows. Water flows in a downhill direction, from high ground to low ground. The colors showing elevation will tell you which part of the river is on high ground, which on low ground.

Look at the Connecticut River on the elevation map. Its source is in New Hampshire near the Canadian border. According to the map, what is the elevation of the river in upper New Hampshire? In Massachusetts the Connecticut River drops in elevation. What is its elevation as it flows through Massachusetts and Connecticut? You can see that the Connecticut River flows southward. It flows from a higher elevation through lower elevations until it reaches the Atlantic Ocean.

Sometimes we describe places in relation to a river as **downstream** or **upstream.** Suppose you are in Springfield, Massachusetts, and you follow the direction in which the Connecticut River flows. You come to Hartford, Connecticut. Hartford is downstream from Springfield. A place reached by going against the river flow is upstream. Springfield is upstream from Hartford.

Physical Maps

Maps that show both relief and elevation are usually called **physical maps.** These maps use shading *and* color to show the shape and height of the land surface.

The combination of shading and color can help you understand the true shape of the land. Find the Catskill Mountains on the map below. The light green color shows that the Catskills have an elevation of between 700 and 3,000 feet (200 and 1,000 m). The shading shows where the Catskills are the steepest.

Uses of a Physical Map

It is much easier to travel on a level trail than on a steep, rough one. Walking up and down mountains is hard work, and it makes for slow traveling. A physical map can show the best travel routes because it shows which areas are flat and which are mountainous.

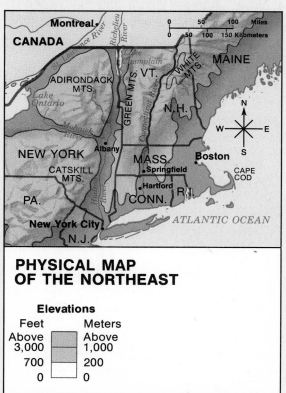

PHYSICAL MAP OF THE NORTHEAST

Elevations

Feet		Meters
Above 3,000		Above 1,000
700		200
0		0

By showing elevation, a physical map can make clear which way rivers flow. Imagine that you are a colonial trader wishing to travel between the St. Lawrence River near Montreal and New York City. With your finger trace the easiest route on the map. You probably would follow the Richelieu (RISH•uh•loo) River to Lake Champlain. Then you would go south until you came to the Hudson River. You could follow the Hudson River all the way to New York City. This route would be much faster and easier than a route straight through the Adirondacks.

CHECKING YOUR SKILLS

Answer the following questions. Use the information in this lesson to help you.

1. To find the elevation of the Green Mountains, should you consult a relief map or an elevation map?

2. Will a relief map tell you if southern Connecticut is generally flat or hilly? Will a relief map tell you the elevation of southern Connecticut?

3. Does the Hudson River flow from north to south or from south to north?

4. How high are the highest areas in northern New Hampshire? Is the land in northern New Hampshire hilly or flat?

5. Imagine you are a Dutch fur trader. You want to set up a trading post so that Indians traveling by canoe from both the Adirondack Mountains and the Catskill Mountains can reach you easily. Would the best place for a trading post be at the mouth of the Connecticut River, at the mouth of the Hudson River, or near Lake Champlain?

6. Is Albany upstream or downstream from New York City?

CHAPTER 6 REVIEW

WORDS TO USE

Use the words below to complete the sentences that follow.

compact   prosper
indentured servants   Puritans
profit

1. The Virginia Company hoped to make a _____ from the Jamestown settlement.

2. People who agreed to work for a certain period of time in return for ocean passage were _____.

3. Tobacco crops helped Virginia to _____, or do well.

4. The Pilgrims made a _____ to form a government and to obey its laws.

5. The _____ established the Massachusetts Bay Colony in 1630.

FACTS TO REVIEW

1. Why was Jamestown founded? Plymouth? New Amsterdam?

2. What problems did Jamestown first face? What helped Jamestown to grow and to achieve prosperity?

3. What leaders were important in the Jamestown and Plymouth colonies? Why was each important?

4. Why was the House of Burgesses important? the Mayflower Compact?

5. How were Pocahontas and Squanto each helpful to early colonists?

IDEAS TO DISCUSS

1. In what ways did tobacco cause Virginia to grow and prosper? How did it affect the need for workers, the growth of slavery, relations with the Indians?

2. What does it mean to be "in a place without government"? Why did the Pilgrims feel it necessary to write and sign the Mayflower Compact?

3. Describing New England, John Smith wrote, "Here every man may be master and owner of his own labor and land." What changes helped the Virginia settlers to reach this goal? the Pilgrims?

4. What changes might one have seen in Jamestown between 1607 and 1619? in Plymouth between 1620 and 1630?

⬤ SKILLS PRACTICE

Using Physical Maps   Use the physical map on page 147 to answer these questions.

1. Which major rivers come together just north of Albany?

2. In what direction does the Mohawk River flow? Would it be easier in a canoe to travel east or west on the Mohawk River?

3. If you lived in the White Mountains, would it be easier to reach Albany by foot or by canoe? Why or why not?

4. Suppose a traveler wished to go from Boston to Albany in the fastest way possible by boat or canoe. What route should the traveler take?

UNIT 2 REVIEW

WORDS TO REMEMBER

Read each sentence. Then replace the underlined words in each sentence with the correct word from this list. Write the new sentences on your paper.

astronomy   expeditions
colonies   journal
compact   missionaries
compass   navigation
conquistadors   profit

1. Prince Henry encouraged a way for sailors to find their way on the seas.

2. An important instrument for sea captains was a tool for finding directions.

3. For sailors to find their way on the seas they need to know something about the study of the stars.

4. After Columbus there were many European journeys to explore the Americas.

5. On Magellan's voyage Pigafetta kept a daily record of what he saw.

6. The Aztec and Inca civilizations were destroyed by Spanish conquerors.

7. After Columbus Europeans started coming to the Americas to live in settlements ruled by a European country.

8. Europeans who came to the new world included people who wanted to bring Christianity to the Indians.

9. The Pilgrims made a written agreement that they would live by laws made for the good of the colony.

10. Traders and businesses in the new world hoped to make a sum of money after meeting expenses.

FOCUS ON MAIN IDEAS

1. Why was the voyage of Christopher Columbus so important?

2. Why did Europeans try to find new routes to Asia?

3. How did Columbus, Balboa, and Magellan each contribute to knowledge about the world?

4. Describe the changes in Mexico as a result of Cortés's conquest.

5. Make a table comparing the explorations of Coronado and Cartier. Where did each explore? When? For what country? Why? What were the results?

6. Why did English sea-dog attacks on Spanish ships help England become a strong nation?

7. Why is the Mayflower Compact important?

8. Give three examples showing the helpfulness of American Indians to the first Europeans. Why did this helpfulness often turn into bad feelings and conflict?

9. How did French settlements in North America differ from English settlements?

10. In what ways did the Pilgrims and the conquistadors differ? Were they alike in any way?

ACTIVITIES

1. **Research/Art** Find out more about one of the first settlements: Plymouth, New Amsterdam, Fort Orange, or Jamestown. Draw a picture of one.

2. **Research/Art/Writing** Find out more about one of these ships: the *Santa Maria,* the *Golden Hind,* the *Mayflower.* Draw a picture of the ship. Write a short report describing the size of the ship, the kind of ship, and its history.

3. **Remembering the Close-Up** Write a menu for lunch or dinner that uses only food native to the Western Hemisphere.

4. **Acting Out** Act out a scene from this unit. Here are some suggestions.

   a. Columbus talking with his sailors
   b. Pocahontas saving the life of John Smith
   c. The Pilgrims arriving at Cape Cod
   d. The first Thanksgiving
   e. Peter Stuyvesant surrendering to the English
   f. An exchange of goods at a French trading post

5. **Writing** Pretend that you were with one of the explorers or settlers. Write either a letter home or a journal entry describing one or two days in your life.

◯ SKILLS REVIEW

1. **Historical Maps** Use the map on this page to answer these questions.

   a. When did Coronado leave Compostela?

   b. When did Cárdenas reach the Grand Canyon?

   c. When did Coronado leave Quivira? In what direction did he then travel?

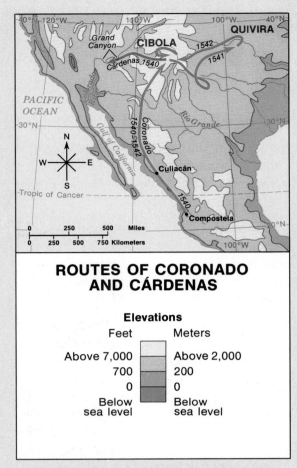

ROUTES OF CORONADO AND CÁRDENAS

Elevations

Feet	Meters
Above 7,000	Above 2,000
700	200
0	0
Below sea level	Below sea level

2. **Latitude and Longitude** Use the map on this page to answer these questions.

   a. What is the approximate latitude and longitude of the place in Quivira where Coronado turned back?

   b. What city is located near 25°N latitude?

   c. What river is near 115°W longitude?

3. **Using Physical Maps** Use the map on this page to answer these questions.

   a. What is the elevation of Cibola?

   b. In what general direction does the Colorado River flow? Where is its mouth?

   c. Why did Coronado not go due north from Compostela?

YOUR STATE'S HISTORY

Explorers from many European lands came to the new world. The early explorers did more than just discover places. They brought their languages, cultures, and ways of life to the areas they found. Every state bears the mark of the people who first settled it. These activities may help you learn about the first Europeans to live in your state.

LEARNING ABOUT PEOPLE

1. Explorers such as Cortés, Coronado, and La Salle helped shape our nation. Find out the name of a famous explorer who discovered or passed through your state. Write a short report on this explorer. Be sure to find out the explorer's native country and language. What hardships did this explorer face in your state?

LEARNING ABOUT GEOGRAPHY

2. Many of the early explorers and settlers dreamed of great riches. They hoped to profit from the gold, beaver fur, and other natural resources they found. Find out which natural resources were discovered by the settlers of your state. Can these resources still be found in your state?

3. Imagine that you are an early explorer of your state. Write a letter to a friend back in Europe and tell about the wild territory you have found. Does it seem like a good place to live? Should your friend come and join you here? Why?

LEARNING ABOUT CULTURE

4. French and Spanish names are common in our country. French names often begin with the words *Saint, Le, La, De,* or *Des.* Spanish names may begin with *San, Santa, Los, El, La,* or *Del.* Look in an atlas of your state. Are there any French or Spanish names?

5. The picture below is a copy, or reconstruction, of the *Mayflower.* There are also reconstructions of the early settlements of Plymouth and Jamestown. Can reconstructions of early ships or settlements be found in your state? If so, learn what you can about a reconstruction and what it shows.

UNIT THREE

LIFE IN THE AMERICAN COLONIES

Key Dates and Events

1632
George Calvert founds colony of Maryland

1636
Roger Williams founds colony of Rhode Island

Thomas Hooker starts settlement in Connecticut

1670
Founding of Charleston, South Carolina

1675
King Philip's War in New England

1682
William Penn founds colony of Pennsylvania

1723
Benjamin Franklin moves to Philadelphia

1733
James Oglethorpe founds Georgia

1743
Eliza Lucas develops indigo

England had one American colony in 1607. By 1733 that number had grown to 13. The population and the prosperity of the colonies grew as well. Imagine visiting a harbor in colonial America. You see sailing ships of every size and for every purpose. There are fishing boats, schooners, whaling ships, and large, ocean-going vessels. The harbors buzz with activity. Lumber, fish, wheat, iron, and tobacco are being loaded onto ships bound for England and other places. Strong workers unload cloth or carriages from England. Worn and weary passengers come ashore in America for the first time. They are about to start new lives for themselves.

The picture at the left shows colonial Philadelphia. It shows how important a harbor was. Ships were the main means of both communication and transportation. Ships linked colonists to each other and to England.

CHAPTER 7

The New England Colonies

New England's geography and history have made it a distinct region of the United States. Religion, schooling, and hard work were important to the New England way of life. At first most people were farmers who lived in villages. Later many worked as shipbuilders, whalers, and traders. These activities helped towns to grow. The experiences and beliefs of the early New Englanders were very important in forming our nation. In this chapter you will read about what life was like in early New England.

1. GEOGRAPHY AND TOWNS OF NEW ENGLAND

To Guide Your Reading

Look for these important words:

Key Words
- deciduous
- navigable
- naval stores
- common
- village green
- meetinghouse
- authority
- meeting
- town meeting
- offices
- official

Places
- Connecticut River

Look for answers to these questions:
1. What are the natural features of New England?
2. How were New England villages laid out?
3. In what ways was religion important to the Puritans?
4. What kind of town government did the Puritan settlers have?

Ten thousand years before the Pilgrims landed at Plymouth, glaciers covered much of New England. As the glaciers melted, they left a new landscape behind. There were gentle hills, sharp mountains, and a rocky, jagged coastline with many harbors. The melting glaciers had left behind huge amounts of stones and boulders.

With the disappearance of the glaciers, great forests took root. These included forests of evergreen trees and **deciduous** (di•SIJ•uh•wus) trees. Deciduous trees are hardwood trees that lose their leaves in the fall. Maple, ash, walnut, and chestnut are deciduous trees that grow in New England.

Clear, fast rivers tumbled down from the mountains to the Atlantic Ocean. Because of the many waterfalls most rivers were not **navigable.** That means they were not wide, deep, or gentle enough for cargo-carrying boats. An exception was the **Connecticut River,** the longest river in New England. Much of this river was navigable, which made the Connecticut valley attractive to early settlers.

Early settlers made good use of New England's natural resources. The fish in the ocean, the forests, the harbors, the rushing streams, and even the rocky fields helped New England to prosper. Because the New Englanders could catch more fish than they needed, they had a surplus. The surplus catch could be sold or traded to the West Indies or Europe. Fishing and trading encouraged ship building.

The forests of New England provided the materials needed for shipbuilding. Logs were floated down rivers to the harbor towns. There the logs were turned into **naval stores.** Naval stores included the planks, masts, pitch, tar, and turpentine used in shipbuilding. Well-built ships encouraged even more trade.

The New Englanders also used the fast streams to turn waterwheels. The waterwheels then turned machinery for grinding grain or sawing wood.

It took hard work to clear the fields of rocks and boulders. The crop that grew best in the rocky soil and short New England summers was corn. The hard-working farmers also grew crops like barley, wheat, rye, and oats. Cows, sheep, and horses grazed in pastures.

The New England Village

Most life in colonial New England centered around the village. Farming was carried on in fields outside the vil-

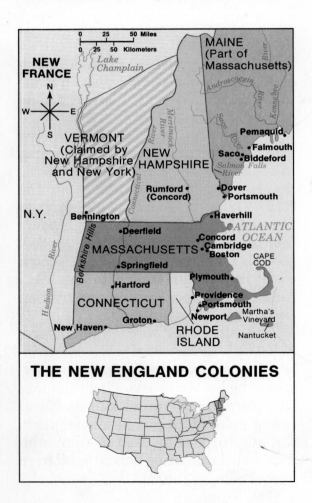

THE NEW ENGLAND COLONIES

lage. Puritan settlers brought this pattern with them from England. They often brought the names of their English villages as well. Boston, Salem, Ipswich, and Groton are some of the New England towns named after English towns.

In the center of the New England village was the **common,** or **village green.** This was a parklike pasture shared by the villagers. At one end was the church, called a **meetinghouse.** Houses lined other sides of the village green. Over the years other buildings were added. Among these were a blacksmith shop, an inn, a school, a village store, and a mill. Beyond the village were the fields and woods.

The Puritans liked the village plan because they thought of themselves as a community. The closeness of village life made it easier for people to help each other. It was easier to get to the meetinghouse.

Village life also made it easier for church ministers to exercise their **authority,** or control. In Puritan New England the minister was the most important person in the village. The Puritans had clear ideas about what was right and what was wrong. The duty of the minister was to help keep people on the right path.

The Meetinghouse

Just as the minister was the most important person, so was the meetinghouse the most important building. Everyone had to attend **meeting,** or church, on Sunday. The major part of meeting was the minister's sermon. A sermon often lasted for several hours. The meeting lasted most of the day, with

Fields

Mill

Minister's house

Craft shops

Blacksmith

Meetinghouse

Stocks

Green or common

Inn

Furniture maker

School

Cooper

Well

Soapmaking

A NEW ENGLAND VILLAGE

A warming box

a break at noon. At noon villagers gathered in nearby homes for warmth, conversation, and a hot meal.

In the meetinghouse each person had an assigned place to sit. Important people had the best seats. Those who failed to sit in their assigned seats were fined. Sometimes people fell asleep during the long sermons. It was the job of one person to awaken them by tickling their faces with a feather.

There was no heat in the meetinghouse. In winter it could be painfully cold. The women and girls often brought metal boxes full of hot coals to meetings. They rested their feet on the boxes to keep warm. Dogs were welcome in the meetinghouse. A dog curled up at his master's feet helped keep him warm, too. Of course, dogs had to behave. One person had the job of Dog Whipper and put out dogs that barked.

The outside wall of the meetinghouse was a kind of a bulletin board. Notices were nailed to the walls announcing livestock and land sales, intended marriages, and auctions. In the early days, wolves' heads might also decorate the outside of the meetinghouse. People were paid for every wolf they killed.

The Town Meeting

Town business was conducted at a **town meeting.** This meeting, usually held in the meetinghouse, was open to everyone. At first, a man had to be a member of the church to vote. By the end of the 1600s, a man could vote if he owned property. At the town meeting all the town's needs and problems were discussed.

Each year men were elected to a number of **offices.** An office in this sense is a job one does for the good of the community. A person holding an office is an **official** (uh·FISH·uhl). Some of the offices in colonial times were constable, drummer, town crier, digger of graves, sweeper of the meetinghouse, and fence viewer. The constable was in charge of keeping the peace. The town crier called out important announcements. The fence viewer made sure that the pasture fences were kept in repair.

There were other tasks. In Haverhill, Massachusetts, the town meeting appointed a man to keep the measles out of town. How he managed that job, we do not know. The Haverhill meeting also appointed a man to run the ferry. He could not charge what he wanted, however. The town meeting set the charges at 3 pence a horse, 1 pence a person, all ministers free. The town meeting also chose the schoolteacher and decided the teacher's salary.

Reading Check

1. In what ways did colonists make use of New England's natural resources?
2. Why did Puritan settlers like the village plan?
3. What are examples of the importance of religion in New England?
4. How did the New England village govern itself?

2. EVERYDAY LIFE IN NEW ENGLAND

To Guide Your Reading

Look for these important words:

Key Words
- Training Day
- militia
- barter

Look for answers to these questions:

1. How did people in New England villages celebrate?
2. What kinds of work did women and girls do?
3. What kinds of work did men and boys do?
4. Why did the Puritans think education important?

The village green was at first used by settlers as grazing land for their livestock. As time passed, the green was used less for livestock and more as a place for village gatherings. On the green, boys would scramble in a rough game of football after their chores were done. Girls would fly kites or play blindman's bluff.

The biggest holiday of the year, **Training Day,** took place on the green. At least once a year all able-bodied men had to report for military drills. A military unit made up of volunteers is called a **militia** (muh•LISH•uh). Men in the militia marched and practiced firing their muskets. After the drill, there were contests and games, and plenty to eat and drink.

Other occasions for celebration included times when people helped one another put up barns or houses. An exciting event in early spring was collecting sap from the maple trees and boiling it down to sugar. Weddings were always a cause for a village celebration.

Home Life

The most important room of a New England house contained the great fireplace. A fire was always kept burning in the fireplace. To let a fire go out

At a house raising, the neighbors would celebrate after the timbers were put up.

In colonial kitchens many activities took place. In the back a woman churns butter. Another spins. One woman cooks while another rolls out dough. A grandfather peels apples. Toddlers play.

caused great trouble because there were no matches. A new fire could be started only by striking flint against metal to make sparks. Most villagers started new fires by borrowing burning coals from a neighbor.

All cooking was done in the fireplace. Baking was done in a small oven in the side of the fireplace. Most food was roasted over the fire or simmered in large iron kettles. Kettles were also used to heat water for cooking and washing.

Women and girls spent long days doing necessary chores. Most of the chores were centered around feeding and clothing the family. Women turned milk into butter and cheese. They dried and preserved fruits such as peaches, pears, and apples. They pickled cabbage and other vegetables from the garden. Pickling vegetables preserved them throughout winter.

The women also made all the clothing for the family. They started with wool from their sheep. They had to spin the wool before weaving it into cloth. From the flax plants in their fields, they spun and wove linen. Pieces of worn-out clothing were used to make patchwork quilts for bedding. Nothing useful was ever wasted.

Farm Work

In New England farmers could raise only enough crops to meet the needs of their families. The men and boys spent long hours working in the fields. They had to remove the rocks, which they used for fences. Once the fields were clear of rocks, the men tilled the soil. To do this, they walked behind oxen pulling a heavy wooden plow. They then planted, weeded, and harvested their crops. Their crops included corn and rye and maybe barley and wheat. Pumpkins and squash grew among the corn.

The men and boys also took care of the cattle, hogs, and sheep. These animals were used as sources of food, leather, and wool. Pig bristles were used to make brushes. Animal fat was turned into soap and candles.

Colonial farmers might make their own barrels or get them from a barrelmaker.

Like the women, the men were skilled in a number of crafts. They made their own work tools, such as plows and rakes. During the evenings a colonial farmer might work leather from his animals into shoes, straps, and work pants. He might also make wooden barrels. Barrels were used to store grain, salted meats, and other foods.

Sometimes a farmer specialized in a craft. A man who was a good blacksmith might make nails for a neighbor. In exchange the neighbor would make barrels for the blacksmith. This system of exchanging goods and services without using money is called **barter.** In the early days of colonial life, money was rarely used.

Schools

It was very important to the Puritans that every person be able to read the Bible. Parents were expected to see that their children and servants learned to read. Every town of 50 families or more had a school.

Both men and women were teachers in these schools, which at first were in homes. As time passed, villages began to build their own schools.

School met all year. There was no summer vacation. The Puritans would have called such a vacation a waste of "God's precious time." Working hard, they believed, was a way to please God.

Even though school was open all year round, many children attended only 10 or 12 weeks a year. At other times their parents needed them to do work at home or in the fields. Parents were expected to pay a small amount each week their children attended school. In some places parents paid one

Children in New England often learned reading, writing, and arithmetic at small schools run by women in their homes.

Making this sampler was the way young Patty Goodeshall learned both her stitches and her letters.

price for a student to learn to read. If a student were to be taught arithmetic, it cost more.

Paper was very scarce and expensive in the colonies. Students often learned to write on pieces of birch bark. Girls might learn both their letters and their needlework by stitching samplers.

Boys could go to grammar schools to prepare for college. Harvard College, in Cambridge, Massachusetts, was founded in 1636. It was the first college in the colonies. The Puritans wanted their leaders and ministers to be well educated. Some women received excellent educations at home, but they were not allowed to attend college.

Reading Check

1. What was Training Day?
2. Name three skills needed by colonial women; by colonial farmers.
3. What does *barter* mean?
4. What were early schools like?

3. NEW ENGLAND GROWS

To Guide Your Reading

Look for these important words:

Key Words
- Pequot Indians
- King Philip's War
- frontier
- exports
- imports
- triangle trade route

People
- Roger Williams
- Anne Hutchinson
- Thomas Hooker
- Metacomet
- Olaudah Equiano

Places
- Providence

- Rhode Island
- Portsmouth
- Hartford
- Connecticut
- Vermont
- Maine
- New Hampshire
- Nantucket

Look for answers to these questions:

1. Which members of the Massachusetts Bay Colony founded new settlements? Why?
2. What caused the Indian wars in the Connecticut valley?
3. In what ways did New England colonists become prosperous?
4. How did the slave trade work?

The early Puritans of Massachusetts did not welcome people with different ideas. They feared change in their lives. When they disapproved of someone's ideas, that person was punished.

Such a person was **Roger Williams.** He had unpopular ideas about the Puritan Church. He also thought that the Indians, not the king, should have power to grant land to the colonists. Williams's ideas angered the Puritan leaders. They voted to expel Williams from the Massachusetts Bay Colony.

Not allowed to stay in Massachusetts, Roger Williams fled south to Narragansett (nar•uh•GAN•suht) Bay. There he received food and protection from the Narragansett Indians. In 1636 he bought land from the Indians and founded the settlement of **Providence.** It later became part of a new colony called **Rhode Island.** People of all religions were welcome to settle there. In this colony the idea of freedom of religion grew.

A strong and spirited woman named **Anne Hutchinson** was also forced to leave the Massachusetts Bay Colony. This happened after she had begun to question the authority of the Puritan ministers. With her family and many followers, she founded a settlement at **Portsmouth,** Rhode Island, not far from Providence.

Thomas Hooker left Massachusetts too, but for another reason. He had looked with longing at the fertile lands of the Connecticut River valley. Hooker and his followers made the move in 1636. They left the rocky fields of the Massachusetts colony to start

Thomas Hooker led his followers to the fertile valley of the Connecticut River.

a settlement at **Hartford.** Later their settlement joined with others to form the colony of **Connecticut.**

Indian Wars

When settlers first moved into the Connecticut valley, the **Pequot** (PEE•kwaht) **Indians** attacked them. The Connecticut settlers, with help from Massachusetts settlers, struck back and soundly defeated the Pequots.

Meanwhile the English tried to keep peace with other Indians of New England by buying their land. But ownership of land meant different things to the English and the Indians. In the Indian view, no one could own the land. People could only use it. When Indians "sold" land, they thought they were sharing, not giving it up. The English, however, thought the Indians would leave the land after they had sold it.

The ill feelings between the English and the Indians broke out in an all-out war in 1675. This war was called **King Philip's War.** King Philip was the name the English gave to **Metacomet,** the leader of the Wampanoags and the son of Massasoit.

For both Indians and settlers, King Philip's War was bloody and cruel. By this time the Indians had become deadly shots with muskets. Indians attacked and destroyed many New England towns. The Indians were defeated only when the English destroyed their grain crops. Without food, they lost their will to fight. They were either killed or sold into slavery. Their lands were given to soldiers.

The Frontier

King Philip's War cleared New England of Indian resistance. Waves of settlers began pushing up the Connecticut River into the Berkshire Hills. Others moved north into the areas of present-day **Vermont, Maine,** and **New Hampshire.**

The **frontier** was moving westward. A frontier is the area that separates settled land and the wilderness. When the Pilgrims arrived in Plymouth, they were on a frontier. As more and more people carved settlements out of the wilderness, the frontier moved westward.

Settlers who left the coastal areas were looking for good farming land. They settled where they liked the land. They did not necessarily settle in villages. They were independent. With an ax, a knife, and a gun, frontier settlers could take care of most of their needs.

Yet it was usually not long before people organized themselves into communities. Laws and rules were needed to protect the rights of people. Militias were needed to defend the new settlements. Even while these new communities were being formed, other settlers were restlessly pushing the frontier westward.

Towns and Trade

As time passed, life in New England became more comfortable. Fewer people had to struggle to make a living. By 1770 the great-grandchildren of early settlers were living in bigger houses. Many could afford luxuries such as tea and fine cloth from England.

This prosperity was based on the success of fishermen, boatbuilders, and traders. By 1700 many of the 12,000 people in Boston earned their living from the sea.

The town of **Nantucket** on Nantucket Island grew quickly in the 1700s because its sailors began catching great whales. Oil made from whale blubber was in great demand because it burned clear and bright. One lamp of burning whale oil gave as much light as three candles. A large whale might have 500 gallons of such oil.

Whaling ships left their home ports on sea voyages lasting up to five years. Whaling was very dangerous and difficult work. When a whale was killed,

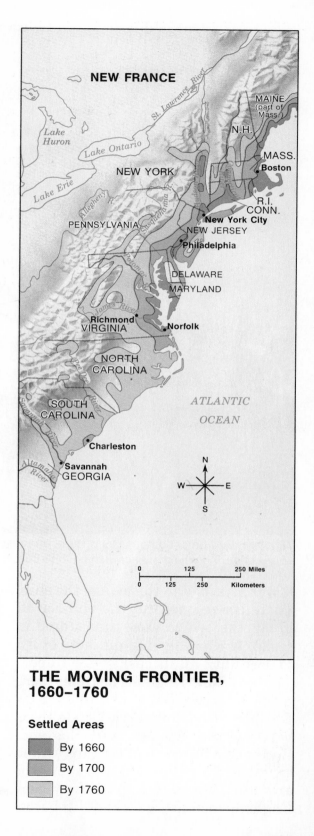

THE MOVING FRONTIER, 1660–1760

Settled Areas

By 1660

By 1700

By 1760

Whaling could be dangerous work. Here, an artist shows an angry sperm whale attacking whalers by crunching their boat.

it was attached to the side of the ship. There the seamen cut the blubber off in chunks, which were then stored in casks. A whaling ship did not return to port until all its casks were filled.

Many New England fortunes were made in trade. Ships owned by New England merchants carried trade goods between the colonies and England. Goods leaving a country are called **exports.** Goods brought into a country are called **imports.** Exports from New England included cargoes of tobacco, furs, lumber, and dried fish. The English expected their colonies to export raw products only to England or English colonies. The English also expected the colonists to buy all manufactured goods from England.

The independent colonists usually ignored this part of English law. Some started small factories where they made iron products and wove cloth. Others made a regular practice of smuggling items not made in England into the colonies.

Trading for Slaves

Some New England trading ships followed the **triangle trade route.** The triangle trade route was one of the most important English trade routes. It looked like a giant triangle on the Atlantic Ocean.

The triangle trade worked this way. Ships carried molasses from English colonies in the West Indies to ports like Boston, New Haven, and New York. In these ports the molasses was turned into rum. Ships then carried cargoes of rum and iron products to the coast of Africa. There ship captains sold their cargo and bought slaves. They then carried the slaves to the West Indies. In the West Indies they sold the slaves for molasses. In the American colonies they might buy rum again. At each point in the trade shipowners and merchants hoped to make a profit.

The trade in slaves was cruel. In 1764, for example, one Yankee captain in the triangle trade sold rum, candles, guns, and iron chains in Africa. With the money he received, the captain then bought 196 slaves. Before the ship reached the West Indies, 109 of those slaves had died. Some died before the voyage began. Some rebelled during the voyage and were shot. Many

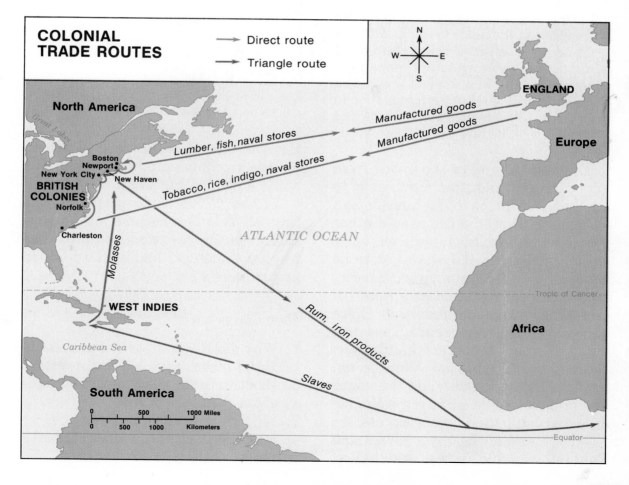

took their own lives by jumping overboard.

Millions of Africans were sold into slavery. Some had been slaves in Africa. Most had been born free. They had come from many different African cultures. Some were highly skilled as leaders, weavers, sculptors, metalsmiths, and storytellers. Most had been either kidnapped or captured in raids on villages.

Their voyage across the Atlantic in stinking, cramped quarters was part of a vast business. It was the business of providing workers for the new world.

Olaudah Equiano (OL•uh•dah eh•kwee•AH•noh) was 11 years old when he was kidnapped from his village. He described the event:

> One day, when all our people were gone out to the fields to work, and only I and my dear sister were left to mind the house, two men and a woman got over our walls. In a moment they seized us both, and without giving us time to cry out, they stopped our mouths and ran off with us into the nearest wood.

Olaudah was soon separated from his sister and sold from one person to another. In time he found himself on a slave ship. There he discovered other people who spoke his language.

"I asked them if I were not to be eaten by those white men with horrible looks, red faces, and long hair."

As the voyage got underway, Olaudah wished he were dead. He saw two men, chained together, jump overboard. He was whipped when he did not feel like eating. He heard the moans and cries of people suffering from disease, hardship, and homesickness.

At the end of the voyage, Olaudah Equiano was sold in the West Indies.

Olaudah Equiano, taken as a slave, wrote a book about his life in 1793.

He was one of those rare slaves to receive an education. In later years he wrote down his life story.

In the 1700s some people in the English colonies became uncomfortable about the slave trade. By 1750 New England colonists had begun to form groups to end slavery.

Reading Check

1. Why did Roger Williams and Anne Hutchinson leave Massachusetts?
2. What were the most important tools of the frontier settler?
3. Why were whales hunted?
4. Describe each of the three stages in the triangle trade.

THE YANKEE WHALERS

A pastry cutter

A carved whale tooth

A whale-oil lamp

"Thar she blows! Thar she blows!" cried the lookout perched on a high tower above the sandy beach. This familiar shout meant that whales had been spotted off the New England coast. At this signal, hardy whalers set out in their small boats to do battle with the great whales.

For generations, whaling was a leading industry of New England. Nearly every part of a whale's body was used. Whale oil provided light for homes and city streets. The oil was also used to lubricate machines. Whalebone was used in umbrellas, buggy whips, skirts, and hairbrushes. Whale meat was eaten. Other whale products helped make fertilizer and perfume.

To get whales, Yankee whalers often sailed far from home. Their boats were often smaller than the whales themselves. Out on the open sea they would try to spear these enormous creatures. Some were over 50 feet (15.2 m) long and weighed more than 100,000 (45,351.5 kg) pounds. Sometimes whales rose up out of the sea and smashed the whale boats. At other times, wounded whales dragged the undersized boats through the water for many miles at great speed. This was known as a "Nantucket sleigh ride."

New England whaling reached its peak during the 1800s. By the twentieth century, whales had become less important. Petroleum oil replaced whale oil for fuel and lubrication. Electric lights soon made oil lamps unnecessary. The demand for whale products dropped.

Yankee whaling died for another important reason. The New Englanders had killed too many whales. Each year they had to travel farther and farther to find whales. Their voyages became increasingly difficult and expensive.

We know today that whales are not fish. Whales, like dolphins and porpoises, are highly intelligent mammals. Most nations now do not allow whaling because people fear whales will become extinct. They want these graceful, intelligent giants of the sea to be part of our world always.

SKILLS FOR SUCCESS

READING BAR GRAPHS

A **graph** makes it easy to compare facts. A **bar graph** compares facts by using solid bars or lines to stand for numbers.

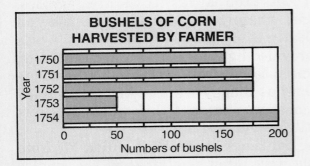

BUSHELS OF CORN HARVESTED BY FARMER

This graph shows how many bushels of corn were harvested by one farmer during a five-year period. Each bar shows the number of bushels harvested in one year. Notice that the lines are labeled *0, 50, 100,* and so on. The bar for the year 1753 ends at the line marked *50.* This means that 50 bushels of corn were harvested by this farmer in 1753. The bar for 1750 extends to the line marked *150.* What does this mean? How many bushels of corn did this farmer harvest in 1752? When did the farmer harvest the most corn?

Sometimes a graph can hint at important events. Find the shortest bar on the graph. This bar tells you that the number of bushels harvested in 1753 was very low. You can guess that something unusual happened that year. Perhaps the crops were ruined by bad weather or fire.

A bar graph is useful because it makes it easy to compare amounts. Yet it often does not give you exact figures. Sometimes you have to guess at actual numbers as you read a bar graph.

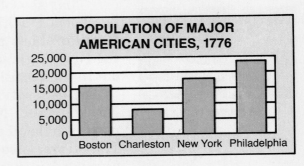

POPULATION OF MAJOR AMERICAN CITIES, 1776

Sometimes a bar graph is to be read from bottom to top. The graph above compares the population of four major cities in the American colonies in 1776. The names of the cities are listed at the bottom of the graph. Population figures are listed on the side of the graph. The first line represents 5,000 people. How many people does the second line represent?

Find Boston. Follow the bar above it. The bar passes through the line marked *15,000* but does not reach the line marked 20,000. You can see that the end of the bar is closer to 15,000 than 20,000. From this you can guess that the population of Boston in 1776 was about 16,000.

CHECKING YOUR SKILLS

Answer these questions.

1. What is a bar graph?

2. Does a bar graph always give exact numbers? Explain your answer.

3. About how many people were there in New York City in 1776?

4. Which city shown on the graph had the smallest population? What was it?

CHAPTER 7 REVIEW

WORDS TO USE

Number your paper from 1 to 10. Use the words below to complete the sentences that follow.

authority	imports
barter	meetinghouse
common	militia
exports	navigable
frontier	officials

1. Most rivers in New England were not _____.

2. In town meetings New England settlers elected _____ to do necessary community jobs.

3. The center of a New England village was its _____, or village green.

4. Puritan ministers had much _____ over early settlers.

5. The most important bulding in a New England village was the _____.

6. The _____ was a group of volunteers organized to defend a settlement.

7. Most early settlers exchanged goods and services by using a system of _____.

8. A _____ is an area between settled land and wilderness.

9. Goods that are sent from a country are called _____.

10. Goods that are brought into a country are called _____.

FACTS TO REVIEW

1. How did colonists use New England's natural resources to make a living?

2. Give three examples that show the importance and authority of Puritan ministers in Massachusetts.

3. What did Roger Williams, Anne Hutchinson, and Thomas Hooker have in common?

4. How did the English and the Indians differ about land ownership?

5. Why was the frontier always moving?

IDEAS TO DISCUSS

1. Early settlers had to work very hard just to meet their basic needs for food, shelter, and clothing. What kinds of skills and crafts did they need to know? How do we meet basic needs today?

2. What kinds of thing happened in a meetinghouse? In what ways did the meetinghouse serve both religious needs and the needs of village governments?

3. What was life like for Puritan children?

◯ SKILLS PRACTICE

Reading Bar Graphs Use the city population graph on page 170 to answer these questions.

1. Which had the greater population in 1776, New York or Boston?

2. Which city had a population of about 3,000?

CHAPTER 8

The Middle Colonies

America's Middle colonies were different from those in New England. Most people who lived in New England had Puritan ancestors from England. Because agriculture was difficult in New England, many people turned to shipbuilding, fishing, and trading.

In contrast, the people who settled the Middle colonies came from many places and held a variety of religious beliefs. The soil and climate of the Middle colonies were good for raising grain and livestock. The large rivers and good harbors encouraged trade in these agricultural products. Trade led to the growth of large cities.

1. THE BREADBASKET COLONIES

To Guide Your Reading

Look for these important words:

Key Words
- fall line
- proprietor
- delegates

Places
- New York
- New Jersey
- Delaware
- Pennsylvania
- New York City
- Philadelphia

Look for answers to these questions:

1. How was the geography of the Middle colonies different from that of the New England colonies?
2. Why were the Middle colonies also called the breadbasket colonies?
3. How were the Middle colonies ruled?
4. What groups of people settled the Middle colonies?

The Middle colonies were **New York, New Jersey, Delaware,** and **Pennsylvania.** These colonies were all alike in an important way. Living in them were people from different countries and of different religions.

Large, navigable rivers flowed through each of these colonies. Near the mouths of these rivers great cities grew. **New York City** grew at the mouth of the Hudson River. The city of **Philadelphia** was founded near the mouth of the Delaware River.

The rivers flowed through plains and gently rolling hills. When the first white settlers arrived, most of the land was covered with deciduous hardwood trees. The land was good for farming. The soil was not as rocky and was more fertile than that of New England. The climate was also better for growing crops. The summers were longer, and the amount of rain, 30 to 50 inches (76.2 to 127 cm) a year, was just right.

One farmer used poetry to describe his feelings about the land:

The fields, most beautiful, yield
such crops of wheat,
And other things most excellent
to eat. . . .

So much wheat was produced in the Middle colonies that they were called the "breadbasket colonies." Ships docked at the ports of Philadelphia and New York City to pick up cargoes of wheat flour. The wheat flour was carried to other colonies and to people across the sea.

As one followed the rivers west to the Appalachian Mountains, the rivers gradually ceased to become navigable at the waterfalls on the **fall line.** The fall line is the point where a river passes from high land to the low, coastal plains. For many years people did not settle beyond the fall line because river transportation was not possible.

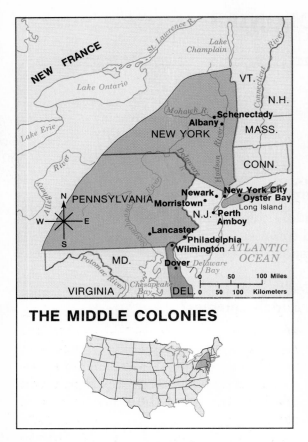

THE MIDDLE COLONIES

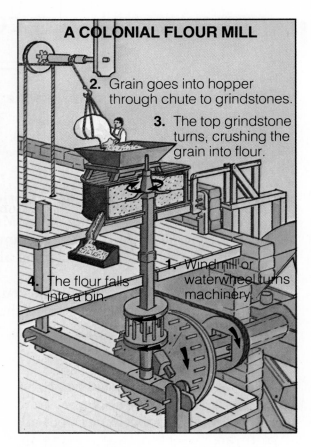

A COLONIAL FLOUR MILL

2. Grain goes into hopper through chute to grindstones.

3. The top grindstone turns, crushing the grain into flour.

1. Windmill or waterwheel turns machinery.

4. The flour falls into a bin.

However, as in New England, frontier settlers began to go into the hills and mountains. There they settled in small clearings, often far from towns.

Rule by Proprietors

Each one of the Middle colonies belonged to an owner who ruled the colony. Such an owner was called a **proprietor** (pruh•PRY•uht•uhr).

At first the proprietor could make all the laws. The proprietor of New York, the Duke of York, ruled as he wished. In 1664 he gave the province of New Jersey to two friends. They in turn became its proprietors. The New Jersey proprietors promised freedom of religion and a lawmaking assembly.

The king, however, had control over each proprietor. In time, King Charles

II of England limited the power of proprietors. The king said that all laws made by proprietors had to be approved by colonial assemblies. These assemblies were made up of **delegates,** people elected by colonists to represent them. In the assemblies the delegates learned valuable lessons in lawmaking and self-government.

Reading Check

1. Describe the geography of the Middle colonies.
2. Why did people usually settle below the fall line?
3. What was a proprietor?
4. How did King Charles II limit the power of the proprietor and at the same time encourage self-government?

2. COLONIAL NEW YORK CITY

╭─ To Guide Your Reading ─────────────────────

Look for these important words:

Key Words
- influence
- stoop

People
- Sarah Knight

Look for answers to these questions:

1. What was travel between Boston and New York City like in the early 1700s?
2. What was colonial New York City like?
3. How does our language reflect a Dutch heritage?

Today it is possible to travel by airplane from Boston to New York City in less than an hour. In colonial times the trip took much longer. By boat the journey from Boston to New York City took from 2 to 14 days, depending on the weather.

A journey by land was also long and often unpleasant. At that time the only way to travel on land was by horseback or on foot. Later, the trails through the forest were widened so that carriages could be used.

In October 1704 Madam **Sarah Knight** made a journey by horseback from Boston to New York City. Madam Knight faced many problems along the way. Of part of her trip she wrote:

> The roads all along this way are very bad, with rocks and mountainous passages. After about eight miles riding, in going over a bridge under which the river ran very swift, my horse stumbled, and very narrowly escaped falling over into the water.

Not all rivers had bridges. Near Providence, Rhode Island, Sarah Knight and her guide came to a wide, swift river. She was afraid to ride her horse into it. A boy with a canoe was found to take her across while her horse swam. The canoe was very small and shallow. Sarah Knight held fast to each side, her eyes steady. She dared not even move her tongue for fear the canoe would tip.

There were few inns along the road. Sometimes it was necessary to travel late into the night before reaching an inn. At night the trail became a scary place. Madam Knight sometimes thought she saw an enemy in the dark shadow of a tree or bush.

When Madam Knight reached New York City, she noted that the city of New York was a "pleasant" place. It was located on a river with a "fine harbour for shipping." She found New York City different from Boston in many ways.

The Dutch had been the first European settlers of New York, but a mixture of people had soon settled there. In addition to the English who came, there were also free blacks, French, and

Jews. New York differed from Boston in part because of this mixture of peoples.

Sarah Knight noted that most people in New York City belonged to the Church of England. "They are not as strict in keeping the Sabbath as in Boston," she observed.

Dutch Influence

When Sarah Knight visited New York, the Dutch influence was still strong. **Influence** is the power of people or things to act on others. Dutch women, she noticed, wore earrings "with jewels of a large size and many in number." Their fingers were "hooped with rings, some with large stones of many colors." Women in Boston did not wear such fancy jewelry.

For winter entertainment the people of New York City rode sleighs to inns about three or four miles (4.8 or 6.5 km) out of town. When Madam Knight was taken on such a ride, she wrote, "I believe we met 50 or 60 sleighs that day—they fly with great swiftness and turn out of the path for none except a loaded cart."

The step-like roofs, the stoops, and the half-doors of these houses all show Dutch influence in colonial New York City.

Some skaters arrive by sleigh, while others warm themselves at a fire in this scene of New York City in about 1700.

Many Dutch houses were built using bricks of different colors. A Dutch house often had a **stoop,** which is a wide, high doorstep. On the stoop were benches where a family could sit on warm evenings. There the family members spent pleasant hours talking with each other and with neighbors passing by.

The door of a Dutch house also made it easy to be friendly to passersby. The door had two parts. The top part could be open while the bottom part stayed closed. A closed bottom door kept dogs and pigs from wandering into the house.

Pigs were common in colonial cities. People threw their garbage into the gutters. The wandering pigs were absolutely necessary to get rid of the garbage.

Today the skyline of New York City is filled with huge skyscrapers. Even in the 1700s New York had an inter-esting skyline. Large windmills stood on top of the highest hills. The windmills provided power for grinding grain into flour.

Our language reflects the Dutch heritage of New York. Words that come from the Dutch are *boss, stoop, cookie, Santa Claus, sleigh,* and *waffle.*

Reading Check

1. Describe the roads Sarah Knight traveled from Boston to New York.
2. Name at least three ways in which New York City was different from Boston.
3. How did the design of Dutch houses encourage friendliness between neighbors?
4. What did the people of New York use as a source of power to grind grain?

3. PENNSYLVANIA

To Guide Your Reading

Look for these important words:

Key Words
- Quakers
- refuge

- immigrants
- Conestoga wagon
- Scotch-Irish

People
- William Penn

Look for answers to these questions:

1. Who was William Penn?
2. What peoples settled in Pennsylvania? What were their reasons for settling there?
3. What things were German settlers known for?
4. How did relations between the Indians and Pennsylvania settlers change?

William Penn became the proprietor of Pennsylvania in 1681. The next year he planned out the town of Philadelphia. *Philadelphia* comes from Greek words meaning "brotherly love." Penn planned out the town so that it had the look of a checkerboard, with straight streets and squares. Philadelphia's location was excellent for shipping and trading. By 1760 it was the largest city in America.

William Penn belonged to a church group called the **Quakers.** The Quakers believed in simple and plain living. They believed that all people were equal and that all people were basically good. The Quakers refused to bear arms or to fight. They believed in the peaceful solution of problems.

For these ideas the Quakers were made to suffer, both in England and in New England. Any Quakers who came to New England were whipped and forced to leave. Some were hanged.

William Penn offered Pennsylvania as a **refuge,** a place of safety, for the Quakers. He also offered land and freedom of religion to any who settled in Pennsylvania.

The early Quakers in Pennsylvania lived simply. People were expected to dress plainly—no bright colors or satin cloth, no jewelry or silver buckles. Their homes were also plain. There was no silver or gold or fancy furniture.

Even their conversation was plain. Quakers frowned on chatter, gossip, or boasting. Dancing, music, and theater were all thought to be sinful. The Quakers agreed with the Puritans in at least one way. They thought that each moment should be spent in a useful task or in good thoughts.

The Quakers also showed great concern for the poor. Penn wrote that he expected the town meetings "to supply the wants of the poor." Further, they were to care for "widows and orphans and such as are helpless." Quakers very early decided that slavery was evil. They freed their slaves and opposed slavery.

The Pennsylvania Germans became famous for the way they decorated everyday objects with pictures of flowers, birds, and animals.

Pennsylvania Germans

Pennsylvania became a refuge not only for the Quakers but also for other groups. These new settlers were **immigrants.** Immigrants are people who come from one country to live in another country.

Among the immigrants were many German-speaking people seeking religious freedom and a better life. The first Germans in Pennsylvania wrote back enthusiastic letters. "If a workman will only work four or five days in a week, he can live grandly," one wrote.

The Germans who came to Pennsylvania included both farmers and skilled workers. Among the skilled workers were bakers, masons, carpenters, shoemakers, tailors, butchers, coopers, millers, and blacksmiths. They often set up craft shops in towns where they engaged in their crafts.

The Germans were great lovers of music. They made musical instruments like zithers, organs, and pianos. At any German gathering there was likely to be music. There was also likely to be large quantities of food. German foods included sauerkraut, sausage, doughnuts, gingerbread, and apple pies.

German gunmakers developed the excellent, long-barrel rifle called the Pennsylvania rifle. In the 1700s it was the most accurate rifle in the world. It was particularly valued on the frontier. Because famous frontiersmen from Kentucky used the rifle, it later became known as the Kentucky rifle.

The excellent and hardworking German farmers built great barns to shelter livestock in winter. These barns, or barns like them, are still found in Pennsylvania.

The German houses were often built over a cellar, or earth basement. In the cellar was a spring or well for water. The earth walls and water helped keep the cellar cool for storing food. Fruit, cheese, milk, and butter could be found there.

The farmers had to figure out how to get their crops and livestock to market. To deal with this problem, the **Conestoga wagon** was invented. This wagon was well suited for carrying heavy freight over bad roads. Pulled by teams of four or six horses, it could carry loads as heavy as 6 tons (5.4 T). The wagon's wheels were wide, which usually kept them from sinking into the mud. A curved floor in the wagon kept the wagon's contents from moving about. A white canvas cover protected the freight from bad weather.

The wagons were painted blue. The horses often wore bows of bells. Farmers were proud to drive these grand and beautiful wagons.

The Scotch-Irish

Scotch-Irish settlers also came to Pennsylvania. These were people from Scotland who had settled in northern Ireland in the 1600s. Many of them and their descendants had then come to America. Like other immigrants, they were looking for religious freedom and opportunities to make a living. They entered the country through the port of Philadelphia. Then they fanned out into the hilly frontiers of the Appalachians from Pennsylvania to Georgia. The Scotch-Irish were among the first to settle beyond the fall line. They lived

Pennsylvania farmers carried their goods to market in Conestoga wagons. Here, they stop for a rest and a chance to exchange news.

This painting shows William Penn and the Delaware Indians making a peace agreement in 1681. Penn never broke the treaty, but others did.

in small clearings, making a living as best they could from farming and hunting.

Relations with Indians

William Penn tried to be very fair in his dealings with the Indians. The Indians respected Penn and looked on him as a friend. "Let them have justice, and you win them," he said.

Despite this early friendship, the pattern of the other colonies repeated itself in Pennsylvania. As the number of settlers increased, the settlers took lands from the Indians. The Scotch-Irish, in particular, were known as "hard neighbors to the Indians." They paid no attention to the agreements the Quakers had made with the Indians.

When the Indians reacted by attacking frontier settlements, the settlers demanded military protection and help. The Quakers, most of whom did not live on the frontier, insisted on peaceful behavior. They refused to provide military help. The settlers on the western frontier then felt great bitterness toward the city Quakers.

Reading Check

1. Why did Philadelphia become an important city?
2. Name at least three Quaker beliefs.
3. Why was the Conestoga wagon developed?
4. Why did bitterness develop between many frontier settlers and the Quakers?

4. BENJAMIN FRANKLIN

To Guide Your Reading

Look for these important words:

Key Words
- apprentice
- lightning rod

People
- Benjamin Franklin

Look for answers to these questions:

1. How did Benjamin Franklin learn to be a printer?
2. Why was Franklin the most important citizen of Philadelphia?
3. What contributions did Franklin make to science?

Benjamin Franklin was the most important citizen of colonial Philadelphia.

Benjamin Franklin was born in Boston, the fifteenth of 17 children. His father was a candlemaker. One of his earliest teachers was Sarah Knight, the lady who went on horseback from Boston to New York.

Benjamin Franklin was always curious and eager to try out new ideas. One hot day when he was a boy, he was flying a kite from the edge of a pond. He tied the kite down so he could go for a swim. Then he decided to try swimming and flying a kite at the same time.

He lay on his back in the water and held on to the kite string. "I began to cross the pond with my kite, which carried me quite over without the least fatigue, and with the greatest pleasure," he wrote.

Franklin Becomes a Printer

Young Franklin showed great interest in reading and books. Because of this, his father made him an **apprentice** (uh•PRENT•uhs) to his older brother, who was a printer. An apprentice worked a certain number of years for a person skilled in a craft. An apprentice lived with the skilled worker's family while he learned the craft.

The apprentice system was the most common way for boys to learn skills. Girls usually learned skills from their mothers. Sometimes girls worked in households as indentured servants.

Franklin was 12 years old when he became an apprentice. As a printer's apprentice, the young Franklin learned how to set type, or put together the letters for the press. He also learned to work the press, which pressed paper onto the type and printed it. In his spare time Franklin read books and worked at improving his own writing.

Benjamin Franklin did not get along well with his older brother. In 1723, when he was 17 years old, he ran away. He sold his books to buy passage on a boat from Boston to New York. When he arrived in New York, Franklin went to a printer to get work. The printer had no work for him, and he suggested that Franklin go to Philadelphia.

Franklin made his way by boat and on foot to Philadelphia. Hungry, tired, and poor, he finally arrived. The first thing he did was ask at a bakery for 3 pence worth of bread. He was given three large loaves, much more than he expected. He ate one and gave the other two to a woman and her child who had been on the boat with him. Then he found work as a printer.

Citizen and Inventor

Franklin did very well as a printer. Yet he said that he would rather live a useful life than die rich. When he could, he worked as a citizen, a scientist, and an inventor.

As a citizen, Franklin left a strong mark on the growing city of Philadelphia. He organized the first trained fire department. He worked to establish the first public library and the first hospital in Philadelphia. He organized a militia to protect Philadelphia and the frontier settlements.

As a scientist, Franklin is most famous for his experiments in electricity. Using the kite of his childhood, he proved that lightning is electricity. A result of his experiments was his invention of the **lightning rod.** A lightning rod is a rod of metal attached to the top of a house, barn, or boat. It conducts lightning bolts into the ground. Until the invention of the lightning rod, buildings or boats struck by lightning were likely to burst into flames.

Franklin's mind was always looking for a better way to do things. Unhappy with smoky fireplaces, he

In Philadelphia Benjamin Franklin oversees the latest printing to come off his press.

invented an iron stove. This stove, called the Franklin stove, threw heat, but no smoke, into a room. It is still in use.

Benjamin Franklin would be famous if he had done no more. However, some of his most important work was still to come. As a statesman, he would help his country become an independent and respected nation.

Reading Check

1. What is an apprentice?
2. What skills did Benjamin Franklin learn as an apprentice?
3. Give three examples that show why Franklin was an important citizen.
4. Why is Franklin also called a scientist?

SKILLS FOR SUCCESS

READING PICTURE, CIRCLE, AND LINE GRAPHS

You have learned that graphs are a way of comparing amounts. Many kinds of graphs exist. In addition to bar graphs, there are picture, circle, and line graphs.

Picture graphs use symbols to stand for numbers. The graph below compares the population of the four Middle colonies in 1760. Each symbol stands for 10,000 people. Half of a symbol stands for about 5,000 people. Three complete symbols are shown for Delaware. To find the population represented by these figures, you must multiply 10,000 by 3. The answer is 30,000. How many symbols are shown for New Jersey? What was the population of New Jersey in 1760?

POPULATION OF THE MIDDLE COLONIES, 1760	
New York	𝕏𝕏𝕏𝕏𝕏 𝕏𝕏𝕏𝕏𝕏𝕩
New Jersey	𝕏𝕏𝕏𝕏𝕏𝕏𝕏𝕏𝕏𝕩
Delaware	𝕏𝕏𝕏
Pennsylvania	𝕏𝕏𝕏𝕏𝕏𝕏𝕏𝕏𝕏𝕏 𝕏𝕏𝕏𝕏𝕏𝕏𝕏𝕩
𝕏 = 10,000 people	

Reading Circle Graphs

A **circle graph** shows parts of a whole. For example, in a flock of 10 chickens, 8 chickens lay eggs and 2 chickens do not. A circle graph shows this fact in this way:

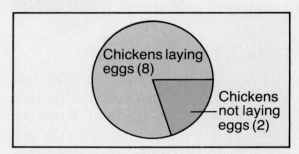

The circle graph below shows how the population of Pennsylvania could be divided up in 1760.

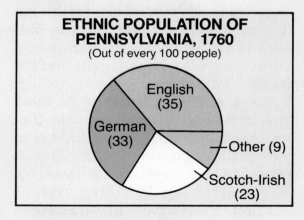

ETHNIC POPULATION OF PENNSYLVANIA, 1760
(Out of every 100 people)

The circle represents 100 people in Pennsylvania in 1760. Of every 100 people, 33 were of German origin and 35 were of English origin. The Germans and the English made up the largest part of Pennsylvania's population. Find the next largest section of the circle. What group is that? How many of every 100 people in Pennsylvania were Scotch-Irish?

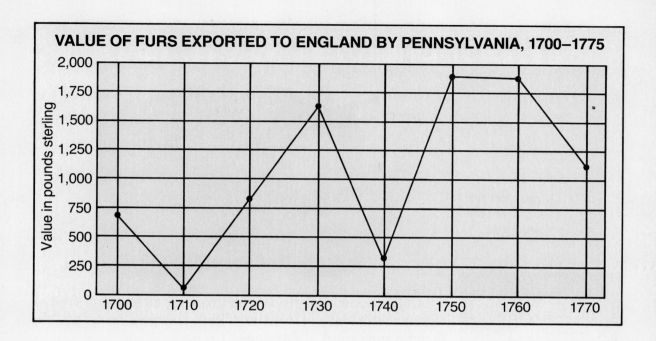

VALUE OF FURS EXPORTED TO ENGLAND BY PENNSYLVANIA, 1700–1775

Value in pounds sterling

Reading a Line Graph

A **line graph** shows change. The graph above shows the value of furs exported to England by Pennsylvania from 1700 to 1770. On the left side of the graph are numbers. These numbers represent the value of the furs in English money called pounds sterling.

Across the bottom of the chart are dates. Years shown here are 10 years apart. Find the year 1720. Trace the line up until you reach the dot. Then move your finger across to the number beside it. You can see that in 1720 the value of furs was about 850 pounds sterling. Now find the year 1730. Move your finger up the line until you come to the dot. What was the value of furs in that year?

Find the highest point on the graph. What year is it?

The lines that connect the dots are there to help you see a pattern in the dots. You can see that the dots drop in 1710 and then rise until 1730. In 1730 they begin to fall, before rising again to values higher than before. These up and down patterns are called **trends.**

The overall trend in the value of Pennsylvania exports was an increase. However, between 1700 and 1770 there were bad years for fur exports. A historian would look at these figures and try to find out what they meant. Perhaps the overall increase was due to an increase in the number of people hunting and trading. What might have happened to cause the sudden drops in exports?

CHECKING YOUR SKILLS

Answer the following questions. Use the information in this skill lesson to help you.

1. What kind of graph makes it easy to see parts of a whole?

2. What kind of graph uses symbols to stand for numbers of things?

3. What kind of graph shows change?

4. What kind of graph could you use to show the trend of your grades on spelling tests between September and January?

THE FIRST FIRE DEPARTMENT

A volunteer fire department battles a large fire.

Benjamin Franklin as a firefighter

A leather fire bucket

Colonists who lived in the growing cities were free of the hardships of the frontier. These city dwellers, though, faced a new kind of danger—fire.

In the cities of colonial America, houses were built close together. Heat came from open wood and coal fires. Light in homes and city streets was produced by oil lamps. These conditions made fires more likely to start. When fires did occur, they could spread quickly.

Benjamin Franklin put his keen mind to work on the problems of fires. As a child, Franklin had watched a huge fire in Boston. He saw the flames run wild. He saw the panic on the faces of his parents and their friends. Later in Philadelphia Franklin watched in fear when a great fire nearly destroyed the entire city. Franklin knew that something had to be done.

As a printer and writer, Franklin began writing articles about how to prevent fires in the home. Then, in 1736, Franklin joined with fellow Philadelphians to organize America's first fully trained volunteer fire department. It was called the Union Fire Company. It was trained to respond quickly to alarms and to put fires out. The men also learned to rescue people trapped in burning buildings. The fire department was able to keep fires from spreading and getting out of control.

Within a few years Boston and New York organized their own fire departments. Ben Franklin and other brave fire fighters helped make cities safer from raging fires.

CHAPTER 8 REVIEW

WORDS TO USE

Explain the meaning of each term below. Then use each in a complete sentence.

1. **apprentice**
2. **delegate**
3. **immigrants**
4. **influence**
5. **lightning rod**
6. **proprietor**

FACTS TO REVIEW

1. How did the geography of the Middle colonies encourage the development of agriculture and trading?

2. Why was shipping the most common way to transport people and goods?

3. How did Dutch influence show in the style of building, the recreation, and the language of New York City?

4. Who founded Philadelphia?

5. How did King Charles II put controls on the authority of the proprietor? What was the result?

6. What groups of people settled in Pennsylvania?

7. Would each of the following more likely be found in New York or in Philadelphia?

    a. sleigh rides   f. Conestoga wagon
    b. stoops   g. gingerbread
    c. windmills   h. waffles
    d. plain furniture
    e. organs and pianos

8. What examples can you give that show Benjamin Franklin's willingness to try out new ideas?

IDEAS TO DISCUSS

1. The Middle colonies were settled by a mixture of people from different countries. What were some of the contributions these groups made? How do our lives today show our heritage from people of many countries?

2. When people face new challenges, they often come up with new ideas and inventions. What examples of this idea are in this chapter? Can you think of other examples?

3. Benjamin Franklin was famous for his curiosity and eagerness to try out new ideas. How was this shown when he was young? What other qualities does a successful scientist and inventor need?

4. Imagine a visit to New York City or Philadelphia 250 years ago. Describe what you might see.

◯ SKILLS PRACTICE

1. **Picture Graphs** Make a picture graph showing the number of ships leaving colonial harbors in the 1750s. Use this information: Boston, 600 ships. New York City, 500 ships. Philadelphia, 650 ships. Charleston, 400 ships.

2. **Circle Graphs** During colonial times hundreds of ships left harbors each year. Draw a circle to represent 100 of those ships. Then make a circle graph showing where the ships went. Use the following numbers: Europe, 25. Caribbean, 25. American colonies, 50.

CHAPTER 9

The Southern Colonies

About
this
chapter

Settlement of the South was first centered in two places. These were the Chesapeake Bay area and the coastal lands of South Carolina. To these regions came mostly English people. Unlike English colonists in Pennsylvania and New England, the Southern colonists were neither Quakers nor Puritans. Instead, most belonged to the Church of England.

Life in the Southern colonies was based on the cultivation of a few important crops. Raising these crops required many workers. With time the landowners depended on large numbers of black slaves to do the backbreaking work. In this way slavery became a part of the Southern way of life.

1. SETTLEMENT OF THE SOUTH

To Guide Your Reading

Look for these important words:

Key Words
- indigo
- cash crops
- economy
- tidewater
- swamps
- piedmont

People
- George Calvert
- Lord Baltimore
- James Oglethorpe

Places
- Maryland

- Virginia
- North Carolina
- South Carolina
- Georgia
- Charleston
- Albemarle Sound
- Savannah

Look for answers to these questions:

1. How did people in the South use the natural resources of the land?
2. Why was the colony of Maryland settled?
3. Why was Carolina founded? Why did it split into two parts?
4. Why was Georgia founded?

In the 1700s the Southern colonies included **Maryland, Virginia, North Carolina, South Carolina,** and **Georgia.** The soil and climate of the Southern colonies was excellent for crops like tobacco, rice, and indigo (IN•di•goh). **Indigo** is a plant that produces a blue dye. Colonial landowners in the South usually grew one of these **cash crops.** Cash crops are crops that people grow in order to sell and make a profit. Cash crops were the most important part of the Southern **economy.** An economy is the way people use resources to produce and sell goods and services.

Tobacco grew best in the rich soil of the Chesapeake Bay **tidewater.** A tidewater is a low, coastal plain full of waterways. The waterways made it easy to use boats to get the tobacco to market in England.

In South Carolina and Georgia many navigable rivers flowed through the coastal plains. Along these rivers were **swamps,** places with soft and wet soil. Rice grew well in the swamplands.

The coastal plains rise gradually until they meet the **piedmont,** or foothills. The piedmont was covered with forests of either pine or hardwood. Settlers in the piedmont raised tobacco, cotton, wheat, and corn.

Founding of Maryland

In 1632 the king of England gave a fruitful piece of Virginia to his friend **George Calvert.** Calvert was a Roman Catholic. Catholics could not worship as they chose in England. Because of this, Calvert intended his colony to be a place where Catholics could settle in safety and freedom.

In this portrait Lord Baltimore hands a map of Maryland to his young son.

After Calvert's death, his dream was carried out by his son, **Lord Baltimore**. He named the new colony Maryland. As proprietor, Lord Baltimore had complete control over the laws in Maryland. In 1649 the Maryland assembly approved his suggestion that Maryland provide religious freedom to all Christians.

The Maryland colony was first centered at St. Mary's City. It was located not far from the mouth of the Potomac River. The colony at St. Mary's City had learned from the experiences of other colonies. The colonists knew no period of starvation and fought no Indian wars. Jamestown was nearby in case the new colony needed supplies or help.

Nature smiled on the settlers at St. Mary's City. One of the first colonists there wrote:

> The soil appears particularly fertile, and strawberries, vines, sassafras, hickory nuts, and walnuts, we tread upon every where, in the thickest woods. There is an infinite number of birds of various colors, as eagles, herons, swans, geese, and partridges.

The mild climate, rich soil, and good river system helped the settlers to prosper. Lord Baltimore granted some people large pieces of land. However, most settlers who came to Maryland were indentured servants. Of these, most were men between the ages of 18 and 22.

The indentured servants in Maryland did better than those in other colonies. When their terms were finished, they were helped to start their own farms. Each was given 50 acres (20.2 ha) of land, a suit of clothes, an ax, two hoes, and three barrels of corn.

The Carolinas

By the end of the 1600s Virginia had neighbors to the south. These were the colonies of North Carolina and South Carolina.

North Carolina and South Carolina were each part of an original grant called Carolina. King Charles II of England had given Carolina to eight men. They hoped to gain wealth through the settlement and development of Carolina. Their idea was to raise silkworms, olives, and wine grapes.

The Carolina proprietors sent three ships from England in 1669. Only one of these ships reached the Carolina coast. Its captain sailed along the coast looking for a suitable place for a settlement. He considered Port Royal but decided that it was too close to the Spanish. The Spanish controlled Florida from their port at St. Augustine.

An Indian whom the English met at Port Royal had a suggestion. He described a wonderful place farther north. Excited, the captain, with the Indian on board, sailed to this place.

There he found a good harbor fed by two rivers. It was a good place to settle. Spanish ships would not be able to see the harbor from the sea. It would be easy to protect. On land between the rivers he established the new settlement. It was named Charles Towne in honor of the king.

Today we call Charles Towne **Charleston,** South Carolina. At first the settlement survived by trading with the Indians for furs and deerskins. Deerskin was valued in Europe for gloves. The early settlers also raised livestock and made barrel parts from timber. It was not long before Charleston became an important trading and agricultural center.

Other settlements in Carolina were in the area of **Albemarle Sound.** These settlements were a long way from the settlement at Charleston. Because of this, the proprietors divided Carolina into two parts: South Carolina and North Carolina. Most of North Carolina was hillier than the Chesapeake Bay tidelands and the flatlands of South Carolina. It did not attract large landholders because it was not as fertile. Most of North Carolina became a land of small farms.

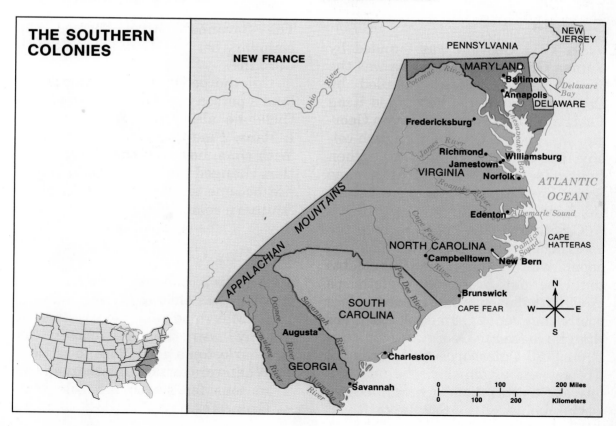

THE SOUTHERN COLONIES

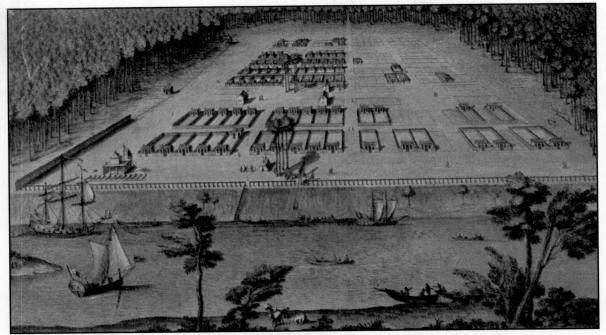

James Oglethorpe laid out a city plan for Savannah, Georgia. The plan called for straight streets and square blocks. The houses were spaced widely apart to guard against the spread of fires.

Georgia

In 1733 Georgia was founded by **James Oglethorpe.** Georgia was the last American colony founded by England. Oglethorpe had urged King George II to approve a colony in Georgia. Oglethorpe hoped an English colony in Georgia would strengthen England's claim to the land. At the time Spain, France, and England all claimed Georgia.

Oglethorpe also hoped to help the poor people of England. In England people who could not pay their debts could be put in prison. Oglethorpe thought that such people needed a place where they could get a fresh start. For that, he looked to Georgia.

In 1733 Oglethorpe and a group of 114 settlers established the new colony at **Savannah,** which was located at the mouth of the Savannah River.

The Savannah River formed the boundary between Georgia and South Carolina.

Oglethorpe limited the amount of land a person could own. To avoid conflicts, he also forbade trading with Indians. Finally, he forbade slavery. With time, however, the Georgia settlers changed these laws. Their way of life became similar to that in other Southern colonies.

Reading Check

1. What is a cash crop?
2. What was George Calvert's dream for Maryland?
3. Why was the site chosen for Charleston a good place to settle?
4. What were James Oglethorpe's two reasons for starting a colony in Georgia?

2. THE WORLD OF THE PLANTER

To Guide Your Reading

Look for these important words:

Key Words
- plantation
- planters
- broker

- public service
- society

People
- William Byrd II

Places
- Annapolis
- Williamsburg
- Richmond
- Baltimore

Look for answers to these questions:
1. What was a plantation?
2. How did the plantation economy work?
3. Why did towns grow slowly in the tidewater region?
4. What was life like on a plantation?

In colonial times the English called any farm a plantation. In later times **plantation** came to mean a Southern farm, particularly a large farm. The people who owned these farms were called **planters.**

In the tidewater region of Virginia and Maryland a plantation was usually located in a clearing along a waterway. The main building was the planter's house, but there were many other buildings as well. Some were cottages for servants or slaves. Others were used for food storage and for cooking. There were sheds for drying and storing tobacco. There were barns for livestock. There was a hen house. Each plantation had a private landing wharf. This allowed boats to dock right at the plantation and to load tobacco.

Surrounding the buildings of the plantation were a vegetable garden, a corn plot, and an orchard. The tobacco fields were farther away. The planters grew or made what they could. Other things they imported from England.

Money was rarely used in the plantation economy. Tobacco was used instead. Ship peddlers from England would travel up the waterways selling English goods. Imagine the delight of the household when the peddlers showed up. Shoes, pretty lace, colorful thread, iron pans, iron hoes, china dishes—all these tempted the planter's household. The planters bartered tobacco for the things the family chose.

Large planters arranged to sell their tobacco through a London **broker.** A broker is a person who gets paid to buy and sell for someone else. Planters sent their tobacco to England with a shopping list of what they wanted for the next year. The list might include carriages, books, and hoes.

The broker in London sold the tobacco, bought what the planter wanted, and sent it back. Sometimes a planter did not make enough money to pay for all the things he wanted. As a result, many planters were often in debt to their English brokers.

Barn

Cattle pen

Slave cabins

Brick making

Blacksmith

Smokehouse

Stable

Vegetable garden

Storage

Carpenter

Spinning and
weaving shed

Office

Laundry

Main house

Kitchen

Tobacco field

Tobacco barn

Dock

A SOUTHERN PLANTATION

Towns in the Tidewater

Towns and cities in the tidewater region grew slowly. Early towns, including **Annapolis,** Maryland, and **Williamsburg,** Virginia, remained small. In New England and the Middle colonies, towns grew where there were good harbors. Towns were a necessary part of trading activities. But in the tidewater, goods could be bought and sold from the plantation docks. Towns were not necessary for the planters to buy and sell.

Planters were always having to clear new land to raise tobacco. Tobacco used up the soil in about four years. As land wore out near the coast, planters began to move up the rivers to higher land.

In time important towns grew at the fall line. They included **Richmond,** Virginia, and **Baltimore,** Maryland. Farmers who lived above the fall line brought their crops to these towns. There the crops were sold and shipped down the river to other markets.

Life on a Plantation

Plantations were often far from each other. Therefore, company was always welcome. When guests came, the men might amuse themselves racing horses. Dancing and card games were favorite pastimes of both men and women.

There were few schools. People lived too far apart. Some plantations had their own small schools for teaching basic reading and writing. Planters often hired teachers from Scotland for their children. When they were about 12 or 13 years old, the young people might attend special town schools. Later students might go to England in order to complete their schooling.

Planters were among the best educated people in the colonies.

Most planters and their families belonged to the Church of England. This was true even in Maryland. To attend church, the family might have to travel an hour by horseback or carriage. Church of England ministers did not have the authority they did in New England. In Southern society planters were more important than ministers. Unlike the Puritans, the members of the Church of England celebrated Christmas. It was the most important holiday in the South.

Plantation Duties

Although slaves did most of the hard work, a planter had important responsibilities. A planter had to see that the crops were planted and harvested. Once the tobacco was harvested, it had to be hung correctly to dry. The planter then had to make arrangements to ship the tobacco to England. He had to keep careful records.

A planter was also responsible for taking care of all those on his plantation. Often the planter or his wife acted as a doctor. Both gave medicines and nursed the sick.

A planter's duties also included **public service.** Public service is doing a job to help the community or **society** as a whole. *Society* means a broad grouping of people who are bound by common laws, traditions, and activities. Public service for a planter could mean serving as a judge or as a representative to the assembly. Some planters served as advisors to the governor, and some did all these things. This tradition of public service may

William Byrd was a Virginia planter who left a diary describing his everyday life.

As part of his public service, William Byrd sat here, in the House of Burgesses.

explain why many planters were leaders in the American colonies.

One of the most famous of early Virginia planters was **William Byrd II.** We know much about him because he kept a diary. Byrd had learned law in England and business methods in Holland. Like many Southern planters, he had a lifelong interest in learning.

Life was often difficult on the plantation. Byrd's diary is full of reports of sickness and death. Sometimes Byrd had servants whipped for lying or for "a hundred faults." Sometimes he heard that the boats carrying his tobacco to London had sunk at sea. His neighbors gave him problems. He wrote:

> In the evening I took a walk about the plantation and found that some of my good neighbors had dug down the bank of my ditch to let their hogs into my pasture, for which I was out of humor.

A planter's wife needed the same skills as other colonial women. She needed to know how to spin and weave, make clothes, and preserve and cook food. Although she did not do all these tasks herself, she had to see that they were done. Her large household—family, servants, and slaves—sometimes numbered in the hundreds. She had to see that all these people had food, clothing, and medical care.

Reading Check

1. What was used for money in the plantation economy?
2. What is a broker?
3. Why did towns at the fall line become important?
4. Name three ways in which a planter might perform public service.

3. SLAVERY IN THE SOUTH

To Guide Your Reading

Look for these important words:

Key Words
- field slaves
- house slaves
- overseer
- almanac

People
- Benjamin Banneker

Look for answers to these questions:
1. Why did planters depend upon slave labor?
2. What kind of life did slaves lead?
3. How were the rights of free blacks restricted?

During the 1600s most plantations in Maryland and Virginia were small. Most used indentured servants from Europe. When tobacco prices were high, everybody did well. When tobacco prices were low, many small planters had trouble. They found it difficult to pay for servants to do farm work.

The big planters could afford to buy slaves to do the work. Slaves cost more than the passage of an indentured servant, but a slave worked for life. An indentured servant worked only for about five years. The more slaves a planter had, the more tobacco he could raise.

By 1700 slaves were becoming an important part of plantation life. Plantations themselves were becoming larger as small planters sold out. The use of slaves changed life in the South. A way of life developed that depended on cheap, plentiful slave labor. Slave labor replaced free labor wherever tobacco, rice, and indigo were raised.

There were generally two kinds of slaves: **field slaves** and **house slaves.** The person directly responsible for field slaves was the **overseer.** He was hired to see that slaves did the work they were supposed to. Some overseers were free blacks. Some were white. Overseers could be harsh and cruel. Whippings and beatings were common.

House slaves had more contact with the planter and his family. They often were clothed, fed, and housed better than field slaves. Women who were house slaves did the work of washing, spinning, cooking, cleaning, and sewing. Men who were house slaves drove carriages, took care of horses, and practiced skills like carpentry. Children of house slaves were often playmates of the planter's children.

Slaves were treated well or cruelly depending on their owners. Some planters took pride in being fair and kind to their slaves. In turn the slaves gave them loyalty and affection. There was no protection, however, for slaves who had cruel masters. A slave owner was free to beat, whip, or insult any slave. However, by law, a slave owner could not willfully kill a slave.

Slaves As Property

The cruelest part of slavery, however, was not whips. It was that one person could own another. The slaves had no direct control over their own lives. Thousands of white people had come to America looking for freedom and opportunity. At the same time, freedom and opportunity were denied to people of black skin.

Slaves were considered property, like horses or cattle. As with other property, slaves could be bought and sold. That meant that slave families were often separated. Husbands were separated from wives. Parents and children were separated, often never to see each other again.

Slave Children

Separated slave families who lived on nearby plantations were more fortunate than most. When family members lived relatively close together, fathers could visit their families. Slavery made it almost impossible, however, to have a family life.

Slave children under the age of ten lived with their mothers. Starting about age eight, they too began to work. Children of field slaves usually worked in the fields with their mothers. Children of house slaves might learn skills. Boys might learn to make barrels or wheels or do carpentry—all important crafts on a plantation. Young girls might learn the skills of sewing, cooking, or weaving. Some helped take care of the planter's children. Slave children were rarely taught to read or write.

Most slave children beyond the age of ten left their mothers. Some went to stay with relatives. Others were sold.

Millions of people were carried in ships from Africa to the Americas. This picture shows how they were wedged into dark, airless spaces between the ship's decks. Thousands of Africans died of disease, suffocation, or misery during the ocean passage.

The Call of Freedom

Slaves made repeated efforts to escape. Many slaves, separated from their families, ran away to return to their loved ones. Others ran away because they wanted to be free.

Ann Joice had come to Maryland as an indentured servant but had been made a slave. Her grandson, Peter Harbard, said that he often heard his grandmother say that she and all her children "ought to be free." In 1748 Peter Harbard ran away twice. Each time he was recaptured. Finally he was able to buy his freedom.

Some slaves were able to buy their freedom because they had learned useful crafts. They had been allowed to earn money by working as skilled workers. These workers often settled in towns and cities.

In folk stories Brer Rabbit, although smaller, outwits larger animals like greedy Brer Fox.

The total number of slaves who gained freedom, however, was small. Most remained on a plantation, toiling from dawn to dusk six days a week. It was a life of sameness, often boredom. It was a life that did not let grown people be adults. They could not make decisions for themselves or be responsible for their own children.

Few slaves ever wrote about their experiences. Most of what we know about how slaves felt comes from their songs and stories. Music, dance, and stories were all ways they expressed their feelings. Their music included work songs, sad songs, and merry songs. Music and dancing were part of Saturday night gaiety and holidays. One such song went:

> Rabbit in the briar patch,
> Squirrel in the tree,
> Wish I could go hunting
> But I ain't free.
>
> Rooster's in the henhouse,
> Hen's in the patch.
> Love to go shooting,
> But I ain't free.

Stories told from one generation to another helped keep alive some memories of family history. Folk stories about Brer Rabbit, Brer Fox, and Brer Bear had their roots in African stories. In these stories Brer Rabbit usually outwits the more powerful animals like Brer Bear. Through music, dance, and stories, blacks held onto their own world of inner feelings.

In time the Christian religion became a source of strength for millions of slaves. At first little effort was made to introduce Christianity to black people. Many of them continued to hold on to African beliefs and traditions. In the late 1700s, however, the Baptists and Methodists began to bring Christianity to the slaves. From then on Christianity became increasingly important in black society.

Free Blacks

At first free blacks had all the rights of citizenship. Free black men could vote. Gradually these rights were taken away in the South. Virginia took away the vote in 1723, and Georgia, in 1761.

Most free blacks, particularly in cities, learned to read and write. To do so was a struggle and sometimes against the law. Both Virginia and Georgia passed laws forbidding education for blacks. Nevertheless, free blacks organized themselves to provide schooling for their children.

Benjamin Banneker was a free black in Maryland. Through education he became an important scientist.

Banneker was the son of a free woman and a slave father. Because his mother was free, Banneker was born free. They lived on a prosperous farm in Maryland. When a Quaker opened a school nearby, Banneker enrolled at the age of 12. A new world opened up to him. He particularly excelled in mathematics. One day he saw a pocket watch for the first time. He was fascinated. He began studying to find out how clocks worked. Banneker then spent his spare time making his own clock. Carved entirely of wood, it was finished in 1753, and was the first clock made in America. It kept perfect time for 48 years.

Later, Banneker gained fame for his **almanac.** An almanac gives information about natural events. When will the sun rise and set on different days of the year in different places? What will the weather be like? How high will the tide be at a certain place at a certain time? Such information is very helpful to farmers and sailors.

Benjamin Bannaker, one of America's first scientists, published an almanac.

Reading Check

1. Name the two main kinds of slaves.
2. What was the responsibility of an overseer?
3. What were three ways that slaves expressed their feelings?
4. Who was Benjamin Banneker?

4. THE GROWTH OF SOUTH CAROLINA

To Guide Your Reading

Look for these important words:

People
- Eliza Lucas

Places
- Columbia

Look for answers to these questions:

1. For what reasons did Charleston become a major city?
2. How did geography influence the life and work of the colonists in South Carolina?
3. Why was slavery important on rice plantations?
4. What contribution did Eliza Lucas make to the economy of South Carolina?

Large numbers of French people came to South Carolina in 1680. These French people were seeking religious freedom. Many of them were skilled in a number of crafts. They also liked town life. As the small colony began to grow, Charleston turned into one of the most beautiful cities of colonial America.

Charleston, South Carolina, was one of the prettiest and busiest of colonial cities.

Visitors called Charleston a neat and pretty town. Flocks of buzzards helped it stay that way. Buzzards were protected by law because they cleaned up the garbage.

Because of its excellent harbor, Charleston became one of the most important colonial ports. Only Boston, New York City, and Philadelphia were larger.

Growing Rice

Charleston grew because it became the center of a rice-growing region. Rice needs land that can be flooded while the rice is growing. When the rice is ready for harvest, the land must be drained of water. The low, flat land of South Carolina with its swamps and streams was ideal for growing rice.

201

Slaves did the hard work on this South Carolina rice plantation. Can you find the overseer in this picture?

Growing rice was not as easy as growing tobacco. The planter had to construct canals to flood and drain the fields. Sometimes a hurricane or a flooded river ruined the canals and the crops.

Many workers were needed to do the backbreaking work of building canals, planting rice, and harvesting it. To do this work the South Carolina planters depended on slaves. Women usually waded in the black muck of the wet fields to plant the rice. Near harvest time children had the job of scaring the birds away.

The watery fields were full of mosquitoes. Often their bites carried the germs of the disease malaria.

The summers in the lowlands of South Carolina could be very hot and humid. The skies opened with great thunderstorms. Mosquitoes and sand flies swarmed everywhere. To escape such summers, the planters went to Charleston. In Charleston they lived in houses that had wide verandas to catch the ocean breezes. The summer months were merry with parties, dances, and musical gatherings.

Eliza Lucas

One of those who enjoyed the summer gaiety of Charleston was **Eliza Lucas.** At the age of 17, she was in charge of three plantations. Her father, who owned the plantations, lived in an English colony in the West Indies. He was afraid of a war with Spain and sent his family to South Carolina for safety.

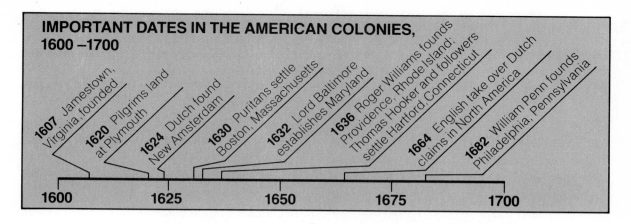

IMPORTANT DATES IN THE AMERICAN COLONIES, 1600 –1700

1607 Jamestown, Virginia, founded

1620 Pilgrims land at Plymouth

1624 Dutch found New Amsterdam

1630 Puritans settle Boston, Massachusetts

1632 Lord Baltimore establishes Maryland

1636 Roger Williams founds Providence, Rhode Island; Thomas Hooker and followers settle Hartford, Connecticut

1664 English take over Dutch claims in North America

1682 William Penn founds Philadelphia, Pennsylvania

1600   1625   1650   1675   1700

Eliza Lucas described her busy life in a letter to a friend:

I have a little library well furnished in which I spend part of my time. My music and the garden, which I am very fond of, take up the rest of my time that is not employed in business.

The business of running three plantations, she wrote, "requires much writing and more business and fatigue of other sorts than you can imagine."

In other letters Eliza described teaching two black girls to read so that they could teach other black children. This was a very advanced idea for that time.

Another of Eliza Lucas's projects was raising indigo plants. People did not learn to make chemical dyes until the 1800s. Until then, indigo was one of the most important dyes. Chemical indigo is widely used today to dye denim for blue jeans.

Using seeds sent by her father, Eliza spent several years growing different types of indigo. In 1743 samples of her dye were judged in London to be of the best quality. Eliza gave indigo seeds to her neighbors and friends. Within a few years South Carolina planters were selling a million pounds (453.6 T) of indigo a year. The South Carolina planters could grow indigo on land where rice did not grow.

Settlers in the Piedmont

While plantations were growing in coastal areas, people were moving into other regions. They spread out beyond the coastal plain. There the soil was good, and people began to establish tobacco and cotton plantations.

Many Scots settled beyond the fall line. The Scots, used to raising cattle, drove their herds to Charleston for export. The way of life of these frontier cowboys did not depend on slaves.

As in other colonies, important towns developed at the fall line. They included **Columbia,** the capital of South Carolina.

Reading Check

1. Give two reasons Charleston became an important city.
2. Why was coastal South Carolina a good place to grow rice?
3. What work did slaves do on rice plantations?
4. What cash crop did Eliza Lucas develop?

SKILLS FOR SUCCESS

USING CLIMATE MAPS

Climate is a word used to talk about the usual weather of a place over a long period of time. Temperatures and the amount of moisture for all seasons are part of climate. Climate maps give information about temperatures and moisture.

A **precipitation map** is one kind of climate map. A precipitation map shows how much moisture falls as rain or snow. The colors on the map tell how much precipitation each area gets. The map key shows that areas tinted dark blue get more than 60 inches (150 cm) of precipitation a year.

A **growing season map** is another kind of climate map. It shows the number of days between the last frost of spring and the first frost of fall. The number of frost-free days is the length of time crops can be grown.

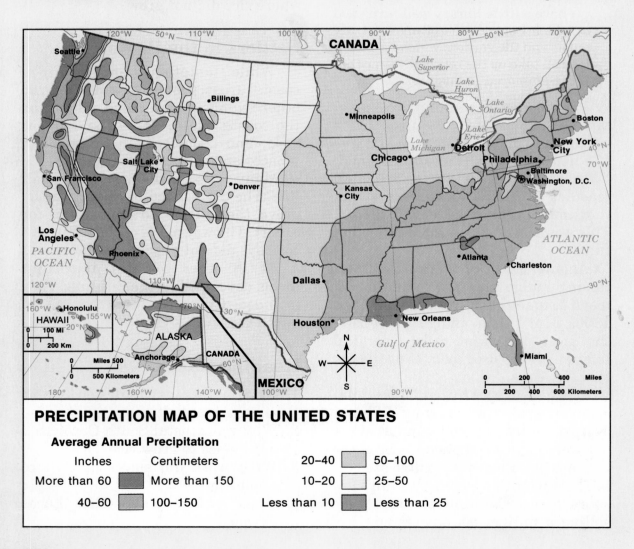

PRECIPITATION MAP OF THE UNITED STATES

Average Annual Precipitation

Inches	Centimeters
More than 60	More than 150
40–60	100–150
20–40	50–100
10–20	25–50
Less than 10	Less than 25

Working with Two Climate Maps

You can use a growing season map and a precipitation map together. This is one way to learn about growing conditions in certain places. Find Phoenix, Arizona, on the growing season map. Nearby areas are colored yellow or purple. You can see from the map key that the area near Phoenix has growing seasons that last from five months to seven months.

Now look at the precipitation map. How much precipitation does the Phoenix area have? The area around Phoenix may be too dry for crops to grow naturally. A farmer there will have to irrigate the crops to make them grow.

CHECKING YOUR SKILLS

Use the precipitation map and the growing season map to answer these questions.

1. Cotton needs a growing season at least 6 months long. Would you be more likely to find cotton growing near Denver, Colorado, or near Atlanta, Georgia?

2. Sugarcane grows in a warm, wet climate. Would you find sugarcane near Salt Lake City, Utah, or near Miami, Florida?

3. In general, are growing seasons longer in northern states or in southern states?

4. In general, is there more rainfall in eastern states or in western states?

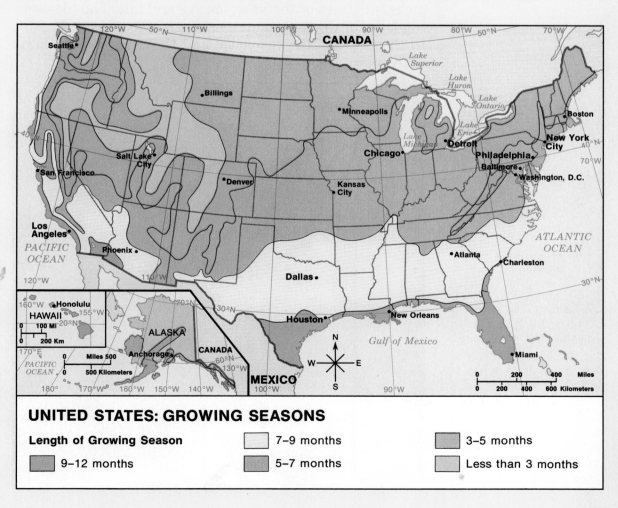

UNITED STATES: GROWING SEASONS

Length of Growing Season

- 9–12 months
- 7–9 months
- 5–7 months
- 3–5 months
- Less than 3 months

CLOSE-UP

A VISIT TO WILLIAMSBURG

In colonial Virginia, a visit to Williamsburg was an exciting event. It was always something to look forward to. Many planter families went twice a year to Williamsburg. They traveled on horseback or in horse-drawn carriages over narrow dirt roads. They went during the most pleasant times of the year, spring and fall. The blossoming trees of woods and orchards perfumed the spring air. In the fall the air was crisp, and the trees were aflame with colors.

On Training Day the militia drilled on the green at Williamsburg. Musicians playing fifes and drums marched in front of the soldiers. Afterwards, sports, races, and other contests were held on the green. At Williamsburg today you can see musicians march as they once did.

At Williamsburg today you can visit the Spinning and Weaving House. At the spinning wheel a woman turns fibers from the flax plant into linen thread. At other times she might turn sheep's wool into yarn. Hanging from the rafters are skeins of wool yarn that have been dyed different colors. Weavers at large looms make fabric using the linen and wool yarns. In colonial times a good weaver could produce about 3 yards (2.7m) of cloth a day.

The blacksmith was one of the most important colonial craftsmen. Today at the blacksmith's forge on Prince George Street, the fire turns the iron red-hot and ready for shaping. As in colonial times, this blacksmith makes horseshoes as well as candleholders, farm tools, and wagon wheels.

207

This candle dipper stands over a kettle of hot fat called tallow. He makes candles just the way they were made in the eighteenth century. He starts with a candle rod, a short metal rod with string twisted around it. The string will become the wick. The candle rod is dipped into the hot tallow, cooled, and then dipped again. The process is repeated until the candle is ready.

On a visit to Williamsburg ladies would come to the Margaret Hunter Shop, which was run by Margaret Hunter and her sister Jane. Today, the Hunter Shop continues to sell ladies' hats, fans, buttons, shoes, and other fine fashions of the colonial period.

208

In 1780 the capital of Virginia was moved from Williamsburg to Richmond. Richmond was on the fall line of the James River. By then more and more people had moved inland. It was easier for them to get to Richmond than to Williamsburg.

After the capital was moved, the village of Williamsburg lost its importance. Plantation owners and government officials no longer had reason to visit. By 1900 historic Williamsburg showed little of its former sparkle.

Then in 1926 the project of rebuilding Williamsburg began. First, old maps and drawings were studied. Then the buildings that remained from the 1700s were **restored,** or returned, to their original appearance. Even the colonial gardens were replated as they had been.

A visit to Williamsburg is like a trip back 250 years in a time machine. Here are all the sights and sounds of colonial life. You hear the hammering of the blacksmith and the clip-clops of horses' hooves. You see the trimmed hedges and the church's high steeple. The sights and sounds of Williamsburg let us experience our colonial heritage.

The Prentis Store was a gas station in the 1920s when this photo was taken.

The Prentis Store today, restored to look as it did in colonial times.

209

CHAPTER 9 REVIEW

WORDS TO USE

Number your paper from 1 to 10. Use the terms below to complete the paragraph that follows. Use each term once.

broker   plantations
cash crop   planters
economy   public service
indigo   society
overseer   tidewater

Large farms were called __(1)__ in the South. Persons who owned these farms were called __(2)__ . In the __(3)__ region tobacco was the main __(4)__ . In South Carolina rice and __(5)__ were grown. Farmers often sold their crops through a London __(6)__ . Among their duties, Southern landowners helped __(7)__ by giving time to __(8)__ . In general, the Southern __(9)__ depended on slave labor. The person in charge of field slaves was an __(10)__ .

FACTS TO REVIEW

1. What were the important cash crops of the Southern colonies?

2. Why was Maryland founded?

3. Why was Carolina divided into two parts?

4. What were James Oglethorpe's reasons for founding Georgia?

5. Why weren't there any large towns in the tidewater region?

6. What responsibilities did a planter have?

7. Why did slave labor replace hired labor where cash crops were grown?

8. How did the buying and selling of slaves affect their family life?

9. Name three important Southern cities that were established at the fall line.

10. Describe the achievements of Benjamin Banneker and Eliza Lucas.

IDEAS TO DISCUSS

1. How were geography, cash crops, and slavery connected? Why was slavery less important where there were smaller farms and fewer cash crops?

2. How was the life of a slave different from the life of a plantation owner? How was it different from that of a small farmer?

3. Four of the first five Presidents were from the planter class of people. From what you have read, can you explain why many of our early leaders came from the South?

◯ SKILLS PRACTICE

Climate Maps   Use the maps on pages 204 and 205 to answer these questions.

1. The tastiest apples are grown in climates that have growing seasons of 3 to 6 months. Would apples grow well near Atlanta, Georgia? near Boston?

2. Oranges need mild temperatures and a growing season of 9 to 12 months. Would oranges grow well near Los Angeles, California? near Seattle, Washington?

3. What is the average precipitation of Billings, Montana? of Houston, Texas?

UNIT 3 REVIEW

WORDS TO REMEMBER

Number your paper from 1 to 15. Use the words below to complete the sentences that follow. Use each term once.

apprentice
authority
barter
cash crops
delegates
economy
exports
frontier
immigrants
meetinghouse
militias
navigable
plantations
proprietor
tidewater

1. There were few _____ rivers in New England.

2. The most important building in New England towns was the _____.

3. Furs, lumber, and fish were all _____ of the American colonies.

4. In New England the church leaders had a great deal of _____.

5. Wars between Indians and colonists happened as settlers continued to push the _____ westward.

6. It was common for American colonists to _____ instead of using money.

7. The _____ of the Middle colonies depended on growing and trading bread grains.

8. William Penn was the _____ of Pennsylvania.

9. The Germans and Scotch-Irish were among the many _____ who settled in Pennsylvania.

10. King Charles II said proprietors had to consult with an assembly of _____ chosen by the colonists.

11. As a boy, Benjamin Franklin served as an _____ to his brother, a printer.

12. In the South the first settlements were in the _____ region of Virginia and Maryland.

13. Farms in the South were called _____.

14. Tobacco, rice, and indigo were the _____ in the South.

15. Colonists everywhere organized _____ to provide for their defense.

FOCUS ON MAIN IDEAS

1. Why did many colonial cities grow near good harbors? Why did other cities develop at the fall line?

2. Compare and contrast agriculture in the New England colonies, the Middle colonies, and the Southern colonies. Discuss the size and fertility of farms, the kinds of crops grown, and the source of farm labor.

3. Religion was an important influence in colonial life. What examples of this statement can you find in the unit?

4. In colonial times fighting was common between the settlers and the Indians. Why? Give two examples of Indian-settler conflict to support your answer.

5. In what ways did the American colonists get experience in self-government?

211

ACTIVITIES

1. **Research/Oral Report** Choose a person in this unit who interested you. Find out more about that person. Share what you learned with the class.

2. **Writing** Imagine you are a girl or a boy living in one of the colonies. Name the place where you imagine you live. Then write what happens during one day in your life.

3. **Research/Art** Benjamin Franklin invented a stove, eyeglasses, and many other things. Find out about one of his inventions. Describe or draw a picture of it.

4. **Art** Describe or draw a picture of an invention you would like to see. Make sure to explain how it would work.

5. **Research/Art** People in the colonies practiced many different crafts, such as candlemaking, weaving, and making musical instruments. Research one of these crafts and share your findings with the class. If you can, give a simple demonstration of the craft.

6. **Past and Present** Compare and contrast today and colonial times with respect to transportation, food, clothing, shelter, schooling, light, and power. Do this by making a chart. If you wish, put pictures on your chart.

7. **Art** Imagine you are coming to America to start a colony. Build a model showing the kind of location you would look for. Show natural features on your model.

8. **Remembering the Close-Up** Imagine that you recently made a visit to Williamsburg. A friend says to you, "Why bother to see that old stuff?" What would you answer? Write your answer or tell it to the class.

○ SKILLS REVIEW

1. **Reading Bar Graphs** This is a graph that shows the number of pelts a fur trapper sold one year. Use the graph to answer the questions that follow.

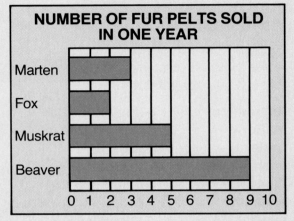

NUMBER OF FUR PELTS SOLD IN ONE YEAR

a. Which animal supplied the most pelts?

b. Which animal supplied the fewest pelts?

c. How many fox pelts did the trapper sell?

2. **Using Climate Maps** Use the maps on pages 204 and 205 to answer these questions.

a. Is the average yearly precipitation of San Francisco, California, more like that of Chicago, Illinois, or New Orleans, Louisiana?

b. Is the average yearly precipitation of Anchorage, Alaska, more like that of Denver, Colorado, or Charleston, South Carolina?

c. What is the growing season of the area near San Francisco? Is it more like that of New Orleans, Louisiana, or Boston, Massachusetts?

d. Does Dallas, Texas, or Kansas City, Missouri, have a growing season of at least eight months?

YOUR STATE'S HISTORY

American colonists learned to use the different natural resources they found. They learned to use the land, the forests, the rivers, the swamps, and the harbors. Most of the activities below can help you learn about the natural resources or economy of your state.

LEARNING ABOUT GEOGRAPHY

1. The table below shows five important resources. Make a copy of this table in your scrapbook. Find out which of these resources your state has. Next to each resource, give information about this resource in your state.

NATURAL RESOURCES IN OUR STATE	
Navigable rivers	
Fertile soil	
Good ports and harbors	
Forests	
Valuable minerals	

2. Most American colonists lived near rivers. Rivers helped communication and shipping and provided water for agriculture. What are the most important rivers in your state? Make a map of your state showing the major rivers.

3. Farming was important to all the colonists. The Southern colonies grew tobacco, cotton, and rice. The Middle and Northern colonies raised wheat, barley, and corn. What crops are grown in your state?

LEARNING ABOUT CULTURE

4. Williamsburg, Virginia, is a town that shows life as it was in colonial America. Have any places in your state been restored or rebuilt to show some period in American history? Find out about these places and share your findings with the class.

LEARNING ABOUT ECONOMICS

5. The English colonies were not the only colonial settlements in what is now the United States. By 1750 there were French settlements in the Mississippi River valley. The Spanish had settled in Texas, New Mexico, and Florida. The Russians had fur trading posts in Alaska. Were there any European settlements in your state by 1750? If so, describe the economy of these settlements.

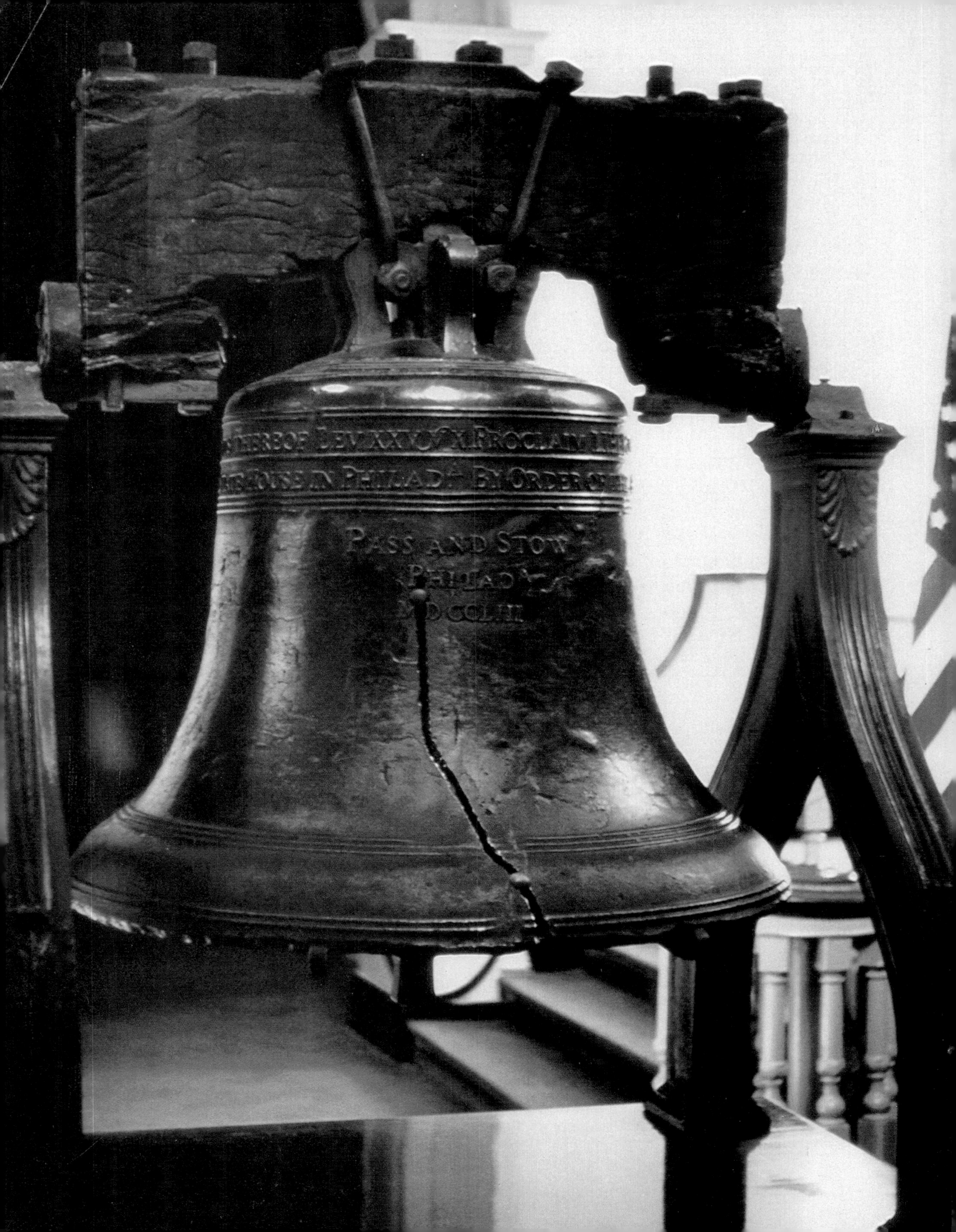
PASS AND STOW
PHILAD

UNIT FOUR

THE AMERICAN REVOLUTION

Key Dates and Events

1754–1763
French and Indian War

1765
The Stamp Act taxes paper

1767
The Townshend Acts tax imports

1770
Boston Massacre

1773
Boston Tea Party

1774
March–June: The Intolerable Acts

September: First Continental Congress meets

1775
April: Battles of Lexington and Concord

May: Second Continental Congress meets

June: Battle of Bunker Hill

1776
July: Declaration of Independence

1777
Victory at Saratoga brings help from France

1781
Battle of Yorktown

1783
Britain and the United States sign a peace treaty

Independence Day, July 4, is our most important national holiday. On that day we celebrate the birth of our nation in 1776. Before then a British king ruled the people of the 13 American colonies. On July 4, 1776, in Philadelphia, Pennsylvania, the Americans declared they would no longer have a king. They would govern themselves from that day forward.

The great bronze bell in this picture is the Liberty Bell. It now rests near Independence Hall in Philadelphia, where the Declaration of Independence was made. On the bell are these words: PROCLAIM LIBERTY THROUGHOUT THE LAND UNTO ALL THE INHABITANTS THEREOF. The Liberty Bell was rung the first time the Declaration of Independence was read aloud to the people of Philadelphia. For years afterward it rang out on every Fourth of July. Today it remains a symbol of American freedom and independence.

CHAPTER 10

Background of the Revolution

About
this
chapter

A **revolution** is a large, sudden change in government and people's lives. In the American Revolution, the 13 American colonies broke away from Britain and became a separate, independent country. In this chapter you will learn why differences grew between the American colonists and the British government. You will learn how these differences finally led to war.

1. THE FRENCH AND INDIAN WAR

To Guide Your Reading

Look for these important words:

Key Words
- revolution
- French and Indian War
- allies

People
- George Washington
- Edward Braddock

Places
- Ohio River Valley
- Fort Duquesne
- Fort Necessity

Look for answers to these questions:

1. What led to the French and Indian War?
2. Why were the French and Indians often able to defeat the British?
3. How did the war end?

By 1750 life was good for most Americans. In the growing cities, merchants and traders were doing well. Carpenters, coopers, smiths, printers, all were busy. Farmers in the settled areas were able to sell their animals and crops for a nice profit. They helped feed the people of the growing cities and towns.

Meanwhile, settlers kept pushing the frontier ever westward. Log cabins and small fields of cleared land were gradually replacing the wilderness. Some people began to think of crossing the Appalachian Mountains and settling in the rich valleys on the other side.

The American colonies were still ruled by England, but England was 3,000 miles (about 4,830 km) away. Each colony had become used to governing itself.

Important events would soon lead to the American Revolution. The first of these was the **French and Indian War.** This war started because both

France and England claimed the land of the **Ohio River valley.**

France had become worried about the growing American colonies. There were a million and a half people in the British colonies and only 80,000 in New France. If colonists started to spill over the Appalachian Mountains, they could threaten French settlements.

The French decided to protect themselves by building a string of forts in the upper part of the Ohio River valley. One of these forts was **Fort Duquesne** (doo•KAYN), where Pittsburgh, Pennsylvania, is now. Fort Duquesne was on land claimed by Virginia.

The governor of Virginia sent young **George Washington,** then 21, to warn the French that they were on Virginia territory. The French replied that they would stay.

The governor immediately sent Washington with an army of 150 men to drive out the French. Near Fort Duquesne, Washington and his men

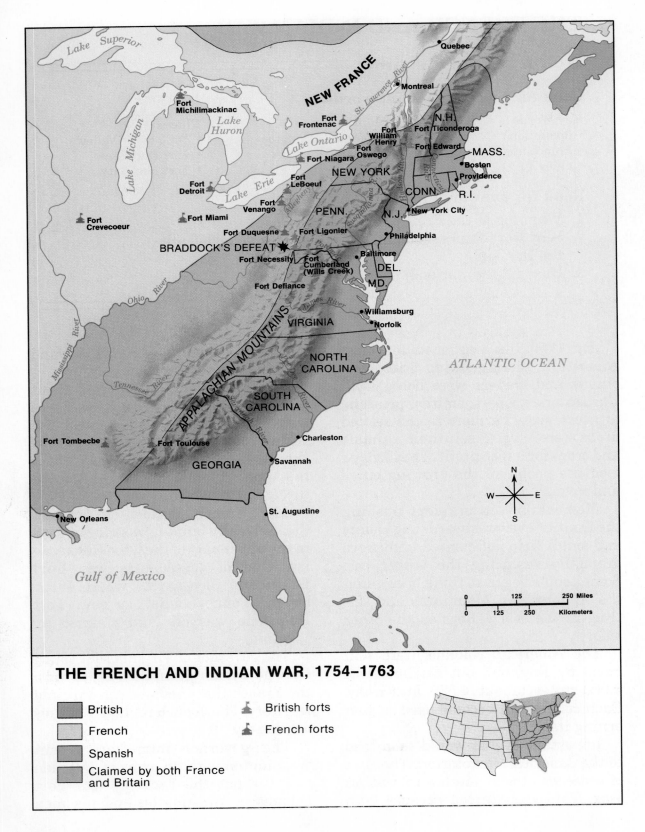

THE FRENCH AND INDIAN WAR, 1754–1763

British

French

Spanish

Claimed by both France
and Britain

British forts

French forts

built a fort called **Fort Necessity.** It lay in a low place. Then the French attacked the fort from woods nearby. Outnumbered, Washington and his men held out until a heavy rainstorm began. Runoff from the storm soaked all the gunpowder. Without dry powder to fire their guns, Washington's small army was forced to surrender.

Washington learned from his experience. He never again built a camp in a low place. Like many Americans, Washington was to learn about war from fighting the French.

Braddock's Defeat

At first it looked as if Britain would lose to France in North America. In 1754 the British general, **Edward Braddock,** led troops through the wilderness to attack Fort Duquesne. His army included British troops in red coats and Virginians in blue coats. George Washington later described the beauty of the red and blue uniforms against the green of the forest. Near Fort Duquesne the French attacked Braddock's troops. His men, numbering 1,459, were badly beaten by about 200 French soldiers and about 600 Indians. The Indians had long been trading partners of the French. Now they were also **allies,** or friends in war, of the French.

Braddock's troops never had fought Indians. The Indians were hard to see in the forest. In contrast, the colorful British made easy targets. Indian war whoops were terrifying to British ears. The British fled in panic. That day almost 1,000 of the British army were wounded or killed. General Braddock was one of those who died.

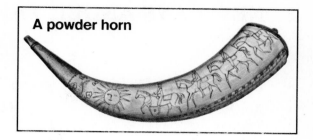

A powder horn

Such British defeats left the frontier without defenses. Even more Indians decided to side with the French. Indian war parties began to attack frontier settlements in Pennsylvania, Maryland, and Virginia. Hundreds of men, women, and children were killed. The colonists blamed the French for these attacks.

In 1757 the war turned in Britain's favor. The British government sent more armies to North America. With fresh generals and thousands more troops, Britain began to win battles against the French and Indians.

In 1763, the French and Indian War ended with victory for Britain. As a result, the French left North America. The British flag now flew over Canada and the Ohio River valley. France gave Spain the rest of its North American territory. Britain now claimed all of North America east of the Mississippi River. Spain claimed all lands west of the Mississippi.

Reading Check

1. What caused the French and Indian War?
2. Why did the Indians help the French?
3. What caused the defeat of General Braddock?
4. What parts of North America did Britain win from France?

2. NEW LAWS ANGER THE COLONISTS

To Guide Your Reading

Look for these important words:

Key Words
- Stamp Act
- trial by jury
- Parliament
- houses
- House of Lords
- House of Commons
- petitions
- repeal
- Sons of Liberty
- liberty
- Townshend Acts
- boycott

People
- Sam Adams

Look for answers to these questions:

1. What were the main disagreements between Britain and the colonies?
2. What kinds of taxes did Britain put on the colonists?
3. Why did these taxes make the colonists angry?
4. What methods did they use to protest the taxes?

The French and Indian War led to disagreements between Britain and its American colonies. They soon disagreed about the frontier and the new lands won from France. Many colonists were eager to move into the Ohio River valley. Britain, however, wanted to keep those lands for the Indians. Britain did not want more Indian wars between its colonists and the Indians. In 1763, Britain passed a law that forbade colonists to settle west of the Appalachian Mountains. This law made many Americans angry.

The next major disagreement between Britain and the colonies was about money. The long war between France and Britain had cost a great deal of money. Britain had borrowed much of the money and now had to pay it back. The British thought the colonists should pay part of the cost. After all, one reason for the war was to defend the colonies.

The Stamp Act

Britain decided to raise money by taxing the colonies. In 1765, the British government passed a tax on paper. Every piece of paper had to carry a stamp to show that the tax had been paid. This law was called the **Stamp Act.** A person could not get a license or a diploma, a newspaper or playing cards, without paying the stamp tax. People who did not obey the new law could be tried in special courts, without **trial by jury.**

Trial by jury had been a right of British people for hundreds of years. A person accused of breaking the law could be tried only by a jury of fellow citizens. Now the colonists felt this basic right was threatened.

The Stamp Act took away another important right, Americans said. That was the right to vote their own taxes. The Stamp Act had not been voted for by the colonists' own assemblies.

220

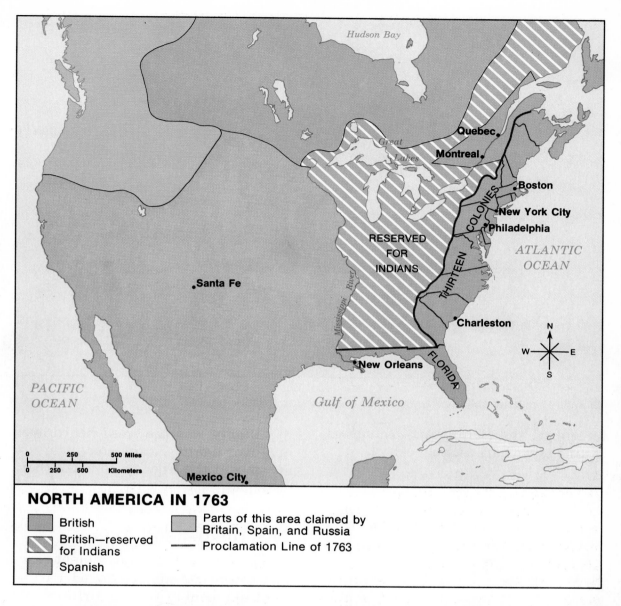

NORTH AMERICA IN 1763

- British
- British—reserved for Indians
- Spanish
- Parts of this area claimed by Britain, Spain, and Russia
- —— Proclamation Line of 1763

The British **Parliament** (PAHR‧luh‧muhnt) had passed the Stamp Act. Parliament was the law-making body of Britain. Parliament had two parts, or **houses.** Members of the **House of Lords** held office because of their noble birth. On the other hand, members of the **House of Commons** were elected by the people in Britain. The British felt that Parliament represented British people everywhere.

Not so, said the Americans. Only colonial assemblies had the right to pass taxes in the American colonies. They had not elected people to Parliament. Therefore, they said, Parliament could not tax them.

The Stamp Act made the colonists furious. Colonial leaders made their feelings known to Parliament in the form of **petitions.** Petitions are written requests. They asked Parliament

221

A protest against the Stamp Act takes place under Boston's Liberty Tree. From the branches swing straw dummies of British tax collectors.

to **repeal** the Stamp Act. *To repeal* means to withdraw or cancel.

Sons of Liberty

At the same time, citizens in every seaport organized themselves into groups called **Sons of Liberty.** The Sons of Liberty burned the stamped paper and attacked British tax officers. A tax officer in New York said he would "cram the Stamp Act down the people's throats." Mobs then attacked his house.

In Boston, a lawyer named **Sam Adams** organized protests around an elm tree in Boston Common. The tree became known as the Liberty Tree. Straw dummies dressed as British officials were often hung from the limbs of the Liberty Tree.

Liberty was the word heard over and over again. To the colonists, *liberty* meant the freedom to make their own laws.

The Townshend Acts

The furious and often violent reaction to the Stamp Act forced Parliament to repeal it in 1766. Britain still needed money, however. The next year, Parliament passed the **Townshend Acts.** These laws raised taxes on many imported goods. Lead, paper, paint, glass, and tea now all cost more to buy.

Once again the colonists were angry.

The British government had paid little attention to its American colonies in 150 years. It had let them do pretty much as they pleased. Then Parliament changed. It seemed to be

In Boston angry citizens make a bonfire of Stamp Act paper.

Merchants who did not boycott British goods were named on lists like this.

A LIST of the Names of *those* who AUDACIOUSLY continue to counteract the UNITED SENTIMENTS of the BODY of Merchants thro'out NORTH-AMERICA; by importing British Goods contrary to the Agreement.

John Bernard,
  (In King-Street, almost opposite Vernon'sHead.
James McMasters,
  (On Treat's Wharf.
Patrick McMasters,
  (Opposite the Sign of the Lamb.
John Mein,
  (Opposite the White-Horse, and in King-Street.
Nathaniel Rogers,
  (Opposite Mr. Henderson Inches Store lower End King-Street.
William Jackson,
  At the BrazenHead, Cornhill, near theTown-House.
Theophilus Lillie,
  (Near Mr. Pemberton'sMeeting-House,North-End.
John Taylor,
  (Nearly opposite the Heart andCrown inCornhill.
Ame & Elizabeth Cummings,
  (Opposite the Old Brick Meeting House, all of Boston.
Israel Williams, Esq; & Son,
  (Traders in the Town of Hatfield.
And, Henry Barnes,
  (Trader in the Town of Marlboro'.

treating the colonies like children. Parliament did not accept the idea that the colonies had grown up and were now able to handle their own affairs. "This is the mother country. They are the children. They must obey," said a member of Parliament.

A Boycott Begins

The colonists began to **boycott** British goods. A boycott is a refusal to buy something in order to show disapproval. A boycott of British goods would cause British merchants to lose money. These merchants might in turn pressure Parliament to repeal the taxes. At town meetings people voted to make things for themselves and not to buy imported goods. Some who did not boycott British goods were covered with tar or molasses and dusted with feathers.

The boycott began to work. Imports decreased by half in several colonies. Women were particularly important in making the boycott a success. Many met in groups to spin and weave as their grandmothers had done.

Again the colonists were successful in forcing Parliament to repeal most of the taxes on imports. King George insisted, however, that the tax on tea remain. He wanted the Americans to remember who was boss.

Reading Check

1. Why did Britain pass the Stamp Act?
2. For what reasons did colonists protest the Stamp Act?
3. Who were the Sons of Liberty?
4. How did the colonists protest the Townshend Acts?

223

3. PROTESTS IN BOSTON

To Guide Your Reading

Look for these important words:

Key Words
- Redcoats
- massacre
- Committee of Correspondence
- monopoly
- Boston Tea Party
- quartered
- Intolerable Acts
- tyranny
- resist
- First Continental Congress

People
- Crispus Attucks
- Paul Revere
- John Adams
- Patrick Henry

Look for answers to these questions:

1. Why did fighting first break out between the colonists and British soldiers?
2. What were the Committees of Correspondence?
3. What was the Boston Tea Party?
4. How did Britain punish the colonies after the Boston Tea Party?
5. What were some achievements of the First Continental Congress?

Ten thousand British soldiers had been sent to America in 1763 to keep peace on the frontier. If these soldiers had gone to the frontier, Americans would not have minded. Instead, the soldiers stayed in the cities. In Boston the soldiers took over a church for their living quarters. They even rode their horses in the church. That kind of thing greatly angered Americans.

British soldiers were paid so little that they were willing to work at odd jobs for low wages. They took jobs away from American workers. That also angered Americans.

Many colonists made fun of the British soldiers in their red jackets. They called them **Redcoats** and "lobster-backs."

The Boston Massacre

In several cities, Americans got into serious fights with British soldiers. The worst fight happened in Boston. On March 5, 1770, an angry crowd of boys and men began throwing snowballs at a British soldier on duty. More soldiers and their captain arrived on the scene. For half an hour they stood their ground listening to the jeers of the mob: "Come on, you rascals, you bloody backs, you lobster scoundrels! Fire if you dare!"

Suddenly one soldier, hit with a club, fired. Other soldiers followed. When the smoke cleared, five American men were dead or dying. The first to die was a black man, **Crispus Attucks** (AT•uhks).

Many Americans in Boston and elsewhere were angered. Now the hated

With this picture of the Boston Massacre, Paul Revere helped create angry feelings against the British.

British soldiers had actually killed people they were supposed to be protecting. At least 10,000 persons turned out for the funeral processions of the dead men. The shops and stores of Boston and neighboring towns were closed. Everywhere church bells tolled.

Paul Revere, a silversmith, made a picture showing the British troops firing on the people of Boston. He titled it *The Bloody Massacre.* A **massacre** (MAS•uh•kuhr) is the killing of large numbers of people who cannot defend themselves. The shooting in Boston was not really a massacre, but to this day we call the event the Boston Massacre.

The British captain in charge of the soldiers was tried for murder. **John Adams,** a cousin of Sam Adams, defended him. It took courage for John

Adams to do this because the British were so unpopular. John Adams was a strong believer in justice. He believed that the British soldiers had fired in self-defense. The Boston jury found the British captain not guilty.

Meanwhile Sam Adams had persuaded Boston's Town Meeting to set up a **Committee of Correspondence.** The job of committee members was to write to colonists in other places to keep track of events. By 1774 most colonies had such committees. The committees did much to bind the colonists together against the British.

Boston Tea Party

The three years following the Boston Massacre were quiet. Historians have called it "the calm before the storm." The storm came when Parliament again passed a law that angered Americans.

The new law of May 1773 gave a **monopoly** (muh.NAHP.uh.lee) on tea to the East India Company. A monopoly is complete control over a product or service. According to the law, only the East India Company could import tea into the American colonies. That meant that American merchants and traders could no longer make money in the tea trade.

Tea would cost less under the monopoly, but Americans did not care. They remembered that they were still paying a tax on tea, and they feared monopolies. Merchants worried that Parliament might establish other monopolies and drive them out of business.

During the Boston Tea Party people cheered when the Sons of Liberty, dressed as Indians, threw chests of tea into the harbor.

Three ships carrying East India tea arrived in Boston Harbor in December, 1773. The colonists refused to let the tea come ashore. The British governor then said that the tea would be unloaded under the protection of cannons and guns.

Now the Sons of Liberty acted. Disguised as Mohawk Indians, they headed for the Boston docks. As they marched to the docks the Sons of Liberty sang a song that started:

Rally, Mohawks! bring out your axes,
And tell King George we'll pay no taxes
On his foreign tea. . . .

The "Mohawks" scrambled onto the British ships. They chopped open the chests of tea with their axes. They threw the tea into the water. Newspapers called this the **Boston Tea Party.**

In Britain the king and Parliament passed laws to punish the colonists. In the spring of 1774, an angry Parliament closed the port of Boston to all shipping until the city paid for the destroyed tea. Shipping was the most important business of Boston. Without shipping, the people of Boston had few goods to buy or sell, including food.

To make things even worse, Parliament did away with the elected assembly of Massachusetts. A British general, Thomas Gage, was named to govern Massachusetts. Town meetings were forbidden without his approval.

Parliament also said British soldiers could be **quartered,** or housed, in American homes. The Americans had to pay for the soldiers' blankets, their food, their cooking pots. People even had to buy rum for the soldiers.

The colonists called these harsh, new laws the **Intolerable Acts.** "Tyr-anny!" they shouted. **Tyranny** (TIR•uh•nee) is harsh and unjust rule.

The Colonists Unite

The Intolerable Acts united the colonies as nothing else had. People in all the colonies sent food, clothing, fuel, and money to Boston. In Philadelphia, a committee of citizens declared, "We consider our brethren, at Boston, as suffering in the common cause of America."

The Philadelphia committee invited the colonies to send delegates to Philadelphia. They wanted to discuss how the colonists could **resist,** or act against, British tyranny. In September 1774, 55 men chosen by committees in 12 states met in the **First Continental Congress.**

The men at the First Continental Congress worked hard to develop a statement of rights. They stated these rights in a petition to Parliament. People had a right to life, liberty, and property, they said. People had a right to trial by jury. People had the right to make laws in their own assemblies. People had the right not to have soldiers living in their homes.

The Continental Congress also voted another boycott of British goods. Americans were asked not to import or use British goods. Furthermore, the Congress asked Americans not to sell anything to the British.

In Virginia, some members of the House of Burgesses thought that Americans and British would end up fighting each other. They suggested that the militias start preparing for war. Others strongly opposed the suggestion. In response, **Patrick Henry**

George Washington strides out of a session of the First Continental Congress. With him are Patrick Henry and William Henry Lee, both from Virginia. Although Washington had not yet taken command of the army, the artist paints him in uniform to show that in spirit, Washington was ready to fight for his country. The Continental Congress met in Carpenter's Hall, later renamed Independence Hall.

rose. He gave the most famous speech of his career. Americans have long remembered its last words:

Is life so dear, or peace so sweet, as to be purchased at the price of chains and slavery? Forbid it, Almighty God! I know not what course others may take; but as for me, give me liberty or give me death!

Reading Check

1. What happened in the Boston Massacre?
2. Why did the Sons of Liberty dump tea in Boston harbor?
3. How did Parliament punish the colonies after the Boston Tea Party?
4. What important rights were stated in a petition to Parliament?

4. LEXINGTON AND CONCORD

To Guide Your Reading

Look for these important words:

Key Words
• Minutemen

Places
• Concord
• Lexington

Look for answers to these questions:

1. Why did the British plan to march to Lexington and Concord?
2. Who warned the countryside that the British were coming?
3. Why were the battles of Lexington and Concord important?

Americans now felt they would have to fight to protect their rights and their liberties. In Massachusetts men took time from their work to practice marching and firing guns. Because these volunteer soldiers were to be ready at a moment's notice, they were called **Minutemen.** The Minutemen began collecting military supplies and storing them at **Concord,** a village about 15 miles (24.1 km) west of Boston.

In Boston the British governor became alarmed at the activities of the Minutemen. He decided to make a quick strike to seize the military supplies at Concord. He also hoped to arrest the American leaders, Sam Adams and John Hancock, leaders of the Minutemen. They were staying in **Lexington,** a town near Concord.

From Boston, the British could get to Concord in two ways. One was to go the long way around by land. The other was to go across the Charles River before starting their march.

Paul Revere had made arrangements to signal the movements of British troops. If the British were to go by water, two lanterns would shine in Boston's Old North Church. If they were to go by land, one lantern would shine. These arrangements were made in case other plans for warning the countryside failed.

On April 17, 1775, William Dawes was sent by the land route to warn that the British would soon be coming. No one knew yet by what route. On the night of April 18, the Minutemen of Boston realized that the British were leaving by boat. With this knowledge, Paul Revere was to go by the water route and alert the countryside.

Making certain two lanterns were shining in the tower of the Old North Church, Revere set off across the Charles River in a small boat. On the other side, friends met him with a good horse. At a gallop, Revere set off to warn that the British were coming. He raced

229

down the dark roads pounding on doors, shouting his warning. As Paul Revere later said, "I alarmed almost every house till I got to Lexington."

In Lexington, Revere warned Hancock and Adams. Joined there by William Dawes, Revere then set off to alert Concord. On the road, a young doctor joined them. The midnight ride of Dawes and Revere came to an end when they were stopped by a British patrol. The doctor, however, escaped by jumping his horse over a low stone wall and reached Concord.

Meanwhile, the Minutemen gathered on Lexington Green. At dawn the first British troops arrived. There were far more soldiers than the Minutemen were prepared to fight. Seeing this, the captain of the Minutemen ordered his men to return to their homes. At about the same time, the British captain, on

his horse, yelled, "Ye villains, ye Rebels, disperse!" As the Minutemen were breaking up, a shot was fired. No one knows who fired first, but each side was soon firing at the other. Within minutes eight Minutemen lay dead or dying.

The smell of gunpowder was still in the air in Lexington Green when the British army marched on to Concord. There they found some wooden carts used to hold cannons. As they burned them, the smoke rose above the town.

Meanwhile, the news of the shots at Lexington had spread. Minutemen from nearby villages began to gather near Concord's North Bridge. The bridge was half a mile (0.8 km) from Concord. When the Minutemen saw the smoke from the gun carts, they thought the British were burning the town. They decided to march to save the town or

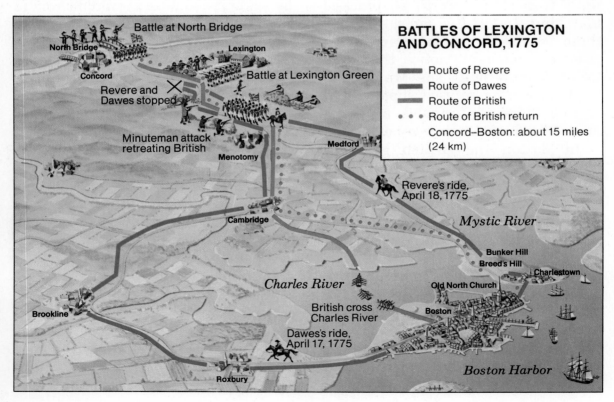

Battle at North Bridge

North Bridge

Lexington

Concord

Battle at Lexington Green

Revere and Dawes stopped

Minuteman attack retreating British

Menotomy

Medford

BATTLES OF LEXINGTON AND CONCORD, 1775

▬▬▬ Route of Revere
▬▬▬ Route of Dawes
▬▬▬ Route of British
• • • Route of British return
Concord–Boston: about 15 miles (24 km)

Revere's ride, April 18, 1775

Mystic River

Cambridge

Bunker Hill

Breed's Hill

Charlestown

Charles River

Old North Church

British cross Charles River

Boston

Brookline

Dawes's ride, April 17, 1775

Boston Harbor

Roxbury

The British Redcoats retreat from Lexington while Minutemen fire on them from behind walls and hedges.

die in the attempt. The Redcoats and Minutemen faced each other and fired in a brief battle at the North Bridge.

After several Redcoats were killed, the British troops fled back into Concord. The Minutemen began to take up positions behind stone walls around Concord. Fearing the numbers of Minutemen they could see gathering, the British started to march back to Boston. Their red coats stood out against the new spring grass, budding trees, and stone fences of the countryside.

Behind the trees and stone fences was hidden an army of Minutemen. These farmers, shopkeepers, craftsmen, and schoolteachers peppered the Redcoats with musket fire. The hail of musket fire created panic in the British troops. "It seemed as if men came down from the clouds," one Redcoat later said. The Redcoats had been trained to fight on a battlefield against an enemy they could see. How could they fight an enemy that hid behind trees and buildings?

It took the British half a day to reach the outskirts of Boston. On the river were British warships with guns ready. At last they were safe.

At least 72 British soldiers were killed that day. Some 49 Americans died. Neither the British governor nor the Americans had looked for battle, but that day it had happened.

The battles of Lexington and Concord on April 19 produced the shots "heard round the world." They announced that Americans meant to fight the British for their rights. They were the shots that started a war.

Reading Check

1. Why did the British decide to march to Lexington and Concord?
2. What did two lanterns in the Old North Church signal?
3. Which men set out to warn the countryside?
4. Why were the Minutemen able to defeat the British?

231

PAUL REVERE

Paul Revere

Silver pitcher

Silver tray

Child's whistle

Listen, my children and you shall hear
Of the midnight ride of Paul Revere.
Henry Wadsworth Longfellow

These are the first lines of a famous poem about Paul Revere's ride to Lexington. Henry Wadsworth Longfellow wrote the poem in 1863, many years after the ride.

Paul Revere was famous in his own day, but not for his daring ride. He was most famous as a silversmith.

Revere had learned to make silver pitchers and bowls from his father. His father had come to Boston from France to find religious freedom. When young Paul was old enough, he became an apprentice to his father.

Paul Revere learned quickly. He soon became one of New England's finest silversmiths. For his wealthy customers, Revere fashioned large silver punch bowls and fancy serving dishes. Paul Revere also made things for everyday use. He made spoons, dog collars, baby rattles, and even false teeth.

In 1765, when the Stamp Act was passed, Paul Revere joined the Sons of Liberty. Some of them served their country by writing or speaking. Revere served as a messenger.

Few people had horses in Boston. Paul Revere kept a horse because he loved to spend free hours galloping through the countryside. Because he had a horse, Revere often carried messages from Boston's Committee of Correspondence to other towns. His most amazing ride took place in December of 1773. He rode to Philadelphia to bring news of the Boston Tea Party. He made the 700-mile (about 1,125-km) round trip in just 11 days.

After making his ride to Lexington on April 18, 1775, Revere could not return to Boston. The British would have jailed him. Instead, he continued to act as a messenger for the Sons of Liberty. Later he served in the Continental Army.

Paul Revere was well known as a silversmith. Today, partly because of Longfellow's poem, he is famous as a rider for liberty.

SKILLS FOR SUCCESS

CAUSE AND EFFECT

Imagine you are waiting for a bus. You discover you have forgotten your homework. You run back home to get it, and you miss your bus.

Something that makes something else happen is a **cause.** What happens is called the **effect.** Forgetting your homework is the cause of your missing the bus. Missing the bus is the effect of forgetting your homework.

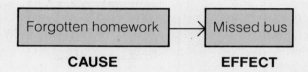

CAUSE   EFFECT

Suppose you kick a ball too high. It flies over a fence and breaks a window. What is the effect? What is the cause?

(*Reading hint:* The word *cause* has two meanings. Its main meaning is "something that makes something else happen." Its second meaning is "goal" or "struggle," as in "fighting for the cause of freedom." Only the main meaning is used in this section.)

Life is full of causes and effects. Because history is about life in the past, history too is full of causes and effects. So are history books!

Sometimes causes or effects are labeled. You might see sentences like this in a history book:

The *cause* of the war was an attack on the fort.
The *effect* of the attack was war.
The attack *caused* a war.

All three sentences mean the same thing. There was an attack. It was the cause of something else. There was a war. The war was an effect of something, the attack.

Often, word clues can help you find causes or effects. Such word clues include *because, as a result of,* and *therefore.* Here are some examples:

a. The French and Indian War started *because* the French and the English both wanted to control the Ohio River valley.

b. *As a result of* General Braddock's defeat, Indians began attacking the frontier settlements.

c. As the British and Minutemen faced each other at Lexington, someone fired a shot. *Therefore,* both sides started shooting.

In sentence a the word *because* signals the cause: The French and the English both wanted the Ohio River valley. The effect is that the French and Indian War started. What is the cause in sentence b? What is the cause in sentence c? What is the effect?

Sometimes, however, there are no word clues. Writers cannot always use word clues, and the reader does not always need them. Let's look at some sentences you have already read.

Imagine you are waiting for a bus. You discover you have forgotten your homework. You run back home to get it, and you miss the bus.

In these sentences, word clues are not needed. You, the reader, put them in. You know that forgetting your homework comes before missing your bus. You figure that what comes first probably *caused* or had an *effect* on what came later.

Events often have more than one cause. Suppose that you are hurrying to school. It is raining, and the sidewalks are slippery. You are wearing shoes with slick soles. There are wet leaves on the sidewalk. Your feet slip on the leaves and you fall.

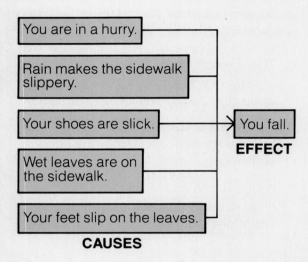

CAUSES

EFFECT

The chart below shows the cause of the Stamp Act. What is it? It shows two effects of the Stamp Act. What are they? Notice the way in which an effect can become a cause of the next event.

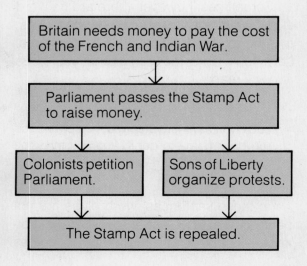

CHECKING YOUR SKILLS

Look at this chart and answer the questions that follow.

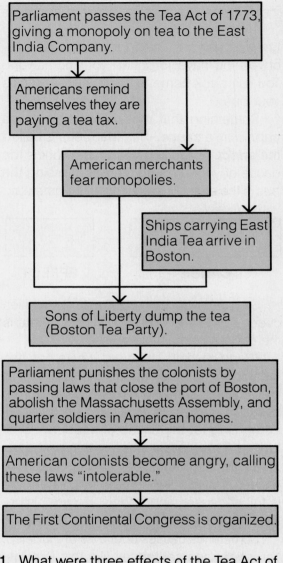

1. What were three effects of the Tea Act of 1773?

2. What was the effect of the Boston Tea Party?

3. What was the cause of Massachusetts losing its assembly?

4. Why did the American colonists become angry? What was an effect of this anger?

CHAPTER 10 REVIEW

WORDS TO USE

Write the numbers from 1 to 10 on your paper. Explain the meaning of each of the words below.

1. **allies**
2. **boycott**
3. **liberty**
4. **massacre**
5. **monopoly**
6. **petition**
7. **quartered**
8. **repeal**
9. **resist**
10. **tyranny**

FACTS TO REVIEW

1. What started the French and Indian War? Who fought whom?

2. How did the colonies and Britain disagree over settlement west of the Appalachians?

3. What was the Stamp Act? Why did Parliament pass it?

4. Give two reasons the colonists were so angry about the Stamp Act.

5. List several ways Americans protested the Stamp Act.

6. How did women help make the boycotts a success?

7. What was the purpose of the Committees of Correspondence?

8. Why did American merchants fear monopolies?

9. What were the Intolerable Acts? Why did they so anger the colonists?

10. What was the effect of the battles of Lexington and Concord?

IDEAS TO DISCUSS

1. Why did it take courage for John Adams to defend the British captain? Can you think of other examples of courage in this chapter? Do you think some things take more courage than others? Why?

2. Do you think it was fair for Parliament to ask the colonies to help pay for the French and Indian War? Explain your answer.

3. Why did Patrick Henry say, "Give me liberty or give me death"? What did liberty mean to the colonists? What does it mean to you?

○ SKILLS PRACTICE

Cause and Effect   Study the chart below. Answer the questions that follow.

Minutemen begin collecting military supplies at Concord.
↓
British set off to seize Minutemen and supplies.
↓
Paul Revere and William Dawes warn the countryside.
↓
Minutemen gather.

1. Why did the British set off for Concord?

2. Why did Paul Revere and William Dawes warn the countryside?

3. What was the effect of this warning?

CHAPTER 11

The Revolutionary War

About
this
chapter

Americans declared their independence of Britain on July 4, 1776. Yet words alone did not make the United States a free country. Americans had to fight for their freedom and independence. They had to make war against the army and navy of Britain, one of the most powerful countries in the world. The Revolutionary War, or War for Independence, was a long, hard war. In the end, Americans won.

In this chapter you will learn how American people defeated the British and won independence for themselves and for us.

1. ON THE ROAD TO INDEPENDENCE

To Guide Your Reading

Look for these important words:

Key Words
- Second Continental Congress
- Patriots
- Loyalists
- declaration
- Continental Army
- earthworks

- Battle of Bunker Hill
- independence
- Olive Branch Petition
- mercenaries
- Declaration of Independence
- Independence Day

People
- George Washington
- Thomas Paine
- Thomas Jefferson

Places
- Mount Vernon

Look for answers to these questions:

1. How did the colonists prepare to fight the British?
2. Why did most Americans want to avoid war with Britain?
3. Why did Americans finally declare independence from Britain?

After the Battles of Lexington and Concord, the Continental Congress met again in Philadelphia. This was the **Second Continental Congress.** Some of the wisest men in America attended. From Massachusetts came Sam Adams, John Adams, and John Hancock. From Pennsylvania came Benjamin Franklin, and from Virginia, Patrick Henry and **George Washington.**

These men were called **Patriots.** Patriots believed that the American colonists were right to stand up for their liberties. About one-third of the American colonists were Patriots. About one-third of the colonists sided with Britain. They were called **Loyalists,** or Tories. Another third of the colonists did not choose either side.

Few members of the Second Continental Congress wanted a complete break with Britain. In a **declaration,** or statement, the Second Continental Congress said, "We fight not for glory or for conquest." Colonists had started fighting, they said, because they felt they had no choice.

Even though it hoped for peace, the Continental Congress created an army and navy to fight the British. It appointed George Washington to be commander in chief of the new **Continental Army.** John Adams had suggested Washington for the job. Washinton's skill, great talents, and excellent character would command the respect of all Americans, Adams said. He proved to be right.

Washington would rather have returned to his Virginia plantation, **Mount Vernon.** Instead, he accepted the position of commander in chief. He felt it was his duty to do so. He wrote Martha Washington, his wife, that he hoped his going would "answer some good purpose."

Battle of Bunker Hill

After the battles at Lexington and Concord, the angry citizens of Massachusetts started to build **earthworks,** or walls of dirt and stone, near Boston. Earthworks would protect Patriot soldiers if there were another battle. The Patriots had taken over control of the countryside. A British soldier was not safe if he tried to leave Boston. The British troops were hemmed in, able to enter and leave Boston only by sea.

The Patriots began to build new earthworks on a small hill near Charlestown on June 16, 1775. At this, the British commander decided the time had come for action. He called out his troops. On June 17, lines of Redcoats started marching up the hill to the roll of drums. Behind the earthworks the Patriots waited, muskets ready. "Don't fire until you see the whites of their eyes," they were told. When the British drew close to the earthworks, the Patriots let loose a deadly hail of shot.

The British were forced back several times. Finally, the Patriots ran out of ammunition and retreated. The British took the hill, but at great cost. On that day about half of the British army were killed or wounded. The Patriot losses were much fewer. The Americans were proud of how well they had done. They felt the victory was really theirs. From this battle, the **Battle of Bunker Hill,** the British learned that it would be no easy job fighting the Americans.

Hopes for Peace

Most Americans still did not want war. They considered themselves loyal

At the Battle of Bunker Hill, Patriot soldiers prepare to defend themselves against lines of British Redcoats.

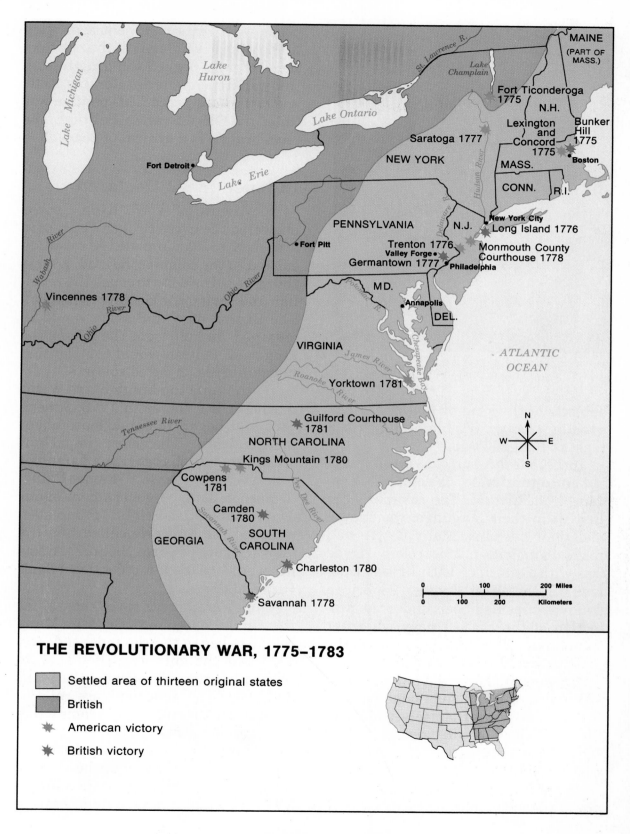

THE REVOLUTIONARY WAR, 1775–1783

Lake Huron

Lake Michigan

Lake Ontario

Lake Erie

St. Lawrence R.

Lake Champlain

MAINE
(PART OF MASS.)

Fort Ticonderoga 1775

N.H.

Saratoga 1777

Lexington and Concord 1775

Bunker Hill 1775

NEW YORK

MASS.

Boston

CONN.

R.I.

Fort Detroit

Wabash River

PENNSYLVANIA

Fort Pitt

Delaware R.

Hudson River

N.J.

New York City

Long Island 1776

Trenton 1776

Valley Forge

Germantown 1777

Philadelphia

Monmouth County Courthouse 1778

Vincennes 1778

Ohio River

MD.

Potomac R.

Annapolis

DEL.

Chesapeake Bay

VIRGINIA

James River

ATLANTIC OCEAN

Roanoke River

Yorktown 1781

Tennessee River

Guilford Courthouse 1781

N

W   E

S

NORTH CAROLINA

Kings Mountain 1780

Cowpens 1781

Pee Dee River

Camden 1780

Savannah River

SOUTH CAROLINA

GEORGIA

Charleston 1780

Savannah 1778

0   100   200 Miles

0   100   200 Kilometers

Settled area of thirteen original states

British

American victory

British victory

239

In his right hand King George III holds the scepter, symbol of his right to rule.

subjects of the king of England. Each evening George Washington drank a toast to King George.

In 1775 few Americans could imagine **independence,** or complete freedom, from Britain. The colonies were British in their language, their laws, and their customs. Many people had relatives in Britain. Most colonial trade was with Britain or with British colonies in the West Indies. American trading ships had been under the protection of the British navy wherever they sailed. The British navy was the most powerful in the world.

If the colonies did fight a war against Britain, how could they hope to win? If the colonies cut themselves off from the king, how would they be ruled? They could not imagine a government without a king.

In July 1775, the Continental Congress made another effort to achieve peace with Britain. It sent a petition to the king of England. In the petition, the Congress begged the king to stop the war, repeal the Intolerable Acts, and bring back peace. This petition was called the **Olive Branch Petition.** The olive branch is a symbol of peace.

Independence Declared

In August of 1775, King George answered the Olive Branch Petition in a speech to Parliament. A rebellion existed in the colonies, he said. Everything would be done to crush the rebellion and "bring the traitors to justice." The British navy and army would be enlarged. To help fight the rebels, the king said, Britain would use German **mercenaries,** or hired soldiers.

By the time the king's harsh words reached the colonies in 1776, Americans had begun to think more about independence. The most important reason for this change was a pamphlet called *Common Sense.* **Thomas Paine,** its author, said, "A government of our own is our natural right." Paine even attacked the king. He called him the "Royal Brute of Great Britain." America would be better off independent, Paine said.

Paine's arguments paved the way for the final break from Britain. Many colonists began to urge independence. That was the only way, they said, to ensure liberty. "By every post [mail] and every day, independence rolls in on us like a torrent," John Adams wrote from the Congress.

In June of 1776, the Congress asked a committee to write a declaration of independence. **Thomas Jefferson,** a Virginia planter and scholar, was a

Thomas Jefferson presents the Declaration of Independence to Congress. On his left is Benjamin Franklin. On his far right is John Adams.

member of this committee. Using a goose quill pen, Jefferson wrote every evening for 17 days. The committee suggested some changes. At last the document was ready.

On July 4, 1776, the members of the Continental Congress voted for the **Declaration of Independence.** Writing to his wife, Abigail, John Adams said that **Independence Day** should be remembered with shows, games, sports, guns, bells, bonfires, and fireworks "from this time forward forever more."

The Declaration of Independence announced to the world why the American colonies had to cut their ties with Britain. Now the colonies were the United States of America. After the declaration was read out loud in Philadelphia, the Liberty Bell rang out.

Yet saying the 13 colonies were the United States of America did not make it so. The United States had to prove their strength and push the British troops off their soil.

Reading Check

1. Why did the Second Continental Congress appoint George Washington commander in chief?
2. Why could few Americans imagine independence in 1775?
3. What was the main idea of *Common Sense?*
4. Who was the main writer of the Declaration of Independence?

SKILLS FOR SUCCESS

READING A DOCUMENT: THE DECLARATION OF INDEPENDENCE

Wars are fought with words as well as with guns. Thomas Jefferson, the main writer of the Declaration of Independence, firmly believed it was right to be fighting against British rule. He wrote the Declaration of Independence to win support for the American Revolution. Jefferson wanted his words to help the new nation win its battle for freedom.

In order to do this, Jefferson had to plan and write carefully. He had to state facts to convince people independence was necessary. He also had to speak to people's hearts. He had to make people *feel* that the Americans were right and the British were wrong.

Jefferson organized the Declaration of Independence into several main parts. In the first part, or introduction, he said why the Declaration was necessary. In the sec-ond part, Jefferson explained the colonists' basic beliefs about rights and government. In the third part, he listed the wrongs done by the king. In the fourth part, or conclusion, Jefferson said that the colonies were now free and independent.

Introduction: When In the Course of Human Events

Jefferson began the Declaration with words that mean this:

Sometimes a group of people must cut themselves off from the country they once belonged to. They find they have no choice but to form a new nation with the same powers of other independent countries. When people do this, they should explain their reasons. In that way, they show respect for the opinions of others.

The modern paragraph above gives the basic meaning of Jefferson's words. The words Jefferson actually used were these:

When, in the course of human events, it becomes necessary for one people to dissolve the political bands which have connected them with another, and to assume, among the powers of the earth, the separate and equal station to which the laws of nature and of nature's God entitle them, a decent respect to the opinions of mankind requires that they should declare the causes which impel them to the separation.

Notice that Jefferson's words form one long sentence. It is a serious, dignified sentence. It moves slowly and surely, like a great

You can view the original Declaration of Independence in the Library of Congress.

river, toward the last word and key idea: *separation.*

This very special sentence may be hard for you to understand. However the declaration was easily understood by the people of 1776. In fact, it was written much more simply and honestly than many other important writings of that time. The people who read the Declaration of Independence found it effective and stirring.

Beliefs: All Men Are Created Equal

In the second part of the Declaration, Jefferson stated the Patriots' main ideas about government. He began with a sentence that means this:

> We believe in certain ideas. Anyone can see how true these ideas are. God has given all people some rights that are a natural part of them. These rights include the right to live, the right to be free, and the right to try to be happy. People cannot give up or take away these rights. In these ways, all people are born equal.

Below are the words Jefferson actually used. They say what Patriots believed in 1776, and what Americans believe today:

> *We hold these truths to be self-evident: that all men are created equal; that they are endowed by their Creator with certain inalienable rights; that among these are life, liberty, and the pursuit of happiness.*

These words are as clear and powerful today as when they were first written. They are among the most famous in history. Since they were written, they have stirred people in many nations to fight against cruel and unfair governments.

Jefferson believed that a government must protect the basic rights of its people.

For him, this was the purpose of government. If a nation's government does not protect these rights, he said, people have the right to change or get rid of the government. Jefferson warned, though, that action against a government is a very serious thing. It should not be done except when a government has treated its people very badly for a long time.

Wrongs: The King Has Wronged Us

In the third and longest part of the Declaration, Jefferson tells how badly the king of England had governed America. Jefferson listed more than 25 ways in which the king had wronged the American colonists. Here are three examples in modern language:

- The king has not let the colonies pass laws of their choice.
- The king has not given any power to representatives from the colonies.
- The king has sent soldiers to live among the colonists. He has not punished these soldiers when they have broken laws.

In this part Jefferson used strong language to make people very angry at the king of England. In his words:

> *He has plundered our seas, ravaged our coasts, burnt our towns, and destroyed the lives of our people.*

Plunder means to take by force. *Ravage* means to destroy. If you had been a colonist, how would you feel about a king who did such things?

Jefferson did not stop there. He pointed out that the king was now doing something even worse. The king was sending German mercenaries, to do even more damage.

243

He is, at this time, transporting large armies of foreign mercenaries to complete the works of death, desolation, and tyranny already begun.

Perhaps, after reading a long list of wrongs, someone might still ask, "But did you try to settle these problems peacefully?" So Jefferson explained that the colonists had often asked the king to correct these wrongs. They had sent many petitions to the king, but he had ignored them. Such a king, Jefferson said, was "unfit to be the ruler of a free people."

Conclusion: We Are Free and Independent

In the last part of the Declaration, Jefferson announced independence in words that mean this:

> We, the representatives of the United States of America, say this: the colonies are now free and independent. They no longer have any connection with the British king or government. As an independent country, we now have the right to make peace or war, and to trade with other nations. We now have all the other rights that other nations have.

Jefferson knew that *saying* such things would not be enough. American patriots now had to fight and win a war with Britain. Only then would the United States be a free and independent country.

Jefferson added one last sentence to the Declaration. He wanted to make clear that he and the other Patriots meant every word.

> *And, for the support of this declaration, with a firm reliance on the protection of Divine Providence [God], we mutually pledge to each other our lives, our fortunes, and our sacred honor.*

Jefferson and other Patriots then signed their names to the Declaration. They were telling the world that they were willing to die for the cause of independence. They wanted to set an example for all Americans who would join them. They made a promise to give their property, even their lives, to the struggle. They promised to do this upon their sacred honor, the most serious and deep promise they could make.

By writing the Declaration of Independence in clear and powerful words, Jefferson helped the Patriot cause. His words also laid the foundation for a new kind of government, one dedicated to protecting the rights of its people.

CHECKING YOUR SKILLS

Copy the sentences below. Use the information in this skill lesson to find the words that best complete each sentence. When the sentences are complete, you will have a list of the main ideas of the Declaration of Independence.

1. The colonists say they are breaking off from _____. They promise to explain their reasons for doing this.

2. The colonists explain their belief that all people have some basic rights. These rights are _____ , _____ , and _____ .

3. They list the _____ the king had done to them. They explain how they tried to settle these problems _____ .

4. They declare their _____ , and they declare that they want the rights of nations.

5. The signers pledge their _____ , their _____ , and their _____ to the cause of freedom.

2. AMERICANS FIGHT FOR LIBERTY

To Guide Your Reading

Look for these important words:

People
- Marquis de Lafayette
- Friedrich von Steuben

Places
- Trenton
- Saratoga
- Valley Forge

Look for answers to these questions:
1. What difficulties did the Continental Army face?
2. How was George Washington able to hold an army together?
3. How did women help in the Revolutionary War?
4. How did Europeans help the Patriots?

In the summer of 1775, George Washington arrived in Massachusetts to take command of the 15,000 soldiers gathered there. Washington's problems were great and would remain so throughout the war.

Washington's major problem was feeding and supplying the Continental Army. Most soldiers in the war never did have uniforms. They fought in the clothes they had. Thousands marched and fought without shoes. Thousands never had blankets or tents. The historian Samuel Eliot Morison has written:

> Altogether, the private soldier of the War of Independence was so badly fed, clothed, and cared for...that one is surprised and grateful that any continued to fight.

Another problem Washington faced was the lack of discipline. The soldiers knew little of drills or marching in lines. The men who came to fight were not used to taking orders. They were independent people—backwoodsmen, fishermen, farmers, and craftsmen. Washington's job was to turn these soldiers into a well-trained army able to take on the British forces.

Another problem was keeping men in the army. Washington's army at times had more than 15,000 men. At other times it shrank to as few as 2,000. Most men served in the army less than a year. Many would go home when it was time to plant or harvest crops. Others joined the army only when the fighting was nearby. They were like the farmer Reuben Stebbins. He had paid little attention to the war until he heard the sounds of a battle near his farm in New York state. Then he saddled his horse and rode off to fight the British. "We'll see who's going to own this farm," he shouted.

Washington was able to hold his army together only because people respected him so much. Soldiers were

These ragged Continental soldiers proudly march forward in this painting by Howard Pyle. In the front line is the drummer, one of the most important persons in the army. Drum beats directed soldiers to advance, to retreat, or to halt.

willing to follow Washington when they were hungry, cold, or even barefoot. Washington's simple presence brought respect, as a boy soldier later remembered.

Israel Trask, at the age of 10, was a cook and messenger boy in Washington's army. He was with the army in Massachusetts when a group of soldiers from Virginia arrived. The Virginia soldiers wore white, fringed shirts that came to their knees.

The New Englanders, who dressed differently, began to make fun of the Virginians. At first the Virginians were patient and took the teasing, but then they scooped up the snow at their feet and started throwing snowballs. Soon the snowball fight turned into a free-for-all with 1,000 soldiers kicking, biting, and hitting each other.

Young Israel watched. Then, Israel Trask remembered, George Washing-

ton appeared. "With the spring of a deer, he leaped from his saddle, threw the reins of his bridle into the hands of his servant, and rushed into the thickest of the fight."

Washington was a strong man, 6 feet 3 inches (190.5 cm) tall. With an iron grip he "seized two tall, brawny, athletic, savage-looking riflemen by the throat, keeping them at arm's length, alternately shaking and talking to them." As soon as the other soldiers saw the general, they ran away as fast as they could. Only Washington and the two soldiers in his grip remained on the field.

Women in the Revolution

The story of the War of Independence may seem to be the story of men. Men made the important battle decisions. Men did most of the fighting. Men did most of the dying. Yet women were as important in winning the war. When the men went off to fight, the women took over the businesses, shops, and farms.

Many women formed groups to raise money for the war. Others worked hard to sew shirts and knit socks for the soldiers.

Women were spies and messengers. Some, left alone in their homes, resisted the British either by wit or by guns. When women at Groton, Connecticut, heard that the British were approaching, they dressed in men's clothes. Armed with pitchforks, sling shots, and guns, they successfully turned back the Redcoats.

Lead for bullets was in short supply during the war. Because lead was an important part of pewter, women gave up their pewter pots and plates, their pewter spoons and forks. Many family treasures were melted down for bullets.

Hundreds of women shared the uncomfortable army life. These women, often with children, followed their husbands. In army camps they cooked food and washed clothes. Some, like Martha Washington, nursed the sick and wounded. On the battlefield women brought water and sometimes loaded cannons. A few dressed and fought as men.

The British knew how important the women were. One officer wrote that even if the British destroyed all the men in America, "we should have enough to do to conquer the women."

Victory at Trenton

By the fall of 1776, Washington and his ragged army moved south from

Molly Pitcher grabs a rammer to load cannon even though an officer tries to order her off the field. "Molly Pitcher" was the nickname of Mary Ludwig Hayes. She earned the nickname by bringing water to troops suffering through a long, hot battle at Monmouth, New Jersey.

This famous painting shows George Washington crossing the icy Delaware River on Christmas Day before the attack on Trenton.

Massachusetts. They went first to New York and then to New Jersey. The British had defeated the army several times and were chasing what remained of it. The Americans were in despair.

Then came new hope. On Christmas Day, 1776, Washington and his army of 2,400 men crossed the Delaware River in boats. By night in freezing weather, the shivering soldiers silently marched toward **Trenton,** New Jersey. There the German mercenaries were celebrating Christmas.

At daybreak the Americans made a surprise attack. Over 900 Germans surrendered. Only four Americans were wounded. Two others froze to death. The Continental Army found many weapons and supplies at Trenton. Patriots everywhere were overjoyed at the news. Perhaps there was hope after all!

Help from Europe

The year 1777 brought help to the Patriots. From Europe came men eager to fight for the idea of liberty. The most important of these was the **Marquis de Lafayette** (mahr•KEE duh lahf•ee•ET), then only 20 years old. A rich Frenchman, he hired French soldiers to come with him to America. Washington liked the young Lafayette and immediately gave him important duties.

Another who came was Johann de Kalb, a German-born professional soldier. From Poland came Casimir Pulaski (KAZ•ih•mihr puh•LAS•kee) and Thaddeus Kosciuszko (THAD•ee•uhs kahs•ih•UHS•koh). Later Kosciuszko returned to Poland to lead a revolution for Polish liberty.

The best news of October 1777 was an American victory at **Saratoga,** New

It is a snowy, cold day at Valley Forge in 1777 as George Washington reviews his hungry and weary troops. Even his horse looks weary.

York. There the Americans soundly defeated a large British army. This victory brought America an ally—France.

Benjamin Franklin had gone to France to try to win help for the Americans. At news of the American victory at Saratoga, the French decided to help the struggling nation. In this way the French hoped to get back at Britain, their old enemy.

Later in 1777, Washington's army faced another hard winter. After losing Philadelphia to the British, Washington established his winter camp at **Valley Forge,** about 20 miles (32 km) away. While the British were warm and comfortable in Philadelphia, the Americans were hungry, cold, and sick at Valley Forge. Things looked bad indeed for the Continental Army.

In these hard times a German soldier showed up to help. **Friedrich von Steuben** (FREE•drihk vahn STYOO•buhn) took on the job of organizing and drilling the army so that it could move quickly on command. He taught the soldiers how to use bayonets. Bayonets were standard equipment for European soldiers but were unknown in America. By spring the troops were marching smartly.

Reading Check

1. What problems did George Washington face as commander in chief?
2. How did women contribute to the Revolution?
3. Name at least three Europeans who helped the Patriots.
4. Why did France decide to help the American Patriots?

3. THE PUSH TO VICTORY

To Guide Your Reading

Look for these important words:

Key Words
• treaty

People
• Nathanael Greene
• John Paul Jones
• George Rogers Clark
• Francis Marion
• Charles Cornwallis

Places
• Yorktown

Look for answers to these questions:

1. What leaders helped win the war? What did each accomplish?
2. What happened at the Battle of Yorktown?
3. Why was the United States able to defeat Britain?

Starting in 1778, most of the fighting shifted to the South, particularly South Carolina. The Americans suffered some terrible defeats, but under the leadership of General **Nathanael** (nuh•THAN•yuhl) **Greene,** they began to hold their own. Victories at Kings Mountain, Cowpens, and Guilford Courthouse gave new heart to the Southern forces.

The British were able to take many important cities in America. But they could not win the war, for no one city was the heart of America. America's heart was in the farms and villages of its 13 states. As the British tried to stamp out the fire of independence in one place, they found that it only sprang up in another place. "We fight, get beat, rise, and fight again," Nathanael Greene wrote.

During the war Americans were cheered by news of many brave people. **John Paul Jones,** a navy commander, battled British ships in their own waters. In one famous battle the British demanded his surrender. He replied, "I have not yet begun to fight."

In the Ohio River valley, **George Rogers Clark** helped safeguard the frontier by attacking the British and their Indian allies. Clark became known as the "Washington of the West."

From bases in the swamps of South Carolina, **Francis Marion** led daring raids against the British. They called Marion the "Swamp Fox" because they could never catch him and his men.

Thousands of blacks, both slave and free, fought on both sides of the Revolution. The British offered freedom and land in Canada to slaves who would join the Loyalists. The blacks who fought for the Patriots did so with courage and skill. Black soldiers from Rhode Island were "the best under arms," a French officer wrote.

In the Revolution's most famous naval battle, John Paul Jones's ship
Bonhomme Richard, left, fought all night against the British *Serapis.*

Francis Marion and his followers cross the Pee Dee River in the swamps of
South Carolina. The British never could catch him.

French troops march toward the battle line in the siege of Yorktown, 1791.
In the distance is Yorktown itself. Behind earthworks, French and American
gunners fire their cannons into the British positions.

Victory at Yorktown

In October 1781, the last major battle of the war was fought at **Yorktown, Virginia.** Yorktown was a small town on Chesapeake Bay, not far from Williamsburg. The British general **Charles Cornwallis** had set up headquarters at Yorktown because it was easy for British ships to bring supplies.

The French and Americans made a plan to defeat Cornwallis. First, the French troops in Rhode Island marched south to join Washington's army. Along the way, Americans turned out to stare at the trim and colorful uniforms of the French. The French soldiers looked so fancy compared to the poorly clothed Continental soldiers. Everywhere the French went they carried war chests full of silver and gold coins. With the coins they could buy all the supplies and food they needed.

The French army joined George Washington's army near New York City. Together, the two armies continued marching toward Virginia. Meanwhile, the French navy gained control of Chesapeake Bay, as planned. Hearing the news, Washington whooped with joy and swung his hat in the air. Now, even the British navy could not help Cornwallis, trapped at Yorktown.

The French and American armies began to surround and bombard the British at Yorktown. To do this, they started on September 28 to dig trenches, or large ditches. The trenches protected the soldiers from most bullets and cannonballs. For two weeks they dug trenches closer and closer to the British. Day and night the two sides fired cannonballs at each other. At night the cannonballs looked like shooting stars.

252

During the battle Sarah Osborn was taking food to her husband and others in the trenches. Each day she brought beef, bread, and a gallon pot of coffee. On one of her trips she met George Washington. "Are you not afraid of the cannonballs?" he asked. "No," she said. "It would not do for the men to starve as well as fight."

Cornwallis, knowing he could not win, decided to surrender. A drummer boy in a red coat appeared on top of a British earthwork. He beat his drums until French and American gunners saw him. One by one they stopped their fire. A British officer then appeared with a white flag, a sign of surrender.

Two days later British and German soldiers marched out of Yorktown to lay down their arms in a field. Their bands played sad music. One of the songs was named "The World Turned Upside Down." Americans were joyful. When news of the victory reached Philadelphia, the Liberty Bell rang out loud and clear.

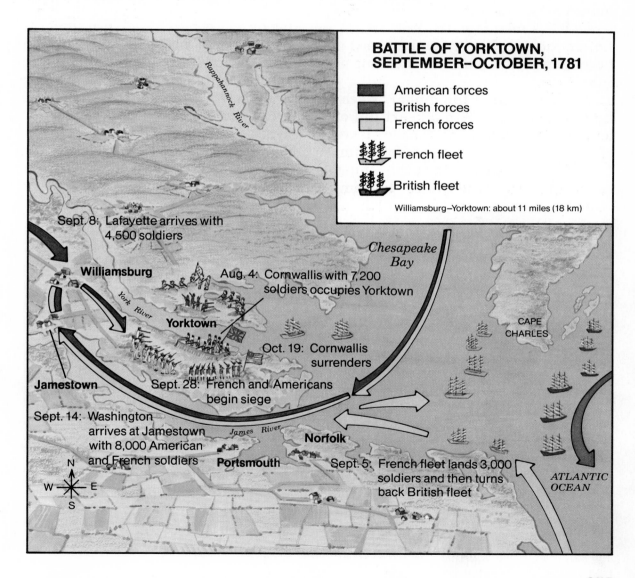

BATTLE OF YORKTOWN, SEPTEMBER–OCTOBER, 1781

- American forces
- British forces
- French forces
- French fleet
- British fleet

Williamsburg–Yorktown: about 11 miles (18 km)

Rappahannock River

Chesapeake Bay

Sept. 8: Lafayette arrives with 4,500 soldiers

Williamsburg

Aug. 4: Cornwallis with 7,200 soldiers occupies Yorktown

York River

Yorktown

CAPE CHARLES

Oct. 19: Cornwallis surrenders

Jamestown

Sept. 28: French and Americans begin siege

Sept. 14: Washington arrives at Jamestown with 8,000 American and French soldiers

James River

Norfolk

Portsmouth

Sept. 5: French fleet lands 3,000 soldiers and then turns back British fleet

ATLANTIC OCEAN

N
W   E
S

The War Is Over

The Battle of Yorktown was the last major battle of the war. Yet a peace **treaty,** or formal agreement, did not become final until 1783. By that time George Washington and his officers had made their headquarters in New York City.

In early December 1783, George Washington and his officers met at the Fraunces (FRAWN•sehs) Tavern for a farewell dinner. Famous for its food, the tavern was in a fine, old New York mansion. Samuel Fraunces, the owner, was a black man from the West Indies. Before the war, his tavern had been a favorite meeting place for the Sons of Liberty.

Near the end of the dinner, Washington stood up. "With a heart full of love and gratitude, I now take my leave of you," he said to the men before him.

One by one, each man at the dinner came up to say good-bye to the commander in chief. Tears streaming down his cheeks, Washington hugged each one. "Such a scene of sorrow and weeping I have never before seen," wrote one of the officers. They were sad because they thought they would never again see George Washington. He was the man who had led them through the long and bloody war. He was the man who had led his country to glory and independence.

After saying his farewells, Washington started home to Mount Vernon. On the way he stopped in Annapolis, Maryland, where the Continental Congress was meeting. He told the Congress that, with peace, his work was done. "I retire from the great theater of action," Washington said. He was leaving public life forever, he thought. Saying his good-byes, Washington mounted his favorite horse, Nelson. By riding hard, he reached Mount Vernon on Christmas Eve.

Great as their joy was in victory, American officers were sad to say good-bye to each other. In Fraunces Tavern in New York City, George Washington bids each of his officers a final, tearful farewell.

After eight years as general, George Washington could at last return to Mount Vernon. This picture of his home was painted about 1792.

Why the Americans Won

The Americans had beaten the powerful British army. How was this possible? All during the war the British army had problems. First of all, it was far from Britain and had to depend on supplies delivered by ship. The army could not set up and hold bases far from the sea. Generals of the British army often did not work together.

On the other hand, the Americans were fighting on their own soil. If they lost the war, many Patriots knew they would be hanged for treason. Americans were also fighting for liberty, an idea dear to their hearts. For these reasons they fought harder, and they would not give up. The Americans also had important help, particularly from the French. Finally, the Americans won because they had fine leaders. Soldiers respected these leaders and followed them even when times were hard. The finest of these leaders was George Washington.

Reading Check

1. Why could the British capture important cities but not win the war?
2. What plan did the French and Americans follow to trap Cornwallis at Yorktown?
3. When was a peace treaty finally signed between Britain and the United States?
4. What problems did the British face during the war? What advantages did the Americans have?

CLOSE-UP

Mercy Otis Warren often met with other Patriots to discuss the Revolution.

AMERICANS FOR FREEDOM

Without great leaders, the American Revolution would have failed. It would also have failed without the courage and skill of many other Americans. In the next pages, you will read about six of these people.

Mercy Otis Warren

In the 1760s few Americans thought seriously about independence from Britain. One who did was Mercy Otis Warren of Plymouth, Massachusetts.

Mercy Otis Warren was the sister of James Otis, a lawyer and Patriot. James and Mercy were educated together until it was time for James to go to college. In the 1700s women did not go to college. Mercy kept up her studies at home, however, and often wrote to James.

James Otis was one of the very first to write and speak against British rule. He was the first to use the phrase "no taxation without representation." Otis was a fiery speaker. His motto was "Where liberty is, there is my country!" Mercy Otis Warren shared her brother's views.

Mercy and her husband, James Warren, opened their house to many of the early Revolutionary leaders. These included Sam Adams, John Hancock, and John and Abigail Adams.

Mercy Warren was also a friend of Thomas Jefferson and Martha Washington. In her letters, Mercy Warren kept these Virginians informed of events in New England.

In 1769 James Otis was seriously injured. He could no longer write and speak for the Patriot cause. Mercy Warren continued her brother's work. She was a fine writer.

Peter Salem fights bravely at the Battle of Bunker Hill.

She could have written as her brother did, with reason and fiery words. Instead, she chose another way of attacking the British and the Loyalists. She chose to make fun of them in her poems and plays. She made the British look like "blockheads" who were too stupid, greedy, or silly to rule a free country.

In 1775 Mercy Warren was almost 50. The American Revolution had begun, and Mercy Warren had helped start it. She began to write a three-volume history of the Revolution. She finished it 30 years later, at the age of 77. It is still read by historians today.

Peter Salem

Of the Minutemen who faced the British soldiers at Concord Green on April 19, 1775, at least five were black. Several were slaves, but all were volunteers. One of them was Peter Salem.

Peter Salem heard Major John Pitcairn (PIHT•kairn), the British commander, shout, "Disperse, ye rebels!" When the death and confusion started, Peter Salem held his ground. He fired again and again.

A few weeks later, Peter Salem was in the Battle of Bunker Hill. He was one of about 20 blacks. The Americans waited as more than 2,000 British soldiers marched toward them. Closer and closer the British came. Three times the British marched up the hill, and three times they were stopped by American musket fire.

Running out of gunpowder, the Americans began to retreat. When a British officer saw the retreat, he ran forward, shouting to his men, "Follow me, the day is ours!"

Peter Salem raised his musket and shot him dead. The British officer was Major John Pitcairn.

After the Battle of Bunker Hill, George Washington asked to meet Peter Salem.

Two years later, Salem fought at the important Battle of Saratoga. In 1779, he took part in a surprise bayonet attack on a British camp at Stony Point, New York.

In 1816 Peter Salem died in his home town, Framingham, Massachusetts.

257

John Honeyman

George Washington thanks John Honeyman for his services.

John Honeyman was a weaver from Ireland who lived near Trenton, New Jersey. As a young man, Honeyman had been taken from his home and forced to serve in the British army. Honeyman hated the British and their king. With all his heart, John Honeyman was a Patriot.

George Washington asked Honeyman to pretend that he was a Loyalist. He asked Honeyman to make fun of the Patriots and to cheer when they lost a battle. He asked him to praise the king of England. George Washington needed a spy in the Trenton area.

Honeyman played his part. His Patriot neighbors came to hate him and even threatened him with death. Their friends scorned his wife and children. Almost no one knew that Honeyman was a secret Patriot. Several times American soldiers tried to kill him.

In the winter of 1776, Washington's army was on the run. It had lost battle after battle. The Patriots were discouraged. Washington needed a victory to keep the war going. John Honeyman made such a victory possible.

Honeyman told Washington that hired German soldiers were planning to celebrate Christmas in Trenton. He made detailed drawings of where all the soldiers and guns were. Honeyman was almost killed by Patriots while trying to get to Washington's camp with this information. Washington asked him to go back to Trenton. Once again, fearful for his life, Honeyman crept through the line of Patriot soldiers.

Finally Honeyman reached Trenton. There he was questioned by the German commander. Was it true that Washington's army was tired, starving, freezing? Yes, said Honeyman. Honeyman convinced the commander that Washington was a fool and was ready to give up. Hearing the news, the Germans went ahead with their Christmas party. They did not even bother to post guards.

George Washington captured Trenton on December 26, 1776. The German soldiers were still asleep after their party. The victory enabled the Americans to get food, clothing, and arms. With these supplies, the army could go on and fight again.

Lydia Darragh overhears the British plan an attack on Washington's army.

John Honeyman told no one that he had helped win the Battle of Trenton. For the rest of the war, his neighbors disliked him. After the war, the state of New Jersey brought him to trial as a traitor. Honeyman was a simple man. He could not bring himself to say that he had worked for the great George Washington. Perhaps he thought no one would believe him. Honeyman was almost hanged as a traitor. In the nick of time, an American officer got to the trial and saved Honeyman's life. Honeyman's neighbors were still suspicious. They still thought he had worked for the British. They refused to trust or like him.

Then one day in 1784, Honeyman's neighbors were astonished to see George Washington himself ride up to Honeyman's house. In a voice that all the neighbors could hear, Washington said to Honeyman: "Thank you, sir, for your service to me and to your country. I am grateful, and your country, sir, is grateful."

Lydia Darragh

Washington's army was camped near Philadelphia in early December 1777. But for one woman, Washington and his army might have been destroyed. Lydia Darragh (DAR•ah) showed great bravery by warning the army of its danger.

Lydia Darragh's family were Quakers. Quakers did not believe in war. They thought it wrong to kill another human being for any reason.

As a Quaker, Lydia Darragh's oldest son also hated violence. But he also believed in the Patriot cause. Finally, he decided he must fight. He joined Washington's army. Early in December 1777, he was with Washington at Whitemarsh about 8 miles (12.8 km) from Philadelphia.

The British had captured Philadelphia. The British asked to have a meeting in the Darragh house. They told Lydia Darragh to put her family to bed early. She did what she was told. Later that night, however, she listened at the keyhole as the officers talked. They were planning a surprise attack on Washington's army. Lydia Darragh heard the whole plan.

259

Charles Cornwallis is surprised to see James Armistead with the Marquis de Lafayette.

Early next morning, Lydia Darragh left her house carrying a flour sack. The British soldiers believed she was only on her way to get flour. She walked five miles (8 km) to the miller's and left her sack to be filled. Then she walked on toward the Continental Army. She finally met a Continental officer on the road and told him of the planned attack.

Lydia Darragh then returned to the miller's. She paid for her flour and quietly returned home. She did not tell her husband what she had done. That day Lydia Darragh had made a choice. In doing so she had bravely supported the Patriots and independence.

James Armistead

The Battle of Yorktown was over. Charles Cornwallis, the defeated British commander, paid a visit to the headquarters of the Marquis de Lafayette. Cornwallis was astonished to see the young French nobleman chatting and laughing with a black man, James Armistead. Armistead had been Cornwallis's servant. Cornwallis had used Armistead as a spy against the Americans. Why hadn't the Americans shot this spy?

Like John Honeyman, James Armistead was what we call a double agent. He had pretended to spy for the British. He had passed false information to them. In reality, Armistead had been working for Lafayette. While he served dinner to Cornwallis and other officers, he listened to their plans. Then he passed these plans on to Lafayette and George Washington. Information from Armistead helped make possible the plan that led to defeat of the British at Yorktown.

Like Washington himself, Armistead admired the dashing young Lafayette. After the war, Armistead changed his name to James Armistead Lafayette. In 1786 the General Assembly of Virginia held a vote. The lawmakers voted to buy the freedom of the slave James Armistead Lafayette. They did so with these words: "At the peril of his life, he found means to visit the British camp, and there perfectly did many jobs."

Mary Katherine Goddard

Mary Katherine Goddard checks a page coming off her printing press.

Two years after the Battle of Yorktown, many Americans were still not sure they had won the war. There were still many British soldiers in frontier forts. To the north, Canada was still British. Would the British try to take back their former colonies?

On February 19, 1783, readers of the *Maryland Journal and Baltimore Advertiser* knew for sure. They learned that Britain had agreed to recognize the new nation. The British would withdraw their soldiers. The *Journal* was a newspaper that went to many readers in many states. It had "scooped" the story. It had got the story to its readers before any other newspaper.

The *Journal* was run by Mary Katherine Goddard (GAHD•uhrd). She gathered the news and decided what stories to print. Then she printed copies of her newspaper one at a time on a big printing press.

During the American Revolution, Mary Goddard kept her readers informed of everything that happened. She was the first to publish reports of the battles at Lexington and Concord. She was the first to print a signed copy of the Declaration of Independence.

Mary Goddard was a Patriot and made no bones about it. She was also a newspaperwoman. She printed whatever she thought would interest her readers. Once during the war, she printed an unsigned letter that poked fun at the Second Continental Congress. Baltimore Patriots thought the letter gave support to the British. They demanded to know the name of the letter writer so they could arrest and punish him.

No, said Mary Goddard. If that happened, people would be afraid to tell newspapers anything. Then the only place to get news would be the government. The government would become too powerful. That, said Goddard, is not the way to have freedom.

Some Patriots threatened to wreck her newspaper. Mary Goddard still refused to name the letter writer. Finally the case went to the Maryland lawmakers. They decided that Mary Goddard was right. It was important to protect the freedom of the press.

261

CHAPTER 11 REVIEW

WORDS TO USE

Explain the meaning of the words below. Then use each word in a complete sentence.

1. **declaration**
2. **independence**
3. **Patriots**
4. **mercenaries**
5. **treaty**

FACTS TO REVIEW

1. Why did Patriots consider the Battle of Bunker Hill to be a victory?

2. How did the Second Continental Congress try to get peace with Britain?

3. What personal strengths did George Washington have?

4. How did Thomas Paine's *Common Sense* influence the Revolution?

5. What did the Declaration of Independence announce to the world?

6. Why was Washington's victory at Trenton important?

7. Why was the Battle of Saratoga a turning point in the war?

8. Name at least four Patriot military leaders in addition to George Washington. Why is each famous?

9. How was French help important at the Battle of Yorktown?

10. Put these events in order: Battle of Yorktown, Declaration of Independence, Battle of Bunker Hill, *Common Sense*, Battle of Saratoga.

IDEAS TO DISCUSS

1. You may know the saying "The pen is mightier than the sword." This means that words can be more powerful than weapons. Do you think the saying is true? Explain your answer by using examples.

2. George Washington faced many problems as leader of the army. Yet he led the army to victory. What other leaders can you think of? What qualities should a good leader have?

3. You have read about the Battle of Yorktown from the point of view of the Americans. Imagine what a British account of the battle might say. How might it be different from the American view?

4. Most leaders of the Revolution were well off. They were people of education and property. Why do you think they risked everything they had for the Revolution?

5. What rights did the Patriots fight for?

◯ SKILLS PRACTICE

Reading a Document Use pages 242–244 to answer these questions about the Declaration of Independence.

1. What methods of persuasion did Thomas Jefferson use in writing the Declaration of Independence?

2. What are the four main parts of the Declaration of Independence?

3. What did the Declaration of Independence achieve?

UNIT 4 REVIEW

WORDS TO REMEMBER

Number your paper from 1 to 10. Complete the sentences below with the words or names in the list. Write the correct answers on your paper.

allies
boycott
independence
Loyalists
monopoly

Patriots
repeal
revolution
treaty
tyranny

In 1763 the British and Americans won a war against the French and their Indian __(1)__ . When the British passed the Stamp Act in 1765, Americans accused them of __(2)__ . Americans asked the British to __(3)__ the Stamp Act. To make their feelings clear, Americans started a __(4)__ of British goods. When Britain gave a __(5)__ to the East India Company to import tea, angry Americans threw tea into Boston harbor. In July 1776, the Continental Congress voted to declare __(6)__ . People who supported the fight against Britain were called __(7)__ . People who supported the British were called __(8)__ . The efforts of American Patriots to overthrow British rule was a __(9)__ . In 1783 a peace __(10)__ recognized American independence.

FOCUS ON MAIN IDEAS

1. How did the French and Indian War lead to the Stamp Act?

2. What events led to disagreements between Britain and the 13 colonies?

3. What rights did the colonists consider important?

4. What caused the British and American colonists to start shooting at each other?

5. What was the Olive Branch Petition? What was the king's response?

6. What was the purpose of the Declaration of Independence?

7. Why is the Liberty Bell a symbol of American freedom and independence?

8. How was each of these battles important?

   a. Lexington and Concord
   b. Bunker Hill
   c. Trenton
   d. Saratoga
   e. Yorktown

9. Why did the Americans win the war?

10. How did each of these people contribute to the American Revolution?

    a. Sam Adams
    b. John Adams
    c. Paul Revere
    d. Thomas Paine
    e. Thomas Jefferson
    f. George Washington
    g. Marquis de Lafayette
    h. Patrick Henry
    i. Friedrich von Steuben
    j. Nathanael Greene
    k. Crispus Attucks
    l. George Rogers Clark
    m. John Paul Jones
    n. Francis Marion

263

ACTIVITIES

1. **Research/Writing** You have read about many people who had the courage to fight for what they believed in. Choose the person who interests you most. Find out more about that person. Share what you learn in a report to the class.

2. **Research/Art** Many famous artists drew or painted scenes from the Revolutionary War. In this book or in your library, find some pictures showing the struggle for independence. Then paint or draw an event from the war that interests you.

3. **Research/Writing** The three main parts of an army in the 1700s were the artillery, the cavalry, and the infantry. Find out what each of these words means. Describe what a soldier did in the artillery, in the cavalry, and in the infantry.

4. **Timeline** Make a timeline showing the major events of the American Revolution. Start your timeline with 1763 and end it with 1783.

⭕ SKILLS REVIEW

1. **Cause and Effect** Read the paragraph below. Then answer the questions.

   Benjamin Franklin went to Paris in 1775 to persuade the French government to help the Americans. In Paris Franklin was well-liked. The French liked Franklin because he dressed plainly. The French also admired his experiments with electricity. Finally, the French enjoyed Franklin's witty sayings. When news of the Battle of Saratoga came in 1777, Benjamin Franklin again urged the French to send help to the United States. This time the French leaders agreed.

   a. What was the cause of Benjamin Franklin going to Paris?

   b. In Paris Franklin was well liked. What were the causes for this?

   c. What effect did the American victory at Saratoga have in France?

2. **Reading a Document** You have learned how and why Thomas Jefferson wrote the Declaration of Independence. You have also read about *Common Sense* by Thomas Paine. In *Common Sense,* Thomas Paine tried to persuade people that America should be independent. Like Thomas Jefferson, Paine used reason to convince people he was right. He also used words and ideas that appealed to people's feelings.

   Here is a part of *Common Sense* rewritten in modern language. Read it and answer the questions that follow.

   Some people say that America has grown rich and strong under the control of Britain. They say that America will continue to grow if it stays under Britain's control. I answer this way: America would have grown rich and strong even without Britain.

   Some people say that Britain is the parent country. If that is true, then the more shame on Britain. Even animals do not make war against their families. People have come here to get away from Britain because it was cruel to them. I believe, too, that Europe, and not Britain, is the parent country of America. America is a home for lovers of liberty from *every part* of Europe.

   a. Name at least one reason Thomas Paine believed America should break away from Britain.

   b. What ideas or words of Paine make people feel good about America? Which of Paine's ideas or words make people dislike Britain?

   c. How does Paine use "parent" as an idea in his argument?

YOUR STATE'S HISTORY

The American Revolution took place mainly in the 13 original states. Is your state one of these? Is it near one of the original states?

During the American Revolution, other things were happening in the places that later became states. West of the Appalachians, people were exploring and settling. Spanish-speaking people were settling an area that stretched from the Mississippi River to California. They were building towns, trading, and exploring. They were naming the mountains, rivers, plains, and deserts of half a continent.

Whaling ships were stopping at Hawaii to get fresh vegetables, fruit, and water. In Alaska, Russian fur traders were setting up trading posts.

To know what else was happening in other places is to have a "sense of history." You can begin to develop this sense by learning more about your own state's history. Here are some things you can do.

LEARNING ABOUT GEOGRAPHY

1. Your state probably looked very different during the Revolution than it does today. What was your state like? Were there towns and cities? What kinds of people lived in your state? What did they do? Try to find a map of your state or region during the time of the Revolution. Use what you have learned about your state to make your own map for the years 1763–1781.

2. Because the American Revolution was so important, many places are named after Patriots. In the United States today, cities, rivers, streets, schools, and even mountains carry the names of Washington, Jefferson, and Adams. Towns carry the names of de Kalb, Lafayette, and Pulaski. Are there streets or schools in your town named after any of the Patriots?

    Find your state in an atlas. What places in your state are named after Patriots of the Revolution?

LEARNING ABOUT PEOPLE

3. You may know about some people of courage who lived in your state during the time of the Revolution. They may be war heroes, traders, explorers, or settlers. Learn more about one of these people. Write a short report on the person you choose. Share your report with the class.

MAKING A TIMELINE

4. Important events may have happened in your state during the Revolution. Make a timeline showing these events. Then add to it some key events of the American Revolution. Start with the French and Indian War. Add the Boston Tea Party; July 4, 1776; the Battle of Yorktown.

UNIT FIVE

THE NEW NATION

Key Dates and Events

1769
Daniel Boone explores Kentucky

1787
Constitutional Convention meets in Philadelphia

1789
The Constitution becomes the law of the land

George Washington is elected President

1793
Eli Whitney invents the cotton gin

1803
The United States buys the territory of Louisiana

1804–1806
Lewis and Clark explore the Louisiana Purchase

1812–1814
The War of 1812

1825
Erie Canal completed

1830
First U.S. railroads using steam locomotives

1836
Texas declares independence

1846–1848
The Mexican War

1848
Gold discovered in California

After winning its independence, the United States grew. It grew in size, stretching clear to the Pacific Ocean. It formed an amazing new government, combining strong powers with great freedoms. While this was going on, people were finding new ways to do things. The use of new inventions was changing American life forever.

Perhaps the best symbol of this growing America was the covered wagon. In covered wagons thousands of families left familiar places to find homes in unknown places. They went into the unknown with a belief that change could be good. Through change they would improve their lives.

People believed in change, in finding new ways to do things and new places to live. This belief left a strong mark on American history.

CHAPTER 12

The U.S. Constitution

About
this
chapter

Winning the Revolutionary War took bravery and skill on the part of the American Patriots. After the war, the United States faced new kinds of problems. American leaders dealt with these problems in ways that helped our country become strong. Their greatest contribution was the **Constitution** of the United States. The Constitution is the framework for our government.

George Washington was the first President under the Constitution. He had helped the country win independence. Now he was to help the new nation get firmly on its feet.

1. THE AMERICAN REPUBLIC

To Guide Your Reading

Look for these important words:

Key Words
- Constitution
- Articles of Confederation
- republic
- creditors
- debtors
- territory
- survey
- townships
- Northwest Ordinance
- compromise
- federal
- Preamble

People
- George Washington
- James Madison

Places
- Northwest Territory

Look for answers to these questions:

1. What problems did the United States face after the American Revolution?
2. Who is called the Father of the Constitution?
3. What form of government did the Constitution establish?
4. What did the writers of the Constitution hope to achieve?

The Constitution did not become law until 1789. Before then, the United States was governed under rules of the **Articles of Confederation** (kuhn•fed•uh•RAY•shuhn). The Articles of Confederation gave most powers of government to the states. The states sent representatives to a congress. It was this congress that conducted the Revolutionary War.

By the end of the war **George Washington** had become the symbol of the new country. He was treated as a hero wherever he went. One general said this of Washington: "First in war, first in peace, and first in the hearts of his countrymen."

Some thought that Washington, not Congress, should run the country. Instead, Washington retired to his beloved Mount Vernon. For this, the American people admired him even more. By retiring to private life, Washington showed that he believed in a **republic.** A republic is a form of government in which people elect representatives. These representatives, sitting in an assembly, make the laws and decisions.

The Nation Faces Problems

Washington had high hopes for the new nation. Soon, however, the government under the Articles of Confederation began to fall apart. War against Britain no longer held the states together. They began to quarrel and bicker with each other. They quarreled over boundary lines. They passed taxes on goods imported from neighboring states. New York had a tax on all farm produce from New Jersey. Connecticut taxed goods coming from Massachusetts. Such taxes discouraged trade between the states. Business owners and merchants disliked the taxes, but Congress had no power to lift them.

Under the Articles of Confederation, Congress had no means of solving the nation's money problems. Congress could not pass taxes. Congress could only ask each state to pay its share toward running the government. Congress could not force the states to pay.

Congress could print paper money, but it printed too much paper money. The result was terrible inflation. A $20 paper bill in 1779 was worth only 2¢ in 1782.

Congress had borrowed a great sum of money to pay for the war. It owed money to the suppliers of food, clothing, and military equipment. It owed money to the soldiers. For three years Congress could not even pay the salaries of its own members.

These money problems greatly upset all kinds of people. **Creditors,** the people who had loaned money, wanted to be paid back in gold or silver, not with worthless paper money. **Debtors,** the people who owed money, could not pay in gold or silver. They wanted to use paper money. Debtors were often jailed for not paying in gold or silver. Some groups of debtors attacked courthouses and local governments.

The young country faced other problems. Britain did not allow American trading ships in its ports. Spain was threatening to close the Mississippi River and the port of New Orleans to American traders.

American statesmen tried to make trade agreements with England and Spain. But these powerful nations had no respect for young America. In England John Adams was asked, "Do you represent one nation or thirteen?"

Governing the Ohio Valley

In this time of troubles, Congress made several decisions of lasting importance. Congress decided how to divide and how to govern America's western lands.

Britain had refused to allow settlement west of the Appalachian Mountains. With independence, the frontier was opened. Settlers poured into the Ohio valley. The land north of the Ohio River and east of the Mississippi River was called the **Northwest Territory. Territory** is an area of land belonging to a government.

In 1785 Congress established a system to **survey** (suhr•VEY) the western lands. *To survey* means to make land measurements. The land was to be marked off in squares called **townships.** Each side of the township measured 6 miles (9.7 km). Each township, in turn, was divided into 36 squares, or sections. This survey system of townships and sections continues to be used in the United States.

In 1787 Congress passed the **Northwest Ordinance** (ORD•uhn•uhns). This law outlined the steps by which new states would be formed. It forbade slavery in the Northwest Territory. It also declared that one section of each township was to be used to support public schools.

The Northwest Ordinance was an excellent plan for America's growth. It was fair and forward-looking. Still, few people took Congress seriously.

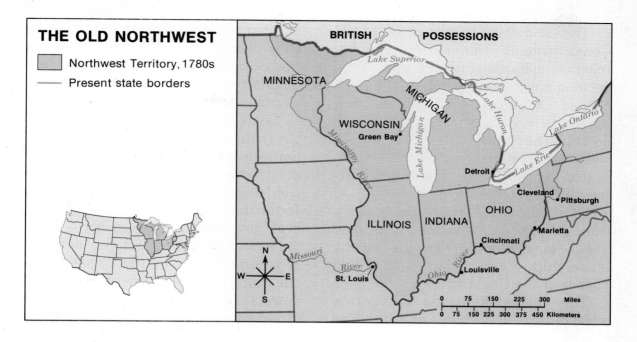

THE OLD NORTHWEST

Northwest Territory, 1780s

Present state borders

BRITISH POSSESSIONS

Lake Superior

MINNESOTA

MICHIGAN

WISCONSIN
Green Bay

Lake Michigan

Lake Huron

Lake Ontario

Mississippi River

Detroit

Lake Erie

Cleveland

Pittsburgh

ILLINOIS   INDIANA   OHIO

Marietta

Cincinnati

Missouri River

Ohio River

Louisville

St. Louis

N
W   E
S

0   75   150   225   300   Miles
0   75   150   225   300   375   450   Kilometers

A Rope of Sand

James Madison was a member of Congress under the Articles of Confederation. In 1779 Madison had been elected to Congress from Virginia. Then 29 years old, he was its youngest member. He was to spend the rest of his life in public service. Madison became a student of government. He read everything he could find about ancient and modern governments.

Madison was disturbed by the weakness of the Articles of Confederation. Under the Articles of Confederation each state was almost a nation by itself. Congress had little power over the states. Madison said he feared Congress had become a "rope of sand."

Such leaders as George Washington, John Adams, and Thomas Jefferson agreed with Madison. Madison began to argue for a stronger national government. Only a strong national government could keep the country from breaking apart, Madison said.

Others, including Patrick Henry, preferred the Articles of Confederation. They were afraid of a strong government. A rope of sand, they said, was better than a rod of iron.

A New Constitution

In 1787 Congress invited the states to a convention in Philadelphia to consider changing the Articles of Confederation. The delegates began to gather in Philadelphia in May 1787. Early to arrive was George Washington. By attending the convention, Washington was again letting Americans know that he supported the republican form of government.

In 1787 Washington was 55 years old. He arrived in Philadelphia in a great black coach pulled by six high-stepping horses. He promptly called on Benjamin Franklin, then 81 years old. At that time Franklin was governor of Pennsylvania.

The 55 delegates who came to the Constitutional Convention quickly reached a surprising decision. They decided not to try to patch up the Articles of Confederation. Instead, they agreed to write a new constitution. To do this, they worked hard six days a week for four months. George Washington served as president, or chairman, of the convention.

Of all the delegates to the convention, James Madison knew the most about government. For his strong leadership, Madison has been called Father of the Constitution.

The delegates to the convention often disagreed with one another. The constitution was written only because they were willing to **compromise** (KAHM•pruh•myz). *To compromise* means to give up some of what one wants in order to reach agreement.

Some delegates wanted the national government to have most of the power. Some wanted the states to have the most power, as under the Articles of Confederation. The compromise was a **federal** form of government. In a federal government powers are shared between the states and the national government. Under the Constitution the national government has some powers and the state governments have other powers. Still other powers are

In this famous painting, George Washington directs the signing of the Constitution. Benjamin Franklin is seated, lower left. James Madison is seated at the table to Franklin's left. Alexander Hamilton is at his right.

THE GREAT SEAL OF THE UNITED STATES

The Great Seal was adopted by Congress in 1789. It appears on dollar bills and important government documents. On one side an eagle holds an olive branch and arrows. On the other side an unfinished pyramid suggests a strong nation not yet complete.

shared by the national and state governments.

The convention delegates thought about the problems the country faced under the Articles of Confederation. They agreed to give the national government the powers it needed to meet these problems. The national government was given strong powers to collect taxes and to regulate trade between states. It was also given the powers to raise an army and to deal with foreign nations.

The Constitution's Purpose

The first part of the Constitution is the **Preamble** (PREE·am·buhl), or introduction. The Preamble tells the purpose of the Constitution.

We the people of the United States, in order to form a more perfect union, establish justice, insure domestic tranquility, provide for the common defense, promote the general welfare, and secure the blessings of liberty to ourselves and our posterity, do ordain and establish this Constitution for the United States of America.

The Preamble is short and dignified, but it may be hard for you to understand. What it means is this:

We the people of the United States have made the Constitution for the following reasons. We wish to bind together our people, our places, and our states in a better way. We wish to set up courts in which people can get fair treatment. We wish to make certain that there will be peace and order within the country. We wish to set up an army and navy so we can defend our country. We wish to be able to do what is necessary to make the lives of our people better. And finally, we wish to make certain that we and those who live after us remain a free people.

Reading Check

1. Name three problems faced by the United States under the Articles of Confederation.
2. Why is Madison called the Father of the Constitution?
3. What is a federal form of government?
4. According to the Preamble, what is the purpose of the Constitution?

2. THE STRUCTURE OF THE GOVERNMENT

To Guide Your Reading

Look for these important words:

Key Words
- legislative
- executive
- judicial
- House of Representatives

- Senate
- President
- Supreme Court
- constitutional
- checks and balances

- veto
- amendments
- democracy
- majority

Look for answers to these questions:

1. How is our government set up?
2. What do we mean by checks and balances in the Constitution?
3. Why is the Constitution a remarkable document?
4. What do we mean by *democracy*?

The new Constitution called for three branches of government. These were the **legislative** (LEJ•uh•slay•tiv), the **executive** (ek•ZEK•yuh•tiv), and the **judicial** (joo•DISH•uhl) branches. The legislative, or lawmaking, branch was the Congress. It was divided into two houses: the **House of Representatives** and the **Senate.** The legislative branch was given the power to pass taxes and make laws.

A **President** would head the executive, or management, branch. The President's main duties were to carry out the laws and head the armed forces.

The judicial branch would be the system of courts, headed by the **Supreme Court.** The President would appoint justices, or judges, to the Supreme Court. The Supreme Court would have power to decide whether laws were **constitutional** (kahn•stuh•TOO•shuhn•ul). *Constitutional* means lawful according to our Constitution.

The framers of the Constitution were afraid to give to any part of government too much power. Therefore, they established a system of **checks and balances.** Each branch of the government would have controls on the power of the other branches.

For example, only Congress can make laws. After Congress has voted for a law, the President shows his approval by signing the law. If the President disapproves of the proposed law, he can **veto,** or refuse, it. The Supreme Court can decide if laws are constitutional or not. If not, then the law ceases to exist.

The States Compromise

A major disagreement at the convention was between small and large states. Small states like Delaware and New Jersey wanted to have an equal voice with the large states. They were afraid that large states like Pennsylvania and New York would have more power because they had more people.

The large states and small states then compromised. Each state would have two senators, so all states would have equal representation in the Senate. In contrast, the number of members in the House of Representatives would depend on the population of each state.

The delegates also disagreed on how people would be elected to Congress. All the delegates believed in a republican form of government. Even so, some were suspicious of letting the people have too much direct influence. They remembered the mobs of angry debtors who had attacked the courts. Others had more faith in the people.

Again a compromise was reached. Members of the House of Representatives would be elected directly by the people. The senators would be elected by state legislative bodies. That part of the Constitution has since been changed. Senators today are elected directly by the people.

A Living Document

Not everyone was satisfied with the new Constitution. Some of the delegates refused to sign it. Most followed the lead of Benjamin Franklin. "I consent . . . to this Constitution because I expect no better, and because I am not sure that it is not the best," he said.

The Constitution as hammered together by the convention in 1787 is

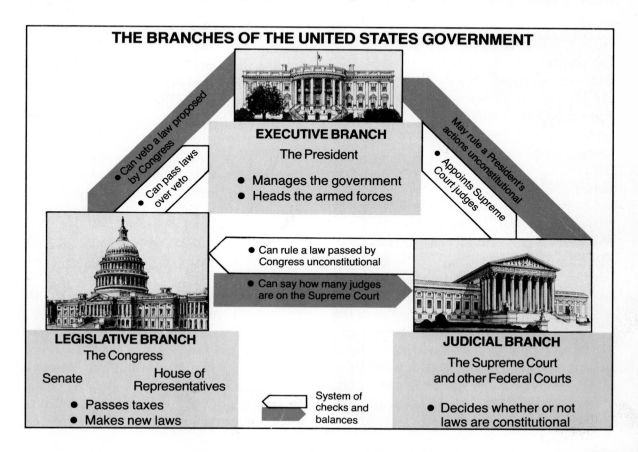

THE BRANCHES OF THE UNITED STATES GOVERNMENT

Can veto a law proposed by Congress
Can pass laws over veto

May rule a President's actions unconstitutional
Appoints Supreme Court judges

EXECUTIVE BRANCH
The President
- Manages the government
- Heads the armed forces

- Can rule a law passed by Congress unconstitutional
- Can say how many judges are on the Supreme Court

LEGISLATIVE BRANCH
The Congress
Senate   House of Representatives
- Passes taxes
- Makes new laws

System of checks and balances

JUDICIAL BRANCH
The Supreme Court and other Federal Courts
- Decides whether or not laws are constitutional

remarkable. It has been the framework of our government for about 200 years. It has been a model for the constitutions of other nations. As the law of the land, it has served the nation well. Over the years there have been **amendments,** or additions, to the Constitution. These have reflected the will of new generations of Americans.

Under the Constitution the 13 United States have become 50 United States. The population has grown from 4 million to 230 million. Americans have gone from horse-and-buggy days to the space age. The Constitution has given us a strong form of government and yet allowed change. For that reason we call it a living document.

The Constitution was the foundation of our government when there were but 13 states. It remains so today.

The Meaning of Democracy

Our form of government under the Constitution remains a republic. We continue to elect representatives to make laws and decisions. The United States is also a **democracy.** *Democracy* is an ancient Greek word meaning "rule by the people." People in a democratic nation like ours can make many choices about their lives. They have many rights and freedoms.

Democracy depends on respecting the wishes of the **majority,** or greatest number. Democracy can be found working all over the United States. In class meetings, in school government, in town meetings, you can find democracy. Whenever and wherever people decide something by voting, democracy is working.

Since the Constitution was written, our country has become more democratic. In 1789 only white men who owned property could vote. Women and poor white men could not vote. Millions of slaves had no rights or representation in government. The Indians were not considered citizens. With time more people were represented in government because they could vote. As more and more people achieved the right to vote, the nation became more democratic.

Reading Check

1. What are the three branches of our government?
2. What does it mean for a President to veto a law?
3. Why is the Constitution called a living document?
4. How has our country become more democratic?

3. A NEW GOVERNMENT BEGINS

To Guide Your Reading

Look for these important words:

Key Words
- Bill of Rights
- Cabinet
- Federalists
- Republicans

People
- John Adams
- Thomas Jefferson
- Alexander Hamilton

Places
- District of Columbia
- Washington

Look for answers to these questions:

1. What is the Bill of Rights? Why did Americans think it necessary?
2. Who were the first men to serve in the government? What were their jobs?
3. In what ways did some of these men disagree about what was best for the nation?

The new Constitution could not become law until two-thirds of the states had approved it. After reading it, many people were upset that the Constitution said nothing about individual rights. Many Americans remembered all too clearly how they had fought for liberty and for their rights. They wanted to make certain that tyranny could not raise its head in America. Never again, they vowed, could the government take away their liberties.

Those who wanted the Constitution promised to add a bill of rights that protected the individual. When the Constitution was approved, Madison wrote the **Bill of Rights,** the first ten amendments to the Constitution.

In 1789 George Washington was elected President, and **John Adams,** Vice President. Leaving Mount Vernon in his shining coach, Washington traveled to New York, the temporary capital. There the most popular man in America took the oath of office as President. As his advisers, he chose **Thomas Jefferson** and **Alexander Hamilton.** Jefferson would be secretary of state and Hamilton would be secretary of the treasury. Such advisers later became known as the **Cabinet.**

Congress faced the task of passing laws to make the government work. "We are in a wilderness without a single footstep to guide us," said James Madison.

Hamilton and Jefferson

Alexander Hamilton and Thomas Jefferson often argued about what each thought was best for the United States. Washington respected and listened to both men. Hamilton thought that the country should encourage manufacturing and the growth of cities. Jefferson thought that the country should continue to depend on agriculture. Like

OUR NATION'S CAPITAL

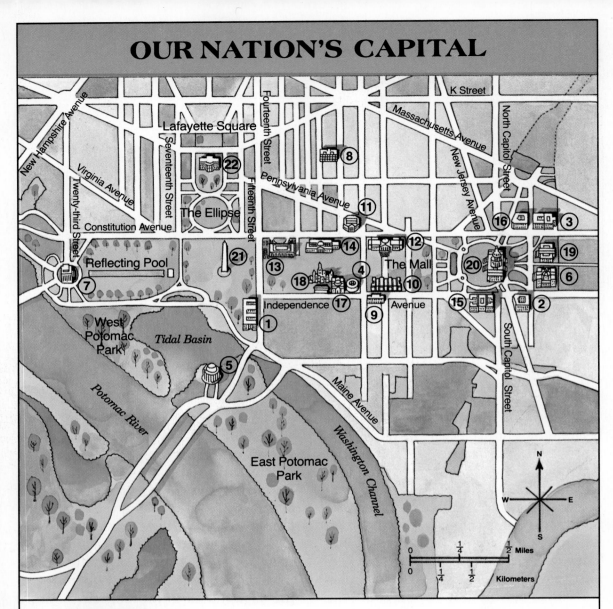

WASHINGTON, D.C.

Index to Buildings and Monuments

1. Bureau of Engraving and Printing
2. Cannon House Office Building
3. Dirksen and Hart Senate Office Buildings
4. Hirshhorn Museum and Sculpture Garden
5. Jefferson Memorial
6. Library of Congress
7. Lincoln Memorial
8. Martin Luther King Memorial Library
9. National Aeronautics and Space Administration
10. National Air and Space Museum
11. National Archives

12. National Gallery of Art
13. National Museum of American History
14. National Museum of Natural History
15. Rayburn House Office Building
16. Russell Senate Office Building
17. Smithsonian Arts and Industries Building
18. Smithsonian Institution building (offices)
    (Smithsonian museums: 4, 10, 12, 13, 14, 17)
19. Supreme Court Building
20. United States Capitol
21. Washington Monument
22. White House

Thomas Jefferson was an important leader during Washington's Presidency.

Adams Becomes President

George Washington served as President for two terms, each term four years long. Many people wanted him to remain President for a third term. Washington refused, saying two terms were enough. In refusing, Washington set an example for future American Presidents.

Washington retired to Mount Vernon for a well-deserved rest. When he left, the nation was on its feet. The government established by the Constitution was working.

John Adams followed Washington as the next President. The government then moved to Washington, D.C. John and Abigail Adams were the first to live in the newly built White House.

At that time the White House was called the President's Palace. When the Adamses moved in, the now-lovely East Room was unfinished. There Mrs. Adams hung the family wash to dry. She complained that she had trouble getting enough firewood. Thirteen fireplaces, all going at the same time, were necessary to keep out the damp cold of the Washington winter. Despite the problems, Mrs. Adams was hopeful. "This House is built for ages to come," she wrote. The same could be said of the Constitution.

many of his day, Jefferson felt that farmers were a better sort than city dwellers. Hamilton wanted a strong national government. Jefferson favored as little government as possible.

From the disagreements of Hamilton and Jefferson were born political parties. The supporters of Hamilton's ideas called themselves **Federalists.** The supporters of Jefferson's ideas called themselves **Republicans.** Political parties are not part of the Constitution. They have, however, become important to the way our government works.

Sometimes Hamilton and Jefferson had to compromise so that laws could get passed. In one compromise, it was agreed that the national capital would be built in the South. It would not be part of any state. Created from land given by Virginia and Maryland, the site would be called the **District of Columbia.** George Washington himself chose the site for the capital city. It would carry his name, **Washington.**

Reading Check

1. Why did people want a bill of rights added to the Constitution?
2. What is the Cabinet?
3. What was the beginning of the first political parties in the United States?
4. Who were the first and second Presidents under the Constitution?

279

ABIGAIL ADAMS

Abigail Adams
at about age 22

Abigail Adams
at about age 40

Only one woman in American history has been the wife of one President and the mother of another President. That was Abigail Adams. Her husband, John, was the second President of the United States. Her son, John Quincy Adams, became our sixth President. Abigail herself was an important person.

We know a great deal about Abigail's life because she wrote and received thousands of letters. Many of these letters still exist. Like most young girls of her day, Abigail did not go to school. She learned reading and writing from her family at home.

In 1764, one month before her twentieth birthday, Abigail married John Adams, then a young lawyer. Because of John's political career, they were separated frequently. During such times Abigail managed the farm, raised the children, and ran the household. Abigail and John wrote frequently to each other during these separations.

In 1776 John Adams was elected to the Continental Congress. Abigail wrote him a long letter expressing her ideas on liberty. "In the new Code of Laws which I suppose it will be necessary for you to make," she wrote, "I desire you would Remember the Ladies, and be more generous and favorable to them than your ancestors. Do not put such unlimited power into the hands of the Husbands." Why could women not have a voice in the making of laws? she asked. This itself was a revolutionary idea.

Abigail Adams taught all her children to think for themselves. She taught them to fight for what they believed. Early in his political career, young John Quincy Adams decided to leave his father's party, the Federalists. His father was upset, but Abigail defended her son for following his conscience. "I pride myself more in being the Mother of such a son," she wrote, "than in all the honors and titles which a Monarch could bestow."

John Quincy Adams could have been equally proud of his mother. Abigail Adams was a capable woman, as well as an independent thinker.

SKILLS FOR SUCCESS

UNDERSTANDING THE BILL OF RIGHTS

In 1791 ten amendments were added to the United States Constitution. These first ten amendments are known as the Bill of Rights. They protect the rights of United States citizens.

Americans had fought long and hard to break free from the unfair laws of the king of England. They wanted to make their hard-won rights part of the new Constitution.

This list tells you what rights each amendment protects.

- **Amendment I** promises freedom of religion, freedom of speech, and the freedom to hold meetings. It also says that Americans have the right to ask the government to correct wrongs.
- **Amendment II** says that the people's right to own weapons cannot be taken away. This is because weapons are needed to maintain militias.
- **Amendment III** says that no one can be forced to give room and board to soldiers.
- **Amendment IV** says that people and their property cannot be searched without good reason.
- **Amendment V** says that no one can be brought to trial twice for the same crime. No one can be forced to be a witness against himself or herself. No one can be punished without a fair trial. The government cannot take a person's property without paying for it.
- **Amendment VI** says that everyone has the right to a fair trial within a short time. A person has the right to defend himself or herself against charges.
- **Amendment VII** says that the right to a jury trial cannot be taken away.
- **Amendment VIII** says that no one should have to pay unreasonable bail or fines. No one should be given cruel and unfair punishment for any crime.
- **Amendment IX** says that the people will have all basic rights. They will have these rights even if they are not mentioned in the Constitution.
- **Amendment X** says that the states will keep all those powers not given to the federal government by the Constitution.

The Important First Amendment

The First Amendment guarantees some of our most important freedoms. Read it as it is written in the Constitution:

> Congress shall make no law respecting an establishment of religion, or prohibiting the free exercise thereof; or abridging the freedom of speech, or of the press; or the right of the people peaceably to assemble, and to petition the government for a redress of grievances.

Look at the first part of this amendment: "Congress shall make no law respecting an establishment of religion, or prohibiting the free exercise thereof." What does this mean? It means that Congress cannot pass a law saying that one religion is the nation's only religion. Congress cannot say that any religion is against the law.

In England there had been fights over religion for centuries. At times people were fined for not attending services of the Church of England. At other times certain churches were forbidden to meet. Americans did not want this to happen in their new nation. The First Amendment guarantees religious freedom. Americans have the right to believe or not to believe whatever they want.

Next, the First Amendment says Congress cannot **abridge** the freedom of speech or of the press. *To abridge* something is to cut it off. In England in the time before the American Revolution, people could not always talk freely. They could be thrown in jail if they complained about the king or the government. Without free speech people cannot talk about ways to change the government.

In a country that allows free speech, some people may express ideas unpopular at first. As people discuss these ideas, they may decide that some of them are wise after all. At one time, for example, it was unpopular to say that women should be able to vote. It was unpopular to say that factories must be safe places to work. After talking about these situations, though, people began to change their minds. They called for laws allowing women to vote and for making factories safer. Acceptance of these once

The right to read what we choose is one of our most precious freedoms.

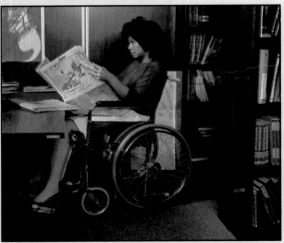

unpopular opinions has made the United States a better place to live.

The last part of the First Amendment says that people have the right to meet peacefully. It says they also can ask the government for help if they think they have been wronged.

CHECKING YOUR SKILLS

Imagine a completely different United States. Imagine that after the Revolution no one had written the Constitution or the Bill of Rights. Imagine that rulers passed only the laws they liked. Read what could happen. Then answer the questions.

1. You want to have a birthday party, but the law says you can have only four people. Why would rulers want to limit the number of people who gather together? What part of the First Amendment keeps this from happening in our country?

2. The rulers of the country have set up the Church of North America. They say you cannot go to public schools unless you belong to this church. You cannot hold a public office unless you belong to this church. What part of the First Amendment keeps this from happening?

3. Imagine that a ruler wants only good things said about him. You draw a cartoon that makes fun of the ruler. A newspaper prints your cartoon. For this you are thrown in jail and the newspaper is shut down. What part of the First Amendment protects you from this sort of thing?

4. You are riding a public bus and you say to someone next to you, "The government has too much power." Someone reports you, and you have to pay a $100 fine for complaining. What keeps this from happening in our country?

CHAPTER 12 REVIEW

WORDS TO REVIEW

Read each sentence. Then replace the underlined words in each sentence with the correct word or phrase from this list. Write the new sentences on your paper.

Bill of Rights   executive
checks and balances   judicial
compromise   legislative
Constitution   republic
democracy   Senate

The form of the United States government is a (1) government in which people elect representatives to make laws and decisions. The United States is also a (2) government by the people. The laws of the nation are based on the (3) framework of government approved in 1789. The organization of our government was based on (4) people giving up some of what they wanted. The government was divided into three parts: the (5) lawmaking branch, the (6) courts branch, and the (7) management branch. The lawmaking branch is divided into two houses: the House of Representatives and the (8) house in which each state has two votes. Important to our system of government are (9) ways each part has controls on other parts. Individual liberties are protected in the (10) first ten Amendments.

FACTS TO REVIEW

1. What decisions did Congress make about the Northwest Territory?

2. Name at least four powers the Constitution gives to the national government.

3. According to the Preamble, what is the purpose of the Constitution?

4. Describe the main purpose of each of the three branches of government.

5. How did Thomas Jefferson and Alexander Hamilton differ about what was best for the country?

IDEAS TO DISCUSS

1. Why did James Madison call the Articles of Confederation "a rope of sand"? Why did others say they preferred a rope of sand to a rod of iron?

2. In what ways did the Constitution make the national government stronger than it had been under the Articles of Confederation?

3. In what ways is the Constitution a document of compromises? Have you ever compromised on the playground or at home?

◯ SKILLS PRACTICE

Understanding the Bill of Rights Answer these questions.

1. What is the purpose of the Bill of Rights?

2. What Amendment says that people cannot be searched without good reason?

3. What Amendment guarantees freedom of speech?

4. What Amendment says that a person has the right to trial by jury?

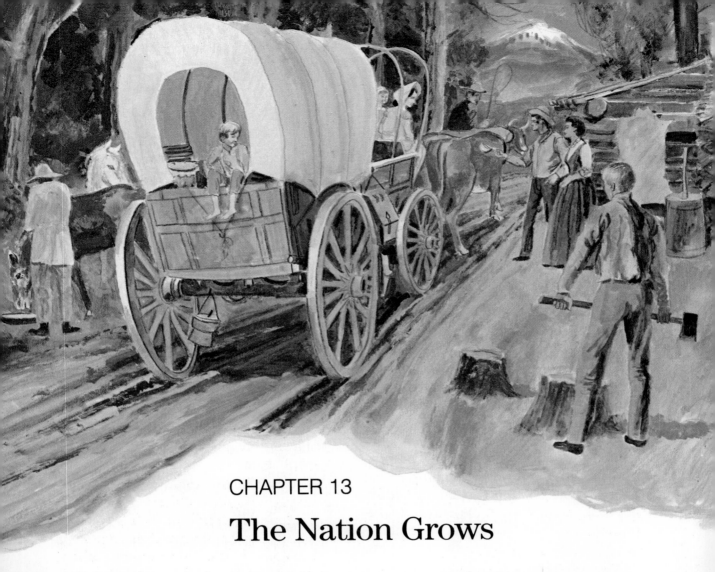

CHAPTER 13

The Nation Grows

About
this
chapter

During colonial times most Americans lived near the Atlantic coast. Then, after the Revolution, Americans began to explore and settle North America at a rapid pace.

As in the past, Indians did not want to lose their hunting and farming lands to the settlers. Yet the power and numbers of the settlers were too great. The Indians had to retreat. Defeated in battles, the Indians were forced to retreat farther west.

During this time the United States fought one more war with Britain. Victories against Britain gave Americans new pride in their growing nation. As the nation grew, so did democracy. Laws were changed, allowing more people to vote.

284

1. EXPLORATIONS WESTWARD

To Guide Your Reading

Look for these important words:

Key Words
• pioneers

People
• Daniel Boone

Places
• Kentucky
• Cumberland Gap
• Wilderness Trail

Look for answers to these questions:

1. What happened to the frontier after the American Revolution?
2. Who was Daniel Boone?
3. Why did the Shawnee and Cherokee Indians resist settlers in Kentucky?
4. How was Kentucky finally settled?

The United States grew rapidly in the 50 years after the Revolution. In those 50 years the frontier moved from the Appalachian Mountains to the Mississippi River. Pushing the frontier ever west were the **pioneers.** Pioneers are the first people to settle or enter a new territory.

Daniel Boone was one of the most famous American pioneers. Born in Pennsylvania, Boone was 16 years old when his family moved to the Yadkin valley of North Carolina. Boone had always loved roaming the woods. In North Carolina he spent months at a time living and hunting in the woods. He was as comfortable in the woods as in a farmhouse, maybe more so.

After marrying, Boone supported his growing family with some farming and much hunting. Deer were so plentiful that venison was a staple food of frontier life. In the winter Boone trapped beaver and otter for their skins. With the money he received for the skins, he bought guns, gunpowder, and lead for bullets.

Daniel Boone drove a wagon for General Braddock's army during the French and Indian War. While serving in the army, Boone met John Finley, a fur trader. Finley told stories about visiting a wonderful land the Iroquois called *Kentake* (kuhn•TUK•ee). *Kentake* is the Iroquois word for "meadowland."

After the war Boone tried to find this land, **Kentucky,** but he could not find a way over the mountains. He looked in vain for the Warrior's Path, an Indian trail that crossed the mountains. Discouraged, he returned home.

Soon after, a wandering peddler came to the door of the Boone house. He was none other than Boone's old friend, John Finley! With Finley to help him, Boone again made plans to find Kentucky. In 1769 a small party of six men started out. This time they found the Warrior's Path. Following the trail, they crossed the Appalachian Mountains at **Cumberland Gap.** On the other side they found the rolling green pastures of the Kentucky River valley. The pastures were thick with buffalo. The woods were full of deer. In the many streams swam numbers of beaver.

Both Cherokee and Shawnee Indians claimed parts of Kentucky as their hunting grounds. Several times the Shawnees captured Boone. Each time they let him go, but with a warning. "Don't come here anymore, for this is the Indians' hunting ground, and all the animals, skins, and furs are ours," said their chief. He told Boone that if he returned, the wasps and yellow jackets would sting him severely. Boone

Daniel Boone may have looked like this frontiersman. Rifle in hand, he wears buckskins and a coonskin cap.

did not listen. He returned again and again to Kentucky to explore and to hunt. His adventures became legends.

Boone tried to lead several families to Kentucky in 1773. The Cherokees attacked them at Cumberland Gap, however. Boone's oldest son was killed. The party turned back.

Kentucky Is Settled

Meanwhile word spread of Kentucky's rich land. People wanted to settle there, but the Indians refused to give up land. Finally, in 1775, the Virginia militia defeated the Indians in battle. They were forced to give up their claims to Kentucky.

As soon as the treaty had been signed, Daniel Boone was hired by a land developer to clear a road to Kentucky. In March 1775 Boone and a group of woodsmen headed for the Warrior's Path. Slashing trees and bushes to make way for wagons, they carved a road out of the wilderness. This road became known as the **Wilderness Trail.**

When the road was finished, Boone returned to North Carolina. He gathered his relatives and neighbors into a party to move to the new land. It was a slow, difficult trip over the mountains. Getting a cow to walk 300 miles was not easy. Sometimes wild animals scared the packhorses so that they scattered in all directions. Indians made surprise attacks. Despite these difficulties, the pioneers were soon busy building the Kentucky settlement of Boonesborough.

Soon thousands of pioneers passed over the Wilderness Trail on their way to the valleys beyond. They went west

Settlers west of the Appalachians shipped their goods by flatboat to New Orleans. Boatmen then returned north on horseback or by foot.

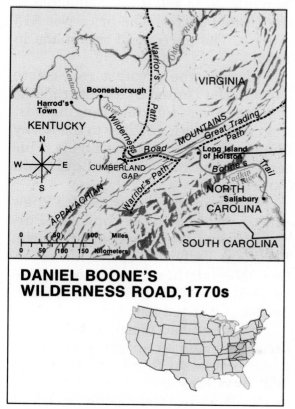

DANIEL BOONE'S WILDERNESS ROAD, 1770s

hoping to find cheap, good land. Land meant new opportunity.

By 1800 Americans were settling as far west as the Mississippi River. Kentucky and Tennessee had become states. Ohio would soon be a state. Farmers in these states shipped their crops and livestock on flatboats down the Mississippi River to New Orleans. From New Orleans the goods went by ship to markets on the east coast and elsewhere. Meanwhile the boatmen returned home on land.

Reading Check

1. What is a pioneer?
2. What land did Daniel Boone explore and later settle?
3. Why did the Shawnee Indians tell Boone to go home?
4. Why did pioneers push west?

287

2. THE LOUISIANA PURCHASE

To Guide Your Reading

Look for these important words:

Key Words
- Louisiana Purchase

People
- Napoleon Bonaparte
- Meriwether Lewis

- William Clark
- Sacajawea

Places
- Louisiana
- Missouri River
- North Dakota

- Montana
- Snake River
- Columbia River
- Arkansas River
- Red River
- Colorado
- New Mexico

Look for answers to these questions:

1. What was the Louisiana Purchase?
2. What did Meriwether Lewis and William Clark achieve?
3. Who explored the Arkansas and Red river valleys for the United States?

Thomas Jefferson, his red hair now gray, became the country's third President in 1801. The country soon faced a major difficulty. Spain closed the port of New Orleans to the farmers of the American West. By closing New Orleans, Spain hoped to stop the westward movement of the U.S. frontier.

After France lost the French and Indian War, it gave Spain its claims to land west of the Mississippi. This land was called **Louisiana.** Then, in 1802, Jefferson learned that Spain had secretly given Louisiana back to France. The French leader, **Napoleon Bonaparte** (nuh•POHL•yuhn BOH•nuh•pahrt), dreamed of again establishing French power in North America.

Jefferson sent representatives to Paris to ask Napoleon to sell New Orleans to the Americans. Jefferson offered $10 million. Napoleon at first refused. Then events in Europe changed his mind. Britain declared war on France.

Needing money to fight the war, Napoleon offered to sell all of Louisiana to the United States. The price was $15 million. The agreement was made in 1803.

This was the greatest real estate bargain the United States ever made. It gained a vast territory ranging west from the Mississippi River to the Rocky Mountains and north to Canada. This territory was known as the **Louisiana Purchase.**

Nobody in the United States knew exactly what lay in the Louisiana Purchase. It was unexplored, an unknown. President Jefferson asked his secretary, **Meriwether Lewis,** to lead an expedition to gather all kinds of information about the new land.

Lewis had had much experience in the wilderness as an army officer in the Northwest Territory. He chose **William Clark,** a good friend, to share the leadership of the expedition. Clark had valuable wilderness experience. He was particularly good at making maps.

Lewis and Clark Head West

The Lewis and Clark expedition left St. Louis, Missouri, in the spring of 1804. It proceeded by canoe up the **Missouri River.** Near the Mandan villages in present-day **North Dakota,** they built a fort in which to spend the winter. While there, they hired a French fur trader to translate some Indian languages for them. The Frenchman was married to a Shoshone named **Sacajawea** (sa•kuh•juh• WEE•uh). Sacajawea had been kidnapped from her people years before. Lewis and Clark hoped that Sacajawea would translate for them when they reached the land of the Shoshones.

In the spring of 1805 the small party of about 40 set out on their historic trip. They had six small canoes and two large ones. "This little fleet, although not quite so respectable as that of Columbus or Captain Cook, was still viewed by us with as much pleasure," wrote Lewis in his journal.

At last the expedition reached the streams that were the source of the Missouri River. The snow-capped peaks of the Rocky Mountains were in sight. The expedition had reached the land we call **Montana.** To cross the high mountains, they would need horses. They put their hopes on the Shoshones. "If we do not find them or some other nation who have horses, I fear the successful issue of our voyage will be very doubtful," Lewis wrote.

Lewis and Clark were so eager to find the Shoshones that they walked

Reaching the Continental Divide, Meriwether Lewis and William Clark gaze across the Rockies into an unexplored land. With the expedition was Sacajawea, a Shoshone Indian. The Shoshones loaned horses to the expedition and showed Lewis and Clark a route to reach the Pacific Ocean.

on land ahead of the slow-moving canoes. They were rewarded only with severe blisters. Their leather moccasins were no match for the sharp rocks and cactuses that were everywhere.

At last the travelers made contact with the Shoshones. Imagine their surprise to learn that the Shoshone chief was Sacajawea's brother! The party was now able to get horses and continue its journey over the mountains.

Once over the Rockies, the expedition built more canoes. They then canoed down the **Snake River** to the **Columbia River.** From there they continued on to the Pacific Ocean. Near the mouth of the Columbia River, they built a small fort. There they stayed the winter of 1805–1806. They had hoped to find an American trading ship anchored offshore. Not finding one, they had to return overland as they had come.

The expedition returned to St. Louis in 1806. Under the expert leadership of Lewis and Clark, the expedition had collected a mass of information. Lewis

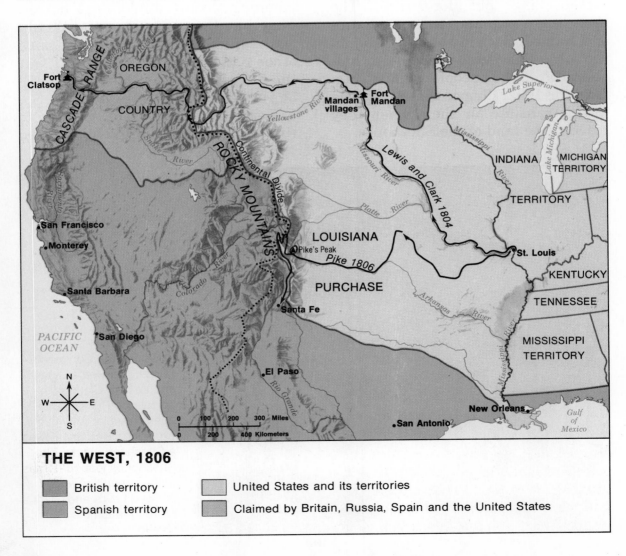

THE WEST, 1806

- British territory
- Spanish territory
- United States and its territories
- Claimed by Britain, Russia, Spain and the United States

Zebulon Pike led a government expedition to explore the Arkansas and Red River valleys. In Colorado he tried unsuccessfully to climb the peak that now carries his name. In New Mexico the Spanish captured him for trespassing. They released him a year later.

and Clark brought back seeds, plants, and animal bones. They brought descriptions of the land and its peoples. They brought back maps locating rivers and mountain ranges. Lewis and Clark even sent two grizzly bears to President Jefferson. He kept the bears in cages on the White House lawn. Jefferson, always curious, spent hours studying the bones brought from the faraway places.

Pike Reaches Colorado

At the same time Lewis and Clark were on their expedition, Zebulon Pike was also leading an expedition. He intended to explore the **Arkansas** and **Red** rivers, which flowed through the middle part of the Louisiana Purchase. Pike reached **Colorado** and then turned south. He hoped to get additional information about Spanish territory. He went too far south, however. In **New Mexico,** he was jailed by the Spanish for trespassing.

After his release about a year later, Pike reported that the people of Santa Fe needed manufactured goods. Soon American traders were heading for Santa Fe.

Reading Check

1. From what nation did the United States buy Louisiana?
2. Who were Lewis and Clark?
3. How did the Shoshones help Lewis and Clark?
4. Which part of the Louisiana Purchase was explored by Zebulon Pike?

3. WAR OF 1812

To Guide Your Reading

Look for these important words:

Key Words
- neutral
- impressment
- War Hawks
- *Constitution*
- *Guerrière*

People
- Henry Clay
- Francis Scott Key
- Andrew Jackson

Places
- Fort McHenry

1. What were some causes of the War of 1812?
2. What American cities did the British attack in the War of 1812? What happened in each case?
3. Who became a national hero after the War of 1812?

After the War of Independence, American relations with both France and Britain were troubled. France and Britain were often at war with each other. Neither country recognized the right of a country to be **neutral,** not to take sides. The British seized American ships to stop trade with the French. The French seized American ships to halt trade with the British. Congress decided to do something. It passed laws forbidding Americans to trade with either power until each stopped seizing American ships.

Americans were also furious with Britain for taking sailors off American ships. The British seized the sailors to put them to work on British ships. This was called **impressment.** Americans felt that they and their nation were not getting the respect they deserved.

In 1810 Napoleon Bonaparte announced that France would respect American ships. By then James Madison was President. He announced that the United States would favor France over Britain. This made Madison popular in the West and South.

In the early 1800s the British seized U.S. sailors for work on British ships.

People in the West and South favored war with Britain. Those who wanted war were called **War Hawks.** The War Hawks blamed the British in Canada for encouraging Indian attacks on the frontier. The War Hawks were eager for more land. They hoped to take Canada from Britain and Florida from Spain. Senator **Henry Clay** of Kentucky was the most famous of the War Hawks. He urged that the United States "take the whole continent."

Meanwhile, Britain agreed that it, too, would no longer seize American ships or sailors. But it was too late. The desire for war with Britain was too strong. At the urging of the War Hawks, the United States declared war on Britain in 1812.

Britain had the strongest navy in the world. Yet the small United States navy won several important victories. Some of these battles took place on the Great Lakes, some on the high seas.

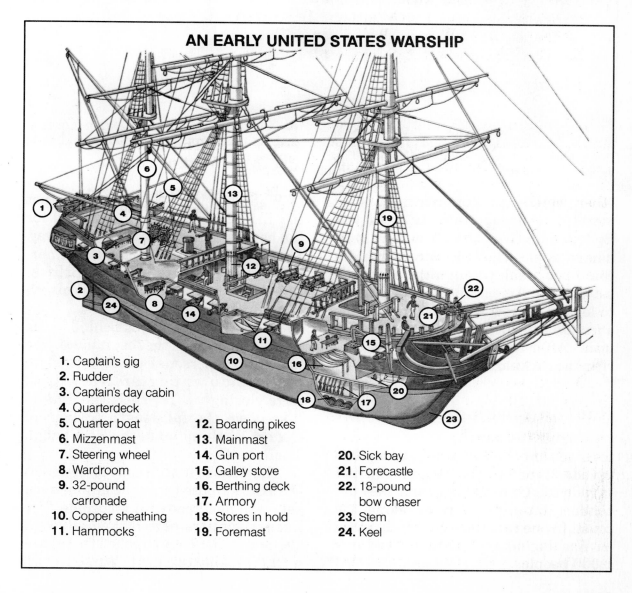

AN EARLY UNITED STATES WARSHIP

1. Captain's gig
2. Rudder
3. Captain's day cabin
4. Quarterdeck
5. Quarter boat
6. Mizzenmast
7. Steering wheel
8. Wardroom
9. 32-pound carronade
10. Copper sheathing
11. Hammocks
12. Boarding pikes
13. Mainmast
14. Gun port
15. Galley stove
16. Berthing deck
17. Armory
18. Stores in hold
19. Foremast
20. Sick bay
21. Forecastle
22. 18-pound bow chaser
23. Stem
24. Keel

Dolley Madison, a quick-witted and patriotic First Lady, rescues George Washington's portrait even as the British march into the Capital.

The U.S. frigate **Constitution,** commanded by Isaac Hull, defeated the British ship **Guerrière** (ge•ri•YAIR) in a hard battle. The British cannonballs could not break through the hard oak sides of the American ship. According to legend, a crew member on the *Constitution* yelled, "Her sides are made of iron." After that the *Constitution* carried the nickname Old Ironsides.

Raid on Washington, D.C.

During the war the American armies made only half-hearted attempts to invade Canada. The British did not invade the United States, but they did conduct hit-and-run raids along the coast. In one raid the British advanced on Washington, D.C., then a city of only 8,000 people.

When President Madison heard that the British were near, he headed for the battlefield 7 miles (11.3 km) away. There, on August 24, 1814, the American army failed to stop the British. The British continued their march toward Washington.

Dolley Madison stayed behind in the White House until the last minute. She had loaded personal goods and state papers into a waiting cart. The British were closing in. Yet she took time to take down the full-length portrait of George Washington in the East Room. Then she fled.

The first British troops to arrive at the White House found the dining room set, with food ready for 40 people. The hungry soldiers helped themselves to the fine foods. They finished their banquet by setting fire to the White House.

The next day Washington was still burning when a great hurricane struck the city. "Roofs of houses were torn off and carried up into the air like sheets of paper," a British soldier wrote. The British lost 30 men buried beneath the ruins. After the storm they quickly retreated to their ships.

Battle at Baltimore

When the British left Washington, they sailed up Chesapeake Bay. The British commander said that he intended to spend the winter in Baltimore. But Baltimore, unlike Washington, was defended by a fort. This was **Fort McHenry.**

The commander at Fort McHenry had earlier requested an American flag. He asked that it be "so large that the British will have no difficulty in seeing it at a distance." Mary Pickersgill and her 13-year-old daughter made an enormous flag for the fort. It measured 42 by 30 feet (12.8 by 9.1 m).

All night of September 13, the British threw a hail of rockets and bombs on Fort McHenry. At dawn **Francis Scott Key,** an American prisoner on a British ship, looked through the reddened sky at the fort. He was overjoyed at what he saw. The Stars and Stripes was still flying! He quickly set down the words to *The Star-Spangled Banner,* our national anthem.

The British bombarded Fort McHenry in Baltimore all night. At dawn the American flag still flew, and the British abandoned their attack.

In New Orleans, Andrew Jackson defeated the British with an army of crack-shot frontiersmen, French-speaking planters, and free blacks.

Battle of New Orleans

Unable to defeat the Americans at Baltimore, the British sailed away to New Orleans. There American soldiers commanded by **Andrew Jackson** were waiting for them.

Earlier that year Andrew Jackson had soundly defeated the Creek Indians at the Battle of Horseshoe Bend in Alabama. The Creeks had sided with the British. By doing so, they hoped to keep Americans off their land.

When word came to Jackson that the British might attack New Orleans, his troops hurried to defend the city. There they withstood an assault of over 5,000 British soldiers. For ten days the British attacked in vain, finally retreating to their ships. For his victories against the Creeks and the British, Jackson became a national hero.

Americans were later to learn that the Battle of New Orleans had not been necessary. Two weeks before the battle, the British and Americans had signed a peace treaty in Europe. However, word that the war was over had not reached New Orleans in time.

Reading Check

1. What troubles did the United States have with Britain and France after the War of Independence?
2. Who were the War Hawks?
3. Who was President during the War of 1812?
4. Who was the hero of the Battle of New Orleans?

JOHN J. AUDUBON

John J. Audubon

The American Eagle

The Wild Turkey

In the early 1800s thousands of young Americans moved into the wild new lands of the West to seek their fortunes. Among them was John J. Audubon, a Frenchman. Audubon ended up making a fortune, but not at all in the way he expected.

Young Audubon tried his hardest to be a successful businessman. He just did not have the right abilities. He tried his luck as a clerk, a salesman, and a store manager. None of these efforts was successful. In 1819, at age 34, he was jailed for having too many debts.

John Audubon's real loves were art and exploration. He was fascinated by the millions of multicolored birds and other wild creatures in the backwoods. Soon he began to devote all his time to watching and drawing wildlife.

Audubon had married Lucy Bakewell. To help support their family, she had become a teacher. Her earnings made it possible for Audubon to pursue his art.

Audubon traveled on foot, horseback, flatboat, stagecoach, and river steamer. His goal was to paint every kind of bird in America.

Audubon faced many hardships. Rats ate 200 of his drawings. Spilled gunpowder stained months' worth of painting. Still, Audubon never gave up his dream. He hoped to offer his country "a monument to the varied splendor of American nature."

Finally, in 1838 Audubon completed his greatest work, *The Birds of America*. People were amazed by Audubon's colorful drawings of nearly every kind of native bird. Audubon made his drawings life-size. The birds seemed ready to fly off the page at any moment. *Birds of America* brought him both fame and money.

Audubon died in 1851. Within a few years many of the birds he had drawn were extinct. Only from his drawings do we know what such birds as the Carolina parakeet and the great auk looked like. Today Audubon's name has become a symbol for preserving what is wild, beautiful, and unspoiled.

4. GROWTH OF THE COUNTRY

To Guide Your Reading

Look for these important words:

Key Words
- Trail of Tears

People
- Davy Crockett
- Sequoya

Places
- Oklahoma
- New Echota

Look for answers to these questions:

1. How did the United States grow in territory in its first 50 years?
2. In what ways did democracy grow?
3. What qualities did Andrew Jackson have?
4. What happened to the Indians of the Southeast?

On July 4, 1826, the United States celebrated its fiftieth birthday. Everywhere Americans rejoiced with parades, speeches, fireworks, and celebrations. Many hoped that those two old Patriots, John Adams and Thomas Jefferson, would live to see the celebration. Both men did live to greet that Fourth of July, but both died before sunset. In Philadelphia the Liberty Bell tolled at their passing.

In the 50 years since the Declaration of Independence, the Union had increased by 11 states. In New England Vermont and Maine had become states. Ohio, Illinois, and Indiana were carved from the Northwest Territory. Kentucky and Tennessee had also become states. Louisiana and Missouri were the first states formed from the Louisiana Purchase. Alabama became a state after the Creek Indians were forced to give up much of their land. The state of Mississippi and the territory of Florida had been created from land once claimed by Spain.

Democracy Grows

The promises of the frontier continued to lure Americans westward. They went, seeking land, adventure, opportunity. On the frontier, people faced the hardships of the wilderness equally. People had to rely on themselves and yet help their neighbors. Democratic ideas grew on the frontier.

In early America voting was a privilege that usually came only with owning property. In most of the new frontier states, this changed. There the vote was given to all white men, not just to those who owned property. Many of the older states began to follow the example of the frontier states.

Today it does not seem democratic that only white men could vote. In the 1820s women and most blacks could not vote. The Indians were not considered citizens. Yet giving the right to vote to all white men was an important step in the growth of democracy. No other country in the world was so advanced at that time.

298

When all white men could vote, there was a change in the kind of man elected. Elected officials were no longer always men of education and property. **Davy Crockett** is an example of the new kind of leader. When Davy Crockett first ran for office, he admitted he knew nothing about the government. "I had never read even a newspaper in my life," he said. When he gave election speeches, he told "laughable stories." His "laughable stories" got him elected.

Davy Crockett was like many on the frontier. By being part of the government, he learned about government. He learned much by listening to others make election speeches. Davy Crockett later became a member of Congress.

Election of Andrew Jackson

Andrew Jackson was elected President in 1828. Until the election of Jackson, Presidents had come from either Massachusetts or Virginia. Now, for the first time, a person from the frontier was elected President. It was also the first election in which most American men could vote. They elected Jackson, the hero of the Battle of New Orleans.

Voters liked Jackson because he was a self-made man of the frontier. Jackson had been born in a log cabin. He had taught himself enough law to become a wealthy lawyer and judge in Tennessee. The new voters felt that Jackson was one of them, one of the common men.

Crowds gather to greet Andrew Jackson on his way to Washington, D. C. The popular frontier hero was elected President in 1828.

Jackson first fought the British in the hills of South Carolina during the Revolutionary War. He was only 13 years old at the time. One day Jackson and his brother were captured while trying to find food in a farmhouse. The British officer in charge ordered young Andy Jackson to shine his boots. When Jackson refused, the officer swung his sword toward Jackson's head. Ducking, Jackson put his arm up for protection. He was cut severely on his hand and forehead. The scars were with him all his life.

As the British officer learned, Andrew Jackson was stubborn. Even as a boy he was known for his toughness. One of his friends later remembered him this way: "I could throw him

At 13, Andrew Jackson had to dodge the sword of a British officer angered by Jackson's refusal to shine his boots.

three times out of four, but he would never stay throwed." Such toughness earned Jackson the nickname of Old Hickory. Hickory was the toughest tree growing in the forests of Tennessee.

When Jackson was elected in 1828, his followers were overjoyed. Thousands streamed into Washington for the inauguration. They showed up at the White House for the reception. Rough frontiersmen with muddy boots stood on the satin-covered chairs to get a glimpse of their hero. To keep from being crushed, Jackson had to escape by a back door.

As President, Jackson continued to be both tough and stubborn. He vetoed a bank law that would favor the rich. Government should not help the rich get richer, he said. Government instead should "shower its favors alike on the high and the low, the rich and the poor."

Indian Removal

Jackson's toughness also resulted in harsh and unfair treatment of the Indians east of the Mississippi. He insisted they be removed to land west of the Mississippi. Explorers had reported that the plains west of the Mississippi were useless to white people. At that time people believed that the soil was good only where trees grew. It became a popular idea that all Indians should move west. Jackson made this idea come about.

Congress passed the Indian Removal Act in 1830. Under the terms of the Indian Removal Act, all Indians east of the Mississippi were forced to leave their land and move west. They were to live in a new Indian territory, present-day **Oklahoma.**

Jerome Tiger, a modern artist, caught the feelings of cold, hunger, and despair of his ancestors' Trail of Tears to Oklahoma.

Not all Americans agreed with Jackson's Indian policy. Senator Henry Clay of Kentucky was one who did not. He pleaded with his fellow senators to honor the Indian treaties. His speech brought tears to the eyes of other senators, but they did nothing to stop the removal.

Many Indians resisted the Indian removal policy. In Illinois the government fought the Black Hawk War. This was to force the Sauk and Fox Indians to move. In the Southeast the removal policy was particularly hard on the Five Civilized Tribes. They were the Choc-taws, the Chickasaws, the Cherokees, the Creeks, and the Seminoles. The Seminoles refused to move. The result was the Seminole War. Thousands of Seminoles lost their lives.

The 15,000 Cherokees in Georgia had 22,000 cattle, 1,300 slaves, and 2,000 spinning wheels. They had 18 schools. Their chief, **Sequoya** (si• KWOI•uh), had invented an alphabet for the Cherokee language. When a Cherokee-language newspaper was printed, the Cherokees quickly learned to read and write their language. They established a republic with the capital at **New Echota** (i•KOHT•uh).

The United States had guaranteed the independence of the Cherokee nation by a treaty in 1791. When gold was discovered on Cherokee lands in 1828, Georgia began to take those lands. The Cherokees appealed for help to the national government, but their pleas went unheard.

Instead of supporting the treaty with the Cherokees, Jackson used the army against them. They too were forced to move. They started westward in the winter of 1838. Almost one-fourth of their number died on the trail from disease, hunger, and cold. This journey, like others taken by Indians forced to move west, has been called the **Trail of Tears.**

Reading Check

1. Why did Davy Crockett get elected?
2. Why did frontier voters like Andrew Jackson?
3. What did the Indian Removal Act of 1830 say?
4. What happened on the Trail of Tears?

301

SKILLS FOR SUCCESS

READING POLITICAL CARTOONS

Talking animals, Presidents who look like vegetables, superheroes leaping over buildings—how are they alike? They can all be found in cartoons!

Cartoons can make you laugh. They can tell a story. They can also poke gentle fun or contain deeper meanings behind their humor. They can express opinions about something. Cartoons that express opinions about politics or government are called **political cartoons.** Political cartoons are most often found in newspapers or news-magazines.

The First American Political Cartoons

Benjamin Franklin drew what is thought to be the first American political cartoon. This famous cartoon appeared in *The Pennsylvania Gazette* in 1754.

In 1754 Benjamin Franklin was representing Pennsylvania at the Albany Congress in New York. At this congress he suggested a "Plan of the Union" for the colonies. He wanted the colonies to unite to defend America's freedom. He used his cartoon to urge union. Each piece of the snake represents one of the colonies. The *Join or Die*

saying was based on a superstition about snakes. The belief was that a snake cut to pieces would come to life again if put back together before sunset. Benjamin Franklin wanted the pieces of the snake (the American colonies) to join together and thus be strong.

Below is another early American political cartoon. It was drawn for a similar reason as Franklin's cartoon: the hope for a united America. This cartoon celebrates New York's approval of the Constitution in 1788. It expressed the hope that North Carolina and Rhode Island would also approve the Constitution.

Symbols in Political Cartoons

Benjamin Franklin's cartoon used a snake to represent the colonies. The second cartoon used pillars of a building to show the states. The snake and the pillars used in these cartoons are **symbols.**

Political cartoons often use symbols. It would be hard to show a picture of colonial unity. How could you show a picture of peace? or war? Symbols are a good way to show these ideas. The use of symbols can make a message easier to understand.

You are probably familiar with some symbols. Many of them are used in political cartoons. Before you read on, try to think of a few symbols you know.

Uncle Sam is probably the best-known symbol of America. The first known cartoon of Uncle Sam was drawn in 1832.

No one knows who first drew Uncle Sam. Yet over the years he developed into the figure we all know. He is the man wearing a blue top hat with stars and red-and-white striped pants. The initials of Uncle Sam are the same as for the United States. In political cartoons Uncle Sam stands for the United States as a whole.

Another symbol often used in American political cartoons was the crown and dress of royalty. America had fought a war to end rule by royalty. Americans wanted to make sure that their leaders did not act like kings. By showing a leader dressed as a king, cartoonists were saying *beware.* This leader's behavior threatened democratic rule. Look at the cartoon below. What do you think this cartoon is saying about Andrew Jackson as President?

GETTIN' BACK AT THE CARTOONISTS.

JIM
BERRY
NEAT

REDEDICATION

CANADA

Animals are often used as symbols in political cartoons. The eagle is used to represent the United States. The dove is used as a symbol of peace. The snail, as in the cartoon on page 303, is a symbol of slowness.

Two of our most famous political symbols are also animals. The donkey represents the Democratic party, and the elephant represents the Republican party. The donkey was probably first used to represent Andrew Jackson. Later, the donkey became a symbol for the entire Democratic party. Cartoonist Thomas Nast introduced the elephant as a symbol of the Republican party in 1874. We are still using these symbols today. Political cartoons may combine many symbols at once. The cartoon at the upper right was published in 1938 to honor friendship between the United States and Canada. The dove as a symbol of peace carries an olive branch in its beak. The olive branch is also a symbol of peace. What other symbol do you recognize in this cartoon?

Political cartoons can make important points. It is up to you, however, to decide whether you agree with them.

CHECKING YOUR SKILLS

Answer the following questions. Use the material in this lesson to help you.

1. How is a political cartoon different from other types of cartoons?

2. Where can you find political cartoons?

3. According to the cartoon on page 302, which states had not yet approved the Constitution?

4. Uncle Sam, a symbol himself, carries several other symbols in his clothing. What are they?

5. Name at least four symbols you might find in political cartoons.

6. What do the donkey and elephant stand for?

CHAPTER 13 REVIEW

WORDS TO USE

Number your paper from 1 to 10. Use the words below to complete the sentences that follow.

Daniel Boone　　**Francis Scott Key**
William Clark　　**Meriwether Lewis**
Columbia River　　**Missouri River**
Andrew Jackson　　**neutral**
Kentucky　　**Sacajawea**

__(1)__ led pioneers on a trail through the Cumberland Gap into __(2)__ . President Thomas Jefferson sent __(3)__ and __(4)__ to explore the Louisiana Purchase. They first proceeded by canoe up the __(5)__ . In North Dakota a Shoshone woman, __(6)__ , joined the expedition. The expedition journeyed down the Snake River and the __(7)__ to the Pacific Ocean.

When war broke out between France and Britain, the United States tried to remain __(8)__ . In the course of events, the United States went to war with Britain. While the British bombarded Fort McHenry at Baltimore, __(9)__ wrote *The Star Spangled Banner*. A hero of that war, __(10)__ , became President in 1828.

FACTS TO REVIEW

1. Why did Napoleon decide to sell the territory of Louisiana?

2. What was the purpose of the Lewis and Clark expedition?

3. Compare and contrast the British attack on Washington, D.C. with the British attack on Baltimore, Maryland.

4. How did voting requirements change in the early 1800s?

5. In what ways was Andrew Jackson a man of the frontier?

IDEAS TO DISCUSS

1. Compare two events: the Shoshones helping Lewis and Clark and the Cherokees on the Trail of Tears. Why were relations between whites and Indians so different in each event?

2. How did the experiences of the frontier encourage the growth of democracy?

○ SKILLS PRACTICE

Reading Political Cartoons Below is a political cartoon of former President Lyndon Johnson. What is the cartoonist's opinion of President Johnson? Explain your answer.

CHAPTER 14

A Nation on the Move

The United States was on the move during the 1800s. As people moved west, new means of transportation developed. First there were canals, then steamboats, and finally the railroads. New means of transportation made it easier for people to travel from place to place. The frontier then moved west even faster. By 1850 thousands of people were settled in Oregon and California.

In the East life was also changing. In the Northeast factories were starting to produce manufactured goods. Cities were growing rapidly. In the Southeast cotton was becoming the most important crop. This was a time of invention, of movement, of excitement.

1. CANALS, STEAMBOATS, AND RAILROADS

To Guide Your Reading

Look for these important words:

Key Words
- engineers
- Yankee know-how
- locks
- flatboats
- steam engine

People
- De Witt Clinton
- Robert Fulton
- Henry Miller Shreve
- Peter Cooper

Places
- Erie Canal

Look for answers to these questions:

1. Why was the Erie Canal important? How was it built?
2. What effects did the invention of the steamboat have?
3. How did the railroad change life in the United States?

The early nineteenth century saw an explosion of energy and confidence in the United States. Nothing seemed too difficult. Americans conquered one problem after another. Where there was a will there was a way, they told themselves.

A grand example of this spirit was the building of the **Erie Canal.** New York's governor, **De Witt Clinton,** had urged the building of a canal. The purpose would be to transport both people and goods between the Hudson River and the Great Lakes.

Settlers in western New York and the Great Lakes region had trouble getting their goods to East Coast markets. Roads crossed the Appalachian Mountains in very few places. Those roads more often than not were designed for pack animals, not loaded wagons.

The proposed Erie Canal would be 363 miles (584.1 km) long, the longest in the world. It would connect Troy on the Hudson River with Buffalo on Lake Erie. It was foolish, said critics of the canal, to try to build something so huge. The longest canal in America at the time was just 27 miles (43.4 km) long. But most New York citizens wanted the canal. In 1816 the New York lawmakers voted to build it.

Two lawyers from New York City were named chief **engineers.** As engineers they would be responsible for designing the canal and seeing that it was built. They had some experience surveying, but they knew nothing about building canals. People assumed that the two men could figure out how to build a canal as they went. Americans called this ability to solve practical problems **Yankee know-how.**

The engineers planned the canal to be 40 feet (12.2 m) wide carrying 4 feet (1.2 m) of water. The towpath would be on one side of the canal. Horses pulling the canalboats would walk along the towpath.

Lake Erie is 568 feet (173.1 m) higher than the Hudson River. The

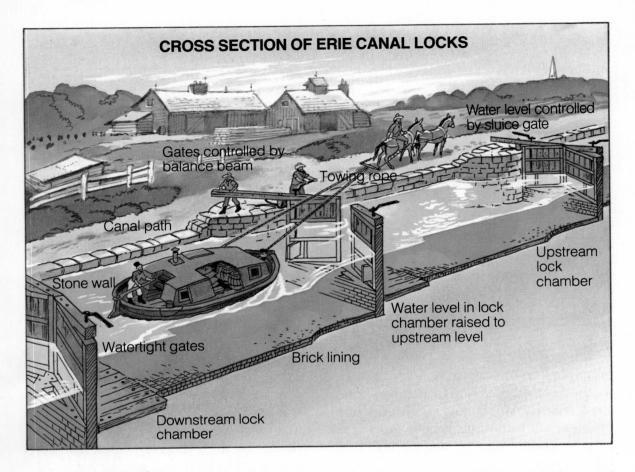

CROSS SECTION OF ERIE CANAL LOCKS

Gates controlled by balance beam

Water level controlled by sluice gate

Towing rope

Canal path

Stone wall

Upstream lock chamber

Watertight gates

Water level in lock chamber raised to upstream level

Brick lining

Downstream lock chamber

main problem they faced was how to get the canal to go uphill. The solution to the problem would be **locks.** The engineers designed 82 locks. A lock is like an elevator of water. In a lock a boat can go to a higher or lower level on the canal.

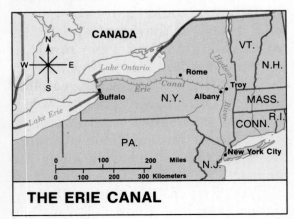

CANADA

VT.

N.H.

Lake Ontario

Rome

Troy

Buffalo

Erie Canal

N.Y.

Albany

MASS.

CONN. R.I.

PA.

New York City

N.J.

0   100   200 Miles

0   100   200   300 Kilometers

THE ERIE CANAL

The builders of the canal invented new machines to deal with their problems. Cutting down each tree in their path took too much time. So they invented a machine that pulled a tree down from its top. The builders also invented a machine that took great roots out of the ground.

Most of the canal was dug by men using shovels, pick axes, and wheelbarrows. Some 3,000 Irish immigrants made up the labor force. Boatloads of Irish immigrants came to New York City. Their hope was to get jobs working on the "Big Ditch." They would be paid 80¢ a day plus meals and lodging. The Irish could hardly believe their luck. Such wages were three times what they could earn at home. The high wages became a magnet that attracted thousands to a new life in America.

The Erie Canal was finished in 1825. Hundreds of canalboats began to haul both passengers and freight. They moved at the grand speed of 4 miles (6.4 km) an hour. People could now travel more easily between the Atlantic Coast and the Midwest. A steady stream of westward moving settlers began to use the Erie Canal.

Freight charges dropped. In 1817 it had taken 20 days to send a ton (907 kg) of wheat from Buffalo to New York City. The cost was $100. By the 1850s it cost $8 and took 8 days. Freight boats hauled grain from Buffalo to the growing cities of the East. On their return journey, the boats carried manufactured goods made in the cities.

The Erie Canal was opening up a transportation route to the heartland of the country. The opening of this route made New York City the leading city in the United States.

Steamboats

While the Erie Canal was being dug, Americans were working on another important problem. This was the problem of moving up mighty rivers. It was easy for farmers to float goods down the Ohio and Mississippi rivers. Farmers used great rafts called **flatboats.** But once the flatboats were downriver,

Horses patiently pulled heavily loaded towboats along the Erie Canal. The boats carried people, grain, and goods.

that was it. They could not return against the river current. The flatboats were sold for lumber in New Orleans. The boatmen had to walk or ride home on horseback. Usually they followed the road called the Natchez Trace.

In 1807 **Robert Fulton** amazed onlookers by chugging up the Hudson River in a steamboat. The **steam engine** had been invented in Britain in the 1700s. A steam engine works by heating water to make steam. The hot steam then drives the machinery. The first steam engines were used to pump water out of mines. Robert Fulton was the first who successfully put a steam engine on a boat. The steam engine turned a paddle wheel, which then pushed the boat through water.

Several years later came the first steamboat trip down the Mississippi. The steamboat *New Orleans* made this first voyage, from Pittsburgh to New Orleans, in 1811. It was probably one of the most difficult trips ever made. Just as the steamboat entered the Mississippi from the Ohio River, it was tossed and thrown about by great waves. The greatest earthquake ever to hit the United States had just struck. The river changed course. Trees toppled pell-mell into the water.

The engine on the *New Orleans* was not powerful enough to drive the boat back up the Mississippi. Yet its voyage showed the possibilities of the steamboat. The man who realized these possibilities was **Henry Miller Shreve.** Shreve designed a more efficient and powerful engine. He installed the engine on a two-deck boat with the paddle wheel in back. Shreve's steamboat could travel up the mighty Mississippi.

By the 1820s great paddle-wheel boats were operating on the Mississippi. They could also be seen on the other large rivers and lakes of the United States. It had taken four months for a flatboat to travel from Pittsburgh to New Orleans. A steamboat could make the trip in a few days.

HOW A STEAM ENGINE WORKS

1. Steam pushes one side of piston.
2. Piston moves flywheel half a turn.

3. Flywheel slides valve. Steam enters and pushes other side of piston.
4. Piston moves flywheel another half a turn. Alternating motion makes power to move other machines.

Coming of the Railroads

Both canals and steamboats were soon challenged by the railroad. Rails had been used for some time to move carts into steep mines. On a Pennsylvania canal, canalboats rode rails to get over hills too steep for locks. Horses and even sails had been used to move rail cars. But it was the steam engine that really made the railroad possible.

The Baltimore and Ohio Railroad was the first American railroad to use a steam locomotive. The railroad switched from horses to steam loco-

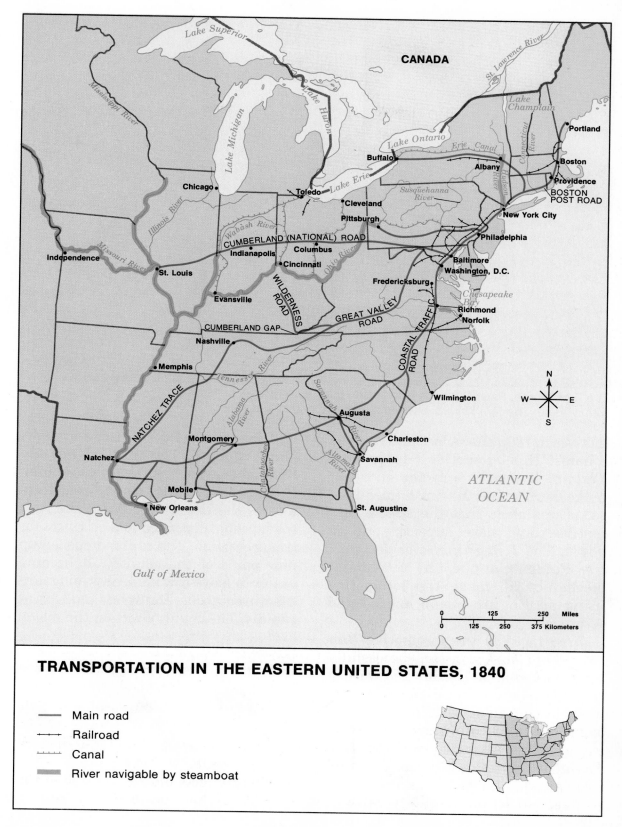

TRANSPORTATION IN THE EASTERN UNITED STATES, 1840

— Main road

+−+− Railroad

···· Canal

▬▬ River navigable by steamboat

CANADA

Lake Superior

Lake Michigan

Lake Huron

Lake Ontario

Lake Erie

St. Lawrence River

Lake Champlain

Connecticut River

Mississippi River

Missouri River

Illinois River

Wabash River

Ohio River

Tennessee River

Alabama River

Chattahoochee River

Altamaha River

Savannah River

Susquehanna River

Hudson River

Erie Canal

BOSTON POST ROAD

CUMBERLAND (NATIONAL) ROAD

WILDERNESS ROAD

CUMBERLAND GAP

GREAT VALLEY ROAD

COASTAL ROAD TRAFFIC

NATCHEZ TRACE

Portland

Boston

Providence

New York City

Philadelphia

Baltimore

Washington, D.C.

Albany

Buffalo

Toledo

Cleveland

Pittsburgh

Chicago

Indianapolis

Columbus

Cincinnati

Independence

St. Louis

Evansville

Nashville

Memphis

Fredericksburg

Richmond

Norfolk

Wilmington

Augusta

Charleston

Montgomery

Savannah

Natchez

Mobile

New Orleans

St. Augustine

Chesapeake Bay

ATLANTIC OCEAN

Gulf of Mexico

N S E W

0 125 250 Miles
0 125 250 375 Kilometers

The *Tom Thumb,* Peter Cooper's locomotive, puffs black smoke in its race with a horse. The *Tom Thumb* lost, but a new age had begun.

motives in 1830 after a locomotive raced a horse. This locomotive was the *Tom Thumb*. It nearly won the race but broke down before the finish line. Even so, it was clear that the steam locomotive could have superior pulling power. The *Tom Thumb* was designed by **Peter Cooper**, a self-taught mechanic. He made the locomotive using an English steam engine and scrap iron.

Also in 1830 the locomotive *Best Friend of Charleston* ran successfully in South Carolina. Doctors had warned that fast speeds would cause human blood to boil. In spite of its speed—up to 30 miles (48.3 km) an hour—the train was a success. After six months the *Best Friend of Charleston* blew up. The train fireman, disliking the hissing of the engine, had sat on the safety-valve.

The coming of the railroad brought many changes. The railroad was the first industry to make heavy use of iron. People, in fact, called the railroad locomotive the Iron Horse. With the railroad, people depended less on rivers for transportation. The railroad opened up new parts of the country. It became easier to move raw materials and manufactured goods. Railroads multiplied rapidly. The country was on the move.

Reading Check

1. Why was the Erie Canal built?
2. What was the effect of the Erie Canal?
3. What were the advantages of river steamboats?
4. What effects did the coming of the railroad have on the country?

2. GROWTH OF MANUFACTURING

To Guide Your Reading

Look for these important words:

Key Words
- technology
- mass production
- interchangeable parts

People
- Samuel Slater
- Francis Cabot Lowell
- Eli Whitney

Look for answers to these questions:

1. What were the first important factories in the United States?
2. How did textile manufacturing develop?
3. What changes did the cotton gin bring about?
4. How did Eli Whitney change American manufacturing?

New methods of transportation made it easier for different parts of the country to specialize. People in the West supplied food crops and raw materials. People in the Northeast began to specialize in manufactured goods.

The textile mills of New England were the first important factories in the United States. These mills turned cotton and wool into thread and the thread into cloth. They were built in New England where swift-running streams turned waterwheels to power machinery.

Getting the right machinery for factories had taken great effort. In the 1700s new inventions in Britain made large textile mills possible. These mills turned out great quantities of thread, yarn, and cloth. The new inventions were secret, however. Britain would allow no one to leave the country with factory designs. It wanted no one else in the world copying its success.

Such laws, however, did not discourage **Samuel Slater,** a young man who worked in the British mills. Hoping to go to America, Slater completely memorized the workings of the machines. His memory was the beginning of the New England textile business. He arrived in America in 1789. From memory he designed a spinning mill for a manufacturer named Moses Brown. In less than two years Brown's mill near Pawtucket, Rhode Island, was in operation. The first workers in this factory were six boys and three girls, all between 7 and 12 years of age.

Later, **Francis Cabot Lowell** of New England developed a new system of organizing factories. Lowell spent two years, from 1810 to 1812, observing British textile mills and factories. Like Samuel Slater, he memorized the workings of the machinery. He also memorized the organization of the spinning, dyeing, and weaving mills.

When Lowell returned to America, he started his own factory. He put the spinning, dyeing, and weaving together under one roof. This was different from the usual practice of having a different factory for each process. In Lowell's mill raw cotton went in one end of the mill and came out as cloth at the other end. Nothing like that had ever been done in Britain or America.

To get workers for the mills, Lowell urged young country women to come work. The women lived in boarding houses and worked 12-hour days. Lowell tried to create healthy and happy living conditions for the women. He was unusual in this, too.

Other manufacturers began to follow Lowell's lead in the way they built factories. They did not, however, show his same concern for people. As the number of factory workers grew, working conditions grew worse.

Eli Whitney's Inventions

American manufacturing was given another important boost by the inventions of **Eli Whitney.** Whitney's inventions led to new **technology.** Technology is using tools and knowledge to achieve practical aims.

A New Englander, Eli Whitney went in 1793 to visit a plantation near Savannah, Georgia. There he heard cotton planters tell how hard it was to prepare cotton for market. The cotton fibers had to be separated from the seeds by hand. It was a slow, tiring process. At that time it took a person all day to clean 1 pound (about 0.5 kg) of cotton. It was like picking burrs from socks and sweaters. As a result, cotton was expensive.

Women and children worked in New England's first textile factories. Here, women are making the looms ready for weaving.

The cotton gin made it easy to separate seed from cotton fiber. It meant profits for the planters as well as a demand for more slaves.

Within ten days Whitney invented the cotton gin. The cotton gin did the work 50 times faster and cleaned the cotton better. Whitney's cotton gin made growing cotton profitable for Southern planters. Soon cotton was "king" of Southern crops. The textile mills of New England wanted all the clean cotton the South could produce.

One effect of Whitney's invention was that slavery became more important than ever. Slavery was dying in other parts of the country. In the South, too, people questioned slavery. But the cotton gin changed all that. The demand for field workers increased.

Another effect of the cotton gin was that cotton cloth became common. People have used and valued cotton for several thousand years. Cotton cloth is soft to the touch and cool to wear. It had always been expensive. After the invention of the cotton gin, cotton cloth was no longer a luxury. It became the commonly used cloth.

Mass Production Started

The cotton gin was only a beginning for the inventive Eli Whitney. Another idea of his would change American manufacturing forever. This

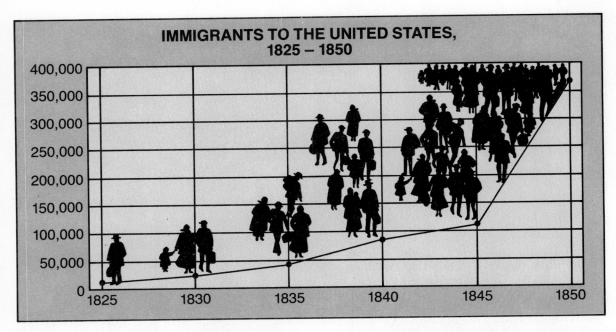

IMMIGRANTS TO THE UNITED STATES, 1825 – 1850

was a new way of manufacturing that could produce huge amounts of goods. We call it **mass production.**

In the old way, a craftsworker made one thing at a time from start to finish. Muskets, for instance, were each made by hand, one at a time. No musket was exactly like any other musket.

Why not make all the musket parts the same and then assemble them? Whitney asked. He presented his idea to the United States government, which then ordered 10,000 muskets. First, Whitney had to make the machines to make the musket parts. When he had 10 muskets, he took them to Washington, D.C. There President John Adams and his Cabinet were amazed at what Whitney showed them. He took the 10 muskets apart, mixed up the parts, then put them back together. These were **interchangeable parts.** Similar parts were identical. Interchangeable parts are the basis of all mass production.

Mass production made it possible to use unskilled workers in factories. No longer was it necessary for a gunsmith to make a musket, or a clockmaker, a clock. Workers could assemble machine-made parts. Using the principle of interchangeable parts, workers could manufacture many more goods than could individual craftsworkers.

By the 1840s thousands of immigrants were taking jobs in the new factories. The populations of cities like New York, Boston, and Baltimore mushroomed. Almost half these immigrants were Irish. Others came from Germany, Poland, and other parts of northern Europe.

Reading Check

1. Where were the first factories in America?
2. Who invented the cotton gin and used the idea of interchangeable parts?
3. Name two effects of the invention of the cotton gin.
4. Why did mass production create jobs for unskilled workers?

3. THE SETTLING OF TEXAS

To Guide Your Reading

Look for these important words:

People
- Stephen Austin
- Sam Houston
- Santa Anna
- William Travis

Places
- Texas
- San Antonio
- Alamo

Look for answers to these questions:

1. Why did Americans first go to Texas?
2. How did relations between the Mexican government and American settlers change?
3. Why is the Battle of the Alamo famous?
4. How did Texas win independence from Mexico?

The thousands heading west on the Erie Canal in 1825 were a trickle compared to what followed. Full of energy, always on the move, people began to push beyond the country's borders.

Land-hungry Americans had looked longingly at **Texas,** which was part of Mexico. In 1821 Mexico won its independence from Spain. In the same year Mexico allowed a group of Americans to settle in Texas. These settlers were led by **Stephen Austin.** The new settlers pledged loyalty to Mexico and became Roman Catholics in return for grants of land.

Texas was larger than the nation of France. It had rich coastal plains, rolling hills, prairies, forests, and deserts. Here was a good place to raise cotton, wheat, and cattle. Soon there were far more North Americans than Mexicans in Texas.

Concerned about the numbers of Americans in Texas, Mexico tried to tighten its control. First it tried to keep people from moving there. Then it tried to stop slavery, which was illegal in Mexico. Finally, Mexican officials tried to make the Texans give up their guns. The Texans revolted. For a leader they turned to **Sam Houston.**

Sam Houston had come to Texas from Tennessee. There he was a close friend of the Cherokees and had been adopted into their tribe. He had fought in the War of 1812 under Andrew Jackson. He had served as governor of Tennessee.

Santa Anna, the president of Mexico, sent troops to Texas to put down the revolt. In early December 1835, 300 Texans entered **San Antonio** late at night. Their plan was to attack the Mexican troops at dawn. The Mexicans flew a red flag. It meant that no mercy would be shown to the enemies of Mexico. After five days of furious fighting, the Mexicans raised a white flag—the flag of surrender. The Mexican forces then departed for Mexico.

Sam Houston became leader of the Texans in their fight for independence from Mexico.

Davy Crockett, famous frontiersman, met death at the Battle of the Alamo.

Fight at the Alamo

A small group of Texans remained in the **Alamo,** an old San Antonio mission. These men were using the mission as a fort. Their commander was **William Travis.** It was not expected that the Mexicans would attack again until spring.

Thus it was a surprise on February 23, 1836, when a guard hollered that thousands of Mexican soldiers were coming. This time Santa Anna himself led the force. There were at least 4,000 soldiers. Santa Anna was a handsome man who sat well on his gold-stamped saddle. He was a man of strong will. The Texans, he had decided, would not get away with their revolt. Again they flew the red flag.

For 11 days fewer than 200 Texans successfully fought off the Mexican assault. Besides Travis, there were Davy Crockett from Tennessee and sharpshooter "Deaf" Smith. Jim Bowie, a famous frontiersman, lay sick in the chapel. Susanna Dickinson, wife of one of the defenders, nursed him and the wounded men.

Travis knew the fort was doomed. The Texans were running out of powder and cannonballs. Calling his men together, Travis drew a line in front of them and challenged them. "I now call upon every man who is determined to stay here and die with me to come across this line. Who will be first? March!" All but one did.

On March 6, the twelfth day of the siege, 2,500 Mexican soldiers attacked the Alamo. They used ladders to scale its walls. Fighting became hand to hand. One after another, the Texans were killed. When the soldiers burst

Fighting for independence, Texans fought to the death when Mexican soldiers attacked them at the Alamo. In this picture of the attack, considered to be quite accurate, the Texas flag still flies.

into the chapel, Jim Bowie defended himself from his sick bed. But he, too, was killed.

Within 24 hours it was all over. The force of 183 Texans had been killed. More than 1,000 Mexicans had also died. Santa Anna spared the lives of Susanna Dickinson, her child, several women servants, and two boy slaves.

Texas Becomes Independent

Six weeks after the fall of the Alamo, the Texans struck back. Sam Houston led Texan troops to attack Santa Anna's forces near the San Jacinto (juh•SINT•oh) River. As they bore down on the Mexican army, the Texans yelled their battle cry: "Remember the Alamo." Santa Anna was captured in the battle. His army was forced to retreat to Mexico.

Texas had declared its independence of Mexico on March 2, 1836. Texas remained an independent republic until it became a state in 1845. Sam Houston served as president and then governor of Texas.

Reading Check

1. Who was Stephen Austin?
2. In what ways did Mexico try to tighten its control over Texas?
3. What happened when Texans refused to obey Mexican laws?
4. What happened at the Battle of the Alamo?

4. OREGON, UTAH, AND CALIFORNIA

To Guide Your Reading

Look for these important words:

Key Words
- Mormons
- forty-niners

People
- Marcus and Narcissa Whitman
- Brigham Young

- James K. Polk
- Johann Sutter
- James Marshall

Places
- Oregon Country
- Cape Horn
- Oregon Trail

- Independence
- South Pass
- St. Louis
- Great Salt Lake
- Utah territory
- California
- Rio Grande
- Sacramento River valley

Look for answers to these questions:

1. How was Oregon Country settled?
2. Who were the Mormons? Where did they settle?
3. What territory did the U.S. acquire from Mexico? By what means?
4. Why did people rush to settle in California?

After Lewis and Clark, the first Americans to go by land to **Oregon Country** were fur traders. Oregon Country included present-day Oregon, Washington, and British Columbia. It was claimed by both Britain and the United States.

The surest way to get to the Pacific coast was to sail around **Cape Horn.** This long and difficult voyage around the tip of South America took six to eight months. Yet Yankee traders regularly sailed this route. They traded for cattle hides and tallow with the Mexican ranchers in California. Farther north they traded with the Indians for furs.

The overland route taken by Lewis and Clark was long and hard. In 1812 an American fur trader found an easier route. The new trail, called the **Oregon Trail,** led northwest from **Independence,** Missouri, to the Platte River. It followed the Platte River to what is now Wyoming. There, at **South Pass,** it crossed the Continental Divide. On the western side of the Rocky Mountains, the trail followed first the Snake River, then the Columbia River. The end of the trail was the Willamette (wuh•LAM•uht) valley of Oregon.

Among the first pioneers in Oregon Country were **Marcus and Narcissa Whitman.** They were missionaries who made the difficult journey west in 1836. They then established a mission in the Walla Walla valley. Their mission was near the homes of the Cayuse (KY•yuhs), Nez Perce (NEZ PUHRS), and Flathead Indians.

The first settlers in Oregon Country reported lush valleys, wooded hills,

News of timberlands, rich soil, and sparkling streams in Oregon lured pioneers like these across the vast spaces of the continent.

and fertile soil. Here was land Easterners could dream of farming. It was not like the treeless Great Plains. Easterners associated good farming land with wooded land. If trees grew, they reasoned, then crops would. In 1843 the first large group of pioneers headed for Oregon. In the next few years thousands more followed.

On the Oregon Trail

Travelers to the West usually gathered in **St. Louis,** Missouri, called the Gateway to the West. From St. Louis they traveled up the Missouri River by steamboat to Independence. In Independence they organized themselves in wagon trains to cross the "prairie ocean." The wagons were similar to Conestoga wagons, but smaller. Travelers were protected by white canvas covers. Because the pioneers thought of the grasslands as a kind of ocean, the covered wagons were nicknamed "Prairie Schooners." A schooner is a kind of sailing ship.

With the coming of spring, the wagon trains headed west across the flower-dotted plains. These plains were "too wide for the eye to measure," wrote one traveler, Francis Parkman. "One day we rode on for hours, without seeing a tree or bush." He saw only an "unbroken carpet of fresh green grass."

What a hard trip this was! The sun was like a fireball. Fresh water was scarce. Sudden storms drenched the

321

travelers. Wagons broke down. Rivers had to be crossed. Valuable farm animals stumbled into prairie-dog holes and broke their legs. Parkman wrote:

When thirsty with a long ride in the scorching sun over some boundless reach of prairie, the traveler comes at length to a pool of water. He alights to drink—only to discover a troop of young tadpoles sporting in the bottom of his cup.

The trip took at least three months and often as long as six months. These pioneers put up with great hardship for the hope of good farmland and a fresh start.

Travelers on the Oregon Trail often stopped at the mission of Marcus and Narcissa Whitman. Some travelers had measles, a disease new to the Indians. By August 1847 half the Cayuse Indians had died of measles. Marcus Whitman did what he could to treat the Cayuse, but they stopped trusting him. They began to believe that his medicine was poison. In November 1847 the Cayuse killed the Whitmans and others at the mission.

The Mormons Settle Utah

In 1846 the **Mormons,** a religious group, joined the migration across America. Under the leadership of Joseph Smith, they had first settled in Nauvoo, Illinois. Their religious beliefs caused problems with neighboring settlers. In 1844 a mob killed Joseph Smith. His successor, **Brigham Young,**

Pulling handcarts containing all their possessions, thousands of Mormons head across the Plains to Utah, which they called Deseret.

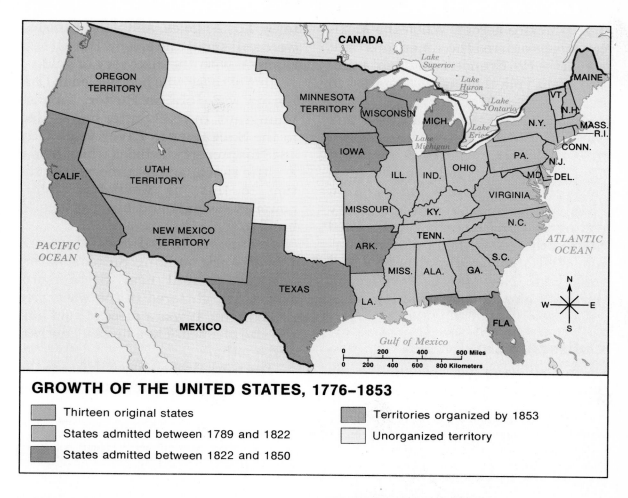

GROWTH OF THE UNITED STATES, 1776–1853

- Thirteen original states
- States admitted between 1789 and 1822
- States admitted between 1822 and 1850
- Territories organized by 1853
- Unorganized territory

decided that the Mormons should move to a place where no one would bother them. In 1846 the first group of Mormons started on the overland route to the **Great Salt Lake.**

Under the stern, strong leadership of Brigham Young, the Mormons quickly organized the **Utah Territory.**

One of the first things the Mormons did was build irrigation canals. The canals brought plentiful water from the mountains to the desert plains surrounding Great Salt Lake. The Mormons made the Salt Lake desert bloom with produce, grain, and grass. Soon they were selling supplies to other pioneers headed west.

The Mexican War

When the Mormons settled near Salt Lake, that land belonged to Mexico. In 1848, only two years later, it would become part of the United States.

James K. Polk had been elected President in 1845. His supporters wanted to see the United States expand to the Pacific Ocean. They thought that Texas, Oregon, and **California** should all be part of the United States. Indeed, Texas became a state soon after Polk's election. Polk and his followers particularly wanted California.

In January 1846 President Polk sent American troops south into Mexico. They crossed the **Rio Grande,** the

Texas-Mexico border. When the Mexican troops ordered the Americans back across the Rio Grande, shooting started. President Polk then asked Congress to declare war on Mexico.

The United States Army won this war with Mexico by invading Mexico in 1847. The army marched from Vera Cruz to Mexico City following the same route Hernando Cortés had taken. In 1848 Mexico signed a peace treaty ending the war. In the treaty the United States acquired far more than California. It also got land that is now Arizona, Utah, New Mexico, Nevada, and parts of Colorado and Wyoming.

California Gold Rush

In California most people lived on sprawling ranches. Towns like Monterey, Los Angeles, and San Francisco were still small and sleepy. But all this changed with the discovery of gold.

One of those who had settled in California was **Johann Sutter,** a Swiss immigrant. In 1839 Sutter had settled in the **Sacramento River valley.** By 1848 his property included wheat fields, a cattle ranch, and a tannery. In addition to this, he wanted a water-powered sawmill and hired people to build it.

In January 1848 **James Marshall** was at work building Sutter's water-powered sawmill near Sacramento. Something glittered in the water. He picked it up. It was a piece of gold half the size of a pea. Then he saw another, and another.

The news flashed like wildfire to the East. Gold! As in times past, this sim-

San Francisco boomed as goldminers poured into California. Along the waterfront, abandoned ships became stores, hotels, and businesses.

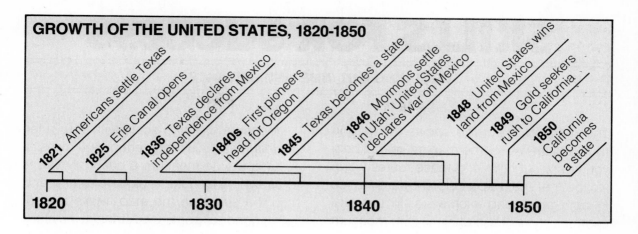

GROWTH OF THE UNITED STATES, 1820-1850

1821 Americans settle Texas
1825 Erie Canal opens
1836 Texas declares independence from Mexico
1840s First pioneers head for Oregon
1845 Texas becomes a state
1846 Mormons settle in Utah; United States declares war on Mexico
1848 United States wins land from Mexico
1849 Gold seekers rush to California
1850 California becomes a state

1820 · 1830 · 1840 · 1850

ple word drew all who were footloose and adventurous, all who dreamed of quick riches.

Sutter's employees themselves caught the fever. They stopped working and started looking for gold. The sawmill was never finished. "Everybody left me from the clerk to the cook," Sutter complained. From his point of view, worse was to come. Soon thousands of people swarmed over his land. They shot and ate his cattle. They claimed his land. They made him into a poor man.

Ninety thousand gold seekers came to California in 1849. These were the **forty-niners.** Most traveled the overland trail and then branched south across the Nevada desert to California. These travelers faced scorching heat of the desert and steep passes in the mountains. The longer but easier way was to come by water around Cape Horn. Forty-niners came in anything that would float. When they arrived in San Francisco Bay, everyone hot-footed it to the gold fields. By 1850 more than 500 ships lay rotting and forgotten in San Francisco Bay. Some were later used as floating hotels, restaurants, and even a prison.

The California gold rush stimulated the building of the clipper ships. These were the fastest and most beautiful ships to sail the seas. The first clipper ships were designed to bring fresh tea from China as quickly as possible. Time was just as important in the gold rush. Gold-seekers were impatient to reach California and would pay to get there faster. Merchants could make huge profits by quickly getting food supplies to San Francisco. Clipper ships reduced the journey around Cape Horn from eight months to three months.

California filled with new people. By 1850, just one year after the gold rush, California had become a state.

Reading Check

1. Why did Marcus and Narcissa Whitman travel west?
2. Describe at least three problems faced by pioneers on the Oregon Trail.
3. By what means did the United States acquire California, Nevada, Utah, and New Mexico?
4. Why did thousands travel to California in 1849?

SKILLS FOR SUCCESS

FIGURING OUT TIME AND DISTANCE

The map on this page shows the wagon routes to the West. The map scale can help you figure out how long these routes were. Notice that the map scale shows distance in both miles and kilometers. In this skill exercise you will use only miles to measure distance.

Measure the map scale with your ruler. On this map 1¼ inches equal 400 miles.

One way to measure a curving route is to use a string. Take a piece of string and hold the string on the map. Make a mark with a pencil or pen on the string at the starting place. Then use the string to follow the

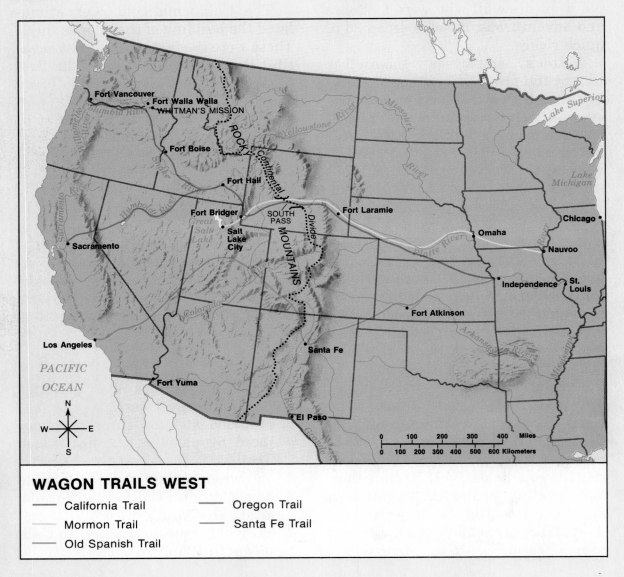

WAGON TRAILS WEST

—— California Trail   —— Oregon Trail

—— Mormon Trail   —— Santa Fe Trail

—— Old Spanish Trail

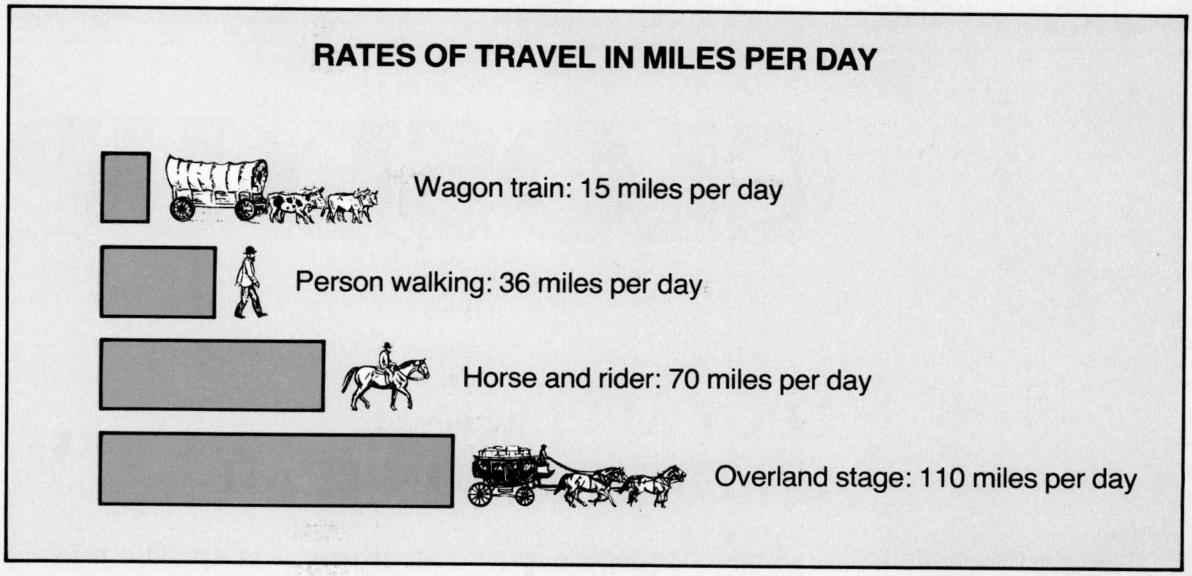

RATES OF TRAVEL IN MILES PER DAY

Wagon train: 15 miles per day

Person walking: 36 miles per day

Horse and rider: 70 miles per day

Overland stage: 110 miles per day

route. Make another mark on the string at the ending place. Place the string against the map scale. You can measure off the distance by making a mark for every 400 miles.

Use a string to measure the distance between Independence and Fort Vancouver along the Oregon Trail. Then mark off the string into 400-mile marks. You should have four 400-mile marks. How many miles does that stand for? The last part of your string measure is less than 1¼ inches. Hold it to the map scale and guess the number of miles it stands for. To figure out the distance between Independence and Fort Vancouver, add the miles represented by each part marked on the string.

The chart above shows travel rates for different forms of transportation.

The first pioneers traveled in covered wagons. They went about 15 miles per day. How many days did it take to get from Independence to Fort Vancouver by wagon? To find out, divide the total number of miles by the rate of travel. Let us assume your mileage figure is 1700 miles. If you divide that by 15, you get a round number of 113. It took pioneers about 113 days to get from Independence, Missouri to Fort Vancouver by wagon.

Use a string to measure the route between Santa Fe and Los Angeles. How long would it take to make this journey by stagecoach?

CHECKING YOUR SKILLS

Use the map and chart to answer these questions.

1. About how long did it take a covered wagon to travel 600 miles?

2. About how many miles was Salt Lake City from Sacramento, California?

3. About how many days would it take a horse and rider to go from Independence to Fort Laramie?

4. About how far was Santa Fe from Fort Atkinson?

5. About how many miles long was the California Trail? About how many days would it take to walk the California Trail?

CLOSE-UP

LUCY APPLEGATE ON THE OREGON TRAIL

Lucy Applegate knew something was up. The minute the Missouri teenager walked into the house, she sensed something special was happening. Her father, Lindsay Applegate, was in the kitchen with Uncle Charles and Uncle Jesse. They all seemed very excited. They were talking about leaving Missouri for the new land of Oregon!

Uncle Jesse, a lanky six-footer, did a lot of the talking. He was going on about how difficult farming had become in Missouri. Bacon prices had dropped. Wheat was down to 15 cents a bushel. You could not give the corn away. Uncle Charles said he had heard the grass grew as high as your eye in Oregon. Lucy heard her dad complain about how Missouri had changed since the slave owners had come. Her family would have nothing to do with slavery.

The decision was made quickly. The families of Jesse, Charles, and Lindsay Applegate were going west on the Oregon Trail! Lucy was thrilled. So were her brothers and her many cousins.

The Applegate families all sold their farms to raise money for the trip. Some of the money was used to buy a few hundred head of cattle. The rest of the money was used to make covered wagons.

The brothers built the wooden boxes for the wagons themselves. They used only well-seasoned hardwoods. Each box measured about 10 feet (3.1 m) long, 4 feet (1.2 m) wide, and 2 feet (0.6 m) deep. The brothers then built arched frames on top of the wagon boxes to support canvas covers. A blacksmith and wheelmaker put together the wagons' moving parts, including the wheels and axles.

Lucy's father placed an advertisement in a local newspaper. The ad invited other families in the area to join the move to Oregon. The idea was to leave from the little town of Elm Grove, Missouri, on May 22, 1843.

On the evening of May 21, the wagons started pouring into Elm Grove. Lucy was astonished to see the huge crowd that had gathered to go west. Uncle Jesse guessed that 1,000 people were going—400 adults and about 600 children. Charles pointed out one of the men to Lucy. His name was Baptiste Charbonneau (SHAHR•bon•noh). He was the son of Sacajawea, the Indian guide. Baptiste had been born on the trail during the Lewis and Clark expedition.

A sea of animals accompanied the wagons. There were horses, mules, oxen, beef cattle, and milk cows, not to mention all the dogs.

Lucy went for an evening walk among the wagons. Their canvas covers looked beautiful in the light of the full moon. Lucy peeked inside one of the wagons her father had built. The sides were packed high with supplies and personal belongings. A narrow walkway remained down the middle of the wagon. The frame was just tall enough for a grown-up to stand in the walkway. Lucy's mother had sewn pockets in the canvas cover to hold ammunition, hairbrushes, medicines, and other things.

The next morning the wagons set out. Uncle Jesse rode on horseback and kept the cattle moving. After a few miles of bouncing around in the slow-moving wagon, Lucy decided to walk. It seemed as if most people in the wagon train agreed with her choice.

In the afternoon Lucy took all the Applegate youngsters on a romp to pick wildflowers. They had no trouble catching up again with the poky wagons.

After a few days the wagons reached the Kansas River. There, where Topeka, Kansas, now stands, the train decided to elect a leader. Lucy watched, fascinated. The men who wanted to be leader started out walking across the prairie. People then followed the person of their choice. The person with the longest line of followers was elected leader. The winner was Peter Burnett. He later became governor of California. Uncle Jesse was chosen to lead the families who had brought large numbers of cattle.

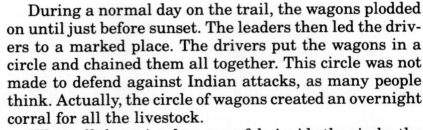

During a normal day on the trail, the wagons plodded on until just before sunset. The leaders then led the drivers to a marked place. The drivers put the wagons in a circle and chained them all together. This circle was not made to defend against Indian attacks, as many people think. Actually, the circle of wagons created an overnight corral for all the livestock.

When all the animals were safely inside the circle, the women started making dinner. Lucy and her friends went to collect fuel for the fire. In the great prairie there was very little firewood. The most common fuel was dried pieces of buffalo dung. These pieces were called buffalo chips.

Lucy was surprised by the bright, clean, odorless flame the buffalo chips made. The biggest problem with the chips was the fights that started during the collections. Sometimes children would steal from each other's piles. That would bring about great fights and shouting matches. Pretty soon the chips would be flying all over the place.

Somehow dinner was cooked every night. Lucy's mother liked to serve potatoes, squash, or rice with buffalo, beef, or deer meat. Occasionally the men would catch trout or catfish. The Applegates always had plenty of dairy products. The jostling wagons turned the milk cows' daily offerings into rich, golden butter.

Sometimes for a special treat, mother baked a pie using dried fruit brought from Missouri. The men all loved to drink coffee with their pie. It seemed as if Uncle Jesse could drink gallons of coffee.

As the evening sky darkened, the sounds of music drifted through the camp. Fiddles, harmonicas, and flutes played "O Susanna" and "She'll Be Comin' Round the Mountain." Lucy and the other young people danced in the twinkling starlight.

By eight o'clock the guards were on duty. By nine, the whole camp was quiet. The only sounds were an occasional whinny or the barking of a dog.

Some mornings Lucy felt she had just fallen asleep when the wake-up shots were fired. Every morning the guards fired their guns into the air at four o'clock. By the time the sun had risen, the wagon train was off again. Making another hard-earned 15 or 20 miles (about 24 or 32 km) was a daily goal.

One day Uncle Jesse rode off in a great hurry with the train's doctor, Marcus Whitman. Jesse returned that afternoon with a big smile on his face. He announced that he and Dr. Whitman had helped Mrs. Stewart deliver a beautiful baby. This baby was the first born on the trail. "Born on the Oregon Trail," Lucy said to herself. "What a baby that will be!"

Lucy was very glad Dr. Whitman was along. When someone was sick or injured, Dr. Whitman always knew what to do. Lucy did not worry about sickness. There was a lot more sickness in the cities than on the Oregon Trail. So her father said.

After many weeks the wagons climbed from the plains into the Rocky Mountains. Buffalo became scarce. Lucy began to collect sagebrush instead of buffalo chips for fuel.

Lucy could feel the air get thinner as the trail continued to climb. The air was so dry! Lucy's lips became chapped and sore. She heard her mother complain about how long it now took to boil rice or potatoes.

Then the wagons passed through a place Jesse called Great South Pass. Lucy noticed that something was strange. All the creeks and streams had started to flow in a new direction. Before, the water had run to the east, toward the rising sun. Now, the water flowed west, toward the setting sun. Lindsay explained that the wagon train had just crossed the Continental Divide. From there on, all the streams flowed into the Pacific Ocean, not the Atlantic Ocean. The Pacific Ocean! Just the name made Lucy dizzy with excitement.

331

After leaving South Pass, the Applegates found the journey even more difficult. The wagons had to struggle over giant boulders, wind through steep canyons, and cross swift rivers. Sometimes Lucy thought they would not make it. Somehow Lindsay, Uncle Jesse, and the others always kept the train moving.

A man named Mr. Eyres drowned while the wagons crossed the mighty Snake River. Lucy felt so sorry for his wife and children. What would she ever do without her father and uncles?

The roughest stretch for the Applegate train was the cruel trek through the Blue Mountains. The forests were thick and scary. The hills seemed impossibly steep. It took 40 men five full days to cut a path. Finally the wagons reached the top. There Stickus, Dr. Whitman's Indian guide, raised his arms thankfully to the heavens. Uncle Jesse pointed excitedly to Mt. Hood and other snowy peaks on the horizon. They had made it to Oregon!

Amazingly, this huge wagon train had stayed together nearly all the way across the country. Then, when the pioneers reached the great Columbia River, the wagon train began to split up.

At Fort Walla Walla the Applegates decided to sell their cattle to a trading post. The brothers then built boats to ride down the river. To do so, they sawed boards from huge driftwood logs.

The river trip started well, but soon disaster struck the Applegate family. Just before reaching a dangerous waterfall, the lead boat crashed into a rock and splintered. Lucy's younger brother and her ten-year-old cousin were both drowned.

Lucy was heartbroken. She cried until she could not cry anymore. She told her father she did not like Oregon. She wanted to go home. Still, the family had to go on. Jesse and Lindsay led their brave little band downriver. They aimed for the fertile Willamette valley, a place they would eventually call home.

They reached the place where the Columbia and the Willamette rivers meet. Lucy was lost in thought, remembering the deaths of her brother and cousin. She thought about how tired she felt, how weary her mother and father looked. She thought about this strange new land. She thought about her friends back in Missouri.

Lucy was also able to realize the joys of her great journey. She remembered the feathery grass of Grand Ronde valley and the buffalo stampede near Fort Laramie. She remembered the boys trying to plug a hot-springs geyser with their hats. She recalled the wildflowers and the spectacular showers of falling stars. She wanted to laugh and to cry at the same time.

Lucy's boat passed an ocean-going schooner of the Hudson's Bay Company. One of the English sailors saw the sad-looking young lady with tears in her eyes. He called out to her, saying she was beautiful. Then he tossed her a red, shiny apple.

Lucy smiled back at the sailor. The darkness of her brother's death left her heart. She wiped away her tears of sorrow and set about starting a new life.

333

CHAPTER 14 REVIEW

WORDS TO USE

Explain the meaning of each of the words below. Then use each word in a complete sentence.

1. **canal locks**
2. **interchangeable parts**
3. **mass production**
4. **technology**

FACTS TO REVIEW

1. Describe three effects of the Erie Canal.

2. How did Robert Fulton and Henry Miller Shreve each contribute to the development of the steamboat?

3. What was the importance of the race between the *Tom Thumb* and a horse?

4. Which two men helped establish textile mills in New England?

5. How did the invention of the cotton gin encourage the growth of textile mills in New England?

6. How did Eli Whitney's idea of interchangeable parts bring about a new way of manufacturing?

7. What happened when Mexican troops attacked the Alamo?

8. Why did people head west on the Oregon Trail?

9. What territory did the United States gain as a result of the Mexican War?

10. Why did the gold rush encourage the development of clipper ships?

IDEAS TO DISCUSS

1. How did the Erie Canal encourage the growth of New York City?

2. Why did the railroad mark the beginning of a new age? How did peoples' lives change with the railroad? In what ways does new technology change our lives today?

3. What was it like to cross the country in a wagon train? What problems did travelers face? Why did people cross the country?

4. How did new inventions help bring about: growth of the country, growth of cities, growth of manufacturing, growth of slavery?

◯ SKILLS PRACTICE

Figuring Out Time and Distance   Use the map on page 326 and the Rates of Travel chart on page 327 to answer the following questions.

1. About how many days would it take a wagon train to travel from Fort Bridger to the Whitman mission?

2. About how long would it take to cover the same distance on horseback?

3. Did it generally take a covered wagon more or less than 35 days to travel from Salt Lake City to Fort Vancouver?

4. About how many days would it take to go on horseback from Independence to Los Angeles?

UNIT 5 REVIEW

WORDS TO REMEMBER

Number your paper from 1 to 10. For each term below select the correct definition from the list that follows.

1. **compromise**
2. **democracy**
3. **executive**
4. **federal**
5. **legislative**
6. **mass production**
7. **neutral**
8. **republic**
9. **survey**
10. **technology**

a. Not taking sides

b. Give up some of what one wants in order to reach agreement

c. A form of government in which power is shared between states and the national government

d. A word meaning "rule by the people"

e. Make land measurements

f. A kind of manufacturing in which unskilled factory workers assemble interchangeable parts

g. A new way of doing things as a result of a new invention

h. A form of government in which elected representatives rule

i. The lawmaking part of a government

j. The part of the government headed by the President

FOCUS ON MAIN IDEAS

1. What compromises did delegates to the Constitutional Convention make when writing the Constitution?

2. What are the main responsibilities of each of the three branches of government?

3. How does the Constitution give strong powers to the national government and yet protect the liberties of the people?

4. Pioneers did not all share the same goals. Tell *where* each of the following people settled and *why*.

   a. Daniel Boone
   b. Stephen Austin
   c. Marcus and Narcissa Whitman
   d. Brigham Young
   e. Johann Sutter

5. The United States had troubled relations with both Britain and Mexico. What was the cause of troubles with Britain? with Mexico? What wars were fought? What was the outcome?

6. Explain how each of these people contributed to the growth of the United States: Samuel Slater, Henry Miller Shreve, DeWitt Clinton, and Eli Whitney.

7. Why was the steam engine so important in the nineteenth century?

8. In what ways did the United States become more democratic by 1850? How was the nation not democratic?

9. How did manufacturing, the growth of cities, and the frontier all create a need for better transportation?

10. How did new methods of transportation help tie parts of the country together?

ACTIVITIES

1. **Research/Art** Learn more about how steam engines work and how they were used. Draw or show pictures of what you learned.

2. **Research/Writing** Learn more about transportation in the early nineteenth century. You might choose canals, flatboats, steamboats, or railroads. Write a report on what you learn.

3. **Mapmaking/Art** Make a picture map of the western United States. On your map include: the Alamo, the Whitman mission, prairie schooners on the Oregon Trail, forty-niners, the Mormon settlement, steamboats on the Missouri River.

4. **Reading/Acting** Many stories have been written about pioneers such as Daniel Boone, Davy Crockett, and Sam Houston. With other students, read more about a pioneer of your choice. Then act out a scene from that person's life.

5. **Creative Writing** Rebecca Boone was Daniel Boone's wife. Imagine what her life was like during Daniel Boone's long absences. What skills and strengths would she need? Write about her life as you imagine it.

6. **Research** Find out more about the naval battles of the War of 1812. You may want to do one of these:

   a. Draw or paint a picture of a battle.
   b. Give a report on a naval battle.
   c. Make a map showing where naval battles were fought.

7. **Timeline** Make a timeline showing *one* of the following:

   a. Major inventions in the United States, 1790–1850

   b. Major steps in the growth of transportation systems, 1790–1850
   c. The Growth of the United States: New States and Territories, 1776–1850

8. **Remembering the Close-Up** With several others, act out a scene from *Lucy Applegate on the Oregon Trail.*

◯ SKILLS REVIEW

Figuring Out Time and Distance   Use the map to answer the questions that follow.

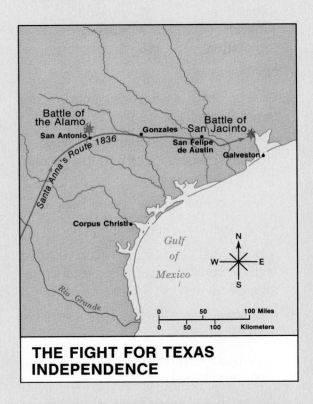

THE FIGHT FOR TEXAS INDEPENDENCE

1. How far did Santa Anna travel between the Rio Grande and San Antonio? At 75 miles a day, how long did it take him?

2. From San Antonio was it farther to Corpus Christi or to San Felipe de Austin?

3. How many miles did Santa Anna travel between San Antonio and the battle site of San Jacinto?

YOUR STATE'S HISTORY

After the American Revolution the young American nation grew by leaps and bounds. The population of the United States jumped from about 4 million in 1790 to about 23 million in 1850. The amount of land in the United States more than tripled.

In the East cities grew as trade and manufacturing increased. In 1790 New York and Philadelphia were the only large cities. By 1840, 13 cities had populations of more than 20,000 people. Thousands of these people were recent immigrants.

In the West settlers advanced into the areas first explored by Lewis and Clark. The discovery of gold in California speeded up the settling of the West. The following activities will help you learn about the history of your state during this exciting time.

LEARNING ABOUT TECHNOLOGY

1. In the early nineteenth century our country experienced a transportation revolution. New roads were built for travel by stagecoach. Canals, like the Erie Canal, helped connect the states by water. Steamboats journeyed on great rivers. Railroads provided a new kind of quick, powerful transportation. They carried both raw materials and manufactured products. Learn about your state's first transportation systems and industries. Were there towns that became important as stops for wagon trains, canals, steamboats, or railroads? Were there towns that grew because of increased trade or manufacturing?

LEARNING ABOUT PEOPLE

2. Was your state settled between 1789 and 1850? Where did people first settle and what did they do? Write a report about the pioneer settlers of your state.

3. Did people settle in your state between 1789 and 1850? If so, where did they come from?

LEARNING ABOUT CULTURE

4. The early years of the westward movement are the source of many wonderful stories. Some of them are real stories. Some of them are tall tales like those told about Pecos Bill or Paul Bunyan. Are there stories about your state in its early days? Draw pictures to go with one of these stories.

LEARNING ABOUT GEOGRAPHY

5. Between 1789 and 1850 many states sent farm products and raw materials to manufacturing states. During these years was your state a manufacturing state or an agricultural state? What were its principal products? How important is agriculture to your state today? manufacturing?

6. In colonial times the trade centers were ocean ports. In the nineteenth century cities developed inland. What were the important towns or cities in your state before 1850? Why were they important? Are they still important? Why?

UNIT SIX

THE NATION DIVIDED

The first half of the nineteenth century was a time of hope and enthusiasm for most Americans. It was a sunny time in American history. Yet there were dark storm clouds on the horizon. People were divided over serious issues, including slavery. In 1861 these divisions turned into the **Civil War.** A civil war is a war between parts of the same country. In the American Civil War, the country was split apart, with North fighting South. The Civil War was one of the saddest, darkest times in American history.

Abraham Lincoln was President during the Civil War. This statue of Lincoln is part of the Lincoln Memorial in Washington, D.C. In Lincoln's face we can see sadness and concern. Like most Americans, he loved his country and grieved when it was torn in two.

In this unit you will read about some of the causes of the Civil War. You will read about the kind of war it was and how the North won.

339

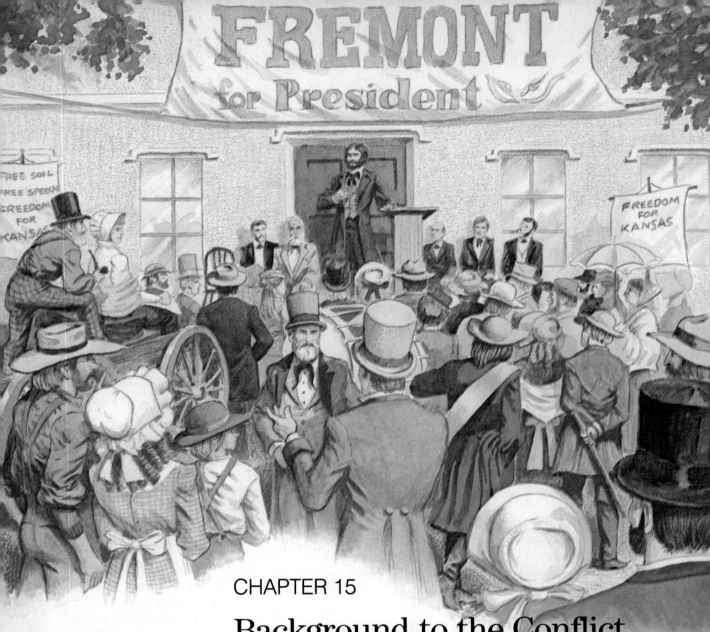

CHAPTER 15

Background to the Conflict

About
this
chapter

The Civil War was fought between the northern and southern sections of our country. The roots of the Civil War went deep into the American experience. Different ways of life had developed in the North and South. North and South tried to work out solutions to their disagreements. These solutions were compromises. They worked for a while, but finally even compromise was impossible.

This chapter describes the disagreements between North and South that led to the Civil War.

1. DIVISIONS BETWEEN NORTH AND SOUTH

To Guide Your Reading

Look for these important words:

Key Words
- tariff
- free states
- abolish

- abolitionists
- fugitives
- Underground Railroad
- stations

People
- Nat Turner
- Frederick Douglass
- Harriet Tubman

Look for answers to these questions:

1. What general concerns divided North and South?
2. How did feelings differ about slavery?
3. What was the Underground Railroad?
4. How did Frederick Douglass and Harriet Tubman each work against slavery?

While the nation was expanding, strong differences were developing between the North and the South. The textile mills and new factories were making the North a center of manufacturing, banking, and trade. Hundreds of thousands of immigrants were arriving from Europe. These immigrants worked in the factories and lived in the cities.

As in colonial days, Southern life continued to center around agriculture. The invention of the cotton gin in 1793 made cotton a profitable crop. Southern planters began growing tens of thousands of acres of cotton. They kept looking for new land on which to raise cotton. By 1830 cotton had become the most important crop in the South. The raw cotton went to textile mills in both Britain and New England.

In Congress, the South favored laws that would help its interests, including agriculture. The North favored laws that would help manufacturing and trade. For instance, the North wanted a high **tariff,** or tax on imported goods. Imported goods would then cost more than goods made in the United States. People would then buy goods made in the United States, and American manufacturing would grow.

The South had little manufacturing of its own. Southerners bought manufactured goods made in Britain or in the northern United States. Southerners wanted to pay the lowest possible price for manufactured goods. Southerners, therefore, did not like tariffs on imported goods.

Division over Slavery

Most planters used slaves to do the hard work. This included planting, hoeing, harvesting, and cleaning cotton. The increasing importance of cotton led to the growth of slavery. In 1820 there were about 1.5 million slaves in the South. By 1860 the number had

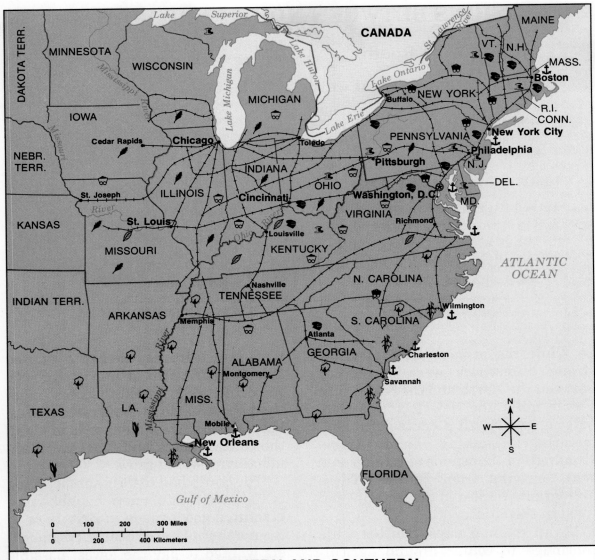

RESOURCES OF THE NORTHERN AND SOUTHERN STATES BEFORE 1860

Northern states and territories	⚓ Port	🦅 Iron ore
Southern states and territories	⚓ Port	🌾 Rice
⚓ Port	🌿 Sugar cane
Railroad	🐚 Textile manufacturing
Coal	Tobacco
Cotton	Wheat
Iron and steel works	

342

increased to nearly 4 million slaves. In 1820 the price of a good field hand was several hundred dollars. By 1860 the price had risen to a thousand dollars. Slaves were extremely valuable. Free blacks everywhere were in danger of being kidnapped and sold into slavery.

Only one of four families in the South owned slaves. Many owned just a few to help in the house and fields. The planter families who owned many slaves, however, were the leaders. Their way of life and their ideas were accepted by most people in the South.

Until the 1820s most Southern people thought slavery was wrong, but necessary. Many, like Thomas Jefferson, hoped that it would disappear. In 1832 the Virginia House of Burgesses argued about whether to end slavery in Virginia.

The argument started because many people had been scared by a slave revolt the year before. The revolt had been led by **Nat Turner.** Turner had been known as a peaceful, God-fearing slave. One August night in 1831, however, he and a band of fellow slaves attacked white families. The slaves, carrying axes and guns, went from house to house, surprising people in their sleep. They killed about 55 people, most of them women and children. Turner was caught, tried, and hanged.

In the end the House of Burgesses voted—73 to 58—not to end slavery. Instead, Virginia joined with other slave states in passing laws that put more controls on slavery. Slaves could not meet in groups after dark. Speaking against slavery became a crime.

Many Southerners began to say that slavery was good. Without slaves, they said, their way of life would be destroyed.

Slavery had gradually disappeared from Northern states. Many of these states had passed laws making slavery against the law. States that did not allow slavery were called **free states.**

As the demand for cotton increased, so did the demand for slaves to work in the cotton fields. These women, up at daybreak to pick cotton, would work in the fields until it was dark. In an ordinary day's work, a slave would be expected to pick 200 pounds of cotton. This painting is by Winslow Homer, a famous American artist.

Some people thought that slavery should be ended everywhere, including the South. Slavery had been stopped in other parts of the world. Mexico had ended slavery in 1829. Britain had ended slavery in 1833. People wishing to **abolish,** or end, slavery were called **abolitionists** (ab·uh·LISH·uh·nuhsts).

Frederick Douglass

One of the most famous abolitionists was **Frederick Douglass.** Frederick Douglass had been born a slave on a Maryland plantation. As a young boy he often asked himself, "Why am I a slave?" Some of his fellow slaves told of being brought from Africa. Others told how their fathers and mothers had been stolen from Africa. When he was seven or eight years old, he learned an exciting fact. There were states in the North where there was no slavery.

As a child Douglass lived with a family in Baltimore. He wanted to learn to read and write. The wife of his owner began teaching Douglass. She had to stop when her husband reminded her that it was against the law. If slaves could read and write, he said, they might get ideas of freedom. Douglass then taught himself to read and write. He did so by asking questions of neighborhood boys who went to school.

When Douglass was a young man, he escaped by riding a train from Baltimore to New York City. In the North, Douglass became friends with William Lloyd Garrison, a well-known abolitionist. Garrison encouraged Douglass to speak out on slavery. Douglass began to give lectures. Later he started a newspaper.

Douglass described his experiences as a slave. He described the masters he had known, both the kind and the cruel. He described the whippings that men and women received for little or no reason. He described the heartbreak of being sold, the separation of families—husbands, wives, and children. He spoke against the evil of slavery.

Underground Railroad

For most slaves, escape to the North meant a difficult and dangerous journey. People who were seeking to escape from slavery were called **fugitives** (FYOO·juht·ivs).

Fugitives from slavery had to hide by day and travel by night. They kept their direction by following the North Star. They had to avoid patrols looking for escaped slaves. Sometimes they had to go for days without food. Other times they lived on wild plants in the woods. Most fugitives tried to get to Canada. Fugitive slaves caught in the Northern states could still be returned to their owners. Only in Canada was a fugitive slave completely safe.

Often the fugitives had help from other people. This help was called the **Underground Railroad.** It was a network of safe places stretching from points in the South to Canada. The safe places were called **stations.** They were the homes and farms of people who wanted to help the fugitives.

The "conductors" on the Underground Railroad guided the fugitives to freedom. They included fearless men and women of both races. One was John Fairfield, a young white man raised in the South. He helped many slaves reach

Weary from the night's travels, fugitives on their way to Canada seek refuge at dawn at a station on the Underground Railroad.

freedom. One of them said, "I never saw such a man as Fairfield. He told us he would take us out of slavery or die in the attempt." Fairfield did not return from one trip to the South. Some think he was killed helping the slaves.

Another famous conductor on the Underground Railroad was **Harriet Tubman.** She had escaped from slavery in Maryland. After that she returned time and time again to the South. She guided 300 people to freedom during daring nighttime journeys.

Harriet Tubman was known as Moses. Some nights slaves could hear the song "Go Down Moses" being quietly sung. This was a sign that Harriet Tubman had arrived. Part of that song ran:

We need not always weep and moan
Let my people go
And wear these slavery chains forlorn,
Let my people go.

Reading Check

1. Why did slavery grow in the South in the early nineteenth century?
2. What were people called who wished to end slavery everywhere?
3. How did Frederick Douglass fight against slavery once he was free?
4. Who were Harriet Tubman and John Fairfield?

SOJOURNER TRUTH

Sojourner Truth

On June 1, 1843, a handsome black woman named Isabella stood looking at the East River in New York City. She was thinking about her future. She had decided to start a new life, but first she wanted a new name.

Isabella had been born a slave in New York state. She was given her freedom after New York abolished slavery in 1827. For some years Isabella had worked as a household servant. Then she had become a religious missionary on the streets of New York City.

Now Isabella had felt a call from God to "travel up and down the land." So she named herself *Sojourner,* which means "traveler." Sojourner wanted to preach, to bring truth to the world. So she chose *Truth* as a last name, calling herself Sojourner Truth.

After crossing the East River that day in 1843, Sojourner Truth followed her calling. She set out to talk, preach, and sing to the American people. Before the year was over, she was also preaching freedom for all slaves. Across her chest she wore a banner. On this banner were the same Bible words as on the Liberty Bell: *Proclaim liberty throughout the land unto all the inhabitants thereof.*

By 1850 women were organizing to get equality under the law. In simple and strong language Sojourner began to speak out for women's rights. Once she heard a man say that women were naturally weak and unequal to men. Sojourner Truth stood up, bared her right arm, and showed her muscles. "Ain't I a woman? Look at me. Look at my arm. I have ploughed, and planted, and gathered into barns." Her strong words gave spirit to the women's rights movement.

For 40 years Sojourner Truth traveled throughout America speaking out for freedom and equality. Once a man tried to tell Sojourner that her speeches were useless. "Why I don't care any more for your talk," he complained, "than I do for the bite of a flea." Sojourner smiled at the man. "Perhaps not," she answered, "but just like the flea, I'll keep you scratching."

2. THE EXTENSION OF SLAVERY

To Guide Your Reading

Look for these important words:

Key Words
- extension of slavery
- Missouri Compromise
- Compromise of 1850
- *Uncle Tom's Cabin*
- Kansas-Nebraska Act

- secession
- debates

People
- Henry Clay
- Harriet Beecher Stowe

- Stephen Douglas
- Abraham Lincoln
- Dred Scott

Look for answers to these questions:

1. How did North and South disagree about slavery in new territories?
2. How did they work out their differences?
3. What led to fighting in Kansas?
4. What brought national attention to Abraham Lincoln?

Most Northerners were not abolitionists. They were content to let slavery remain in the South. Northerners were generally opposed, however, to the **extension of slavery.** That means they opposed slavery in the new territories of the West. They wanted new states to be free states.

People in slave states felt they had the same rights as other Americans. These included the right to move to new territory. Slaves were their property, they said. Why couldn't they take their property with them?

Important Compromises

In 1820 the North and South reached a compromise. **Henry Clay,** a senator from Kentucky, worked hard on this agreement. It was called the **Missouri Compromise.** The Missouri Compromise said that the new state of Missouri would be a slave state.

The new state of Maine, formerly a part of Massachusetts, would be admitted as a free state.

The Missouri Compromise set an imaginary line running through the Louisiana territory. It said that new states north of this line would be free states. New states south of this line would be slave states.

The Missouri Compromise worked to keep peace for almost 30 years. In 1849 there were 15 slave states and 15 free states.

Then, after the Mexican-American War, the question came up again. How would the new territories be organized? California wanted to be admitted to the Union as a free state. The South did not like that. It would mean 16 free states to 15 slave states. It would mean the free states would have more power in Congress. They could pass laws that favored the North. The Missouri Compromise no longer worked.

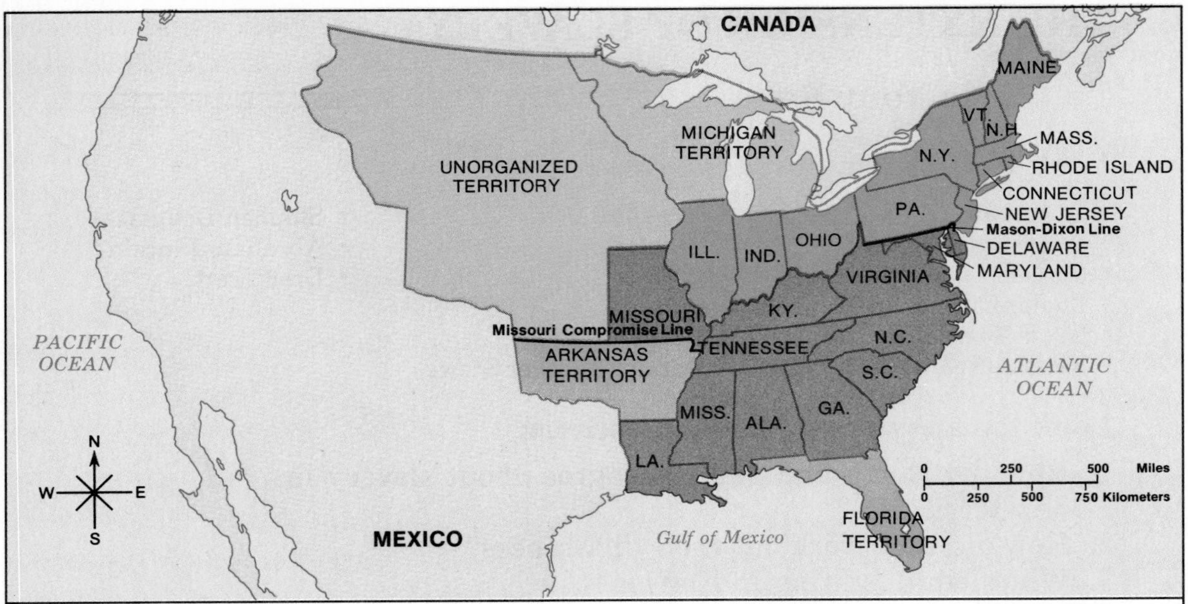

THE UNITED STATES IN 1821

Free states | Slave states
Free territories | Slave territories

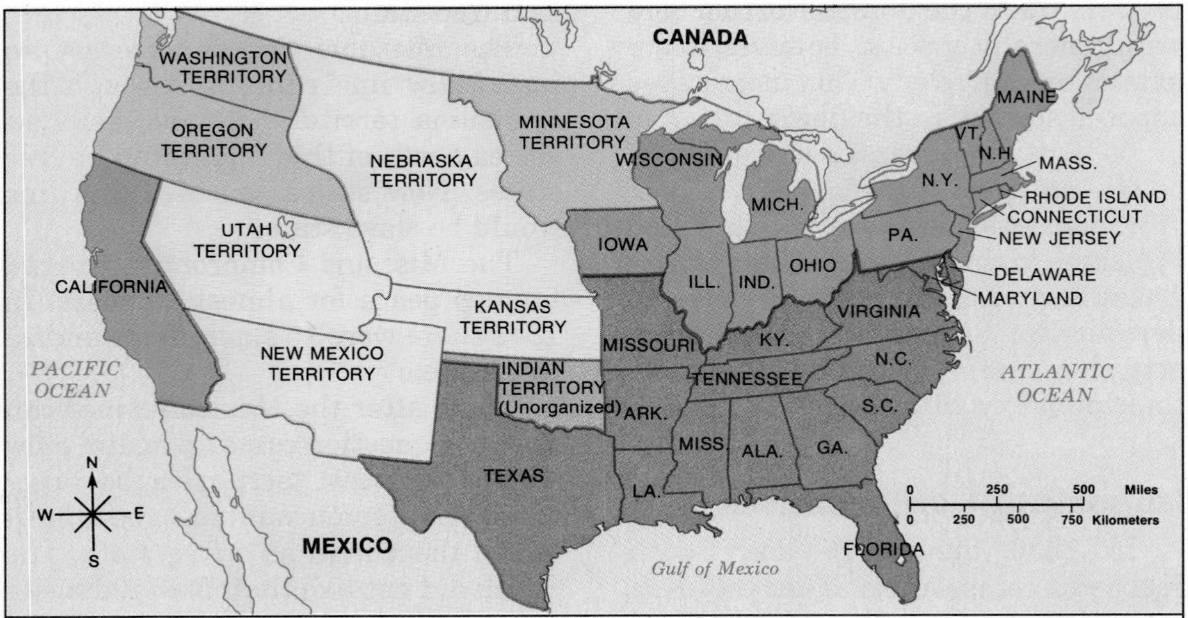

THE UNITED STATES IN 1854

Free states | Slave states | Free or slave by popular vote
Free territories | Slave territory

In 1850 Congress again hammered out a compromise. The **Compromise of 1850** included several parts:

- California would be a free state.
- The people in the territories of Utah and New Mexico could decide themselves to be free or slave states.
- Any slaves escaping to the North would have to be returned.
- Anybody helping slaves to escape would be punished.

This last part of the compromise was particularly important to the South. Slaves were worth a great deal of money. Southerners were getting quite angry about the help Northerners were giving runaway slaves.

The Compromise of 1850 did not last long. Feelings in both the North and South grew stronger and hotter. Many Northern leaders urged people to disobey the new law by helping runaway slaves. Southerners believed that abolitionists were encouraging slaves to revolt as well as to escape. They remembered Nat Turner. They were afraid of the bloodshed that could be part of a slave revolt.

Feelings Grow Stronger

In 1852 **Harriet Beecher Stowe** wrote a novel, **Uncle Tom's Cabin.** She wrote the book based on stories heard from fugitive slaves. It brought tears to the eyes of millions of Northern readers.

Uncle Tom's Cabin did more than anything else to turn people in the North against slavery. Northerners who had paid no attention to the abolitionists now saw slavery as an evil.

Southern people said the stories of slavery in *Uncle Tom's Cabin* were not true. Southern writers also said that slaves were generally better off than most Northern factory workers. Wage earners, they said, had to work longer hours under worse conditions.

Uncle Tom's Cabin convinced millions of Northerners that slavery was evil.

Bloodshed in Kansas

Feelings in both North and South were inflamed even more by a new law, the **Kansas-Nebraska Act** of 1854. The Kansas-Nebraska Act said there would no longer be a line to separate slave states and free states. Instead, in each new state the people themselves would decide.

The Kansas-Nebraska Act was written by **Stephen Douglas,** a senator from Illinois. A short man, Douglas was known as the Little Giant. He was a popular man and well known in both North and South.

The people against slavery were furious with the Kansas-Nebraska Act. They agreed with an Illinois lawyer, **Abraham Lincoln.** Lincoln said, "Slavery must be kept out of Kansas." Lincoln did not believe in ending slavery where it existed, but he did not want slavery to expand.

Kansas was one of the places where people would vote to decide whether it was to be a free state or a slave state. Therefore people both for and against slavery rushed into Kansas. As these two groups fought for control of Kansas, that territory became known as Bleeding Kansas. More than 200 settlers were killed in the first year. After elections were held, Kansas was finally admitted as a free state in 1861.

The bloodshed in Kansas was a sign of things to come. People on both sides of the slavery issue no longer saw compromise as possible. Some in the South began to speak of **secession.** By *secession,* they meant withdrawing from the United States.

Dred Scott Decision

The clouds over North and South became even stormier in 1857. In that year the Supreme Court handed down its decision in the **Dred Scott** case. Dred Scott, a slave, had asked for his freedom because his master had taken him to a free territory.

The Supreme Court ruled that Congress could not keep slavery out of the territories. The Court also said that the Declaration of Independence did not really mean "all men are created equal." Black people were not meant to be included, the Court said. Black people had no rights under the Constitution. Therefore, the Supreme Court said, Dred Scott must remain a slave.

In Illinois, Abraham Lincoln disagreed. Congress did have the power to

A cannonball rips through a pioneer home in eastern Kansas as people for and against slavery fight each other. Kansas would be free or slave depending on how the majority of its people voted. In the end, they voted for Kansas to be a free state.

Thousands came to hear Abraham Lincoln, standing, and Stephen Douglas, at his right, debate about the extension of slavery. Their debates received national attention.

keep slavery out of the territories, he argued. And, he said, when the writers of the Declaration of Independence said "All men are created equal," they meant it. There could be no exceptions.

Lincoln-Douglas Debates

In 1858 Lincoln ran against Stephen Douglas for the office of United States senator from Illinois. Lincoln and Douglas each expressed their ideas in a series of **debates,** or arguments. They debated each other in towns throughout Illinois. Crowds of 15,000 often came to hear them. Newspapers printed what each man said. Their arguments were eagerly read by thousands more.

Douglas argued, "Let each state mind its own business and let its neighbors alone." He said, "This republic can exist forever divided into free and slave states."

Lincoln responded that Douglas's arguments were thin. They were like soup "made by boiling the shadow of a pigeon that starved to death." Lincoln said: "I believe this government cannot endure, permanently half slave and half free. . . . It will become all one thing or all the other."

Douglas won the election, but Lincoln won national fame. People began to talk of the tall man from Illinois.

Reading Check

1. What was the main disagreement between North and South over the extension of slavery?
2. Name the two important compromises over the extension of slavery.
3. What book turned many in the North against slavery?
4. How did Abraham Lincoln win national fame?

SKILLS FOR SUCCESS

One special kind of map is a population map. A population map shows where people live. Sometimes population maps are called maps of **population density.** *Density* means the amount of crowding. A map showing population density shows how many people live in different areas. The map at the top of page 353 shows population density of much of the United States in 1860.

To read this map, first look at the key. There you see that a different color has been given to different population densities. The yellow color is a symbol for fewer than 2 people per square mile (2.6 km). People who lived in parts of the country with this density might have been quite far from their neighbors. It would take 20 minutes to walk to a neighbor's house 1 mile (1.6 km) away. Many lived much farther apart than that.

What does the dark orange color stand for? This population density shows much more crowding. It is an area of smaller farms and many towns. In such an area there is usually a large city.

The map key also shows a dot (●) for cities of over 50,000 people. An even larger dot stands for cities of over 100,000 people. The largest dot is for cities of over 500,000 people.

Special Population Maps

Some population maps show density for only a particular part of the population. The map at the bottom of page 353 shows where slaves lived in 1860.

The key helps you read this map. It tells you that the lightest area had no slaves or

was unsettled. The remaining color symbols tell you how many slaves there were for every 100 people. The word to describe this way of looking at numbers is *percent.* For instance, find the color that stands for 10 to 30 percent. Ten to 30 percent means that there were 10 to 30 slaves for every 100 people.

CHECKING YOUR SKILLS

Use the maps and keys to answer these questions.

1. What does *density* mean?

2. Was the population density greater or less as one moved west?

3. Where were the greatest number of cities?

4. Locate South Carolina on the maps. Describe its population density in 1860.

5. How many cities in the United States had more than 500,000 people?

6. Was there greater density of slaves in northern or southern United States?

7. Locate Texas on the maps. Were there more slaves in eastern or western Texas?

8. Describe the slave population density of South Carolina in 1860.

9. Were slaves more likely to live in areas of greatest population density? Explain.

10. Were areas of low population density always areas of low slave density? Explain.

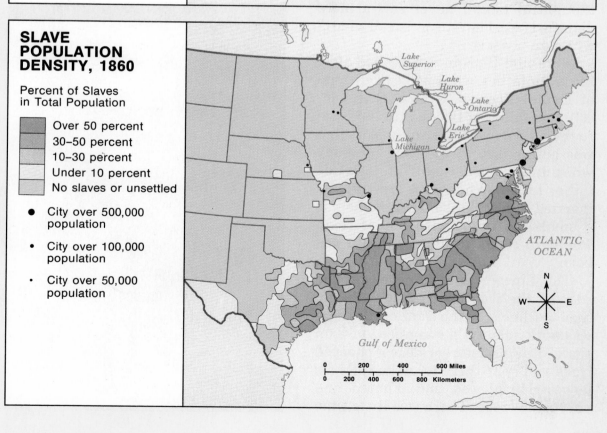

POPULATION DENSITY, 1860

People per square mile	People per square kilometer
More than 45	More than 18
18–45	8–18
2–18	1–8
Less than 2	Less than 1

● City over 500,000 population

• City over 100,000 population

· City over 50,000 population

Lake Superior
Lake Huron
Lake Ontario
Lake Michigan
Lake Erie

ATLANTIC OCEAN

Gulf of Mexico

| 0 | 200 | 400 | 600 Miles |
| 0 | 200 | 400 | 600 | 800 Kilometers |

SLAVE POPULATION DENSITY, 1860

Percent of Slaves in Total Population

Over 50 percent
30–50 percent
10–30 percent
Under 10 percent
No slaves or unsettled

● City over 500,000 population

• City over 100,000 population

· City over 50,000 population

Lake Superior
Lake Huron
Lake Ontario
Lake Michigan
Lake Erie

ATLANTIC OCEAN

Gulf of Mexico

| 0 | 200 | 400 | 600 Miles |
| 0 | 200 | 400 | 600 | 800 Kilometers |

3. ABRAHAM LINCOLN BECOMES PRESIDENT

To Guide Your Reading

Look for these important words:

Key Words
- Union
- secede
- Confederate State of America

- Confederacy
- inauguration

People
- Jefferson Davis

Places
- Fort Sumter

Look for answers to these questions:

1. What personal qualities did Abraham Lincoln have?
2. What views did the Republican Party hold?
3. How did the South react to Lincoln's election as President?
4. Why did a war begin between North and South?

Abraham Lincoln had a face one could not forget. "I never saw a more thoughtful face. I never saw a more dignified face. I never saw so sad a face," wrote an observer.

Abraham Lincoln was named after his grandfather, who had been a friend of Daniel Boone's. Grandfather Lincoln had followed Boone into the Kentucky wilderness. His young son Tom was beside him in the fields one day when Indians attacked. Tom saw his father killed. When Tom grew up, he married Nancy Hanks. Their home was a small log cabin with a dirt floor. There, in 1809, Abraham Lincoln was born.

The Lincoln family moved on the edge of the frontier first to Indiana, then to Illinois. In the frontier life there was work aplenty. "I was raised to farm work," Lincoln later wrote. He chopped trees and split them to make rails for fences. He plowed and planted and harvested crops. There was little time

After a long day of farmwork, young Abraham Lincoln read at night by firelight.

Eastman Johnson, American 1824-1906
Boyhood of Lincoln, 1868, oil on canvas, The University of Michigan Museum of Art, bequest of Henry Lewis, © 1983, The Regents of the University of Michigan.

for school. When he could, Lincoln borrowed books to read. He could only read during a lunch break or after finishing his evening chores.

As a young man Lincoln worked taking flatboats loaded with cargo down the Mississippi River. For a time he kept a store. Then he became a surveyor. All the while, he was reading. He taught himself law. In 1836, at age 27, he became a lawyer.

Lincoln became known for his honesty, his fairness, his humor. He was known as the best storyteller around. Once Lincoln was carrying home his two sons Willie and Tad, both crying. A neighbor asked, "Why, Mr. Lincoln, what's the matter?" Lincoln answered, "Just what's the matter with the whole world. I've got three walnuts and each wants two."

Lincoln had great respect for work. He felt that all people had the right to the rewards of their own labor. No matter how hard slaves worked, they had no hope for a better life. Wage earners might work under conditions as bad, but they had hope that life would improve for themselves and their children. Lincoln supported shoe-factory workers in New England who went on strike for higher wages. Lincoln said, "Thank God that we have a system of labor where there *can* be a strike."

Election of Lincoln

The next year, 1860, the Republican party made Abraham Lincoln its candidate for President. The Republican party had been born in 1854. Its members stood against the extension of slavery and for the preservation of the **Union.** *Union* refers to the union of states that is the United States of America. Republicans did not think that states had the right to **secede,** or withdraw, from the Union. Abraham Lincoln frightened the South. If he were elected, Southerners said, their way of life would come to an end.

Abraham Lincoln was elected in 1860. South Carolina then chose to secede. South Carolina leaders argued that the state had the right to secede. Their reasoning was simple. Because the state had voted to join the Union, it could vote to secede from the Union. Other cotton states quickly followed: Mississippi, Alabama, Georgia, Florida, Louisiana, and Texas. The seceding states formed a new nation, the **Confederate States of America.** It was also called the **Confederacy.**

Jefferson Davis of Mississippi was chosen president of the Confederacy. Davis was a cotton planter. He had fought in the Mexican-American War and had been a United States senator. Like Lincoln, he was known for his honesty.

North and South watched to see what Lincoln would do as President. Lincoln's **inauguration** (in•O•guh•ray•shun), or taking the oath of office, was March 4, 1861. The first thing he did as President was to make a speech, an inaugural (in•O•guh•ruhl) address. In this speech Lincoln took a strong stand. He said that slavery would be left alone in the slave states. Slavery should not, however, be extended to any new places. Lincoln also gave notice that he would do all he could to preserve the Union. He would "hold, occupy, and possess" all property belonging to the United States government. Finally, he pleaded for peace

The Battle of Fort Sumter in the harbor of Charleston, South Carolina, was the first battle of the Civil War. It resulted in a Confederate victory.

and asked the Confederate states to return to the Union. "We are not enemies, but friends," he said. "We must not be enemies."

People in the Confederacy did not trust Lincoln. They had not voted for him. They did not feel Lincoln represented them. Confederate leaders insisted that the states had the right to secede from the Union.

Battle at Fort Sumter

For one month after Lincoln's inauguration, the tension built. People asked, what would Lincoln do about the seceding states? The first test was in South Carolina at **Fort Sumter.** When South Carolina seceded from the Union, government troops were stationed at Fort Sumter. Fort Sumter was located on an island in the harbor of Charleston, South Carolina. Lincoln sent word that ships would be bringing food to the soldiers at Fort Sumter.

On April 12 the Confederate leaders demanded that the fort surrender. The fort's commander refused. Confederate troops then fired their cannon. They bombarded the fort for 30 hours until, at last, Fort Sumter surrendered. War between North and South had begun.

Reading Check

1. Describe at least three qualities for which Abraham Lincoln was famous.
2. Why did Southern states secede when Lincoln was elected?
3. Name three ideas Lincoln expressed in his inaugural address.
4. Where did the Civil War begin?

CHAPTER 15 REVIEW

WORDS TO USE

Choose the correct word from the list below to complete the sentences that follow.

abolish   secession

abolitionists   tariff

fugitives

1. Frederick Douglass wanted to _____ slavery.

2. The _____ wanted to end slavery.

3. A tax on imported goods is a _____.

4. People escaping from slavery were _____.

5. The act of withdrawing from the Union was called _____.

FACTS TO REVIEW

1. Explain why the North favored a tariff and the South opposed a tariff.

2. Compare how Frederick Douglass and Harriet Tubman worked against slavery.

3. Compare how the North and South differed about the extension of slavery.

4. What were the beliefs of the Republican party when it was formed?

5. What event caused Southern states to secede from the Union?

IDEAS TO DISCUSS

1. How did North and South try to compromise on the extension of slavery? Why did compromise finally fail to work?

2. Compare how Frederick Douglass and Harriet Beecher Stowe each fought against slavery? Who had the greater effect? Why?

3. What problems did fugitive slaves face? Why were people like Harriet Tubman and John Fairfield important to the fugitives?

4. What kind of person was Abraham Lincoln? What were some of his beliefs? How might his early life had an effect on those beliefs?

5. Imagine two people, one a planter in South Carolina and one a small farmer in Illinois. How might they disagree with each other over these subjects:

   a. The extension of slavery
   b. *Uncle Tom's Cabin*
   c. The election of Abraham Lincoln

◯ SKILLS PRACTICE

Using Population Maps Answer these questions.

1. What is a population density map?

2. If a map shows a population density of more than 45 people per square mile (1.6 per sq km), what kind of place is that likely to be?

3. If a map shows a population density of less than 2 per square mile (1.6 per sq km), what kind of place is that?

4. If a special population map shows that 30 percent of the people were slaves, what does that mean?

CHAPTER 16

The Civil War

About this chapter

The shots fired at Fort Sumter started a war between two parts of the nation. The cotton states of the South had left the Union to form the Confederate States of America. They were going to fight for independence. President Abraham Lincoln had declared that the states had no right to leave the Union. The Union would fight to force the seceding states back into the Union.

The Union finally won the war in 1865, primarily because it had more soldiers, more money, more guns, and more food. For both sides the cost in lives was great. For the nation, the scars from the Civil War remained for a long time.

1. THE FIGHTING BEGINS

To Guide Your Reading

Look for these important words:

Key Words
• regiments

People
• West Virginia
• Robert E. Lee
• Stonewall Jackson

Places
• Bull Run

Look for answers to these questions:

1. What was the mood of Americans at the beginning of the Civil War?
2. What happened at the Battle of Bull Run?
3. What effect did the Battle of Bull Run have?

After the battle of Fort Sumter, four more states joined the Confederacy. They were Virginia, North Carolina, Tennessee, and Arkansas. The western counties of Virginia refused to join the Confederate effort. Later they became another state, **West Virginia.** The slave states of Delaware, Maryland, Missouri, and Kentucky stayed with the Union. In these states, which bordered on free states, slavery was not so important a part of the economy.

Both North and South began preparations for war. Men and boys eagerly joined **regiments,** or organized groups of soldiers, made up of their neighbors and friends. In the North the foreign-born organized their own regiments. The Irish, the Italians, the Germans, and the British all had their regiments. Some wore colorful uniforms of red baggy trousers, yellow sashes, and blue coats.

The new soldiers left their homes in a riot of enthusiasm. There were cheers, speeches, and the rousing music of fife-and-drum bands. "On to Washington," cried young soldiers in the South. "On to Richmond," they shouted in the North. Richmond, Virginia, was the Confederate capital.

Those who stayed home formed committees to help with the war effort. They collected funds. Women in both North and South formed societies. They busied themselves making bandages and knitting and sewing for the soldiers. "I do not know when I have seen a woman without knitting in her hand. Socks for the soldiers is the cry," Mary Chesnut, a Southerner, wrote in her diary.

Spirits were high in the South. "Secession is the fashion here," wrote a British newspaper reporter. "Young ladies sing for it. Old ladies pray for it. Young men are dying to fight for it. Old men are ready to demonstrate it."

Spirits were high in the North as well. "We shall crush out this rebellion as an elephant would trample on a mouse," wrote one Northerner. Eager as Northerners were to join the army, they did not always know why. Nathaniel Hawthorne, a writer, was one such man. "Though I approve the war as much as any man, I don't quite understand what we are fighting for," he wrote to his wife.

President Lincoln had hoped that **Robert E. Lee** would command the Union army. Lee had fought bravely in the Mexican War. By the time Lincoln asked Lee to take command, Lee's home state of Virginia had seceded. Lee refused Lincoln's offer. His choice was hard. Lee disliked slavery and had no slaves of his own. He was devoted to the Union. But, Lee wrote, he could not fight "against my relatives, my children, my home."

Robert E. Lee, left, on his horse Traveller, meets with Stonewall Jackson.

First Battle of Bull Run

In the light-hearted days after the battle at Fort Sumter, people thought the war would soon be over. Neither North nor South understood how strongly the other side felt.

The first battle between armies of the North and South was fought in July 1861. The site was near **Bull Run,** a small stream near Manassas Junction, Virginia. Shouting "On to Richmond," the Union army gaily left Washington on July 16. The sun was very hot. Soon clouds of dust covered the bright new uniforms of the marching soldiers. On their backs the soldiers carried their bedding, clothing, muskets, and personal items. As it grew hotter their loads seemed heavier. They began to leave unneccessary items beside the road.

These soldiers showed little discipline. Whenever they felt like it, they wandered off to pick berries or rest. On the day of the battle, July 21, crowds of sightseers came out from Washington in carriages. They brought picnic baskets of food and drink. They carried bright umbrellas to protect themselves from the sun.

Now the two armies found each other. Some soldiers had trouble telling friend from enemy because there were so many different uniforms. In time the Union army would wear blue uniforms. The Confederates would wear gray.

In the fighting at Bull Run that hot July day, the Confederates began to weaken. Then a Confederate general saw a group of Virginians shooting well and standing firm. At their head was Thomas Jackson, a former teacher in a military school. "There is Jackson

At Bull Run, two untrained armies clashed in a confusing, bloody battle. Defeated by the South, Union troops retreated to Washington, D. C.

standing like a stone wall," cried the general. "Rally behind the Virginians!" The Confederates were able to hold their line. Ever after Jackson was known as **Stonewall Jackson.** He became one of the South's best generals.

The Union attack failed. The soldiers began to retreat. The picnickers decided it was time they, too, picked up and went home. The road back to Washington became jammed with carriages, wagons, and running soldiers. Everywhere people were in panic. The fleeing troops left behind 8,000 muskets, many cannons, and quantities of supplies. The Confederates could have followed their victory with a march on Washington. Instead, they chose to celebrate.

The city of Washington was shocked by Bull Run. More than 4,700 men were killed, wounded, or missing. The First Battle of Bull Run, according to a Civil War historian, "ended the rosy time in which men could dream that the war would be short, glorious, and bloodless." The war now became a serious, deadly business. The North would win the war only after four long years of bloody and bitter fighting.

Reading Check

1. What slave states did not join the Confederacy?
2. Why did Robert E. Lee refuse to command the Union army?
3. Where was the first battle between armies fought?
4. Why did people on each side change their minds about the war ending quickly?

2. PLANS, STRENGTHS OF EACH SIDE

To Guide Your Reading

Look for these important words:

Key Words
- strategy
- Anaconda Plan
- blockade
- cavalry

People
- Jeb Stuart
- Ulysses S. Grant
- Mary Ann Bickerdyke
- Sally Tompkins

Look for answers to these questions:

1. What was Lincoln's plan for winning the Civil War?
2. What was the Confederate plan for winning the war?
3. What were the strengths of the South? of the North?
4. How were the sick and wounded treated during the war?

Lincoln's **strategy,** or long-range plan, for winning the war was first to weaken the South, then to invade it. To weaken the South, Lincoln and his advisors adopted a plan the newspapers called the **Anaconda Plan.** An anaconda is a large snake that kills its prey by squeezing. The Union would squeeze the South by not letting it ship its cotton or get necessary supplies. The South was a farming economy. It needed to sell its cash crops and buy manufactured products like cloth, shoes, sugar, and guns. To block the imports was the purpose of the Anaconda Plan. It called for winning control of the Mississippi River and for a naval **blockade** of Confederate seaports. A blockade is the use of warships to prevent other ships from entering or leaving a harbor.

The Confederate strategy rested on the belief that Britain and France would help the South. Both countries depended on Southern cotton to keep their cotton mills going. The South hoped to hold out against the North until European help came. The other hope of the South was that the North would tire of the war. At first, the fighting strategy of the Confederacy was to defend its own territory. Later this strategy was expanded to include brief invasions of the North.

Strengths of the South

Going into the war, the North and South each had different strengths. Southern soldiers had the will and fire that came from fighting on their own soil. They were fighting for a cause clear to them—the independence of the Confederacy. Most Confederate soldiers came from the countryside. They were in better physical shape than the city boys who joined the Union forces. Southern boys learned to ride and shoot at an early age. Soldiers joining the Union army often had to be taught to sit on a horse and how to shoot.

Dashing Jeb Stuart, wearing a feathered cap, led the Confederate cavalry. He reported to General Lee on the movements of Union troops.

One of the South's greatest strengths was its generals. These generals had had experience fighting for the United States in the Mexican-American War. Robert E. Lee became the greatest of the Confederate generals. Lee was a kind and courteous man. He was a capable and skilled leader. Confederate soldiers cheered wildly when Lee appeared before them riding his huge iron-gray horse, Traveller.

Many of Lee's military successes depended on other fine generals. They included Stonewall Jackson, Joseph Johnston, and **Jeb Stuart.** Jeb Stuart was in charge of the **cavalry,** the soldiers on horses. Stuart was a dashing man, who wore a large feather in his hat. Stuart and his men acted as the "eyes" of Lee. The cavalry could travel the countryside quickly, leaping walls and fences. It often circled the whole Union army. Stuart then reported the movements of the Union troops.

Strengths of the North

The North went into the war with a greater population. There were 22 million people in the 23 states of the North. The 11 states of the Confederacy had only 5.5 million free people. The North had greater industrial strength. It had at least six times as many factories as the South. It had 22,000 miles (35,398 km) of railroad track to the South's 9,000 miles (14,481 km). The North had most of the nation's coal and iron. Both coal and iron were necessary in the modern age of factories, steam engines, and railroads.

The North also had the money to build factories, railroads, and ships. It had the money to pay soldiers' wages and purchase war supplies. The gold and silver discovered in California and Colorado were making the Union rich.

Even with all these strengths, the North needed the will to achieve victory. In his speeches Abraham Lincoln gave people this will to fight. Lincoln was a great strength of the Union, perhaps its greatest strength.

When the war started Lincoln had difficulty finding good generals. Toward the end of the war, excellent generals were in command of Union troops. They included **Ulysses S. Grant.** Grant had fought in the Mexican-American War but had retired. He was a store clerk in Illinois when the war broke out.

Nursing Care in the War

The Civil War claimed more than half a million lives before it ended. Most of those who died were between the ages of 15 and 21. Almost every home, North and South, lost someone in the war.

Thousands upon thousands lost their lives either on the battlefield or from battle wounds. In his diary the poet Walt Whitman described the wounded after a battle on a cold winter day. The

A Catholic nun dies on a Civil War battlefield. Those who braved battlefields to care for the wounded were often innocent victims of stray gunfire.

wounded were lying on the ground, which was frozen hard. The wounded were lucky, Whitman said, if their blankets were spread on layers of pine or hemlock twigs, or even small leaves.

Medical service was poor. Little was then known about germs. Nothing was used to kill germs. Many soldiers died of infections. Painkillers were hard to get. Army doctors sawed off mangled limbs often without giving patients any sort of painkiller.

Thousands of soldiers who survived battle conditions died from disease. The army camps were often dirty and unclean. Water became infected. Disease spread quickly. Twice as many died from disease as from battle.

At that time many people still thought it improper for women to care for sick men. Most nurses were men. But the need for nursing care soon changed peoples' ideas. In the North and South over 600 trained nurses from Catholic religious orders helped. Several thousand other women also served as volunteer nurses.

One of the most famous of these nurses was **Mary Ann Bickerdyke.** Her church minister asked for a woman to take supplies to the sick and wounded. She volunteered. Arriving at the Union camp at Cairo, Illinois, she was shocked by the conditions. Sick soldiers were lying in dirt and filth.

Mary Ann Bickerdyke announced that no one would get food until he had a bath. On the spot she had barrels sawed in half to make bathtubs. Within hours each sick man was washed, shaved, and dressed in clean clothing. The muck they had been lying on was carted away. Each man was given a mattress filled with clean straw. Only

Mother Bickerdyke, known for her stern tongue and plain dress, scolds an army surgeon for disobeying orders. Thousands of soldiers survived the war thanks to her standards of cleanliness and nursing care.

then did Mary Ann Bickerdyke hand out the fried chicken she had brought.

Mary Ann Bickerdyke came to be called Mother Bickerdyke by the soldiers she cared for. She ended up directing kitchens, rounding up supplies, and starting army laundries. She became the terror of lazy officers and doctors. She was present at a total of 19 battles.

Mother Bickerdyke would do anything to help the sick and wounded under her care. She was with the Union army when it was camped in Tennessee in December 1863. A bitter, cold storm blew in. The sick and wounded were in danger of freezing to death. There was no firewood. The storm was too fierce to send soldiers to chop down trees.

In the camp were walls built of logs. They had been constructed to provide for protection in a recent battle. It was against army orders for anyone to destroy these walls. Mother Bickerdyke did not care. At her command soldiers used mules and chains to tear the logs from the walls. The logs were then used for a great fire that saved many lives.

In the South **Sally Tompkins** gained fame for her private hospital in Richmond, Virginia. There, she took excellent care of both Yankee prisoners and Confederate soldiers. The fine care of her hospital made it different from most. At the end of the war only 73 of 1,333 of her patients had died. In contrast, a visitor described another Richmond hospital. Mary Chesnut wrote in her diary that there were "long rows of them dead, dying. Awful smells, awful sights."

Reading Check

1. What was the Anaconda Plan?
2. Name at least three strengths of the South.
3. Name at least three strengths of the North.
4. How did Mary Ann Bickerdyke and Sally Tompkins each help the soldiers?

SKILLS FOR SUCCESS

CHOOSING BETWEEN FACT AND OPINION

When we speak, listen, and read, we need to be able to tell the difference between **fact** and **opinion.** Facts are statements that can be proved true. Opinions are statements that cannot be proved true. You can find exam-ples of both facts and opinions in the letter below. The letter is based on an actual letter a Confederate soldier, James Chesnut, Jr., wrote to his wife during the Battle of Richmond.

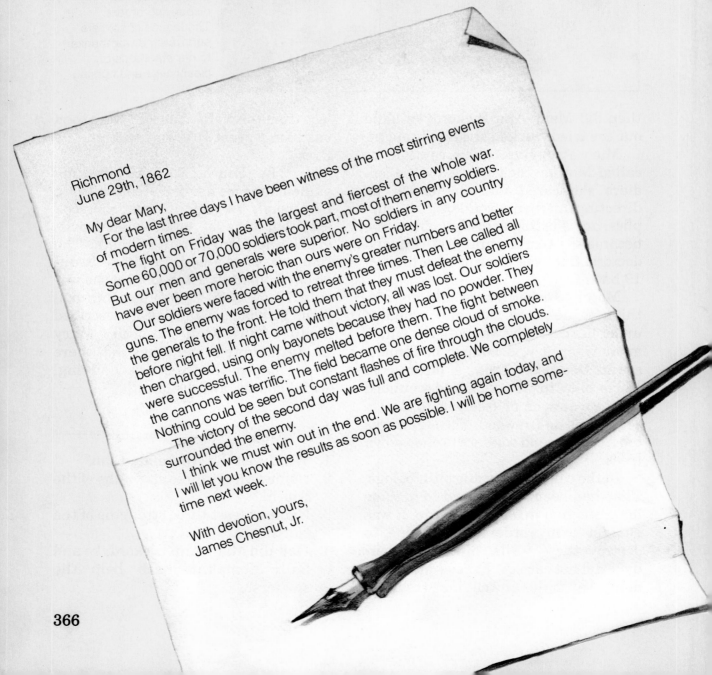

Richmond
June 29th, 1862

My dear Mary,
For the last three days I have been witness of the most stirring events of modern times.
The fight on Friday was the largest and fiercest of the whole war. Some 60,000 or 70,000 soldiers took part, most of them enemy soldiers. But our men and generals were superior. No soldiers in any country have ever been more heroic than ours were on Friday.
Our soldiers were faced with the enemy's greater numbers and better guns. The enemy was forced to retreat three times. Then Lee called all the generals to the front. He told them that they must defeat the enemy before night fell. If night came without victory, all was lost. Our soldiers then charged, using only bayonets because they had no powder. They were successful. The enemy melted before them. The fight between the cannons was terrific. The field became one dense cloud of smoke. Nothing could be seen but constant flashes of fire through the clouds.
The victory of the second day was full and complete. We completely surrounded the enemy.
I think we must win out in the end. We are fighting again today, and I will let you know the results as soon as possible. I will be home some-time next week.

With devotion, yours,
James Chesnut, Jr.

Mary Chesnut kept the letter her husband wrote her from the Battle of Richmond.

Look for facts in the letter. For instance, it was a fact that the Confederates were outnumbered by Union soldiers at Richmond. It was a fact that the Union had more guns.

Some statements in this letter however, are opinions. Sometimes an opinion is a guess. Sometimes it is a conclusion drawn from certain facts. An opinion can be sensible or foolish. It often expresses the wishes or hopes or fears of the speaker.

In the last sentence in the second paragraph, James Chesnut, Jr., says: "No soldiers in any country have ever been more heroic than ours were on Friday." This is an opinion. Being heroic, or brave, cannot be measured, as height and weight can.

Even if hundreds of people agreed with Chesnut's statement, it would still be an opinion. There is no way to show that soldiers in one battle were braver than other soldiers anywhere ever.

How can you recognize an opinion? Certain expressions such as *I think, I believe,* and *in my opinion* give a hint. They tell you that someone is about to give an opinion. An expression such as *I doubt* tells you that someone is giving a negative opinion.

Words such as *beautiful, wonderful, terrible,* and *terrific* are expressions of opinion. There is no way for everybody to agree on what is wonderful or terrible. A wonderful book to one person may be a terrible book to someone else. Experts may agree that something is wonderful or terrible, but they are still giving opinions.

No one can see into the future, so any statement about it is an opinion. Some people are expert enough to tell what is likely to happen in the future. But these statements do not become facts until the events have taken place.

When James Chesnut, Jr., wrote his letter, he could not know who would win the battle. Chesnut thought the South would win. He expresses this opinion in the fourth paragraph: "I think we must win out in the end."

We now know that Chesnut's opinion was right. The South did win the Battle of Richmond.

CHECKING YOUR SKILLS

Which of these statements are facts, and which are opinions? Explain why.

1. Most Confederate soldiers were skilled horsemen.

2. Union soldiers will quit fighting as soon as winter comes.

3. The South won many battles during the first year of the Civil War.

4. I think the South would have won the war if it had had more industries.

5. Many Union newspapers printed articles saying that the war would not last long.

3. THE FIRST PART OF THE WAR

═ To Guide Your Reading ═

Look for these important words:

Key Words
- casualties
- Emancipation Proclamation
- Pickett's charge
- Gettysburg Addres

Places
- Antietam
- Chancellorsville
- Gettysburg

Look for answers to these questions:

1. What were some of the important battles of the first part of the war? Why was each important?
2. What were the effects of Lincoln freeing the slaves?
3. How was the fighting in the Civil War different from that in the Revolutionary War?
4. Why is the Gettysburg Address important?
5. For what goals was the North fighting?

For more than a year the Union army tried to march on the Confederate capital of Richmond. Each time it failed. Union troops were well armed and well organized, but they seemed no match for the Southern troops. Particularly outstanding were those led by Stonewall Jackson.

In May 1862 Jackson and his troops marched 245 miles (394 km), fought four battles, and won them all. As a result, one-third of the Union army in Virginia was busy chasing Jackson instead of attacking Richmond.

Jackson was a beloved general, who showed great concern for his men. On long marches he made the soldiers lie down and rest ten minutes every hour.

The Northerners had hoped for a short war. They began to be discouraged by the long lists of **casualties.** Casualties are people who have been killed or wounded. Some people began to ask, Why keep fighting?

Union Victory at Antietam

Then, in September 1862, the North won a major victory at **Antietam** (an•TEET•uhm). By then Robert E. Lee was commander of the Southern troops. He had led his army across the Potomac River into Maryland, aiming for Harrisburg, Pennsylvania. There the Confederates planned to cut off railroad communication between the Eastern states and the West. Lee's troops were badly in need of food, shoes, and clothing. They hoped to find these supplies in the North.

Union troops stopped the Confederate army near Sharpsburg, Maryland, at Antietam Creek. The loss of life on that mild September day was great. "Never before or after in all the war were so many men shot on one day," the historian Bruce Catton wrote. Having lost one-fourth of his army, Lee finally retreated back across the Potomac River.

Union and Confederate troops blaze away as each side seeks to control the bridge at Antietam Creek. By dusk, at least 22,500 men had died.

Union victory at Antietam had an important result. The South, besides losing the battle, lost possible help from Britain and France. Both British and French leaders had shown sympathy for the Confederacy. Now it was not certain that the South would win independence. Neither Britain nor France wanted to help a loser.

Slaves Are Freed

By this time Lincoln had decided to free the slaves. He wanted to wait to make the announcement, however, until after a Union victory. After the victory at Antietam, Lincoln issued the **Emancipation Proclamation.** *Emancipation* means freedom. Lincoln announced freedom for the slaves of the Confederacy as of January 1, 1863. The Emancipation Proclamation gave new spirit to the North. It gave Union troops a cause for which to fight. Abolitionists were overjoyed. Their goal had now become the North's goal.

Black Soldiers

When the war started, blacks had not been welcome as soldiers in the army. Runaway slaves who came to Union camps were often returned to their owners. After the Emancipation Proclamation, regiments of black soldiers were organized. Before the end of the war about 180,000 blacks fought in the Union army. Another 30,000 served in the navy.

The black soldiers fought in regiments commanded by white officers. At first black soldiers were paid only half the salary of white soldiers. Some therefore refused to take any pay. By

Proud to be in uniform, this soldier rushed to have his picture taken with a new invention—the camera.

the end of the war, pay for black soldiers and white soldiers was equal. Black soldiers often had to fight with weapons of poor quality. Their hospital care was usually worse than that of whites.

Yet the spirit of black soldiers was high. They were fighting for freedom. Frederick Douglass, the abolitionist, urged free blacks to volunteer for the army. With their help, he said, "four million of our brothers and sisters shall march out into liberty." The secretary of war wrote to Lincoln about the courage of the black soldiers. He said they had "proved themselves among the bravest of the brave."

Lee's Important Victory

Most of the fighting in the East was in northern Virginia. There, for most of the war, Robert E. Lee and his army held back the Union army. General Lee's most brilliant victory was at **Chancellorsville,** Virginia, in May 1863. Lee's army defeated a Union force twice the size of his. In winning, however, Lee lost his right-hand man. In the confusion of battle, Stonewall Jackson was shot by some of his own soldiers.

The victory at Chancellorsville gave the Confederacy confidence to try again to invade the North. The Confederate goal was to win a clear victory on Northern soil. If they could do so, they hoped the war might end. In June, one month after the victory at Chancellorsville, Lee's troops started north.

The Battle of Gettysburg

The Union army met Lee's army near the town of **Gettysburg,** Pennsylvania. The greatest battle of the war was fought there on the first three days of July 1863. Lee was forced into the battle before he was quite ready. Jeb Stuart and the cavalry had taken off to ride around the Union army. The ride took much longer than they had planned. The "eyes of Lee" had not yet arrived when the battle started. Lee did not have the information he needed about the position of Union troops.

The high point of the fighting came the afternoon of July 3. That morning all had been quiet. The main line of the Union army lay behind a stone wall on a ridge. Across a large field were the Confederates. At one o'clock Confederate guns began firing, all their fire power directed to the ridge. A Union officer on the ridge described the scene: "How the long streams of fire spout from the guns, how the rifled shells hiss, how the smoke deepens and rolls."

The "great ceaseless roar of the guns" lasted two hours. Men and horses lay dead. Gun carriages and wagons were destroyed.

Then "an ocean of armed men" started toward the Union line on the ridge. Marching shoulder to shoulder, 15,000 Confederate troops in a line half a mile (0.8 km) wide moved steadily. This moving wall of Confederate soldiers, led by General George Pickett, is called **Pickett's charge.** "Here they come," shouted the Union soldiers, guns ready.

When the Confederates were within musket range, the Union soldiers fired. "Men were falling all around us, and cannon and muskets were raining death upon us," remembered a Con... officer. "Still on and up the slop... the stone fence our men steadil... Pickett's men reached the wall but were stopped by the murderous fire of Union guns. Pickett's charge had failed. The Confederate troops retreated, leaving half their number dead and wounded. Lee had to order a retreat.

When Lee's army reached the Potomac, the river was flooding. The troops had to wait for the waters to go down. President Lincoln sent this message to the Union general: "Do not let the enemy escape." While the Union general tried to make plans, the flood waters went down. Lee's army escaped back into Virginia.

This painting shows a part of Pickett's Charge at Gettysburg. The Confederates lost so many men that General Lee was forced to retreat.

The battle had cost thousands of lives. Each side lost more than 20,000 men. For Lee, that amounted to one-third of his army.

Battlefield Technology

Casualties were particularly high in the Battle of Gettysburg. The main reason for this was an advance in war technology. There were new kinds of cannons and guns. Most of the cannons could fire a 12-pound (5.4-kg) ball a distance of a mile (1.6 km). The cannons fired not only cannonballs but also special cans filled with nails and shot. When fired, the can would fly into pieces. Nails and shot sprayed murderously in all directions.

In the Revolutionary War bayonets had been a very important part of the fighting. The fighting was often "eyeball to eyeball" because guns were not very accurate and often misfired. There was none of this kind of fighting at Gettysburg. Most of the soldiers on both sides used the rifle musket, a new kind of gun. The new rifle musket had very good aim and firing power. It could kill a person half a mile (0.8 km) away. The gun could also be loaded faster than the old kind. Charging across an open field in the face of such weapons was deadly. Yet some generals continued to order such charges. Pickett's charge failed because it was an old way of fighting a new kind of war.

The Gettysburg Address

In November 1863 President Lincoln went to Gettysburg to honor those who had died there. The speech he gave has become known as the **Gettysburg**

This photograph of Abraham Lincoln shows him tired, but determined.

Address. In his speech Lincoln spoke to the heart of the war-weary North. These thousands had died, Lincoln said, so that "government of the people, by the people, for the people shall not perish from the earth." Lincoln made clear that democracy had become part of the Northern cause. The North was now fighting for three goals. These were preservation of the Union, freedom for the slaves, and defense of democracy.

Reading Check

1. What was an important effect of the Union victory at Antietam?
2. What was the Emancipation Proclamation?
3. Why were the casualties so high at the Battle of Gettysburg?
4. What is the importance of the Gettysburg Address?

THE GETTYSBURG ADDRESS

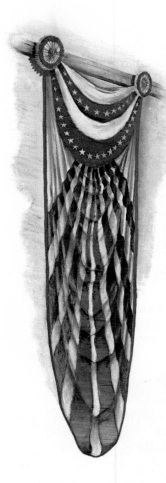

Thursday, November 19, 1863, was a mild day at Gettysburg, Pennsylvania. At least 15,000 people had come to Gettysburg that day for the dedication of a national soldiers' cemetery. There, lay buried thousands who had died five months before at the Battle of Gettysburg.

Abraham Lincoln rode to the site on a large chestnut horse. Bands played. When it was Lincoln's turn to speak, he stood up and took two pages of notes from his pocket. In five minutes he delivered the speech known as the Gettysburg Address.

In the Gettysburg Address Lincoln gave clear and noble expression to the nation's democratic ideals.

Four score and seven years ago, our fathers brought forth on this continent a new nation, conceived in liberty and dedicated to the proposition that all men are created equal.

Now we are engaged in a great civil war, testing whether that nation—or any nation, so conceived and so dedicated—can long endure.

We are met on a great battlefield of that war. We have come to dedicate a portion of that field as a final resting place for those who here gave their lives that that nation might live.

It is altogether fitting and proper that we should do this.

But, in a larger sense, we cannot dedicate, we cannot consecrate, we cannot hallow, this ground. The brave men, living and dead, who struggled here, have consecrated it, far above our poor power to add or detract.

The world will little note nor long remember what we say here, but it can never forget what they did here.

It is for us, the living, rather, to be dedicated, here, to the unfinished work which they who fought here have thus far so nobly advanced. It is rather for us to be here dedicated to the great task remaining before us—that from these honored dead we take increased devotion to that cause for which they gave the last full measure of devotion; that we here highly resolve that these dead shall not have died in vain; that this nation under God, shall have a new birth of freedom; and that government of the people, by the people, for the people, shall not perish from the earth.

4. THE SECOND PART OF THE WAR

┌─ To Guide Your Reading ─────────────────────

Look for these important words:

Key Words
• assassination

People
• William Tecumseh Sherman

Places
• Vicksburg
• Atlanta
• Appomattox Court House

Look for answers to these questions:
1. Why was the Union victory at Vicksburg important?
2. How did William Tecumseh Sherman wage war against the South?
3. How did the Civil War end?
4. Why did the North win?
5. What event brought grief to the nation?

In the West, by 1863, the Union forces were in control of New Orleans. Other points along the Mississippi River above **Vicksburg,** Mississippi, were also under their power. But Vicksburg itself belonged to the South. It was on a high bluff overlooking the mighty river. There powerful guns protected that part of the river for the Confederacy. Soldiers, food, and supplies crossed the river from Texas, Louisiana, and Arkansas.

General Ulysses S. Grant started to lay siege to Vicksburg in late May 1863. For 47 days Union guns pounded the city. The people of Vicksburg lived in caves for protection. Finally, on July 3, the Confederate commander at Vicksburg sent up the white flag of surrender. This was about the same time of Pickett's charge at Gettysburg.

Grant's victory at Vicksburg was the worst blow the South had yet received. It cut the South in two. The Union now

Ulysses S. Grant had common sense and a talent for military strategy.

had complete control of the Mississippi River. The Anaconda Plan was working. For his brilliant victory Lincoln would name Grant as his top general.

With the Union now controlling the Mississippi, Grant planned an invasion of the South. In 1864 Union troops started marching from Chattanooga, Tennessee, into Georgia. They destroyed everything that the South could use to fight the war. This army, led by General **William Tecumseh Sherman,** attacked and then occupied **Atlanta,** Georgia.

Sherman's March to the Sea

Until 1864 the war was fought between armies. In 1864 the Union army began destroying farms in Virginia. The purpose was to keep food from the Confederate armies. With Grant's permission Sherman marched his army from Atlanta toward the sea to Savannah. His goal was to destroy everything that could help the Southern war effort. Sherman's army burned crops, wrecked bridges, and tore up railroad tracks. Sherman hoped to destroy the spirit and will of the South to keep fighting.

Mrs. Thomas Burge, who lived near Covington, Georgia, was in the path of Sherman's march. She described in her diary what happened.

To my smokehouse, my dairy, pantry, kitchen and cellar, like famished wolves they come, breaking locks and whatever is in their way. The thousand pounds of meat in my smoke-house is gone in a twinkling. My flour, my meat, my lard, butter, eggs, pickles, wine, jars, and jugs are all gone. My eighteen fat turkeys, my hens, chickens, and fowls, my young pigs are shot down in my yard.

Union soldiers under Sherman's command tore up railroad tracks as they marched through Georgia. This was a new kind of warfare.

375

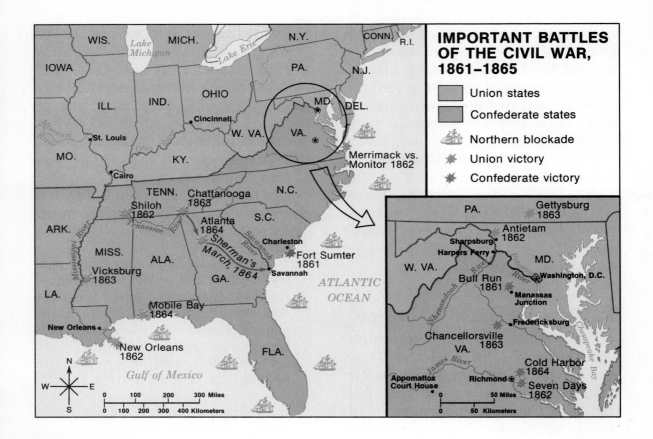

IMPORTANT BATTLES OF THE CIVIL WAR, 1861–1865

- Union states
- Confederate states
- Northern blockade
- Union victory
- Confederate victory

Lincoln's Second Term

In March 1865 Lincoln took the oath of office for a second term as President. The end of the war was in sight. Lincoln's words had given will and spirit to the North to carry on the war. Now his words, in the Second Inaugural Address, aimed at healing the nation's wounds. Lincoln said he hoped to see a "just and lasting peace." It would be "with malice toward none, with charity for all."

Surrender at Appomattox

General Grant was now in charge of the Union army fighting in northern Virginia. There Lee's troops were ragged and starving. Grant's soldiers were well armed and well fed. Grant kept pushing the Confederate troops. Lee could no longer protect Richmond. At last Lee was put in a position where he could neither fight nor retreat. He surrendered his army to Grant at the town of **Appomattox Court House** on April 9, 1865.

There in the parlor of a private home, Grant met with Lee. They discussed the terms of the surrender.

Grant told Lee the Confederate soldiers were to lay down their arms. They were also to return to their homes. The men who owned their own horses and mules could keep them, Grant said. They would need the animals to plant enough crops to get through the next winter. After they had signed the surrender papers, Lee asked Grant for food for his soldiers. Grant told Lee to take all he wanted from Union supplies.

Grant later wrote about that meeting with Lee. He said he could not tell whether Lee was glad or sad the end had come.

Despite Lincoln's Second Inaugural Address, not everyone in the North approved of the kindness Grant showed Lee. Many wanted to see Confederate leaders hanged as traitors. Grant's surrender terms made that impossible.

The North had won the war for several reasons. Lincoln's strategy of keeping supplies from the South had worked. Northern manufacturing supplied the needs of the Union army. Lincoln had been a strong leader who inspired the Union to fight.

In winning the war the North had preserved the union of the United States. It had ended slavery. The war encouraged Northern industries to grow. The North was even stronger at the end of the war than before.

Tired, hungry, and war-saddened, these Confederate soldiers weep as the Confederate flag is furled for the last time.

The Death of Lincoln

Less than a week after the surrender at Appomattox, President Lincoln was attending the theater. There John Wilkes Booth, an actor, shot him. Booth thought he was helping the Confederates. After shooting Lincoln, Booth leaped to the stage. Then he escaped on horseback. He was followed, and 12 days later he was shot while hiding in a barn.

Lincoln was taken to a house across the street. Early the next morning, April 15, his heart stopped. "Now he belongs to the ages," said Lincoln's secretary of war, Edwin Stanton. It was a cold, rainy day. Strong and brave people wept.

The North mourned Lincoln's death. A railroad train carried Lincoln's body from Washington to Illinois. Millions gathered along the route. They grieved for the man who had led the nation through its darkest time.

Secretary of War Stanton blamed Jefferson Davis for the **assassination** (uh•SAS•uhn•ay•shun). An assassination is murder for a political reason. In grief and anger many Northerners wanted to see the South punished. "Hang Jeff Davis," many shouted. Confederate leaders had nothing to do with Lincoln's death, but bad feelings remained. The North forgot Lincoln's words, "with malice toward none, with charity for all." As a result, the nation's wounds were slow to heal.

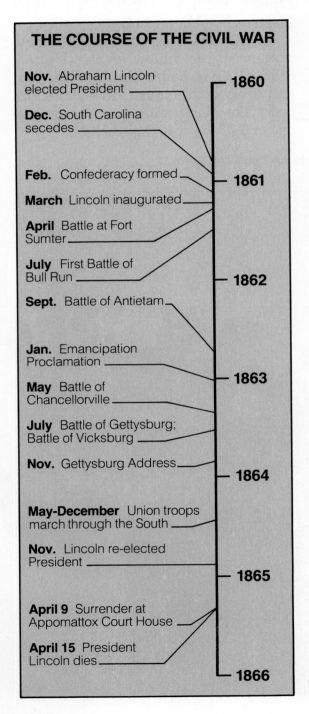

THE COURSE OF THE CIVIL WAR

Nov. Abraham Lincoln elected President — 1860

Dec. South Carolina secedes

Feb. Confederacy formed — 1861

March Lincoln inaugurated

April Battle at Fort Sumter

July First Battle of Bull Run — 1862

Sept. Battle of Antietam

Jan. Emancipation Proclamation

May Battle of Chancellorville — 1863

July Battle of Gettysburg; Battle of Vicksburg

Nov. Gettysburg Address — 1864

May-December Union troops march through the South

Nov. Lincoln re-elected President — 1865

April 9 Surrender at Appomattox Court House

April 15 President Lincoln dies — 1866

Reading Check

1. Why was the Union victory at Vicksburg a terrible blow to the South?
2. How was Sherman's march a different kind of warfare?
3. In what way did General Grant show kindness in the surrender terms?
4. Name three reasons the North won the war.

CLOSE-UP

THE CIVIL WAR AT SEA

The Confederate ironclad *Merrimac* (right) does battle with the *Monitor* on March 9, 1862.

The *Congress,* a wooden Union warship, was on patrol in the waters near Norfolk, Virginia. An officer on board scanned the horizon with his spyglass. He was looking for Confederate ships. Suddenly he cried out, "That thing! That thing is coming!" It was March 8, 1862.

The other crewmen of the *Congress* gathered to see a strange vessel coming toward them. It looked, one of them thought, like a runaway hay barn.

379

A Confederate sailor

This strange ship was called the *Merrimac*. It was America's first metal warship, then called an *ironclad*. The Confederacy had created it starting with the hull of an old wooden frigate. On the top of the hull a fortress had been built. This fortress had 2-inch (5.1-cm) iron sheets placed on slanted walls of thick pine and oak. The *Merrimac* was slow and very hard to steer, but that did not matter much. The *Merrimac* was almost unsinkable. No one had yet invented a shell or cannonball able to pierce iron. The *Merrimac* easily destroyed the *Congress* and another union warship that day. Then it went away for the night. Its intention was to return the next day and finish off the remaining Union vessels.

Fortunately for the Union, its navy had an ironclad of its own. Stephen Mallory built the *Merrimac* for the South. At the same time a Swedish immigrant, John Ericsson, designed an iron-covered ship for the North. Ericsson named his creation the *Monitor*.

The *Monitor* had already left New York when President Lincoln heard about the *Merrimac*'s success. He ordered the *Monitor* to rush to Norfolk.

When the *Merrimac* returned on March 9, its crew stared at the strange vessel guarding the harbor. One Confederate officer described it as "an immense shingle floating in the water, with a gigantic cheesebox rising from its center."

For four hours the "runaway barn" battled the "floating cheesebox." They fought side by side, each ship landing direct hits on the other. Neither ship was seriously damaged, but eventually the *Merrimac* was forced to retreat. A telegram announced the news to President Lincoln. "*Monitor* is uninjured and ready at any moment to repel another attack." Lincoln was overjoyed. The *Monitor* had saved the small Union fleet.

Violent sea battles between Union and Confederacy took place throughout the war. The Union won most of these battles. As brave as its sailors were, the South could not match the Union navy.

UNION ADVANTAGES   At the time of the war, the South depended on agriculture. Cotton, tobacco, and rice were the major crops. There was little industry.

The North had the lion's share of factories and ironworks. Most trading ships and merchant seamen were based in the North. Annapolis, the training school for naval officers, was in Maryland, a Union state.

The North's strategy was a blockade of Southern ports. Unable to trade, the South ran short of many necessary items. In fact, the South ran short of almost everything but tobacco, rice, and cotton.

FIGHTING THE BLOCKADE   The South fought against the blockade with all the might and wit at its command. Southern inventors used beer kegs and other metal cases to make exploding underwater bombs. These bombs, called mines or torpedoes, were placed in Southern harbors to sink or scare off Union vessels.

Most blockade runners were built in England. They could use either sails or steam engines for power.

Special Confederate ships called **blockade runners** learned to sneak through the blockade. These steamers were painted gray to blend with the coastal fog. Cotton was loaded onto the runners for export to England and other countries. The blockade runners returned carrying food, guns, and luxuries.

BATTLE AT MOBILE BAY As the war dragged on, the South found itself strangled by the blockade. By 1864 only a few Southern ports remained open. The most important of these ports was Mobile, Alabama.

A Union admiral, David Glasgow Farragut, intended to close the port. In August 1864 he led his fleet to the entrance of Mobile Bay. Two years earlier Farragut had cleverly slipped his ships past two Confederate forts to capture New Orleans. Two Confederate forts also guarded the entrance to Mobile Bay. This time, however, Farragut would have no chance to slip by.

This picture of the Union fleet at the Battle of Vicksburg shows how ships changed during the war. Notice that they are powered by steam engines and have metal decks.

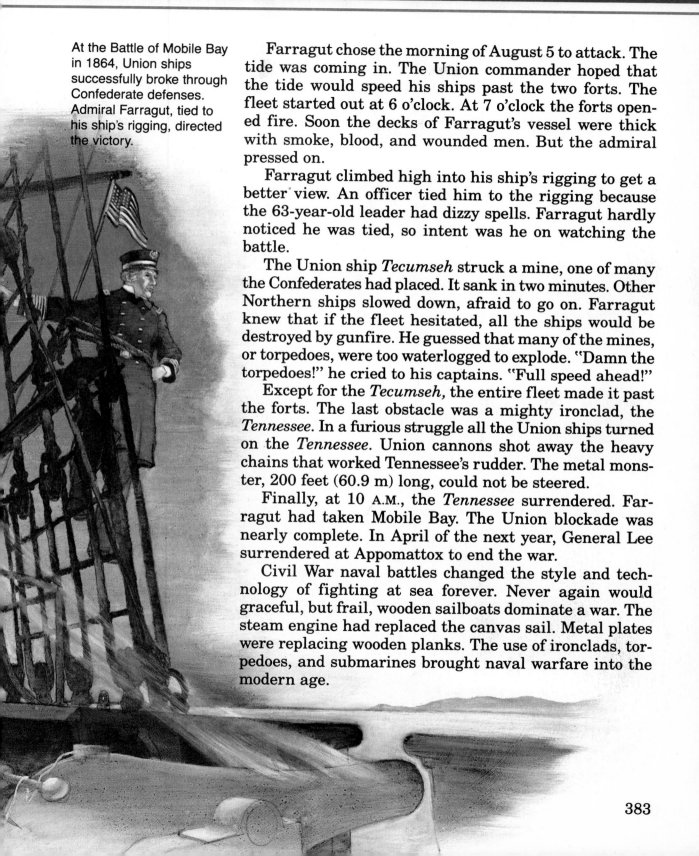

At the Battle of Mobile Bay in 1864, Union ships successfully broke through Confederate defenses. Admiral Farragut, tied to his ship's rigging, directed the victory.

Farragut chose the morning of August 5 to attack. The tide was coming in. The Union commander hoped that the tide would speed his ships past the two forts. The fleet started out at 6 o'clock. At 7 o'clock the forts opened fire. Soon the decks of Farragut's vessel were thick with smoke, blood, and wounded men. But the admiral pressed on.

Farragut climbed high into his ship's rigging to get a better view. An officer tied him to the rigging because the 63-year-old leader had dizzy spells. Farragut hardly noticed he was tied, so intent was he on watching the battle.

The Union ship *Tecumseh* struck a mine, one of many the Confederates had placed. It sank in two minutes. Other Northern ships slowed down, afraid to go on. Farragut knew that if the fleet hesitated, all the ships would be destroyed by gunfire. He guessed that many of the mines, or torpedoes, were too waterlogged to explode. "Damn the torpedoes!" he cried to his captains. "Full speed ahead!"

Except for the *Tecumseh,* the entire fleet made it past the forts. The last obstacle was a mighty ironclad, the *Tennessee.* In a furious struggle all the Union ships turned on the *Tennessee.* Union cannons shot away the heavy chains that worked Tennessee's rudder. The metal monster, 200 feet (60.9 m) long, could not be steered.

Finally, at 10 A.M., the *Tennessee* surrendered. Farragut had taken Mobile Bay. The Union blockade was nearly complete. In April of the next year, General Lee surrendered at Appomattox to end the war.

Civil War naval battles changed the style and technology of fighting at sea forever. Never again would graceful, but frail, wooden sailboats dominate a war. The steam engine had replaced the canvas sail. Metal plates were replacing wooden planks. The use of ironclads, torpedoes, and submarines brought naval warfare into the modern age.

CHAPTER 16 REVIEW

WORDS TO USE

For each word below select the correct definition from the list that follows.

1. **assassination**   4. **regiments**
2. **blockade**   5. **strategy**
3. **casualties**

a. Organized groups of soldiers

b. Long-range plan

c. Persons killed or wounded in war

d. Murder for a political reason

e. Using a navy to prevent ships from entering or leaving a harbor.

FACTS TO REVIEW

1. Describe the feelings of both North and South before the Battle of Bull Run.

2. Compare and contrast the war strategies of both the North and South.

3. How did the strengths of the South give it an early advantage in the war?

4. How did the strengths of the North make an important difference in the long run?

5. In what way did women, North and South, help the soldiers?

6. How did black soldiers help the North? How were they treated?

7. In what ways was the Civil War a different kind of war from the Revolutionary War?

8. What were the three goals of the North? When did Lincoln express each goal?

9. How did the North carry out the Anaconda Plan?

10. What did the North accomplish by winning the war?

IDEAS TO DISCUSS

1. How did technology make a difference in the war's outcome?

2. How was Abraham Lincoln a strong and great leader? What are the marks of leadership? Who else discussed in this chapter showed leadership?

3. Which slave states did not join the Confederacy? What reasons might they have had for staying in the Union?

4. What did Lincoln mean when he said "with malice toward none, with charity for all"? Did General Grant carry out that idea at the war's end?

○ SKILLS PRACTICE

Fact and Opinion   Decide which of the statements below is fact and which is opinion.

1. I think Robert E. Lee was the greatest general in American history.

2. Much property was destroyed when Sherman marched through Georgia.

3. General Sherman was a terrible man.

4. Abraham Lincoln was reelected in 1864.

5. The South would have won if Britain and France had come to its aid.

UNIT 6 REVIEW

WORDS TO REMEMBER

Replace the underlined words in the sentences below with the correct word or words from this list. Write the new sentences on your paper.

abolitionists　**fugitives**
assassination　**regiments**
a blockade　**secession**
casualties　**strategy**
emancipation　**tariff**

1. North and South had long disagreed over a tax on imported goods.

2. Frederick Douglass and William Lloyd Garrison both were people who wanted slavery ended everywhere.

3. Harriet Tubman helped runaway slaves reach freedom in Canada.

4. After the election of Abraham Lincoln many Southern states voted for withdrawing from the Union.

5. President Lincoln ordered warships to prevent other ships from entering or leaving harbors of Southern ports.

6. Men and boys from both North and South joined with friends and neighbors to form organized groups of soldiers.

7. The Anaconda Plan was the name given to Lincoln's long-range plan for winning the war.

8. The battles of the Civil War resulted in great numbers of people killed or wounded.

9. President Lincoln declared freedom for all slaves in the Confederacy as of January 1, 1863.

10. The North mourned at news of the murder for a political reason of President Lincoln.

FOCUS ON MAIN IDEAS

1. The causes of the Civil War were rooted in the different ways of life in North and South. How did North and South differ?

2. Why was the extension of slavery so important to both North and South?

3. How did North and South use compromise to keep the peace for years?

4. What was the purpose of the Underground Railroad? How did it get its name?

5. Why was the fighting in Kansas a sign of the coming Civil War?

6. Describe Abraham Lincoln's ideas on slavery:

   a. when he first ran for President
   b. when he issued the Emancipation Proclamation

7. When the war started, what were the Confederate states fighting for?

8. Many changes happened during the Civil War. What changes occurred in:

   a. the goals of the North?
   b. technology of guns and cannons?
   c. medical care on the battlefield?

9. What were the important ideas of the Gettysburg Address? How did it give the North yet another goal to fight for?

10. What was Lincoln's strategy for winning the Civil War? Did his strategy work? Explain your answer.

ACTIVITIES

1. **Research/Writing** Choose one of the people discussed in this unit. Find out more about that person and write a report.

2. **Research/Oral Report** With a friend read more about the Lincoln-Douglas debates. Then one of you take the point of view of Douglas, and one take the point of view of Lincoln. Each explain your point of view to your class.

3. **Making a Chart** Make a chart of the major battles of the Civil War. On the chart name the battles in the order they happened. Tell when and where each battle was fought. Tell the importance of the battle.

4. **Reading/Writing** Read a book about Civil War times. It could be a biography of a person or a fiction book. Write a report telling how the book helped you understand more about this time in history.

5. **Writing** Imagine that you are serving in one of the armies in the Civil War as either a soldier or a nurse. Write a letter home about your feelings and experiences.

6. **Timeline** Make a timeline with 1850 as the beginning date and 1865 as the ending date. On your timeline put the main events leading to the Civil War. Put the major battles and events of the Civil War.

7. **Research/Art** Choose an event from this unit. Read more about it. Then draw or paint a picture of the event.

8. **Remembering the Close-Up** After you have read about the navies during the Civil War, do one of the following:

   a. Make a map showing the locations of important naval battles.
   b. Read more about one of the naval battles and write a report on it.

9. **Research/Oral Report** Learn more about one of these subjects and give an oral report on what you learn.

   a. Civil War cavalry
   b. Civil War artillery
   c. Civil War medicine and nursing
   d. Famous generals of the Civil War
   e. Black soldiers in the Civil War

◯ SKILLS REVIEW

1. **Using Population Maps** Find Florida and Louisiana on the population density maps on page 353. Use the maps to answer these questions.

   a. What was the average population density of northern Florida in 1860? of southern Florida?
   b. Did Florida or Louisiana have a city of over 100,000 people?
   c. In 1860 were there probably more slaves in Louisiana or Florida? Explain.

2. **Fact and Opinion** Which of the following sentences is fact and which is opinion?

   a. Savannah is a much older city than Atlanta.
   b. Atlanta is a transportation center of the South.
   c. I think Georgia peaches are better than any others.
   d. West Point Lake is more fun to visit than Lake Sinclair.

YOUR STATE'S HISTORY

Most of the fighting in the Civil War took place in the southeastern states. The whole nation, however, felt the effect of this war. The following activities may help you learn about your state during this stormy, difficult time.

LEARNING ABOUT GOVERNMENT

1. Did your state join the Union between 1820 and 1860? If so, did it join the Union as a free state or a slave state? Did people in your state vote whether it would be a free or slave state?

LEARNING ABOUT ECONOMICS

2. How did the economy of your state change during the Civil War? Was there an increase in manufacturing? What happened to agriculture? Was your state generally richer or poorer at the end of the war? Why?

MAKING A TIMELINE

3. What important events happened in your state between 1850 and 1865? Make a timeline showing these events. Include on the timeline important Civil War events.

LEARNING ABOUT GEOGRAPHY

4. Were any Civil War battles fought in your state? If so, locate the battle sites on a blank map of your state.

5. Many places in the United States are named after people who were important during the Civil War. What places in your community or state are named after people you have studied in this unit?

6. Do you live in a state that had stops on the Underground Railroad? If so, what towns in your state were stops on the Underground Railroad?

LEARNING ABOUT PEOPLE

7. When the Civil War started, Clara Barton began to carry supplies to the wounded. She was called the Angel of the Battlefield. After the war she organized a search for missing persons. Even later, she founded the American Red Cross. Today the Red Cross is important in every state. Find out what services the Red Cross provides in your state. Find out how volunteers are important to the Red Cross and other service organizations.

UNIT SEVEN

MODERN TIMES BEGIN

After the Civil War the number of factories in the nation greatly increased. Cities grew larger and larger. People in great numbers moved west. All this growth and movement were due to new technology.

Perhaps the leading symbols of the new technology were the telegraph line and the railroad. Running side by side, the railroad track and the telegraph line knitted the country together. They changed where and how people lived.

In this unit you will read about how America changed after the Civil War. These changes were the beginning of modern technology and of life as you know it.

Key Dates and Events

1865
Civil War ends
Freedmen's Bureau started

Steel railroad tracks manufactured

1866
Fourteenth Amendment passes Congress

1867
Military rule in Southern states

First Texas cattle drive to Kansas

1869
Transcontinental railroad completed

1872
Yellowstone becomes the first national park

1877
Reconstruction ends

1876
Battle of the Little Bighorn

1877
Chief Joseph surrenders

1886
American Federation of Labor founded

Geronimo surrenders

1890s
Populist movement

CHAPTER 17

Changes in North and South

After the Civil War people in the South struggled to get their farms working again. They needed to rebuild towns, factories, and railroads. One by one the former Confederate states came back into the Union. One of the biggest challenges faced by the South was to establish new relations between whites and former slaves.

During the years of the Civil War, the Northern cities were booming. Their growth was based on earlier inventions, new factories, and war production. This growth continued after the Civil War. It resulted in great wealth for some people. In contrast, the poor of the cities worked and lived in miserable conditions. Before the century was over, workers had begun to organize. Their aims were better wages and working conditions.

1. RECONSTRUCTION IN THE SOUTH

To Guide Your Reading

Look for these important words:

Key Words
- Reconstruction
- Freedman's Bureau
- sharecroppers
- tenant farmers
- legislatures
- Black Codes
- second-class citizens
- Fourteenth Amendment
- ratify
- carpetbaggers
- scalawags
- Fifteenth Amendment
- secret ballot
- segregation
- Jim Crow laws
- poll tax

Look for answers to these questions:

1. What problems did freed slaves face after the Civil War?
2. What was the Freedman's Bureau?
3. Why was military rule established in the South?
4. How did Southern states discourage black people from voting?

The end of the Civil War in 1865 brought the nation three main problems.

- The war had freed millions of slaves. The freed slaves were overjoyed to be free, but what would they do for housing, clothing, and food? How would they earn a living?
- The South was in economic ruin. There was no money. Banks were closed. Stores had little to sell. Railroads, bridges, plantations, and crops had been destroyed. How would the South be rebuilt?
- With the defeat of the Confederacy, the South no longer had any government. How would the Southern states be brought back into the government of the United States?

The government plan for dealing with these problems was called

Reconstruction. The word *reconstruction* means rebuilding. Reconstruction had two distinct parts. The first part was Lincoln's Reconstruction plan. The second part was Congress's Reconstruction plan.

President Lincoln's Reconstruction plan called for a **Freedmen's Bureau.** The Freedmen's Bureau would provide help and education to the former slaves. After Lincoln's death, Andrew Johnson, the new President, started to carry out Lincoln's Reconstruction plan.

The Freedmen's Bureau provided food, clothing, and fuel to both black and white people. It set up law courts. It established schools, perhaps its most important work. The Freedmen's Bureau built more than 4,000 schools and hired teachers for them.

The newly freed blacks were eager for education. "The tiniest children are

Freed blacks were eager to learn. Children and grandparents sit side by side in this Freedman's school in Vicksburg, Mississippi.

delighted to get a book in their hands," one teacher wrote. Another observer said that they would "starve themselves, and go without clothes, in order to send their children to school." Learning, they knew, was a key to another kind of freedom.

Freed blacks had hoped that they would be given 40 acres (16.2 ha) and a mule. That did not happen, so most worked for their former masters as **sharecroppers** or **tenant farmers.**

Sharecropping worked like this. A landowner gave a sharecropper mules, plows, farming tools, and food. In return, the sharecropper gave the landowner one-third to one-half his crop. Unlike a sharecropper, a tenant farmer owned his animals and tools. He paid rent to the landowner in either crops or money. As sharecroppers or tenant farmers, millions of freed blacks were now able to earn a living. Southern farms began again to produce crops.

As part of Lincoln's Reconstruction plan, elections were held in the South and state governments were soon back in operation. However, the new state **legislatures,** or lawmaking bodies, soon began to pass laws called **Black Codes.** These laws made newly freed blacks into **second-class citizens.** This meant that blacks did not have the full rights of citizenship. In some states they could by law do only household or field work. Blacks could not vote.

Many members of Congress were upset about what the South was doing. They did not think that blacks should be second-class citizens. Congress replaced Lincoln's Reconstruction plan with one of its own.

Congress's Plan

As part of its plan, Congress proposed the **Fourteenth Amendment** to the Constitution. The Fourteenth Amendment declared that all people born in the United States were citizens. All were to be given equal protection under the law.

Southern states refused to **ratify,** or approve, the Fourteenth Amendment. In response, Congress ordered military rule in the South, beginning in 1867. The South would be governed by the army until each state ratified the Fourteenth Amendment. In a region already torn apart by war, Southern political life was turned upside down.

New people, blacks as well as whites, became leaders in the South. Some were Northerners who had come south to teach school or start factories. Southern whites called these Northerners **carpetbaggers.** A carpetbag was a kind of cheap suitcase made of carpet scraps. It was said the carpetbaggers came south carrying everything they owned in a carpetbag. White Southerners who worked with the Northerners in the Reconstruction governments were called **scalawags.**

Blacks held important positions in the state governments set up under military rule. Many were elected to seats both in state legislatures and in Congress.

The Reconstruction legislatures approved the Fourteenth Amendment, which became law in 1868. They also ratified the **Fifteenth Amendment.** The Fifteenth Amendment says that no citizen shall be denied the right to vote because of color or race.

The Reconstruction legislatures made some important and lasting contributions. They set up schools. They repaired damage to bridges and roads. They had railroads rebuilt. They repealed the Black Codes. They set up new state constitutions that gave the vote to all men. No longer did a person have to own property to vote. Under the state constitutions, a person could no longer be put in prison for debt. This helped the poor.

The End of Reconstruction

The Reconstruction legislatures passed heavy taxes on land. The taxes were used for schools, road repairs, and railroads. The taxes hurt landowners who were trying to get their farms and plantations going again. Many farms had to be sold for unpaid taxes. Planters believed the heavy taxes were strangling them.

Southern landowners began to organize to get back power. One way to achieve such power was to control the way people voted.

At that time there was no **secret ballot.** A secret ballot is a way to vote without anyone knowing how one has voted. Before the secret ballot was used, the names of voters and how they voted were published in newspapers.

Secret societies were formed to keep blacks from voting or to make certain they voted only in certain ways. Those who joined the secret societies included white people who resented the equality of black people.

Members of one secret society, the Ku Klux Klan, wore white hoods and robes. Dressed like this, they delivered

Here a black man casts his first vote. Later, new laws took away this right.

nighttime warnings to blacks who voted. Klan members also threatened white people with whom they disagreed. They sometimes burned schools and churches. At election time Klan members whipped and even killed black leaders. It was a time of terror for blacks throughout the South. Appeals to Congress fell on deaf ears.

Reconstruction was over by 1877. By then military rule had ended in the South. State governments were controlled by white landowners. Congress no longer showed an interest in protecting the rights of black people.

Blacks in the New South

In the 1870s many Southern blacks were kept from voting or forced to vote in certain ways. In some places, however, they continued to be elected and serve in city, state, and national offices.

In the 1880s practices were established that again made black people second-class citizens. One of these practices was **segregation,** or separation, of the races. Segregation came about gradually. The laws and customs that brought about segregation became known as **Jim Crow laws.** Jim Crow laws established segregation by race in all public places. Schools, theaters, trains, buses, even drinking fountains were segregated. This pattern of segregation lasted for more than 50 years.

At the same time, Southern states began to pass laws that in effect took away the right of black people to vote. One law was that a **poll tax** be paid in order to vote. In Mississippi each adult male had to pay two dollars in order to vote. A poor person might have to work four days to earn two dollars. The poll tax discouraged poor people, both black and white, from voting.

Another law in Southern states said that a person had to prove he could read or understand the state constitution. Officials who gave the tests rarely passed a black person. White people could vote whether or not they could read or understand the constitution. Unable to vote, blacks had little power to bring about changes they wanted. By 1899 there were few black officeholders.

Reading Check

1. How did the Freedmen's Bureau help Reconstruction?
2. Why did Congress propose the Fourteenth Amendment?
3. What were Jim Crow laws?
4. How did new state laws keep blacks from voting?

2. NEW TECHNOLOGY, NEW INVENTIONS

To Guide Your Reading

Look for these important words:

Key Words
- Industrial Revolution
- Bessemer process
- smelt
- coke
- slag
- industrial
- telegraph
- Morse Code
- invested
- reaper

- guarantee
- petroleum
- monopoly

People
- Samuel F. B. Morse
- Andrew Carnegie
- Cyrus McCormick
- John D. Rockefeller
- Alexander Graham Bell

Places
- Pittsburgh
- Lake Superior
- Chicago
- Gary
- Cleveland
- Detroit
- Birmingham

Look for answers to these questions:

1. What happened during the Industrial Revolution?
2. Why did places like Chicago become large cities?
3. What inventions and improvements depended on iron and steel?
4. Why did petroleum become an important resource in the nineteenth century?

The great growth of technology and business in the nineteenth century changed American life forever. Taken together, these changes are called the **Industrial Revolution.** During the Industrial Revolution, machines replaced hand tools. Factories replaced craft shops. Coal replaced wood as a fuel. Iron became the basis of new technologies.

In 1779 the British built the first all-iron bridge. Soon iron was being used for buildings and railroad tracks as well. The development of railroads depended on iron tracks. As locomotives got bigger and heavier, not even iron tracks were strong enough. Many lasted only about three years.

Steel tracks were harder and lasted longer, but steel was very expensive to make. Steel is made from iron with a small amount of carbon added. Other metals like nickel may also be added. Because of the expense, steel was used only for such objects as knives and swords.

By 1856 inventors in both England and the United States discovered a new way to make steel. It was both cheaper and easier than the old way. Named after the English inventor Henry Bessemer, this new method was called the **Bessemer process.** By 1865 factories in the United States were turning out steel railroad tracks. They were expected to last at least 20 years.

Making steel requires a fuel that burns hot enough to **smelt** the iron ore. *To smelt* means to melt ore to separate out the metal. The best fuel, steelmakers discovered, was **coke.** Coke is made from coal and burns much hotter than coal itself.

Steelmaking also requires the use of limestone. Mixed with the molten iron ore, limestone helps remove the **slag.** Slag is the part of the ore that is not iron. After the smelting process, slag is left over as a waste product.

New Cities

New cities were started as the United States became an **industrial** nation. *Industrial* means having many

In the hot glare of the blast furnaces, workers made steel for the nation.

factories. Before this time, important cities were located on good harbors near the ocean. The new industrial cities were built inland. They developed close to resources needed for iron and steel manufacturing.

The Appalachian Plateau, an area west of the Appalachian Mountains, had many such resources. It was rich in iron, coal, and limestone. Because of this, the first iron and steel industry developed in western Pennsylvania. **Pittsburgh** became a great steelmaking center. It remains so today.

The nation's greatest iron ore deposits were found in the 1850s near **Lake Superior** in Michigan. The ore was transported by barge across Lake Superior to Chicago and other Great Lakes cities. To the same cities, trains brought coal from the Appalachian region. **Chicago,** Illinois; **Gary,** Indiana; **Cleveland,** Ohio; and **Detroit,** Michigan, all became centers of iron and steel manufacturing. Other manufacturers who used iron and steel to make their products built their factories nearby.

In the South, **Birmingham,** Alabama, also became a large city. It too was close to iron and coal deposits. It was not on the water, like the older cities of Charleston and New Orleans.

Manufacturers were able to build factories near resources because of the railroads. Railroads could be built almost anywhere. Manufacturers could use them to bring necessary raw materials to their factories. Manufactured goods could be transported by railroad to distant markets. Cities such as Chicago, Illinois; Pittsburgh, Pennsylvania; St. Louis, Missouri; and Atlanta, Georgia, became railroad centers.

The Telegraph

The inventions and improvements of the nineteenth century depended on iron and steel. The **telegraph** was one of the most important of these inventions. Both Europeans and Americans had experimented with ways to send messages over long distances. An American inventor, **Samuel F. B. Morse,** experimented with sending electricity along iron wires. To send messages along the wires, Morse invented a code. The code was a system of dots and dashes standing for letters of the alphabet. This system became known as the **Morse code.**

With money from Congress, Morse built the first telegraph line between Washington, D.C. and Baltimore, Maryland. On May 24, 1844, Morse tested the telegraph line. He sat in the Capitol and sent a series of electrical dots and dashes along the iron wire to Baltimore. There his assistant translated the dots and dashes to read, "What hath God wrought!"

The country quickly recognized the importance of the telegraph. Telegraph lines were strung along railroad tracks. With the telegraph, railroads could keep track of train schedules. With the telegraph, news could flash quickly from one part of the country to the next.

By 1861 telegraph poles reached across the continent to California. In

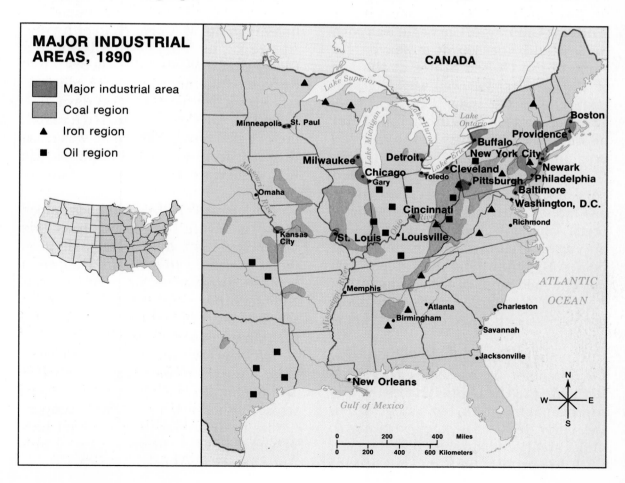

MAJOR INDUSTRIAL AREAS, 1890

- Major industrial area
- Coal region
- ▲ Iron region
- ■ Oil region

1866 a telegraph cable was successfully laid under the Atlantic Ocean. Within hours people on either side of the Atlantic could communicate with one another. Time had speeded up.

After the Civil War most of America's energy was directed to inventing, manufacturing, and selling. In this, inventors were important, but it was businessmen who made fortunes. Huge fortunes were made in new industries, including steel, oil, flour milling, railroads, and lumber. The richest and most important businessmen were called captains of industry.

Andrew Carnegie

The captain of the steel industry was **Andrew Carnegie.** Carnegie was born in Scotland, the son of a weaver. He came to the United States at the age of 12. His first job was working in a textile mill. He then became a telegraph operator on a railroad line. Later he worked as secretary to the railroad president.

As a young man, Carnegie **invested** part of his wages. *To invest* means to use money with the hope of making a profit. Carnegie invested his money by buying shares of stock in new businesses. By buying shares of stock, Carnegie owned parts of these companies. As these companies grew and made profits, stockholders like Carnegie prospered.

Carnegie visited England and saw the Bessemer process for making steel. Returning to the United States, he and several partners started a steel mill in the early 1870s. He kept working to make steel at a lower and lower cost. With his profits, he built and bought more steel mills. Carnegie became one of the richest men in America.

Cyrus McCormick

Cyrus McCormick, both an inventor and businessman, changed life on the farm. For centuries there had been only one method of harvesting grains. This was to use a hand-held scythe (SYTH). It was hard, backbreaking work. A better way to harvest the grain was needed. Many tried to develop a good **reaper,** or harvester, but Cyrus McCormick succeeded.

Cyrus McCormick grew up on a Virginia farm. As a boy he liked to spend time in his father's tool shop. His father had tried to invent a reaper but had given up. McCormick kept trying. At age 22, in 1831, he finally made a reaper that worked. Within hours it had harvested as much grain as could be cut with a scythe in several days.

In 1848 McCormick started a reaper factory in Chicago. There he was close to wood, iron, and steel supplies. He was also close to the grain-growing prairies.

McCormick's selling methods helped make a revolution in business. He advertised his reaper widely. He gave demonstrations to farmers. He gave a written **guarantee,** or promise, that the machine would work. He even let farmers buy reapers by paying a little at a time instead of all at once.

All the while, McCormick was improving the reaper, making it better and bigger. By the 1880s farmers were using 30-horse teams to pull reapers across their fields. Tons of wheat harvested this way were sold to feed millions of city dwellers.

Near Steele's Tavern, Virginia, a crowd gathers to see an invention that will change their lives: Cyrus McCormick's reaping machine. With this invention, farmers could cut as much wheat in one day as they had been able to cut in two weeks using a hand-held scythe.

New Uses for Oil

For years people had been aware of the black oil, or **petroleum,** that gathered on ponds in western Pennsylvania. In the early 1800s the oil was collected and sold in bottles as "American oil." Drinking it was supposed to cure everything from cough to toothache. Yet there seemed to be more oil than Americans could ever take as medicine.

What else could one do with the oil? Scientists were asked to study it. They reported that the oil burned well and was a good grease. Soon more and more uses for petroleum were discovered. Greater efforts were made to collect it from the tops of ponds.

Then in 1859 Edwin Drake started to drill for oil as one drills for water. This was in Titusville, Pennsylvania. People thought he was crazy. But when his well filled up with oil, an oil rush started. Oil towns sprang up all over western Pennsylvania. About 250 refineries in Pittsburgh and Cleveland began processing the oil for grease and kerosene.

John D. Rockefeller

John D. Rockefeller became a captain of the oil industry. Rockefeller lived in Cleveland. He was 23 years old in 1863 when he invested in an oil refinery. He steadily expanded his investment and ended up buying other refineries.

Rockefeller was known as a shrewd businessman who looked after pennies as well as dollars. "To drive a good bargain was the joy of his life," said a writer of the time.

Rockefeller hated to let anyone make a profit off his business. Therefore, his company bought forests to get its own lumber. It bought a barrel factory to make its own barrels. It bought ships and railroad cars to carry its products. Rockefeller set out to get a **monopoly,** or complete control, of the oil business. He succeeded, but he made many enemies. He put out of business many companies that were unable or unwilling to follow his business practices. Many began to question the fairness of these practices.

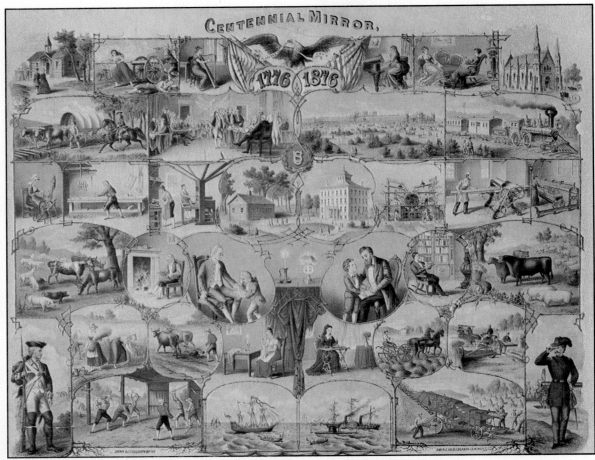

This picture was made in 1876 to show the changes in American life since 1776. Look at it carefully. How many things do you see compared?

The 1876 Exposition

The United States celebrated its one-hundredth birthday in 1876 with a world's fair in Philadelphia. At this fair, the 1876 Exposition, countries from all over the world exhibited their products. The United States did the same. American exhibits included sewing machines, iron cookstoves, locomotives, a knitting machine, and canned food. The center of American pride was a giant steam engine.

Getting less attention at the fair was one new machine. Yet this machine would change communication as much as the telegraph had. **Alexander Graham Bell,** a teacher of the deaf, demonstrated his invention of the first telephone. A professor in Scotland who heard of the invention declared, "It is all humbug, for such a discovery is physically impossible."

Reading Check

1. Name three resources needed by steelmakers.
2. Who invented the telegraph?
3. Name three captains of industry and tell the business of each.
4. Why was the reaper an important invention?

400

3. THE WORKERS OF THE NATION

To Guide Your Reading

Look for these important words:

Key Words
- tenements
- piecework
- sweatshops
- reformers

- Hull House
- labor union
- federation
- American Federation of Labor

- queue
- prejudice

People
- Jane Addams
- Samuel Gompers

Look for answers to these questions:

1. How did thousands of immigrants live in the cities?
2. How was life made better for immigrants and workers?
3. Who was Samuel Gompers? What did he achieve?
4. Why did Asians come to the United States?

The new age of steam and iron created thousands of jobs. People were needed to mine coal, build railroads, cut timber, and keep the smelters going. To fill these jobs came millions of immigrants from Europe. Between 1865 and 1900, 12 million people came from overseas. They came from such countries as Britain, Ireland, Germany, Sweden, Italy, Russia, and Hungary. The immigrants came to get away from poverty, war, or tyranny.

Millions of these immigrants lived in the cities and worked in factories, mines, and mills. Life was hard for them. They lived crowded together in run-down apartment houses called **tenements.** Salaries were so low that everyone in a family had to work. Children had to work from an early age to keep the family fed.

Many children worked at home helping their parents do **piecework.** *Piecework* is work done and paid for by the piece. Piecework was usually sew-

ing of some kind. A family doing piecework might do nothing but sew seams.

To help feed his family, this New York boy carried heavy loads of piecework.

They got paid a few pennies for each piece they sewed.

Children had always helped their parents when they lived on farms. Children who worked on farms got plenty of exercise and fresh air. They learned how to do many things. Children who worked 12 hours a day in stuffy, poorly lit rooms were not healthy. They did not learn new skills.

Long Days in Sweatshops

Often piecework was done in small factories called **sweatshops.** Sweatshops had terrible working conditions. Workers were pushed to work faster and harder and longer. Twelve-hour days were common. So were accidents. "Sometimes in my haste I get my finger caught and the needle goes right through it." This was said by Sadie Frowne, a worker in a sweatshop. "We all have accidents like that," she said. "Sometimes a finger has to come off."

If workers complained about conditions or went on strike, as many did, they were fired. Employers found it easy to hire new immigrants to work at the lowest possible wages.

Help for the City Poor

Many Americans became concerned about the growing problems of the city poor. In Chicago, for example, a group of women forced changes that resulted in better treatment in Chicago's jail and mental hospitals. These women were **reformers,** people who wish to bring about change for the better.

Jane Addams was a reformer who started **Hull House** in 1889. Hull

Jane Addams worked to help immigrants.

House was a community center where immigrants received education and training.

Reformers also worked to improve conditions in tenements. They demanded an eight-hour working day for women. They worked to outlaw child labor and to improve health and safety conditions in factories.

Samuel Gompers

As business grew more powerful, working conditions seemed to grow worse. Workers organized to fight against the power of what was now called "big business." Leading that fight was **Samuel Gompers.**

Samuel Gompers was 13 years old when his family left the tenements of London for America. America sounded good to Samuel's father, a cigar maker. It was hard to make a living in London. Samuel had quit school at the age of 10 to help his father make cigars.

In New York City the Gompers family found life similar to life in London. The whole family worked hard making cigars at home. When he was 16 years old, Samuel Gompers started to work in a cigar maker's shop. There the cigar makers worked from dawn to sunset.

Gompers had joined a cigar makers **labor union.** A labor union is an organization of workers that seeks to protect their interests. Soon Gompers was union leader of the workers in his shop. Then he organized one big union of all the cigar makers. They went on strike for a ten-hour day and better wages, but the strike failed. Tobacco buyers owned many of the tenements where the workers lived. They forced the cigar makers to move. Some ended up begging on the streets.

From this experience Gompers decided that cigar makers should get other workers to join them. All skilled workers in trades like carpentry, plumbing, and bricklaying should get together. They should form one large **federation,** Gompers said. A federation is an organization formed of many member groups. Gompers felt that only skilled workers should be in this federation. If they went on strike, it would be harder to replace them. The strike would have a better chance of success.

Gompers' dream came true in 1886. Representatives of skilled workers formed the **American Federation of Labor,** or AFL. Gompers was elected president of the AFL every year but one until his death in 1924.

Under the wise and strong leadership of Gompers, the AFL grew. Government and business leaders began to listen to its demands. The demands included higher wages and an eight-hour day. The AFL also wanted better working conditions, an end to child labor, and accident insurance. The insurance would pay the salary and medical bills for workers injured on the job. Whenever people asked what the unions wanted, Gompers answered "More."

Immigrants from Asia

The Chinese first came to America in great numbers after the California gold rush. Like others who flocked to California, they hoped to strike it rich.

About 25,000 Chinese had arrived in San Francisco by 1852. To get there, they had suffered terrible conditions on board ship. Most, however, felt they had no choice. China was a poor country, yet taxes were high. To survive, parents sometimes sold one or more of their children into slavery.

Most of the Chinese immigrants were men. They left their families behind in China and sent back money to them.

Chinese men wait to board ship for "Gold Mountain," their name for California.

To American miners in the goldfields, these Chinese immigrants seemed very strange. They looked different. They wore their hair in one braid called a **queue** (KYOO). Wearing a queue was an important part of Chinese culture. A man without a queue was in disgrace. The Chinese language and religion were also completely unfamiliar to Westerners.

The American miners tried to force the Chinese out of the goldfields. Many Chinese were beaten and even killed.

But the Chinese felt they had no choice but to persist. To go home would mean starvation for their families. Some Chinese began to specialize in meeting two important needs. They began to supply good food and clean clothes. They opened restaurants and laundries all over California. Other Chinese continued mining. In 1870 one-third of the miners in California were Chinese.

As the goldfields gave out, the Chinese did other work. They worked building railroads, draining swamps, and growing crops. They were known as hard workers.

Numbers of Chinese immigrants continued to come to this country looking for opportunity. But by the 1870s many white people wanted to keep out the Chinese. Workers were particularly upset that the Chinese were willing to work for low wages. In 1882 Congress passed a law that stopped the immigration of Chinese workers.

For Chinese in this country, life could be difficult. They continued to

Chinese immigrants, eager for opportunity and willing to work for low pay, laid down the tracks of the Central Pacific Railroad.

Japanese people, like immigrants before them, found opportunity in the United States. Many, like this family, were farmers.

face **prejudice** on the part of white Americans. Prejudice means making negative judgments about people because of their race or religion.

In western states, mobs sometimes attacked the Chinese, even killing them. Sometimes bullies amused themselves by cutting off queues. The police usually looked the other way.

Meanwhile numbers of Japanese had also come to the United States as agricultural workers. Many of these Japanese were able to save enough money to buy small farms. In California they became known as excellent farmers. In time they, too, experienced prejudice as did the Chinese.

The first Asian immigrants faced hard times. However, Asian-Americans today have distinguished themselves in all walks of life. One of these people is Hiram L. Fong, a former United States senator. Fong's parents left China to work on sugarcane plantations in Hawaii. Life in the tenements of Honolulu was hard. The Fong family was very poor.

To earn money, young Hiram Fong started shining shoes and selling fish and newspapers. He worked hard to earn money to attend school. In time he graduated from law school. Fong became rich by practicing law and investing in business. He also gave time to public service and was elected to Hawaii's legislature. Later he served four terms in the United States Senate.

Reading Check

1. What were conditions like in a sweatshop?
2. What was the purpose of Hull House?
3. Why did Samuel Gompers urge trade unions to join together?
4. Why did people wish to exclude Chinese and Japanese immigrants?

SKILLS FOR SUCCESS

USING TIME ZONES

People used to figure time based only on the sun's position. Noon was the hour when the sun reached its **zenith,** or highest point, in the sky. Yet the sun is not at its zenith in all places at the same time. When it is noon in Kansas City, Missouri, it is still morning in San Francisco, California. It is afternoon in Baltimore, Maryland.

Telling time from the sun was not a problem until the railroads began to cross the United States. Railroad managers could not set up train schedules because of the time differences from place to place.

Sandford Fleming of Canada and Charles F. Dowd of the United States had an idea. They proposed that the world be divided into 24 time zones. The time zones would be laid out along every fifteenth meridian from the Prime Meridian at Greenwich, England. Each time zone would be one hour different from neighboring time zones. Each time zone to the west would always be one hour earlier than the time zone to the east. All towns in a time zone would use the same time. In the 1880s railway managers began to adopt this plan. Most countries in the world today follow this plan for figuring time.

On the next page is a time zone map of the mainland United States. Most of the United States is divided into four time zones. Much of Alaska and all of Hawaii are in other time zones. Notice that the lines between time zones are not as straight as meridians. That is because time zone boundaries may follow state borders or geographic areas.

How can you figure out what time it is in cities in different time zones? First, figure out what time zone each city is in. Find New York City on the map. It is in the eastern time zone. Now find Kansas City in the central time zone, the next time zone to the west. To find the time in Kansas City, subtract one hour from the time in New York. If it is noon in New York, it is 11:00 A.M. in Kansas City. Find Denver on the map. It is in the mountain time zone. It is one hour earlier in Denver than it is in Kansas City. It is two hours earlier in Denver than in New York City.

Move west to Los Angeles. What time zone is Los Angeles in? It is one hour earlier in this zone than it is in Denver. It is two hours earlier than in Kansas City. It is three hours earlier than in New York. When it is noon in New York City, what time is it in Los

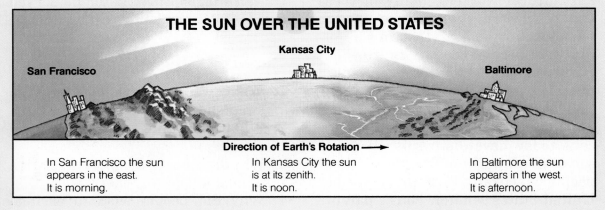

THE SUN OVER THE UNITED STATES

Kansas City

San Francisco

Baltimore

Direction of Earth's Rotation ⟶

In San Francisco the sun appears in the east. It is morning.

In Kansas City the sun is at its zenith. It is noon.

In Baltimore the sun appears in the west. It is afternoon.

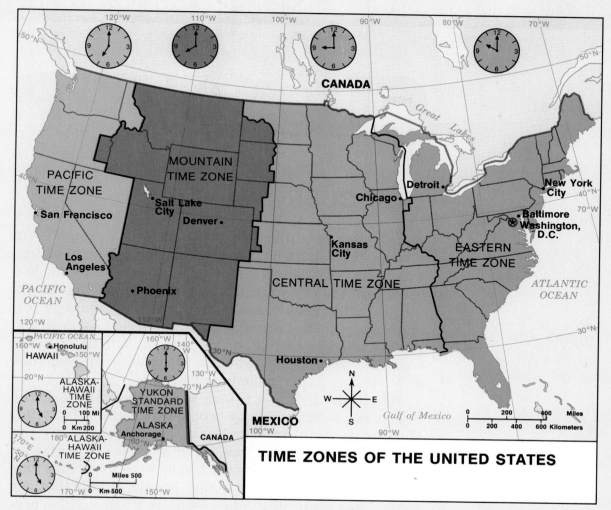

TIME ZONES OF THE UNITED STATES

Angeles? When it is noon in Los Angeles, what time is it in Hawaii?

The time in each zone is often abbreviated. *EST* stands for Eastern Standard Time. *CST* stands for Central Standard Time. *MST* stands for Mountain Standard Time. *PST* stands for Pacific Standard Time. When a newspaper announces that the President will speak at 7:00 P.M. (EST), people in other parts of the country have to figure the time for their zone.

From the end of April to the end of October, most places operate on daylight time. This means that the clocks are set ahead an hour. Daylight time lets people have more hours of light at the end of the day. During daylight time the abbreviations in each time zone are *EDT, CDT, MDT,* and *PDT.*

CHECKING YOUR SKILLS

Use the map to answer these questions.

1. In what time zone is Salt Lake City?

2. What time is it in Salt Lake City when it is 4:00 P.M. in New York City?

3. What time is it in Salt Lake City when it is 6:00 A.M. in San Francisco?

4. In what time zone is Houston?

5. When it is 2:00 P.M. in Houston, what time is it on the West Coast?

CLOSE-UP

HOW BUSINESS WORKS

Did you ever think about how many things you use in a single day? Imagine it is a school day. In the morning, when you wash your face, you use soap and water. You use a towel to dry yourself. When you brush your teeth, you use a toothbrush and toothpaste. For breakfast you might eat a bowl of cereal with milk. To get to school, you might use your bicycle, or ride a bus, or ride in a car. Once you get to school, you use many other things, such as books and paper, pencils and pens.

Where do all these things come from? Many of the things we use are made by people who work in factories. Most of these things they make are sold in shops and stores. Factories and offices, shops and stores are all part of business. Business provides people with the things they want or need. Business provides **goods,** things that are made, like this book you are reading. Business also provides **services.** A service is any kind of work that helps people. People who cut hair, fix cars, or trim trees are all providing services.

In the United States, businesses can offer for sale many kinds of goods and services. This freedom is called **free enterprise.** In a free enterprise system, people can buy almost anything they may need or want.

Today there are millions of businesses in our country. A small shoe store and a large airline are both called businesses. Many small businesses, such as shoe stores and bicycle shops, are owned by one person. Very large businesses, such as automobile makers and airlines, are usually owned by many people.

How does business work? To answer this question, let's meet some people. They are in the business of making and selling something you might use every day—bicycles.

Edna Jones' bicycle shop features a variety of bicycles for her customers to choose from.

A Bicycle Shop

Edna Jones owns a small bicycle shop called Wheels and Deals. Her shop is filled with many different kinds of bicycles, everything from tricycles to ten speeds. "I'm very proud of my business," she says. "I have one of the most successful bike shops in the city."

Edna Jones explains that her shop did not always have so many bicycles on display. "To start my shop, I needed money," she says. "The money used to start a business is called **capital.** I needed capital to buy a cash register and to get my shop ready for business. I also needed capital to buy my first shipment of bicycles from the factory. At first I had only a few bicycles. Now I have more than 100."

How does Edna Jones run her business?

"First of all, it costs money to run a shop like this. I have three people who work for me, and I pay them wages. I pay money each month to rent this building. Even the electricity for the lights and heat costs money."

The amount of money it takes to run a business is called **overhead.** Overhead can be costly.

409

A customer responds to an advertisement.

People make bicycle parts in a factory.

If it costs so much to run a shop, how does Edna Jones make money?

"I sell bicycles for more than they cost to buy from the factory," Edna Jones explains. "That means that I make some money on each bicycle I sell. With that money I pay my overhead. If business is good, there is money left over after I have paid my overhead." In business the money left over after all expenses are paid is called **profit.**

Edna Jones shows an advertisement for her bicycle shop that appeared in the local newspaper. "I use advertisements like this to bring in new customers," she explains. "You see, there are other bicycle shops in the city. We are all trying to offer the best price or the best service. That way we will find new customers." Trying to get new customers is called **competition.** One shop competes with another for business.

Just then a customer comes into the shop. He has come because he saw the advertisement in the newspaper.

"You see, my advertisement is working!" Edna Jones says happily. "And now, please excuse me. In a business like mine, the customer is always the most important person."

A Bicycle Manufacturer

We have seen how bicycles are sold. Now let's look at one business that makes bicycles, the Putnam Bicycle Company. Walter Putnam started the company, but he only owns part of it. The company is a **corporation.** A corporation is owned by stockholders who have each invested money in the company. Mr. Putnam is president of the company but he must make reports to the stockholders.

Mr. Putnam is happy to show people how bicycles are produced. Big machines clank and rumble inside the factory. "More than 100 people work in my company," Walter Putnam says. The people who work in a business are called **employees.** The work they do is called **labor.** "In a company like mine, labor is very important," Mr. Putnam says. "I try to make sure my employees are happy and safe at work."

410

A factory employee checks that each bicycle is put together correctly.

Walter Putnam points out some of the machines. One large machine shapes the metal bicycle frames. Another machine makes the metal handlebars. Some employees tighten the spokes of the bicycle wheels.

In any business, the materials used to make something are called **resources.** "To make a bicycle," Mr. Putnam says, "we use several different kinds of metals, including aluminum and steel. We use rubber for the brakes and for the tires. To make the bicycle seats we use plastic or leather. In our company the yearly costs of resources and overhead run into millions of dollars."

"We are always trying to improve our bikes," he explains. "We sell our product to bicycle shops. They are our customers, just as you might be a customer in a bicycle shop. We want to sell as many bikes as we can. To do that, we try to make the kinds of bicycles our customers will want. The more customers we have, the more profit we will make." The company's profit may be invested in new machinery or divided among the stockholders.

In business the job of finding and keeping customers is called **marketing.** "To market a bicycle, you have to

411

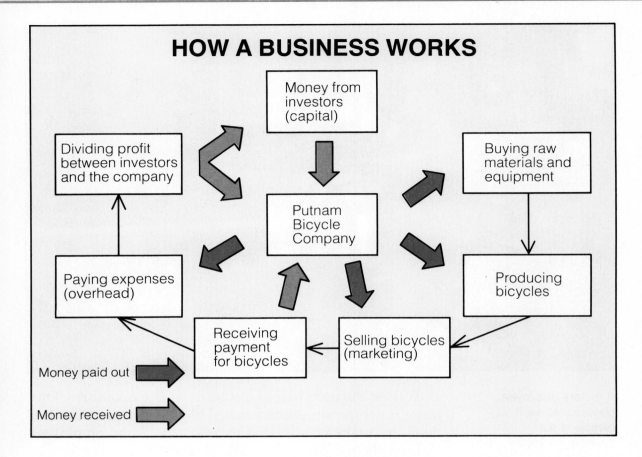

HOW A BUSINESS WORKS

talk to the owners of bicycle shops. Then you have to make sure that your customers are happy. That's what running a business is all about," Mr. Putnam says.

A bicycle might seem like a simple thing at first. However, producing and selling a bicycle takes many people in many different kinds of businesses. Walter Putnam, Edna Jones, and their employees are only some of the important people. The employees of a steel mill must produce the steel for the bicycle frames. Workers in a rubber company make the rubber for the bicycle tires. A trucking company delivers these resources to Walter Putnam's factory and then deliver the bicycles to stores.

Can you see why business is one of the most important activities in our country? Just think about the number of businesses involved in making one thing, a bicycle! Then remember how many different things you use in a single day. Each one is made by people in business.

CHAPTER 17 REVIEW

WORDS TO USE

Write the words below on a piece of paper. Next to each word, write its definition.

1. **federation**
2. **industrial**
3. **invest**
4. **legislatures**
5. **monopoly**
6. **prejudice**
7. **reconstruction**
8. **segregation**
9. **sweatshop**
10. **tenements**

FACTS TO REVIEW

1. What problems did the nation face after the Civil War?

2. What was the purpose of military rule in the South during Reconstruction?

3. What were some achievements of the Reconstruction legislatures?

4. Describe the position of Southern blacks in 1900.

5. What changes were part of the Industrial Revolution?

6. Why did inland cities such as Gary, Pittsburgh, Cleveland, Detroit, and Birmingham become centers of iron and steel manufacturing?

7. Why was the telegraph such an important invention?

8. Why were there so many immigrants from Europe during the last half of the nineteenth century?

9. What problems were Jane Addams and Samuel Gompers concerned about? What did they do about these problems?

10. Why did Chinese immigrants stay in the United States, even though they were often badly treated?

IDEAS TO DISCUSS

1. How did the people discussed in this chapter contribute to American society? Do you think some were more important than others? Why or why not?

2. Imagine living in the 1870s and working 12 hours a day in a sweatshop. Describe the working conditions. How might this affect your future?

3. How is learning a key to another kind of freedom? What examples can you think of to support your answer?

4. What were forms of racial prejudice in the decades after the Civil War?

◯ SKILLS PRACTICE

Using Time Zones   Use the time zone map on page 407 to answer these questions.

1. Suppose you live in California and want to call your grandmother in New Jersey at 8:00 P.M. her time. At what time would you have to telephone from California?

2. The Olympics are going to be broadcast at 10:00 A.M. (PDT). What time would that be if you lived in these cities?

   a. Kansas City
   b. New York City
   c. Denver
   d. San Francisco

CHAPTER 18

A Nation Settled and Strong

About
this
chapter

In 1860 few people lived on the Great Plains. The grasslands stretched as far as the eye could see. At least 15 million buffalo roamed the prairies. There, Plains Indians led an independent and rich way of life.

By 1890 the Great Plains were settled. Fenced pastures and farms had been carved out of the grassy plains. Farmers often could see railroad locomotives chugging across the continent. Fewer than 600 buffalo were left. The Plains Indians now lived on reservations set aside for them by the government.

1. SETTLING THE GREAT PLAINS

To Guide Your Reading

Look for these important words:

Key Words
- Pony Express
- transcontinental railroad
- stockyards
- Chisholm Trail
- stampede
- Homestead Act

- homesteaders

Places
- Kansas City
- St. Louis
- Omaha
- St. Joseph

- Sacramento
- Promontory
- Nueces River valley
- Abilene
- Dodge City
- Ogallala
- Cheyenne

Look for answers to these questions:

1. How did the railroad bring about new ways of life on the Great Plains?
2. Why did cattlemen in Texas drive their herds north?
3. What inventions were necessary to settlers of the Great Plains? What problems did these pioneers face?

In the 1850s freight wagons and stagecoaches were making regular trips between California and such cities as **Kansas City, St. Louis,** and **Omaha.** In 1860 a private company started the **Pony Express.** Its purpose was to carry letters between **St. Joseph,** Missouri, and **Sacramento,** California.

The Pony Express rider rode as fast as he could. He stopped only when he reached one of the 190 relay stations. There he might get a fresh horse to continue the journey. If not that, he would hand the mail sack to another rider ready to go. In this manner the Pony Express was able to deliver letters quickly. A letter could travel the 1,900 miles (about 3,057 km) from Missouri to California in just ten days.

Galloping across the West was difficult and dangerous work for the Pony Express riders. In a San Francisco newspaper, the Pony Express advertised for riders this way:

> Young skinny wiry fellows, not over eighteen. Must be expert riders, willing to risk death daily. Orphans preferred.

The Pony Express lasted only 18 months. In October 1861 a telegraph line across the country was completed. It put the Pony Express out of business.

Transcontinental Railroad

When Abraham Lincoln ran for President in 1860, the Republican Party promised a **transcontinental railroad.** This was to be a railroad that linked the East with the Pacific Coast. When Lincoln was elected, the Republicans kept their promise. In 1862 Congress granted two railroad companies

415

the right to build this railroad. The government gave them land and loaned them money. The Union Pacific would build west from Omaha, Nebraska. The Central Pacific would build east from Sacramento, California.

Each railroad raced to see which could lay the most track before they met. The ribbons of steel were laid at the rate of one or two miles (1.6 or 3.2 km) a day. The Union Pacific used Irish immigrants as laborers. The Central Pacific used Chinese immigrants.

On May 10, 1869, the two railroads met at **Promontory,** Utah. Only the distance of two pieces of track separated them. The last steel spike to be driven in was attached to a telegraph wire. When the spike was hit, an electric charge would announce that the rail line was complete. All over the country people waited for the news.

Then the spike was hit. Within seconds, the country began to rejoice. Chicago held a parade seven miles (11.3 km) long. Church bells pealed across the nation.

The Union Pacific–Central Pacific did not long remain the only railroad across the West. By the 1890s four more railroads had been built from Midwestern cities to the Pacific.

The telegraph had carried messages across the Great Plains. But it was the steam-belching locomotive on steel tracks that changed the Plains. In the East the railroad had followed settlement. In the West settlement would follow the railroad.

The railroad made possible great cattle ranches. The railroad opened up the Plains to farmers. By the 1890s these farmers were turning the Great Plains into seas of wheat.

Westward-bound settlers, many of them from Europe, travel by railroad to new homesteads on the Plains.

A cowboy gallops to head off a stampeding herd of cattle. This was one of the cowboy's most dangerous jobs.

Railroads and Cowboys

The cowboy is one of the most popular figures of the American past. In his pointed-toe boots, wide-brimmed hat, and leather chaps, the cowboy has become legend. Yet cowboy life lasted a rather short time—about 25 years. The railroads helped make the cowboy an important figure. The railroads also brought the settlement that ended the cowboy way of life.

For years Texans had raised longhorn cattle in the **Nueces** (nyoo. AY.suhs) **River valley** below San Antonio. They had learned from the Mexicans the techniques of rounding up cattle, roping, and branding them. The cattle were longhorn cattle that had been raised for years in northern Mexico. Longhorns were wild, tough beasts that did well on the prairie. Only men on horseback—the cowboys—could control them.

Thousands of cattle grazed in Texas while people in northern cities were hungry for beef. Prices for cattle were low in Texas. Cattlemen could get nearly 20 times as much money for the cattle if they could get them to the cities. The question was how?

Railroad lines moving into Kansas provided the answer. Joseph McCoy, a cattle trader, built large cattle pens called **stockyards** in **Abilene**, Kansas. He built them near the railroad tracks. Then he sent word to Texas that he would buy herds of cattle. In 1867 Texas cattlemen started driving huge herds of cattle north to Abilene. Later **Dodge City**, Kansas; **Ogallala**, Nebraska; and **Cheyenne**, Wyoming, became important cow towns.

417

The most famous of the cattle trails was the **Chisholm** (CHIZ•uhm) **Trail.** On the long cattle drives, cowboys rode with the herd. They had a hard job. A constant danger was that the cattle would **stampede,** or run away out of control. Other dangers included prairie fires, flash floods, or attacks by bandits.

In the cow towns the cattle were loaded onto freight cars and shipped to Chicago. There the cattle were butchered. The meat was then sent in refrigerated freight cars to all parts of the East.

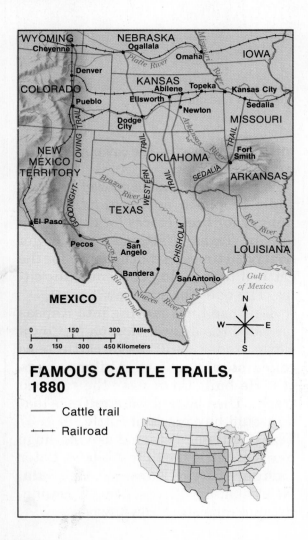

FAMOUS CATTLE TRAILS, 1880

—— Cattle trail
+—+—+ Railroad

Cattlemen soon started grazing cattle on the ranges of the Great Plains. By this time most of the buffalo had been killed off by sharp-shooting buffalo hunters. The grasslands did not belong to the cattle ranchers, but they used millions of acres for their herds.

Railroads and Homesteaders

The railroads wanted more settlement on the Plains because it would mean more business. They advertised for people to come settle the Plains.

In 1862 Congress had passed the **Homestead Act.** This law gave 160 acres (64.8 ha) of land to anyone willing to live on it for five years. The people who settled the land in this way were called **homesteaders.** Many settlers also bought land from the railroads or the government.

Even with the railroad, settlement of the Plains would have been impossible without three inventions. These important inventions were the steel plow, the windmill, and barbed wire.

In the 1830s a steel plow had been designed that could turn over the tough sod. The invention of the windmill let settlers pump necessary water from hundreds of feet below the surface. The windmill was first used by the railroads. Windmills provided water for the steam lomotives. Soon, windmills marked each new town on the Plains. By the 1890s homesteaders had their own windmills.

The use of barbed wire brought the open range to an end. Barbed wire was invented in 1873. Before then farmers had no way to keep cattle out of their fields. When farmers started enclosing their land with barbed wire,

This pioneer Nebraska family poses outside its sod "dug-out" house. Why do you suppose the wagon and team of horses is in the picture?

ranchers often cut the wire. Some bitter fighting took place between the cattle ranchers and the farmers.

In the end, however, ranchers found barbed wire to be as useful as farmers did. With barbed wire they could make pastures to enclose their cattle. The windmill provided water for the cattle. Pastured cattle meant that fewer cowboys were necessary. Cowboys now needed to be as skilled at digging fence-post holes as roping calves.

With the steel plow, barbed wire, and hard work, pioneer homesteaders conquered the Great Plains. For fuel they used buffalo chips. For houses they used sod. Sod houses were cool in summer and warm in winter, but housekeeping was a problem. Dirt often fell from the sod ceiling. Sometimes snakes did too!

These pioneers faced other hardships. In the years of drought nothing grew. When crops did grow, farmers worried about prairie fires, hailstorms, hot winds, or grasshoppers.

Grasshoppers attacked in force for the first time in 1874. They came in clouds by the millions, eating every green thing. One pioneer woman, Adelheit Viets, was wearing a white dress with a green stripe the day the grasshoppers came. "The grasshoppers settled on me and ate up every bit of green stripe in that dress before anything could be done about it," she remembered.

As hard as life could be on the Great Plains, the settlers had fun, too. Picnics, dances, horseback riding, and fairs were common events.

Reading Check

1. How did the government help bring about the transcontinental railroad?
2. What was the most famous cattle trail?
3. Why did cowboys drive cattle north?
4. What inventions made settlement possible on the Great Plains?

SKILLS FOR SUCCESS

TRANSPORTATION AND RESOURCE MAPS

Transportation Maps

A **transportation map** shows transportation routes. It may show railways or the regular routes of ships and airlines. It may also show major highways. The map below is a historical transportation map. It shows how people and goods traveled to western states during the 1870s.

Look at the map key. What types of transportation routes are shown on this map? Can you find four rivers on which people journeyed by boat? Notice that many trails on

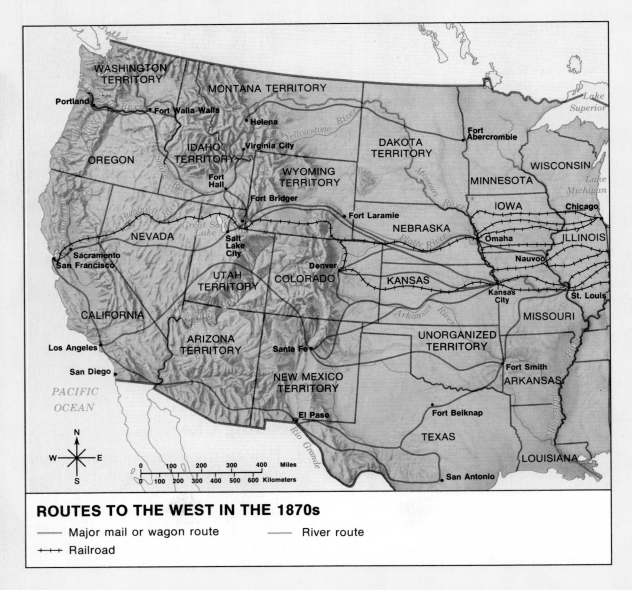

ROUTES TO THE WEST IN THE 1870s

—— Major mail or wagon route —— River route
+++ Railroad

the map follow along rivers. They followed trails near rivers because they were level and easy to travel.

The railroads went west much later than the wagons and stagecoaches. Trace the routes of the railroad from east to west. Notice that in places the railroads followed the wagon routes.

The railroads were an improvement over wagons and ships. They speeded up the development of the West. Railroads were faster than wagons and stagecoaches. They could carry more people in greater comfort and safety. They could carry goods at a lower cost. They could also carry the products of the West back to eastern markets. This encouraged people to go west to make a living.

Resource Maps

How could people make a living in the West? A **resource map** shows the location of natural resources and regions. It also may show the manufactured goods of an area. Often resource maps show which crops and livestock do well in certain areas. The map on this page is a historical map that shows some of the natural resources and products of the state of Colorado. It also shows the railroad routes that existed in 1881.

Look at the map key. What mineral regions are shown? What other resources and products are shown on this map? Both sheep and cattle were raised in Colorado. Where was one likely to find the most cattle? Where were sheep generally found?

Study the railroad routes shown on the map. The tracks that run to the edges of the state continue to cities elsewhere. Compare these railroad routes to the ones shown in the map at left. Notice that more routes are shown on the 1881 map. Why might there be more railroads in 1881 than in 1870?

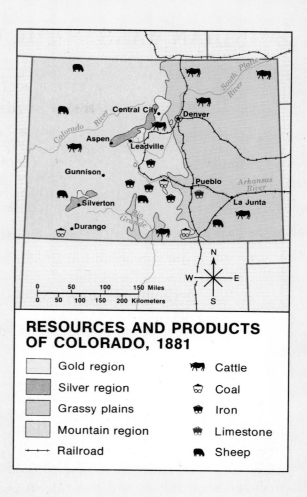

RESOURCES AND PRODUCTS OF COLORADO, 1881

☐ Gold region	🐂 Cattle
◼ Silver region	⬙ Coal
▨ Grassy plains	🐖 Iron
☐ Mountain region	🐗 Limestone
┼─── Railroad	🐏 Sheep

CHECKING YOUR SKILLS

Use the two maps and their keys to answer these questions.

1. Which methods of transportation could someone use to travel from Denver to San Francisco in 1870?

2. Coal, limestone, and iron are needed to make steel. Which town in Colorado was best located for steel mills?

3. Ranchers drove their cattle each year to a town where the cattle could be shipped east by train. Which town in Colorado was likely a cattle center?

4. Could a traveler get to Denver from Kansas City by a water route?

421

2. INDIAN WARS IN THE WEST

=To Guide Your Reading=

Look for these important words:

Key Words
- Sioux
- Nez Perce
- Apaches

People
- Chief Red Cloud
- George Custer
- Crazy Horse
- Chief Joseph
- Geronimo

Places
- Black Hills
- South Dakota
- Sierra Madre

Look for answers to these questions:

1. What did settlement of the Great Plains mean for the Indians who lived there?
2. Why did Indians attack wagon trains, homesteads, and army forts?
3. Who were some of the outstanding Indian leaders of this time?

From the time the Spanish had introduced the horse to the plains, the Plains Indians had become superb horsemen. The Indians used the horse to carry themselves and their belongings. Riding fleet horses, the Indians hunted buffalo. As in the past, they depended on buffalo to satisfy most of their needs. With settlement of the Plains, Plains Indian culture came to a rather quick and violent end.

The familiar pattern of conflict between settlers and Indians was repeated in the Great Plains. There, Indians were distressed to see their hunting grounds invaded. Unable to hunt, the Indians lost their economic base. Their whole way of life had depended on hunting. Westward-moving settlers forced one Indian group after another to leave their homes and hunting grounds. Angry about the loss of their hunting grounds, the Indians began to fight back. They attacked wagon trains and homesteads.

In 1865 the **Sioux** (SOO) attacked wagon trains on the Bozeman Trail. This trail led from the Platte Valley Overland Trail to Montana. It also cut through some of the best Sioux hunting grounds. For three years the Sioux, led by **Chief Red Cloud,** fought army troops. The Sioux even forced the army to abandon forts along the trail.

Then, in 1868, Red Cloud signed a peace treaty. The treaty recognized the right of the Sioux to the **Black Hills** of **South Dakota.** The Sioux triumph was short-lived. In 1874 General **George Custer,** ignoring the treaty, led government troops into the Black Hills. Custer was looking for gold, and he found it. With the discovery of gold, the government could not keep miners out of the Black Hills. It was easier to force the Sioux to leave.

In the 1870s the Sioux fought to hold their land in the Black Hills. This picture shows George Custer demanding that the Sioux settle on a reservation.

Crazy Horse was now, in 1876, leader of the Sioux. Groups of Sioux and Cheyennes were camped together on the Little Bighorn River in Montana. Custer, at the head of a scouting party, learned about the encampment. He attacked and found his party surrounded by at least 2,500 Indians. In the battle that followed Custer and all his men were killed. The Battle of the Little Bighorn was the last Sioux victory. The army hounded the Sioux until hunger forced them to give up. Crazy Horse surrendered in 1877. He was killed by guards while in prison.

The Nez Perce and Apaches

The **Nez Perce** (NEZ PUHRS) lived on the Columbia Plateau in Washington. They had lived in peace with white people since the coming of Lewis and Clark. Their valley was beautiful. Then settlers began to stream onto their land by the wagonload. The Nez Perce were told to leave.

Some of the young men wanted to fight, but **Joseph,** their chief, said no. He said that there were not enough warriors—only 100. "We were like deer," he said later. The white settlers "were like grizzly bears." Joseph's hopes to lead his people away peacefully were ruined. A settler killed one of Chief Joseph's people. The son of the murdered man in turn led an attack, killing some settlers. The army came in pursuit.

During the summer of 1877 Chief Joseph led his people away. They traveled over 1,700 miles (about 2,735 km) through the states of Idaho, Montana, and Wyoming. Time after time the Nez Perce defeated army troops. Deciding they would never be left in peace, the Nez Perce headed for Canada. Forty miles (64.4 km) south of the border, they were stopped by soldiers. Chief Joseph was forced to surrender. These words he spoke:

> I am tired of fighting. Our chiefs are killed. . . . The old men are killed. It is the young men who say yes or no. He who led the young men is dead. It is cold and we have no blankets. Our little children are freezing to death. I want time to look for my children and see how many of them I may find. Maybe I shall find them among the dead. Hear me, my chiefs, I am tired. My heart is sick and sad. From where the sun now stands, I will fight no more forever.

Chief Joseph and his people failed to find the peace they longed for.

For his bravery, the people of Bismarck, North Dakota, honored Chief Joseph with a dinner. Many Americans, particularly Easterners, began to demand that Congress provide better treatment for the Indians.

Between 1869 and 1874 there were more than 200 major battles. In the end, starvation made the difference. It became government policy to kill as many buffalo as possible. This was to destroy the Indian way of life. Starved and defeated, most Indians had no choice but to move onto government reservations.

In the Southwest a small band of **Apaches** (uh·PACH·ees) held out longer than other Indian groups. These Apaches, led by **Geronimo,** rebelled against conditions on the hot, dry San Carlos Reservation. There it was hard to grow or find food. Government food given to the reservation was often wormy. Geronimo and his followers fled to the **Sierra Madre** of Mexico. From bases in these mountains they made attacks on Arizona settlers. For ten years they escaped capture by United States soldiers. At last, an Apache scout working for the soldiers led them to Geronimo's hiding place. In 1886 Geronimo was forced to surrender.

Reading Check

1. Why did the Indians feel they had to fight?
2. Why did General George Custer break the treaty with the Sioux Indians?
3. Who led the Nez Perce on their long march?
4. Who led the Apaches in their rebellion?

3. CHANGES IN AMERICAN LIFE

To Guide Your Reading

Look for these important words:

Key Words
- conservation
- reforms
- Populist

People
- John Muir
- Gifford Pinchot
- Thomas Edison
- Guglielmo Marconi

Places
- Yellowstone
- Yosemite
- Sequoia

Look for answers to these questions:

1. Why did Americans become interested in protecting some of America's wilderness?
2. What kinds of changes did farmers ask for?
3. How did women's lives change?
4. What sports did people enjoy in the 1890s?

The 1890 census reported there was no longer a frontier. The United States was now settled. New states had been organized. These included Colorado, Wyoming, Montana, Idaho, Washington, North Dakota, and South Dakota. Oklahoma had been set aside for American Indians, but it was opened to settlement in 1886. Utah would become a state in 1898, Oklahoma in 1907, Arizona and New Mexico in 1912.

As long as there was a frontier, there was always a place to go. The frontier had been a place for people in trouble, people looking for opportunity, people starting a new life. These kinds of people had often gone to the frontier during the settlement of the continent.

With the frontier gone, Americans began to see their country in a new way. They wanted to protect some of the wild beauty of America. One such place was **Yellowstone.** This part of Wyoming had been visited in 1807 by the Lewis and Clark expedition. Shortly afterward fur trappers and traders began to visit Yellowstone. They told stories of boiling mud pots and steaming geysers, but few believed them. Then in 1870 General Henry Washburn, a government surveyor, led an expedition to Yellowstone. The trappers' stories, he learned, were true. Soon afterward, in 1872, Yellowstone became our first national park.

In California the naturalist **John Muir** wrote about the beauty of **Yosemite** (yoh•SEM•uh•tee) and **Sequoia** (si•KWOI•uh). These places too became national parks in 1890. As with Yellowstone, they were to be preserved for the enjoyment of future generations.

For most of their history, Americans had acted as if the forests would always be there. They had cut trees freely wherever they grew. As early as the 1870s some people began to warn of the danger of using up the forests.

425

Four-fifths of the nation's forests had already been chopped down. In 1891 Congress responded to the concern by creating national forests. The forests would be managed so they would produce a steady supply of timber.

Gifford Pinchot (PIN•shoh) became the nation's chief forester. He had studied how Europeans had used and maintained forests for hundreds of years. Pinchot was the first to use the word **conservation.** *Conservation* means using a natural resource so as to keep it from being wasted or destroyed.

Here a cedar with a 17-foot diameter dwarfs the lumberjacks about to fell it. Concerned that America's trees would disappear, Congress established in 1891 a system of national forests.

Reforms from the West

The railroad had opened up the West, but farmers came to hate the railroad. Railroads charged as much as they could. Farmers had to pay. There was no other way to get their crops and livestock to market. In California the Central Pacific was called "the octopus." When farmers complained, neither Congress nor state legislatures listened.

People began to organize to bring about **reforms,** or changes. They wanted to get rid of the wrongs. This movement was called the **Populist,** or People's, movement. Most Populists were farmers who wanted more control over the large corporations. For instance, they wanted railroad rates controlled so that they were fair.

The Populists also wanted government to do more for the farmers. They demanded free mail delivery to rural areas and a parcel post service. The Populists were the first to demand direct election of senators and the secret ballot. They also wanted ways to remove officials who acted improperly. In time many of their demands became laws.

Changes in Women's Lives

One result of the Industrial Revolution was that women had machines to help with housework. Sewing machines reduced the time needed to make clothes. Washing machines reduced the toil of washday. Women no longer had to spend hours growing or storing food. Grocery stores offered canned food and fresh fruits and vegetables. These fresh fruits and vegetables were brought by railroad from California and Florida.

For women, the bicycle meant more than holiday fun. Inexpensive and easy to ride, it offered a new freedom and independence.

Ice was now available year round. The iceman delivering ice was a common sight all over America. The icebox made it easier to keep milk and meat cool. The availability of ice helped make ice cream a favorite American treat.

At the end of the nineteenth century, growing numbers of women went to college. Many of these educated women became teachers. Others, like Jane Addams, worked for reform and change.

Still other women entered industry and business. In business offices women at typewriters replaced male clerks. In the growing number of department stores, women were used to run the new cash registers. Women by the thousands began to operate the switchboards of the expanding telephone industry.

Sports

As people spent more of their time working indoors, outdoor sports became popular. One of the most popular pastimes was playing baseball on city streets or vacant lots. Baseball had developed from a children's game. The Knickerbocker Baseball Club of New York was organized in 1845. It wrote down the rules of the game. During the Civil War, New Yorkers taught baseball to other Union soldiers. The game soon grew in popularity.

The invention of the bicycle gave city dwellers a new freedom. Bicycling to the country on holidays became a favorite pastime.

Sports that first became popular in the 1890s were golf and tennis. Basketball was invented in 1891 as a winter sport that could be played in gymnasiums.

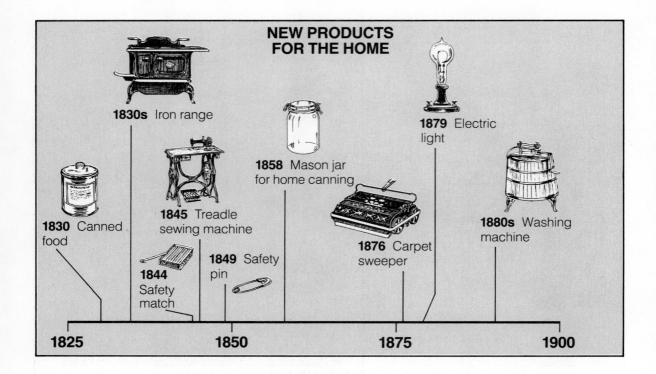

NEW PRODUCTS FOR THE HOME

1830s Iron range

1858 Mason jar for home canning

1879 Electric light

1845 Treadle sewing machine

1830 Canned food

1880s Washing machine

1849 Safety pin

1844 Safety match

1876 Carpet sweeper

1825   1850   1875   1900

New Inventions

New inventions of the 1890s were about to cause even greater changes in American life. The kind of gasoline engine used today had been invented in 1876 by a German engineer. Soon people were putting the engines on horse carriages. In 1895 the first important race between "horseless carriages" was held. It took place on a road between Chicago and Evanston, Illinois. It took these first automobiles almost eight hours to go 54 miles (86.9 km). By 1898, however, there were 50 automobile manufacturers in the United States.

The invention of the telephone by Alexander Graham Bell in 1876 had started a revolution in communications. **Thomas Edison** carried this revolution even further with his invention in 1877 of the phonograph. Edison's first phonograph looked very different from today's stereo systems, but it worked. In the first recording, Edison recited "Mary had a little lamb."

In September 1899 **Guglielmo Marconi** (goo•LYEL•moh mahr•KOH•nee) tried out a new invention to report from sea on a sailing race. Marconi was an Italian inventor. His reports of the race from sea were the first use of radio in America.

The gasoline engine, the automobile, and the radio all were important inventions. They would bring as many changes as the steam engine, the railroad, and the telegraph had.

Reading Check

1. Why were national parks created?
2. Name at least three demands of the Populists.
3. Name three new inventions of the 1890s.

428

THOMAS EDISON

Thomas Edison

Edison's electric light

An early phonograph

Try to imagine a world without electric lights, phonographs, movie cameras, and microphones. All these marvelous things were invented by an American named Thomas Edison. Edison may have been the greatest inventor of all time.

Most of Edison's inventions turned out to be important. The most important of all, however, was the electric light. He perfected the electric light in 1879, more than 100 years ago.

Inventors had known since 1808 that electricity could provide light. Many people had tried to make a small, practical electric light, but all had failed. After many embarrassing failures and more than a few explosions, Edison finally perfected his electric lamp. The first public demonstration of the miracle invention was given on New Year's Eve, 1879. Three thousand people flocked to Edison's New Jersey laboratory. Edison flipped a switch, and dozens of lamps lit up the darkness. A reporter called the light "a little globe of sunshine." Edison formed a company to sell his invention. He quickly became one of the richest men in America.

Edison started early as an inventor. At the age of ten, he set up a laboratory in the basement. To get money to buy supplies for his experiments, he sold newspapers on a train. At the age of 12, he set up a laboratory in the train's baggage car. Working on the railroad, young Edison learned how to operate the telegraph. As a telegrapher, Edison learned much about electricity. He drew on that knowledge of electricity when he started to invent an electric light.

What made Thomas Edison such a superb inventor? For one thing, he refused to give up in the face of failure. One failure did not stop him, neither did 20, or even 100 failures. "I'll never give up," Edison said once, "for I may have a streak of luck before I die." When we turn on lights, see a movie, or play a record, we can be glad Edison just kept trying.

CHAPTER 18 REVIEW

WORDS TO USE

Write the meaning of each word below. Then use each word in a complete sentence.

1. **conservation**
2. **homesteaders**
3. **reforms**
4. **stampede**
5. **stockyards**

FACTS TO REVIEW

1. How did the transcontinental railroad change the West?

2. How did the railroad both create and destroy the cowboy's way of life?

3. What were some of the problems homesteaders faced?

4. How did the invention of the steel plow, the windmill, and barbed wire help people live on the Great Plains?

5. Why did the Plains Indians attack wagon trains and settlers' homes?

6. Compare and contrast the experiences of the Sioux led by Chief Crazy Horse with those of the Nez Perce led by Chief Joseph.

7. What happened that finally forced the Indians to move onto reservations?

8. Why did Americans become interested in conservation in the 1890s?

9. How did new inventions change women's lives?

10. What inventions of the 1890s would cause major changes in the twentieth century?

IDEAS TO DISCUSS

1. How did the Indians, cowboys, and homesteaders differ from each other in their use of the Great Plains? How would each feel about the buffalo, the railroad, and the steel plow? Which way of life on the Great Plains would you choose if you could? Why?

2. How did census of 1890 cause Americans to see their country in a new way?

3. The railroad in the West could be viewed as both good and bad. Why?

4. Imagine city life in the 1890s. What things might you use in the house? What recreation would be important?

◯ SKILLS PRACTICE

Transportation and Resource Maps Use the two maps on pages 420 and 421 to answer the following questions.

1. In 1870 what method of transportation would a traveler use to get from Santa Fe to Los Angeles?

2. If you were building a meat processing plant in Colorado, near what city would you locate it?

3. An early traveler from Omaha, Nebraska, wants to go into the Montana territory. What method of transportation would a traveler use to begin this trip?

4. If you wanted to work on a sheep ranch in Colorado, would you go to eastern or western Colorado?

UNIT 7 REVIEW

WORDS TO REMEMBER

Number your paper from 1 to 10. Use the words below to replace the underlined words in the sentences that follow.

conservation
federation
homesteaders
invested
prejudice

reaper
reconstruction
segregation
sharecroppers
stampede

1. A plan for the rebuilding of the South provided help for freed slaves, for repairing war damage, and for restoring state governments.

2. Most freed blacks could not own land, so they became farmers on rented land.

3. Cyrus McCormick invented a harvester that made it possible to harvest much more grain than formerly.

4. Andrew Carnegie used some of his money to buy shares in growing companies.

5. Samuel Gompers organized unions of skilled workers into a single organization representing them all.

6. By 1900 separation of the races was common throughout the South.

7. Chinese and Japanese immigrants faced problems caused by people making negative judgments based on race.

8. Many settlers on the Great Plains were people who were given 160 acres (64.8 ha) of land by the government.

9. Gifford Pinchot was one of the first Americans to promote the idea of using natural resources wisely.

10. A danger faced by cowboys on the cattle trails was that the cattle might rush off wildly.

FOCUS ON MAIN IDEAS

1. How did the Freedmen's Bureau and Reconstruction legislatures try to rebuild the South?

2. As businesses grew larger, what reforms did Jane Addams, Samuel Gompers, and Western farmers work for?

3. How did inventions change transportation and communication in the nineteenth century? What are examples in which one invention led to another?

4. Compare and contrast the treatment of the blacks, the Indians, and the Chinese during the late nineteenth century.

5. How did the Industrial Revolution change the way work was done? How are people's lives continuing to change?

ACTIVITIES

1. **Research/Oral Report** With a partner research the Battle of the Little Bighorn. Prepare a class presentation. One of you describe the battle from the point of view of General Custer. The other describe the battle from the point of view of Chief Crazy Horse.

431

2. **Art** Draw a picture of the Great Plains as it might have been before the railroad. Draw another picture showing how it changed after the railroad brought settlers.

3. **Research/Art/Writing** Choose your favorite national park. Prepare a display or bulletin board with pictures or photographs. Write a paper about why the park is a special place.

4. **Timeline** Make a timeline of important inventions using 1830 as the first date and 1900 as the last date.

5. **Remembering the Close-Up** With your teacher or parent, visit a business in your community. Find out what kinds of goods the business sells. Who are the customers of this business? Does the business advertise? Talk with the manager or owner of the business. Find out what he or she likes about the business. What kinds of decisions does that person make? Make an oral or written report on what you learn.

6. **Research/Writing** Find out more about a person, invention, or problem discussed in this unit. Write a report about what you learn.

⬤ SKILLS REVIEW

Transportation and Resource Maps

Look at the map at the bottom of the page to answer these questions.

1. If you were driving cattle north through Oklahoma to Kansas, what river would you have to cross?

2. If you wanted to look for oil, would it be wiser to look in eastern or western Kansas?

3. If you wanted to raise pigs, which eat a lot of corn, would Garden City or Topeka be a better place to settle?

4. What towns likely had stockyards near the railroad station? Explain your answer.

5. What products could be found in western Kansas in 1880?

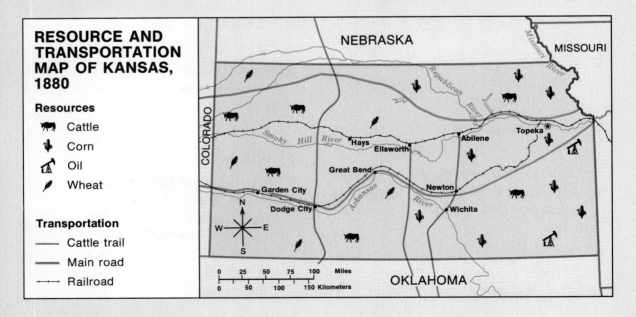

RESOURCE AND TRANSPORTATION MAP OF KANSAS, 1880

Resources

🐃 Cattle
🌵 Corn
⛽ Oil
🌾 Wheat

Transportation

— Cattle trail
— Main road
+—+ Railroad

YOUR STATE'S HISTORY

Before the Civil War the United States was mainly a land of small towns and farmland. In the years between 1860 and 1900, our nation changed a great deal. Across America great factories sprang up. Little towns sprouted into large cities. Railroads reached out across the land. Great inventions changed the way of life for all Americans.

Each state faced a different challenge during this period. The Eastern states tried to handle the problems of rapid industrial growth. The Southern states tried to recover from the Civil War. On the Great Plains, farmers worked to tame the endless stretches of rolling grassland. In the West people were discovering and developing new resources. The following activities will help you learn about your state as it entered the modern industrial age.

LEARNING ABOUT GEOGRAPHY

1. By the year 1900 most states had one or more large cities. What is the largest city in your state? What year was this city founded? If you can, find out its population in 1860 and in 1900. How many live there today?

2. In many states the largest city is also the state capital. In other states, however, the capital city is not the largest city. Write a short report on your state's capital city. How did it get its name? How far is it from your hometown? Why was it chosen as the capital?

3. Make a resource and transportation map of your state. Show the major railroads, highways, and airports. Show the major rivers. Use picture symbols to show the important mineral, manufacturing, and agricultural resources.

LEARNING ABOUT ECONOMICS

4. With the Industrial Revolution, mineral resources such as iron, coal, oil, and copper became very important. Make a table of mineral resources that your state has. Tell where they are to be found. Give examples of manufactured products that use these minerals.

MINERAL RESOURCES IN OUR STATE				
Coal	Oil and Gas	Iron	Gold and Silver	Copper

5. What are the major industries in your state today? Why is your state a good location for these industries?

LEARNING ABOUT TECHNOLOGY

6. Draw a picture of a scene in your town or state as it might have been in 1850. Show the same scene as it might have been in 1900. The two pictures should contrast changes in technology.

UNIT EIGHT

THE TWENTIETH CENTURY

A hundred years from now, textbooks will probably still include the picture to the left. Men landing on the moon may be the most important event of the twentieth century. Going to the moon was a great technological achievement. It was also an achievement in cooperation. It was a symbol of a nation saying that exploration, knowledge, and skill are important.

In this unit you will read about other major events of the twentieth century. They include United States involvement in world affairs. They include efforts to achieve justice and equality for all Americans.

Key Dates and Events

1901
Theodore Roosevelt becomes President

1903
First successful air flight

1917
The United States enters World War I

1920
Women get the right to vote

1930s
The Great Depression

1932
Franklin D. Roosevelt elected President

December 7, 1941
Japan bombs Pearl Harbor

1941–1945
World War II

1945
United Nations organized

1963–1973
Vietnam War

July 20, 1969
Astronauts land on the moon

1980
Ronald Reagan elected President

CHAPTER 19

Our Century Begins

About
this
chapter

During the early twentieth century the United States became a major world power. It gained both territory and influence.

During these times the face of America changed. Bicycles, automobiles, high-rise buildings, and electric lights changed how America looked. The first airplanes drew crowds wherever they went.

These were also years of reform that made the nation more democratic. One of the most important reforms was a Constitutional amendment granting women the right to vote.

1. BECOMING A WORLD POWER

To Guide Your Reading

Look for these important words:

Key Words
- Spanish-American War
- tyranny
- Rough Riders
- Battle of San Juan Hill
- armistice
- Polynesians

People
- Theodore Roosevelt
- King Kamehameha I
- Queen Liliuokalani

Places
- Cuba

- Philippine Islands
- Manila Bay
- Guam
- Puerto Rico
- Hawaiian Islands
- Alaska
- Klondike

Look for answers to these questions:

1. Why did the United States go to war with Spain?
2. What territories did the United States acquire from Spain?
3. How did the United States acquire Hawaii? Alaska?

By 1900 American settlement and influence extended far beyond America's shores. One reason for this was the **Spanish-American War.**

The Spanish-American War was fought in part because Americans took the side of **Cuba** against Spain.

Cuba was Spain's largest colony in the Western Hemisphere at the time. In 1898 Cubans rebelled against Spain. American newspapers were full of stories about Spanish **tyranny,** or harsh rule, in Cuba. After Americans read such stories, they wanted to help the Cubans win independence.

Spain was close to granting Cuba independence. Then, in February 1898, an American battleship, the *Maine,* exploded in the harbor at Havana. More than 200 sailors were killed. It was not clear why the ship blew up. The United States, however, blamed Spain and declared war.

No American war had ever been more popular. Americans saw themselves as defenders of Cuba against old-world tyranny. Soon after war was declared, the American navy in the Pacific steamed to the **Philippine Islands.** There the navy destroyed the Spanish fleet and captured **Manila Bay.** George Dewey was the American naval commander. Overnight he became a hero.

In the United States thousands joined up to fight in the war. One of these was **Theodore Roosevelt.** Roosevelt collected a fighting company made up mostly of Western cowboys and sheriffs. They called themselves the **Rough Riders.** Roosevelt hoped to find both action and glory in the war.

At the **Battle of San Juan Hill** in Cuba, Roosevelt found the action and glory he was seeking. The Spanish commanded the top of a hill that lay

CUBA DURING THE SPANISH-AMERICAN WAR, 1898

between the Americans and the city of Santiago. With bullets ripping the grass around him, Roosevelt yelled "Charge!" and started up the hill. But only five men followed. Mad as could be, Roosevelt retreated. The Rough Riders, it turned out, had not heard his battle cry. Up the hill Roosevelt charged again. This time the Rough Riders followed. Regiments of professional soldiers also charged. After heavy fighting, Santiago at last surrendered.

The Spanish-American War lasted less than four months. In August 1898 Spain signed an **armistice.** An armistice is an agreement to stop fighting.

A peace treaty followed the armistice. The treaty gave the United States control of Cuba, **Guam, Puerto Rico,** and the Philippine Islands. By giving up Cuba and Puerto Rico, Spain gave up the last of its territory in the Western Hemisphere.

This is an artist's idea of Teddy Roosevelt's charge into a rain of Spanish bullets at the Battle of San Juan Hill. In truth, Roosevelt made the charge on foot.

The United States was now a world power. Control of the Philippines meant that Americans became important in the Far East. In the Caribbean, the United States was now the most powerful nation. European nations showed new respect for the United States.

The United States gave Cuba its independence in 1902. In 1946 the Philippines became an independent country. Puerto Rico and Guam remain territories of the United States.

The Hawaiian Islands

The **Hawaiian Islands** also came under American control in 1898. These tropical islands are 2,000 miles west of the Pacific coast. The original inhabitants of Hawaii were **Polynesians** (pahl•uh•NEE•zhuhns). In the eighth century they had migrated from other Pacific islands to the Hawaiian Islands. Expert navigators, they sailed in double-hulled ships able to carry as many as 100 people. They carried with them dogs, chickens, and pigs as well as banana and coconut trees.

The Hawaiian Islands were explored in 1778 by Captain James Cook, an Englishman. Whaling and trading ships started making regular stops. American missionaries arrived about 1820. Soon after, cattle ranches and sugar plantations were started.

Other people came to live and work in the islands. They included Mexicans, Asians, Filipinos, Portuguese, and Americans.

The Hawaiian Islands had been united under **King Kamehameha I** (kuh•may•uh•MAY•hah) in the early nineteenth century. The sugar planters and missionaries came to have much

Queen Liliuokalani failed in her effort to restore royal authority in Hawaii.

influence in the government. In 1893 the Hawaiian ruler, who was **Queen Liliuokalani** (li•lee•uh•woh•kuh•LAHN•ee), tried to change things. She wanted to restore the ruler's traditional power.

The sugar planters did not want Queen Liliuokalani to get back power. The planters took over the government and set up a republic. They asked to be part of the United States.

Alaska

In 1867 the United States had bought **Alaska** from Russia. Most native Alaskans were Aleuts and Eskimos. Their way of life depended on hunting and fishing. Many Americans thought the purchase extremely foolish. Why should the United States buy a piece of land so far north? "Polar Bear Garden," some called it.

439

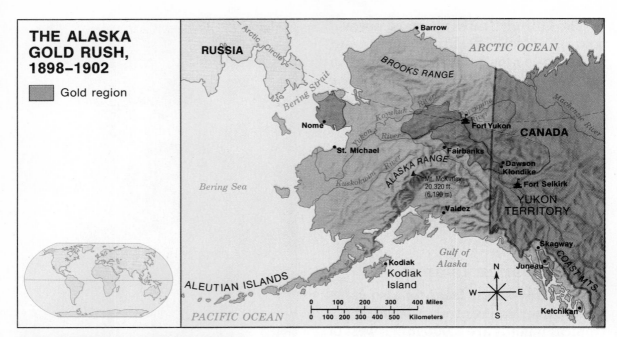

THE ALASKA GOLD RUSH, 1898–1902

Gold region

Gold—and lots of it—was the message of the Klondike News in 1898.

Alaska was almost forgotten. Then in 1896 gold was discovered in the **Klondike** region. The Klondike was in Yukon Territory, near the Canadian-Alaskan border. The discovery of gold opened up Alaska for settlement. About 100,000 people left by boat from Seattle to head into this newfound land of riches. It was a harsh frontier. Thousands died from sickness, starvation, and the extreme cold of winter.

The Alaska purchase turned out to be a very good bargain. The land is full of valuable mineral resources, including silver, copper, lead, and petroleum.

Reading Check

1. Why did Americans side with Cuba?
2. What territories did the United States gain as a result of the Spanish-American War?
3. How did the Hawaiian Islands become part of the United States?
4. What caused people to become interested in settling Alaska?

2. THEODORE ROOSEVELT AND HIS TIME

To Guide Your Reading

Look for these important words:

Key Words
- isthmus
- Progressives
- regulate
- tuberculosis

Places
- Panama Canal
- Colombia

Look for answers to these questions:

1. What were some of Theodore Roosevelt's qualities?
2. Why did Roosevelt urge the building of the Panama Canal?
3. What kinds of reforms did Roosevelt work for?

Theodore Roosevelt returned from Cuba a well-known and popular man. He was immediately elected governor of New York. Two years later Roosevelt was chosen to be President William McKinley's running mate.

Roosevelt had been rather skinny and sickly as a child. When he found he could not defend himself against some bullies, he took boxing lessons. For the rest of his life, Roosevelt was a man of action. He loved outdoor activity—hiking, riding, hunting.

On September 6, 1901, President McKinley was shot in Buffalo, New York. Eight days later McKinley died. Roosevelt was now President.

As President, Theodore Roosevelt was the most popular man in America. Americans liked the athletic, outspoken "Teddy" Roosevelt. They chuckled over stories about his six children romping through the White House. They approved when they heard that the President and his children had pillow fights. On one of his hunting trips, Roosevelt refused to shoot a bear cub. Overnight a new toy came into being—the teddy bear.

This loveable, stuffed toy was Theodore Roosevelt's own Teddy bear.

441

Roosevelt believed that the United States should use its power and influence in the world. He believed that what happened in the rest of the world affected the United States.

When Russia and Japan fought a war in 1904–1905, President Roosevelt offered to help the two nations work out peace terms. For his peace work Roosevelt became the first American to receive the Nobel Peace Prize. First awarded in 1901, the Nobel Peace Prize is given to a person or organization helping to bring peace to the world.

The Panama Canal

The way to get things done, Roosevelt once said, was "to speak softly and carry a big stick." He meant that the nation should try to achieve its aims quietly and properly. If that did not work, however, the nation should be prepared to be forceful. It should be prepared to use a strong navy and army.

Roosevelt used a big stick to get the **Panama Canal.**

For years people had talked about building this canal. It would cut across the **isthmus,** or neck of land, joining South and North America. Such a canal would save ships the hard and lengthy travel time around South America. It would greatly speed up the journey between the Atlantic coast and the Pacific coast. In the 1880s a French company had tried to build such a canal. The jungle and disease had defeated its efforts.

From the White House, Roosevelt urged the building of a canal. The canal could serve both merchant ships and the growing United States Navy.

Congress voted to build the canal. It did so, although the Isthmus of Panama belonged to **Colombia.** The United States offered $10 million to Colombia for the right to build a canal. But Colombia delayed making a decision.

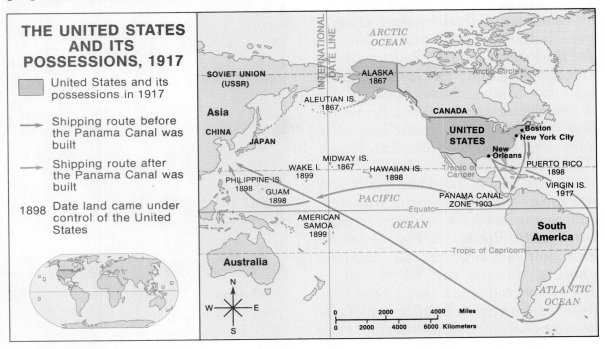

THE UNITED STATES AND ITS POSSESSIONS, 1917

- United States and its possessions in 1917
- Shipping route before the Panama Canal was built
- Shipping route after the Panama Canal was built
- 1898 Date land came under control of the United States

Railroads hauled away the dirt while the Panama Canal was being built as a link between two oceans.

Roosevelt then made it known that he would welcome a revolution in Panama against Colombia. Roosevelt sent the navy to protect the isthmus. If revolution broke out, the navy was to keep Colombian troops from landing. Within three months such a revolution came about. Roosevelt immediately recognized the new nation of Panama. Panama then gave the United States the right to build the canal. The United States would control a zone on either side of the canal 5 miles (8.5 km) wide.

Work on the canal began at once. Great earth-moving machines began to tame the jungle. Engineers designed canal locks.

Unlike the Frenchmen, American workers were able to stay healthy. Doctors had learned that mosquitos car-ried both malaria and yellow fever. Controlling the mosquito helped the Americans succeed where the French had failed.

Building the canal was a tremendous feat. It took ten years. Roosevelt went to visit the canal site in 1908. It was the first time a President had left the United States while in office.

The first ships steamed through the canal on August 15, 1914. Today, the canal continues to be of great importance. It helps world trade as well as American defense.

Progressives and Reform

Roosevelt used his popularity and the power of his office in other ways. One of them was to bring about needed

The Grand Canyon, with its colorful rock formations and mile-deep gorge, became a national park at the urging of Theodore Roosevelt.

reform at home. Roosevelt and his supporters were called **Progressives.** The Progressives wanted government to **regulate,** or set rules for, business, transportation, and banking.

One business that needed reform was the meat-packing industry, according to a government report. Shredded rope had been found mixed with canned meat. Many of the workers in packing plants had the lung disease **tuberculosis** (too•buhr•kyuh•LOH•suhs). Tuberculosis could spread through the food the sick workers handled. The packing plants were dirty. Roosevelt supported new laws that let the government set standards for purity. Government officials could inspect packing plants to make sure these standards were followed.

New National Parks

When Roosevelt became President, he made conservation popular with Americans. Roosevelt added 194 million acres (78.5 ha) to the national forest system. He successfully pushed for five new national parks. Among them were the Grand Canyon, Mesa Verde, and Glacier national parks.

Reading Check

1. Why did the United States want to build the Panama Canal?
2. What happened after Colombia refused to let the United States build a canal?
3. What did Progressives want?
4. Why were reforms needed in the meat-packing business?

444

3. STEPS IN TECHNOLOGY AND DEMOCRACY

┌─ To Guide Your Reading ─────────────────────────

Look for these important words:

Key Words
- glider
- assembled
- assembly line
- suburbs
- suffrage
- Nineteenth Amendment

People
- Orville and Wilbur Wright
- Henry Ford
- Lucretia Mott
- Elizabeth Cady Stanton

- Lucy Stone
- Susan B. Anthony
- Abigail Duniway

Places
- Kitty Hawk

Look for answers to these questions:

1. What processes did Orville and Wilbur Wright go through before achieving powered flight?
2. What were important effects of the automobile?
3. Who were the leaders in the women's rights movement?
4. What does the Nineteenth Amendment say?

The twentieth century has been a time of major achievements in technology. For one, people began to travel through the air in flying machines. **Orville and Wilbur Wright** were the first to achieve the long-held dream of powered flight.

The Wright brothers were bicycle makers in Dayton, Ohio. Like many others of the time, they became fascinated with the possibility of flying. They started out by reading everything already known about flight. They even spent hours studying flying birds.

Then the Wright brothers constructed a **glider,** an aircraft that has no engine. On a windy stretch of beach at **Kitty Hawk,** North Carolina, the Wright brothers experimented with the glider. They developed ways to control and turn the glider in the air. Next they designed a gasoline engine and propellors to power the plane.

Orville and Wilbur Wright took the parts of this new aircraft to Kitty Hawk in September 1903. For the next several months they worked feverishly to get the new aircraft ready for flight. Propellors broke and had to be remade. The brothers raced against time. Winter was near, and they feared others might succeed before them.

At last, on December 17, the Wright brothers were ready. Orville was at the controls. He started the engine and headed into the high winds. The plane flew 120 feet (30.5 m). Orville and Wilbur made three more flights that day. After the last flight they were taking the plane back to its shed. Just then a gust of wind tossed it about. The plane was smashed, but no matter. History had been made that day.

The Wright brothers continued to make improvements, testing them in a cow pasture near Dayton. When

Theodore Roosevelt became President, powered flight was still a dream. Before his presidency was over, the army had ordered an airplane from the Wright brothers. A new age had begun.

The Automobile

In Detroit, Michigan, another revolution in transportation was in the making. Until 1908 only the rich could afford automobiles. **Henry Ford,** who sold his first car in 1903, wanted to make a cheaper car. Before 1908 cars had been made one at a time. Workers **assembled,** or fitted together, the many parts. Ford changed this system. His workers stayed in one place, each worker with a specific task to do. The automobile being assembled moved on a conveyor belt from one work station to another. This system was called an **assembly line.**

The first Model Ts came off Ford's assembly line in 1908. They were made in the old way, one at a time, and sold for about $850. Five years later, after introducing the assembly line, Ford was able to sell a Model T for about $450.

Even though a Model T cost under $500, many Americans could not afford to buy one. To help people buy automobiles, installment buying became common for the first time.

The automobile gave Americans a freedom of movement they had never known. People could use the automobile for vacations or for getting to work. People were no longer dependent on city streetcars. Able to live farther from their work, people began to move to the **suburbs,** communities near a city.

The automobile created a need for new business and industry. The need for tires led to the growth of the rubber industry. The oil refining business expanded in order to supply gasoline. Gas stations began to replace blacksmith shops. People began to demand that government build good roads.

Henry Ford, a self-taught engineer, believed that every American could own a car. His Model Ts, or "Tin Lizzies," rolled off the assembly lines by the thousands. Ford, in the driver's seat of this Model T, is accompanied by naturalist John Burroughs, left, and Thomas Edison.

446

By 1910, 1 of every 200 persons owned a car. By 1930, 1 of every 53 persons owned a car. Today 1 out of 2 persons owns a car, van, or truck. Now it is difficult to imagine life without automobiles.

The Rights of Women

Another major achievement of the twentieth century has been the continuing growth of democracy. In 1920 women got the right to vote.

The right of women to vote had first been proposed in 1848 at a women's rights meeting. This meeting, which was held in Seneca Falls, New York, was organized by **Lucretia Mott** and **Elizabeth Cady Stanton.** They had met each other while working for the abolition of slavery. At the meeting Elizabeth Cady Stanton read a Declaration of Sentiments. It was modeled on the Declaration of Independence. "We hold these truths to be self-evident: that all men and women are created equal," she said. The declaration demanded that women be given full rights of citizenship, including the right to vote.

From then on, a small group of outstanding women worked for the right to vote. In addition to Stanton and Mott, they included **Lucy Stone** and **Susan B. Anthony.**

Lucy Stone, like Stanton and Mott, was both an abolitionist and a defender of women's rights. As a young woman, she traveled the country giving speeches. "She was the first who really stirred the nation's heart on the subject of women's wrongs," according to Stanton.

Susan B. Anthony became a close friend of Elizabeth Cady Stanton.

Anthony and Stanton started a national organization to promote women's rights.

In 1872 the Supreme Court had supported Illinois in its refusal to let women practice law. Women, said the Court, were naturally timid and delicate. Therefore they were unfit for many occupations. This was a popular idea among people of the time. The facts, however, did not support it.

Settling America would have been impossible without numbers of strong and brave women. The American Revolution would not have been won without the active help of women. Women worked to end slavery and bring about reforms. At telephone switchboards, at typewriters, at cash registers, women were helping American business to grow. Other women became teachers, scientists, writers, and doctors.

Yet in 1900 one-fourth of the states would not let a wife own property. One-third of the states said a woman had no right to her own earnings. They belonged to her husband.

Working for the Vote

In Oregon **Abigail Duniway** felt this system was most unfair. Why, she asked her husband, was the law so one-sided? "Because," he said, "men made the laws."

In 1871 Abigail Duniway started a newspaper to promote **suffrage** for women. Suffrage means the right to vote. If women could vote, then they could change unfair laws. Susan B. Anthony journeyed to Oregon to help her. For years Abigail Duniway wrote and spoke about women's right to vote.

By 1910 the suffrage movement had gained the support of most American

447

Thousands of women marched in New York City to demand the right to vote. In the Nineteenth Amendment that right was finally recognized.

women. Women started wearing yellow, the color of the cause. Women started holding rallies and parades. Their demands became bolder and stronger. In 1912, 15,000 women marched up Fifth Avenue in New York in a demand for women's suffrage.

A woman who marched in a parade talked about it several years later:

> I didn't walk in New York's first suffrage parade because my mother wouldn't let me. Next year, in 1913, I wanted to march, but my husband asked me not to. This fall I decided that it was up to me to suffer for democracy.

The **Nineteenth Amendment** to the Constitution became law in 1920. For the first time adult women could vote nationwide for President. Another step toward a fuller democracy had been taken.

Reading Check

1. Why are the Wright brothers famous?
2. Who developed an assembly line method of making cars?
3. Why was the 1848 Seneca Falls meeting important?
4. What was the result of the women's suffrage movement?

WOMEN IN THE SKIES

Harriet Quimby

Ruth Law

Amelia Earhart

Seven years after the airplane was invented, a handful of hardy women were flying. They soared across America in the open, rickety contraptions that were the first airplanes.

In 1912 Harriet Quimby was the first woman to fly across the English Channel. Five minutes before she took off into the foggy skies, a friend showed her how to read a compass. Following the compass, she flew safely across the Channel. This brave lady died several months later when her airplane crashed near Boston.

Ruth Law was also a flier. On the day of her first plane ride, she saw Harriet Quimby plunge to her death. Nevertheless, Ruth Law was determined to fly. Within six months she was doing stunt flying, making graceful loops in the air. In 1916 Ruth Law took off from Chicago for New York City. She flew until her sputtering engines told her she was out of gas. She landed in Hormel, New York, setting a long-distance air record of 590 miles (804.5 km). Why did Ruth Law risk danger and death in the air? "My flight was done just purely for the love of accomplishment," she told people.

The most famous of the early women fliers was Amelia Earhart. She was a military nurse in Canada in 1918 when she saw her first airplane. Thrilled at the sight, she started taking flying lessons. In 1932 she was the first woman to fly alone across the Atlantic Ocean. Near the end of the flight, she faced grave problems. Her instruments were out of order and her engine was failing. Gasoline was leaking into the cockpit. Just as she feared she would go into the ocean, the coast of Ireland appeared. She sputtered to a landing in a cow pasture near Londonderry. To an amazed farmer working nearby, she said, "I've come from America." Her flight of 15 hours, 18 minutes was then the fastest crossing on record.

On an around-the-world flight in 1937, Amelia Earhart disappeared in the South Pacific. At the news, America grieved for this spirited and courageous flier.

449

SKILLS FOR SUCCESS

LEARNING FROM A NEWSPAPER

Some newspapers have hundreds of pages, and others have just a few. Even so, almost all newspapers are divided into the same parts.

The News Section

The first part of most newspapers is the **news section.** This section begins on the front page. Here you will find the most important international, national, and local stories.

If a story was written someplace besides the newspaper's hometown, it carries a **dateline.** A dateline gives the name of the place where the story was written. At the top or bottom of such a story, you may see the words *Associated Press* or *United Press International.* These are the names of large news agencies that send reporters all over the world. Sometimes only the initials are used—*AP* or *UPI.* The stories written by news agency reporters are sold to many newspapers.

A **by-line** gives the name of the person who wrote the story. Not all newspaper stories have by-lines.

The Editorial Page

Most papers have a special page or section for **columns** and **editorials.** A column is an article that gives the views of a particular writer. An editorial is an article that gives the opinion of the **editor.** The editor directs the newspaper.

Columns and editorials are very different from news stories. News stories present facts and tell what happened. Editorials and columns present opinions. An editorial usually judges something that happened and argues whether it was right or wrong. An editorial may also give advice to leaders or citizens.

The editorial section also presents letters that are written by the paper's readers. In these letters the readers give their opinions about recent events. Political cartoons in the editorial section express opinions about news events.

Other Sections

You will find both news stories and columns in other sections of a newspaper. These include sports, entertainment, and business sections.

You can locate parts of the paper by looking in the paper's table of contents. The table of contents is usually printed on the bottom half of the front page.

Almost all newspapers have a section of small advertisements. These ads are **classified,** or grouped, by what they are offering. Some ads list jobs that are available. Others list cars or boats for sale. Still others list houses for rent or for sale.

Scanning a Newspaper

Very few people have time to read every word in a newspaper. Most people just read articles about things they think are important or interesting. They **scan,** or quickly look through, the newspaper to find articles to read. They do this by looking at **headlines.** The headline is in big type and tells the main

PEARY REACHES THE POLE

April 7, 1909

BATTLE HARBOR, Labrador—Commander Robert E. Peary of the United States Navy has reached the North Pole. Peary wired this message yesterday—"I have the pole, April sixth."

For 23 years Peary has explored the Arctic regions. Since 1898 Peary has searched for routes to the North Pole. Now his ambition has been realized.

The ship *Roosevelt* landed the Peary expedition in September near Cape Columbia on Ellesmere Island. In March Peary's expedition left Cape Columbia for the North Pole.

"I decided that I should strain every nerve to make five marches of fifteen miles each," Peary said in his wire. At the end of the fifth march, on April 6, there was a break in the clouds at noon. Peary made his observation. He was at 90°N—the North Pole.

Ready for the Pole, Commander Robert E. Peary posed with his huskies last fall on board the steamer *Roosevelt*.

Peary quoted his original entry for that day:

"The pole at last! The prize of three centuries, my dream and goal for twenty years, mine at last!"

---

idea of a story. After you read the headline, you may then decide to read the story.

News stories are usually written according to one rule: the first paragraph should give all the basic facts. It should answer the questions *Who?*, *What?*, *When?*, and *Where?*. Depending on the story, the answers to *How?* or *Why?* may also be included. The paragraphs of a news story are arranged in order of importance. The basic facts are always in the first paragraph or two. Each paragraph that follows gives more details. The least important details are at the end.

Read the news story above. It is based on a 1909 newspaper account.

The first sentence tells *who* did *what* and *where.* Robert Peary discovered the North Pole. The second sentence tells *when*—on April 6.

The paragraphs that follow each give additional information about the facts in the first paragraph. The second paragraph tells that Peary had tried for several years to reach the pole. The third paragraph quotes Peary about the march to the pole. The last paragraph expresses how Peary felt when arriving at the pole.

With each paragraph a reader gets more information. Yet the reader could stop after the first paragraph and have the most important facts. This way of organizing facts lets the reader scan. It lets the reader decide how much of the story to read.

CHECKING YOUR SKILLS

Write the answers to these questions.

1. Where will you find major news stories in a newspaper?

2. What is an editorial?

3. Why is a news story different from an editorial?

4. What should the headline of a news article do?

5. What questions should the first paragraph of a news story answer?

4. WORLD WAR I

To Guide Your Reading

Look for these important words:

Key Words
- Allied powers
- Allies

- Central powers
- no-man's-land
- League of Nations

People
- Woodrow Wilson

Look for answers to these questions:

1. Why did the United States fight in World War I?
2. Where was most of World War I fought?
3. What kinds of jobs did women do during the war?
4. How did the United States make a difference to the outcome of the war?

In 1914 war broke out in Europe. On one side were Russia, France, Britain, and Italy. These were known as the **Allied Powers,** or **Allies.** On the other side were the **Central Powers** —Germany, Austria, and Turkey. Of these, Germany was the strongest nation.

The United States as a country tried to stay neutral in the war. But the feelings of Americans were not in the least neutral. Most Americans favored Britain. The Americans and the British shared the same language and many of the same traditions. Americans were comforted by British control of the seas. On the other hand, people with roots in Germany or Austria favored those nations.

The strategy of Britain was to win the war with a blockade of German ports. German strategy, on the other hand, was to end the blockade and destroy the British navy by using submarines. In 1915 German submarines sank the British passenger ship *Lusitania* with great loss of life. Americans

were outraged. Such an attack was against the rules of the sea.

The U.S. Enters the War

Woodrow Wilson was President of the United States at this time. He had hoped to keep America out of the war, but this proved impossible.

In the spring of 1917 Germany announced that its submarines would go after any ships in British waters. The German submarines then sank three ships. American passengers aboard these ships were killed. President Wilson asked Congress to declare war on Germany. It was necessary to fight, he said, for the peace of the world. "The world must be made safe for democracy," he said.

After the United States declared war, a wave of anti-German feeling ran through the country. Schools and colleges stopped teaching the German language. German music was no longer played. Sauerkraut was called "liberty

452

TRENCH WARFARE DURING WORLD WAR I

To enemy lines
Front line
No-man's-land
Barbed wire
Headquarters dugout—
30 ft. (9 m) down
Area between support line and
front line—200 yds. (180 m)
Support line
Communication trench
Area between reserve line and
support line —300 yds. (270 m)
Reserve line
Field artillery—500–1000 yds.
(about 469–910 m) to the rear

cabbage." Even German measles were renamed "liberty measles."

Trench Warfare

In Europe the war had bogged down into deadly trench warfare. Most of this warfare was in northern France. The soldiers who lived and died in these trenches were separated by a **no-man's-land.** No-man's-land was the land separating opposing armies. It was laced with barbed wire and mines. The Germans used poison gas for the first time to kill enemy troops.

The English developed a new secret weapon they called a tank. By the end of the war, tanks could cross the no-man's-land, crushing barbed wire. Bullets could not pierce tanks.

Overhead, observation balloons were used to spy on the enemy. During the war each side developed an infant air force. Flying "aces" gained glory for their skill and bravery. They included Germany's "Red Baron," Manfred von Richthofen (RIK•toh•vuhn), and America's Eddie Rickenbacker.

Women in the War

American women went to Europe to serve as nurses and ambulance drivers. Katherine Stinson of San Antonio, Texas, wanted to become a combat pilot in the war. The army refused her. Instead she flew across the United States raising money for the Red Cross. Then she went to Europe as an ambulance driver. Katherine's sister Marjorie taught many Canadian and American men to fly.

Thousands of women joined the navy and army as clerks and telegraph

453

During World War I women stepped forward to do all kinds of work formerly done by men. Here these women take on the job of delivering blocks of ice— an important job before most people had refrigerators.

operators. Thousands more took over jobs left vacant by men going to war. They worked in fields and factories. They became auto mechanics. As police officers they directed traffic and patrolled the streets.

The War Comes to an End

In Europe the Americans made a difference to the outcome of the war. Enthusiastic American soldiers gave important military help. Shiploads of American wheat, hay, canned goods, and guns poured into France. Working together, the Allies, which now included the United States, began to push back the German army.

On November 11, 1918, an armistice was declared. The war was over, and American troops started coming home. Meanwhile world leaders gathered together to make peace terms. Wilson urged these leaders to accept his idea for a **League of Nations.** The League of Nations would be a worldwide organization to which all nations could belong. The league would work to find peaceful solutions to problems among nations.

The League of Nations was established, but the United States refused to join. The United States Senate must vote approval of all treaties. It voted not to approve the League of Nations treaty. Many senators believed that America should not get involved any more in world affairs.

Reading Check

1. Who was President during World War I?
2. Why did the United States enter World War I?
3. How did the United States help its allies in World War I?
4. What was the League of Nations?

454

CHAPTER 19 REVIEW

WORDS TO USE

Match each word with the correct definition.

1. **armistice**
2. **assembled**
3. **assembly line**
4. **isthmus**
5. **no-man's-land**
6. **regulate**
7. **suburbs**
8. **suffrage**
9. **tuberculosis**
10. **tyranny**

a. A narrow piece of land connecting two larger areas

b. A lung disease

c. Right to vote

d. Communities near a city

e. Fitted parts together

f. Harsh and unjust rule

g. The land separating opposing armies

h. An agreement to stop fighting

i. Set rules for

j. Moving a product from one work station to another in manufacturing

FACTS TO REVIEW

1. What caused the Spanish-American War?

2. How did the United States defeat Spain in the Spanish-American War?

3. How did the United States gain control of Hawaii? of Alaska?

4. Name three major achievements of Theodore Roosevelt as President.

5. Why was the Panama Canal important?

6. What was an example of government regulation of business?

7. How did new technology in transportation bring changes to American life?

8. How did American women show their support of the suffrage movement?

9. For what reasons did the United States join Britain's side in World War I?

10. How was the Spanish-American War similar to World War I? How was it different?

IDEAS TO DISCUSS

1. What beliefs delayed women's suffrage? What did some women do to focus attention on their right to vote?

2. How did the United States use its power and influence in world affairs? Use examples from this chapter.

3. If you could choose to relive a part of the history you have read about in this chapter, which part would it be? Why?

◯ SKILLS PRACTICE

Reading a Newspaper Look in a newspaper and bring to class an example of these:

- A news article with a by-line
- A column
- An editorial
- A letter to the editor
- A political cartoon
- A sports column

CHAPTER 20

The Jazz Age, the New Deal, and World War II

About this chapter

In the decades after World War I, American culture, technology, and influence received growing recognition. American music, sports, literature, and entertainment became known around the world. Technology had more influence on the way Americans lived. Radios, airplanes, giant dams—all were part of this new growing technology. The national government grew larger and more powerful. In the world the United States became a leader of democratic nations and fought another war to defend democracy.

1. THE JAZZ AGE

To Guide Your Reading

Look for these important words:

Key Words
- Jazz Age
- Roaring Twenties
- jazz
- spirituals
- stock market
- stocks

People
- Charles Lindbergh
- Charlie Chaplin
- Will Rogers
- Herbert Hoover

Look for answers to these questions:

1. What was life like for many Americans in the 1920s?
2. Why did Charles Lindbergh become an American hero?
3. What forms of entertainment were popular in the 1920s?
4. What was the Great Crash?

The **Jazz Age** and the **Roaring Twenties** are both names given to the 1920s. After the serious days of World War I, Americans were ready for good times. Many had more money than ever before. They spent their money on many of the new products becoming available. Such products included cars, washing machines, phonographs, and radios.

A Pennsylvania radio station was the first to make regular broadcasts in 1920. People who wanted to listen to the station had to make their own radios. Soon companies began to sell manufactured radios. By 1922 more than 500 stations were broadcasting. By 1925, 5 million families had radios.

Radio made possible an audience of millions of people. Listening to the radio, Americans shared in the exciting events of the decade. One of these, in 1926, was a fight for the heavyweight boxing title. Millions listened as Gene Tunney beat Jack Dempsey in a ten-round boxing match. Baseball games were also popular. Yankee fans cheered when Babe Ruth hit his sixtieth home run during the 1927 season.

This listener strains his ears to catch the faint, scratchy sounds of early radio.

Charles Lindbergh

In 1927 Americans listened eagerly when **Charles Lindbergh** flew across the Atlantic Ocean toward Paris. Lindbergh wanted to win a $25,000 prize. The prize was offered to the first person to fly nonstop from New York to Paris. Lindbergh had designed his own small plane, the *Spirit of St. Louis*. On May 20, 1927, Lindbergh climbed into his plane with five sandwiches and a canteen of water. Alone, battling fatigue, he tried to keep his course over the wide ocean. Lindbergh wrote in his journal: "My back is stiff; my shoulders ache; my eyes smart. It seems impossible to go on longer."

Go on he did. Thirty-three and one-half hours after leaving New York, he landed in Paris. The French greeted him as a hero. In that hour Lindbergh became the most popular person in America.

Jazz and the Movies

Over their radios Americans could also hear a new sound of music. It was **jazz.** Jazz grew out of the heritage of the American blacks. That heritage included West African music brought by their ancestors. In America blacks were introduced to the hymns of the Christian missionaries. They gradually changed the hymns. These new versions of hymns became known as **spirituals.** From this tradition of African music and spirituals, jazz was born.

Americans everywhere began to go to the movies. The invention of the

After flying nonstop from New York to Paris, Charles Lindbergh became a national hero. A navy ship brought him and his plane home from France.

Louis Armstrong, born in New Orleans, moved to Chicago in the 1920s. Playing his trumpet or the piano, he was one of the great performers of American jazz.

458

Looking cold and forlorn, Charlie Chaplin huddles against a door in "A Dog's Life."

movie camera was the basis of the new industry. Based in Hollywood, California, the movie business first turned out silent films. By 1927 Edison had come up with another invention, the talking picture. Soon movies with sound replaced silent films.

Charlie Chaplin was one of the most popular movie stars of the silent films. One of his most famous roles was the "little tramp."

Will Rogers became one of the most popular stars of the "talkies." Will Rogers kept America laughing. Rogers was a cowboy, a stage entertainer, a radio and movie star, and a newspaper writer. He was part Cherokee and had been born in the Indian Territory of Oklahoma. "My ancestors didn't come on the *Mayflower,* but they met the boat," he quipped.

The Good Times End

In 1928 **Herbert Hoover** was elected President. Hoover had gained fame for the excellent way he organized relief after World War I. The poor, the hungry, and the displaced of Europe were helped because of Hoover's efforts.

The good life of the 1920s, many thought, would go on forever. Hoover shared those hopes. "We in America today are nearer to the final triumph over poverty than ever before in the history of any land," he said.

Thousands pinned their hopes on a rich future by investing in the **stock market.** The stock market is a place where people can buy and sell **stocks.** Stocks are shares of ownership in business corporations. If more people want to buy than sell, the price of shares goes up. The reverse is also true. If more people want to sell than buy, the price of shares goes down. During the 1920s the prices on the New York Stock Exchange kept going higher. People began to borrow money to buy stocks. "How can you lose?" they asked.

On October 29, 1929, nearly everyone lost. Prices on the stock market crashed down like a house of cards. This was called the Great Crash. It marked the end of the good times of the Twenties. It was the beginning of hard times ahead.

Reading Check

1. How do we know radio became very important in the 1920s?
2. Who was the first person to fly alone from New York to Paris?
3. How did jazz music come about?
4. What happened in the Great Crash?

459

2. DEPRESSION AND NEW DEAL

═══ **To Guide Your Reading** ═══

Look for these important words:

Key Words
- Great Depression
- depression
- New Deal
- bureaucracy
- unemployment
- Dust Bowl

- hydroelectric dams
- Tennessee Valley
  Authority
- Social Security

People
- Franklin Delano
  Roosevelt

- Eleanor Roosevelt

Places
- Hoover Dam
- Grand Coulee
- Bonneville

Look for answers to these questions:

1. What was life like for many Americans in the 1930s?
2. What qualities did Franklin D. Roosevelt have?
3. What was the New Deal?
4. What was the effect of the government building huge dams?

The hard times of the 1930s were called the **Great Depression.** During a **depression** there is little money and no economic growth.

Most people who had invested in the stock market lost their money. Banks that had lent too much money had to close. When the banks closed, great numbers of people lost their savings.

Because people had little money, they bought few goods. Manufacturers could not sell what they had made. Workers then lost their jobs. Millions of these people had borrowed money to buy cars, radios, and washing machines. When they lost their jobs, they could not pay their debts. This caused even more banks and businesses to fail.

"We saw bank failures everywhere," an Arkansas man remembered. "The most valuable thing we lost

A rich man in the 1920s, Fred Bell sold apples in the 1930s.

was hope. A man can endure a lot if he still has hope."

The farmers had not shared in the boom times of the 1920s. Crop and livestock prices had dropped so low that farmers could make no profit. When they could not pay off loans to the banks, they lost their farms.

Poverty and hardship settled on the face of the land.

There had been hard times in the past. Always the country had come out of them. These hard times too would pass, President Hoover said. The government gave loans to businesses and some aid to the poor. But it was not enough.

Times got even worse. By 1932 one-fourth of American workers were without jobs. Farmers could not afford to ship their goods to market. In the cities, people were starving. Soup kitchens and breadlines gave some relief. There poor people could get free soup and bread.

Studs Terkel is a writer who interviewed people about their memories of the 1930s. One woman he talked to remembered:

> There were many beggars who would come to your back door, and they would say they were hungry. I wouldn't give them money because I didn't have it. But I did take them in and put them in my kitchen and give them something to eat.

Another person told Studs Terkel that her mother used to feed hungry men at the back door. This made the neighbors angry at her mother. "They said it would bring others, and then what would she do? She said, 'I'll feed them till the food runs out.' "

Roosevelt Elected President

In 1932 the American people rejected Hoover as President and elected **Franklin Delano Roosevelt.** Roosevelt was a hearty, likable person. He was married to **Eleanor Roosevelt,** a niece of Theodore Roosevelt.

Eleven years before his election as President, Roosevelt had come down with polio. The disease left him crippled, unable to use his legs. While fighting to get well, Roosevelt made a decision not to feel sorry for himself. Though crippled, he would do something worthwhile with his life. Before getting sick, Roosevelt had gained some experience in public service. He reentered politics and was elected governor of New York. Then, in 1932, the Democratic party chose Roosevelt as its Presidential candidate. "I pledge myself to a new deal for the American people,"

Franklin Roosevelt, with Eleanor at his side, gave new hope to many people.

Roosevelt told the Democrats. The words stuck. Roosevelt's program was called the **New Deal.**

Ending the depression, Roosevelt decided, needed bold, new actions from government. On inauguration day Americans listened on the radio to Roosevelt's rich, confident voice. "The only thing we have to fear is fear itself," he said. In those dark days Roosevelt gave people new hope. Things would be all right. The government would do something.

Growth of Government

The new Congress quickly began to pass Roosevelt's proposals. The programs of the New Deal greatly expanded the power of the federal government. These programs were to bring help to the American people. A large **bureaucracy,** or body of government officials, developed along with the government programs.

Help for the Jobless

The New Deal aimed at getting people back to work. The government hired thousands of young men. Their jobs were to build bridges, plant trees, and do other worthwhile things.

Another New Deal program trained unemployed people in new skills. The government hired others to use the skills they had. Librarians, artists, and writers were given jobs. Even with these programs, **unemployment,** the number of people without jobs, remained high. At least unemployment did not increase.

Drought, dust storms, and depression led farmers to abandon their homes, load up their Model Ts, and head to California to look for work.

Help for Farmers

The New Deal gave loans to farmers so they would not lose their farms. Another program limited production. If farmers produced less, then prices would rise. The government began to pay farmers not to plant crops.

On the Great Plains farmers faced another problem. A drought came to the area early in the 1930s. The dry, plowed land blew away in the strong winds. Wind-blown dirt covered fences and roads. The arrival of a dirt storm could turn daylight into the black of night. The western Great Plains became known as the **Dust Bowl.**

To deal with this problem, the New Deal started a conservation program. The aim was to stop the dust storms and preserve the land. An important part of the program was planting trees to serve as windbreaks. In time, better plowing methods, more rainfall, and the new windbreaks ended the Dust Bowl.

Government-built Dams

Until the New Deal, the development of energy was generally left to private business. But Senator George Norris of Nebraska had a different idea. He wanted the government to build **hydroelectric dams,** dams that produce electricity. The government would then sell the electricity at low rates to users. This idea became another part of the New Deal.

In 1933 Congress created the TVA, or **Tennessee Valley Authority.** The purpose of the TVA was to tame the Tennessee River. The plan called for the construction of hydroelectric dams, for locks to help navigation, and for fertilizer factories. The TVA has made the Tennessee valley a productive and prosperous place.

Other large dams were built by the government during the New Deal. The **Hoover Dam** on the Colorado River was one. Others included the **Grand Coulee** and **Bonneville** dams on the Columbia River. The electricity generated by the Hoover Dam helped southern California and Arizona to grow. The dams on the Columbia River encouraged the agricultural development of eastern Washington and Oregon.

Support for Labor

The New Deal brought new support for the American labor movement. There had often been bitter strikes and conflicts over the right of workers to organize into unions. Roosevelt gave his support to labor unions. New laws gave workers the right to form unions and the right to a minimum wage.

Workers were further helped by **Social Security.** It was one of the most important reforms of the New Deal. Social Security is a kind of insurance program for retired workers. Workers and employers each contribute to Social Security. In turn workers can count on an income when they retire.

Reading Check

1. What kinds of hardships did people face during the Great Depression?
2. How did the New Deal help the jobless? the farmers?
3. What was the purpose of the Tennessee Valley Authority?
4. How did the New Deal help workers?

3. WORLD WAR II

To Guide Your Reading

Look for these important words:

Key Words
- Nazi party
- storm troopers
- dictator
- World War II
- military draft
- Axis powers
- Allies
- rationing
- relocation camps
- civilians

- carriers
- D day
- Holocaust

People
- Adolf Hitler
- Benito Mussolini
- Dwight D. Eisenhower
- Harry S. Truman

Places
- Japan
- Austria
- Czechoslovakia
- Poland
- Pearl Harbor
- English Channel
- Normandy
- Berlin
- Hiroshima
- Nagasaki

Look for answers to these questions:

1. What events led to World War II?
2. Why did the United States enter World War II?
3. What was Allied strategy in World War II?
4. What was the Holocaust?
5. What forced Japan to surrender?

Roosevelt was reelected in 1936. Problems at home seemed to be getting better, but world news was bad. Great changes were taking place in Europe. Americans who listened to the radio or read the newspaper were aware of these. In 1936 the news often reported on **Adolf Hitler** in Germany.

After World War I Germany was expected to pay back the costs of the war. Germany did not have the money to pay this huge debt. Its economy suffered. Inflation in Germany was terrible.

Hitler played on German feelings that Germany had not been treated fairly after World War I. In addition, Hitler said that Germans were superior to other peoples of the world.

Hitler joined a political party, the National Socialists, or **Nazi party.** Soon he became a leader of the party. The Nazis promised to make Germany a powerful nation once again. They blamed many of Germany's problems on Jews. The Nazis set up a private army called **storm troopers.** The storm troopers burned books they did not like and attacked Jewish people.

In 1933 the Nazis took over, and representative government in Germany came to an end. Only Hitler ruled. Hitler began to prepare Germany for another war. He had plans for Germany to rule the world.

In Italy **Benito Mussolini** (buh-NEET-oh moo-suh-LEE-nee) had come to power. Like Hitler, Mussolini was

464

all-powerful. We call such a ruler a **dictator.** A dictator has no respect for individual rights. A dictator has no respect for democracy or representative government.

On the other side of the world, military officers had started to rule **Japan.** Japan did not have all the resources necessary to become an industrial country. The military leaders said Japan could get oil, rubber, iron, and tin only by conquest. The United States, which controlled the Philippines, stood in the way of Japanese expansion.

War Begins in Europe

In 1938 Germany invaded **Austria** and **Czechoslovakia.** The next year Germany invaded **Poland.** Britain and France declared war on Germany but were almost powerless against the German armies. German armies quickly took over most of Europe. German bombers attacked Britain, but Britain fought on. In 1941 Germany invaded the Soviet Union. **World War II** had begun.

In the United States many people felt that the country should stay out of European conflicts. Few citizens wanted to see the United States fight another war. Yet, as Roosevelt said, war was a disease that could spread. The United States, said Roosevelt, should prepare itself in case war came. The United States started making war equipment such as tanks and bombers. It began to send equipment and supplies to Britain. To build up an army of trained soldiers, Congress started a **military draft.** A military draft is a way of bringing people into the army.

In 1940 German troops marched into Paris passing through the Arc de Triomphe.

America Enters the War

On Sunday, December 7, 1941, World War II came to the United States. At 7:55 A.M. 100 Japanese bombers swooped through the clouds above **Pearl Harbor.** Pearl Harbor was the American naval base in the Hawaiian Islands. A deadly load of bombs was dropped on the American ships and airfield. It was a day, Roosevelt said, that would "live in infamy." *Infamy* (IN•fuh•mee) means remembered for being evil.

The United States had been attacked. That meant war. Japan was an ally of Germany and Italy. These countries were known as the **Axis powers.** The United States joined Britain and Russia. They were called the **Allies.**

A Japanese surprise attack on December 7, 1941, brought death and destruction to the American military base at Pearl Harbor, Hawaii.

The United States immediately speeded up production of airplanes, ships, submarines, jeeps, and tanks. Now, instead of there not being enough jobs, there were not enough workers. As in World War I, women took over many jobs in factories, fields, and offices. Other women joined the army and navy to do nonfighting jobs.

The demands of fighting a world war led to further growth in government. Never had Americans experienced so much control over their lives. Controls were established over prices, wages, and rents. This became necessary in order to produce war supplies and feed thousands of troops. Government rules called for **rationing,** or limiting, what people could buy. Each citizen had a coupon book. It was impossible to buy most goods without coupons. Coupons were needed for such items as shoes, sugar, and gasoline.

The Japanese Americans

When the United States went to war with Japan, prejudice against the Japanese grew. This was particularly true in California.

Military officials believed that the Japanese Americans could not be trusted. They believed they would help Japan invade the United States.

The United States government therefore decided to put Japanese Americans in **relocation camps.** These camps were like prisons. Barbed wire fenced in the camps. Soldiers with guns guarded the camps to keep people from leaving. About 120,000 Japanese Americans spent the war years in these camps.

For them it meant heartache, bitterness, and loss of property. They were forced to leave their land, their businesses, and their homes.

Arrival at the camps themselves was a fearful time, as one woman remembered: "Can you imagine the despair and utter desolation of all of us? Everybody was weeping, youngsters hanging onto parents, fear and terror all around."

While their parents were in the camps, Japanese American soldiers served bravely and well. The Japanese American regiment was, for its size, the most decorated unit in World War II.

Not all Americans agreed with the way Japanese Americans were treated. One who did not was Eleanor Roosevelt. Free societies do not do such things, she said.

Fighting the War

World War II was a different kind of war. Armies did not spend years in trenches as in World War I. Instead, armies moved quickly by tank, ship, and airplane. Radio helped them stay in touch with each other and make quick decisions.

Both sides bombed cities, killing hundreds of thousands of **civilians.** A civilian is a person who is not a soldier.

Bombs dropping from the air destroyed factories, hospitals, apartment houses. They often destroyed old and beautiful buildings, great churches, and museums. Whole cities were destroyed.

The strategy of the Allies called for the following:

- Getting control of the Mediterranean Sea. The Allies would fight the Germans and Italians in North Africa and then invade Italy.
- Landing armies on the coast of France to start pushing back the Germans. At the same time the Russians would push the German armies from the east.
- Forcing the Japanese back from the Pacific lands and islands they had conquered.

Much of London was destroyed by bombs dropped during German air raids.

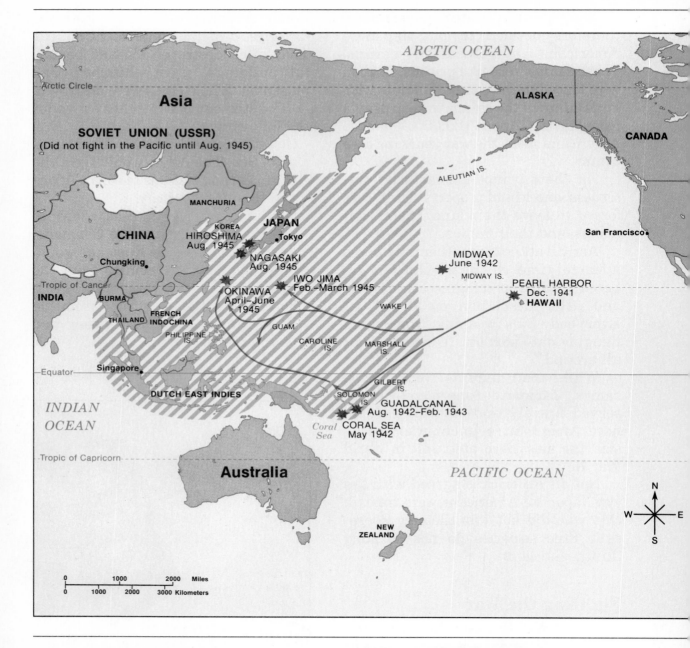

In the Pacific important air battles were fought by planes based on aircraft **carriers.** Carriers are huge ships that serve as bases for fighter planes. American victories at sea began to force the Japanese back. Fighting was fierce as the United States began pushing the Japanese from the Pacific islands.

Victory in Europe

The Allies invaded North Africa in 1942. They started pushing north through Italy in 1943.

On June 6, 1944, the Allies worked together in the greatest seaborne invasion in history. We call it **D day.** General **Dwight D. Eisenhower** led

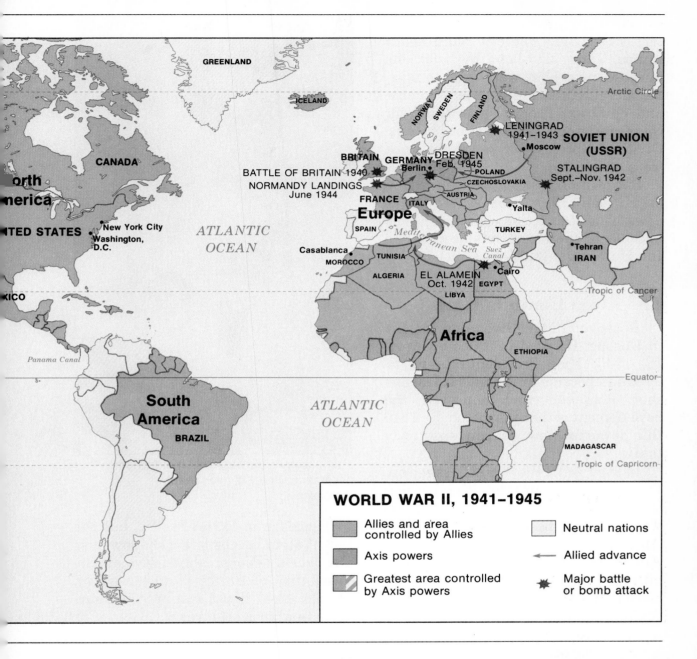

WORLD WAR II, 1941–1945

- Allies and area controlled by Allies
- Axis powers
- Greatest area controlled by Axis powers
- Neutral nations
- ← Allied advance
- ✶ Major battle or bomb attack

the invasion. Allied forces crossed the **English Channel** to land on the beaches of **Normandy** in France. They were met by murderous gunfire from German soldiers, but the invasion was successful. Technology made the difference. The Americans had 6,000 aircraft. The Germans had 900.

The Allies started pushing back the Germans. In May 1945 Allied troops met near **Berlin,** the German capital. There they found out that Hitler had killed himself. The Allied victory in Europe was complete.

Only then did people understand fully the evil nature of Hitler and the

Nazis. Throughout former German territory Allied soldiers found death camps. These had been built for one purpose only. They were used to murder more than 12 million men, women, and children. People were killed for their religious or political beliefs. Civilian captives who could not work were also killed.

Six million people were murdered on Hitler's orders because they were Jews. This destruction of Jewish people because of their race has been called the **Holocaust** (hahl•uh•KOST).

The Atom Bomb Is Used

Roosevelt did not live to see victory in Europe. He died in office on April 12, 1945. Vice President **Harry S. Truman** became President. He learned that Roosevelt had approved the development of the atom bomb. By 1945 this powerful new weapon was ready to use.

In the Pacific the war still raged on. President Truman made the decision to drop the atom bomb on Japan. He wanted to end the war quickly and save American lives. On August 6, 1945, an American bomber, the *Enola Gay,* took off and flew high over the industrial city of **Hiroshima** (hir•uh•SHEE•muh). A single bomb was dropped. There was a flash like an exploding sun. Then a great mushroom cloud rose from the destruction. On that day or soon after, nearly 100,000 people died.

As terrible as the bomb was, Japan did not surrender immediately. On August 9 another atom bomb was dropped on **Nagasaki** (nahg•uh•SAHK• ee). Only then did Japan make plans to surrender.

The mushrooming cloud of an atom bomb became a symbol of new, deadly technology.

Peace came to the Pacific, but the use of atom bombs left a shadow over the world. People shuddered at the possibility of future atomic warfare. People asked if civilization could survive another world war.

Reading Check

1. What was a cause of World War II in Europe?
2. Why did the Japanese attack the United States at Pearl Harbor?
3. How did the way World War II was fought affect civilians?
4. What happened on D day?

ALBERT EINSTEIN

Albert Einstein

Einstein as a scientist

Einstein as a musician

Albert Einstein was one of the great scientific thinkers of modern times. His ideas have helped us understand our universe. Because of him, we know more about the tiniest atom and the most distant star. Einstein's ideas explained how stars like our sun can give off heat and light. His ideas also explained how people could use uranium, a metal, to make an atom bomb.

Albert Einstein grew up in Germany. His parents worried because Albert did not talk until he was almost 4 years old. One of his teachers wrote on his report card, "You will never amount to anything." By the time he was 26 years old, however, Einstein had become a world-famous scientist.

In 1933 Einstein realized he would have to leave his homeland. Adolf Hitler and the Nazis had come to power. They were mistreating Jewish people. Einstein was Jewish, so he took his family to the United States.

When World War II started, many scientists feared that Germany would build an atom bomb. The scientists sent a letter to President Franklin Roosevelt. The letter warned that "extremely powerful bombs of a new type may be constructed." Einstein was one of those who signed the letter. He knew that America had to do everything possible to defeat Hitler. Because of the letter, Roosevelt created a highly secret project to make the first atom bomb.

Albert Einstein was a peaceful man. He loved to play the violin and sail his small boat. He loved the grace and beauty of science. He did not like using his ideas to make bombs. He was sad when the United States dropped atom bombs on Hiroshima and Nagasaki. Before his death in 1955, Einstein said that signing the letter to Roosevelt was the greatest mistake of his life.

Now many nations have atom bombs. We have the power to destroy the whole planet. A continuing challenge for the peoples of the world is to use atomic energy wisely. Science in the service of people—that was Einstein's hope.

SKILLS FOR SUCCESS

CONDUCTING AN INTERVIEW

Interviewing means questioning people about what they have done or what they think. You can learn about events in recent history by interviewing people who took part in them.

Interviewing takes careful planning. You must first decide what event or period you want to learn about. For instance, you might want to learn what it was like to live during the depression. Perhaps you have a relative or a neighbor who lived at that time. If so, ask the person for an interview. Explain why. You might say, "We are studying the depression in school. I would like to find out what it was like to live then."

If the person agrees to an interview, set up an exact time for the meeting. You should also ask for permission if you want to use a tape recorder. Some people do not like to have their words recorded on tape.

Several days before the interview, think about the main questions you want to ask. Try to ask questions that start with *How, What kind of, Where, When,* or *Why.* Write your questions on a sheet of paper. Questions about the Great Depression might include:

- *Where did you live during the depression?*
- *Were you then in school?*
- *How did your family live?*
- *Did you hear Franklin Roosevelt speak?*
- *What kind of entertainment did you have?*
- *Did you have a job? What was it?*

On the day of the interview, be ready well ahead of time. Get out your notebook and have several pens or pencils ready. Dress neatly.

Be on time for the interview. You may spend a few minutes chatting just to relax.

Start by asking the first questions on your list. Remember that a good interviewer listens rather than talks. Do not argue with the person or interrupt.

It is not important that you ask your questions in order. Often your questions will be answered without your asking them. Sometimes, however, the conversation will stop. You can start it up again asking certain kinds of questions. "What happened then?" and "How did you feel when you saw that?" are good for this purpose.

After the interview go over the notes you have taken. Add to them if necessary.

To turn your notes into a report, first look for three or four topics. Use these topics to organize your report. When you are finished, you may want to send a copy of your report to the person you interviewed. You can ask if the information is correct. If there are any corrections, make them in your report. Finally, send a thank-you note to the person you interviewed.

CHECKING YOUR SKILLS

Use the information in this lesson to answer these questions.

1. What are some of the things you should explain in making an appointment for an interview?

2. What kinds of questions should you ask?

3. What should you bring with you to the interview?

4. What should you do after the interview is over?

CHAPTER 20 REVIEW

WORDS TO USE

Number your paper from 1 to 10. Use the words below to complete the sentences that follow.

bureaucracy
civilians
depression
dictator
jazz

Holocaust
military draft
rationing
stock market
unemployment

1. A music called _____ grew out of the heritage of American blacks.

2. The _____ is where people buy and sell shares of ownership in large corporations.

3. In a _____ there is little money and no economic growth.

4. During the Great Depression, there was much _____, or many people without jobs.

5. A large body of government officials is called a _____.

6. Adolf Hitler was a _____, an all-powerful ruler, of Nazi Germany.

7. When war began in Europe, Congress started a _____, a way to bring people into the army.

8. To provide supplies during the war, government regulations called for _____ to limit what people could buy.

9. Many _____ were killed during the bombing of cities in World War II.

10. The name given to the Nazi murder of millions of people in death camps is _____.

FACTS TO REVIEW

1. What new forms of entertainment did technology create?

2. How did Roosevelt's New Deal get some people back to work?

3. Describe at least three ways in which government under the New Deal took over new responsibilities.

4. What were three parts of the Allied strategy in World War II?

5. Why did Japan surrender to the United States?

IDEAS TO DISCUSS

1. Compare the 1920s with the 1930s. Use the pictures in this chapter to help you.

2. How was World War I a different kind of war from World War II?

3. Would you agree with the statement "A man can endure a lot if he has hope"? Why or why not?

4. What might life be like under a dictator?

○ SKILLS PRACTICE

Conducting an Interview If you were to interview someone, in what order would you do each of the following? Write the phrases in the correct order.

- Ask for an interview
- Write a report on the interview
- Tape or take notes of the interview
- Decide whom you want to interview
- Send a thank-you letter to the person you interviewed

CHAPTER 21

Meeting New Challenges

About this chapter

The years since World War II are recent history. These are times that your parents and grandparents remember. These have been years of new challenges. Exploration of space has been a challenge. Achieving greater equality and opportunity for all Americans has been another challenge. Achieving peace in the world and prosperity at home continues to challenge us.

474

1. EISENHOWER, KENNEDY, AND JOHNSON

To Guide Your Reading

Look for these important words:

Key Words
- *Sputnik*
- satellite
- NASA
- ideals
- Peace Corps

- Great Society
- Vietnam War
- inflation

People
- Dwight D. Eisenhower
- John F. Kennedy

- Lyndon B. Johnson

Places
- South Vietnam
- North Vietnam

Look for answers to these questions:

1. What was life like for many in the 1950s?
2. What goals did President Kennedy set forth?
3. What were the purposes of the Great Society programs?

Dwight D. Eisenhower, the famous general of World War II, was elected President in 1952. Raised in Abilene, Kansas, Eisenhower had been a professional soldier. As a leader, he inspired confidence. With his broad grin and fatherly manner, he was one of the most popular Americans.

The decade of the 1950s was a time of prosperity for most Americans. This prosperity could be seen in the increasing numbers of goods—automobiles, houses, and household items. Among these goods were televisions. For millions of Americans, television began to replace radio as a source of both news and entertainment.

The Eisenhower years saw the birth of the Space Age. In October 1957 the United States was stunned at the news that the Soviet Union had launched **Sputnik** (SPOOT·nik) in orbit around Earth. *Sputnik* was a **satellite.** A satellite is a natural or man-made body that revolves around a planet. The moon is a natural satellite of Earth.

Sputnik was a challenge to Americans. The Russians were obviously more advanced in space technology. Americans asked why? Maybe, they sug-

Dwight Eisenhower, famous World War II general, was President in the 1950s.

gested, students in the Soviet Union were better educated. There followed major changes in the ways science and mathematics were taught in our country. In addition, more money was made available for education.

The United States also speeded up its own space efforts. In 1958 Congress formed the National Aeronautics and Space Administration, also known as **NASA.** Its purpose was to develop and oversee United States efforts in the new frontier—space. NASA continues today to be the agency in charge of space programs.

Kennedy Elected President

In 1960 **John F. Kennedy** was elected President. Kennedy was the son of a wealthy Massachusetts family. During World War II Kennedy had fought in the Pacific. As a newspaper reporter, Kennedy reported the founding of the United Nations in San Fran-

cisco. In 1946 he began his career in politics by running for a seat in Congress.

At age 43, Kennedy was the youngest man elected President. Kennedy was particularly popular among young people. He brought dash, humor, and energy to the job of President.

In his inaugural address Kennedy asked that people join the struggle against the common enemies of mankind. These were "tyranny, poverty, disease and war itself." To Americans he said, "Ask not what your country can do for you—ask what you can do for your country."

Americans responded to the **ideals** set forth by Kennedy. An ideal is a worthwhile goal. One such ideal was helping people in the rest of the world. To do this, Congress founded the **Peace Corps** (KOHR). Thousands of Americans joined the Peace Corps. They carried know-how, help, and concern to far parts of the world.

Since the 1960s, members of the Peace Corps have shared American technology and know-how with people around the world. Here an American Peace Corps volunteer teaches modern farming methods in North Borneo, a part of Indonesia.

When John F. Kennedy was assassinated, Lyndon Johnson, left, became President.

On November 22, 1963, the President and his wife Jacqueline visited Dallas, Texas. They were waving to crowds as the President's car moved through the streets. Suddenly shots rang out. President Kennedy was assassinated. Hours later, Vice President **Lyndon B. Johnson** took the oath of office of President.

In the dark days that followed, the nation mourned. American hearts went out to Jacqueline Kennedy and her two young children. At the same time Jacqueline Kennedy's dignity gave a calm tone to the nation's grief.

Johnson as President

Lyndon Johnson was a tall, energetic Texan. He had years of experience in Congress. There he was known for his ability to get laws passed by Congress. As President, he used this same skill.

Johnson was particularly concerned with helping America's poor. He used his skill with Congress to bring about new government programs. These programs were part of Johnson's dream of the **Great Society.** The Great Society programs included medical aid to the aged and aid to education. They included help to the poor with education, housing, and jobs.

At the same time, the United States was fighting in another war. This was the **Vietnam War.** In 1964 the United States had sent thousands of troops to southeast Asia. Their purpose was to help **South Vietnam** in its fight against the invading soldiers of **North Vietnam.**

President Johnson said that the nation could pay for both guns and butter. That meant that the nation could afford both a war and prosperity at home. As it turned out, Johnson was wrong. To pay for both the Great Society programs and the Vietnam War, the government had to borrow a great deal of money. This led to **inflation,** or the steady rise of prices. Where there is inflation, people can buy less and less with the money they earn.

Reading Check

1. How did *Sputnik* bring change to the United States?
2. What is the ideal behind the Peace Corps?
3. What skill did Lyndon Johnson have?
4. Why did the government borrow a great deal of money? What was the result?

477

SKILLS FOR SUCCESS

BEING A WISE CONSUMER

Unlike in earlier times, Americans today buy most of the goods they need. A person who buys and uses goods is a **consumer.** You have been a consumer since the day you spent your first quarter by yourself. How can you be a wise consumer? How can you get the most out of the money you have to spend?

Use Advertisements Wisely

Businesses tell the public about products through messages called **advertisements.** These appear on television, in newspapers and magazines, on billboards, and in store displays. Advertisements are also broadcast on radio stations. Some are sent directly to people through the mail.

The purpose of most advertising is to convince people to buy particular products. Because of this, advertisements only say good things about what they are offering. You must keep this in mind when you hear or read advertisements. Sometimes it is helpful to ask yourself questions:

- *What is this advertisement not telling me about this product?*

- *Does this product offer something others don't?*

Advertisements can be helpful. They can tell you about new products and about special sales. You can use advertisements to learn what kinds of products are available. You probably do not need most of the products shown or talked about in advertisements. It is up to you to decide what you really need. Then, with the help of information in advertisements, you can buy wisely.

Plan Your Spending Carefully

A **budget** can help you learn to plan your spending. A budget is a plan for controlling how much money you spend. Imagine that you are going to buy a birthday present. First, you must decide how much you want to spend. This is your shopping budget. You do not want to spend more than you can afford.

How can you begin budgeting? If you have a certain amount of money, you might plan how much to spend each week. It usually helps to write out your budget on paper. That way you can check it before spending money. Then stick to your plan.

My Budget This Week	
Income	
Allowance	$ 5.00
Earnings	$ 5.00
Total	$ 10.00
Expenses	
Savings	$ 1.00
Movie	$ 2.00
Popcorn	.75
Bus fare	.50
Ann's birthday gift	$ 3.50
Paperback or magazine	$ 1.50
Miscellaneous	.75
	$10.00

This is one way to make a budget. You first figure how much you have to spend. Then you figure what your expenses will be. You make certain that your expenses do not exceed your income.

Compare Prices and Quality

To get good value in what you buy, pay attention to prices. **Comparison shopping** means checking prices and qualities of goods at different stores. Suppose you want to pick out a pair of running shoes. Take a notebook with you and go to several stores. Write down the brands of shoes they carry. Also write down how much each style of shoes costs. Note the good and bad points of each brand. Finally, buy the pair of shoes that gives you good quality at the best price.

It is wise to shop at stores that stand behind what they sell. Even when you choose carefully, you may buy a product that does not work right. Stores that care about their customers will repair or replace products that are not right.

Products that have names known across the United States are called **brand-name products.** Most well-known companies try to make products that are of good quality. They know what might happen if one of a company's products turns out bad. Customers may stop buying *all* that company's products. That is why brand-name products generally are dependable. Brand-name products may cost more than products made by smaller companies. Sometimes products made by smaller companies are just as good and less expensive.

You can sometimes find out about product quality by asking a friend. If your friend likes a product, it may be a good one.

Look for a Warranty

If you are buying something with moving parts, look for a **warranty.** A warranty is a manufacturer's promise to fix or replace a product that stops working. Usually a warranty is good only for a certain period of time. A warranty tells you that the company stands behind its product.

> ### WARRANTY
> This product is guaranteed to be free of defects in materials or workmanship for a period of one year from the date of purchase. If any defect occurs within that time, the product will be repaired or replaced at no charge. To obtain warranty service, the defective product or part must be taken either to the retail store where it was purchased or sent to one of the company's service centers.

Buy Wisely at Sales

Finally, if you are buying something expensive, try to wait for a sale. Most items are put on sale at least once a year. They go on sale for several reasons. Sometimes it is because the factory no longer makes the product. Sometimes a store has bought more goods than it can sell at the regular price. Sometimes the store must make room for new goods.

You can sometimes buy sale items at half the normal price. However, when you buy something on sale, be sure it is exactly what you want. Sale items usually cannot be returned. This is so even if they turn out to be the wrong size or model.

CHECKING YOUR SKILLS

Write answers to the questions below.

1. How can you use advertisements to help you shop?

2. What is a budget?

3. What is one way to be sure you are not paying too much for a product?

4. What are brand-name products?

5. What is a warranty?

2. THE STRUGGLE FOR CIVIL RIGHTS

To Guide Your Reading

Look for these important words:

Key Words
- segregation
- civil rights
- integration
- Civil Rights Act of 1964

People
- Rosa Parks
- Martin Luther King, Jr.
- César Chavez

Places
- Montgomery
- Birmingham

Look for answers to these questions:

1. What was Martin Luther King's idea about the way to bring about change?
2. What methods were used to bring about equal treatment of the races?
3. What was the goal of many farm workers in California?

On December 1, 1955, **Rosa Parks** sank wearily to her seat on the bus in **Montgomery,** Alabama. She was sitting in the back of the bus. This was where black people were supposed to sit. If white people filled the front of the bus, blacks then had to give up their seats in the back. This was one of the Jim Crow laws in Alabama.

As the bus filled up, Rosa Parks was asked to give up her seat. She refused. The bus driver called the police, and she was taken to jail.

By her action Rosa Parks had challenged **segregation,** the practice of separating the races. In the South there were laws that supported segregation. In other parts of the nation, segregation existed by custom and practice. The result was that black people often were denied their **civil rights.** Civil rights are the rights of citizens to equal treatment both in law and practice.

Yet things were gradually changing. In 1948 President Truman ended segregation in the armed forces. In 1954 the Supreme Court declared that separate schools for black children were illegal. Such schools did not provide equality of education, the Court said.

Martin Luther King, Jr.

Martin Luther King, Jr., was a young minister in Montgomery when Rosa Parks was arrested. He was angry when he heard what happened. He called a meeting in his church. Furious also, the people at the meeting decided to let the bus owners know how they felt. Bus owners and downtown stores depended on the money of black people. What would happen if they did not ride the buses or go downtown? "Don't take the bus on Monday" was the word passed from person to person. In their churches black ministers gave the same message. A bus boycott began.

Martin Luther King led this protest. For 381 days black people in

From his pulpit Martin Luther King, Jr. urged an end to segregation.

Montgomery boycotted the buses. Often they did so with great hardship to themselves. At last the bus owners agreed that black people could sit where they wanted. Black people had learned that by working together they could bring about change peacefully.

Change in a peaceful, or nonviolent, way was important, Martin Luther King said. Nonviolence, he said, would change people's minds and hearts. Violence would only make matters worse.

Thousands of white people of all ages began to join the civil rights movement. Together, both black and white people worked to break down segregation. Their targets were public places—lunch counters, bus stations, schools, and public buildings.

Voting is an important way people bring about peaceful change. If more black people could vote in the South, then they could bring about further change. Knowing this, civil rights workers helped to register black voters.

Support for Civil Rights

Despite the 1954 Supreme Court decision, most schools in the South remained segregated. In April 1963 King led a march in **Birmingham,** Alabama. The marchers demanded an end to all segregation. In its place they wanted **integration,** or full equality of the races. For eight days there were marches and police arrests of the marchers. Millions of people watched on television.

The peaceful behavior of the marchers gained nationwide sympathy for the civil rights cause. The President demanded that Congress pass a civil rights law to end segregation in public places.

To let Congress know how they felt, 200,000 civil rights supporters held a huge march. This was in Washington, D.C., in August 1963. As the marchers gathered before the Lincoln Memorial, Martin Luther King spoke to them of his hopes:

I have a dream that one day, on the red hills of Georgia, sons of former slaves and the sons of former slave owners will be able to sit down together at the table of brotherhood. . . .

I have a dream that my four little children will one day live in a nation where they will not be judged by the color of their skin but by the content of their character.

481

Civil Rights Law Is Passed

President Kennedy had pledged his support to a civil rights law. President Johnson carried out that promise. He pushed Congress until it passed the **Civil Rights Act of 1964.** Under the new law, segregation in public places was illegal. Communities with segregated schools could lose government funds.

Martin Luther King received the Nobel Peace Prize in 1964. King had been effective in using nonviolent means to bring about change.

King, the man who preached nonviolence, himself died by violence. He was killed in April 1968 by an assassin.

In the South the walls of segregation tumbled down. At the same time Americans became aware that segregation also existed outside the South. During the 1970s the courts ordered busing of students in many places. This was an attempt to bring about nationwide integration of schools.

Others Seek Rights

Following the lead of the civil rights movement, other groups of Americans began to organize. They too wanted to achieve more rights in American society. American Indians organized to achieve the rights they had been granted in earlier treaties. They began to take more control over their lands, their mineral resources, and their education.

In California **César Chavez** worked for the right of farm workers to organize a union. Farm workers, many of them Mexican American, had never been able to form a union. Farm workers, said Chavez, had the same rights

César Chavez led his fellow farm workers in a strike for recognition of their union.

as other workers. They had the right to organize a labor union.

In 1965 Chavez led a strike of the United Farm Workers Union against grape growers in California. For five years growers refused to recognize the union. During this time the union received much public support. Like Martin Luther King, Chavez emphasized nonviolence as a way to bring about change. In 1970 an agreement was at last signed between growers and the United Farm Workers.

Reading Check

1. How did Rosa Parks challenge segregation?
2. What was the purpose of the Montgomery bus boycott?
3. How did civil rights workers try to bring about peaceful change?
4. What did César Chavez work for?

482

3. THE UNITED STATES IN THE 1970s

To Guide Your Reading

Look for these important words:

Key Words
- scandals
- Watergate
- resigned
- OPEC
- Equal Rights Amendment

People
- Richard Nixon
- Gerald Ford
- Jimmy Carter

Places
- Israel
- Egypt

Look for answers to these questions:

1. Who were the Presidents between 1968 and 1980?
2. Why did the cost of oil present an important challenge?
3. What caused inflation in the 1970s?
4. What gains have women made in achieving equal treatment with men?

In 1968 **Richard Nixon** was elected President. Nixon had run for President in 1960, but Kennedy had defeated him.

As President, Nixon achieved outstanding success in foreign relations. Nixon became the first President to visit both China and the Soviet Union.

In 1972 Nixon was reelected President. In his second term Nixon's fine record in foreign relations was darkened by a **scandal**. A scandal is any action that brings disgrace. This scandal was called **Watergate**. The Watergate scandal was caused by Nixon knowing about the improper and illegal activities of people working for him. Some of the illegal activities took place in a building named Watergate. Because of the scandal, Nixon **resigned** (ri•ZYN•d) as President in August 1974. *Resign* means to give up an office or position. Vice President **Gerald Ford** became President as soon as Nixon resigned.

Vietnam War Ends

Ford was president when the Vietnam War came to an end. Massive bombing and thousands of soldiers had not brought a quick end to the war. Increasing numbers of Americans had died in the jungles of South Vietnam. Opposition to the war had grown. Finally Congress refused to approve any more money to fight the war. The United States withdrew from Vietnam in 1973. The North Vietnamese had established control over all of Vietnam by 1975.

An Energy Challenge

In the 1970s the nation faced a new challenge. Petroleum supplies became scarce. Americans were importing much oil from other countries. Oil-exporting countries belonged to an organization called **OPEC,** the Organization of Petroleum Exporting Countries. OPEC began to set the price of a barrel of oil. A result was that prices of oil rose rapidly. This caused economic hardship for many. In response to the rising prices, millions of Americans began to conserve oil. They started driving smaller cars and turning down the heat.

Carter's Presidency

In 1976 American voters chose **Jimmy Carter** of Georgia over Ford. As President, Carter earned worldwide acclaim for arranging a peace agreement between **Israel** and **Egypt,** both nations in the Middle East.

A continuing problem faced by President Carter was what to do about inflation. During the 1970s rapidly increasing prices were hurting the buying power of most Americans. A major cause of this inflation was that the government was spending too much money. It was spending more money than it took in. Another major cause of inflation was the rapidly rising cost of oil and energy.

Equality for Women

An important challenge of the 1970s was achieving equal treatment for both women and men. Before the 1970s many jobs had not been available to women. Few women were in business. When women and men did have the same kind of job, women were often paid less than men. In the 1970s women organized to bring about changes. New

Sandra Day O'Connor became the first woman on the Supreme Court when appointed in 1981.

laws were passed saying that employers must treat men and women equally. Jobs were no longer limited to men only or women only. Women began to do all kinds of work. Some now drive trucks. Others are bank managers.

Many women worked hard for the **Equal Rights Amendment.** This proposed amendment to the Constitution would have recognized the equality of men and women under the law. It failed because the necessary number of state legislatures did not vote for it. Even without the amendment, however, the United States has done much to achieve equal rights for women.

Reading Check

1. Which President was the first to visit both China and the Soviet Union?
2. What was Watergate?
3. What was an economic challenge of the 1970s?
4. What changes occurred in the 1970s in the kinds of jobs women did?

4. TECHNOLOGY IN THE SPACE AGE

To Guide Your Reading

Look for these important words:

Key Words
- synthetic
- pesticides
- recycle
- astronauts

- Apollo
- module
- space shuttle
- spin-offs
- solar cells

People
- Neil Armstrong
- Edwin Aldrin, Jr.
- Michael Collins

Look for answers to these questions:

1. How has recent technology changed American life?
2. What environmental challenges do Americans face?
3. What have been the major achievements of the American space effort?
4. How has space technology brought changes to everyday life?

Since the 1950s Americans have seen continuing changes in their lives. One of the biggest changes has been television. In 1950, 9 of every 100 families had a black-and-white television set. By 1960, 87 of 100 families had television in their homes. Today 98 of 100 families have television sets. Half the homes have two or more sets. Millions depend on television for entertainment and for news.

Computers have become increasingly important in American life. At first only large businesses and government offices had computers. Today computers are in many homes and schools. They are the workhorses of the future.

Recent decades have seen changes in the kinds of materials used. Before World War II most materials were used in their natural state. Fabrics were silk, cotton, linen, and wool. Dishes were made of clay. Tires were made of rubber. Drinking glasses were made of glass.

Today many of the materials we use are **synthetic,** or man-made. Synthetic materials are very different from the raw materials they are made from. Plastic, detergent, and nylon are all synthetics made from petroleum. Yet they do not look at all like black oil.

Before World War II the large cities of the United States were in the Northeast. Since then there has been rapid growth in the southern half of the country. This area is now known as the Sun Belt. In the Sun Belt many new industries and new jobs are tied to airplane technology, space exploration, and the development of computers. Five of the nation's ten largest cities are in the Sun Belt. These cities are Los Angeles, Houston, Dallas, San Diego, and Phoenix.

The Environment

Technological growth also brought problems. The air over American cities and factories was becoming polluted. America's streams and rivers had also become polluted. The water in polluted rivers was not safe for drinking or swimming. The increasing use of **pesticides,** or bug killers, was creating harmful effects on birds, animals, and people.

Rachel Carson pointed out some of these problems in her book *Silent Spring*. This book, published in 1962, caused people to think about the balance of nature. *Silent Spring* started a debate in the United States. How could the needs of the environment be pro-

tected while technology and the economy went forward?

As Americans became more aware of the problems of the environment, Congress responded. It passed new laws regulating what could be put in the air or water. The pesticides most dangerous to human and animal health were banned.

To save natural resources, more Americans began to **recycle,** or return for further use, their newspapers, cans, and bottles. In recent years technology has been used to help preserve the environment. Factory smoke is cleaner and sewage treatment is more efficient. Pollution caused by cars has been somewhat controlled.

Scientist Rachel Carson caused people to think about the balance of nature.

Space Exploration

The most spectacular technological achievement of recent decades has been the exploration of space. Under the guidance of NASA, the United States first launched a series of satellites. Orbiting satellites provide information about weather on Earth. They relay radio and television signals. They have become an important part of the way we use and get information.

In 1961 President Kennedy set a new space goal. It was to put a man on the moon by the end of the decade. Throughout the decade the American space effort was directed toward putting people into space. There was so much that was not known. There were the problems of getting a spaceship out into space and then back again. A spaceship must break away from Earth's gravity. To do this, it has to reach an enormous speed, almost 25,000 miles (40,225 km) an hour. Away from Earth, a spaceship experiences either deadly heat or freezing cold. How could a spaceship be designed to withstand such extreme temperatures? How could people travel safely in an environment where there was no air to breathe?

The men and women working for NASA tackled these and other problems during the 1960s. By 1963 manned American spacecraft had orbited Earth. The people going into space were called **astronauts.** Then a series of explorations called **Apollo** prepared for a moon landing. In 1968 *Apollo 8* circled around the moon.

On July 16, 1969, the American team blasted off from Cape Canaveral, Florida, for the moon. On board the spaceship were astronauts **Neil Armstrong, Edwin Aldrin, Jr.,** and **Michael Collins.** As they approached the moon, Armstrong and Aldrin left the spacecraft in a small landing unit. This vehicle, called a **module,** looked like a big spider. The module landed gently on the moon's surface on July 20.

Millions watched on television as Neil Armstrong climbed from the

As seen from space, Earth is a special and beautiful place.

Astronauts left this plaque on the moon.

module onto the moon. "One small step for a man, one giant leap for mankind," he said.

Wilbur and Orville Wright had flown for the first time less than 70 years before. Some people watching the moon landing could remember a time when people traveled only by train, ship, and horse. In one lifetime the world had changed more than in any other time of history.

For the first time Earth could be seen as it appears in space. It looks like a pretty blue-and-white marble. People began to consider Earth as a kind of spaceship shared by everyone. One astronaut called Earth "a grand oasis in the vastness of space."

After a total of six moon landings, NASA launched a new series of explorations. Unmanned spaceships were sent to get information about the other planets in the solar system. As a result of these efforts, scientists now know

487

These 1981 stamps honor America's space achievements. The center four stamps show the space shuttle. The corner stamps show the moon landing, Skylab, Pioneer-Saturn spacecraft, and a new space telescope.

much more about Mars, Venus, Saturn, and Jupiter.

The **space shuttle** is one of the most recent space programs. A shuttle is something that goes back and forth. The space shuttle will allow people to travel between Earth and an orbiting space station. Space stations will be used for scientific research and even manufacturing.

Space Spin-Offs

American achievements in space have affected technology on Earth. New inventions and new products coming from the space program are called **spin-offs.** Space exploration made necessary the development of tools and materials that are both lightweight and very efficient. Such tools and materials have now become part of our life.

The spin-offs include very lightweight fabrics that are fireproof. To feed the astronauts, new methods of drying and packing food were developed. Today grocery store shelves carry many foods packed in this way. Cordless tools such as drills and saws were first developed by NASA. They are now used by doctors and craftworkers.

Solar cells were first developed for spacecrafts. Solar cells use the sun's rays to make electricity. Now solar cells are used to provide electricity for large buildings as well as small watches and calculators.

Reading Check

1. What are examples of synthetic materials?
2. How have people showed concern for the environment?
3. When did the first astronauts land on the moon?
4. How has space exploration resulted in new inventions and products?

488

SKILLS FOR SUCCESS

SAVING ENERGY

The United States has always been rich in natural resources. Natural resources include oil, coal, natural gas, water, and timber. As our country has grown, we have used increasing amounts of resources to support our technology. Now we face a challenge. How can we keep the world's natural resources from being used up? How can we save resources for the use of future generations? The answer is, save energy.

How can you save energy? One way is to cut down energy use in your home.

Most home energy is used for heating in winter and cooling summer. You can save energy by using the heater less during cold months. When you feel cold, put on a sweater instead of turning up the heat. Turn the heat down or off when you go to bed at night. After sunset, close the curtains. This will keep the warm air inside from cooling off as it hits the cold windows. Open and close outside doors quickly so that cold air does not sweep inside. Keep windows tightly shut.

In hot months, try not to use the air conditioner unless the temperature is over 90°F (32°C). Close the curtains in the daytime to keep the sun out.

There are many ways to save on electricity use at home. Turn lights off as you leave a room. Check to be sure outdoor lights are not left on all night. Turn off radios, stereos, and television sets if no one is using them.

Washing and drying clothes uses up a lot of energy. Always wash enough laundry at one time to make a full load. You can save energy by drying clothes on a clothesline instead of in a dryer.

A refrigerator also uses up a lot of energy. This is especially so when warm air gets inside and has to be cooled. Holding the refrigerator door open for several minutes lets a lot of warm air in. Open and close the door quickly and not often.

You can help cut down on energy use outside your home, too. Many people waste gas by making unnecessary car trips. Walk or ride your bicycle whenever you can. Take public transportation for longer trips.

The best way to save energy is not to waste anything. When a product is manufactured, energy and raw materials are used. When you no longer have use for things, give them to organizations that take such things. Then they can be used again.

Recycling also saves energy. Using recycled materials to make new products usually takes less energy than using raw materials. Recycling also saves such resources as iron, aluminum, and timber.

CHECKING YOUR SKILLS

Write the answers to these questions.

1. What is an important reason for saving energy?

2. What are some ways you can save energy during the cold months?

3. What are some ways you can cut down on electricity use in your home?

4. What are some ways you can save energy in transportation?

5. How can you save the energy used to manufacture things?

5. THE 1980s AND THE FUTURE

To Guide Your Reading

Look for these important words:

Key Words
- quality of life
- robots

People
- Ronald Reagan

Look for answers to these questions:

1. What economic problems have Americans faced in recent years?
2. What kinds of challenges does the United States face?
3. How can technology help meet some challenges?
4. How can other challenges be met?

In 1980 **Ronald Reagan** was elected President. Reagan had been a movie actor and then governor of California.

Under Reagan's Presidency, that problem of the 1970s—inflation—almost disappeared, but it was replaced by another problem. This was unemployment. Unemployment resulted partly from the efforts to control inflation. Unemployment in the automobile industry was also caused by another reason. Millions of people had been buying foreign-made rather than American-made cars. Areas where automobiles were manufactured were particularly hard hit. Detroit, Michigan, the center of the automobile industry, was one of these. There, one of four people was unemployed in 1981. In Detroit and elsewhere, people spoke of a return to hard times just like in the 1930s.

By the middle of the 1980s, however, things were getting better. Employment increased in the automobile industry with more car sales.

The United States now heads into the last decades of the twentieth century. It is like a traveler with three

Aboard the President's jet, *Air Force One*, President Ronald Reagan studies a report.

490

suitcases. In one suitcase are packed future challenges. In a second suitcase is the technology of the present. In the third suitcase are successful experiences in solving past problems.

In coming years the United States faces the challenge of achieving a high **quality of life** for its people. This includes providing equal job opportunities and full civil rights for American citizens. It includes helping people achieve education, satisfying jobs, and pleasant places to live and work.

Americans face the challenge of protecting Earth's resources and environment. Clean air and clean water will continue to be a goal. Americans value the wilderness lands. They too are part of the history of our country. A continuing challenge will be to protect the wilderness and its wildlife.

Other challenges of the future include exploration of new frontiers. These frontiers include space and the depths of the ocean. With further exploration, people may meet future needs for energy, food, and raw materials.

For 100 years we have depended on oil as our principal source of energy. The amount of oil is limited, scientists say. In the future we may want to use oil only for making synthetics. It may become too valuable to burn for energy.

Meeting Challenges

Meeting the challenges of the future will depend on people with skills and education.

Routine jobs of the future will likely be performed by **robots.** Robots are machines that do human tasks. Robots are beginning to replace human workers on assembly lines. Companies are developing robots that can vacuum the house, wash the dishes, and even make coffee.

New jobs almost always come out of new technology. Some people think that a million new jobs will exist in the computer industry by 1990. Training people for those jobs is an immediate concern and challenge.

Technology is already helping Americans meet some of the challenges of the future. For instance, scientists and engineers are now developing other sources of energy. They include solar power, wind energy, and nuclear power plants.

Not all the challenges facing Americans can be solved by technology. People will have to think about what is important. American ideals have always included democracy, equality, and opportunity. Americans have protected the rights of the individual. They have compromised and cooperated to achieve a better society. They have been willing to fight to support their ideals. These same ideals are important in our future.

There have always been challenges. There always will be. In the past Americans met challenges with skills, knowledge, and a belief in their ideals. In such ways we can also meet the challenges of the future.

Reading Check

1. What was a problem of the early 1980s?
2. Name at least three challenges of the future.
3. How is technology helping to meet the energy challenge?

CLOSE-UP

Now an architect, Jonathan Hammond designs homes that use solar energy.

PEOPLE FINDING SOLUTIONS

Throughout our history Americans have faced many difficult challenges. Imagine the first settlers arriving on an unknown continent. Their problems were many. They had to build houses, plant crops, and protect themselves.

In the years ahead Americans will face many new challenges. Americans must find ways to protect and conserve our precious natural resources. As our future grows, we must meet the need for new housing. By learning new skills and by working together, people are finding solutions to some of these challenges.

Conservation in Davis, California

The first settlers in America must have imagined themselves in a land of unlimited resources. Today we know that our resources are indeed limited. Natural resources such as coal and petroleum cannot be replaced once used up. Other resources, such as soil and water, must be protected if they are to last.

In 1973 some students and teachers at the University of California at Davis started looking for ways to save energy. "We knew that the cost of energy was going up and up," explained Jonathan Hammond. He was a teacher at the university. "We discovered that the city of Davis was using more than the average amount of electricity. So we began to look for ways to save electricity and other energy sources in Davis."

The group found ways that buildings could be constructed to use less energy. For example, they studied the

At a building site, Mr. Hammond checks plans against the work already done.

492

With moveable awnings, the amount of sun entering windows can be controlled.

Bicyclists in Davis have their own left-hand turn lane. This is one way the city has encouraged bicycling.

effect of sunlight on an apartment building. They discovered that apartments facing north or south stayed cooler during hot days. They learned that apartments facing east or west used six or seven times more electricity for air conditioning.

Then Jonathan Hammond had an idea. "I was walking across campus one day," he explains, "and suddenly the idea struck me. A city like Davis could create a **building code** designed especially to save energy." A building code is a set of rules about constructing new buildings and repairing old ones. A committee set out to create a new building code. Local citizens, teachers, and members of the city government sat on the committee.

The committee agreed that new buildings should be constructed to face north or south. Windows that were not shaded by trees had to be covered by awnings. These would keep the buildings cooler by day.

To keep houses warm at night, the committee decided that old and new houses alike had to have special **weather stripping.** Weather stripping is a material placed around doors and windows. It keeps the cold air out and the warm air in. The committee recommended that water heaters be covered with special blankets to keep in the heat.

The city government turned the committee's suggestions into a new building code for Davis. As the result of other suggestions, the city government also built 10 miles (16 km) of bike paths. This encouraged the people of Davis to use bicycles instead of cars. A program was started to recycle glass, newspapers, and aluminum cans.

Today energy use is cut in half in houses built according to the new building code. Thanks to the bike paths, bicycles outnumber cars by two to one. For people who cannot ride bicycles, there are special buses. By using bicycles or buses instead of cars, the residents of Davis are saving gasoline.

"Our programs have succeeded because people were willing to give some new ideas a chance," says Warren Williams. "And now that we've learned that we *can* solve some of our energy problems, we are working on new and even better solutions."

One of the first jobs in building a house is to make accurate measurements.

The two houses below are homes recently built by people in the Owner Built Housing Project of Oakland.

Building a House Themselves

Oscar and Marianne Coffey faced a serious problem of their own. They wanted to buy a house. For almost a year they had looked, but the houses they saw cost too much. "Finally we just gave up the idea of owning our own home," says Oscar Coffey.

People in many parts of the country have found it difficult to buy a house. In some cities there simply are not enough houses for the number of people who desire them.

A group of people in Oakland, California, found a solution—building their own houses.

They were part of a special program called the Owner Built Housing Project. Working together, nine families built their own houses. Together, the families poured concrete for the foundation of each house. Step-by-step they built the floors, constructed the walls, and raised the roofs. In this way they could afford their own homes.

"Many people working together have made the Owner Built Housing Project work," says Kenneth Nunn. A community developer in Oakland, he first began the project. "We needed local banks to agree to lend money to the families. Many people in different departments of city government helped with planning. Architects studied

Digging trenches for the foundation and utility lines is hard work.

which kind of house was most practical. It took a good year to get the project started."

"Each family worked 40 hours a week on the houses," Oscar Coffey, one of the new owners, said. "Most of us had never built a house before. There was all kinds of work to be done. You find the work you do best. I did most of the power-saw cutting. Marianne [his wife] was good at drawing out where the foundations would be."

Working together, the families became good friends. "We saw one another all week long, and then on the weekends," says Loreeca Banks. She worked with her husband Raymond to build their own house. "Everybody got along just fine. I think we will be good neighbors."

In Oakland, California, nine families have found a solution to the high cost of housing. All of them worked very hard. They all tried things they had never done before. Oscar Coffey said, "It wasn't easy. But I always wanted my own home. It makes me very proud to look at the work we've done. I have learned one very important thing. If you use your brains, and if you put your back to it, you can do almost anything."

Americans have been learning such lessons since the first settlements at Jamestown, Santa Fe, and Plymouth. It has become the American way.

CHAPTER 21 REVIEW

WORDS TO USE

Explain the meaning of each word or phrase below. Then use the word or phrase in a complete sentence.

1. **civil rights**
2. **ideals**
3. **inflation**
4. **integration**

FACTS TO REVIEW

1. What is the purpose of NASA?

2. What were some of the Great Society programs?

3. What did President Johnson mean when he said the nation could afford both guns and butter?

4. What were Martin Luther King's ideas about how to bring about change?

5. What is the importance of the Civil Rights Act of 1964?

6. What was the space goal of the 1960s? When was it achieved?

7. What did President Nixon achieve in foreign policy?

8. Why did people begin to conserve oil?

9. Name two causes of inflation during the 1970s.

10. What changes have come about in American life since the 1960s?

IDEAS TO DISCUSS

1. How has the space program helped American society?

2. Both Martin Luther King, Jr. and César Chavez believed in nonviolence to achieve their goals. What does *nonviolence* mean?

3. What changes have occurred in American life since the 1950s? Which do you think are most important?

4. What are challenges of the future?

5. What is the meaning of the statement "Ask not what your country can do for you—ask what you can do for your country"?

⃝ SKILLS PRACTICE

1. **Saving Energy**   Use the skill on page 489 to answer these questions.

   a. Why is it important to conserve natural resources?

   b. How can you help save energy during winter months? during summer months?

   c. What is recycling?

2. **Being a Wise Consumer**   Suppose you need to buy a pair of shoes. Are the statements below true or false? Turn each false statement into a true statement.

   a. Advertisements can be helpful to let you know what products are available.

   b. Advertisements tell you all you need to know to buy a product.

   c. A budget is a plan for controlling how much money you spend.

   d. It is wise to compare prices.

UNIT 8 REVIEW

WORDS TO REMEMBER

Read each sentence. Then replace the underlined words in each sentence with the correct word from the list. Write the new sentences on your paper.

armistice
astronauts
bureaucracy
dictators
ideals

inflation
integration
resigned
synthetics
unemployment

1. In 1918 the fighting in World War I stopped when the warring nations signed an agreement to stop fighting.

2. During the Great Depression there was a large amount of people out of work.

3. A result of the growth of government since the 1930s has been a large group of government officials.

4. Adolf Hitler and Benito Mussolini were both all-powerful rulers.

5. Martin Luther King, Jr. headed protests to bring about full equality of the races in public places.

6. A problem of the 1970s was that the prices of goods were rapidly rising.

7. Neil Armstrong, one of the travelers in space, landed on the moon in 1969.

8. Many of the things we use every day are made from chemicals such as petroleum.

9. Richard Nixon gave up his office because of the Watergate scandal.

10. Democracy and equality of opportunity are two worthwhile goals held by Americans.

FOCUS ON MAIN IDEAS

1. How did the United States use its power and influence in the Caribbean in the late nineteenth and early twentieth centuries? What were the results?

2. What major achievements have been made in the twentieth century in the struggle for justice and equality for all Americans?

3. How did the United States use its power and influence

   a. in World War II?
   b. to work for peace among nations?

4. What are some of the great technological achievements of this century? How have they affected American life?

5. What challenges does the United States face today? Which of these challenges might be solved by technology? Which may depend on the values of people for solutions?

ACTIVITIES

1. **Research/Writing** What will go in history books in the future? Look through newspapers and magazines to collect information you think future historians might use. Choose one major event and write it up as it may appear in a history book.

2. **Timeline** Make a timeline beginning with the year 1900 and ending with the current date. Put at least 20 events on your timeline. If you wish, illustrate your timeline.

3. **Remembering the Close-Up** Think of your neighborhood, school, or city. Give an example of a problem people have solved. Write a paragraph explaining the problem and a paragraph explaining the solution. Share it with the class.

4. **Research/Art** Research the equipment that was used to put man on the moon. Make a picture of the module, an astronaut in a space suit, the control center, or any of the other equipment used for moon exploration.

5. **Research/Writing** Who do you think is the most interesting or important person of the twentieth century? Write a report on this person.

6. **Making a Chart** Make a chart listing all the Presidents since 1928. On your chart tell the years each President served. Describe one or more of each President's accomplishments.

7. **Newspaper Reading** Read newspapers to find articles that tell about changing technology. For each article you find, write several sentences in your own words telling what it is about.

8. **Research/Oral Report** Find out about Sally Ride, the first American woman astronaut. What was her training and education? Have there been other woman astronauts since? Report to the class on what you learn.

9. **Research/Report** Give a report on a famous black American of the twentieth century.

◯ SKILLS REVIEW

1. **Interviewing** To do a report, you want to interview an expert on solar energy. You call the expert, ask for an interview, and make an appointment. Write down at least three questions you might ask the expert.

2. **Reading a Newspaper** Use the information on pages 450–451 to answer these questions.

   a. Where would you find a story about a school using solar energy to provide heat?

   b. What questions would you expect the story to answer?

   c. Where would you find the editor's opinion that the decision to use solar energy is a good one?

   d. Where would you look to find out if any solar energy businesses need workers?

3. **Being a Wise Consumer** Write the words below on a sheet of paper. Next to the word or words, write the correct definition from the list that follows.

   advertisements
   brand-name products
   budget
   comparison shopping
   warranty

   a. Products that have names known across the country
   b. A plan for controlling how much money you spend
   c. A promise that the company will fix or replace the product if it stops working within a certain time
   d. Commercial messages
   e. Checking prices and quality of goods at different stores

YOUR STATE'S HISTORY

In the twentieth century Americans have been involved in four wars. They have lived through the country's worst depression and have traveled in outer space. These events may have changed your state and your hometown a great deal.

Perhaps the Western states have been changed the most by this century. Sleepy little towns like Los Angeles and Phoenix have grown into large cities. Forgotten lands in Nevada, Utah, and Wyoming have become important because of their mineral wealth. All our states have been brought closer together by radio, television, and air travel.

The following activities may help you learn how your state has changed in this century.

LEARNING ABOUT PEOPLE

1. Women have made great progress toward gaining equality in our society. One hundred years ago women did not even have the right to vote. Today women are judges, business leaders, police officers, construction workers, and athletes. Write a short report on a woman from your state whom you admire for her achievements.

2. The Great Depression, beginning in 1929, affected life in every state. It is hard to know what the depression was like if you did not live then. One way to learn more about it is to talk to someone who lived through it. Find a member of your family or community who lived in your state during the depression. Interview that person and give a talk to your class on what you learned.

LEARNING ABOUT GEOGRAPHY

3. Teddy Roosevelt and others have had the wisdom to preserve beautiful areas as national parks. Find out if there are national parks in your state. Write to one of the parks for more information. Write a short report about the animals, plants, and natural features of the park. Draw pictures to go with your report.

4. Are there places in your state named after any of the people you studied in this unit? If so, make a list of some of them. Tell where they are.

LEARNING ABOUT ECONOMICS

5. Find out more about how technology has changed your state in the twentieth century. Are there industries in your state that have developed because of automobiles, airplanes, movies, television, synthetics, computers, or space travel? On a map of your state, show where some of the new-technology industries are located.

6. Are there hydroelectric dams in your state? If so, where are they? How have they helped the economy of your state?

UNIT NINE

CANADA AND MEXICO

Our country has particularly strong ties to our two closest neighbors, Canada and Mexico. Both Canada and Mexico share long borders with the United States. These borders run for thousands of miles. A great deal of travel and business goes on among the three nations.

At the left is a view of the border between the United States and Canada at Niagara Falls. Connecting the two nations is the Rainbow Bridge. It is a symbol of the connections we have with our northern and southern neighbors. In this unit you will learn about the people, the land, and the history of both Canada and Mexico.

Key Dates and Events

1519
Hernando Cortés conquers the Aztecs

1600s
French first settle in Canada

1610
Henry Hudson discovers Hudson Bay

1754–1763
French and Indian War

1763
France loses its territory in North America

1810
Miguel Hidalgo leads a revolution in Mexico

1821
Mexico wins its independence from Spain

1863
France takes control of Mexico

1867
France driven out of Mexico

1910–1917
Mexican revolution for land and liberty

1931
Statute of Westminster gives more independence to Canada

1959
St. Lawrence Seaway completed

1982
Canada gets control over its Constitution

CHAPTER 22

Canada—Neighbor to the North

About this chapter

Canadian lands and waters border on 14 American states, including Alaska. Our two countries share the longest undefended border in the world, 5,525 miles (8,890 km). Much of Canada's history and culture is linked to that of the United States. Americans and Canadians are partners in many businesses, including mining, oil exploration, finance, and international trade. In this chapter you will learn about Canada's geography, its history, and its government.

1. CANADA'S GEOGRAPHICAL REGIONS

To Guide Your Reading

Look for these important words:

Places
- Appalachian Highlands
- Halifax, Nova Scotia
- St. Lawrence River Lowlands
- Montreal
- Toronto
- Ottawa
- St. Lawrence Seaway
- Canadian Shield
- Interior Plains
- Winnipeg
- Western Mountains
- Vancouver
- Arctic Islands
- Baffin
- Victoria

Look for answers to these questions:

1. How does Canada compare to the United States in size?
2. What is Canada's greatest natural resource?
3. What are the natural regions of Canada?
4. Where do most people in Canada live?

Canada, our neighbor to the north, is a huge country. It is the second largest nation on earth. Only the Soviet Union is larger. Canada is slightly bigger than China or the United States. Canada extends from almost the North Pole south to the United States border. It stretches 3,223 miles (5,186 km) between the Pacific Ocean and the Atlantic Ocean.

The population of Canada, over 24 million people, is about one-ninth that of the United States. Most Canadians live in southeastern Canada within 200 miles (320 km) of the American border.

Canada is rich in natural resources. It has large areas of fertile soil, forests, oil and gas reserves, and mineral deposits. Canada's largest industries take advantage of this natural abundance. The leading industries are wood products, farming, fishing, mining, and the production of electrical power.

Canada's greatest natural resource is water. Almost one-half of all the world's fresh water lies in Canada. This country has more lakes than the rest of the world combined. No one has ever been able to count all the lakes in Canada.

There are six natural regions in Canada. They are the Appalachian Highlands, the St. Lawrence River Lowlands, the Canadian Shield, the Interior Plains, the Western Mountains, and the Arctic Islands. The geography of these regions determines much of Canadian life. In fact, a past leader of Canada called it "a nation of regions."

Appalachian Highlands

The **Appalachian Highlands** are a rugged area of low hills and dense woods. Summers are cool. Winters are

503

long with lots of snow. Most of the people in this region live near the coast. Off the coast lie the rich fishing areas of the Grand Banks. Near the coast the soil is more fertile than farther inland. Farmers grow hay and raise chickens, pigs, and dairy cows. Minks, foxes, and raccoons are raised for fur. The Appalachian forests are used to make wood pulp for newspapers and other products. Iron, coal, copper, asbestos, and zinc are mined.

There is no large city in this region. The port of **Halifax, Nova Scotia,** is important, however, because it remains free of ice all year.

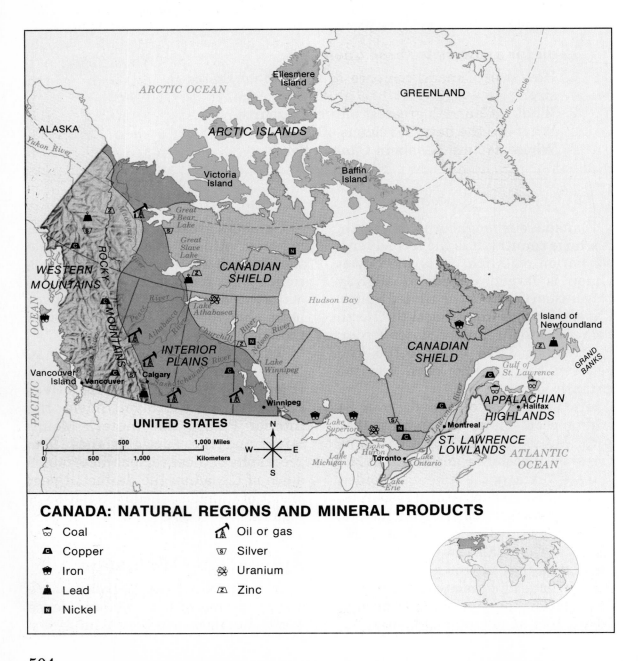

CANADA: NATURAL REGIONS AND MINERAL PRODUCTS

Coal		Oil or gas	
Copper		Silver	
Iron		Uranium	
Lead		Zinc	
Nickel			

St. Lawrence Lowlands

Canada's smallest natural region, the **St. Lawrence River Lowlands,** is also the most heavily populated. At least 40 Canadian cities have populations of over 50,000 people. Twenty-four of those cities are in the St. Lawrence River Lowlands. Among them are **Montreal** and **Toronto,** Canada's two largest cities. Montreal has a population of over 1 million. More than 600,000 people live in Toronto, the second largest city. **Ottawa,** the capital of Canada, is also in the St. Lawrence River Lowlands.

In 1959 Canada and the United States completed the **St. Lawrence Seaway.** The St. Lawrence Seaway is a series of canals and locks between Montreal and Lake Erie. Using the Seaway, ships can travel from the Atlantic Ocean as far as Duluth, Minnesota, on Lake Superior.

Canadian Shield

The **Canadian Shield** is a vast, horseshoe-shaped region in the north of Canada. It makes up about one-half of Canada, an area larger than most countries. Fewer than 2 million people live in the Shield. The surface area is made of the oldest rock mass on the continent. The soil is thin.

During the Ice Age enormous glaciers covered the Shield. The movement of glaciers over the years created many small hollows. Water collected in these hollows, and they are now lakes and swampy areas. The Shield is rich

This glacier, like a freeway of ice, cuts a wide path as it inches downhill. Melting ice forms a glacial lake at its foot.

in uranium, gold, copper, iron, and nickel. The numerous lakes and rivers of the Shield provide much of Canada's hydroelectric power. Great forests in the southern part supply wood for lumber and paper products.

Interior Plains

In the United States, the **Interior Plains** stretch from Iowa to the Rocky Mountains. The Interior Plains also extend north into Canada. In Canada this area of deep, fertile soil is one of the best areas in the world for growing wheat. Large deposits of oil, gas, and coal are also found in this region. Alto-

gether, 3.5 million people live on the Interior Plains. **Winnipeg,** Canada's third largest city, is on the plains.

Western Mountains

The Rocky Mountains and Pacific Coast ranges of the United States also extend into Canada. In Canada this mountainous region is called the **Western Mountains.** Thousands of tourists visit the Western Mountains. There they find natural beauty, clean air, lofty mountain peaks, and rushing rivers. Giant trees abound, including sweet-smelling cedars and stately Douglas firs.

Vast fields of wheat spread across Canada's fertile Interior Plains. Wheat is one of Canada's major exports.

The Western Mountains of Canada offer spectacular scenery of snow-peaked mountains, forests, and lakes.

The leading industries of the Western Mountains are logging, mining, farming, and the production of hydro-electric power. **Vancouver,** Canada's sixth largest city, has a population of nearly half a million. It is located where the north arm of the Fraser River meets the Pacific Ocean.

The climate along Canada's southern Pacific coast is one of the country's wettest. More than 100 inches (254 cm) of rain fall yearly in some coastal areas. In winter, the climate is also warmer than other parts of Canada. Normal January temperatures in Vancouver range from 32 to 41°F (0 to 5°C).

Arctic Islands

Few people live in Canada's cold and rugged **Arctic Islands.** This chain of islands extends far to the north. The northern tip of Ellesmere Island is within 500 miles (805 km) of the North Pole. Some of the islands, like **Baffin** and **Victoria,** are very large. Baffin Island is larger than California.

The Canadian government thinks that there may be large oil deposits in the area. It will be very hard to recover this oil. The waters around the islands are frozen much of the time. Some people want to use submarines as freighters to move the oil.

Reading Check

1. What are some of Canada's natural resources?
2. Name the six natural regions of Canada.
3. What is Canada's largest city?
4. In what region do most Canadians live?

2. CANADA'S HISTORY

To Guide Your Reading

Look for these important words:

Key Words
- Hudson's Bay Company
- French and Indian War
- Quebec Act
- British North America Act
- Statute of Westminster

- Commonwealth of Nations

People
- Count Frontenac
- Pierre Radisson
- Medard Groseilliers
- Louis Montcalm

- James Wolfe
- Alexander MacKenzie
- Simon Fraser
- David Thompson

Places
- New France
- Quebec

Look for answers to these questions:

1. Why does Canada have both a French and a British heritage?
2. What caused France to give up its claims in the new world?
3. Who were some important explorers of Canada?
4. When did Canada become completely independent of Britain?

Until 1763 the French controlled Canada. French missionaries, explorers, farmers, and fur traders helped settle the rugged northern land. They called it **New France.** The city of **Quebec,** on the St. Lawrence River, was the capital of New France. New France included the Mississippi River valley.

One of the great leaders of New France was **Count Frontenac.** He came to Quebec from France in 1672. He established a peaceful relationship between the settlers and nearby Indians. Frontenac made regular visits to Indian camps and participated in Indian activities. Sometimes he danced with the braves around the ceremonial fires, his face covered with paint. The Indians called him Great Father. His leadership helped the settlers protect their villages and their fur trade.

Count Frontenac, both dashing and clever, helped New France to prosper.

Traders traveled far into the North American interior in search of the wealth to be found in animal furs. The traders got along well with the Indians, who exchanged pelts for beads, knives, and iron products.

English Claims

England also had claims to northern Canadian lands. Most British colonists had settled in what was to become the United States. Some, however, had gone to Canada. Since the voyage of John Cabot in 1497, the English had fished off Newfoundland. Henry Hudson's discovery of Hudson Bay in 1610 established English claims to the Canadian north.

Surprisingly, England's strongest interest in Canada started with two Frenchmen. **Pierre Radisson** (ra•dee•, SAWN) and **Medard Groseilliers** (may•DAR groh•ze•YAI) were fur traders. Most Canadian traders made the difficult journey to the north woods by land. There they would trap beaver and other animals. Radisson and his partner had a clever idea. They realized they could reach the fur country more easily by sailing into Hudson Bay.

Their first voyage yielded them a fortune in furs. They asked the French king to put up the money for more expeditions. He refused. Then he placed Groseilliers in jail for trading without a license.

In 1666 the two partners went to England. These rugged explorers became very popular with the English nobles. The nobles nicknamed them "Mr. Radishes and Mr. Gooseberry." King Charles of England agreed to help the young traders. In 1670 the king granted them permission to start a fur-trading business called the **Hudson's Bay Company.** The business proved to be very successful. As a result the English king became even more interested in Canadian lands.

The French and Indian War

Relations between France and Britain became increasingly difficult. Both claimed the Ohio River valley as well as the Hudson Bay area. The **French and Indian War** broke out in 1754. In the war many Indians fought on the side of the French.

The British sent large numbers of men, ships, and arms to Canada. They hoped to defeat the French easily. They had not counted, however, on the brilliant leadership of the French general **Louis Montcalm.** Time and again Montcalm's forces turned back the British.

In the summer of 1759, the British general **James Wolfe** decided on a new plan. With 8,000 men he traveled up the St. Lawrence River to the city of Quebec. His intention was to capture Quebec. From June until September, Wolfe tried, but failed, to take the city. The steep and rocky cliffs made it difficult for the British to attack. Winter was coming on. General Wolfe realized that the St. Lawrence River would soon freeze over. If that happened, they could not leave by ship. With time running out, Wolfe settled on a last, desperate attempt.

In darkness Wolfe and his men rowed upriver past Quebec. They scaled the difficult cliffs in the dead of night. They reached a flat plain behind the city. At sunrise the British attacked. The British won the fierce battle that followed, but both Wolfe and Montcalm were killed. The rest of Canada soon fell to the British.

In 1763 a peace treaty was signed. France gave its North American lands east of the Mississippi to Britain. Madame Pompadour, a friend of the French king, was not upset. "Canada," she announced, "was useful only to provide me with furs." French Canadians did not agree with her at all. Sixty thousand French settlers stayed on in Canada.

British Rule

In 1774 the British Parliament passed the **Quebec Act.** This law allowed French Canadians to keep their laws, to speak their own language, and to practice their own religion.

In 1776 the 13 American colonies rebelled against British rule. The British watched anxiously to see if Canada would also have its revolution. It never happened. Most Canadians were happy with British rule. The Quebec Act helped maintain French-Canadian loyalty.

Westward Movement

In the decades before and after 1800 explorers were pushing across the North American continent. In Canada three men stand out as brave explorers.

Alexander MacKenzie led the first expedition to cross Canada all the way to the Pacific. His epic journey was made in 1793. In 1808 **Simon Fraser** followed Canada's wildest river, now called the Fraser, to the Pacific Ocean.

David Thompson may have been Canada's greatest explorer. He was a master surveyor, astronomer, and mapmaker. The Indians respected him very much. They called him "Koo-koo-sint," the man who looks at the stars.

Thompson worked for the North West Company, a fur trading business. In 1810 his employers gave him a dif-

David Thompson, an astronomer and expert surveyor, explored much of western Canada.

ficult job. They knew the Americans were trying to reach the mouth of the Columbia River. Thompson was to get there before the Americans did. Thompson and his crew traveled by horse, on foot, and finally by canoe. Through the Canadian Rockies and down the mighty Columbia they struggled. The trip was long and hard. At last they saw the bright shoreline of the Pacific Ocean. There on the water's edge stood a rugged log fort— Fort Astoria. The Americans had arrived first!

Thompson continued to explore the West for 25 years. His huge map of western Canada was very accurate.

A canoe of the Hudson's Bay Company shoots the rapids. This picture was painted by Frances Ann Hopkins, who was married to a company agent. You can see her in the canoe hanging on to her hat.

Becoming a Nation

The British Parliament passed the **British North America Act** in 1867. This law united all of Canada into one nation. It gave Canada a representative government. Under the law Britain held the final word in Canadian affairs. The British North America Act provided a framework for the new Canadian nation. Canada grew and prospered.

In 1931 Parliament passed the **Statute of Westminster.** This law gave Canada more independence. It could conduct its own foreign affairs. However, Canada still remained partly under British rule.

In 1982 Queen Elizabeth signed the papers giving Canada its constitution.

In 1965 Canada adopted its own flag, with the symbol of a maple leaf. The new flag showed Canada's growing independence from Britain.

Canada's constitution had been the British North America Act of 1867. This yellowing old document, tied up with a scarlet ribbon, rested in the House of Lords in Britain. The British Parliament, not the Canadian Parliament, made changes in the constitution.

In 1982 the British Parliament passed its last law dealing with Canada. At the request of Canada, the British voted to send the constitution to Canada. Canada also requested that a Charter of Rights and Freedoms be added to the constitution. This statement of rights is similar to our own Bill of Rights. In addition, it recognizes the equality of men and women under the law.

Now completely independent, Canada still holds to part of its British heritage. It remains a member of the **Commonwealth of Nations.** This is the name given to territories that give allegiance to the British crown. Many members of the Commonwealth are territories formerly ruled by Britain. Others remain under British control. Canadians are loyal to Elizabeth II, queen of Great Britain and head of the Commonwealth.

Reading Check

1. Why did both France and England claim parts of Canada?
2. Why was the 1759 battle at Quebec important?
3. Name three Canadian explorers.
4. When did Canada achieve independence of the British Parliament?

THE MOUNTIES

A Mounty on parade

Alick Pennycuick

A Mounty at work

By the 1870s crime and violence were everywhere in northwestern Canada. The Canadian government sent a scout to this wild, unsettled area to investigate. The scout reported that "the region is without law, order or security for life or property. Robbery and murder for years have gone unpunished. Indian massacres are unchecked." The scout recommended that men on horseback be sent to keep the peace.

In 1873 the Canadian government took his advice. It organized a force called the North West Mounted Police. Later it would be called the Royal Canadian Mounted Police. More simply, the police were known as the Mounties.

There were 300 men in the first group of Mounties. They rode the finest horses in the land. They were dashing in scarlet jackets and blue trousers with gold stripes.

The job of bringing peace to the Canadian West was huge. "No more wildly impossible undertaking was ever staged," said a leader of the time. Yet the Mounties succeeded. Many people—traders, prospectors, and Indians—owed their lives to these mounted men.

The Mounties had help in their huge task. Indian leaders cooperated with them. One such leader was Crowfoot, chief of the Blackfeet. "The Mounted Police have protected us as the feathers of the bird protect it from the frosts of winter," he said.

The Mounties became famous for never giving up in their pursuit of a criminal. One man was very famous because he solved so many difficult crimes. This man, Alick Pennycuick (pen•ee•KWIK), became known as the Sherlock Holmes of the Mounted Police.

Today the Royal Canadian Mounted Police use horses only on parade. To do their work, they now use cars, trucks, even snowmobiles. In addition, they use airplanes and boats. Women joined the Mounties in 1974.

The tradition of the Mounties is the same today as it has always been. Throughout Canada's vast spaces, the Mounties maintain the peace and see that justice is done.

SKILLS FOR SUCCESS

READING A ROAD MAP

A road map shows you where places are. It also shows you how to get from place to place. This road map shows part of Washington state and Canada.

Road maps may be large or small. They may show a nation or just part of a city.

All road maps, however, use a grid of letters and numbers. They also have an index. The index gives the grid location for each listing. You can look up the name of a city in the map index. Then you can use grid numbers and letters to find the city on the map. For example, Bellingham is listed with the letter and number *B-4*. It is found in the square formed by the intersection of the "B" column and the "4" column.

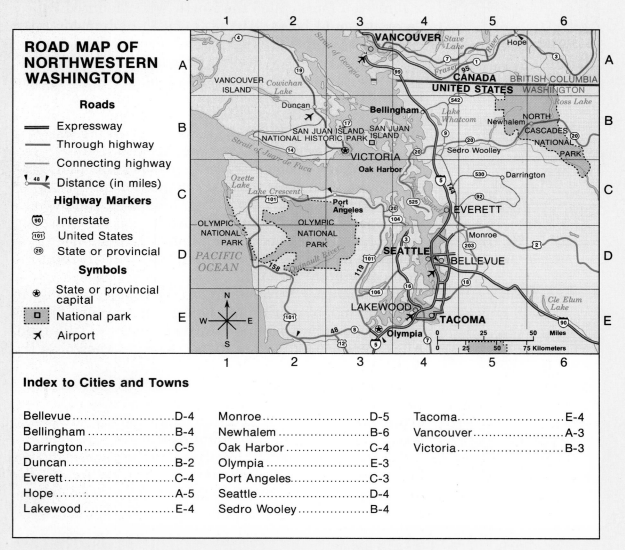

Index to Cities and Towns

Most road maps have a distance scale so you can measure distances between places. The scale on this map is in the lower right-hand corner. Most maps also show the actual number of miles between places. These places are marked by black wedges called distance markers. You can look at the legend to see what the distance markers look like. How far is it from Vancouver (A-3) to Bellevue (D-4)?

The map key also gives information about the kinds of roads shown on the map. It can help you plan the quickest route from one place to another. Look at the map key. It tells you that expressways are printed in blue. In some parts of the country expressways are also called freeways or turnpikes. Travel on expressways is usually quick because it is not interrupted by stoplights or crossroad traffic.

What color are through highways on the map? Through highways are main roads but, unlike expressways, they may have stoplights and crossroads.

A connecting highway is usually a two-lane road. What color does this map show for a connecting highway?

Symbols as well as colors are used to mark highways on road maps. Find the symbol for **interstate highways.** Interstate highways are expressways that cross several states. Find the symbol for United States highways. These highways also cross several states. They may be either broad expressways or two-lane roads. The symbols used for state or provincial highways identify roads that begin and end in one state or province. They often connect with roads in a bordering state or province.

The route numbers make it easy to talk about travel plans. For example, someone might say: "Here's how you get from Tacoma to North Cascades National Park. Take Interstate 5 north until you come to state highway 20. Take highway 20 east. Follow it to the park."

Try following this route on the map. Find Hope, British Columbia, in square A-5 of the map. With your finger, trace highway 1 west until it reaches Vancouver. Now find highway 99 and move your finger south until you come to the Canadian–United States border. What is the number of this expressway in the United States?

Usually road maps identify certain kinds of places with symbols. On this map the symbol of the airplane helps you locate airports. One airport shown on this map is near Seattle. In what squares are there other airports?

Another symbol on this map identifies a national park. According to the symbol, national parks are shown in a light green color. You will notice a small box within the national park symbol. This means that a small box will be used instead of a color if the park is very small. The symbol of the small box is used on this map to show San Juan Island National Historic Park.

CHECKING YOUR SKILLS

Use the map to answer these questions.

1. What state highways pass into Darrington?

2. What is the shortest route from Bellingham to Monroe?

3. In what square is San Juan Island?

4. What national park is nearest Port Angeles?

5. Find Olympia. What two routes could you take to reach Bremerton? Which is probably the fastest? Why?

6. What is the distance between Port Angeles and Olympia?

3. CANADA TODAY

To Guide Your Reading

Look for these important words:

Key Words
- provinces
- House of Commons
- Senate
- prime minister
- ministers
- Separatists
- acid rain

Places
- Newfoundland
- Nova Scotia
- New Brunswick
- Prince Edward Island
- Quebec
- Ontario
- Manitoba
- Saskatchewan
- Alberta
- British Columbia
- Yukon
- Northwest Territories
- Georges Bank

Look for answers to these questions:

1. How is the nation of Canada organized?
2. What is the structure of Canada's government? What is the head of government called?
3. What are examples of the cooperation between Canada and the United States?

Today Canada has one of the highest standards of living in the world. Canada has become a modern industrial power. It is a democratic nation respected around the globe.

Ottawa, Canada's capital, is Canada's eighth largest city. Ottawa is not the center of any important industry. Like Washington, D.C., Ottawa is important primarily because it is the center of government. Canada's Parliament is housed in three large stone buildings. These buildings stand high on a hill overlooking the Ottawa River.

The Provinces

Canada today is a federation of ten **provinces** and two territories. A Canadian province is a political region like one of our states. The provinces are **Newfoundland, Nova Scotia,** **New Brunswick, Prince Edward Island, Quebec, Ontario, Manitoba, Saskatchewan** (suh•SKACH•uh•wuhn), **Alberta,** and **British Columbia.** The territories are the **Yukon** and the **Northwest Territories.** These are large areas in the far north with small populations.

Each province has its own government. Each provincial government makes laws about education, health, working conditions, and the use of natural resources. It also handles other matters within the province. Canadian provinces have a great deal of power and authority.

Canada's Parliament

Canada has a Parliament with two houses, the **House of Commons** and the **Senate.** The House of Commons is

516

the more powerful and important of the two houses. This group has 282 members. Elections to choose members of the House of Commons are held at least every five years. New elections may be called at any time by the political party in power. The party in the majority in the House of Commons is in power.

The leader of the party in power is the **prime minister.** The prime minister is the most important elected official in Canada. Like our President, the prime minister heads the executive branch of government. Unlike our President, the prime minister is not elected nationwide. The prime minister is elected as a representative to the

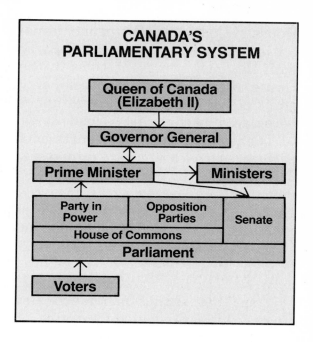

CANADA'S PARLIAMENTARY SYSTEM

Queen of Canada (Elizabeth II) → Governor General → Prime Minister → Ministers

Party in Power | Opposition Parties | Senate

House of Commons

Parliament

Voters

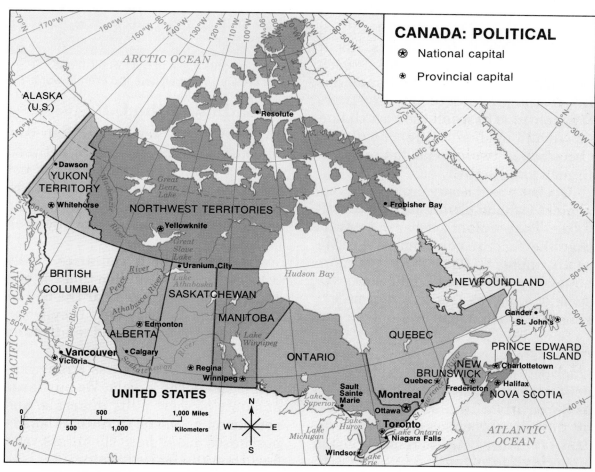

CANADA: POLITICAL

⊛ National capital

✳ Provincial capital

House of Commons. The prime minister is the leader of the political party with the most representatives in the House of Commons. If another party gains power, then the prime minister is replaced by that party's leader.

The people who head departments of the executive branch are **ministers.** They include the minister of national defense, the minister of agriculture, and the minister of transport. They are also members of the House of Commons.

The French Canadians

Once the armies of French and English kings struggled for control of Canada. Today some of that conflict remains.

Almost half of Canada's 24 million people are British descendants. About one-third of Canadians are French descendants. Most French Canadians live in the province of Quebec. There they continue to speak the French language and hold on to French culture. Canada has two official languages— French and English.

Quebec was the only province to vote against Canada having its own constitution. The people of Quebec were afraid that the federal government's power would increase. They feared a more powerful government might take away some of Quebec's freedom to preserve French-Canadian culture.

Some French Canadians want Quebec to secede from Canada. They want Quebec to become a separate, independent nation. These people are known as **Separatists.** In 1980 a vote was held on the question of secession. The citizens of Quebec voted to remain part of Canada.

Canada prints signs in both English and French. Can you translate the French words?

Canada and the U.S.

The United States–Canadian border shows the close friendship between our two countries. The border is not protected in any special way. There are no fences. Visitors crossing the border are given a friendly welcome by each nation.

Citizens of both countries freely cross the border 70 million times a year. Some people who live near the border cross it almost every day. They work, shop, and visit friends and relatives on both sides.

The United States has strong economic ties with Canada. We buy large amounts of wood pulp, minerals, and petroleum products. In return Canada purchases machines, chemicals, and food from the United States.

Together the United States and Canada built the St. Lawrence Seaway, finished in 1959. This project demanded close cooperation.

The United States and Canada have also cooperated in space programs. With help from NASA, Canada launched its first satellite in 1962. Since then Canada has sent up other satellites for research and communication purposes.

More recently Canada and the United States have worked together on the space shuttle program. One of the most important parts of the space shuttle is a huge mechanical arm. This arm can pick up and place objects in space. It was developed by Canadian scientists.

Although a lasting friendship exists between the United States and Canada, we have some disagreements.

Canadians are particularly upset about the air pollution caused by industries. Many of these are coal-burning power plants in the United States. When air pollutants combine with moisture in the atmosphere, **acid rain** results. Acid rain can cause fish to die in lakes and rivers. Acid rain may slow down growth of forests. Acid rain is affecting large parts of Canada and the United States. Both countries have been doing research on acid rain. New laws may be passed to control air pollution.

Canada and the United States have also disagreed about fishing rights on the **Georges Bank.** This is a huge area off the coasts of Nova Scotia and Maine. It is on the southern edge of the Grand Banks. Georges Bank is bigger than Massachusetts, Connecticut, and Rhode Island combined. It is also one of the

What do you think this political cartoon is saying about acid rain? What do you think the cartoonist's views might be on stopping acid rain?

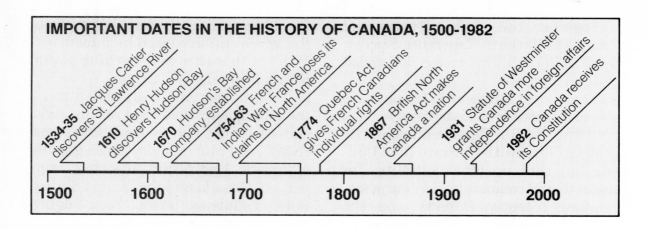

IMPORTANT DATES IN THE HISTORY OF CANADA, 1500-1982

1534-35 Jacques Cartier discovers St. Lawrence River

1610 Henry Hudson discovers Hudson Bay

1670 Hudson's Bay Company established

1754-63 French and Indian War; France loses its claims to North America

1774 Quebec Act gives French Canadians individual rights

1867 British North America Act makes Canada a nation

1931 Statute of Westminster grants Canada more independence in foreign affairs

1982 Canada receives its Constitution

1500   1600   1700   1800   1900   2000

Terry Fox runs in Quebec as part of his fund-raising marathon across Canada.

richest fishing grounds in the world. Both Canada and the United States claim Georges Bank.

Canada's government allows its citizens to catch a limited number of fish and scallops yearly. The United States lets Americans catch whatever they can. Canadians think that Americans are taking too many fish and scallops. The problem is being considered by an international court. It may be many years before the issue is settled.

There will always be challenges, both for nations and for individuals. The challenge met by one brave man, Terry Fox, has inspired Canadians. Terry, who had lost his right leg to cancer, ran 3,339 miles (5,372 km) across Canada in 1980 to raise funds for cancer research. He became a hero to all Canada.

Reading Check

1. What is Canada's capital city?
2. What is the name of Canada's most important lawmaking body?
3. How is Canada's prime minister chosen?
4. Why are Canadians upset about acid rain?

CHAPTER 22 REVIEW

WORDS TO USE

Number your paper from 1 to 10. Use the words below to complete the sentences that follow.

Canadian Shield **provinces**
House of Commons **Quebec**
Ottawa   **Vancouver**
prime minister **Winnipeg**
St. Lawrence Seaway
St. Lawrence River Lowlands

1. Most people in Canada live in the _____.

2. Ocean-going ships can travel as far as the Great Lakes because in 1959 the United States and Canada built the _____.

3. Most French Canadians live in the province of _____.

4. _____ is the largest city in the Prairie region of Canada.

5. The capital of Canada is _____.

6. The natural region that covers half of Canada and is known for its lakes, poor soil, and timber is called the _____.

7. _____ is a large city on the Pacific coast in British Columbia.

8. Canada's most important lawmaking body is the _____.

9. Political regions in Canada that are similar to our states are called _____.

10. The most important elected official in Canada is the _____.

FACTS TO REVIEW

1. What is Canada's greatest natural resource?

2. What was the basis of British claims to Canada?

3. How did the French and Indian War affect Canada?

4. How did Canada gain full independence from Britain in 1982?

5. How is the Canadian prime minister similar to the American President? What differences exist?

IDEAS TO DISCUSS

1. Why did Canadians not join the rebellion against British rule during the American Revolution?

2. What qualities and skills must David Thompson have had?

3. In what ways has the French influence remained strong in Canada?

◯ SKILLS PRACTICE

Reading a Road Map Use the road map on page 514 to answer these questions.

1. In which square is Victoria?

2. How would you get from Newhalem to Tacoma?

3. How far is it from Hope to Vancouver?

4. What highway passes through Sedro Woolley?

CHAPTER 23

Mexico—Neighbor
to the South

Mexico is a land of fiery volcanoes, steamy jungles, and dazzling beaches. It is also a land with a unique culture, the product of both Indian and Spanish heritages.

The history of every country is special and unique. Mexico's history is as stormy, colorful, and interesting as its geography. In this chapter you will read about Mexico's geography, history, and government.

1. MEXICO'S GEOGRAPHY

To Guide Your Reading

Look for these important words:

Key Words
- Ring of Fire

Places
- Parícutin
- El Chichón
- Gulf Coast
- Yucatán Peninsula

- Rio Grande
- Monterrey
- Veracruz
- Sierra Madre
- Durango
- Puebla
- Oaxaca
- Central Plateau

- Mexico City
- Pacific Coast
- Mazatlán
- Puerto Vallarta
- Acapulco
- Baja California
- Ensenada
- Tijuana

Look for answers to these questions:

1. Why does Mexico have a great variety of climates?
2. What kinds of natural regions are there in Mexico?
3. Where do most people in Mexico live?

Americans like to vacation at Mexico's sunny beaches and other resort areas. For this reason some Americans think of Mexico as a warm and gentle place. Mexico actually is a land of great variety and contrast.

Mexico is about one-fourth as large as the United States. Its population is over 70 million.

Mexico is one of the most mountainous countries in the world. Only one-third of the country is level land. In the early sixteenth century, the Spanish conquistador Hernando Cortés was asked about Mexico's geography. He crumpled up a piece of paper and threw it down on a table. "That," he exclaimed, "is the map of Mexico!"

We know that climate changes as we move north or south away from the equator. Canada, for example, is generally colder than the United States because it is farther north. Climate also changes with elevation. Low-lying lands tend to be warmer than high, mountainous areas. Air in mountain regions does not hold heat as well as air at lower elevations.

Because of its many mountains, Mexico has a great variety of climates. They vary from the lowland rain forest climate to the cool air of the mountains.

Mexico also has great extremes of precipitation. In the northwest desert only a few drops of rain fall each year. In the eastern jungles 100 inches (254 cm) of rain may fall. One area, the Grijalva (gree•HAHL•vuh) River valley in the south, can receive 200 inches (508 cm) a year.

Ring of Fire

Perhaps the most awesome natural force in Mexico is the volcano. Mexico lies in a region called the **Ring of Fire.** This is a circular band of volcanoes located on or near both coasts of the

Pacific Ocean. The Ring of Fire contains many active volcanoes and thousands of extinct ones.

In 1943 a farmer was working in his cornfield in western Mexico. He noticed a strange crack in his field. Out of the crack arose hot, smelly smoke. The next day the farmer returned to find a mound of volcanic lava.

For nine years smoke and lava poured from the center of the mound. The lava piled up to a height of 2,000 feet (609.6 m) above the valley floor. It buried all villages and farms in the area. Now only the broken tower of a church sticks out through the lava. The name of this volcano is **Parícutin** (puh•REE•kuh•teen).

In 1982 an ancient volcano again erupted. This was **El Chichón** (chee•CHON) in the state of Chiapas in southern Mexico. There were two eruptions of El Chichón, each a week apart. Gas and ashes from the volcano shot 10 miles (about 16 km) into the sky. Rocks hailed on the surrounding countryside. One man reported, "Rocks came through the roof like bullets." Everywhere roofs were crushed, trees turned to charcoal, and fields covered with rock and ash. A fertile valley was turned into a wasteland. It is feared that thousands were killed fleeing the violent eruptions.

The gasses from the El Chichón eruptions produced the largest volcanic cloud in the Northern Hemisphere since 1912. This cloud circled the globe and prevented the usual amount of sunlight from reaching Earth. As a result, said scientists, Earth's weather would be slightly cooler and stormier for several years.

Five Natural Regions

Mexico has five natural regions. The natural features, climate, and products are different for each of these regions.

The **Gulf Coast** region of Mexico, consisting of lowlands, is thinly pop-

A church steeple among hardened lava is all that remains of this Mexican village. It was destroyed in the 1940s by the erupting volcano Parícutin.

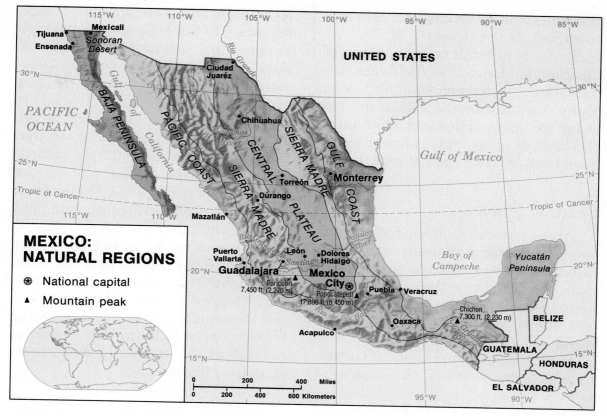

**MEXICO:
NATURAL REGIONS**

⊛ National capital

▲ Mountain peak

ulated. The region stretches from the jungles of the **Yucatán Peninsula** to the mouth of the **Rio Grande.** The Gulf Coast climate is quite warm. The northern part is a desert. The southern coast is a tropical rain forest. In this part of the Gulf Coast region farmers grow coffee, sugarcane, and bananas. Henequen, a plant used to make rope, is grown in Yucatán.

Monterrey is this region's largest city. It is home to Mexico's large steel and automobile industries.

Much of the region's economic activity centers on the oil industry. Rich supplies of oil are found in the Gulf of Mexico.

The developing oil industry has led to the growth of the whole region, particularly the seaport of **Veracruz.** In earlier days Veracruz was surrounded by swamps and marshes. These areas harbored hordes of mosquitoes and other insects. The insects carried many deadly diseases. Veracruz was known as the City of Death.

Today Mexican people are clearing jungles and draining swamps along the Gulf Coast. This work has made Veracruz a safe place to live. It has also created more usable farmland in the region.

The Sierra Madre

Three mountain ranges combine to form the Y-shaped **Sierra Madre** (see•ER•uh MAHD•dray) region. These ranges are known as the Eastern, Southern, and Western Sierra Madre. This rugged region includes the cities of **Durango, Puebla,** and

Oaxaca (wuh•HAHK•uh). All Mexico's volcanoes lie in the Sierra Madre.

Travel is difficult in many parts of the Sierra Madre. Tiny villages are connected by narrow, winding trails. Many of these mountain trails are too rough for automobiles and other vehicles. People often travel on foot or on horseback in the Sierra Madre.

Central Plateau

About two-thirds of Mexico's people live in the **Central Plateau** region. The capital of Mexico, **Mexico City,** sits at the southern edge of the plateau. Mexico City has an elevation of about 7,000 feet (2,134 m). No major city in the world has a higher elevation.

In 1968 the Summer Olympic Games were held in Mexico City. Some athletes, especially runners, had trouble adjusting to the high elevation. Other athletes took advantage of the location. An American named Bob Beamon participated in the long-jump event. He jumped 29 feet, 2½ inches (8.9 m) through the thin air of Mexico City. This was two feet (0.6 m) farther than anyone had ever jumped before.

Temperatures on the plateau are much cooler than in the lowlands. It has a more comfortable climate. The average altitude of the whole region is more than a mile (1.6 km) above sea level. Some of Mexico's best farmland is here. Volcanoes in the Sierra Madre have dumped volcanic ash on the Central Plateau for years. This has created large areas of rich soil. Here farmers raise crops of corn, beans, and wheat, as well as livestock.

The volcano Popocatépetl (poh•puh•KAT•uh•pehtl) is now serenely quiet. Once it showered forth the ash and lava that now make fields fertile.

Sunny Acapulco on Mexico's Pacific Coast is a popular tourist resort.

The giant saguaro cactus grows as high as 60 feet in Baja California.

Pacific Coast

Tourists from around the world enjoy Mexico's **Pacific Coast.** Its weather is sunny, and it features many white-sand beaches. The cities of **Mazatlán, Puerto Vallarta** (PWER·toh vuh·YAHR·tuh), and **Acapulco** (ahk·uh·PUL·koh) are among the region's most popular resort communities. Farmers in this region grow corn, cotton, coffee, and cocoa.

The northern section of the Pacific Coast consists of the Sonora Desert. The Morelos Dam on the Colorado River has changed part of this desert into good farmland.

Baja California

The peninsula of **Baja** (BAH·hah) **California** is 800 miles (1,287 km) long. *Baja* means "lower" in Spanish. The Pacific Coast Range forms the mountainous backbone of the Baja peninsula.

Baja California is a land of desert, rugged mountains, and wind-swept beaches. It attracts tourists and people who like to fish in the ocean. Nature lovers come to see the great gray whales in the shallow waters along the coast. The largest communities in this region are **Ensenada** and the border town of **Tijuana** (tee·uh·WAHN·uh).

Reading Check

1. What is the Ring of Fire?
2. What are the five natural regions of Mexico?
3. In what natural region is Mexico City located?
4. Why is there rich soil in the Central Plateau region?

2. MEXICO'S HISTORY

To Guide Your Reading

Look for these important words:

Key Words
- conquistadors
- *encomiendas*
- *ejidos*
- mestizos
- liberals
- La Reforma
- peasants
- Cinco de Mayo

- estates
- Mexican Constitution of 1917

People
- Hernando Cortés
- Miguel Hidalgo
- Santa Anna
- Benito Juarez

- Porfirio Díaz
- Francisco Madero
- Pancho Villa
- Emiliano Zapata

Places
- Chihuahua

Look for answers to these questions:

1. Why did Mexican people rebel against Spain?
2. What troubles and successes did Mexico have after independence from Spain?
3. Why did Mexico go through a second revolution in the twentieth century?

Hernando Cortés conquered the Aztec rulers of Mexico in 1519 and claimed their land for Spain. Cortés and other conquistadors were given large pieces of Mexican land by the Spanish king. These land grants were called **encomiendas** (en•ko•MYEN•dahs). The Spanish forced the Indians to work on these lands. At first the Indians were treated as slaves, but Spain outlawed Indian slavery in 1542. After that, the Indians had to work on the *encomiendas* only about 45 days every year. Some Indians were forced to work in the mines. Gold and silver from the mines made Spain rich.

The Indians were allowed to farm small communal plots on poor land. These plots, owned in common by a village rather than by individuals, were called **ejidos** (e•HEE•dohs).

The Catholic Church became a powerful force in New Spain. It was because of church leaders such as Bartholomé de las Casas that Indian slavery was ended. The church also became very wealthy. During 300 years of Spanish rule, the church acquired about half of all the Mexican lands. At one point the church also held two-thirds of all the money in Mexico.

Independence Achieved

Life in New Spain was hard and cruel for Indians. Life was also harsh for **mestizos,** people of mixed Indian and Spanish ancestry. Neither Indians nor mestizos had much chance for education and prosperity. Most of the wealth and power belonged to people of pure Spanish ancestry.

In the early 1800s this situation began to change. Mestizo priests and lawyers started reading books about freedom and democracy. They had heard about the American and French revolutions. Many had read the American Declaration of Independence. Some of these priests and lawyers dreamed of liberty and equality for Mexico. They wanted to see mestizos have as much power as the Spaniards. Others dreamed of a new prosperity. Many of them dreamed of revolution.

Finally, many Mexican people could take no more of Spanish rule. In 1810 a revolution started. A mestizo priest, **Miguel Hidalgo,** rang a church bell to call for a people's revolt. Thousands of mestizos and Indians joined him. Hidalgo himself was captured and executed by the Spanish in 1811. The revolution continued, however, for ten more years. In 1821 Mexico finally won its freedom from Spain.

Juarez Brings Reforms

Independence failed to solve many of Mexico's problems. Mexico was poor, with the church holding most of the money. Mexicans had no experience in ruling themselves. The Aztecs had obeyed one ruler. Then for 300 years a viceroy, the king's representative, had ruled. With independence came outbreaks of violence and civil war. Mexico was ruled off and on by one man, General Antonio Lopez de **Santa Anna.** More change was necessary if Mexico was to achieve peace and unity.

The person who did the most to create change in Mexico was **Benito Juarez** (HWAH•rays). In 1857 he became president of Mexico.

Benito Juarez brought about reforms, including a new constitution.

Juarez was a Zapotec Indian. He did not learn to speak Spanish until the age of 12. Juarez was a strong, honest leader, a man often compared to Abraham Lincoln. Juarez was supported by people calling themselves **liberals.** They believed in representative government and in laws based on a constitution. They also wanted private ownership of land.

The changes that Juarez and the liberals brought about were called **La Reforma**—"the reform." They established a new constitution. They took away the large landholdings of the church. They broke up the *ejidos.* The land was divided among the Indian and mestizo **peasants.** Peasants are people who live and work on the land.

In 1862 the government of Benito Juarez ran out of money. Mexico owed a large amount of money to Britain, Spain, and France. Juarez told these nations that they would not be repaid for a few years. France then decided to invade Mexico. The French were supported by Mexican generals and others who did not like the reforms.

On May 5, 1862, a battle was fought at the city of Puebla. In this battle a small band of Mexicans defeated a large French army. The leader of the Mexican forces sent a telegram to Benito Juarez. It said, "The arms of the nation are covered with glory!" This battle is celebrated today as the Mexican national holiday **Cinco de Mayo.** *Cinco de Mayo* means "fifth of May."

The French returned with even more soldiers. They were able to control Mexico for a few more years. Juarez finally drove them out in 1867.

After the French left, Benito Juarez returned to office as president. He was determined to make his country a better place to live. Under his leadership free public schools were established. New roads, railroads, and bridges were built. Juarez served as president until his death in 1872.

At Puebla, on May 5, 1862, Mexicans defeated the rich and powerful French army. Although the victory gave Mexicans new hope, the French sent more troops. They governed Mexico for five years before the Mexicans at last drove them out.

The effort to achieve democracy and equality in Mexico came to an end in 1876. In that year **Porfirio Díaz** (DEE•ahz) led a revolt and took over as ruler of Mexico. Under Díaz the people stayed poor. They had little say in their government. Workers had to labor for low wages and could not form labor unions. Much of the land again ended up in the hands of large landholders. Large landholdings are called **estates.**

A Revolution Begins

In 1910 a Mexican writer named **Francisco Madero** ran for president against Díaz. During the election Díaz had Madero arrested and jailed. Many thousands of people voted for Madero anyway. Díaz announced, however, that Madero had received only 176 votes. Díaz declared that he himself had gathered over 1 million votes. The Mexican people were furious. They knew that Díaz had lied about the results of the voting. Within a few months a revolution had begun.

The first combat started in the rugged backcountry of **Chihuahua** (chee•WAH•wah). This area is in the northern part of the Western Sierra Madre. The leader there was named **Pancho Villa** (PAHN•cho VEE•yah). Villa was a cruel and violent man, but he was an excellent commander of soldiers. Before long, no train, estate, or government official was safe in the northern mountains.

Another leader of this Mexican revolution was fighting in the south of the country. His name was **Emiliano Zapata** (ay•mi•LYAH•noh sah•PAH•tah). Like Benito Juarez, Zapata was a man of high ideals and honesty. He wanted

Land for the peasants was a goal of Mexican revolutionary Emiliano Zapata.

nothing for himself. He wanted only that the land be owned by the people who worked on it. The slogan of his revolt was "Land and Liberty!"

Zapata had another favorite saying. He said, "It is better to die on your feet than to live on your knees." He was not afraid to die fighting for what he believed in.

Zapata and his men swarmed out of the mountains. They drove many rich landowners off their land, dividing up the great estates among the people. Zapata and his men often helped people farm land on the estates they had conquered.

531

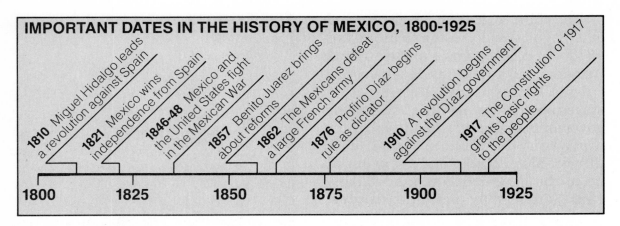

IMPORTANT DATES IN THE HISTORY OF MEXICO, 1800-1925

1810 Miguel Hidalgo leads a revolution against Spain

1821 Mexico wins independence from Spain

1846-48 Mexico and the United States fight in the Mexican War

1857 Benito Juarez brings about reforms

1862 The Mexicans defeat a large French army

1876 Profirio Diaz begins rule as dictator

1910 A revolution begins against the Diaz government

1917 The Constitution of 1917 grants basic rights to the people

1800   1825   1850   1875   1900   1925

Zapata's colorful band of peasants marched across the country to Mexico City. There they met up with Pancho Villa and his men. Two ragtag armies of peasants, all Indians and mestizos,

The green, white, and red flag of Mexico is sold to people celebrating Constitution Day, an important national holiday.

had brought the Mexican government to its knees.

Terrified, Díaz resigned as president and fled to Europe. Zapata was eventually killed in an ambush, but the revolution went on. In 1917 Mexico's new political leaders called for a constitutional convention. They wanted to turn the ideals of Zapata and the other revolutionaries into law.

The Constitution of 1917

The **Mexican Constitution of 1917** gave workers the right to form labor unions. It gave the government control over education, farmland, and the oil industry. It limited the time a president could serve to just one term. This constitution is the heart and soul of Mexico's revolution.

Reading Check

1. Describe the influence of the Catholic Church in New Spain.
2. Why did Father Hidalgo call for a people's revolt?
3. What was *La Reforma?*
4. How did Mexico's Constitution of 1917 bring greater justice to Mexico's people?

FATHER HIDALGO

Father Hidalgo

Silk worms
on mulberry leaves

A church bell

In 1810 a Mexican priest rang a church bell and changed history. That priest was Father Miguel Hidalgo. Today he is known as the Father of Mexican Independence.

Father Hidalgo was the priest for the small village of Dolores. Most of the people who lived in Dolores were poor Indians and mestizos. Father Hidalgo had helped them plant mulberry bushes, olive trees, and grapevines. With mulberry bushes, silkworms could be raised for spinning silk thread. Olive trees could produce olive oil. Grapevines could produce wine. Father Hidalgo then brought in beehives so that honey could be gathered. Father Hidalgo hoped that the people of Dolores could rid themselves of poverty. They would sell silk, olive oil, wine, and honey.

Father Hidalgo's plan was good, but the Spanish government ruling Mexico had other ideas. The Spanish wanted the Indians and mestizos to remain poor. They were suspicious that Father Hidalgo might have other ideas—ideas of democracy and independence. Indeed, Father Hidalgo belonged to a secret society that planned a revolution against Spain. This the Spanish authorities learned and arrested one of the leaders.

When he discovered what had happened, Father Hidalgo acted. He rang the bell of his church to call the people of Dolores together. He told them that they would have to fight to win their freedom. "Down with bad government!" he cried out to them. "Long live Mexico!"

The men of Dolores armed themselves with axes, knives, shovels, and pitchforks. Father Hidalgo was a peaceful man and a deeply religious man. Suddenly he found himself leading a great army. This army swept through Mexico, seizing villages and burning the estates of wealthy Spaniards. Thousands joined Hidalgo's forces.

Father Hidalgo was captured and executed in 1811. The Spaniards hoped this would end the fighting, but they were wrong. For ten more years, the Mexican people fought on. Finally, in 1821 the last of the Spanish army fled the country. Mexico had won its independence!

3. THE NATION OF MEXICO TODAY

═To Guide Your Reading═

Look for these important words:

Key Words
• PRI

People
• Miguel de la Madrid

Look for answers to these questions:

1. What is the structure of Mexico's government?
2. What is Mexico's most important political party?
3. What problems does Mexico face today?
4. What are relations like between Mexico and the United States?

Mexico City today is the second largest urban area in the world. Only New York City is larger. Mexico City has a population of about 14 million people. Like the country itself, Mexico City is a place of great variety and contrasts. Modern skyscrapers cast shadows on lovely old colonial churches. Under the churches may lie the ruins of ancient Aztec structures. Horses and burros share the streets with automobiles. There are neighborhoods of beautiful homes, and there are tenements overcrowded with poor people.

Mexico City stands on the same site as did Tenochtitlán, the capital of the Aztecs. Tenochtitlán was built in the fourteenth century. This makes Mexico City the oldest city in the Western Hemisphere. As in Aztec times, the power and population of Mexico is centered in the capital.

Mexico's Government

In many ways Mexico's government is like that of the United States. Mexico is a democratic federation of 31 states. Like our country, Mexico has legislative, judicial, and executive branches of government. The president, as chief executive, is particularly powerful.

Traffic in Mexico City flows around the towering Independence Monument.

534

Mexico's government is also different from ours. In the United States the two leading political parties are the Democrats and the Republicans. During the last 50 years we have had five Democratic Presidents and five Republican Presidents.

In Mexico there is only one strong political party. This party is called the **PRI**, the Institutional Revolutionary Party. The PRI has not lost a presidential election since 1929. Nine Mexican presidents in a row have belonged to the PRI.

In the United States 13 colonies came together to form a federation of states. These states preserved many powers for themselves. In Mexico the federal government divided the country into 31 states. These states have very little power. Much of the country's political power is in the hands of its president.

Mexico and the World

Mexico's plans for the future have depended on oil. Vast new fields of

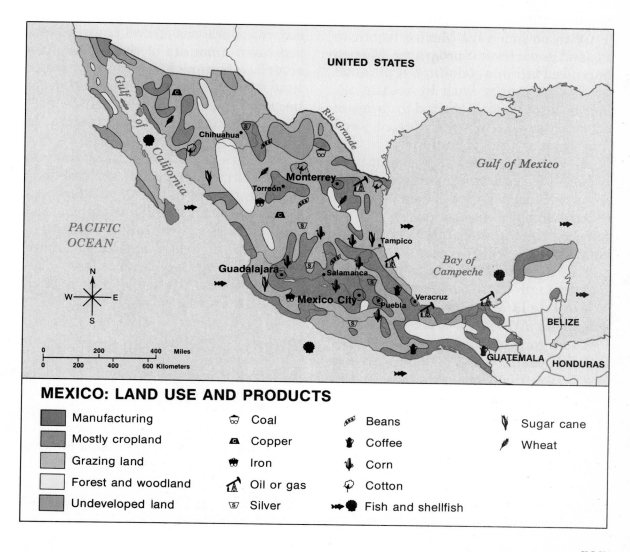

MEXICO: LAND USE AND PRODUCTS

- Manufacturing
- Mostly cropland
- Grazing land
- Forest and woodland
- Undeveloped land

- Coal
- Copper
- Iron
- Oil or gas
- Silver

- Beans
- Coffee
- Corn
- Cotton
- Fish and shellfish

- Sugar cane
- Wheat

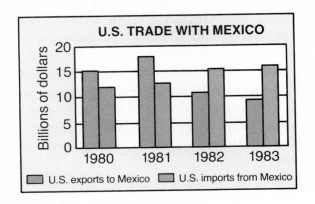

U.S. TRADE WITH MEXICO

Billions of dollars

■ U.S. exports to Mexico ■ U.S. imports from Mexico

Mexican oil were found in 1976. Mexico is now the fourth-leading producer of oil in the world. Some experts believe that Mexico will be the largest producer in the world by 1999.

With so much oil Mexico began to expand government programs. Mexico borrowed billions of dollars. It planned to pay the money back by selling oil. When the price of oil started to go down, so did Mexico's income. Mexico owed more money than it could pay.

Mexico now must tighten its belt, reduce its borrowing, and pay back some of its debt. This will mean a period of hard times for many Mexicans. There will be high unemployment and inflation. Poverty will increase.

The man who will try to lead Mexico through these difficult times is **Miguel de la Madrid.** He was elected president in 1982 for a six-year term. "We are going to have a couple of very difficult years," he said. "These are not the first difficult years we have had in the history of Mexico."

Mexico and the U.S.

The United States wants Mexico to be prosperous. To help Mexico develop its industries, American banks have loaned money to Mexico. If Mexico cannot repay its loans, this will hurt the American economy.

Mexico is an important trading partner of the United States. Only Canada and Japan carry on more trade with the United States. We purchase Mexican cotton, sugar, coffee, shrimp, beef, minerals, and oil. Mexico buys machinery, automobiles, and chemicals from our country. Prosperity in Mexico will lead to even more trade.

We still have disagreements with Mexico, just as we do with Canada. Mexico has complained that American farmers are taking too much water from the Colorado River. American farmers, ranchers, cities, and power plants use huge amounts of this water. The river has become low and salty by the time it reaches Mexican soil. If the river becomes much saltier, it will be useless for drinking and irrigation in Mexico.

Leaders of both countries want to settle their shared problems. Mexican presidents have had many conferences with American Presidents in the last few years. They have talked about fishing rights, oil prices, and illegal immigration. If our political leaders continue talking to each other, such problems may be solved.

Reading Check

1. In what ways is Mexico City a city of contrasts?
2. What is the name of Mexico's leading political party?
3. What is an important cause of Mexico's economic problems?
4. Give two examples showing how the economies of Mexico and the United States are connected.

UNDERSTANDING CLIMATE

Latitude and Climate

The Earth is divided into three major climate zones, depending on latitude. Separating these zones are **parallels,** or lines of latitude, with special names. The equator is the parallel that divides the world into its northern and southern hemispheres. North of the equator are the **Tropic of Cancer** and the **Arctic Circle.** South of the equator are the **Tropic of Capricorn** and the **Antarctic Circle.**

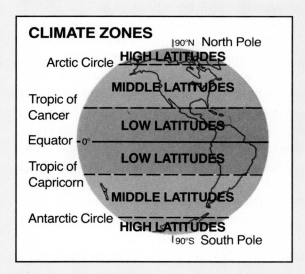

CLIMATE ZONES

North Pole 90°N

Arctic Circle — HIGH LATITUDES

MIDDLE LATITUDES

Tropic of Cancer

LOW LATITUDES

Equator — 0°

LOW LATITUDES

Tropic of Capricorn

MIDDLE LATITUDES

Antarctic Circle — HIGH LATITUDES

90°S South Pole

The Tropics

The area between the Tropic of Cancer and the Tropic of Capricorn is the **tropics.** In the tropics the sun is almost directly overhead at noon all year long. The sun's rays produce high temperatures on the ground. For that reason the tropics are the warmest part of Earth.

Areas between the Tropic of Cancer and the Tropic of Capricorn are sometimes called **low latitude** areas. The latitude of the equa-

HOW THE SUN'S RAYS AFFECT THE EARTH'S CLIMATE ZONES

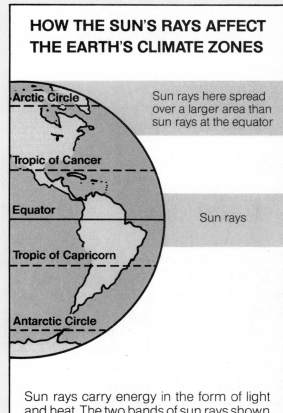

Arctic Circle

Sun rays here spread over a larger area than sun rays at the equator

Tropic of Cancer

Equator

Sun rays

Tropic of Capricorn

Antarctic Circle

Sun rays carry energy in the form of light and heat. The two bands of sun rays shown in the diagram have the same width and the same amount of energy. The tropics are the warmest climate zone because sun rays are more concentrated near the equator. Because of the way the Earth curves, sun rays that strike farther away from the equator cover a larger area of the Earth's surface. Therefore, regions farther from the equator are cooler because they receive less of the sun's heat and light.

tor is 0°. Latitudes closest to the equator have low latitude numbers.

The state of Hawaii and southern Mexico are in the tropics. The latitude of Honolulu, Hawaii, is about 21°N.

The Middle Latitudes

The **middle latitudes** are the second major climate area. There are two areas of middle latitudes. One is between the Tropic of Cancer and the Arctic Circle. The other is between the Tropic of Capricorn and the Antarctic Circle. The middle latitudes are also called the **temperate zone.**

In general, regions in the middle latitudes have warm summers and cold winters. This is because the angle of the sun's rays varies during the year. In summer the sun's rays are more direct and therefore are warming. In winter the sun's rays are slanted and do not heat the ground very much.

The mainland United States lies within the middle latitudes of the Northern Hemisphere.

The Polar Regions

The **polar regions,** or **high latitudes,** form the third major climate area on Earth. The high latitudes are the latitudes closest to the North Pole and the South Pole. The region to the north of the Arctic Circle is called the **Arctic.** The region to the south of the Antarctic Circle is the **Antarctic.** The Arctic and Antarctic have the coldest climate on Earth.

These areas are so cold because the sun's rays are the most slanted there. Even in summer the sun does not appear far from the horizon. In winter near the poles the sun does not appear at all.

Parts of Alaska and northern Canada are within the Arctic region.

Precipitation

Latitude has a general effect on precipitation. Warm air can hold more moisture than cold air. The warmer the air, the more moisture it picks up from the ocean. Much moisture then falls as rain. The tropics have more precipitation than other areas because they are warmest. Mount Waialeale (weye‧ahl‧ee‧AHL‧ee) in the Hawaiian Islands has the most rainfall in the world. The average rainfall there is 460 inches (1,168 cm). The Arctic and Antarctic have little precipitation—fewer than 5 inches (12.7 cm) a year.

Winds

Latitude also has an effect on winds. Winds are caused by the uneven heating of the air. Warm air tends to rise. Cold air then moves to take its place. This action usually takes place in great circular movements. The winds near the equator generally blow from east to west. In the middle latitudes the winds generally blow from west to east.

Winds that generally blow in one direction are called **prevailing winds.** Prevailing winds can affect climate. Consider what happens on the west coast of North America. Winds blowing from the west bring much moisture from the Pacific Ocean. Average yearly rainfall in the coastal parts of northern California, Oregon, Washington, and western Canada ranges from 60 to 80 inches (152 to 203 cm).

In winter the prevailing winds on the east coast of North America are from the northwest. Therefore, they often bring cold, arctic air. In summer the prevailing winds on the east coast come from the southwest. They bring warm, moisture-filled air.

Look at the map on page 539. Notice that the interior of North America is drier than either the west or the east coasts. If prevailing winds from the west carry moisture, why does much of the west have low precipitation? One reason is that winds usually drop moisture when they run into mountains. Therefore, with winds from the west, most moisture falls on the western sides of the mountains.

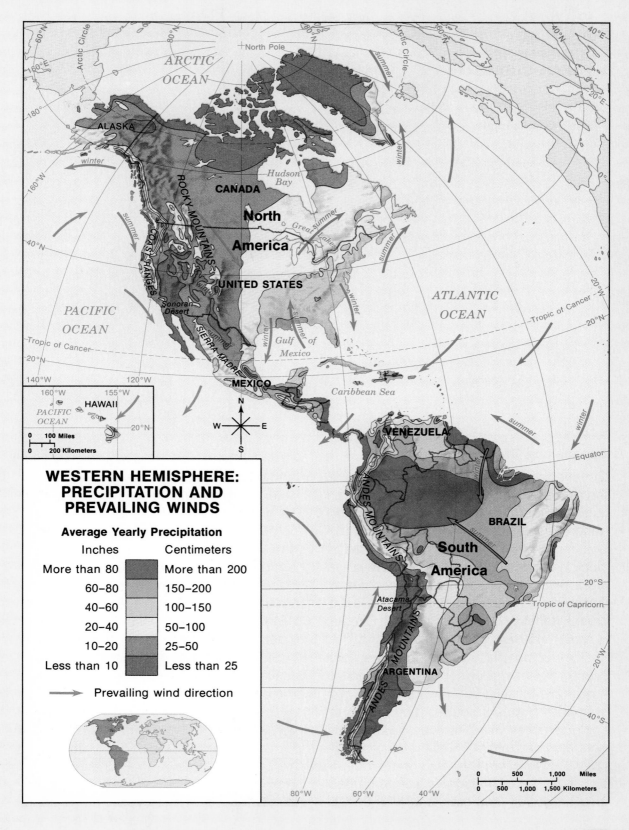

WESTERN HEMISPHERE: PRECIPITATION AND PREVAILING WINDS

Average Yearly Precipitation

Inches		Centimeters
More than 80		More than 200
60–80		150–200
40–60		100–150
20–40		50–100
10–20		25–50
Less than 10		Less than 25

→ Prevailing wind direction

ARCTIC OCEAN

North Pole

ALASKA

CANADA

North

America

Hudson Bay

ROCKY MOUNTAINS

COAST RANGES

UNITED STATES

Great Lakes

ATLANTIC OCEAN

PACIFIC OCEAN

Sonoran Desert

SIERRA MADRE

Tropic of Cancer

Gulf of Mexico

MEXICO

Caribbean Sea

VENEZUELA

ANDES MOUNTAINS

BRAZIL

South

America

Atacama Desert

ANDES MOUNTAINS

ARGENTINA

ANDES MOUNTAINS

Equator

Tropic of Capricorn

HAWAII

PACIFIC OCEAN

0 100 Miles

0 200 Kilometers

0 500 1,000 Miles

0 500 1,000 1,500 Kilometers

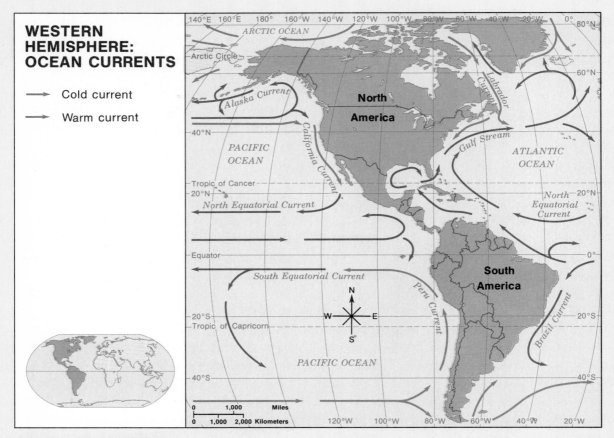

WESTERN HEMISPHERE: OCEAN CURRENTS

→ Cold current

→ Warm current

Oceans and Climate

Oceans can affect climate in two ways. Like the air, oceans have great circular currents. In the Northern Hemisphere these currents generally go in a clockwise direction. In the Southern Hemisphere they go in a counterclockwise direction. The **Gulf Stream** is the name of the current along the east coast. It sweeps from south to north. Because it comes from tropical areas, the Gulf Stream is a warm current.

The current that sweeps down the west coast of North America comes from the north. It is a cold current. When warm air hits the cold water, fog is produced. Fog results in cooler temperatures. The average July temperature of Eureka, California, is 56°F (13.3°C). New York City, also on the ocean and at the same latitude, is warmer. It has an average July temperature of 77°F (25°C).

Water heats and cools more slowly than land does. For this reason, great bodies of water affect climate. In summer, oceans do not get as warm as the land. In winter they do not get as cool. Land near an ocean is warmer in winter and cooler in summer than land far from an ocean. Temperatures of places near an ocean do not vary as much as temperatures of places inland. The Canadian cities of Vancouver, British Columbia, and Winnipeg, Manitoba, are located on about the same latitude. Vancouver is on the ocean. Winnipeg is inland. The chart below shows the difference.

AVERAGE TEMPERATURES		
	January	July
Winnipeg	−4°F (−18°C)	68°F (20°C)
Vancouver	35.6°F (2°C)	62.6°F (17°C)

540

Elevation

The elevation of a place can affect its climate. Generally, the higher the elevation, the cooler the climate. In very hot climates, areas of high elevation are usually the most comfortable places to live.

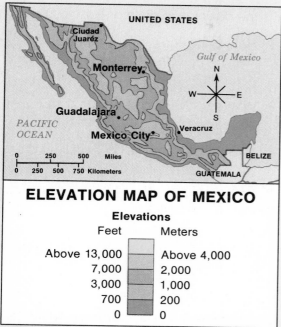

ELEVATION MAP OF MEXICO

Elevations

Feet		Meters
Above 13,000		Above 4,000
7,000		2,000
3,000		1,000
700		200
0		0

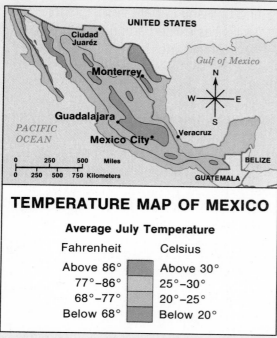

TEMPERATURE MAP OF MEXICO

Average July Temperature

Fahrenheit		Celsius
Above 86°		Above 30°
77°–86°		25°–30°
68°–77°		20°–25°
Below 68°		Below 20°

Look at the map of Mexico showing July temperatures. What is the average July temperature of Mexico City? of Veracruz?

Now look at the elevation map of Mexico. What is the elevation of Mexico City? What is the elevation of Veracruz? Why would Mexico City have cooler temperatures than Veracruz?

CHECKING YOUR SKILLS

Use what you have learned to answer these questions.

1. Which of the three major climate zones best fits each of these descriptions?

   a. The sun is low in the sky in summer. There is very little precipitation.

   b. The sun is overhead at noon. It is likely to be warm and rainy.

   c. It is warm in summer and cold in winter. Precipitation and temperature vary greatly.

2. What kind of winter climate is a city in the interior of Canada likely to have?

3. What kind of climate are you likely to find along a tropical coast? How would it compare to a place at the same latitude but at a higher elevation?

4. Look at the map of prevailing winds on page 539. Why does Nevada have less precipitation than most of California? Why does northern California have more precipitation than southern California?

5. If a town is at 50°N latitude, what is its climate likely to be?

6. What is the name of the warm ocean current off the east coast of North America?

7. How does the ocean temperature make coastal areas warmer in winter than places far from the ocean?

CHAPTER 23 REVIEW

WORDS TO USE

Number your paper from 1 to 5. For each word below select the correct definition from the list that follows.

1. *ejidos*
2. *encomiendas*
3. **estates**
4. **mestizos**
5. **peasants**

a. Land owned in common by Mexican Indians or peasants

b. Poor people who live and work on the land

c. Large landholdings

d. Large grants of land given to the conquistadors

e. People who have both Indian and Spanish ancestors

FACTS TO REVIEW

1. Why is Mexico described as a land of great variety and contrast?

2. What kinds of farming and manufacturing take place in the Gulf Coast region of Mexico?

3. How is the Pacific Coast region different from the Central Plateau region? from the Sierra Madre region?

4. How was the Catholic Church a powerful force in New Spain?

5. How was life in New Spain difficult for mestizos and Indians?

6. What reforms did Benito Juarez bring to Mexico?

7. How did Emiliano Zapata bring about the downfall of dictator Porfirio Díaz?

8. How is Mexico's government similar to that of the United States? How is it different?

9. Why does Mexico now face a period of hard times?

10. What disagreements do Mexico and the United States need to work out?

IDEAS TO DISCUSS

1. How is Mexico's government like that of the United States? How is it different?

2. How did the colonial influence of Spain shape Mexico's history?

3. What did Miguel Hidalgo, Benito Juarez, and Emiliano Zapata each fight for? What similarities existed among the three men? What differences?

◯ SKILLS PRACTICE

Understanding Climate Use pages 537 to 541 to answer these questions.

1. What are the three major climate zones on the Earth?

2. In which climate zone is the United States?

3. Why do the tropics have more rain than other areas?

4. Name two ways in which the ocean affects climate.

5. How does elevation affect climate?

UNIT 9 REVIEW

WORDS TO REMEMBER

Number your paper from 1 to 5. Use the words below to replaced the underlined words in the sentences that follow.

encomiendas   **provinces**
mestizos   **Separatists**
ministers

1. Canada is a federation of ten <u>political divisions similar to states</u>.

2. In Canada <u>people who are in charge of executive departments</u> are usually members of the House of Commons.

3. A number of Canadians with French ancestors and customs are <u>people who wish Quebec to be independent</u>.

4. Life in New Spain was hard for Indians and <u>people of mixed Indian and Spanish heritage</u>.

5. The conquistadors were given <u>large grants of land</u>.

FOCUS ON MAIN IDEAS

1. What are the major natural resources of Canada? of Mexico?

2. Compare the climates of Mexico and Canada.

3. Who were the first Europeans to claim land in Canada? in Mexico?

4. How did Canada gain independence from Britain?

5. How did Mexico gain independence from Spain?

6. What is the Commonwealth of Nations?

7. How is the economy of the United States tied to that of Mexico? of Canada?

8. Why is it significant that the United States borders with Canada and Mexico are undefended?

9. How are the governments of Mexico and Canada alike? How are they different?

10. How have history and geography made Canada and Mexico different?

ACTIVITIES

1. **Research/Writing** Choose an important person, place, or event of Mexico or Canada. Do more research in the library. Write a report and share it with the class.

2. **Map Reading/Writing** Find a road map of Mexico or Canada. Plan a trip across the country. What highways will you travel? What sights will you see? Write down the plan of your trip.

3. **Research/Art** Make a poster or mural of Mexico or Canada. Include the flag, people, important resources, products, national holidays or festivals.

4. **Reading/Writing** In your library find a fiction book about life in Canada or Mexico. Read the book and write a report telling what you learned.

5. **Making a Table** Make a large table comparing Mexico and Canada. Compare the national flags, languages spoken, holidays, resources, and products.

6. **Making a Timeline** Put these events in the correct order on a timeline.

- Mexico wins independence from Spain
- Mexican Constitution of 1917
- Jacques Cartier arrives in Canada
- Britain gains control of Canada
- Canada achieves independence of the British Parliament
- English land at Jamestown
- United States wins independence from Britain
- Cortés conquers Mexico

◯ SKILLS REVIEW

1. **Reading a Road Map** Use the map below to answer the questions that follow.

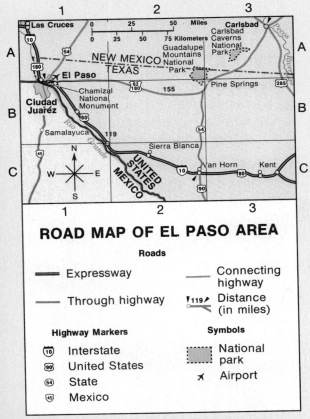

ROAD MAP OF EL PASO AREA

a. What town can be found in square C-3?
b. What kind of road connects Pine Springs (B-3) to El Paso (A-1)?
c. What route would you follow to go from Las Cruces, New Mexico (A-1), to Samalayuca (B-1) in Mexico?
d. What would be the best route to follow to travel from Sierra Blanca, Texas, (C-2) to Guadalupe Mountains National Park?
e. How far is it from El Paso (A-1) to Carlsbad, New Mexico (A-3)?

2. **Understanding Climate** Number your paper from 1 to 10. Choose the best word or phrase from the list below to complete the sentences that follow. You will use each term once.

Antarctic	**middle latitudes**
cooler	**prevailing winds**
equator	**Tropic of Cancer**
Gulf Stream	**tropics**
latitude	**warmer**

a. The __(1)__ is the parallel that divides the Earth into its northern and southern hemispheres.
b. Winds that usually blow in one direction are __(2)__ .
c. The __(3)__ is a warm ocean current along the east coast of the United States.
d. Regions in the __(4)__ , such as the United States, have warm summers and cold winters.
e. The __(5)__ is located in the polar region and has one of the coldest climates.
f. The warmest part of the Earth is in the low latitudes, or __(6)__ .
g. Land that is near an ocean is __(7)__ in summer and __(8)__ in winter than places inland.
h. The Earth is divided into three major climate zones based on __(9)__ .
i. The __(10)__ is a parallel that divides the low latitudes from the middle latitudes.

544

YOUR STATE'S HISTORY

Fourteen American states border on Canadian lands. Four states border on Mexico. Every day thousands of people cross the borders to work, shop, or visit. Mexican Americans and Canadian Americans live in all parts of the United States.

The following activities will help you learn about connections between your state and our neighbors, Canada and Mexico.

LEARNING ABOUT GEOGRAPHY

1. How far is your town from the Mexican border? the Canadian border? Which is closer?

2. Longitude is a measure of the distance east or west of a point in Greenwich, England. Find a map or an atlas with lines of longitude. Look for a Canadian town that is nearly the same longitude as your hometown. Use an atlas to write a short report about the town you choose. What is the population of the town? What is its elevation? What is its climate like?

3. Using a map or an atlas, find the Mexican town that is at the same longitude as your town. If there is none, select a Mexican town or city of your choice. Write a short report on that town.

4. Use a road atlas and plan the route you would follow to reach either Canada or Mexico from your hometown. About how many miles would you have to travel?

LEARNING ABOUT ECONOMICS

5. World trade is important. Are there products you use in your community or state that come from Canada or Mexico? What are they? Does your state export products or goods to Canada or Mexico?

LEARNING ABOUT PEOPLE

6. The picture below shows a dancer performing a traditional dance of Mexico. Mexican folkdances often take place in the United States where there are large numbers of Mexican Americans. These citizens influence the life of the state where they live. Is there a Mexican-American influence in your state? If so, explain what form it takes.

UNITED STATES OF AMERICA: POLITICAL

CANADA

WASHINGTON
- Seattle
- Olympia⊛ •Tacoma
- Spokane•

- •Portland
- ⊛Salem
- •Corvallis
- Eugene• •Springfield

OREGON

- •Medford

•Lewiston

•Missoula
Helena⊛
•Butte

MONTANA
•Great Falls

•Billings

IDAHO
⊛•Boise

Idaho Falls•
•Pocatello

Snake River

•Eureka

NEVADA

•Reno
⊛Carson City

Sacramento⊛
San• •Stockton
Francisco •Oakland
•San Jose

CALIFORNIA

•Fresno

*PACIFIC
OCEAN*

•Bakersfield

•Santa Barbara
Los Angeles
•San Bernardino
Long•
Beach

San Diego•

WYOMING
•Casper

Great Salt Lake
•Ogden
Salt Lake City⊛
Provo•

UTAH

Green River

Colorado River

Las•
Vegas

ARIZONA

Phoenix⊛

Tucson•

Gila River

•Laramie
Cheyenne•⊛

•Boulder
⊛•Denver

COLORADO
•Grand Junction
Colorado• Springs

Pueblo•

⊛Santa Fe
•Albuquerque

NEW MEXICO

Roswell•

Las Cruces•
⊛El Paso
Ciudad Juarez

NORTH DAKOT
⊛Bismarck

•Rapid City ⊛Pierre
SOUTH DAKOT

NEBRASKA
North• Grand
Platte Island•
Platte River

KANS

OKLAH
•Amarillo Oklah

•Lawton

•Lubbock

Pecos River

TEXAS

MEXICO
•Chihuahua

SOVIET
UNION

ARCTIC OCEAN
•Prudhoe Bay
Arctic Circle

ALASKA
•Fairbanks

Yukon River

•Anchorage

Juneau⊛

CANADA

546

| 0 | 250 | 500 | Miles |
| 0 | 250 | 500 | 750 | Kilometers |

Tropic of Cancer

PACIFIC OCEAN

Kauai•

Oahu• **HAWAII**
Honolulu•
Maui•

•Hilo
Hawaii

•Monterrey

San• Antonio

Corp
Chr

| 0 | 100 | 200 | Miles |

CANADA

Lake of the Woods

Duluth

MINNESOTA

Minneapolis • ⊛ St. Paul

Lake Superior

Sault Sainte Marie

Quebec •

St. John •

MAINE

Bangor •

Augusta ⊛

Montreal •

Lewiston •

Ottawa ⊛

Montpelier •

Burlington •

Portland •

MICHIGAN

WISCONSIN

Green Bay

Lake Michigan

Lake Huron

Toronto •

VERMONT

NEW HAMPSHIRE

Concord ⊛

Manchester •

Boston •

Grand Rapids

Flint •

Lansing ⊛

Syracuse •

Rochester •

Buffalo •

Albany ⊛

Springfield •

Hartford •

MASSACHUSETTS

Providence •

Madison ⊛

Racine •

Detroit •

NEW YORK

RHODE ISLAND

CONNECTICUT

Bridgeport •

Cedar Rapids

Rockford •

Chicago •

South Bend •

Toledo •

Erie •

Newark •

Trenton •

New York City •

IOWA

Des Moines ⊛

Davenport •

Hammond • Gary •

Fort Wayne •

Cleveland •

Youngstown •

PENNSYLVANIA

Harrisburg ⊛

Pittsburgh •

Philadelphia •

NEW JERSEY

Omaha •

Peoria •

INDIANA

OHIO

Akron •

Dover •

DELAWARE

Lincoln •

ILLINOIS

Indianapolis ⊛

Columbus ⊛

Dayton •

Wheeling •

MARYLAND

Baltimore •

Annapolis ⊛

Springfield ⊛

Cincinnati •

WEST VIRGINIA

Washington, D.C. ⊛

Kansas City •

St. Louis •

Louisville •

Frankfort ⊛

Huntington •

Charleston ⊛

VIRGINIA

Topeka •

Jefferson City ⊛

Evansville •

Lexington •

Richmond ⊛

MISSOURI

KENTUCKY

Roanoke •

Norfolk •

Virginia Beach •

Springfield •

Greensboro •

Raleigh ⊛

Nashville ⊛

Knoxville •

Winston-Salem •

Tulsa •

TENNESSEE

Asheville •

NORTH CAROLINA

ARKANSAS

Chattanooga •

Spartanburg •

Charlotte •

Fort Smith •

Memphis •

Huntsville •

Greenville •

Columbia ⊛

Little Rock ⊛

SOUTH CAROLINA

Pine Bluff •

Atlanta ⊛

Charleston •

Greenville •

Birmingham •

GEORGIA

MISSISSIPPI

ALABAMA

Macon •

Columbus •

Savannah •

Shreveport •

Monroe •

Vicksburg •

Montgomery ⊛

Albany •

Jackson ⊛

Meridian •

LOUISIANA

Hattiesburg •

Jacksonville •

Baton Rouge •

Biloxi •

Mobile •

Tallahassee ⊛

Lake Charles •

Pensacola •

Houston

New Orleans •

FLORIDA

Orlando •

Tampa •

St. Petersburg •

ATLANTIC OCEAN

Gulf of Mexico

Miami •

Nassau ⊛

BAHAMAS

Havana ⊛

CUBA

Lake Ontario

Lake Erie

Mississippi River

Missouri River

Ohio River

Tennessee River

Savannah River

St. Lawrence River

Tropic of Cancer

Legend:
— National boundary
— State boundary
⊛ National capital
⊛ State capital
• Other cities

N
W — E
S

0 100 200 300 Miles
0 100 200 300 400 Kilometers

547

UNITED STATES OF AMERICA: PHYSICAL

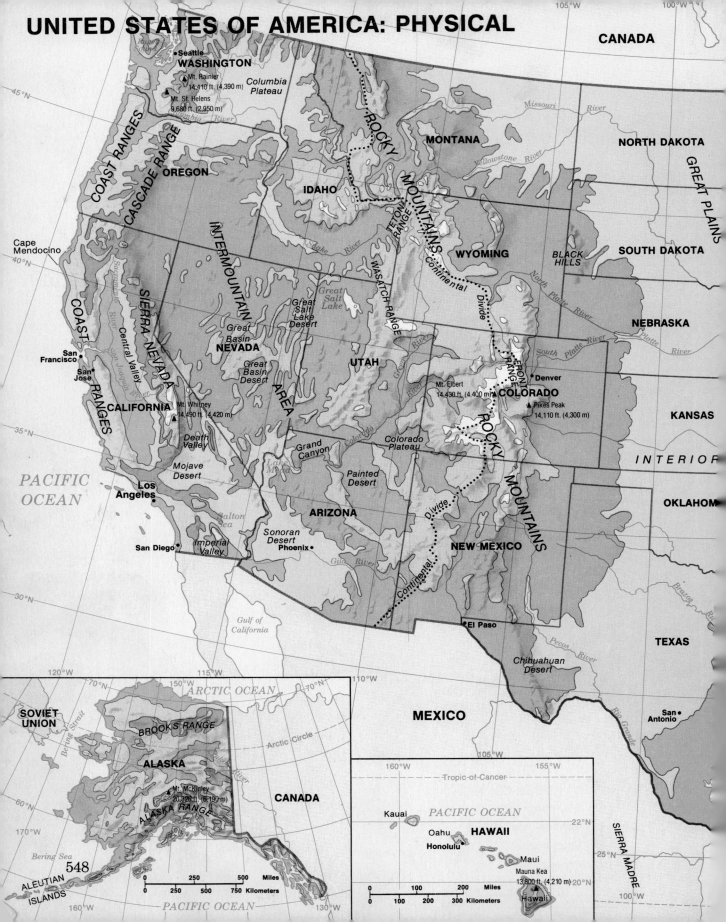

CANADA

WASHINGTON
· Seattle
▲ Mt. Rainier
14,410 ft. (4,390 m)
▲ Mt. St. Helens
9,680 ft. (2,950 m)

Columbia Plateau

MONTANA

NORTH DAKOTA

Missouri River

COAST RANGES

CASCADE RANGE

OREGON

IDAHO

ROCKY MOUNTAINS

Yellowstone River

GREAT PLAINS

TETON RANGE

WYOMING

SOUTH DAKOTA

BLACK HILLS

Cape Mendocino

INTERMOUNTAIN

WASATCH RANGE

Continental Divide

Snake River

Great Salt Lake

Great Salt Lake Desert

Great Basin

NEVADA

COAST RANGES

SIERRA NEVADA

San Francisco ·

San Jose ·

Central Valley

Sacramento River

San Joaquin River

CALIFORNIA

▲ Mt. Whitney
14,490 ft. (4,420 m)

AREA

Great Basin Desert

UTAH

FRONT RANGE

Mt. Elbert
14,430 ft. (4,400 m)

· Denver

COLORADO
▲ Pikes Peak
14,110 ft. (4,300 m)

North Platte River

South Platte River

NEBRASKA

Platte River

KANSAS

INTERIOR

Death Valley

Mojave Desert

Los Angeles

Grand Canyon

Lake Mead

Colorado River

Painted Desert

Colorado Plateau

ROCKY MOUNTAINS

Divide

PACIFIC OCEAN

Salton Sea

San Diego ·

Imperial Valley

ARIZONA

Sonoran Desert

Phoenix ·

Gila River

NEW MEXICO

OKLAHOMA

Gulf of California

Continental

· El Paso

Pecos River

TEXAS

Chihuahuan Desert

Rio Grande

Brazos River

San Antonio ·

MEXICO

Alaska inset

SOVIET UNION

ARCTIC OCEAN

BROOKS RANGE

Arctic Circle

ALASKA

▲ Mt. McKinley
20,320 ft. (6,190 m)

ALASKA RANGE

CANADA

Bering Strait

Bering Sea

548

ALEUTIAN ISLANDS

PACIFIC OCEAN

0   250   500 Miles
0   250   500   750 Kilometers

Hawaii inset

Tropic of Cancer

Kauai

PACIFIC OCEAN

Oahu **HAWAII**

Honolulu

Maui

Mauna Kea
13,800 ft. (4,210 m) ▲

Hawaii

0   100   200 Miles
0   100   200   300 Kilometers

SIERRA MADRE

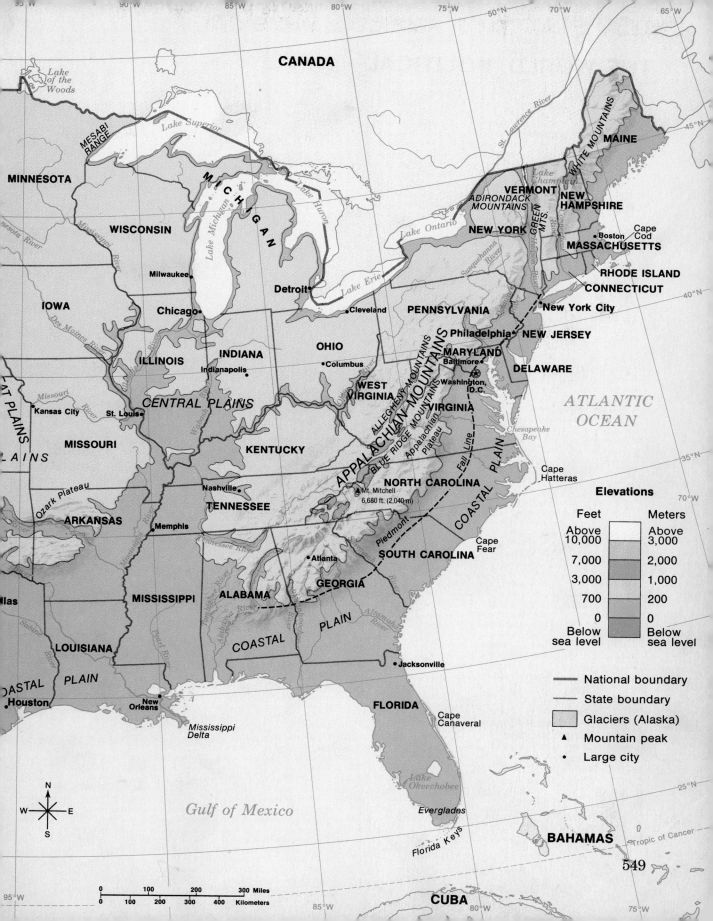

CANADA

Lake of the Woods

MESABI RANGE

Lake Superior

MINNESOTA

WISCONSIN

MICHIGAN

Lake Michigan

Lake Huron

IOWA

Milwaukee

Detroit

Chicago

Cleveland

ILLINOIS

INDIANA

OHIO

St. Lawrence River

Lake Champlain

WHITE MOUNTAINS

MAINE

VERMONT

NEW HAMPSHIRE

ADIRONDACK MOUNTAINS

GREEN MTS.

NEW YORK

Lake Ontario

Boston

Cape Cod

MASSACHUSETTS

RHODE ISLAND

CONNECTICUT

Lake Erie

PENNSYLVANIA

New York City

Philadelphia

NEW JERSEY

MARYLAND

DELAWARE

Columbus

Baltimore

Indianapolis

WEST VIRGINIA

Washington, D.C.

CENTRAL PLAINS

Kansas City

St. Louis

MISSOURI

KENTUCKY

Nashville

TENNESSEE

Memphis

ARKANSAS

Ozark Plateau

GREAT PLAINS

ALLEGHENY MOUNTAINS

APPALACHIAN MOUNTAINS

BLUE RIDGE MOUNTAINS

Appalachian Plateau

VIRGINIA

Fall Line

Chesapeake Bay

ATLANTIC OCEAN

Cape Hatteras

Mt. Mitchell 6,680 ft. (2,040 m)

NORTH CAROLINA

COASTAL PLAIN

Piedmont

Cape Fear

SOUTH CAROLINA

Atlanta

GEORGIA

ALABAMA

MISSISSIPPI

COASTAL PLAIN

Jacksonville

LOUISIANA

Houston

New Orleans

Mississippi Delta

FLORIDA

Cape Canaveral

Gulf of Mexico

Lake Okeechobee

Everglades

Florida Keys

CUBA

BAHAMAS

Tropic of Cancer

Elevations

Feet	Meters
Above 10,000	Above 3,000
7,000	2,000
3,000	1,000
700	200
0	0
Below sea level	Below sea level

— National boundary

— State boundary

▢ Glaciers (Alaska)

▲ Mountain peak

• Large city

0   100   200   300 Miles

0   100 200 300 400 Kilometers

N W E S

549

THE WORLD: POLITICAL

—— National boundary

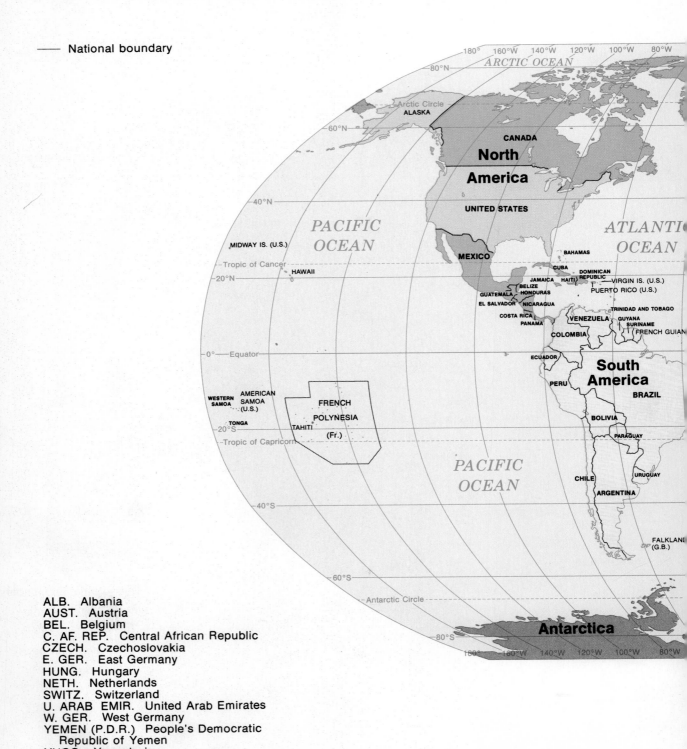

ALB.   Albania
AUST.   Austria
BEL.   Belgium
C. AF. REP.   Central African Republic
CZECH.   Czechoslovakia
E. GER.   East Germany
HUNG.   Hungary
NETH.   Netherlands
SWITZ.   Switzerland
U. ARAB EMIR.   United Arab Emirates
W. GER.   West Germany
YEMEN (P.D.R.)   People's Democratic
   Republic of Yemen
YUGO.   Yugoslavia

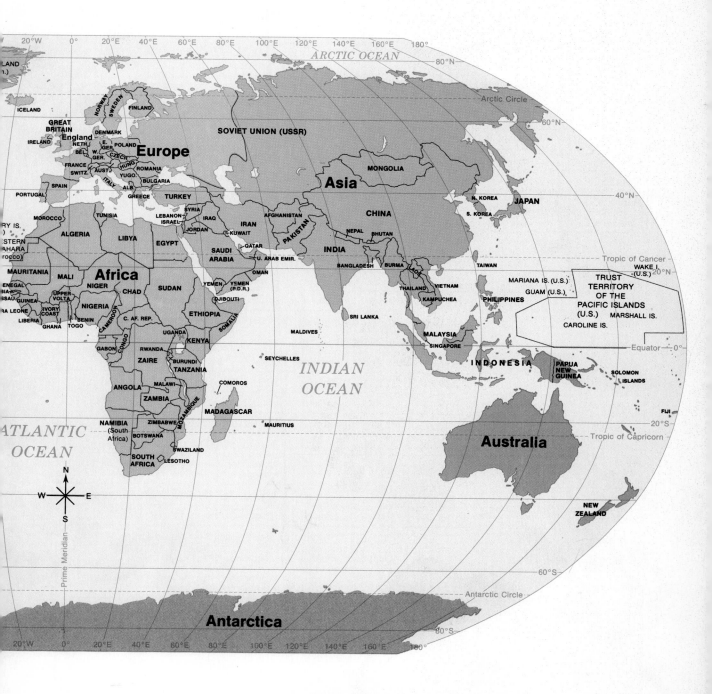

20°W | 0° | 20°E | 40°E | 60°E | 80°E | 100°E | 120°E | 140°E | 160°E | 180°

ARCTIC OCEAN

80°N

Arctic Circle

60°N

ICELAND

NORWAY SWEDEN FINLAND

GREAT
BRITAIN
IRELAND   England   DENMARK
                    NETH.   I.E.   POLAND
                    BEL. W.   GER. CZECH.
            FRANCE   GER.   HUNG.
                 SWITZ. AUST.   ROMANIA
                      ITALY YUGO. BULGARIA
PORTUGAL   SPAIN   ALB.
                    GREECE   TURKEY

Europe

SOVIET UNION (USSR)

Asia

MONGOLIA

N. KOREA   JAPAN
S. KOREA

40°N

MOROCCO   TUNISIA
                    LEBANON   SYRIA
                    ISRAEL   IRAQ   IRAN
ALGERIA   LIBYA   JORDAN   KUWAIT
                              QATAR
EGYPT   SAUDI   U. ARAB EMIR.
            ARABIA
                    OMAN

AFGHANISTAN
            PAKISTAN
                  NEPAL BHUTAN
            INDIA
                  BANGLADESH   BURMA
                                    LAOS
                              TAIWAN

CHINA

Tropic of Cancer

WAKE I.
(U.S.)

20°N

RY IS.
(   )
STERN
SAHARA
(rocco)

MAURITANIA
                  MALI   NIGER
SENEGAL   CHAD   SUDAN
BIA   UPPER
SSAU   GUINEA   VOLTA
RA LEONE   IVORY   NIGERIA
LIBERIA   COAST   BENIN
        GHANA TOGO   CAMEROON
                    CONGO   C. AF. REP.

Africa

YEMEN   YEMEN
            (P.D.R.)
DJIBOUTI

ETHIOPIA

UGANDA
            KENYA
GABON
        RWANDA
ZAIRE   BURUNDI
            TANZANIA

THAILAND
            KAMPUCHEA
VIETNAM

PHILIPPINES

MARIANA IS. (U.S.)
GUAM (U.S.)

MARSHALL IS.

CAROLINE IS.

MALDIVES

SRI LANKA

SEYCHELLES

MALAYSIA
SINGAPORE

TRUST
TERRITORY
OF THE
PACIFIC ISLANDS
(U.S.)

Equator   0°

ANGOLA   MALAWI
ZAMBIA

COMOROS

**INDIAN
OCEAN**

INDONESIA

PAPUA
NEW
GUINEA

SOLOMON
ISLANDS

MOZAMBIQUE
MADAGASCAR

NAMIBIA
(South
Africa)   ZIMBABWE
BOTSWANA
        SWAZILAND
SOUTH   LESOTHO
AFRICA

MAURITIUS

FIJI

20°S

ATLANTIC
OCEAN

Australia

Tropic of Capricorn

N
W   E
S

NEW
ZEALAND

60°S

Antarctic Circle

Antarctica

80°S

20°W | 0° | 20°E | 40°E | 60°E | 80°E | 100°E | 120°E | 140°E | 160°E | 180°

Prime Meridian

0   500   1,000   1,500   2,000 Miles
0   1,000   2,000   Kilometers

551

ALMANAC ★★★★★★★★★★★★★★★★★★★★★★★★★★★★★★★★★★★★★

FACTS ABOUT THE STATES

STATE	YEAR OF STATEHOOD	1980 POPULATION	AREA (sq. mi.)	CAPITAL	ORIGIN OF STATE NAME
Alabama	1819	3,890,061	51,609	Montgomery	Choctaw, *alba ayamule*, "one who clears the land and gathers food from it"
Alaska	1959	400,481	586,412	Juneau	Eskimo, *alayeksa*, "great land"
Arizona	1912	2,717,866	113,909	Phoenix	Papago, *arizonac*, "place of the small spring"
Arkansas	1836	2,285,513	53,104	Little Rock	Sioux, "land of the south wind people"
California	1850	23,668,562	158,693	Sacramento	Spanish, "an earthly paradise"
Colorado	1876	2,888,834	104,247	Denver	Spanish, "red land; red earth"
Connecticut	1788	3,107,576	5,009	Hartford	Mohican, *quinnitukqut*, "at the long tidal river"
Delaware	1787	595,225	2,057	Dover	Named for Lord de la Warr
Florida	1845	9,739,992	58,560	Tallahassee	Spanish, "land of flowers"
Georgia	1788	5,464,265	58,876	Atlanta	Named for King George II of England
Hawaii	1959	965,000	6,450	Honolulu	Polynesian, *Hawaiki* or *Owykee*, "homeland"
Idaho	1890	943,935	83,557	Boise	Shoshone, "light on the mountains"
Illinois	1818	11,418,461	56,400	Springfield	Algonquian, *iliniwek*, "men" or "warriors"
Indiana	1816	5,490,179	36,291	Indianapolis	Indian + a = "land of the Indians"
Iowa	1846	2,913,387	56,290	Des Moines	Dakota, *ayuba*, "beautiful land"
Kansas	1861	2,363,208	82,264	Topeka	Sioux, "land of the south wind people"
Kentucky	1782	3,661,433	40,395	Frankfort	Iroquois, *Kentake*, "meadow land"
Louisiana	1812	4,203,972	48,523	Baton Rouge	Named for King Louis XIV of France
Maine	1820	1,124,660	33,215	Augusta	Named after a French province
Maryland	1788	4,216,446	10,577	Annapolis	Named for Henrietta Maria, Queen Consort of Charles I of England
Massachusetts	1788	5,737,037	8,257	Boston	Algonquian, "at the big hill; place of the big hill"
Michigan	1837	9,258,344	58,216	Lansing	Chippewa, *mica gama*, "big water"
Minnesota	1858	4,077,148	84,068	St. Paul	Dakota Sioux, "sky-blue water"
Mississippi	1817	2,520,638	47,716	Jackson	Chippewa, *mici sibi*, "big river"
Missouri	1821	4,917,444	69,686	Jefferson City	Algonquian, "muddy water" or "people of the big canoes"
Montana	1889	786,690	147,138	Helena	Spanish, "mountainous"
Nebraska	1867	1,570,006	77,227	Lincoln	Omaha, *ni-bthaska*, "river in the flatness"
Nevada	1864	799,184	110,540	Carson City	Spanish, "snowy; snowed upon"
New Hampshire	1788	920,610	9,304	Concord	Named for Hampshire County, England
New Jersey	1787	7,364,158	7,836	Trenton	Named for the Isle of Jersey
New Mexico	1912	1,299,968	121,666	Santa Fe	Named by Spanish explorers from Mexico
New York	1788	17,577,288	49,576	Albany	Named after the Duke of York

STATE	YEAR OF STATEHOOD	1980 POPULATION	AREA (sq. mi.)	CAPITAL	ORIGIN OF STATE NAME
North Carolina	1789	5,874,429	52,586	Raleigh	Named after King Charles II of England
North Dakota	1889	652,695	70,665	Bismarck	Sioux, *dakota*, "friend; ally"
Ohio	1803	10,797,419	41,222	Columbus	Iroquois, *oheo*, "beautiful, beautiful water"
Oklahoma	1907	3,025,266	69,919	Oklahoma City	Choctaw, "red people"
Oregon	1859	2,632,663	96,981	Salem	Algonquian, *wauregan*, "beautiful water"
Pennsylvania	1787	11,866,728	45,333	Harrisburg	Penn + *sylvania* meaning "Penn's woods"
Rhode Island	1790	947,154	1,214	Providence	Dutch, "red-clay island"
South Carolina	1788	3,119,208	31,055	Columbia	Named after King Charles II of England
South Dakota	1889	690,178	77,047	Pierre	Sioux, *dakota*, "friend; ally"
Tennessee	1796	4,590,750	42,244	Nashville	Name of a Cherokee village
Texas	1845	14,288,383	267,338	Austin	Indian, *texia*, "friend; ally"
Utah	1896	1,461,037	84,916	Salt Lake City	"Land of the Ute" (an Indian tribe)
Vermont	1791	511,456	9,609	Montpelier	French, *vert*, "green" and *mont*, "mountain"
Virginia	1788	5,346,279	40,817	Richmond	Named after Elizabeth I of England
Washington	1889	4,130,163	68,192	Olympia	Named for George Washington
West Virginia	1863	1,949,644	24,181	Charleston	From the English-named state of Virginia
Wisconsin	1848	4,705,335	56,154	Madison	Possibly Algonquian, meaning "grassy place" or "place of the beaver"
Wyoming	1890	470,816	97,914	Cheyenne	Algonquian, *mache-weaming*, "at the big flats"
District of Columbia		637,651	67		Named after Christopher Columbus

PRESIDENTS OF THE UNITED STATES

NAME	YEARS IN OFFICE	HOME STATE	NAME	YEARS IN OFFICE	HOME STATE
George Washington (1732–1799)	1789–1797	VA	Chester A. Arthur (1830–1886)	1881–1885	NY
John Adams (1735–1826)	1797–1801	MA	Grover Cleveland (1837–1908)	1885–1889	NY
Thomas Jefferson (1743–1826)	1801–1809	VA	Benjamin Harrison (1833–1901)	1889–1893	IN
James Madison (1751–1836)	1809–1817	VA	Grover Cleveland	1893–1897	NY
James Monroe (1758–1831)	1817–1825	VA	William McKinley (1843–1901)	1897–1901	OH
John Quincy Adams (1767–1848)	1825–1829	MA	Theodore Roosevelt (1858–1919)	1901–1909	NY
Andrew Jackson (1767–1845)	1829–1837	TE	William Howard Taft (1857–1930)	1909–1913	OH
Martin Van Buren (1782–1862)	1837–1841	NY	Woodrow Wilson (1856–1924)	1913–1921	NJ
William Henry Harrison (1773–1841)	1841	OH	Warren G. Harding (1865–1923)	1921–1923	OH
John Tyler (1790–1862)	1841–1845	VA	Calvin Coolidge (1872–1933)	1923–1929	MA
James K. Polk (1795–1849)	1845–1849	TE	Herbert Hoover (1874–1964)	1929–1933	CA
Zachary Taylor (1784–1850)	1849–1850	LA	Franklin D. Roosevelt (1882–1945)	1933–1945	NY
Millard Fillmore (1800–1874)	1850–1853	NY	Harry S. Truman (1884–1972)	1945–1953	MO
Franklin Pierce (1804–1869)	1853–1857	NH	Dwight D. Eisenhower (1890–1969)	1953–1961	KA
James Buchanan (1791–1868)	1857–1861	PA	John F. Kennedy (1917–1963)	1961–1963	MA
Abraham Lincoln (1809–1865)	1861–1865	IL	Lyndon B. Johnson (1908–1973)	1963–1969	TX
Andrew Johnson (1808–1875)	1865–1869	TE	Richard M. Nixon (1913–)	1969–1974	CA
Ulysses S. Grant (1822–1885)	1869–1877	IL	Gerald R. Ford (1913–)	1974–1977	MI
Rutherford B. Hayes (1822–1893)	1877–1881	OH	Jimmy Carter (1924–)	1977–1981	GA
James A. Garfield (1831–1881)	1881	OH	Ronald Reagan (1911–)	1981–	CA

Glossary

This glossary contains important social studies words and their definitions. Each word is pronounced as it would be in a dictionary. When you see this mark ′ after a syllable, pronounce that syllable with more force than the other syllables. The page number at the end of the definition tells where to find the word in your book.

add, āce, câre, pälm; end, ēqual; it, īce; odd, ōpen, ôrder; took, pool; up, bûrn;
yoo as u in *fuse*; oil; pout; ə as a in *above*, e in *sicken*, i in *possible*, o in *melon*, u in *circus*;
check; ring; thin; this; zh as in vision

---

abolitionist (ab•ə•lish′ə•nist) A person wishing to end slavery. (p. 344)

acid rain (as′id rān) A condition that occurs when air pollutants combine with moisture in the atmosphere. (p. 519)

agriculture (ag′rə•kul•chər) Farming. (p. 23)

Allies (al′īz) The countries that fought together on one side during World War I and World War II. (p. 452)

ally (al′ī) A friend in war. (p. 219)

amendment (ə•mend′mənt) An addition to the Constitution. (p. 276)

apprentice (ə•pren′tis) Someone who works for a person skilled in a craft in order to learn that craft. (p. 182)

archaeologist (är•kē•ol′ə•jist) A scientist who studies remains and artifacts to learn about the past. (p. 31)

archaeology (är•kē•ol′ə•jē) The scientific study of artifacts and remains. (p. 31)

armistice (är′mə•stis) A written agreement to stop fighting. (p. 438)

artifact (är′tə•fakt) An object used by people in the past. (p. 31)

assassination (ə•sas•ə•nā′shən) Murder for a political reason. (p. 378)

assembly (ə•sem′blē) A lawmaking body. (p. 50)

assembly line (ə•sem′blē līn) A system of work where the product to be assembled moves on a conveyor belt from one work station to another, while the worker stays in one place. (p. 446)

astronaut (as′trə•nôt) An explorer of the moon and outer space. (p. 83)

astronomy (ə•stron′ə•mē) The study of the stars. (p. 83)

barter (bär′tər) A system of exchanging goods and services without using money. (p. 161)

Bill of Rights (bil uv rīts) The first ten amendments to the Constitution. (p. 277)

blockade (blo•kād′) The use of warships to prevent other ships from entering or leaving a harbor. (p. 362)

boycott (boi′kot) To refuse to buy something in order to show disapproval. (p. 223)

broker (brō′ker) A person who gets paid to buy and sell for someone else. (p. 193)

bureaucracy (byoo•rok′rə•sē) A body of government officials and employees. (p. 462)

Cabinet (kab′ə•nit) People chosen by the President to be his advisers and to head executive departments. (p. 277)

caravel (kar′ə•vel) An ocean-going sailboat. (p. 75)

carpetbagger (kär′pit•bag•ər) A Northerner who moved to the South to make a new life soon after the Civil War. (p. 393)

cash crop (kash krop) A crop grown to sell and make a profit. (p. 189)

casualty (kazh′oo•əl•tē) A person who has been killed or wounded in a war. (p. 368)

cavalry (kav′əl•rē) A group made up of soldiers who ride horses. (p. 363)

century (sen′chə•rē) A period of 100 years. (p. 33)

checks and balances (chekz and bal′ənsz) A system where each branch of the government has controls on the power of the other branches. (p. 274)

civilian (sə•vil′yən) A person who is not a soldier. (p. 467)

civilization (siv•ə•lə•zā′shən) A way of life that has large cities, complex government, and highly developed arts and sciences. (p. 23)

civil rights (siv′əl rīts) The rights of citizens to equal treatment, both in law and in practice. (p. 477)

colonist (kol′ə•nist) A person who comes from a mother country to live in a colony. (p. 103)

colony (kol′ə•nē) A settlement ruled by a faraway country. (p. 103)

compact (kom′pakt) A written agreement. (p. 136)

compass (kum′pəs) An instrument used for finding directions. (p. 75)

compromise (kom′prə•mīz) To give up some of what one wants in order to reach an agreement. (p. 272)

conquistador (kon•kis′tə•dôr) A Spanish conqueror. (p. 91)

conservation (kon•sər•vā′shən) Using a natural resource in a way that keeps it from being wasted or destroyed. (p. 426)

constitutional (kon•stə•too′shən•əl) Lawful according

to the United States Constitution. (p. 274)

corporation (kôr•pə•rā′shən) A company owned by stockholders who have each invested money in the company. (p. 410)

creditor (kred′i•tər) A person to whom money is owed. (p. 270)

culture (kul′chər) The way of life shared by a group of people. (p. 24)

debate (di•bāt′) A formal, public argument. (p. 351)

debtor (det′ər) A person who owes money. (p. 270)

decade (dek′ād) A period of ten years. (p. 32)

declaration (dek•lə•rā′shən) A formal statement. (p. 237)

delegate (del′ə•gāt) A person elected by people to represent them. (p. 174)

democracy (di•mok′rə•sē) Rule by the people. (p. 276)

dictator (dik′tā•tər) A ruler who has no respect for individual rights. (p. 465)

economy (i•kon′ə•mē) The way people use resources to produce and sell goods and services. (p. 189)

editorial (ed•i•tôr′ē•əl) An article that gives the opinion of the editor. (p. 450)

engineer (en•jə•nir′) A person who is responsible for designing something and seeing that it is built. (p. 307)

equator (i•kwā′tər) The imaginary line that circles the Earth halfway between the North Pole and the South Pole. (p. 2)

executive (ig•zek′yə•tiv) The management branch of the government. (p. 274)

export (eks′ pôrt) A product sent out from a country to another country. (p. 166)

fact (fakt) A statement that can be proved true. (p. 366)

fall line (fôl līn) The point where a river drops from the foothills to the plains, forming a waterfall. (p. 12)

federal (fed′ər•əl) A form of government where powers are shared between the states and the national government. (p. 272)

federation (fed•ə•rā′shən) An organization formed of many related groups, for instance, skilled workers in different trades. (p. 403)

flint (flint) A hard stone commonly used for tools during the Stone Age. (p. 20)

frontier (frun•tir′) The area that separates settled land and the wilderness. (p. 164)

fugitive (fyōō′jə•tiv) A person seeking escape, such as from slavery. (p. 344)

geography (jē•og′rə•fē) The study of the surface of the Earth and how people use the Earth. (p. 6)

glacier (glā′shər) A large sheet of ice. (p. 19)

graph (graf) A visual way of comparing amounts. (p. 170)

guarantee (gar•ən•tē′) A written promise that something will work. (p. 398)

hemisphere (hem′ə•sfir) Half a sphere. (p. 2)

heritage (her′ə•tij) A common way of thinking, believing, and doing things. (p. 1)

historian (his•tôr′ē•ən) A person who studies the past. (p. 1)

history (his′tə•rē) The study of past events. (p. 1)

homesteader (hōm′ste•dər) A person who was given 160 acres of land by the government after living on it for five years. (p. 418)

House of Representatives (hous uv rep•ri•zen′tə•tivz) One of the two parts of Congress. (p. 274)

immigrant (im′ə•grənt) A person who comes from one country to live in another country. (p. 179)

import (im′pôrt) A product brought into a country from another country. (p. 166)

inauguration (in•ô•gyə•rā′shən) The ceremony at which the President takes the oath of office. (p. 355)

indentured servant (in•den′chərd sur′vənt) A person who agreed to work for a period of time in the colonies in exchange for ocean passage. (p. 132)

independence (in•di•pen′dəns) Freedom from control by others (p. 240)

indigo (in′də•gō) A plant that produces a blue dye. (p. 189)

industrial (in•dus′trē•əl) An area having many factories. (p. 396)

Industrial Revolution (in•dus′trē•əl rev•ə•lōō′shən) The great growth of technology during which factories and machines replaced craft shops and hand tools. (p. 395)

inflation (in•flā′shən) A situation that occurs when prices rise faster than wages. (p. 142)

influence (in′flōō•əns) The power of people or things to act on others. (p. 176)

integration (in•tə•grā′•shən) Full equality of the races in the use of public facilities. (p. 481)

interchangeable part (in•tər•chān′jə•bəl pärt) A part that can be taken out of one machine or object and put into another similar one. (p. 316)

invest (in•vest′) To use money with the hope of making a profit. (p. 398)

journal (jûr′nəl) A daily record. (p. 83)

judicial (jōō•dish′əl) The branch of government that is the court system. (p. 274)

labor union (lā′bər yōōn′yən) An organization of workers formed to protect their interests. (p. 403)

land bridge (land brij) A piece of land connecting Asia and North America during the Ice Age. (p. 19)

league (lēg) A union of people joined for a common purpose. (p. 44)

legend (lej'ənd) A story about the past that may or may not be true. (p. 92)

legislative (lej'is•lā•tiv) The lawmaking branch of government. (p. 274)

legislature (lej'is•lā•chər) A state lawmaking body. (p. 392)

liberty (lib'ər•tē) Freedom. (p. 222)

lines of latitude (līnz uv lat'ə•tood) The imaginary lines on the Earth that run in an east-west direction. They are used to locate points on the Earth. (p. 124)

lines of longitude (līnz uv lon'jə•tood) The imaginary lines on the Earth that run in a north-south direction. They are used to locate points on the Earth. (p. 124)

locks (lokz) A system that allows boats to go higher and lower within a canal. (p. 308)

majority (mə•jôr'ə•tē) The greater number of people. (p. 276)

mercenary (mûr'sə•ner•ē) A hired soldier. (p. 240)

militia (mə•lish'ə) A military unit made up of volunteers. (p. 159)

minister (min'is•tər) A person who heads a department of the executive branch within the Canadian system of government. (p. 518)

mission (mish'ən) The settlement of a missionary that included a church and the buildings necessary for farming and ranching. (p. 105)

missionary (mish'ən•er•ē) A priest who hoped to convert the Indians to the Christian faith. (p. 105)

monopoly (mə•nop'ə•lē) Complete control over a product or service. (p. 226)

naval stores (nā'vəl stôrz) The planks, masts, pitch, tar and turpentine used in shipbuilding. (p. 155)

navigable (nav'ə•gə•bəl) Rivers that are wide, deep, and gentle enough for cargo-carrying boats. (p. 155)

navigation (nav•ə•gā'shən) The science of figuring out a ship's direction and location and the distance it travels. (p. 75)

neutral (noo'trəl) Not taking sides in a war. (p. 292)

New Deal (noo dēl) The plan of President Franklin Roosevelt designed to end the depression through new government programs. (p. 462)

nomad (nō'mad) A person who has no fixed dwelling but generally moves and lives within a defined territory. (p. 47)

no-man's-land (nō•mans•land) The land separating opposing armies in trench warfare. (p. 453)

office (ôf'is) A job held to achieve the good of the community. (p. 158)

official (ə•fish'əl) A person either elected or appointed to do a community or government job. (p. 158)

opinion (ə•pin'yən) A statement that cannot be proved true. (p. 366)

Parliament (pär'lə•mənt) The lawmaking body of England. (p. 221)

Patriot (pā'trē•ət) A person who believed that the American colonists had the right to stand up for their liberties. (p. 237)

petition (pə•tish'ən) A written request, such as to Parliament. (p. 221)

piecework (pēs'wûrk) Work done and paid for by the piece. (p. 401)

piedmont (pēd'mont) Gently rolling hills at the base of mountains. (p. 2)

Pilgrim (pil'grim) A person who makes a journey for a religious reason; a person from England who settled at Plymouth. (p. 135)

pioneer (pī•ə•nir') One of the first people to settle or enter a new territory. (p. 285)

plantation (plan•tā'shən) A large, Southern farm. (p. 193)

poll tax (pōl taks) A tax paid in order to vote. (p. 394)

population density (pop•yə•lā'shən den'sə•tē) The number of people living in an area. (p. 352)

prejudice (prej'oo•dis) Making negative judgments about people because, for instance, of their race or religion. (p. 405)

President (prez'ə•dent) The head of the executive, or management, branch of government. (p. 274)

Prime Meridian (prīm mə•rid'ē•ən) The line of longitude that is labeled zero degrees. (p. 125)

profit (prof'it) The money left over after expenses have been paid. (p. 129)

proprietor (prə•prī'ə•tər) A person who owned and ruled a colony. (p. 174)

prosper (pros'pər) To do well. (p. 131)

province (prov'ins) A political region in Canada, like a state in the United States. (p. 516)

public service (pub'lik sûr'vis) Doing a job to help the community. (p. 195)

Puritan (pyoor'ə•tən) A person who disapproved of many practices of the Church of England and wished to make it more "pure." For this reason many Puritans left England to settle in New England. (p. 141)

Quaker (kwā'kər) A person belonging to a religion that believes in a simple, peaceful life and in the equality and goodness of all people. (p. 178)

quartered (kwôr'tərd) To be housed. (p. 227)

ratify (rat'ə•fī) To approve by voting. (p. 393)

rationing (rash'ə•ning) Limiting what people can buy. (p. 466)

reaper (rē'pər) A machine used to harvest grain. (p. 398)

Reconstruction (rē•kən•struk'shən) The government plan for rebuilding the South after the Civil War. (p. 391)

reform (ri•fôrm′) A change for the better. (p. 426)

refuge (ref′yōōj) A place of safety. (p. 178)

region (rē′jən) A part of the country that is alike in some way, for instance in geography. (p. 13)

regulate (reg′yə•lāt) To set rules for something. (p. 444)

repeal (ri•pēl′) To withdraw or cancel. (p. 222)

republic (ri•pub′lik) A form of government in which people elect representatives. (p. 269)

reservation (rez•ər•vā′shən) A piece of land on which Indians live. (p. 57)

restore (ri•stôr′) To return something, such as a building, to its original appearance. (p. 209)

revolution (rev•ə•lōō′shən) A large, sudden change in government and people's lives. (p. 216)

robot (rō′bot) A machine that can do human tasks. (p. 491)

saga (sä′gə) A story about the deeds of the Vikings. (p. 71)

satellite (sat′ə•līt) A natural or man-made body that revolves around a planet. (p. 475)

scandal (skan′dəl) Any action that brings disgrace. (p. 483)

scurvy (skûr′vē) A disease caused by lack of vitamin C. (p. 84)

sea dog (sē dôg) A pirate commander of an English warship. (p. 116)

secede (si•sēd′) To withdraw from the union of the United States. (p. 355)

secession (si•sesh′ən) A state withdrawing from the United States. (p. 350)

second-class citizen (sek′ənd•klas′ sit′ə•zən) A person who does not have the full rights of citizenship. (p. 392)

secret ballot (sē′krit bal′ət) A way to vote without anyone knowing how one has voted. (p. 393)

segregation (seg•rə•gā′shən) Separation of people by race. (p. 394)

shaman (shä′mən) An Indian leader who is a priest and a healer. (p. 37)

sharecropper (shâr′krop•ər) A person who farms a rented piece of land and pays the landowner with a share of his crops. (p. 392)

slash and burn (slash and bûrn) A method of agriculture where a field was burned, cleared, and used, then abandoned for a new field. (p. 42)

society (sə•sī′ə•tē) A broad grouping of people who are bound by common laws, traditions, and activities. (p. 195)

space shuttle (spās shut′l) A spacecraft that can travel from Earth into space and back again. (p. 488)

specialize (spesh′əl•īz) To spend most of one's time doing one kind of job. (p. 23)

sphere (sfir) Anything shaped like a ball. (p. 2)

staple food (stā′pəl fōōd) The food that people depend on most for nourishment. (p. 50)

stock (stok) Shares of ownership in a company. (p. 129)

stock market (stok mär′kit) A place where people can buy and sell stocks. (p. 459)

stockyard (stok′yärd) A large cattle pen. (p. 417)

stoop (stōōp) A wide, high doorstep. (p. 177)

strait (strāt) A narrow passageway between two bodies of water. (p. 19)

strategy (strat′ə•jē) A long-range plan. (p. 362)

suffrage (suf′rij) The right to vote. (p. 447)

Supreme Court (sə•prēm′ kôrt) The court within the judicial branch of the government that has the power to decide whether laws are constitutional. (p. 274)

surplus (sûr′plus) An amount more than what is needed. (p. 23)

survey (sər•vā′) To measure the land. (p. 270)

sweatshop (swet′shop) A small factory that has poor working conditions. (p. 402)

synthetic (sin•thet′ik) A man-made material. (p. 485)

technology (tek•nol′ə•jē) Using tools and knowledge to achieve practical aims. (p. 314)

tenant farmer (ten′ənt fär′mər) A person who farms a rented piece of land, owns his animals and tools, and pays the landowner with either crops or money. (p. 392)

tenement (ten′ə•mənt) A crowded, run-down apartment house. (p. 401)

territory (ter′ə•tôr•ē) An area of land belonging to a government. (p. 270)

tidewater (tīd′wô•tər) A low, coastal plain full of waterways. (p. 189)

totem (tō′tem) A spirit being. (p. 52)

township (toun′ship) A square of land measuring 6 miles on each side. (p. 270)

treaty (trēt′ē) A formal agreement to maintain peace. (p. 254)

trial by jury (trī′əl bī jōōr′ē) A trial in which a person accused of breaking the law is judged by a group of fellow citizens. (p. 220)

tributary (trib′yə•ter•ē) A stream or river that flows into another river. (p. 11)

tyranny (tir′ə•nē) Harsh and unjust rule. (p. 227)

unemployment (un•im•ploi′mənt) The number of people without jobs. (p. 462)

veto (vē′tō) To refuse to sign a proposed law. (p. 274)

viceroy (vīs′roi) A ruler appointed as a representative of a king. (p. 93)

warranty (wôr′ən•tē) A manufacturer's promise to fix or replace a product that stops working. (p. 479)

Index

George III, King of England, 223, 240
George's Bank, 519–20
Georgia, 102, 189, 192, 355
Germany
  in American Revolution, 240, 248–49, 258
  in World War I, 452–54
  in World War II, 464–65, 467, 469–70
German immigrants, 179–80, 316, 359, 401
Geronimo, 424
Gettysburg Address, 372, 373
Gettysburg, Battle of, 370–72
Glaciers, 19, 69, 155
Gold, 97, 270
  in Black Hills, 422
  in California, 324–25, 363
  Chinese seeking, 403–04
  English seeking, 116–18
  French seeking, 113
  in Georgia, 301
  in Klondike, Alas., 440
  Spanish seeking, 81–82, 91–105
Gompers, Samuel, 402–03
Government
  of Britain, 221
  of Canada, 512, 516–18
  of colonies, 132, 134, 136, 138, 143, 158, 174, 190, 195
  of Mexico, 534–35
  of U.S., 272–73, 274–76
  See also Articles of Confederation; Constitution; Political parties; Presidents; Self government;
Grand Banks, 111, 114, 504, 519
Grand Canyon, 12, 99, 444
Grant, Ulysses, S., 364, 374–77
Great Britain
  See Britain
Great Lakes, 12, 24, 293, 307
Great Plains
  See Plains
Great Salt Lake, 323
Greene, Nathanael, 250
Greenland, 69, 70, 72
Guam, 438–39
Guilford Courthouse, Battle of, 250
Gulf Stream, 540

H
Hamilton, Alexander, 277–79
Hancock, John, 229–30, 237, 256
Hartford, Conn., 146, 164
Hawaii, 265, 405, 439
Henry, Patrick, 227–28, 237
Henry, Prince of Portugal, 75–76
Hiawatha, 44
Hidalgo, Miguel, 529, 533
Hiroshima, Japan, 470, 471
Hitler, Adolf, 464, 469–70, 471
Hohokam culture, 28–29
Holocaust, 470
Homestead Act, 418
Honeyman, John, 258–59
Hooker, Thomas, 163
Hoover, Herbert, 459, 461
Hopewell culture, 24–25
Hopi Indians, 51, 57
Horses, 19, 21, 37, 48
  in battle, 91, 422
Horseshoe Bend, Battle of, 296
House of Burgesses, 132, 134, 343
House of Commons, British, 221
House of Commons, Canadian, 516–18
House of Lords, British, 221
House of Representatives, 274, 275
Houston, Sam, 317, 319
Hudson Bay, 120, 509
Hudson, Henry, 120–121, 509
Hudson River, 2, 120, 147, 307
Hudson's Bay Company, 509
Hull, Isaac, 294
Huron Indians, 112–14
Hutchinson, Anne, 163
Hydroelectric dams, 10, 463

I
Ice Age, 19, 505
Idaho, 425
Illinois, 298
Immigrants, 179, 401–05, 416, 439
  Asian, 439
  British, 401
  Chinese, 403–05, 416

in Civil War, 359
  Filipino, 439
  German, 179–80, 316, 359, 401
  Hungarian, 401
  Irish, 258, 308, 316, 359, 401, 416
  Italian, 359, 401
  Japanese, 405
  Mexican, 439
  Polish, 130, 316
  Portuguese, 439
  Russian, 401
  Scotch-Irish, 180–81
  Swedish, 401
Imports, 166, 223, 226, 227, 269, 341, 362
Inca Empire, 23–24, 95
Indentured servants, 132, 190, 197
Independence Day, 215, 241, 298
Indiana, 298, 396
Indians, American, 36–53, 57–61
  ancestors of, 19–21, 23–31
  and British, 133–34, 219, 220, 250
  of California, 50
  civil rights of, 276, 298, 482
  and French, 121–22, 219
  of Great Basin, 49
  and Indian Removal Act, 300–01
  in Kentucky, 286
  and Jamestown, 130
  map of cultural areas, 38
  of Northwest, 52
  and Pennsylvanians, 181
  and Pilgrims, 137–39
  of Plains, 46–48, 422
  of Plateau, 49–50
  and Quakers, 181
  ravaged by disease, 39, 103, 130, 137
  religion of, 17, 37, 45, 105
  of Southwest, 27–29, 51, 105
  of today, 57–61
  treaties with, 301, 422, 482
  and Williams, Roger, 163
  Woodland, 41–45
  See also names of particular groups
Indian wars, 37, 134, 164, 181, 217–19, 220, 285, 301, 510

in Kentucky, 286
  after Revolution, 284
  in the West, 422–24
Indies, 74, 83
Indigo, 189, 203
Industrial Revolution, 395–96, 426
Industry
  growth of in U.S., 306, 313–16, 341, 363, 389, 390, 395–400, 446, 490, 491
  See also Business; Economy; Trade
Inflation, 142, 270
  in Germany, 464
  in Mexico, 536
  in U.S., 477, 484, 490
Interchangeable parts, 316
International Date Line, 125
Intolerable Acts, 227
Inventions, 267, 310, 314–15, 398, 400, 428, 429, 435, 456
  Bessemer process, 395–96
  Edison's, 428, 429
  Franklin's, 183
  since 1950, 485–88, 491
  See also particular inventors or inventions; Technology
Iowa, 506
Irish immigrants, 258, 308, 316, 359, 401, 416
Iroquois Indians, 43–44, 61, 120, 285
Irrigation, 14–15, 28–29, 51, 323
  in Mexico, 536
  and Tennessee Valley Authority, 463
  See also Hydroelectric dams
Israel, peace agreement with Egypt, 484
Italy, 73–74, 79, 452, 464, 465, 467, 468

J
Jackson, Andrew, 296, 299–301, 303–04
Jackson, Thomas (Stonewall), 360–61, 363, 368, 370
James River, 129, 209
Jamestown, Va., 129–31, 132–33
Japan, 73–74, 442, 465, 466, 470, 536

PHOTOGRAPH ACKNOWLEDGMENTS

KEY: T, Top; B, Bottom; L, Left; C, Center; R, Right.
HBJ PHOTOS by Alec Duncan: 282BL, 409T, 410T, 410B.
HBJ PHOTO by Sal Fiorella: 61B
HBJ PHOTO by Dick Leonard: 59B.
HBJ PHOTO by Andrew Rakoczy: 545BR.
HBJ PHOTO by Elliot Varner Smith: 57B.

RESEARCH CREDITS: Tom Tracy: 8B. Wheelwright Museum of the American Indian, Herb Lotz Photography, *The Mountainway: Painting for the First Day,* collected by Franc J. Newcomb, ca. 1930, Cat. No. P9 #6: 16. Arizona State Museum, University of Arizona, LB91544, Helga Tiewes, photographer: 21BL. David Muench: 28B. Arizona State Museum, University of Arizona, Helga Tiewes, photographer: 29T. Milwaukee Public Museum: 39T. Museum of the American Indian, Heye Foundation: 44TL. The Granger Collection: 45T. Historical Pictures Service, Inc.: 46BR. Thomas Gilcrease Institute of American History & Art, Tulsa, Oklahoma, *Hunting Under Buffalo Skins*, George Catlin: 47T. National Museum of American Art, Smithsonian Institution, gift of Mrs. Joseph Harrison, Jr.: 48T. Edward Curtis: 50TL. Courtesy of Farm Journal, David O. Born: 58BL. Weiglen Photo: 60B. Jerry Jacka: 65BR. The British Library: 66. The Granger Collection: 70B. Parks, Canada: 71T. Historical Pictures Service, Inc.: 75BL. Scala/Art Resource: 80TL. The Granger Collection: 82T, 85T, 94BR. Stock, Boston, Eric Simmons: 95TL, 95TR. Historical Pictures Service, Inc.: 96T. Woodfin Camp & Associates, John Blaustein: 97TL. Woodfin Camp & Associates, Adam Woolfitt: 97LC. Photo Researchers, Inc., George Holton: 97TR. Remington Art Museum: 99B. National Park Service, painting by Robert Giese: 101TR. The Granger Collection: 102T. The Bettman Archive, Inc.: 103BR. The Granger Collection: 114T. The Bettman Archive, Inc.: 117TR, 118B. The Granger Collection: 119T. Tate Gallery, *The Last Voyage of the Henry Hudson*, John Collier: 121T. The Bettman Archive, Inc.: 122B. The Granger Collection: 123T, 130BR. Jamestown Yorktown Foundation: 131B. Colonial Williamsburg Photograph: 133B. Colonial National Historical Park, National Park Service: 143T. The Granger Collection: 136B, 137TR. Plimoth Plantation: 140T. American Antiquarian Society: 141BL. Museum of the City of New York, J. Clarence Davies Collection: 142B. The Bettman Archive, Inc.: 143T. Old Sturbridge Village: 144T. Plimoth Plantation: 151BL. The Granger Collection: 160T. Old Sturbridge Village, Robert Arnold, photographer: 161BL. The Bettman Archive, Inc.: 162T. Sampler, NYC-TE-64, Index of American Design, National Gallery of Art, Washington: 162BL. The Granger Collection: 164TL. Old Dartmouth Historical Society: 166T. Schomberg Collection for Research in Black Culture, New York Public Library, Lenox-Tilden Foundation: 168TR. Old Dartmouth Historical Society: 169T. Mystic Seaport Museum: 169C. Old Sturbridge Village, Henry Peach, photographer: 169B. Albany Institute of History & Art: 176B. Courtesy of Title Guarantee-New York: 177T. Metropolitan Museum of Art, Rogers Fund, 1923: 179T. Maryland Historical Society, Erik Kvalsvik, photographer: 180B. Courtesy of Shelburne Museum, Shelburne, Vermont: 181T. Compliments of Hercules Incorporated, Wilmington, Delaware, *Franklin the Printer*, Stanley Arthurs: 183TR. CIGNA Corporation, Philadelphia, Pennsylvania: 186TL. Museum of the City of New York: 186TC. The Smithsonian Institution, Brenda Gilmore, photographer: 186B. Enoch Pratt Free Library of Baltimore: 190TL. The Granger Collection: 192T. Colonial Williamsburg Photograph: 196TL. "Illustrations on pages 196BL, 206T, & 208B are reproduced from *A Window on Williamsburg*, published by the Colonial Williamsburg Foundation and distributed by Holt, Rhinehart and Winston." American Antiquarian Society: 198B. Library of Congress: 199B. Maryland Historical Society: 200BL. Colonial Williamsburg Photograph: 201BL, 207T, 207B, 208T, 209BL, 209BR. Historical Pictures Service, Inc.: 202T. The Image Bank, Jules Zalon: 214. Brown Brothers: 222T. The Granger Collection: 223T. New York Public Library, Manuscripts & Archives Division: 223B. Library of Congress: 225T. The Bettman Archive, Inc.: 226B. Historical Society of Pennsylvania: 228T. Historical Picture Services, Inc.: 231T. The Museum of Fine Arts, Boston, *Paul Revere*, John Singleton Copley: 232T. The Historical Collection of the Paul Revere Life Insurance Co.: 232TC, 232BC, 232B. The Bettman Archive, Inc.: 240TL. Yale University Art Gallery, *The Declaration of Independence*, John Trumbull: 241T. Woodfin Camp & Associates, William S. Weems: 242BL. Courtesy of Christie Manson and Woods International, Inc. *The Nation Makers*, Howard Pyle: 246T. Historical Picture Services, Inc.: 247B. The Metropolitan Museum of Art, gift of John Stewart Kennedy, 1897, *Washington Crossing the Delaware*, Emmanuel Gottlieb: 248T. Valley Forge Historical Society, *Washington at Valley Forge*, William Trego: 249T. United States Naval Academy Museum, *The Action Between His Majesty's Ship, Serapis and the Bonhomme Richard*: 251T. Brown University Library, Anne S.K. Brown Military Collection, *Marion Crossing the Peedee River*: 251B. Cliche Musees Nationaux, Paris, *Siege of Yorktown*, Louis-Nicholas Van Blarenberghe: 252T. National Gallery of Art, Washington, D.C., gift of Edgar William and Bernice Chrysler Garbisch, *A View of Mt. Vernon*, artist unknown: 255T. The Bridgeman Art Library: 266. Architect of the United States Capitol, Washington, D.C.: 272B. The Granger Collection: 276T, 276B. Massachusetts Historical Society, *Abigail Adams, Wife of John Adams*: 280T. New York State Historical Association, Cooperstown, *Abigail Adams*, Ralph Earle: 280B. The Granger Collection: 286BL, 287T. Lafayette College Art Collection: 289BR. Courtesy of Colorado Historical Society: 291T. The Granger Collection: 292BR. Maryland Historical Society: 295T. The Granger Collection: 296T. Office of Tourist Development, Frankfort, Kentucky: 297T. Field Museum of Natural History: 297C. The Granger Collection: 299B, 300BL. Jerome Tiger Art Co.: 301TL. Library of Congress: 302TR. Courtesy of the New York Historical Society: 302B. Library of Congress: 303BR. Reprinted courtesy of The Boston Globe: 305BR. New York Public Library, Lenox-Tilden Foundation: 309B. The Bettman Archive, Inc.: 312T. Yale University Art Gallery, Barfoot for Darton, *Progress of Cotton #9 Reeding or Drawing In*, The Mabel Brady Garven Collection: 314B. The Granger Collection: 315T. San Jacinto Museum of History Association: 318T. The Bettman Archive, Inc.: 318B. Library of Congress: 319T. The Granger Collection: 321T. Latter Day Saints Church, Museum of Church History & Art: 322B. New York. Historical Society: 324B. The Image Works, Mark Antman: 338. The Bettman Archive, Inc.: 343B. The Cincinatti Art Museum, *The Underground Railroad*, T. Webber: 345. The Bettman Archive, Inc.: 346T. The Granger Collection: 349BL. Brown University Library, Anne S.K. Brown Military Collection, *Battle of Hickory Point*: 350B. Courtesy of Illinois Secretary of State, Jim Edgar, *Lincoln-Douglas Debate, 1858*, Robert Marshall Root: 351T. The Granger Collection: 356T. *Lee and Jackson*, E.B.D. Fabrino Galio, owned by Mr. & Mrs. Charles J. Sinnott: 360BL. The Granger Collection: 361T. Virginia Historical Society, *The Four Seasons of the Confederacy, The Autumn Mural*, Charles Hoffbauer: 363T. *The Innocent Victim*, from the collection of Dr. Josephine A. Dolan, Ph.D., from "Nursing in Society, a Historical Perspective," W.B. Saunders Company (14th ed., 1978): 364B, 365T. National Portrait Gallery, Smithsonian Institution, on loan from Serence Williams, *Mary Chestnut Boykin*, Miles Van Rennselaer: 367TL. The Granger Collection: 369B. Lane Studio and Gettysburg National Military Park: 371B. Library of Congress: 372TR. National Archives: 374BR. The Bettman Archive, Inc.: 375B. West Point Museum Collection, U.S. Military Academy, *Furling the Flag*, Richard N. Brooke, 1872: 377B. The Granger Collection: 379B. The Mariners Museum: 382B. Official U.S. Signal Corps Photograph: 387BR. Museum of the City of New York, Harry T. Peters Collection, *Across the Continent, Westward the Course of the Empire Takes Its Way*, Currier & Ives: 388. The Granger Collection: 392T, 394TL, 396BL. Library of Congress: 400T. Brown Brothers: 401BR. The Bettman Archive, Inc.: 402TR. California Historical Society: 403BR. The Granger Collection: 404B. Visual Communications Photo Archive, Los Angeles, California: 405T. The Murray Ohio Manufacturing Company: 411T. Thomas Gilcrease Institute of American History & Art, Tulsa, Oklahoma, *The Stampede*, Frederic Remington: 417T. Nebraska State Historical Society, Solomon D. Butcher Collection: 419T. Thomas Gilcrease Institute of American History & Art, Tulsa, Oklahoma, *Custer's Demand*, Charles Schreyvogel: 423T. The Bettman Archive, Inc.: 424BL. Whatcom Museum Archive: 426BL. The Granger Collection: 427T. National Portrait Gallery, Smithsonian Institution, *Thomas Alva Edison*, Abraham Anderson: 429T. National Park Service, Edison National Historic Site: 429C. NASA: 434. Remington Art Museum, *Charge of the Rough Riders at San Juan Hill*, Frederic Remington: 438B. Bishop Museum, Hawaii: 439TR. The Bettman Archive, Inc.: 440BL. Smithsonian Institution: 441BR. The Bettman Archive, Inc.: 443T. Tom Tracy: 444T. Culver Pictures, Inc.: 446B. The Bettman Archive, Inc.: 448T. Wide World Photos: 451T. National Archives: 454T. The Bettman Archive, Inc.: 457BR. Wide World Photos: 458BL. The Bettman Archive, Inc.: 458BR. Wide World Photos: 459TL, 460BR. United Press International Photograph: 461BR. The Bettman Archive, Inc.: 462B. Wide World Photos: 465TR. Culver Pictures, Inc.: 466T. The Bettman Archive, Inc.: 467BR, 471C, 471B. Wide World Photos: 470TR. Black Star, Tor Eigeland: 476B. United Press International Photograph: 477TL. Black Star, Flip Schulke: 481TL. Wide World Photos: 484TR. Magnum Photos, Erich Hartmann: 486BL. NASA, LBJ Space Center: 487BL. NASA: 487TR. The White House, Michael Evans: 490BL. Black Star, John deVisser: 506B. Stock, Boston, Robert Hammond: 507T. Historical Pictures Service, Inc.: 508BR. The Granger Collection: 509T. The Picture Division, The Public Archives of Ottawa, Canada, *David Thompson Taking an Observation*, C.W. Jeffreys: 511TL. *Shooting the Rapids*, Frances Ann Hopkins, C-277A, 33-1-24: 511B. Courtesy of the Royal Canadian Mounted Police: 513T, 513C, 513B. Wide World Photos: 520B. Courtesy of Fred M. Bullard, University of Texas at Austin: 524BL. Instituto Nacional de Belles Artes, Mexico City: 529B. Historical Pictures Service, Inc.: 530B. Brown Brothers: 531TR. Museo Nacional de Historia, Mexico City: 533T.

ART ACKNOWLEDGMENTS

Art Source, James Barkley: 456, 502. Art Source, Bob Berry: 268, 340, 474. Art Source, Karen Bauman: 1. Walter Brooks: 27, 48B, 57T, 58T, 59T, 60B, 61L, 87B, 88T, 154, 158, 172, 188, 219, 273, 293. Art Source, Vince Caputo: 68, 90. Art Source, Bob Handville: 113, 284, 358, 414. Terry Hoff: 306, 436. Larry Hughston: 107, 144C, 144B, 366, 373, 380, 381, 383, 449, 533C, 533B. Intergraphics: 2, 32, 33, 34, 54, 55, 64, 75, 78, 93, 106–108, 123B–125, 145L, 159, 170, 174R, 184, 185, 230, 233, 234, 235, 275, 278, 308T, 316, 327, 378, 406, 412, 428, 433, 453, 478, 479, 517T, 520, 532, 536, 537, 540B. Eric Joyner: 18, 36, 216, 236, 256–261, 390, 522. Daniel Mooney: 86, 87T, 87TC, 87BC, 88C. Art Source, Dan Osycka: 110, 128. Intergraphics, Stephanie Pershing: 104, 157, 194. Kazuhiko Sano: 26, 238. Carla Simmons: 22, 30, 115T. Kirchoff/Wohlberg, Arvis Stewart: 327–333. Michael Sullivan: 77. Bill Walker: 253, 310.

MAP CREDITS

R.R. Donnelley Cartographic Services: 3–6, 9, 11, 13, 15, 20, 24, 29, 38, 40 (Adapted with permission from *Indians of North America*, © 1961, 1969 by the University of Chicago. All rights reserved.), 72, 76, 84, 100, 112, 117L, 126, 145R, 146, 147, 150, 156, 165, 167, 174L, 191, 203–205, 218, 221, 239, 271, 287B, 290, 308B, 311, 323, 325, 326, 336, 342, 348, 353, 376, 397, 407, 418, 420, 421, 432, 438T, 440, 442, 468–469, 504, 514, 517B, 525, 535, 539, 540T, 541, 544.

COVER CREDIT

Woodfin Camp & Associates, © George Hall, 1982

A 4
B 5
C 6
D 7
E 8
F 9
G 0
H 1
I 2
J 3